Informatik-Fachberichte 152

Subreihe Künstliche Intelligenz

Herausgegeben von W. Brauer in Zusammenarbeit mit dem Fachausschuß 1.2 „Künstliche Intelligenz und Mustererkennung" der Gesellschaft für Informatik (GI)

K. Morik (Ed.)

GWAI-87
11th German Workshop on Artificial Intelligence

Geseke, September 28 – October 2, 1987

Proceedings

Springer-Verlag
Berlin Heidelberg New York
London Paris Tokyo

Herausgeber

Katharina Morik
Technische Universität Berlin, Projektgruppe KIT, Sekr. FR 5-8
Franklinstraße 28/29, D–1000 Berlin 10

GWAI-87 (11th German Workshop on Artificial Intelligence)

Der Fachausschuß 1.2 „Künstliche Intelligenz und Mustererkennung"
der Gesellschaft für Informatik bildete das Programmkomitee:

Karl-Hans Bläsius (AEG Konstanz)
Thomas Christaller (GMD Birlinghoven)
Wolfgang Hoeppner (Erziehungswissenschaftl. Hochschule Koblenz)
Egbert Lehmann (Siemens München)
Kai von Luck (TU Berlin)
Bernd Neumann (Universität Hamburg)
Bernd Radig (TU München)
Claus-Rainer Rollinger (IBM Stuttgart)
Herbert Stoyan (Universität Konstanz)

Vorsitzende des Programmkomitees: Katharina Morik

Die Fachtagung wurde von den Firmen
Actis GmbH, Digital Equipments, EAI Electronic Associates GmbH,
IBM Deutschland, Mannesmann-Kienzle, NCR, Nixdorf
Computer AG, Siemens, Symbolics
und dem Land Nordrhein-Westfalen finanziell unterstützt.

CR Subject Classifications (1987): I.2.0

ISBN 978-3-540-18388-4   ISBN 978-3-642-73005-4 (eBook)
DOI 10.1007/978-3-642-73005-4

CIP-Kurztitelaufnahme der Deutschen Bibliothek. GWAI: GWAI ... / ...
German Workshop on Artificial Intelligence. – Berlin; Heidelberg; New York;
Tokyo: Springer
11. 1987. Geseke, September 28 – October 2, 1987. – 1987.
(Informatik-Fachberichte; 152: Subreihe künstliche Intelligenz)
ISBN 978-3-540-18388-4

NE: GT

2145/3140–543210

Vorwort

Die 11. deutsche Fachtagung über Künstliche Intelligenz fand vom 28.9. – 2.10.1987 im Schloß Eringerfeld bei Geseke statt. Sie spiegelt das seit Jahren stetig anwachsende Interesse an der Künstlichen Intelligenz (KI) ebenso wider wie die deutsche Forschungssituation in diesem Bereich.

Um trotz Größenwachstums in Teilnehmerzahl und Anzahl eingereichter Papiere den bisher so fruchtbaren Arbeitscharakter der Tagung zu bewahren, wurde ein Tag für spezielle Sektionen eingerichtet. Spezielle Sektionen bieten einen Rahmen für intensive Diskussionen über ein abgrenzbares Thema. Alle 13 Beiträge der speziellen Sektionen wurden sowohl von dem Sektionsleiter als auch vom Programmkomitee begutachtet und sind in dem vorliegenden Tagungsband enthalten. Vielfachen Wünschen einer Öffnung der KI gegenüber dem Bereich "Datenbanksysteme" kommt **Rudi Studer** (IBM Stuttgart) mit seiner Sektion "Künstliche Intelligenz und Datenbanksysteme – Systemarchitektur, konzeptuelle Modellierung" nach. Gio Wiederhold leitet die Sektion mit einem von Rudi Studer eingeladenen Vortrag ein. **Christian Freksa** (TU München) organisierte die Sektion "Kognition – Wissensstrukturen beim Aufgabenlösen". Er konnte Barbara Becker gewinnen, über die Rolle der Wissensrepräsentation beim Aufgabenlösen zu sprechen, und Gerhard Strube über menschliche Repräsentationsformen beim Problemlösen. Gleich zwei spezielle Sektionen stammen aus dem Bereich natürlichsprachlicher Systeme: **Günther Görz** (Universität Erlangen) leitet die Sektion über "Repräsentationssysteme für Grammatik und Lexikon", **Wolfgang Hoeppner** (EWH Koblenz) die über "Generierung in natürlichsprachlichen Systemen".

Das Tagungsprogramm zeigt zwei deutliche Themenschwerpunkte: natürlichsprachliche Systeme und deduktive Systeme. In diesen beiden Bereichen kann die deutsche KI auf eine Forschungsentwicklung zurückgreifen, die in anderen Bereichen noch aussteht. Der Bereich "natürlichsprachliche Systeme" ist nicht nur durch 7 Beiträge in speziellen Sektionen, sondern auch durch 7 Beiträge im 'regulären' Programm vertreten sowie durch den eingeladenen Hauptvortrag von Christa Hauenschild über maschinelle Übersetzung. Aus dem Bereich "deduktive Systeme" kommen 9 Beiträge, wobei nicht-monotones Schließen und 'reason maintenance' besonders intensiv diskutiert werden. Damit der Bereich "deduktive Systeme" verstärkt auch für auf anderen Gebieten der KI Arbeitende zugänglich wird, hat Karl-Hans Bläsius zusammen mit Hans-Jürgen Bürckert, Norbert Eisinger, Hans-Jürgen Ohlbach und Dieter Hutter ein Tutorium zur Einführung in dieses Gebiet veranstaltet.

Das Größenwachstum der deutschen KI zeigt sich auch daran, daß 100 Papiere eingereicht wurden, von denen allerdings nur 36 Beiträge vom Programmkomitee angenommen wurden, um den hohen Standard der Tagung zu erhalten. Mit den drei eingeladenen Hauptvorträgen im 'regulären' Programm – **Leonie Dreschler-Fischer** (Universität Hamburg) über Stereo-Bildverarbeitung, **Christa Hauenschild** (TU Berlin) über maschinelle Übersetzung und **Pattie Maes** (Universität Brüssel) über Reflexion in Systemarchitekturen – und den drei zu speziellen Sektionen eingeladenen Vorträgen sind 42 Papiere in diesem Tagungsband enthalten.

Mein Dank gilt natürlich dem Programmkomitee und den Nebengutachtern, allen Autoren, die ein Papier eingereicht haben, und denjenigen, die bei der Organisation der Tagung tätig geholfen haben. Insbesondere sei aber **Dimitris Karagiannis** (TU Berlin), dem Organisationsleiter der GWAI-87, für seine phantasievolle Überwindung organisatorischer Probleme gedankt.

September 1987   Katharina Morik

Nebengutachter

C. Beckstein

C. Beierle

H. Bergmann

W. Bibel

R. Block

U. Block

G. Brewka

S. Busemann

R. Cunis

J. Diederich

G. Dirlich

L. Dreschler-Fischer

E. Eder

M. Eimermacher

N. Eisinger

W. Emde

K. Estenfeld

M. Fidelak

R. Frederking

B. Fronhöfer

U. Furbach

M. Gehrke

M. Gerlach

H.-W. Gisgen

G. Görz

E. Groß

A. Günter

H. Gust

C. Habel

C. Hauenschild

H. Haugeneder

J. Hertzberg

S. Hölldodler

B. Hohlfeld

H. Horacek

W. Horn

R. Hunze

J.M. Janas

J. Kindermann

A. Kobsa

T. Käufl

R. Letz

V. Linnemann

W.-M. Lippe

S. Lüttringhaus

H.-D. Lutz

H. Marburger

W. Mellis

B.S. Müller

J. Müller

B. Nebel

S. Noack

H.-J. Novak

H.J. Ohlbach

B. Owsnicki-Klewe

P. Padowitz

C. Peltason

U. Pletat

M. Poesio

F. di Primio

F. Puppe

B. Radig

D. Rösner

M.-J. Schachter-Radig

L. Schmid

A. Schmiedel

C. Sielaff

D. Solecki

W. Stephan

P. Struß

P. Suda

I. Syska

M. Thielemann

H. Voss

I. Wachsmuth

B. Walter

C. Walther

J. Walther

D. Wermser

S. Wermter

T. Wetter

K.-H. Wittur

S. Wrobel

Bildverstehen

Leonie Dreschler-Fischer 1
"Das 'Bootstrap-Problem' bei der geometrischen Szenenrekonstruktion – eine
Übersicht"

Gerda Stein 16
"Konfliktlösung auf statistischer Basis bei der Bildanalyse mit
Produktionsregeln"

Ingrid Walter 21
"EPEX: Bildfolgendeutung auf Episodenebene"

Michael Mohnhaupt 31
"On Modelling Events with an 'Analogical' Representation"

Natürlichsprachliche Systeme
und
die Verarbeitung gesprochener Sprache

Christa Hauenschild 41
"KI-Methoden in der Maschinellen Übersetzung?"

Jochen Dörre, Stephan Momma 54
"Generierung aus f-Strukturen als strukturgesteuerte Ableitung"

Martin Emele 64
"FREGE - Ein objektorientierter FRont-End-GEnerator"

Dekai Wu 74
"Concretion Inferences in Natural Language Understanding"

Hans Haugeneder, Manfred Gehrke 84
"Modelling Heuristic Parsing Strategies"

Peter Bosch (lag zum Druck nicht vor)
"Deeper Reasons for Shallow Processing"

Massimo Poesio 94
"An Organization of Lexical Knowledge for Generation"

R. Gemello, E. Giachin, C. Rullent 104
"A Knowledge-Based Framework for Effective Probabilistic Control Strategies in
Signal Understanding"

Wissensrepräsentation und KI-Programmierung

Bernhard Nebel, Kai von Luck 114
"Issues of Integration and Balancing in Hybrid Knowledge Representation Systems"

Klaus Groth 124
"Der Aspekt der Zeitstruktur in zeitlogischen Formalisierungen der KI"

Stefan Wrobel 129
"Higher-order Concepts in a Tractable Knowledge Representation"

Helmut Simonis, Mehmet Dincbas 139
"Using Logic Programming for Fault Diagnosis in Digital Circuits"

Expertensysteme

Michael Beetz 149
"Specifying Meta-Level Architectures for Rule-Based Systems"

Werner Konrad, Andreas Jaeschke, Helmut Orth, Ono Tjandra 160
"Guiding the Maintenance of a Model-Based Advisory System by Explanation-based
Learning"

Deduktive Systeme

Hartmut Freitag, Michael Reinfrank 170
"An Efficient Interpreter for a Rule-Based Non-Monotonic Deduction System"

Frank Puppe 175
"Belief Revision in Diagnosis"

Oskar Dressler 185
"Erweiterungen des Basic ATMS"

Ulrich Furbach 195
"Oldy but Goody - Paramodulation Revisited"

Marita Heisel, Wolfgang Reif, Werner Stephan 201
"Program Verification by Symbolic Execution and Induction"

R. Ulf Schmerl 211
"Resolution on Formula Trees"

Rainer Manthey, Francois Bry 221
"A Hyperresolution-based Proof Procedure and its Implementation in PROLOG"

Alexander Herold 231
"Narrowing Techniques Applied to Idempotent Unification"

Jürgen Müller 241
"THEOPOGLES - A Theorem Prover Based on First-order Polynomials and a Special
Knuth-Bendix Procedure"

Selbstrepräsentierende Systeme

Pattie Maes 251
"Computational Reflection"

Kognitives Modellieren

Ab de Haan 266
"Cognitive Modelling and Education"

Spezielle Sektionen

Kognition – Wissensstrukturen beim Aufgabenlösen

Christian Freksa **277**

Barbara Becker 278
"Wissen und Können: Anmerkungen zur Wissensrepräsentation beim Aufgabenlösen"

Gerhard Strube 287
"Repräsentationsformen beim menschlichen Problemlösen"

Klaus Rehkämper 296
"Mentale Bilder und Wegbedeutungen"

Generierung in natürlichsprachlichen Systemen

Wolfgang Hoeppner **306**

Dietmar Rösner 307
"Generation of Content vs. Generation of Form: A Review of Recent Work in the SEMSYN Project"

Norbert Reithinger 315
"Ein erster Blick auf POPEL: Wie wird was gesagt?"

Helmut Horacek 320
"How to say WHAT - IT or SOMETHING"

Elisabeth Andre, Thomas Rist, Gerd Herzog 330
"Generierung natürlichsprachlicher Äußerungen zur simultanen Beschreibung von zeitveränderlichen Szenen"

Repräsentationssysteme für Grammatik und Lexikon

Günther Görz **339**

Dietrich Paulus 340
"Endliche Automaten zur Verbflexion und ein spezielles deutsches Verblexikon"

Ulrich Heid 345
"Zur lexikalischen Wissensquelle des Generierungssystems SEMSYN"

Stephan Busemann 355
"Generierung mit GPSG"

Künstliche Intelligenz und Datenbanksysteme –
Systemarchitektur und konzeptuelle Modellierung

Rudi Studer 365

Gio Wiederhold, Surajit Chaudhuri, Waqar Hasan, Michael G. Walker,
Marianne Winslett 366
"Architectural Concepts for Large Knowledge Bases"

Heinrich Jasper 386
"Interfacing PROLOG and External Data Management Systems: A Model"

Theo Härder, Nelson Mattos, Bernhard Mitschang 396
"Abbildung von Frames auf neuere Datenmodelle"

Das "Bootstrap-Problem" bei der geometrischen Szenenrekonstruktion — eine Übersicht

Leonie S. Dreschler-Fischer

Fachbereich Informatik der Universität Hamburg
Bodenstedtstraße 16
D-2000 Hamburg 50

Kurzfassung: Die Aufgabe der geometrischen Szenenrekonstruktion besteht darin, anhand von Bildvorlagen für die Objekte einer Szene ihre Oberflächen und ihre relative Anordnung zu rekonstruieren. Da bei der Bildentstehung durch die Projektion auf die Bildebene die Tiefeninformation verlorengeht, besteht das Hauptproblem der geometrischen Rekonstruktion darin, allgemeine Prinzipien zu finden, die es ermöglichen, die Tiefeninformation wiederzugewinnen. Ein Ansatz hierzu ist die Kombination mehrfacher Objektansichten, wodurch eine Tiefenmessung mittels trigonometrischer Parallaxe ermöglicht wird.

Der erste Teil des Vortrags gibt eine Einführung zum Stand der Kunst bei der geometrischen Szenenrekonstruktion und diskutiert die Probleme, die durch die Komplexität natürlicher Szenen verursacht werden, wobei vor allem das "Bootstrap-Problem" eingeführt wird.

Im zweiten Teil des Vortrags wird am Beispiel des Projektes Stereo-Bildfolgen gezeigt, wie durch die Kombination einer Vielzahl von Tiefenhinweisen Szenenteile rekonstruiert werden können, ohne unnatürliche einschränkende Annahmen machen zu müssen.

1 Lernen durch Beobachtung

1.1 Ziele und Motivation

Sowohl in den U.S.A. als auch in Europa hat in den letzten Jahren das Forschungsgebiet der autonomen mobilen Roboter zunehmende Beachtung gefunden. Dies zeigt sich in neuen Grossforschungsprojekten wie PROMETHEUS und neuen internationalen Konferenzen wie der IAS. Die Forderung nach Mobilität von autonomen Systemen verursacht komplexe Probleme, die über den augenblicklichen Stand der Kunst weit hinausgehen. Ein Hauptproblem der autonomen Fahrzeuge ist, daß diese sich, im Gegensatz zu stationären Robotern, nicht mehr unbedingt an abgeschlossenen Arbeitsplätzen mit wohldefiniertem Aufbau aufhalten. Autonome Fahrzeuge können sich in Szenen hineinbewegen, in denen ihnen bisher unbekannte Objekte begegnen oder bekannte Objekte neue, unerwartete Verhaltensweisen zeigen.

Ein wichtiger Meilenstein auf dem Weg zu autonomen mobilen Systemen wäre daher die Entwicklung eines Gesichtssinns für Maschinen, der ähnlich universell und leistungsfähig wie das menschliche Sehsystem ist. Wir Menschen können uns in der Regel sehr schnell in einer fremden Umgebung orientieren, sei es in einem fremden Zimmer, einer unbekannten Straße oder einer nie zuvor gesehen Landschaft. Ebenso leicht fällt es uns, durch Betrachten eines unbekannten Objektes von allen Seiten, uns davon eine ungefähre räumliche Vorstellung zu machen, auch wenn wir vorher nie etwas Vergleichbares gesehen haben. Hiervon kann man sich leicht in einer Ausstellung mit modernen Plastiken überzeugen. Die Fähigkeit unseres Gesichtssinns zum räumlichen Sehen ermöglicht es uns, die relative Anordnung und Entfernung von Gegenständen wahrzunehmen und den Verlauf ihrer Oberflächen abzuschätzen.

Das Anliegen dieser Arbeit ist es, den Stand der Kunst beim räumlichen Maschinensehen zu dokumentieren, die grundlegenden Probleme zu analysieren und zu diskutieren und Lösungswege aufzuzeigen, die einen Schritt weiter in Richtung auf ein universelles Sehsystem für Maschinen führen.

1.2 Leitlinien und Abgrenzung gegen andere Arbeiten

1.2.1 Maschinensehen versus Kognition

Um Mißverständnissen vorzubeugen: Auch wenn zur Motivation dieser Arbeit auf die erstaunlichen Fähigkeiten des menschlichen Sehsystems verwiesen wird, so liegt die Betonung hier auf *Maschinensehen*, nicht auf den kognitiven Aspekten. Das menschliche Sehsystem dient als Maßstab für die Leistungsanforderungen, aber nicht als operationales Vorbild, wie es von einer Reihe von Forschern, vor allem am MIT, angestrebt wird. Die Entschlüsselung des menschlichen Sehsystems ist sicherlich ein wichtiges und faszinierendes Projekt der KI, durch welches für das Problem des Maschinensehens viele Anregungen gewonnen werden können — aber gerade aus der Sicht der Robotik erscheint es als vordringliche Aufgabe, zunächst einmal die dem räumlichen Sehen zugrundeliegenden Probleme zu verstehen. Dieses wäre eine der Voraussetzungen dafür, je nach Aufgabe und Anforderungen, für jedes Problem einen maßgeschneiderten Sehapparat zu entwerfen.

Auch die Natur hat Sehsysteme in den unterschiedlichsten Ausstattungen entwickelt. Das menschliche Sehsystem ist zwar das flexibelste, das wir kennen, wird aber in jedem einzelnen Aspekt von dem anderer Lebewesen übertroffen: Greifvögel haben eine größere Sehschärfe, Katzen und andere nachtaktive Tiere können besser im Dunkeln sehen, einige Wasservögel können durch spiegelnde Wasseroberflächen hindurch sehen, indem sie die Polarisation des reflektierten Lichtes ausnutzen, Libellen und Heuschrecken lösen Bewegungsabläufe zeitlich sehr viel feiner auf, Schmetterlinge und andere Nektar-saugende Tiere wie Bienen nehmen ein breiteres Farbspektrum wahr und viele Tiere haben ein erheblich größeres Gesichtsfeld. Wir Menschen sind auf technische Hilfsmittel angewiesen, sobald wir Wahrnehmungsaufgaben haben, für die uns die Natur nicht konstruiert hat. Wir benötigen Mikroskope, Teleskope, Zeitlupe, Zeitraffer, Bildverstärker, UV- und IR-Kameras, Polarisationsfilter, Sonnenbrillen als Schutz vor grellem Licht oder Schutzbrillen, um die Augen vor mechanischen Beschädigungen zu bewahren. Kurzum, es gibt Aufgaben und Situationen, für die das menschliche Sehsystem nicht optimal ausgelegt ist; das vorrangige Ziel der Robotik sollte es meiner Meinung nach aber sein, solche Maschinen zu schaffen, die diejenigen Aufgaben übernehmen können, denen der Mensch bisher nicht gewachsen ist. Deshalb kann das menschliche Sehsystem zwar ein interessanter Ideenlieferant, aber nicht die alleinige Leitlinie für das Maschinensehen sein. Eine Maschine mit genau den Fähigkeiten des Menschen zu schaffen, kommt für mich dem faustischen Streben nach dem Homunculus gleich, ein Ehrgeiz, der mir in Anbetracht von Massenarbeitslosigkeit und Überbevölkerung nicht angebracht erscheint. Auch Marr und Nishihara, zwei Hauptvertreter des kognitiven Paradigmas der Bilddeutung, haben festgestellt:

> For human vision to be explained by a computational theory, the first question is plain:
> What are the problems the brain solves when we see?
> *Marr + Nishihara 78*

1.2.2 Szenenspezifisches Wissen

Ein weiteres Leitmotiv dieser Arbeit, das sie von anderen Ansätzen unterscheidet, ist der Verzicht auf szenenspezifisches Wissen und unnatürliche einschränkende Annahmen — beides sind Hilfsmittel, die häufig herangezogen werden, um bei der Komplexität natürlicher Szenen auf heute verfügbaren Rechnerarchitekturen mit vertretbarem Aufwand zu einer heuristischen, wenn auch nicht unbedingt korrekten, Lösung zu kommen. Hier dagegen geht es gerade darum, die Komplexität des Problems der räumlichen Wahrnehmung zu analysieren und bezüglich der Lösungsmöglichkeiten die Grenzen des Machbaren auszuloten. Es steht also nicht die Entwicklung eines heute schon umsetzbaren Verfahrens im Vordergrund, sondern die Klärung der grundlegenden Prinzipien.

Der Verzicht auf szenenspezifisches Wissen ist eine wichtige Voraussetzung dafür, daß ein Verfahren für eine Vielzahl von Szenen geeignet sein kann. Nagel hat die ersten Ansätze hierzu für die Auswertung von Bildfolgen diskutiert *Nagel 78*. Im MORIO-System [*Dreschler + Nagel 82b*, *Dreschler-Fischer u.a. 83*] wurde das Objektkonzept von *Nagel 78* dazu eingesetzt, für einen bewegten starren Körper aus einer Folge von perspektivischen Projektionen eine grobe räumliche Beschreibung zu errechnen. Nagel nennt diesen Vorgang "Lernen durch Beobachtung", da szenen*unspezifisches* Wissen, ein allgemeines Objektkonzept, dazu ausgenutzt wird, während der Beobachtung der Bewegungsabläufe in einer Szene szenen*spezifisches* Wissen, nämlich geometrische Beschreibungen konkreter Objekte, zu erwerben.

2 Geometrische Szenenrekonstruktion

2.1 Das Bootstrap-Problem

Das zentrale Problem des räumlichen Sehens, der *geometrischen Szenenrekonstruktion* besteht nun darin, daß bei der Bildentstehung durch die Projektion auf eine Ebene die Tiefeninformation verloren geht und der Projektionsvorgang daher nicht eindeutig umkehrbar ist. Zur Rekonstruktion einer Szene müssen daher einschränkende Randbedingungen herangezogen werden; das sind typischerweise die Gesetze der projektiven Geometrie, der Photometrie und die physikalischen Eigenschaften von Objekten und ihren Oberflächen. *Neumann 82* gibt eine lesenswerte einführende Übersicht zum Problem der geometrischen Szenenrekonstruktion. Das kürzlich erschienene Buch von Shirai [*Shirai 87*] faßt die wichtigsten Standardverfahren zusammen.

Das Ziel der geometrischen Szenenrekonstruktion ist es, eine *geometrisch-temporale Szenen-beschreibung* zu ermitteln, die die relative räumliche Anordnung der Objekte einer Szene, den räumlichen Verlauf ihrer Oberflächen und deren photometrische Eigenschaften, die Bewegungs-abläufe und die zeitlichen Veränderungen der Objekte beschreibt. Im Gegensatz zur Definition der "geometrischen Szenenbeschreibung" von *Neumann 82* wird bei dieser Definition der temporale Aspekt betont, aber die Erkennung von Objekten als Instanzen von Objektmodellen nicht mit einbezogen, da hierfür szenenspezifisches Wissen erforderlich wäre.

Während des letzten Jahrzehnts wurden beim Verständnis der Probleme der geometrischen Sze-nenrekonstruktion beachtliche Fortschritte erreicht. Die entwickelten Verfahren lassen sich unter dem Namen "Shape-from..." zusammenfassen — "Shape-from-Shading", "Shape-from-Texture", "Shape-from-Contour", "Shape-from-Stereo" usw. Einige dieser Verfahren sind auf Einzelbilder an-wendbar, während andere mehrfache Objektansichten erfordern. "Shape-from-Shading" ermöglicht es, die Orientierung von Oberflächenelementen zu ermitteln, wenn deren bidirektionale Reflektanz-funktion und die Beleuchtung bekannt sind [*Horn 75*]; ebenso läßt sich die Orientierung von Ober-flächen relativ zum Betrachter durch "Shape-from-Texture" ermitteln, wenn die Texturgradienten auf perspektivische Effekte zurückzuführen sind; "Shape-from-Texture" wurde beispielsweise von *Bajcsy + Lieberman 76, Ikeuchi 84* und *Blostein + Ahuja 87* erprobt. Stereoskopie ermöglicht absolute Tiefenmessungen mittels der trigonometrischen Parallaxe, wenn zwei unterschiedliche An-sichten der Szene zur Verfügung stehen, und eignet sich vor allem für die Vermessung von genau lokalisierbaren Objektstrukturen, wie Kanten und Eckpunkten. Eines der bekanntesten Stereo-Verfahren stammt von Marr und Poggio [*Marr + Poggio 79*], das in eindrucksvoller Weise die Aussagekraft der Stereo-Information mittels Zufallspunkt-Stereogrammen demonstriert.

Jedes dieser Verfahren geht von einer impliziten Modellvorstellung von den zu rekonstruierenden Objektmerkmalen aus und ist daher nur unter bestimmten Voraussetzungen anwendbar. Bevor ein "Shape-from..."-Verfahren eingesetzt werden kann, muß daher verifiziert werden, daß diese Voraussetzungen gegeben sind. Diese Verifikation ist bei szenenspezifischen Verfahren und einge-schränkten Szenen in der Regel unproblematisch, aber bei natürlichen Szenen ein noch ungelöstes Problem. Beispielsweise ist einer Textur mit einer systematischen Variation der Dichte nicht ohne weiteres anzusehen, ob diese Dichtevariation durch perspektivische Effekte verursacht wird oder die Oberfläche von sich aus unterschiedlich stark texturiert ist, wie beispielsweise das Fell eines Leoparden. Um zu prüfen, ob "Shape-from-Texture" anwendbar ist, müßte man zuvor die Orien-tierung der Oberfläche im Raum ermitteln. Dasselbe trifft in ähnlicher Form auch auf die anderen 'Shape-from...' Methoden zu. Das heißt:

> Um Objektstrukturen aus Bildstrukturen geometrisch zu rekonstruieren, müssen die erzeugenden Objektstrukturen zumindestens qualitativ schon bekannt sein.

Da natürliche Szenen in der Regel komplex sind und Objektstrukturen der unterschiedlichsten Art vorkommen können, stellt das Problem der Verifikation einen Teufelskreis dar, der nicht einfach zu durchbrechen zu sein scheint. Ich habe dieses Problem *Bootstrap-Problem* genannt, da Rekon-struktionen nur auf Rekonstruktionen aufbauen können und irgendwie ein Einstieg in den Kreis der gegenseitigen Abhängigkeiten gefunden werden muß.

Der erste Meilenstein auf dem Wege zu einer Theorie der niederen Bilddeutung war die Formulierung des *Generalitätsprinzips*, das vor allem auf die Arbeiten von Binford [*Binford 81*] und Marr [*Marr 82*] zurückgeht. Dieses Prinzip besagt[1], daß alle Bildstrukturen jeweils durch das allgemeinste mögliche Modell erklärt werden sollten. Dahinter verbirgt sich die Annahme, daß wir ein Objekt in der Regel von einem allgemeinen Betrachterstandort bei allgemeiner Beleuchtung beobachten und daß die Objektoberflächen keine speziellen Schattierungen und Texturen aufweisen. Das Generalitätsprinzip bildet inzwischen ein allgemein akzeptiertes Fundament für eine sich allmählich entwickelnde Theorie der niederen Bilddeutung. Aus dem Generalitätsprinzip folgt beispielsweise, daß eine durchgehende Linie im Bild als Bild einer durchgehende Linie in der Szene zu interpretieren ist, und nicht etwa als Bild zweier getrennter Linien, die zufällig als verbundene Linie projiziert werden, denn diese Deutung würde einen speziellen Betrachterstandort erfordern.

Bei genauerer Betrachtung zeigt sich jedoch, daß auch das Generalitätsprinzip kein Gesetz, sondern eine Heuristik ist, die verletzt sein kann, und zwar nicht nur durch "böswillig" konstruierte künstliche Objekte, wie z.B. die Bilder von Escher oder Vasareli, sondern auch durch natürliche Objekte, wie das Beispiel des texturierten Leopardenfells zeigt. Variationen in der Oberflächenschattierung und der Textur scheinen bei Lebewesen eher die Regel als die Ausnahme zu schein, und die Lichtquelle oder der Betrachter können sehr wohl spezielle Positionen relativ zu einzelnen Objekten der Szene haben. Besonders in Szenen mit bewegten Objekten muß damit gerechnet werden, daß diese kurzzeitig während eines längeren Bewegungsablaufs spezielle Positionen einnehmen, so daß beispielsweise Flächen genau streifend gesehen werden. Hier zeigt sich ein Ansatzpunkt, um, zumindest bei der Auswertung von Bildfolgen, das Generalitätsprinzip verifizieren zu können, denn unter der Annahme einer *allgemeinen Bewegung* sollten die kurzzeitigen Verletzungen des Generalitätsprinzips zu entdecken sein. Diese erweiterte Fassung des Generalitätsprinzips nenne ich das "*Prinzip der allgemeinen Bewegung*".

Im nächsten Abschnitt wird ein wissensbasiertes Bootstrap-Verfahren vorgestellt, um den circulus vitiosus des Bootstrap-Problems zu umgehen.

2.2 Lösungsansatz

Der Lösungsansatz zum Bootstrap-Problem geht davon aus, daß die einzelnen Bildstrukturen, für sich allein betrachtet, in der Regel mehrere Interpretationen zulassen, sich diese Mehrdeutigkeiten aber durch den räumlichen und zeitlichen Kontext reduzieren lassen sollten, denn die geometrische Interpretation einer Bildstruktur darf nicht der Interpretation von damit verbundenen Strukturen widersprechen. Je nach Art der Bildmerkmale werden unterschiedliche Rekonstruktionsmethoden eingesetzt — trigonometrische Verfahren für genau lokalisierbare Strukturen, wie Kanten und Eckpunkte, und photometrische oder statistische Verfahren für flächenhafte Bildstrukturen. Mittels trigonometrischer Verfahren lassen sich absolute Tiefenmesungen für Punkte und linienhafte Objektstrukturen vornehmen, während die photometrischen Verfahren eher relative Tiefenhinweise geben und sich für flächenhafte Bildelemente eignen. Diese flächenhaften Bildelemente stellen Randbedingungen für die Deutung der sie begrenzenden Linienstrukturen dar und umgekehrt.

---

[1] in der Formulierung von Binford

Das Ziel des Rekonstruktionsverfahrens ist es nun, aus den vielfältigen Interpretationsmöglichkeiten für die einzelnen Bildelemente diejenigen auszuwählen, die im Kontext der Nachbarstrukturen einen möglichst großen Teil des Bildes widerspruchsfrei erklären. Damit stellt sich das Rekonstruktionsproblem als ein Suchproblem in einem extrem großen Suchraum dar, das dadurch erschwert wird, daß die optimale Lösung nur im Vergleich zu allen Alternativen definiert ist. Keine Teilinterpretation kann abgelehnt werden, solange nicht klar ist, daß es eine Lösung gibt, die einen noch größeren Teil des Bildes konsistent erklärt.

Die Definition des Rekonstruktionsproblems als Suchproblem bedeutet nicht unbedingt, daß es auch durch ein Suchverfahren gelöst werden muß. Gerade wegen des extrem großen Suchraums sind heuristische Ansätze, wie Relaxationsververfahren, denkbar, um zu tragbaren Rechenzeiten zu kommen. Bei dem hier vorgestellten Ansatz kommt es jedoch vor allem auf die Untersuchung des Zusammenspiels von einer Vielzahl von Tiefenhinweisen an, so daß ein Ansatz gesucht wurde, der es ermöglicht, alle verwendeten Rekonstruktionsregeln und das Wissen über ihr Zusammenwirken explizit zu repräsentieren. Das führte zu der folgenden Lösung:

Das Suchproblem wird durch ein wissensbasiertes Verfahren zu lösen versucht, das zwei Kategorien von Wissen verwendet: Zum einen physikalische Gesetze und zum anderen Heuristiken. Die Heuristiken dienen zur zielgerichteten Steuerung der Suche, um schnell tragfähige Hypothesen zu finden, während die physikalischen Gesetze zur Verifikation dieser Hypothesen eingesetzt werden. Da das Verfahren im Sinne des "Prinzips der kleinsten Verpflichtung" defensiv angelegt ist, wird keine Hypothese alleine aufgrund von Heuristiken zurückgewiesen, solange keine physikalische Evidenz dagegen vorliegt, sondern allenfalls zugunsten anderer Hypothesen zurückgestellt.

Um ein möglichst breites Spektrum an Tiefenhinweisen zur Verfügung zu haben, baut das Verfahren darauf auf, daß als Ausgangsdaten stereoskopische Folgen von Farbbildern zur Verfügung stehen. Die *Farbbinformation* scheint hilfreich zu sein, um gute Hypothesen über die erzeugenden Strukturen von Bildstrukturen zu finden — beispielsweise verraten sich Glanzlichter dadurch, daß sie die Farbe der Lichtquelle reflektieren, während die Farbe der Umgebung durch die Reflektanzfunktion der Oberfläche bestimmt wird [*Gershon u.a. 87, Klinker u.a. 87*]. Die *mehrfachen Objektansichten* dagegen sind wichtig für die trigonometrische Rekonstruktion: Aus den stereoskopischen Bildpaaren können direkte Tiefenmessungen mittels Triangulation gewonnen werden, während aus den Bewegungsfolgen für starre Körper eine Rekonstruktion mittels Bewegungsstereos [*Ullman 79*] oder des optischen Flusses [*Clocksin 78*] abgeleitet werden kann. Damit wird die Lösung des Korrespondenzproblems (siehe nächster Abschnitt) ein zentraler Punkt des Verfahrens, da dies eine notwendige Voraussetzung zur trigonometrischen Auswertung von mehrfachen Objektansichten ist. Im Gegensatz zu *Ullman 79*, der Korrespondenzproblem und geometrische Rekonstruktion als getrennte Probleme definiert hat, werden sie hier als zwei Aspekte desselben Problems gesehen, die ebenso wie die anderen Rekonstruktionsmethoden durch das Bootstrap-Problem gekoppelt sind und deshalb gemeinsam mit den anderen Verfahren in das wissensbasierte Lösungsverfahren eingehen.

3 Wissensbasierte Korrespondenzanalyse

3.1 Das Korrespondenzproblem

Das Korrespondenzproblem ist seit seiner Definition durch Ullman in unterschiedlicher Weise angegangen worden: Visuelle Korrespondenz, Grauwertverschiebungen und physikalische Korrespondenz (siehe [*Dreschler-Fischer 86a*, *Dreschler-Fischer 86b*] für eine detaillierte Diskussion dieser drei Begriffe). Da das Anliegen dieser Arbeit die geometrische Rekonstruktion von physikalischen Objekten ist, wird hier nach einem Verfahren zur Ermittlung von *physikalischen Korrespondenzen* gesucht. Eine sehr ausführliche Übersicht zur Ermittlung und Interpretation von *Grauwertverschiebungen* findet sich bei *Nagel 85a* und *Nagel 86*.

Für eine geometrische Rekonstruktion anhand von Bildern liegt es nahe, vor allem diejenigen Oberflächenstrukturen zu rekonstruieren, die visuell markant sind. Da der einzige Hinweis auf Strukturen auf den Oberflächen der zu rekonstruierenden Objekte Strukturen in ihren Abbildungen sind, bietet es sich an, das physikalische Korrespondenzproblem merkmalsbasiert zu lösen und nach korrespondierenden Abbildungen von körperfesten Oberflächenstrukturen zu suchen. Bei diesem Ansatz schlägt das Bootstrap-Problem in dreifacher Weise zu:

Merkmalsdetektion: Die Segmentation eines Bildes impliziert Merkmalsmodelle, die einer Annahme über das Vorhandensein von Kanten, Regionen oder markanten Punkten zugrunde-liegen.

Merkmalsinterpretation: Physikalische Korrespondenz ist nur für körperfeste Oberflächenstrukturen definiert. Nicht alle Bildstrukturen entsprechen solchen körperfesten Objektstrukturen, sondern entstehen beispielsweise durch Beleuchtungseffekte oder Verdeckung. Eine Aussage über die Art der Bildstrukturen impliziert eine zumindest qualitative Vorstellung von den erzeugenden Parametern der Bildentstehung.

Mehrdeutigkeit der Korrespondenz: Wegen der fehlenden Tiefeninformation ist die Korrespondenz für einzelne Bildstrukturen in der Regel mehrdeutig. Hypothesen über korrespondierende Bildelemente implizieren räumliche Interpretationen, während umgekehrt Hypothesen über den geometrischen Aufbau von Objekten die möglichen Korrespondenzen einschränken.

Wegen dieser Komplexität des physikalischen Korrespondenzproblems werden hier "Shape-from-Stereo", "Structure-from-Motion", "Shape-from-Shading" usw. nicht als unabhängige Methoden zur Ermittlung von 3-D Information betrachtet, sondern als verschiedene Sichtweisen desselben Problems der geometrischen Szenenrekonstruktion. Während *Crowley 84a* ein Verfahren zur Auswertung von stereoskopischen Bildfolgen vorschlägt, bei dem eine Vielzahl von "Shape-from..." Methoden parallel und unabhängig voneinander eingesetzt werden, sollen bei dem hier verfolgten Ansatz nicht erst die Ergebnisse der Interpretation durch verschiedene Methoden kombiniert werden, sondern auch die impliziten Hypothesen über die Anwendbarkeit im Kontext der Interpretation der Bildstrukturen durch konkurrierende Methoden überprüft werden.

3.2 Das Verfahren

Folgende Kategorien von Tiefenhinweisen können zur Lösung des Korrespondenzproblems beitragen:

Physikalische Gesetze: Bei der Stereoskopie gilt die epipolare Geometrie[2], und für bewegte Objekte gilt, daß sie sich glatt entlang glatter Bahnen bewegen.

Strukturelle Zusammenhänge: Verbindende Kanten zwischen Bildstrukturen ermöglichen das Propagieren von Zwangsbedingungen.

Heuristiken: Häufig angewendete Heuristiken sind: "Sich ähnlich sehende Bildstrukturen korrespondieren." oder "Benachbarte Bildelemente haben ähnliche Verschiebungen von Bild zu Bild."
Diese Heuristiken treffen in einer Vielzahl von Fällen zu, können aber verletzt sein. Daher werden Heuristiken eingesetzt, um schnell tragfähige Hypothesen zu bilden und die Suche zu steuern, aber nicht zum Verifizieren von Hypothesen.

Szenenspezifisches Wissen: Beispielsweise Teilrekonstruktionen aus früheren Beobachtungen.

Das Korrespondenzverfahren segmentiert zunächst die Bilder und baut eine symbolische Beschreibung aus Bereichen, Kanten und markanten Punkten auf [*Bartsch u.a. 86*, *Dreschler-Fischer + Gnutzmann 87b*]. Für diese Merkmale werden aufgrund des Ähnlichkeitskriteriums Korrespondenzhypothesen gebildet, die mithilfe der anderen Regeln verifiziert werden. Zunächst werden für markante Punkte und Vertices stereoskopische Korrespondenzen ermittelt, die mit der epipolaren Geometrie verträglich sind. Für diese Korrespondenzkandidaten werden die 3-D Koordinaten errechnet. Jeweils drei solcher Punkte im Raum aus drei aufeinanderfolgenden Bildern werden zu Bewegungsketten kombiniert, die einer glatten Bewegung im Raum entsprechen [*Jenkin + Tsotsos 86*]. Schließlich werden diese Kandidaten für korrespondierende Punkte mittels der verbindenden Kanten zu strukturell konsistenten Teilinterpretationen erweitert.

3.3 Das SISSY-System

An der Universität Hamburg wird zur Zeit ein Programmsystem entwickelt, in dem das oben beschriebene Korrespondenzverfahren erprobt werden kann (SISSY steht für Stereo Image Sequences SYstem). Das Korrespondenzverfahren ist als Blackboard-System ausgelegt, wobei die Korrespondenzregeln als prozedurale Wissensquellen realisiert sind. Diese Architektur hat den Vorteil, daß das eingesetzte Wissen explizit repräsentiert ist und das Experimentieren mit unterschiedlichen Regeln erleichtert wird. Außerdem wird so eine datengesteuerte Analyse ermöglicht, wobei die Bildstrukturen selbst die Art und Reihenfolge der Analyse bestimmen.

---

[2]Jeder Bildpunkt bestimmt eine Gerade im Raum, auf das Urbild liegt. Der korrespondierende Bildpunkt im anderen Bild muß auf dem Bild dieser Geraden liegen.

BLOCKS←0←H1.GEO

Abbildung 1: Beispielszene (Grünauszug des Farbbilds)

4 Beispiele und Ergebnisse

Wenn auch das SISSY-System noch nicht fertiggestellt ist, so lassen sich doch schon eine Reihe von Experimenten durchführen, wobei Teile des Rekonstruktionsverfahrens erprobt werden können.

Abbildung 1 zeigt eine einfache Szene mit farbigen Blöcken auf einem Drehteller. Durch systematisches Drehen um jeweils 10 Grad wurde eine Stereo-Bildfolge aufgenommen und die Einzelbilder segmentiert. Diese Bildfolge ist in Abbildung 2 zu sehen. Die Bilder in der linken Spalte entsprechen den Bildern der linken Kamera und die der rechten Spalte denen der rechten Kamera. Die beiden Zeilen entsprechen unterschiedlichen Zeitpunkten. Abbildung 2 illustriert die Suchraumbeschränkung durch die epipolare Geometrie: In den beiden linken Bildern ist ein Eckpunkt des Pyramidenstumpfes markiert, für den in den beiden rechten Aufnahmen die epipolaren Linien eingetragen sind. Abbildung 3 zeigt Kandidaten von korrespondierenden Punkten aufgrund der epipolaren Geometrie. Im unteren Bildpaar sind zwei Arten von Mehrdeutigkeiten zu sehen: Zum einen befinden sich zwei Eckpunkte in der Nähe der epipolaren Linie und zum anderen wurden an der Spitze der Pyramide vom Punktefinder zwei Punkte gefunden. Die erste Mehrdeutigkeit kann durch die epipolare Linie im ersten Bildpaar aufgelöst werden und die zweite durch die verbindende Kante.

Abbildung 4 und 5 zeigen Kandidaten für zeitliche Korrespondenzen aufgrund der Persistenz-Annahme (bewegte Objekte befinden sich im Folgebild in der Nähe der alten Position). In Abbildung 6 und 7 sind sind die stereoskopischen und zeitlichen Korrespondenzen kombiniert, so daß die konsistenten Zuordnungszyklen sichtbar werden.

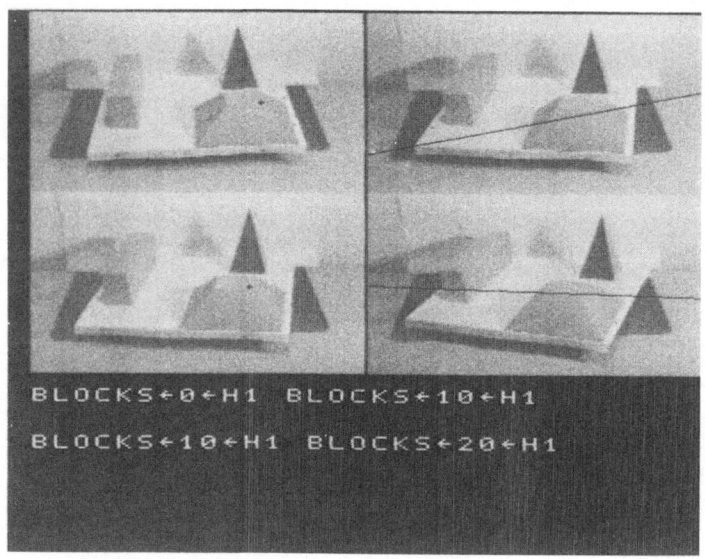

Abbildung 2: Epipolare Linien: Durch Drehen der Klötzchen auf einem Drehteller wurde eine Stereo-Bildfolge simuliert. In den beiden rechten Bildern sind die epipolaren Linien für den in den linken Bildern markierten Eckpunkt des Pyramidenstumpfs eingetragen.

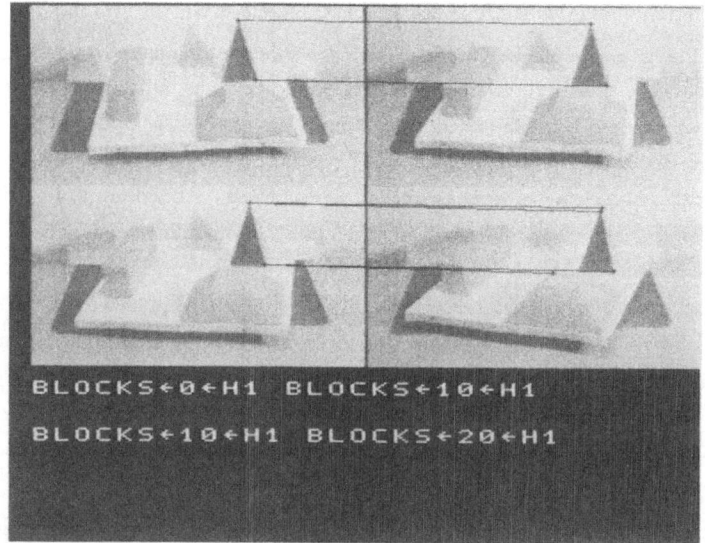

Abbildung 3: Korrespondenzen aufgrund der epipolaren Geometrie: Die dunklen Linien verbinden manuell ausgewählte Punkte aus den linken Bildern mit Kandidaten für korrespondierende Punkte entlang den dazugehörigen epipolaren Linien in den rechten Bildern. Nur eine der potentiellen Korrespondenzen ist konsistent mit den verbindenden Kanten am rechten Pyramidenrand.

Abbildung 4: Eindeutige Korrespondenzen aufgrund der räumlichen Nachbarschaft (Persistenz)

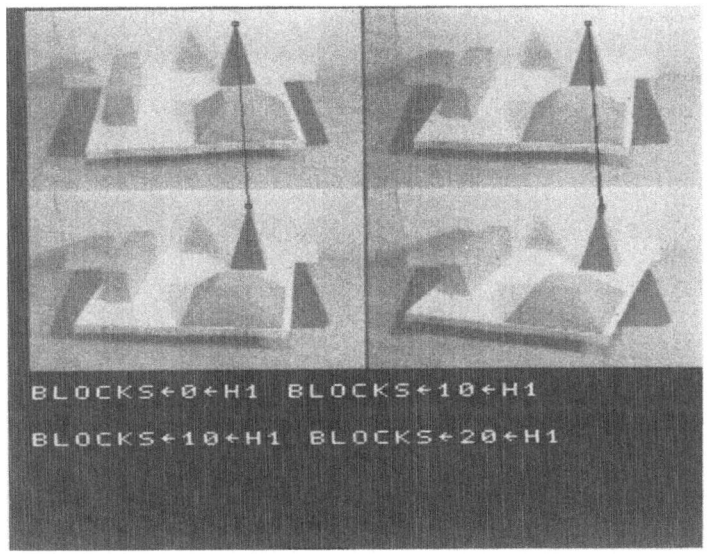

Abbildung 5: Mehrdeutige Korrespondenz aufgrund der räumlichen Nachbarschaft. Hier wird die Mehrdeutigkeit durch eine Schwäche des Punktefinders verursacht, der im linken unteren Bild die Pyramidenspitze nicht eindeutig isolieren konnte.

Abbildung 6: Ein geometrisch konsistenter Korrespondenzzyklus

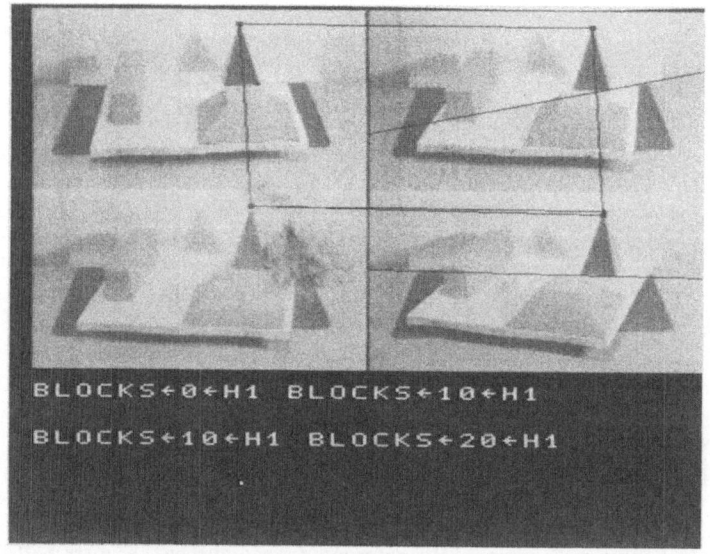

Abbildung 7: Geometrische und strukturelle Konsistenz im Zusammenspiel

5 Zusammenfassung

Es wurde gezeigt, daß das Bootstrap-Problem bei der geometrischen Szenenrekonstruktion eine wichtige Rolle spielt und daß das Problem der physikalischen Korrespondenz als eine spezielle Sichtweise des Rekonstruktionsproblems gesehen werden kann. Weiterhin wurde ein wissensbasierter Ansatz vorgestellt, um das Bootstrap-Problem zu umgehen.

Literatur

Bajcsy + Lieberman 76 : *Texture Gradient as a Depth Cue*, R. Bajcsy und L.I. Lieberman, *Computer Graphics and Image Processing* **5**, 52–67 (1976).

Bartsch u.a. 86 : *Merkmalsdetektion in Farbbildern als Grundlage zur Korrespondenzanalyse in Stereo-Bildfolgen*, Thomas Bartsch, Leonie S. Dreschler-Fischer und Carsten Schröder, *DAGM-86*, pp. 94–97.

Binford 81 : *Inferring Surfaces from Images*, Thomas O. Binford, *Artificial Intelligence* **17**, 205–244 (1981)
siehe auch:
Brady 81, pp. 75–116.

Blostein + Ahuja 87 : *Representation and Three-Dimensional Interpretation of Image Texture: An Integrated Approach*, Dorothea Blostein und Narendra Ahuja, *ICCV-87*, pp. 444–449.

Brady 81 : *Computer Vision*, J.M. Brady (Hrsg.), *North Holland Publ. Comp. Amsterdam 1981, reprinted from Artificial Intelligence 17 (1981)*.

Clocksin 78 : *Determining the Orientation of Surfaces from Optical Flow*, W.F. Clocksin, Proc. AISB/GI-78 on Artificial Intelligence, Hamburg, July 18-20, 1978, pp. 73–102.

Crowley 84a : *A Computational Paradigm for Three Dimensional Scene Analysis*, James L. Crowley, *Technical Report* **CMU-RI-TR-84-11** The Robotics Institute, Carnegie-Mellon University, Pittsburgh, PA (April 1984).

Dreschler + Nagel 82b : *Volumetric Model and 3D-Trajectory of a Moving Car Derived from Monocular TV Frame Sequences of a Street Scene*, L. Dreschler und H.-H. Nagel, *Computer Graphics and Image Processing* **20**, 199–228 (1982).

Dreschler-Fischer 86a : *A Knowledge Based Approach to the Correspondence Problem in Sequences of Stereo Images*, L.S. Dreschler-Fischer, *AIMSA-86*, short papers.

Dreschler-Fischer 86b : *A Blackboard System for Dynamic Stereo Matching*, L.S. Dreschler-Fischer, *IAS-86*, (im Druck).

Dreschler-Fischer u.a. 83 : *Lernen durch Beobachtung von Szenen mit bewegten Objekten: Phasen einer Systementwicklung*, Leonie S. Dreschler-Fischer, Wilfried Enkelmann und Hans-Hellmut Nagel, *DAGM-83*, pp. 29–34.

Dreschler-Fischer + Gnutzmann 87b : *Feature Selection in Colour Images for Token Matching*, L.S. Dreschler-Fischer und F. Gnutzmann, *IJCAI-87*, (im Druck).

Gershon u.a. 87 : *Highlight Identification Using Chromatic Information*, Ron Gershon, Allan D. Jepson und John K. Tsotsos, *ICCV-87*, pp. 161–170.

Horn 75 : *Obtaining Shape from Shading Information*, B.K.P. Horn, in: *Winston 75*, pp. 115–155.

Ikeuchi 84 : *Shape from Regular Patterns*, K. Ikeuchi, *Artificial Intelligence* **22**, 49–55 (1984).

Jenkin + Tsotsos 86 : *Applying Temporal Constraints to the Dynamic Stereo Problem*, Michael Jenkin und John K. Tsotsos, *Computer Vision, Graphics, and Image Processing* **33**, 16–32 (1986).

Klinker u.a. 87 : *Using a Color Reflectance Model to Separate Highlights from Object Color*, Gudrun J. Klinker, Steven A. Shafer und Takeo Kanade, *ICCV-87*, pp. 145–150.

Marr 82 : *Vision*, David Marr, Freeman & Co. San Francisco/CA 1982.

Marr + Nishihara 78 : *Visual Information Processing: Artificial Intelligence and the Sensorium of Light*, David Marr und H. Keith Nishihara, Technology Review, Oktober 1978, pp. 28–49.

Marr + Poggio 79 : *A Theory of Human Stereo Vision*, David Marr und T. Poggio, *Proc. of the Royal Society of London* **B 204**, 301–328 (1979).

Nagel 78 : *Formation of an Object Concept by Analysis of Systematic Time Variations in the Optically Perceptible Environment*, H.-H. Nagel, *Computer Graphics and Image Processing* **7**, 149–194 (1978).

Nagel 85a : *Analyse und Interpretation von Bildfolgen*, H.-H. Nagel, *Informatik-Spektrum* **8** (1985) 178–200 und 312–327.

Nagel 86 : *Image sequences — Ten (octal) Years — From Phenomenology towards a Theoretical Foundation*, Hans-Hellmut Nagel, *ICPR-86*, pp. 1174–1185.

Neumann 82 : *Knowledge Sources for Understanding and Describing Image Sequences*, Bernd Neumann, *GWAI-82*
siehe auch:
Mitteilung **IfI-HH-M-103** Universität Hamburg, Fachbereich Informatik, Hamburg, Bundesrepublik Deutschland (November 1982).

Shirai 87 : *Three-Dimensional Computer Vision*, Yoshiaki Shirai, *Springer Verlag Berlin Heidelberg New York London Paris Tokyo 87*.

Ullman 79 : *The Interpretation of Visual Motion*, S. Ullman, *The MIT Press Cambridge/MA 1979*.

Winston 75 : *The Psychology of Computer Vision*, P.H. Winston (Hrsg.)

AIMSA-86 : Proc. 2nd Int. Conf. on Artificial Intelligence, Methodology, Systems, Applications, Varna, Bulgaria, September 1986, (im Druck).

DAGM-83 : Proc. 5. DAGM-Symposium "Mustererkennung", Karlsruhe, Bundesrepublik Deutschland, Oktober 1983,H. Kazmierczak (Hrsg.), *VDE-Fachberichte, VDE-Verlag Berlin Offenbach 1983.*

DAGM-86 : Proc. 8. DAGM-Symposium, Paderborn, Bundesrepublik Deutschland, September 1986, G. Hartmann (Hrsg.), *Informatik Fachberichte* **125***, Springer Verlag Berlin Heidelberg New York London Paris Tokyo 1986.*

GWAI-82 : 6. Fachtagung über künstliche Intelligenz GWAI-82, Bad Honnef, Bundesrepublik Deutschland, September 1982, W. Wahlster (Hrsg.), *Informatik Fachberichte* ?*, Springer Verlag Berlin Heidelberg New York London Paris Tokyo 1982.*

IAS-86 : Proc. 1st Int. Conf. on Intelligent Autonomous Systems, Amsterdam, The Netherlands, Dezember 1986, (im Druck).

ICPR-86 : Proc. of the 8th Int. Conf. on Pattern Recognition, Paris, France, 1986.

IJCAI-87 : Proc. of the 10th Int. Joint Conf. on Artificial Intelligence, Milano, Italy, August 1987, *Morgan Kaufmann Publishers Inc. Los Altos/CA 1987.*

ICCV-87 : 1^{rst} International Conference on Computer Vision, June, 8–11, London, England, (J. Michael Brady, Whitman Richards und Azriel Rosenfeld (Hrsg.)), IEEE Computer Society Press, Washington, D.C. 1987.

Das Projekt Stereo-Bildfolgen wird von der Deutschen Forschungsgemeinschaft unter dem Titel Dr176/2 gefördert.

Frank Christl hat freundlicherweise die Abbildungen zur Verfügung gestellt, die mittels Programmen und Datensätzen der am SISSY-Projekt beteiligten Studenten erzeugt wurden.

KONFLIKTLÖSUNG AUF STATISTISCHER BASIS

BEI DER BILDANALYSE MIT PRODUKTIONSREGELN

Gerda Stein
Fraunhofer-Institut für Informations-und Datenverarbeitung
IITB Karlsruhe

ZUSAMMENFASSUNG

Zur Analyse von Werkstückszenen mit einem Produktionensystem wurde ein statistisches Konfliktlösungsverfahren entwickelt und erprobt. Die Erfolgsbewertung einer Produktionsregel ist der Quotient aus der relativen Häufigkeit, mit der sie zur Bildinterpretation beiträgt, und der normierten Anzahl der dabei insgesamt erforderlichen Regelanwendungen. Diese Erfolgsbewertung wird in einer Lernphase in Abhängigkeit von der jeweils vorliegenden Konfliktmenge und den zuletzt angewendeten Regeln gewonnen. Anhand der aktuell auftretenden Konfliktmenge und den aktuell zuletzt angewendeten Regeln kommt dann die Produktionsregel mit der für diese Situation höchsten Erfolgsbewertung zur Anwendung. Bei einem Mißerfolg wird die Regel mit der nächst-höchsten Erfolgsbewertung für diese Situation ausgewählt. Bereits bei kleinen Lernstichproben läßt sich mit diesem Konfliktlösungsverfahren der Suchaufwand bei der Zuordnung von Bilddaten zur Interpretation verringern. Der Erfolg des Verfahrens ist abhängig von der Interpretationsaufgabe und von dem in der Lernphase verwendeten Suchverfahren.

PROBLEMSTELLUNG

Fast jedes System, das mit Produktionsregeln arbeitet, wendet Verfahren zur Konflikt-lösung an. Die Menge der in einer Situation jeweils anwendbaren Produktionsregeln ist die Konfliktmenge. Sie ist abhängig vom Zustand der Datenbasis. Werden stets alle Produktionsregeln der Konfliktmenge ausgeführt, wird die Anzahl der neuen Elemente in der Datenbasis so groß, daß die Rechenzeit für praktische Anwendungen zu lang wird. Deshalb muß in regelbasierten Systemen eine Konfliktlösung erfolgen, bei der Produk-tionsregeln aus der Konfliktmenge ausgewählt werden.

Anhand eines bereits vorhandenen Produktionensystems zur Analyse von Werkstückszenen wurde deshalb ein statistisches Konfliktlösungsverfahren entwickelt und erprobt, das die Erfolgswahrscheinlichkeiten der Produktionsregeln in Abhängigkeit von der jeweils vorliegenden Konfliktmenge und den Vorgängerregeln berücksichtigt. Die Entwicklung des Produktionsregelsystems und seine Arbeitsweise ist ausführlich in [6] darge-stellt. Das Produktionensystem arbeitet folgendermaßen:

* Ein Vorverarbeitungsprogramm extrahiert aus Grauwertbildern Strecken und Kreis-

bögen, sogenannte Grundelemente, mit denen der Verlauf von Objektkanten stück-
weise approximiert werden soll. Es können Kantenstücke nicht berücksichtigt sein
wegen zu schwachen Kontrasts, und es können fälschlicherweise Bildbereiche, die
keine Kanten sind, wie z.B. Schatten, Glanzlichter und Aufkleber, durch
Grundelemente approximiert sein.

Produktionsregeln geben an, wie die Grundelemente einer Werkstückszene zu
Zwischenelementen und zu lokalen Formmerkmalen zusammengefaßt werden, mit denen
für örtlich begrenzte Bereiche der Verlauf von den Kanten eines Werkstücks
beschrieben wird. Anhand der Formmerkmale wird, ebenfalls mit Produktionsregeln,
die Werkstückbeschreibung erstellt.

Auswahl des Verfahrens

Methoden zur Konfliktlösung bei Produktionensystemen können in drei Kategorien
eingeteilt werden:

1. Heuristische Maßnahmen, bei denen der Wissensingenieur aufgrund seiner Kennt-
   nisse über das Aufgabengebiet die Produktionsregeln problem- oder auch situa-
   tionsspezifisch nach ihrer Priorität sortiert (einige sind z.B. in [3]
   aufgeführt).

2. Auswahl von Produktionsregeln anhand statistischer Erfolgsbewertungen, wobei die
   Erfolgswahrscheinlichkeiten der Regeln [1] bzw. die Rückschlußwahrscheinlichkei-
   ten für den Erfolg der Regeln bei den verschiedenen Zuständen der Datenbasis [2]
   zugrunde gelegt werden.

3. Bewertung der Daten in der Datenbasis mit Gütemaßen, um eine problemspezifische
   Fokussierung auf kleine Teilmengen der Daten zu ermöglichen (z.B. [4] und [5]).

Lediglich die zweite Methode führt zu analytisch handhabbaren Konzepten, die unabhängig von der Aufgabenstellung übertragbar sind. Die hierzu existierenden Ansätze
machen jedoch Voraussetzungen über statistische Unabhängigkeiten von Regelanwendungen
und von Daten in der Datenbasis, die oft nicht erfüllt sind, oder sie erfordern eine
für praktische Anwendungen nicht vertretbare Anzahl verschiedener Lernstichproben.
Deshalb wurde ein Verfahren entwickelt und erprobt, bei dem die Erfolgswahrschein-

lichkeiten der Produktionsregeln zur Konfliktlösung herangezogen werden, ohne daß unzutreffende Unabhängigkeitspostulate vorausgesetzt werden müssen und bei dem eine Lernstichprobe ausreichend ist.

Statistisches Konfliktlösungsverfahren

In einer Lernphase werden die relativen Häufigkeiten ermittelt, wie oft die Anwendung einer bestimmten Produktionsregel beim Vorliegen einer bestimmten Konfliktmenge einen Beitrag zur Bildung eines Formmerkmals liefert, und wie hoch der Aufwand war (Anzahl der Knoten, die bei der Suche für die Zuordnung von Modell zu Daten bis zum Erreichen des Zielknotens durchlaufen werden müssen). Dabei wird registriert, welche Vorgänger-regeln angewendet wurden. Vorgängerregeln sind die Regeln, die angewendet wurden, um die Zwischenelemente zu erzeugen, aus denen das neue Element aufgebaut werden soll. Die Quotienten aus relativen Häufigkeiten und dem normierten Aufwand (bezogen auf den längsten Weg) sind die Erfolgsbewertungen und werden mit den dazugehörigen Situationen in eine Konfliktdatei eingetragen.

Nach [1] ist die optimale Strategie in Hinblick auf ein Kostenkriterium die Entscheidung für die Regel, bei der der Quotient aus Erfolgswahrscheinlichkeit und Ausführungskosten maximal ist, ohne daß dort die aktuell vorliegende Konfliktmenge und die Vorgängerregeln berücksichtigt werden. Voraussetzung ist jedoch dann die Unabhängigkeit der Regelanwendungen voneinander und daß jede Regelanwendung ein Schritt zum Erreichen des Zieles ist.

In der Anwendungsphase werden die Erfolgsbewertungen der Produktionsregeln für die jeweiligen Konfliktmengen und Vorgängerregeln zur Konfliktlösung verwendet. In der Konfliktdatei aus der Lernphase wird nach der größten gemeinsamen Schnittmenge bezüglich der aktuellen und der abgespeicherten Konfliktmengen und Vorgängerregeln gesucht. Es wird diejenige Produktionsregel ausgewählt, der die größte Erfolgsbewer-tung zugeordnet ist. Bei Mißerfolg wird jeweils die Produktionsregel mit dem nächstniederen Wert ausgewählt oder es wird nach der Situation mit der nächstgrößten Schnittmenge gesucht.

Ergebnisse und Bewertung

Das Verfahren zur Konfliktlösung wurde anhand zweier verschiedenr Szenen erprobt:

1. Ein metallisches Werkstück, das bei unterschiedlichen Beleuchtungen aufgenommen wurde, und dessen Position und Drehlage erkannt werden soll.

2. Porzellanteller mit Oberflächenfehlern, die ebenfalls bei unterschiedlicher Beleuchtung aufgenommen wurden. Hier soll der Fehlertyp klassifiziert werden.

Die Bilder der Szenen sind in [6] gezeigt. Folgende Suchverfahren für die Zuordnung von Modell zu Daten kamen in der Lernphase zur Anwendung:

* Eine Breitensuche mit unterschiedlicher Bergrenzung der maximal zulässigen Tiefe.

* Eine Tiefensuche mit Rücksetzmöglichkeit und unterschiedlicher Qualitätsbewertung eines Zustands im Suchbaum.

Tabelle 1 zeigt den Vergleich bei einer Tiefensuche mit Rücksetzmöglichkeit. Die Tabelle für die Ergebnisse der unterschiedlichen Breitensuchen hat keinen Platz und wird nur qualitativ diskutiert.

Anzahl der Produktionsregeln		Werkstück: 22		Teller: 18			
Anzahl der Formmerkmale		Werkstück: 3		Teller: 8			
Anzahl der Grundelemente		Werkstück: 123±37		Teller: 83±27			
Lernstichprobe		Werkstück: 50		Teller: 42			
Teststichprobe		6					
Anzahl der Regelanwendungen	Werkstück	873±112	906±109	716±82	664±96	761±128	687±142	644±122
	Teller	401±112	337±96	285±81	305±62	387±92	312±74	341±87
Regelanwendungen Grundelement	Werkstück	7.1±3.0	7.4±3.0	5.8±2.2	5.4±2.6	6.2±3.5	6.0±3.8	5.2±3.3
	Teller	4.8±4.1	4.0±3.6	3.4±3.0	3.7±2.3	4.7±3.4	3.8±2.7	4.1±3.2
Qualitätsbewertung eines Zustands im Suchbaum	Tiefe n im Suchbaum	$q_1(x)$ Konturlänge ideal	$q_2(x)$ Konturlänge real	$q_3(x)$ Konturlänge gewichtet	$q_4(x)$ Flächeninhalt ideal	$q_5(x)$ Flächeninhalt real	$q_6(x)$ Flächeninhalt gewichtet

Tabelle 1: Ermittlung der Erfolgsbewertungen von Produktionsregeln in der Lernphase mit einer Tiefensuche mit Rücksetzmöglichkeit für zwei verschiedene Szenentypen. Mit den Qualitätsbewertungen $q_1(x)$ bis $q_6(x)$ werden die Vollständigkeit, geometrische Korrektheit und Fortgeschrittenheit eines Zustands (Bildelements) erfaßt. In der Anwendungsphase werden die Erfolgsbewertungen als heuristische Funktionen $h^*(x)$ in einer A-Suche verwendet.

Wird in der Lernphase eine Breitensuche verwendet, so verringert sich der Suchaufwand in der Anwendungsphase umso mehr, je ausführlicher die Breitensuche in der Lernphase erfolgt. Dieses Ergebnis ist an beiden Szenentypen unterschiedlich ausgeprägt zu sehen. Wegen der kombinatorischen Explosion muß in der Lernphase die Tiefe, bis zu der jeweils in voller Breite gesucht wird, beschränkt werden. Es wurden zwei Qualitätsmaße $q_2(x)$ und $q_5(x)$ (siehe Tabelle 1) verglichen, mit denen in der maximal zulässigen Tiefe eine Auswahl der weiterhin verfügbaren Knoten im Suchbaum vorgenommen wurde. Die Maße zeigen keine signifikanten Auswirkungen auf den Suchaufwand in der Anwendungsphase.

Wird in der Lernphase eine Tiefensuche mit Rücksetzmöglichkeit verwendet, so verringert sich der Suchaufwand in der Anwendungsphase weniger als bei einer Breitensuche jeweils bis zur 5. Ebene, jedoch mehr als bei einer Breitensuche jeweils bis zur 3. Ebene. Ist also die Konfliktmenge im Mittel stets groß (hoher Verzweigungsfaktor), so ist die Tiefensuche mit Rücksetzmöglichkeit besser geeignet als die stark eingeschränkte Breitensuche, um zuverlässige Erfolgsbewertungen der Produktionsregeln zu ermitteln.

Auffällig ist, daß die Definition der heuristischen Maße zur Bewertung der Qualität eines Zustands keine größere Auswirkung auf die jeweils ermittelten Erfolgsbewertungen hat. Bei den Werkstückszenen scheint die Berücksichtigung von Störungen in der Qualitätsbewertung einen positiven Einfluß auf der Zuverlässigkeit der Erfolgsbewertungen zu haben. Dieser Trend läßt sich jedoch anhand der Tellerszenen nicht bestätigen.

Literatur

[1] J.A.Barnett: How Much is Control Knowledge Worth? A Primitive Example. Artificial Intelligence, 22, 1984, S. 77-89.

[2] E.Charniak: The Bayesian Basis of Common Sense Medical Diagnosis. AAAI 83, Nat. Conf. on Art. Intelligence, Washington DC, Aug. 1983, S. 70-73.

[3] J.McDermott, C.Forgy: Production System Conflict Resolution Strategies. In: Pattern-Directed Inference Systems. Ed.: D.A.Waterman, F.Hayes-Roth, Academic Press, New York, 1978, S.177-199.

[4] J.Pearl: Knowledge versus Search: A Quantitative Analysis Using A*. Artificial Intelligence, 20. 1983, S. 1-13.

[5] L.A.Rendell: Toward a Unified Approach for Conceptual Knowledge Acquisition. The AI Magazine, Winter 1983, S. 19-27.

[6] G.Stein: Automatische Strukturanalyse von Bildsignalen aufgrund recherinterner Modelle aus lokalen Formmerkmalen. DFG IITB Bericht Nr. A 3030, 1986, IITB Karlsruhe.

EPEX: BILDFOLGENDEUTUNG AUF EPISODENEBENE

Ingrid M. Walter
Fakultät für Informatik, Universität Karlsruhe
Postfach 6980, 7500 Karlsruhe 1

Kurzfassung: Die Extraktion von Episoden aus Bildfolgen erfordert Wissen über Objekte und Abläufe sowie über deren Verknüpfung. Da bei dem Umfang der Datenmengen für die Episodenextraktion der Einsatz von Datenbanken sinnvoll erscheint, sollten die Formalismen zur Darstellung von Objekten und Abläufen so gewählt werden, daß sie sich auf Datenbankschnittstellen abbilden lassen und mit dem Verknüpfungsmechanismus verträglich sind. Die hier vorgestellten Repräsentationsformen für Objekte und Abläufe basieren auf Ideen von KL-ONE, Inferenzen werden mittels ATN-ähnlichen Regeln durchgeführt. Das Zusammenspiel der einzelnen Teile wird erläutert.

1. Einleitung

Ziel des hier vorgestellten Ansatzes ist es, Inhalte von *zeitlichen* Bildfolgen [Nagel 85] auf einer Abstraktionsebene beschreiben zu können, die über die rein geometrische hinausgeht. Zu diesem Zweck wurden von [Nagel 83] die beiden Abstraktionsebenen Ereignis und Geschichte eingeführt. Eine Erweiterung dieser Abstraktionshierarchie um die mittlere Abstraktionsebene der *Episode* [Walter et al. 86a] soll hier zur Beschreibung von Bildfolgeninhalten dienen.

Episoden lassen sich für die Zwecke der Bilddeutung durch eine Reihe von Eigenschaften charakterisieren [Walter et al. 86a]. Eine dieser Eigenschaften ist, daß sich Episoden aus *Vorgängen* zusammensetzen, die entweder elementar (direkt auf der geometrischen Beschreibung aufbauend) oder selbst wieder aus anderen Vorgängen zusammengesetzt sind. Eine weitere Eigenschaft von Episoden betrifft die Variabilität der eine Episode bildenden Vorgänge. Das bedeutet zum einen, daß gewisse Vorgänge in einer Episode zwar möglich aber nicht notwendig sind. Zum anderen können sich zeitliche Beziehungen zwischen Vorgängen in unterschiedlichen Ausprägungen einer Episode unterscheiden.

Für das System zur Episodenextraktion aus Bildfolgen (*EPEX*) gehen wir davon aus, daß sämtliche in der zu untersuchenden Bildfolge vorkommenden geometrischen *Objekte* beschrieben und ihre Koordinaten zu jedem Zeitpunkt bekannt sind. Zusätzlich sind noch allgemeine Informationen über potentiell vorkommende Objekte vorhanden, z.B. ob sie beweglich sind. Die Gesamtheit aller Daten über Objekte wird *Objektbereich* genannt. Innerhalb des Objektbereichs wird zwischen *Objektgattungen* und *Objektausprägungen* unterschieden. Eine Gattung beschreibt Eigenschaften, die für gleichartige Objekte einheitlich sind. Eine Ausprägung beschreibt ein zu einer Gattung gehörendes einzelnes Objekt. Ausprägung und Gattung sind durch eine *Gattungszugehörigkeitsbeziehung* miteinander verbunden.

Aufbauend auf den Daten des Objektbereichs sollen Episoden mit den oben erwähnten Eigenschaften extrahiert werden. Elementare Vorgänge sowie zusammengesetzte Vorgänge bis hinauf zu Episoden werden innerhalb von EPEX einheitlich als *Abläufe* bezeichnet. Die Gesamtheit der Daten über potentielle und tatsächlich in der Bildfolge vorkommende Abläufe wird im *Ablaufbereich* zusammengefaßt. Analog zum Objektbereich wird auch innerhalb des Ablaufbereichs zwischen *Ablaufgattungen* und *Ablaufausprägungen* unterschieden, die wiederum durch Gattungszugehörigkeitsbeziehungen verbunden sind.

Für die Extraktion von Ablaufausprägungen aus den Daten des Objektbereichs werden *Regeln* benutzt. Der *Regelbereich* bildet die dritte Komponente des EPEX-Systems. Regeln werden mit Hilfe eines Regelinterpretierers ausgewertet, der durch Benutzeranfragen angestoßen wird. Die Zusammenhänge innerhalb von EPEX sind in Bild 1 dargestellt.

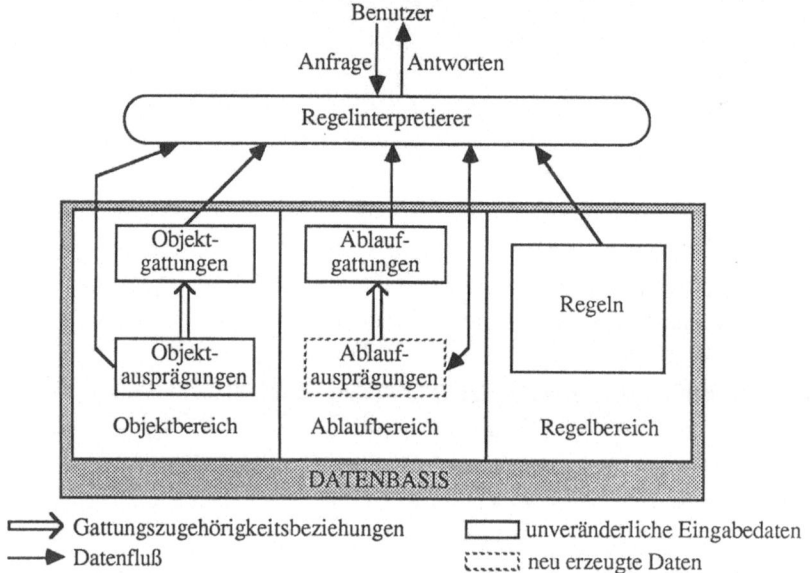

Bild 1: Das EPEX-System und der Datenfluß in EPEX

EPEX betrachtet den gesamten Objektbereich, alle Regeln sowie die Ablaufgattungen als Eingabedaten, die während der Bearbeitung einer Benutzeranfrage nicht verändert werden. Die Ablaufausprägungen dagegen sind Ausgabedaten, mit deren Hilfe die Anfragen beantwortet werden können. Ablaufausprägungen sind zunächst nicht explizit vorhanden, sondern müssen mittels der Regeln aus dem Objektbereich und den Ablaufgattungen hergeleitet werden. Es können nur solche Abläufe hergeleitet werden, für die eine entsprechende Ablaufgattung existiert. Dieses Vorgehen bedeutet, daß EPEX Verifikationen von vorgegebenen Hypothesen durchführt.

Ausgehend von der EPEX-Struktur und den in [Walter et al. 86b] dargestellten Eigenschaften der einzelnen EPEX-Bereiche sind geeignete Darstellungsmöglichkeiten zu entwickeln. Der Umfang der bei der Bildfolgendeutung anfallenden Daten läßt es sinnvoll erscheinen, Datenbanken zur Verwaltung der Daten und zur Unterstützung der Auswertung zu benutzen. Arbeiten aus dem Bereich der Entwurfs-datenbanken ([Dittrich et al. 85]) legen es allerdings nahe, daß die bei konventionellen Datenbanken vorhandenen Ausdrucksmittel (Datenmodelle) für eine natürlich interpretierbare Darstellung der EPEX-Daten nicht ausreichen. Deshalb wird ein Repräsentationsformalismus unabhängig von vorhandenen Datenbankmöglichkeiten entwickelt und dann auf konventionelle Datenmodelle abgebildet. Später kann eine Übertragung auf möglicherweise geeignetere objektorientierte Datenmodelle erfolgen.

Der im folgenden vorgestellte EPEX-Repräsentationsformalismus für den Objekt-und Ablaufbereich baut auf einigen grundlegenden Ideen von KL-ONE [Brachman und Schmolze 85] auf. Die Darstellung der Regeln basiert auf Erweiterten Übergangsnetzen (Augmented Transition Networks (ATN) [Woods 70]). Es wird vorausgesetzt, daß KL-ONE und ATN sowie ihre graphische Veranschaulichung bekannt sind, so daß nur die Grundsätze erläutert werden. Beispiele sind neben der angegebenen Literatur in [Walter et al. 86b], [Walter et al. 87b] und [Ikker 87] zu finden.

2. Der Repräsentationsformalismus für Objekt- und Ablaufbereich

Das EPEX-System benötigt Repräsentationsmittel sowohl für Gattungen als auch für Ausprägungen. Ein geeigneter Formalismus soll die Modellierung beliebiger Diskursbereiche erlauben. Zur Zeit benutzen wir den Diskursbereich „Straßenverkehr" als Validierungshilfsmittel für die Adäquatheit des Ansatzes. Die Beispiele kommen deshalb auch aus diesem Bereich.

Die oben beschriebene Sichtweise des zu modellierenden Wissens hat gewisse Ähnlichkeiten mit objektorientierten Ansätzen, so daß sich die Verwendung bestehender Werkzeuge wie LOOPS [Stefik et al. 83] anbietet. Dagegen spricht aber vor allem die von uns angestrebte Integration mit einem Datenbanksystem, die Eingriffe in den Interpretierer des Werkzeugs selbst erfordert. Wir benutzen deshalb eine eigene Repräsentationsform, deren Grundelemente sich an KL-ONE orientieren.

Im EPEX-Formalismus werden Gattungen durch *generische Begriffe* (generic concepts) und Ausprägungen durch *Individuen-Begriffe* (individual concepts) modelliert. Die Gattungszugehörigkeitsbeziehung entspricht der *Individuierungsbeziehung* (individuation) aus KL-ONE. Zwischen generischen Begriffen bestehen Unter-/Oberbegriffs-Beziehungen, womit sich ein hierarchisches Vererbungsnetzwerk ergibt. Andere zweistellige Beziehungen zwischen generischen Begriffen werden durch *Rollen* dargestellt. Da diese gerichtet sind, kann man die Menge aller von einem generischen Begriff ausgehenden Rollen auch als „slots" des Begriffs auffassen und Begriffe so als „Frame"-ähnliche Strukturen betrac.. n. Rollen werden durch Rollendeskriptoren spezifiziert, die Angaben über Definitionsbereich, Wertebereich, Kardinalität enthalten. Rollen können auch durch Restriktion und Differenzierung anderer Rollen definiert werden.

KL-ONE enthält eine Inferenzkomponente, den Klassifikator, zum automatischen Einfügen neuer Begriffe an der richtigen Stelle des Netzes. Der Objektbereich wird in EPEX als fest vorgegeben vorausgesetzt und benötigt keine Inferenzkomponente. Die für den Ablaufbereich erforderlichen Inferenzen zur Bestimmung von Ausprägungen würden dagegen die Fähigkeiten von bisher bekannten

Klassifikatoralgorithmen bei weitem übersteigen und müssen außerdem durch komplexe diskurs-bereichsabhängige Kontrollinformation gesteuert werden. Aus diesem Grund führen wir Inferenzen mit einem eigenen Regelbereich durch. Die Unterscheidung zwischen primitiven und definierten generischen Begriffen in KL-ONE ist für unsere Zwecke (bisher) nicht erforderlich.

EPEX benutzt noch folgende Beschreibungsmittel, die sich aus Erfordernissen der Anwendung ergeben und in dieser Form nicht in KL-ONE vorhanden sind:
- Standardwertangabe beim Rollendeskriptor
- generische Rollenfüller
- zeitabhängige Individuierungsbeziehung
- zeitabhängige Rollenfüller
- abhängige Rollen
- abhängige Rollen als Strukturbedingungen.

Im folgenden gehen wir auf die Eigenschaften einiger Beschreibungsmittel näher ein, insbesondere auf die Zeitabhängigkeit und die abhängigen Rollen. Bild 2 zeigt die Verwendungsmöglichkeiten verschiedener EPEX-Konstrukte an einem Beispiel, auf das später mehrfach Bezug genommen wird.

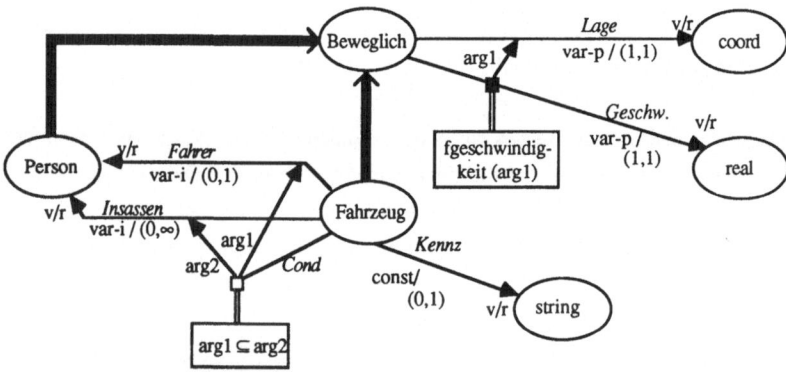

Bild 2: Modellierung mit dem EPEX-Formalismus

EPEX befaßt sich mit der Auswertung zeitlicher Bildfolgen, denen ein diskreter Zeitbegriff zugrundeliegt. Eine inhärente Eigenschaft jeder Ablaufausprägung ist es, daß sie für ein Zeitintervall definiert ist, das auch geeignet modelliert werden muß. Eine zunächst plausible Lösung bieten die *Kontexte* aus KL-ONE an, die ebenfalls eine Vererbungshierarchie bilden können. Da die Zeit diskret ist, würde der endliche Verband aller Teilintervalle des Bildfolgenintervalls gerade den möglichen Kontexten entsprechen. Diese Lösung wäre aber problematisch, da viele Abläufe zusammengesetzt und nicht durativ sind, so daß die Vererbung auf Teilintervalle unzulässig ist. Eine Parkplatzsuche ist beispielsweise in hinreichend kleinen Teilintervallen allenfalls ein Bewegungsvorgang. Außerdem würden bei dieser Lösung sämtliche Ausprägungen den Kontexten zugeordnet und das Netz selbst würde überhaupt keine Information mehr über die Ausprägungen enthalten. Aus diesen Gründen haben wir diese Lösung verworfen und verwalten die Zeitabhängigkeiten auf andere Weise.

Zeitabhängigkeit tritt in EPEX auf zwei Arten auf. Zum einen können Ausprägungen zu verschiedenen Zeitpunkten/Zeitintervallen zu unterschiedlichen Gattungen gehören. Beispielsweise kann eine Ausprägung „Müller" zur Gattung „Person" und eine Zeitlang zur Gattung „Fahrradfahrer" gehören. Innerhalb des EPEX-Formalismus wird dies dadurch realisiert, daß die Individuierungsbeziehung prinzipiell zeitabhängig ist, d.h. sie wird um die Angabe eines Zeitintervalls erweitert. Dadurch werden natürlich auch die Inferenzen beeinflußt, die nun die verschiedensten zeitbezogenen Aussagen über den Zustand der bekannten Fakten ableiten können müssen.

Zum anderen können Rollen zeitveränderlich sein. Beispielsweise trifft dies auf die Rolle „Fahrer" in Bild 2 zu. Während des Zeitraums der Zugehörigkeit einer Ausprägung zu „Fahrzeug" kann der Rollenfüller für „Fahrer" wechseln, zu jedem Zeitpunkt/Zeitintervall darf aber höchstens ein Rollenfüller existieren. Zeitabhängige Rollen ermöglichen somit eine Historienbildung. Im Datenbankbereich werden verschiedene Arten von Zeitveränderlichkeiten unterschieden [Klopprogge und Lockemann 83], wobei die Unterscheidung im wesentlichen auf „Retrieval-Eigenschaften" beruht. Für die Inferenzen sind in EPEX zwei der bekannten Arten relevant, die wir *Zeitintervall-veränderlich* (var-i) und *Zeitpunkt-veränderlich* (var-p) nennen. Bei Zeitintervall-veränderlichen Rollen wird bei Anfrage nach dem Rollenfüller zu einem Zeitpunkt, für den der Wert nicht explizit abgespeichert ist, der zuletzt vor diesem Zeitpunkt bekannte Wert benutzt. Bei Zeitpunkt-veränderlichen Rollen ist der Rollenfüller in einer solchen Situation nicht bekannt und kann allenfalls durch eine Extrapolationsfunktion geschätzt werden. Von diesem Typ ist die Rolle „Lage" von „Beweglich" in Bild 2.

Das Beschreibungsmittel *abhängige Rolle* im EPEX-Repräsentationsformalismus erlaubt die Darstellung funktionaler Abhängigkeiten zwischen den Rollen eines Begriffs. Dazu wird im Rollendeskriptor die Angabe einer Funktion erlaubt, die als Eingabeparameter die Füller anderer Rollen desselben Begriffs benutzt und als Wert Individuen-Begriffe des im Rollendeskriptors angegebenen Wertebereichs liefert. Rollenfüller der Rolle „Geschw." in Bild 2 werden auf diese Weise aus Füllern der Rolle „Lage" berechnet. Berechnete Rollenfüller müssen nicht explizit gespeichert werden, sondern können bei Bedarf jedesmal neu erzeugt werden. Die Semantik des Beschreibungsmittels Rolle wird durch diese Erweiterung nicht verändert, insbesondere sind Kardinalität und Wertebereich unabhängig davon spezifizierbar und auch die Vererbung an Spezialisierungen bleibt unverändert.

Diese Erweiterung zur Darstellung funktionaler Abhängigkeiten erlaubt auch eine natürliche Darstellung von Strukturbedingungen, die in KL-ONE (mit Ausnahme der „role value maps") selbst relativ kompliziert beschrieben werden. Im EPEX-Formalismus sind nur Strukturbedingungen zugelassen, die Abhängigkeiten zwischen den Rollen eines Begriffs beschreiben. Eine Strukturbedingung („Cond") ist durch eine Funktion gegeben, die zu gegebenen Rollenfüllern einen Wahrheitswert liefert. In Bild 2 wird durch die Strukturbedingung „⊆" festgelegt, daß ein Füller von „Fahrer" auch Füller von „Insassen" sein muß. Ist der Wahrheitswert „false", kann die Rollenbeziehung und gegebenenfalls die Individuierungsbeziehung nicht etabliert werden. Strukturbedingungen entsprechen im Prinzip abhängigen Rollen, wobei die Kardinalität stets eins ist und der Rollenfüller dem Wahrheitswert „true" entspricht, der jedoch nicht explizit gespeichert wird. Strukturbedingungen werden wie andere Rollen vererbt.

Neben den angeführten allgemeinen Konstrukten stellt der EPEX-Repräsentationsformalismus noch einige vordefinierte Begriffe zur Verfügung. Dies sind zum einen Standardvorgaben wie „integer", „real", „boolean" und „string". Daneben existieren Vorgaben, die direkt auf die Erfordernisse der Bilddeutung zugeschnitten sind. Für den Objektbereich sind dies geometrische Gebilde wie „Polygon", „Fläche", „Körper", „3-D-Koordinaten". Für den Ablaufbereich werden Abläufe vorgegeben, die elementaren Vorgängen entsprechen, d.h. direkt auf der geometrischen Bildfolgenbeschreibung aufsetzen. Einige davon entsprechen „Primitives" der Conceptual-Dependency-(CD)-Theorie von Schank [Schank und Abelson 77]: „bewegen" („ptrans"), „bewegen eines Teils" („move"), „vereinnahmen" („ingest"), „ausstoßen" („expel"). Zusätzlich werden die zu „bewegen" und „bewegen eines Teils" komplementären Abläufe „verharren" und „verharren eines Teils" sowie die Abläufe „vereinigen" und „separieren" vorgegeben. „vereinigen" und „separieren" entsprechen in gewisser Weise „vereinnahmen" und „ausstoßen", wobei jedoch alle beteiligten Objekte stets sichtbar sind. Außerdem stehen einige vordefinierte Strukturbedingungen zur Verfügung. Dazu gehören Vergleiche wie „gleich" und „ungleich" sowie Beziehungen zwischen Zeitintervallen wie „vorher" und „gleichzeitig". Die zeitlichen Beziehungen in EPEX entsprechen den in [Allen 84] eingeführten.

3. Aufbau von Objekt- und Ablaufbereich

In diesem Abschnitt wird aufgezeigt, wie Objekt- und Ablaufbereich mit den in Abschnitt 2 bereitgestellten Mitteln modelliert werden können. Dabei unterscheidet sich der Objektbereich nicht von dem, was man aus in der Literatur gängigen Beispielen kennt: Objektgattungen enthalten Information über die Zusammensetzung von Objekten aus anderen und über die Beziehungen zwischen ihnen (siehe auch Bild 2). Im Diskursbereich „Straßenverkehr" stehen in der Generalisierungshierarchie unmittelbar unter der Gattung „Objekt" die Gattungen „beweglich", „unbeweglich" und „abstrakt". Unter „abstrakt" fallen alle Gattungen, die allgemeines Hintergrundwissen beschreiben, z.B. Vorfahrtsregeln, zulässige Höchstgeschwindigkeiten.

Bei der Beschreibung einer Ablaufgattung muß zunächst angegeben werden, welche Objekte in welcher Weise an einer Ausprägung der Ablaufgattung beteiligt sind. Kasusrahmen, wie die von [Fillmore 68] verwendeten, reichen für den Zweck der Zuordnung aus. Außerdem wird bei einer Ablaufgattung angegeben, aus welchen anderen Abläufen sich eine Ausprägung zusammensetzen kann und welche wesentlichen Beziehungen zwischen ihnen und zwischen den beteiligten Objekten bestehen. Die allgemeinste Modellierung von „Parkplatzsuchen" könnte z.B. wie in Bild 3 dargestellt aussehen.

Für eine Weiterverarbeitung interessante Varianten von Ablaufgattungen werden durch die Generalisierungshierarchie modelliert. Es gibt Varianten, die sich lediglich durch Restriktionen der Kasusrahmen-Rollen unterscheiden, z.B. könnte man „Parkplatzsuchen" aus Bild 3 durch eine Wertrestriktion der Rolle „Location" von „unbebaute Fläche" zu „Straße" zu „Parkplatzsuche - Straßenrand" spezialisieren. Unabhängig davon können aber auch die zugelassenen Teilabläufe weiter spezialisiert werden. Beispielsweise könnte die Rolle „Teil1" aus Bild 3 zu Rollen mit den Wertebereichen „langsam-fahren" und „rangieren" differenziert werden.

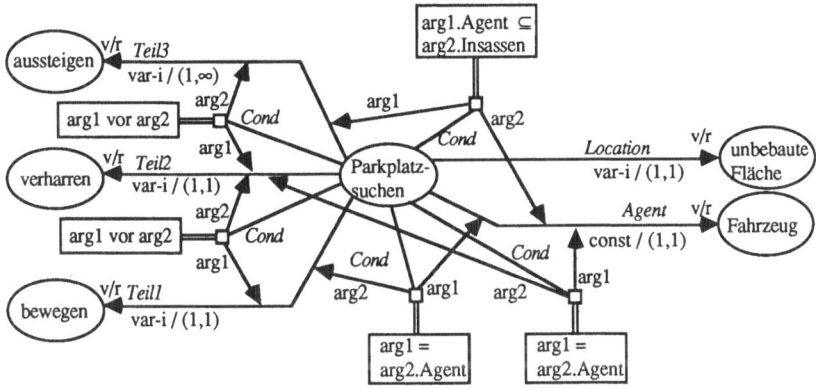

Bild 3: Modellierung der Ablaufgattung „Parkplatzsuchen"

Ablaufgattungen beschreiben die Eigenschaften, die in einer aufbauenden Weiterverarbeitung der gefundenen Abläufe verwendet werden können. Für EPEX steht aber der Gesichtspunkt im Vordergrund, die Bildfolgeninformation zu Ablaufausprägungen zusammenzusetzen. Dies erfordert über die Ablaufgattungen hinausgehende Informationen, etwa über mögliche aber nicht unbedingt notwendige Teilabläufe oder über Variabilitätstoleranzen. Da dieses Wissen nur dem Extraktionsprozeß dient, nicht aber einer späteren Weiterverarbeitung der Ergebnisse, werden diese Informationen nicht im Ablaufbereich sondern im Regelbereich dargestellt. Die in der maschinellen Sprachverarbeitung verwendete Darstellung von Abläufen durch skriptartige Strukturen [Schank und Abelson 77] findet sich somit in unserem Ansatz in verteilter Form wieder: Die Ablaufgattungen enthalten den für die Weiterverarbeitung wichtigen statischen Anteil der Skripts, die Regeln den für den Extraktionsprozeß erforderlichen Rest, wie Alternativen oder Auswertungsreihenfolge der Teilabläufe. Je nach Anwendungsfall kann die Aufteilung der Skripts zwischen den beiden Teilen verschieden sein.

4. Repräsentation von Regeln

Der Regelbereich in EPEX enthält die Information, wie Ablaufausprägungen aus den Daten des Objekt- und Ablaufbereichs extrahiert werden können. Grundlage für die Darstellung von Regeln in EPEX sind die Erweiterten Übergangsnetze (Augmented Transition Networks - ATN) [Woods 70]. Ein ATN besteht aus einem Satz von Registern, die die innerhalb des ATN zugänglichen lokalen Daten enthalten, sowie aus einer Menge von Zuständen und Zustandsübergängen. Den Übergängen sind Tests und Aktionen zugeordnet, die auf den Registern operieren. ATN-Übergänge können von einem der folgenden Typen sein: Cat(egory), Seek, Jump, Send. In EPEX wird vorausgesetzt, daß zu jeder Ablaufgattung auch ein ATN existiert, das die Extraktion von Ausprägungen der Gattung steuert.

Beim Abarbeiten liefern Cat- und Seek-Übergänge jeweils einen Datensatz als „Ergebnis", der von den Tests des Übergangs auf Zulässigkeit überprüft werden kann und dessen Bestandteile von den Aktionen des Übergangs ganz oder teilweise in den Registersatz des aktuellen ATN übernommen werden können. In EPEX-ATN sind Cat-Übergänge mit Zugriffen auf den Objektbereich assoziiert. Das Ergebnis eines

Cat-Übergangs ist eine Objektausprägung oder eine Menge von anderen Daten aus dem Objektbereich. Ein Seek-Übergang entspricht wie üblich dem Aufruf eines anderen ATNs. Ist das aufgerufene ATN einer Ablaufgattung zugeordnet, so kann das Ergebnis des Aufrufs eine Ablaufausprägung sein, die entweder durch das ATN neu erzeugt oder durch Zugriff auf den Ablaufbereich besorgt wird. Seek-Übergänge sind also mit dem Ablaufbereich assoziiert. Cat- und Seek-Übergänge sind weiter klassifiziert nach Zugriff auf Ausprägungen, Gattungen oder negierenden Zugriff auf Ausprägungen (negation as failure). Die Semantik der Jump- und Send-Übergänge wird beibehalten. Zusätzlich wird ein *Initial*-Übergang eingeführt, der zum Anfangszustand eines ATN führt. Dabei wird unter anderem überprüft, ob das ATN einer Ablaufgattung zugeordnet ist. In diesem Fall werden die die Ablaufgattung beschreibenden Strukturen als Teil des ATN-Registersatzes übernommen (siehe [Walter et al. 87b]).

Der ATN-Formalismus beschreibt zwar die Existenz von Aktionen und Tests, nicht aber deren Form und Inhalt. In EPEX sind für Tests und Aktionen beliebige Lisp-Ausdrücke zugelassen, die aber nur auf den Registerinhalten des zugehörigen ATNs arbeiten. Datenaustausch zwischen verschiedenen ATNs sowie zwischen ATNs und Objekt- und Ablaufbereich ist nur über in EPEX vorgegebene Funktionen möglich. Im folgenden werden einige der vorgegebenen Aktionen und Tests beschrieben.

Zur Erzeugung von Ablaufausprägungen existiert eine Aktion „erzeuge-ablauf" für Send-Übergänge. Sie benützt dafür die aktuellen Registerdaten sowie die Gattungsinformation im Ablaufbereich. Die erzeugte Ablaufausprägung kann im Ablaufbereich abgelegt werden.

Alle bei einer Ablaufgattung angegebenen Teilabläufe sind notwendige Bestandteile einer zugehörigen Ablaufausprägung. Es kann bei der Ablaufextraktion allerdings vorkommen, daß der Ablauf nur unvollständig extrahiert werden kann, weil z.B. die Bildfolge vorher endet. Wurden bis dahin jedoch schon genügend viele Merkmale für eine Zuordnung gefunden, sind hypothetische Aussagen über die fehlenden Teilabläufe möglich. Als fehlende und zu ergänzende Teilabläufe werden nur diejenigen betrachtet, die in der Ablaufgattung angegeben sind. Am Beispiel „Parkplatzsuchen" aus Bild 3 ist dies leicht zu sehen. Für eine Ausprägung „Parkplatzsuchen" müssen Ausprägungen von „bewegen", „verharren" und „aussteigen" extrahiert werden. Sind im Rahmen der Auswertung von „Parkplatzsuchen" Ausprägungen von „bewegen" und „verharren" extrahiert worden, und endet z.B. damit die Bildfolge, kann man davon ausgehen, daß „aussteigen" als Fortsetzung zu erwarten ist. In diesem Fall kann man aus der Information in der Ablaufgattung und den Ausprägungen eine hypothetische Fortsetzung erzeugen: Ausprägungen von „aussteigen", wobei als „Agent" jeweils ein Füller von „Insassen" des Fahrzeugs benutzt wird, das als Ausprägung von „Fahrzeug" ermittelt wurde. Die Erzeugung solcher hypothetischer Ausprägungen wird durch die Aktion „erzeuge-hypothetischen-ablauf" durchgeführt.

Beim Zugriff auf den Objekt- bzw. Ablaufbereich macht EPEX von den Zugriffsmöglichkeiten auf Datenbanken besonderen Gebrauch. Zugriffe sind mit Bedingungen für die gesuchten Daten verknüpft. Diese Bedingungen entsprechen Tests, die bereits bei der Gewinnung des Ergebnisses angewandt werden und nicht erst hinterher die gelieferten Ergebnisse wieder verwerfen. Alle Tests, die direkt beim Zugriff durchgeführt werden können, sind von EPEX vorgegeben. Dazu gehören Vergleichsbedingungen wie „kleiner", „gleich", außerdem Zeitbedingungen wie „gleichzeitig", „vorher", ..., die auf zeitabhängigen Rollen arbeiten. An geometrischen Bedingungen sind Angaben wie „innerhalb-Kreis" vorhanden, die mögliche Positionen von Objekten einschränken. Genauere Angaben enthält [Ikker 87].

Neben diesen Bedingungen existieren noch vordefinierte Tests, die nur auf den Registern eines ATN arbeiten. Ein großer Teil dieser vorgegebenen Tests hat die gleiche Bedeutung wie die schon erwähnten Bedingungen. Allerdings sind diese Tests nicht mehr auf eine Ausprägung beschränkt, sondern können Mengen von Ausprägungen bearbeiten. Vor allem für geometrische Beziehungen werden umfangreichere Tests vorgegeben, z.B. „gleicher-Abstand(objekt1, objekt2, tmin, tmax)". Daneben existieren noch Tests wie z.B. „vollständig". Dieser überprüft, ob auch über jeden Zeitpunkt der Dauer einer Ablaufausprägung Aussagen vorhanden sind.

5. Einordnung des Projekts und gegenwärtiger Entwicklungsstand

Ansätze zur Beschreibung von Bildfolgen durch Bewegungsverläufe sind noch relativ selten. Arbeiten finden sich z.b. im medizinischen Bereich. Die Arbeitsgruppe um Tsotsos [Tsotsos et al. 80] baut aus einfachen Grundbegriffen wie „Flächenänderung" kompliziertere Begriffe wie „zusammenziehen" auf. Damit werden Bewegungsänderungen von linken Herzventrikeln qualitativ beschrieben. Mit der Analyse von Herzzyklen befaßt sich auch die Gruppe um Niemann [Niemann et al. 85]. Aufbauend auf den Grundbewegungen Kontraktion, Stagnation und Expansion werden für bestimmte Krankheiten typische Bewegungsabläufe modelliert, die als Grundlage für eine Diagnosekomponente dienen. Die Gruppe um Neumann [Neumann und Novak 86] dagegen arbeitet im System NAOS mit Straßenszenen. Ausgangspunkt ist eine geometrische Szenenbeschreibung (GSB), Ergebnis sind Bewegungsverben wie „abbiegen", die zeitliche Entwicklungen in der Straßenszene beschreiben. Ähnlich wie bei Tsotsos bilden die Bewegungsverben bei Neumann eine Hierarchie, wobei komplexere aus einfacheren zusammengesetzt sind. Die Arbeit [Retz-Schmidt 85] erweitert den NAOS-Ansatz um eine durch Skripts modellierte erwartungsgesteuerte Extraktion von Bewegungsverben, die negative Aussagen erlaubt.

Teile des in EPEX verfolgten Ansatzes zeigen Gemeinsamkeiten mit den in NAOS entwickelten Komponenten. Objektausprägungen enthalten etwas mehr Information als die GSB, sind aber damit vergleichbar. Bewegungsverben und Episoden haben einen gemeinsamen Überlappungsbereich, Episoden sind jedoch im allgemeinen abstrakter und lassen vor allem mehr Variabilität zu [Walter et al. 86a]. Skriptartige Strukturen finden sich in allgemeinerer Form im Regelbereich wieder. Ein wesentlicher Gesichtspunkt unserer Arbeit besteht in der Entwicklung einer systematischen Repräsentationsform für die in EPEX auftretenden Anforderungen. Damit ist jetzt eine einheitliche Darstellung von Objekten und Abläufen möglich. Außerdem haben wir die Repräsentation von weiterverarbeitbaren Abläufen klar von der Repräsentation der sie erzeugenden Regeln abgegrenzt. Dadurch wird unter anderem die Verwendung von Datenbanken erleichtert, was ebenfalls ein wichtiges Ziel unserer Arbeit ist.

Zur Validierung des EPEX-Ansatzes benutzen wir zunächst den Diskursbereich „Straßenverkehr". Die Objektdaten für EPEX werden von einem am Fraunhofer-Institut (IITB) in Karlsruhe entwickelten

Bildverarbeitungssystem bereitgestellt. Die unserer Arbeit zugrundeliegende Bildfolge enthält Szenen der Straßenkreuzung „Durlacher Tor" in Karlsruhe, für die wir im Moment die Episoden „Parkplatzsuchen" und „wenden" modellieren. Mehr Datenbank-orientierte Aspekte werden in [Walter et al. 87a] beschrieben, die Übertragung des Repräsentationsformalismus auf ein relationales Datenmodell ist im Rahmen einer Diplomarbeit [Ikker 87] durchgeführt worden.

Anmerkungen: Die dem Beitrag zugrundeliegenden Arbeiten werden von der Deutschen Forschungsgemeinschaft im Rahmen des Schwerpunktprogramms „Modelle und Strukturen bei der Auswertung von Bild- und Sprachsignalen" gefördert. Die Autorin bedankt sich bei Herrn Prof. Lockemann und Herrn Prof. Nagel für ihre Unterstützung durch zahlreiche Diskussionen.

Literatur

Allen, J.F. (1984) „Towards a General Theory of Action and Time." Artificial Intelligence 23, 123-154

Brachman R.J., Schmolze J.G. (1985) „An Overview of the KL-ONE Knowledge Representation System." Cognitive Science 9, 171-216

Dittrich, K.R., Kotz, A.M., Mülle, J.A., Lockemann P.C. (1985) „Datenbankunterstützung für den ingenieurwissenschaflichen Entwurf." Informatik-Spektrum 8:3, 113-125

Fillmore, C. (1968) „The case for case." in: E. Bach, R. Harms (eds.): Universals in linguistic theory. Holt, Rinehart and Winston, New York, 1-88

Ikker, M. (1987) „Modellierung einer Datenbankschnittstelle für die Bildfolgenauswertung." Diplomarbeit, Fakultät für Informatik, Universität Karlsruhe

Klopprogge, M.R., Lockemann, P.C. (1983) „Modelling Information Preserving Databases: Consequences of the Concept of Time." Proc. Conf. Very Large Data Bases VLDB-9, Florenz, 399-416

Nagel, H.-H. (1983) „Overview on Image Sequence Analysis." in: T.S. Huang (ed.): Image Sequence Processing and Dynamic Scene Analysis. NATO Advanced Study Institute Series F2, Springer-Verlag Berlin, Heidelberg, New York, Tokio, 2-39

Nagel, H.-H. (1985) „Analyse und Interpretation von Bildfolgen I." Informatik-Spektrum 8:4, 178-200

Neumann, B., Novak, N.-J. (1986) „NAOS: Ein System zur natürlichsprachlichen Beschreibung zeitveränderlicher Szenen." Informatik Forschung und Entwicklung 1, 83-92

Niemann, H., Bunke, H., Hofmann, I., Sagerer, G., Wolf, F., Feistel, H. (1985) „A Knowledge Based System for Analysis of Gated Blood Pool Studies." IEEE Trans. Pattern Analysis and Machine Intelligence PAMI-7, 246-259

Retz-Schmidt, G. (1985) „Script-Based Generation and Evaluation of Expectations in Traffic Scenes." Proc. GWAI-85, Springer Informatik-Fachberichte 118, 197-203

Schank, R.C., Abelson, R. (1977) „Scripts, Plans, Goals, and Understanding." Lawrence Erlbaum, Hillsdale, N.J.

Stefik, M., Bobrow, D.G., Mittal, S., Conway, L. (1983) „Knowledge Programming in LOOPS: Report on an Experimental Course." The AI Magazine, Fall 1983, 3-13

Tsotsos, J.K., Mylopoulos, J., Covvey, H.D., Zucker, S.W. (1980) „A Framework for Visual Motion Understanding." IEEE Trans. Pattern Analysis and Machine Intelligence PAMI-2, 563-573

Walter, I. (1986) „Ein Datenmodell für die Extraktion von Episoden aus Bildfolgen." Proc. Mustererkennung 1986, 8. DAGM-Symposium, Springer Informatik-Fachberichte 125, 196-200

Walter, I., Lockemann, P.C., Nagel, H.-H. (1986a) „Untersuchung von Datenbank-Schemata zur Modellierung von Episoden bei der algorithmischen Deutung von Bildfolgen."Interner Bericht 2/86, Fakultät für Informatik, Univ. Karlsruhe

Walter, I., Lockemann, P.C., Nagel, H.-H. (1986b) „Ein Datenmodellentwurf für die Extraktion von Episoden aus Bildfolgen." Interner Bericht 3/86, Fakultät für Informatik, Univ. Karlsruhe

Walter, I., Lockemann, P.C., Nagel, H.-H. (1987a) „Database Support for Knowledge-Based Image Evaluation", Proc. Int. Conf. on Very Large Data Bases VLDB-13, Brighton

Walter, I., Lockemann, P.C., Nagel, H.-H. (1987b) „Die EPEX-Wissensbasis und ihre Auswertung." Interner Bericht (in Vorbereitung), Fakultät für Informatik, Universität Karlsruhe

Woods, W.A. (1970) „Transition Network Grammars for Natural Language Analysis." CACM, 13:10, 591-606

ON MODELLING EVENTS WITH AN 'ANALOGICAL' REPRESENTATION

M. Mohnhaupt

Fachbereich Informatik, University of Hamburg

Bodenstedtstr.16, D-2000 Hamburg 50

mohnhaupt@rz.informatik.uni-hamburg.dbp.de

1. Introduction

This paper is concerned with representing observed trajectories of moving objects. By modelling such spatio-temporal events we want to support certain tasks involving knowledge about typical object motion, such as trajectory prediction. We consider this problem in the context of a natural-language guided scene analysis task where simple questions like "Did a car turn off Schluterstreet?" are used to start top-down controlled image sequence analysis. For an effective control of the vision processes it is essential to provide knowledge about the spatio-temporal constraints implied by the verb 'turn-off' and other verbs for that matter. Previous work (NEUMANN and NOVAK 83, NEUMANN 84) has dealt with the bottom-up path, i.e. assigning meaning to observed object motions in terms of verbal descriptions. To this end event models have been defined which capture the spatio-temporal meaning of locomotion verbs by qualitative predicates which must be conjunctively true for - say - a turn-off event to take place. Propositional event models have been shown to provide an effective means for computing natural language scene descriptions (NOVAK and NEUMANN 86) but cannot be used effectively for the inverse: generating visualizations from verbal descriptions. For this we need an explicit representation of the spatio-temporal knowledge associated with verbs. As there is no unique trajectory which would serve for this purpose, we are faced with the problem of devising a representation for 'typical' trajectories, possibly involving uncertainty, incompleteness and fuzzyness.

There is much literature in cognitive science and related disciplines which provides evidence for explicit spatial representations (often called 'analogical representations') in the human mind. For a recent survey see BLOCK 81 or KOSSLYN 80. Unfortunately we did not find any suggestions concerning a computational representation of motion experience. Nevertheless our thinking has been influenced by the imagery debate and cognitive models proposed for the representatic of visual information. The main purpose of our work, however, is not to explain psychophysical findings but to develop a representation with the following functional properties:

(i) Learnability

It is desirable that the representation is learnable from experience. In other words, we want to consider knowledge about typical object motions as accumulated (and possibly abstracted) from concrete observations. Using the same basic data structure for both concrete experience and the knowledge gained thereby will allow for a meaningful interpretation of the latter. In particular, visualizations may be generated using the same data structure as visual input. There is evidence that this is also the case with humans (FINKE 80, 85).

(ii) Fuzzyness

Propositions about typical object motions tend to be fuzzy. For example, one turning-off trajectory may be considered 'more typical' than another. On the other hand, certain features - e.g. the direction of motion - may be represented with certainty. We seek a representation in which various degrees of typicality can be expressed in a natural (i.e. experience-based) way.

(iii) Generalization

Learning from experience will necessitate generalizing from individual examples. We want our representation to cover situations which must not have been experienced before in every detail. For example, if a car begins its turning-off trajectory slightly different from all we have experienced so far, we still want to be able to predict its approximate course. Another aspect of generalization concerns the stationary environment. We want to generalize turning-off experience w.r.t. the particular location, making it applicable to other street crossings with different street shapes.

(iv) Grouping

As experience accumulates, distinct patterns of behavior may emerge, e.g. objects turning off left and objects turning off right. Such patterns may be thought of as groupings among individual trajectories. Groupings may be useful for distinguishing between alternatives in a prediction task or for conceptual clustering. Our representation should support grouping for these reasons.

The representation we propose is a 'trajectory accumulation frame' (TAF). Roughly speaking, a TAF is an accumulator array for motion state vectors. Each entry corresponds to the number of times a certain state vector has been observed. In section 2 the idea of a TAF will be developed in detail for the task of memorizing and recalling individual trajectories. Section 3 will deal with the more interesting situation where individual trajectories may not be separated any longer and a TAF is used for predicting typical behavior. It is shown that the algorithm used for recall can be employed for the prediction task without change. Prediction follows a skeleton of local counter maxima which provides a pattern of typical behavior. Local operations are proposed which generate smoothed views of the same data, suppressing detail and filling in for missing experience.

In section 4 we discuss situations where obstacles constrain possible predictions. We demonstrate that meaningful predictions can be computed although our representation was accumulated in the absence of any obstacle.

The representation has been implemented on a Symbolics 3640 and examples are simulated to illustrate the performance of a TAF. Conclusions and further work will be outlined in section 5.

2. Trajectory Accumulation Frames

In this section we introduce a TAF as the basic data structure for recording trajectories (i.e. object motions) in a fixed environment. Our domain of interest is street traffic, hence we will restrict ourselves to planar motion.

A TAF is a four-dimensional accumulator array $C(x,y,d,v)$ covering a certain subfield of the xy-plane. For each xy-pair there are counter cells for all possible velocity vectors, each represented by direction d and velocity value v. The vector $\underline{S} = (x\ y\ d\ v)$ describes the motion state of an object at a given time. Note that it is composed of quantities which may be perceived by the observer of a visual scene. For each object trajectory, a trace of state vectors is registered in the TAF by incrementing the associated counters. As more objects are entered, more cells (possibly the same) are incremented without discriminating between different objects.

Let us consider now the recall of individual trajectories from a TAF. Given a starting cell the obvious operation to perform is to look for a nonzero counter in the four-dimensional vicinity. This reflects the assumption that the trajectory has been continuous and sufficiently densely sampled. Hence successive state vectors must be similar. Note that not all xy-neighbors may be reached if the velocity direction is restricted to vary smoothly. To be more specific we introduce the following discretization (which has also been used in the experiments):

- xy-pairs are taken from a rectangular grid
- directions are multiples of 45 degrees corresponding to the chain code
- velocity values are quantized independently.

The 'smooth 4D-neighborhood' N($\underline{S}$) of a cell $\underline{S}$ contains all cells $\underline{S}$'

(a)   which are in the 3 x 3 x 3 x 3 cube centered around $\underline{S}$,

(b)   whose direction d' corresponds to the direction from (x y) to (x' y')

(c)   and whose direction d' differs from d no more than 45 degrees.

Hence N($\underline{S}$) contains alltogether 9 elements, involving 3 different successor locations (x' y'). Any nonzero counter in N($\underline{S}$) indicates a possible successor of $\underline{S}$. In general there may be more than one nonzero cell, hence we define the successor of $\underline{S}$ to be the maximal value cell in N($\underline{S}$).

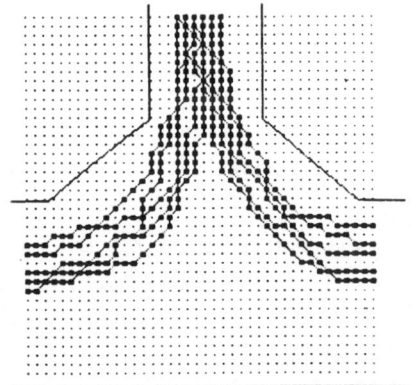 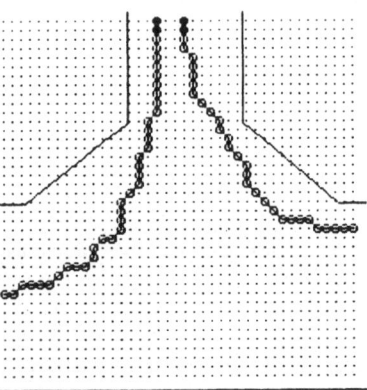

Fig. 1a: A TAF with ten trajectories   Fig. 1b: Two recalled trajectories

Figure 1a shows the xy-projection of a TAF containing ten trajectories. Note that cells with equal xy-location but different velocities are distinct in a TAF but cannot be distinguished in the figure. Figure 1b illustrates the recall of two trajectories given two starting points (solid).

The number of individual trajectories which may be recalled from a single TAF depends on the similarity of the trajectories as compared with the coarseness of the quantization. Trajectories are inseparable if they meet in state space, i.e. have similar velocities at close locations. In this case the recall algorithm may continue with the 'wrong' trajectory. As we are interested in predicting typical behavior rather than individual trajectories, we do not worry about this and turn to the multiple trajectory situation.

3. Typical Trajectories and Prototypes

We consider now the case where trajectory predictions are no longer determined by individual examples but depend on the experience gained from observing a possibly very large number of trajectories. We shall also introduce a blurring operation which spreads out the counter function over a local neighborhood. The combined effect of having many trajectories and of blurring will produce a counter function which is nonzero throughout the approximate area covered by the observed trajectories. Hence the TAF may be considered a four-dimensional density field with high values indicating experience supported by many observations.

In addition we shall discuss a convergence operation. This operation computes an abstraction of the current TAF by emphasizing trajectories with high probability and by suppressing trajectories with lower probability.

Traces along density maxima define a pattern of typical behavior, called the skeleton of the TAF. Predictions will essentially follow this pattern. In the remainder of this section we shall outline the general ideas (for a more detailed discussion see MOHNHAUPT + NEUMANN 87).

Blurring
Blurring is a generalization operation to the effect that experience represented by a counter cell is propagated to its neighbors. This is accomplished by replacing the value of each cell by the weighted average of all neighbors orthogonal to the direction of motion. Cells along the direction of motion contribute according to their positive difference.

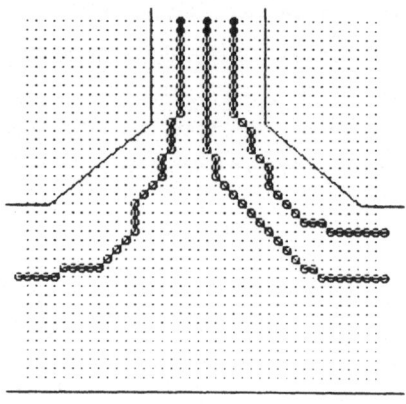

Fig. 2a: Predictions after   Fig. 2b: Predictions after
     1x blurring   3x blurring

The Figures 2a and 2b show predictions after different degrees of blurring. Note that predictions are possible at coordinates where no experience was accumulated and that predictions do not necessary follow any of the recorded individual trajectories (compare to Fig. 1a).

Convergence

While blurring is an operation which generalizes information into the neighborhood, convergence is an operation which abstracts the most relevant information from TAFs by suppressing details and making the most important information explicit. Roughly speaking each cell S supports all the neighbor cells from where one can reach the cell S. The support is proportional to the own counter value.

We show the effects of the convergence operation after discussing why skeletons play an important role for our representation.

Skeletons

Predictions are computed by picking maximum counter value cells for successors (according to the recall algorithm introduced in section 2), hence cells which are relative maxima play a special part. They form a pattern of typical trajectories in the sense that they outline distinct paths which are maximally supported by experience. We call this pattern a skeleton.

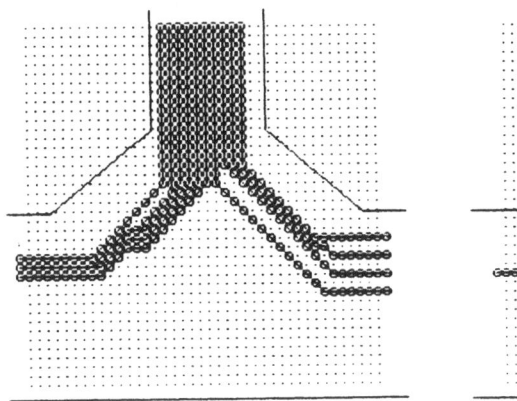 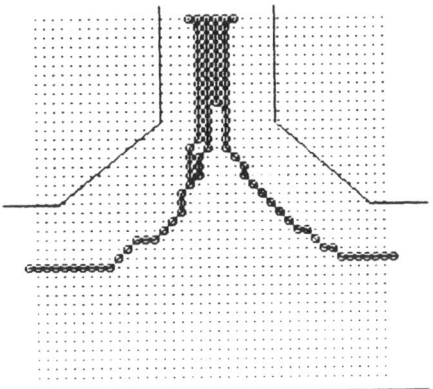

Fig. 3a: Skeleton of the TAF in figure   3b: Skeleton of the same TAF
           2b (3x 'blurring')   after 1x 'convergence'

The figures demonstrate the different effects of the blurring and the
convergence operations. The skeletons show typical behaviour irrespective of
starting points. Figure 3a shows that the blurring operation has generalized
the information by propagating it into the neighborhood. After applying the
convergence operation in figure 3b one obtains the skeleton which makes the most
important paths explicit. Local maxima constitute two conceptual clusters
('turning right' and 'turning left').

Skeletons have the following properties:

(a)   The (predicted) successor of any skeleton cell is again a skeleton cell.

(b)   A skeleton defines a finite set of trajectories, called trajectory
       prototypes.
       Tracing through the skeleton, the largest maximum defines the primary
       continuation, while the other relative maxima lead into secondary
       branches. The set of all such paths is the set of prototypes defined by a
       TAF. Prototypes are useful for grouping, i.e. for decomposing experience
       into conceptual clusters.

(c)   Predictions starting in the vicinity of the skeleton tend to follow the
       skeleton.

4.   TAFs in constrained situations

In this section we want to show how TAFs can be adjusted to cope with slightly

different situations, e.g. situations with obstacles. We assume that obstacles
have been absent when the experience was accumulated. We show that a TAF is
flexible enough to allow meaningful predictions in situations which are slightly
different to the underlying experience.

An obstacle is a subspace of the 4-dimensional TAF where activities are not
allowed e.g.   due to a parking car or due a forbidden range of velocities (in
case of snow on the street). We introduce an obstacle into the TAF by setting
the counter values of the appropriate subspace to zero. Then we propagate this
information through the TAF by using a local inhibition operation.

Inhibition
We inhibit a cell S by setting its counter value to zero under the following
conditions:

  - All the counter cells in the 'smooth 4D-neighborhood' are equal to zero,
  - or all the counter cells from which S can be reached are equal to zero.

This operation is performed repeatedly for all cells until no more changes
occur.   Thus one is sure that all cells which have no active predecessor or no
active successor are set to zero . We demonstrate the inhibition operation with
an example.

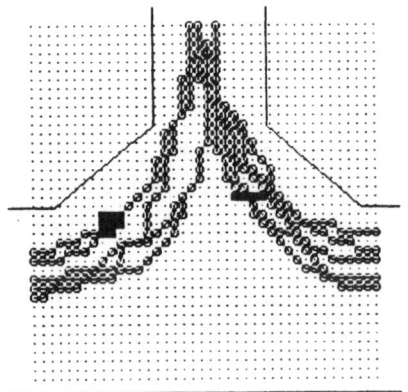
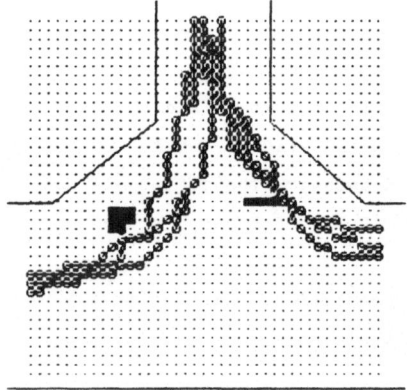

Fig. 4a: Skeleton for the TAF in   Fig 4b: The same Skeleton after
         Fig.1a with obstacles   inhibition

Fig. 4a shows the TAF of Fig.1a after introducing two obstacles. The effects of
the inhibition operation are visible in Fig. 4b. All trajectories which would

pass through the obstacle are inhibited.

5. Conclusions

We have considered the problem of representing observed object trajectories with the objective of making typical behavior explicit and providing means for predicting trajectories from experience. We have proposed a computational model consisting of a TAF as a data structure and several local processes operating on this structure. Our model has the following interesting properties. First, it provides for a natural transition from individual to accumulated experience. There is no epistemological discontinuity between concrete examples and prototypical knowledge. To consider knowledge as accumulated and abstracted from experience may also be a fruitful approach to other problems. Second, in a TAF one can distinguish between more or less typical behavior, thus it captures an important dimension of experience. In the context of top-down controlled image sequence analysis, for example, high-value areas of a TAF can be used to define primary search areas for - say - discovering a turn-off event. Third, a TAF can be used for generalizing observations w.r.t. location and velocity. This is an essential means for making experience apply to novel but similar situations. TAFs are also able to deal with obstacles which where not present during knowledge acquisition. Fourth, a TAF may be characterized by its skeleton and by the trajectory prototypes as defined by the skeleton. This provides the possibility to refer to and reason about typical motion behavior in terms of a finite set of alternatives.

The flexibility of the representation was achieved by using an 'analogical', 'scenic' mapping from the world into the model and by applying local operations to make certain information explicit. We believe that for efficient solutions in the domain discussed in this work an analogical representation is needed and more appropriate than a propositional one. Although the cognitive representations of time-dependent events are far from being clear, we believe that our work also provides some arguments for the usefulness of an analogical representations in humans. It seems to be very difficult to achieve functional properties like fuzzyness, uncertainty, grouping and generalization with propositional descriptions of events.

Several aspects of the problem area have not yet been fully investigated and will be tackled in the near future. One is the problem of generalizing w.r.t. the stationary environment. How should a TAF be transformed to make it applicable to other locations with different street shapes?

Another problem concerns the limits of separability. How can one attain the separation of trajectory bundles which share common parts? One way to deal with this problem is to extend the state vector $\underline{S}$ to contain other useful features such as object characteristics or - to improve separation - global trajectory characteristics. As the usefulness of such features would depend on the situation, a theory of how to select useful features must be developed. This, again, is left for future work.

6. References

BLOCK 81, Imagery, N. Block (ed.), MIT Press, Cambridge/Mass., 1981
FINKE 80, Levels of Equivalence in Imagery and Perception, R.A. Finke, Psychological Review 1980, Vol.87, Nr.2, 113-132
FINKE 85, Theories Relating Mental Imagery to Perception, R.A. Finke, Psychological Bulletin 1985, Vol.98, Nr.2, 236-259
KOSSLYN 80 Image and Mind, Stephen M. Kosslyn, Harvard University Press 1980
MOHNHAUPT and NEUMANN 87, Szenenhafte Modelle fuer zeitabhaengige Ereignisse, M. Mohnhaupt und B. Neumann, Bericht 127, Fachbereich Informatik, University of Hamburg, February 1987
NEUMANN and NOVAK 83, Event Models for Recognition and Natural Language Description of Events in Real-World Image Sequences, B. Neumann und H.-J. Novak, Proc. IJCAI-83, Karlsruhe 1983, pp. 724-726
NEUMANN 84, Natural Language Description of Time-Varying Scenes, B. Neumann, Technical Report, University of Hamburg, IfI-HH-B-105/84, 1984
NOVAK and NEUMANN 86, Text Generation based on Visual Data: Descriptions of Traffic Scenes, H.-J. Novak und B. Neumann, Proc. of the 2nd International Conference on Artificial Intelligence, Methodology, Systems, Applications, September 1986, Varna, Bulgaria

Acknowledgements

This work was done in collaboration with Bernd Neumann. I would like to thank him for many very useful suggestions and comments. The work has been financially supported by the DFG (German Science Foundation).

KI-METHODEN IN DER MASCHINELLEN ÜBESETZUNG ?

Christa Hauenschild

Technische Universität Berlin
Computergestützte Informationssysteme (CIS)
Projektgruppe KIT
Sekr. FR 5-8
Franklinstr. 28/29
D-1000 Berlin 10

0 Interpretation der Titelfrage - Zusammenfassung

Die Frage "KI-Methoden in der maschinellen Übersetzung?" [1] ist mindestens in einer Hinsicht mehrdeutig, nämlich bezüglich dessen, was der "Fokus" der Frage (also das eigenlich Erfragte) sein soll. Um nicht den Eindruck einer unkooperativen oder ungeschickten Sender(innen)-Strategie aufkommen zu lassen, will ich in diesem Einleitungsabschnitt die von mir intendierten Interpretationen erläutern, um diese dann zur Strukturierung des gesamten Beitrages zu benutzen. Angesichts der Tatsache, daß die Adressaten dieser Ausführungen Mitglieder der KI-Gemeinde sind, ist es naheliegend, "KI-Methoden" (oder zumindest "KI") als bekannt vorauszusetzen und also als potentiell thematisch anzusehen. Die Interpretation der Titelfrage, die die höchste Präferenz für den besagten Adressatenkreis haben dürfte, wäre demzufolge etwa so zu paraphrasieren: *"Was macht das Anwendungsgebiet der maschinellen Übersetzung (MÜ) für die KI interessant?"* Diese Lesart der Frage wird das Thema von Abschnitt 1 bilden.

Die umgekehrte Fokussierung der Frage liegt ebenfalls nicht besonders fern: *"Was macht KI-Methoden für die maschinelle Übersetzung interessant?"* Dies ist zwar zunächst einmal eine Frage, die sich MÜ-ler stellen sollten; sie ist aber m.E. durchaus auch für KI-ler relevant. Um nicht von vornherein in eine ganz allgemeine Diskussion über KI-Methoden an sich verstrickt zu werden, will ich zur Beantwortung dieser Frage in Abschnitt 2 einen spezifischen Gegensatz zwischen zwei derzeit aktuellen Alternativen behandeln, nämlich den zwischen KI-Ansatz einerseits und computerlinguistischem Ansatz andererseits. M.E. hat diese Erörterung durchaus auch einen Nährwert für die Diskussion über die Spezifik von KI-Methoden im allgemeinen,

[1] Dieser Beitrag ist entstanden im Rahmen der Projekte KIT-NASEV und KIT-FAST (NASEV = Neue Analyse- und Syntheseverfahren zur maschinellen Übersetzung; FAST = Funktor-Argument-Struktur für den Transfer - beide Projekte innerhalb der Projektgruppe KIT = Künstliche Intelligenz und Textverstehen, Leitung: Prof. Dr. H.-J. Schneider), die vom BMFT im Rahmen der EUROTRA-D-Begleitforschung gefördert wurden bzw. werden. Ich danke meinen Kolleginnen und Kollegen aus der KIT-Gruppe für zahlreiche Diskussionen zum Thema des Vortrages und zu angrenzenden Themen. Mein besonderer Dank gilt meinem KIT-FAST-Kollegen Stephan Busemann.

etwa im Sinne einer "Meta"-Frage: *"Was macht die Diskussion über KI-Methoden in der MÜ für die KI-Gemeinde interessant?"* Diese Frage wird in Abschnitt 3 gestellt und (partiell) beantwortet.

1 Was macht den Anwendungsbereich MÜ für die KI interessant ?

Wenn man von der Hypothese ausgeht, daß maschinelle Übersetzung etwas mit Übersetzung (durch Menschen) zu tun hat oder haben sollte (was durchaus nicht unumstritten ist, s.u.), dann ist die MÜ aus verschiedenen Gründen ein interessantes Anwendungsgebiet für KI-Methoden:

- die zu beschreibenden Einzelkomponenten des komplexen Phänomens Übersetzung decken einen großen Teil der Phänomene ab, die allgemein als für die KI relevant gelten (vgl. z.B. den Katalog in Habel 1986: 6, wo die folgenden Fähigkeiten genannt werden: natürliche Sprache zu verwenden, d.h. Äußerungen zu verstehen und zu generieren, Pläne zu entwerfen und Entscheidungen zu treffen, Schlußfolgerungen durchzuführen, optische und akustische Wahrnehmungen zu verarbeiten (zu verstehen)); [2] alle diese Punkte spielen für die Übersetzung eine Rolle, in der MÜ wird allerdings i.a. zumindest vom letzten Phänomenbereich abstrahiert;
- damit lassen sich die charakteristischen Probleme der KI (nach Schefe 1986 etwa das Repräsentationsproblem, das Inferenzproblem und das Suchproblem) im Problem der Übersetzung wiederfinden und die in der KI bereits entwickelten und noch zu entwickelnden Lösungen für diese Probleme auf die MÜ erfolgversprechend anwenden;
- somit konstituiert die MÜ (genauer: die Entwicklung von MÜ-Systemen) einen geeigneten Testfall für die Adäquatheit von Repräsentationen unterschiedlicher Wissenstypen sowie für die Leistungsfähigkeit der Vorschläge zur Manipulation dieser komplexen Wissensbestände.

Diese stichwortartigen Bemerkungen sollen im folgenden etwas genauer ausgeführt werden.

1.1 Der Katalog der interessanten Phänomene

Daß Übersetzen etwas mit dem *Verstehen und Generieren von natürlichsprachlichen Äußerungen* zu tun hat, dürfte offensichtlich sein (es sei denn, man würde Übersetzen als einen irgendwie mystisch-kreativen, ganzheitlichen und daher nicht in Einzelkomponenten zerlegbaren Prozeß auffassen).

----

[2] Die genannten Phänomene bilden natürlich keinen vollständigen Katalog der KI-relevanten Fähigkeiten des Menschen; sie sind überdies z.T. voneinander abhängig (vgl. dazu auch Habel 1986:6).

Daß Übersetzen auch *das Entwerfen von Plänen und das Treffen von Entscheidungen*
impliziert, ist vielleicht weniger evident; es ist aber in der Übersetzungstheorie
durchaus geläufig, die Herstellung des zielsprachlichen Textes als einen komplexen
Entscheidungsprozeß aufzufassen (vgl. etwa Levý 1967) in dem Sinne, daß aus mehreren
zielsprachlich möglichen Alternativen diejenige ausgewählt wird, die dem
ausgangsprachlichen Text in der jeweils entscheidenden Hinsicht am besten
entspricht. Die "jeweils entscheidende Hinsicht" ist natürlich der springende Punkt:
es kann von Textsorte zu Textsorte ganz verschieden sein, worauf es am meisten
ankommt, d.h. welcher Aspekt der Äquivalenz der entscheidende ist: bei einem Gedicht
kann es z.B. eher das Versmaß und der Reim sein als der genaue Inhalt, bei einem
Informationstext kommt es mehr auf den Inhalt als auf irgendwelche formalen
Kriterien an – wobei allerdings bestimmte Textbildungskonventionen auch essentiell
sein können. In der Übersetzungstheorie gibt es einen langen und heftigen Streit
darüber, ob man bei Übersetzungen überhaupt von "Äquivalenz" reden kann und welche
Aspekte ggf. zu unterscheiden sind (vgl. dazu etwa Koller 1979, Kap. 7).

Das dritte der o.g. Phänomene, nämlich *das Durchführen von Schlußfolgerungen*, läßt
sich in der Übersetzung wieder relativ leicht auffinden: das ergibt sich schon
daraus, daß der zu übersetzende Text bis zu einer "Tiefe" verstanden worden sein
muß, daß eine korrekte Auswahl zwischen verschiedenen systematisch möglichen
Übersetzungsvarianten (z.B. zu einem mehrdeutigen Wort) getroffen werden kann, und
das setzt wiederum komplexe Schlußfolgerungen sowohl über den Inhalt des (ganzen)
Textes als auch aufgrund von faktuellem Vorwissen voraus.

Ein menschlicher Übersetzer hat darüberhinaus natürlich auch mit den Problemen der
optischen bzw. akustischen Wahrnehmung zu tun (wenn man den Begriff des Übersetzens
so weit faßt, daß auch das Dolmetschen mit darunterfällt); von diesem Problem wird
in der MÜ bisher noch weitgehend abstrahiert (allerdings haben die Japaner
inzwischen langfristige Projekte zur Simultan-Übersetzung von Telefongesprächen
angekündigt). M.E. sind die durch den Prozeß des Übersetzens aufgeworfenen Probleme
auch ohne diesen letzten Punkt hinreichend komplex, um einen interessanten
Anwendungsbereich für KI-Methoden zu bieten.

1.2 Die charakteristischen Probleme der KI im Lichte der MÜ

In bezug auf die charakterischen Probleme der KI im Lichte ihrer Anwendung auf MÜ
greifen wir auf den Abschnitt 1.6 "Probleme des Entwurfs von KI-Systemen" in (Schefe
1986: 46 ff.) zurück"

- *das Repräsentationsproblem* ergibt sich, wenn man (wie die Autorin dieses
  Beitrages) der Auffassung ist, daß die verschiedenen Aspekte der Äquivalenz, die
  beim Übersetzen offensichtlich eine wichtige Rolle spielen, durch Operationen auf
  unterschiedlichen Typen von Informationen simuliert werden sollten – das setzt
  nämlich voraus, daß es für die verschiedenen Informationstypen geeignete (formale)

Repräsentationen gibt (ein solches Mehr-Ebenen-Konzept der MÜ wurde im Projekt KIT-NASEV entwickelt, vgl. Hauenschild 1986);

- *das Inferenzproblem* ergibt sich aus der Notwendigkeit, für die Anwendbarkeit bestimmter übersetzungsrelevanter Operationen (Transfer-Regeln) die Input Bedingungen zu überprüfen, was häufig nur mit Hilfe von Schlußfolgerungen möglich ist, weil die Bedingungen erst aus dem Zusammenspiel von sprachlichem und außersprachlichem Kontext abgeleitet werden können (vgl. etwa die Ausführungen in Hauenschild 1986 zur Übersetzung des mehrdeutigen Verbs *fahren* ins Englische);

- *das Suchproblem* ergibt sich im gleichen Zusammenhang: um z.B. herauszufinden, welche Lesart eines mehrdeutigen Wortes im Ausgangstext vorliegt (und welche der möglichen lexikalischen Transfer-Regeln demzufolge anzuwenden ist), muß ein Weg gesucht werden, irgendeine Art von Evidenz für die eine oder andere Lesart zu beschaffen.

- *das Implementationsproblem* stellt sich ganz offensichtlich, wenn man nicht nur ein theoretisches Modell des Übersetzungsprozesses erstellen, sondern ein System entwickeln will - und sei es auch nur zum Zwecke der Theorie-Überprüfung.

1.3 MÜ als Testfall für KI-Konzepte und -Methoden

Da in der Übersetzung viele der für die KI interessanten Phänomene und dementsprechend auch die charakteristischen Probleme der KI wiederzufinden sind, ist anzunehmen, daß das Entwickeln von Modellen und Systemen der MÜ einen geeigneten Testfall für die Anwendung von Lösungsvorschlägen der KI abgibt, die zu den genannten Problemen entwickelt wurden oder werden. Das gilt allerdings m.E. nur unter der Voraussetzung, daß man bei der Entwicklung von MÜ-Systemen von der Hypothese ausgeht, daß Übersetzen mit dem Computer etwas mit Übersetzen allgemein zu tun hat bzw. haben sollte. Diese Ansicht setzt sich im Bereich der MÜ erst in der letzten Zeit durch und ist durchaus (noch) nicht allgemein akzeptiert. Es gibt viele MÜ-Forscher, die der Ansicht sind, daß es zweckmäßiger ist, ein MÜ-System aufgrund von Regeln zu entwickeln, die einer linguistischen Theorie entsprechen oder sonst irgendwie effizient sind, ohne daß sie auch nur das Geringste mit menschlichen Übersetzungsstrategien zu tun haben müßten.

Für die Entwicklung von MÜ-Systemen, die in absehbarer Zeit praktisch anwendbar sein sollen und daher von vornherein auf mehr oder weniger umfangreiche Nachredaktion durch menschliche Bearbeiter angewiesen sind, mag das durchaus zutreffen. Wenn man sich jedoch für die MÜ als Grundlagenproblem interessiert in dem Sinne, daß man herausfinden will, wieweit sich die komplexen Vorgänge des Übersetzens von einer natürlichen Sprache in eine andere in Einzelkomponenten zerlegen, präzisieren und einer formalen Rekonstruktion mithilfe eines Rechners zugänglich machen lassen (um dabei ggf. auch genauere Aufschlüsse über diese Vorgänge selbst zu erhalten), scheint mir der Versuch, KI-Methoden für die MÜ einzusetzen, der bei weitem vielversprechendere Weg zu sein.

Es ist in diesem Zusammenhang natürlich auch wichtig, daran zu erinnern, daß der MÜ am Anfang ihrer Geschichte gar nicht die methodischen Hilfsmittel zur Verfügung standen, um einen solchen Weg mit einiger Aussicht auf Erfolg einschlagen zu können (vgl. zur Geschichte der MÜ etwa Bátori 1986). Erst mit der Entwicklung der KI konnte ernsthaft ins Auge gefaßt werden, das (Wenige), was man bisher über den menschlichen Übersetzungsprozeß weiß, in die Entwicklung von MÜ-Modellen und -Systemen mit einzubeziehen.

2 Was macht KI-Methoden für die MÜ interessant ?

In diesem Abschnitt wird die Fokussierung der Frage umgedreht; den Ausgangspunkt bilden nun die Gegebenheiten der MÜ. Es soll hier darauf verzichtet werden, die Geschichte der MÜ mit den verschiedenen, durch bestimmte grundlegende Ansätze gekennzeichneten Phasen in extenso darzulegen; das ist inzwischen mehrfach geschehen (z.B. sehr übersichtlich in Bátori 1986 oder - aus einem mehr praxisorientierten Blickwinkel - in Slocum 1985). Es sollen vielmehr zwei gegenwärtig virulente "Paradigmen" der MÜ dargestellt werden, nämlich das computerlinguistische und das KI-orientierte; anschließend sollen die charakteristischen Unterschiede anhand eines Beispiels für ein Übersetzungsproblem erläutert werden.

2.1 Zwei Paradigmen der MÜ: Computerlinguistik vs. KI-Orientierung

Laut (Bátori 1986) lassen sich drei Phasen der MÜ unterscheiden:
1. die Computer-Phase,
2. die computerlinguistische Phase,
3. die Phase der KI-Modelle.

Die erste Phase, die die aus der Kryptologie stammenden Anfänge der MÜ umfaßt, kann inzwischen als überwunden angesehen werden; auch in MÜ-Systeme, die eigentlich noch aus dieser ersten Phase stammen (wie z.B. SYSTRAN) hat sich im Laufe der Zeit eine stärker linguistische Orientierung durchgesetzt, weil sich herausgestellt hat, daß man seinerzeit einfach von viel zu simplizistischen Annahmen über die sprachlichen Strukturen ausgegangen ist. (Bátori 1986) stellt dar, daß der ALPAC-Report, der allgemein als das erste große Desaster der MÜ aufgefaßt wurde, im Grunde die (computer-)linguistische Orientierung eingeleitet hat, indem er entsprechende Forschungen förderte (Mitte der 60er Jahre). Die computerlinguistische Phase der MÜ steht im engen Zusammenhang mit der Entwicklung der Generativen Grammatik durch Chomsky.

Charakteristisch für den computerlinguistischen (CL-) Ansatz der MÜ, der heute noch in vielen MÜ-Systemen und -Projekten die zentrale Rolle spielt, sind folgende Gesichtspunkte (vgl. Bátori 1986: 14ff):

- es gibt eine voll ausgeprägte Syntax-Komponente und es wird eine vollständige syntaktische Analyse der zu übersetzenden Sätze angestrebt;
- durch die Entwicklung von Parsern wird eine Trennung von Grammatik und Programm (also von Daten und Verfahren) ermöglicht, was einer Arbeitsteilung zwischen Linguisten und Informatikern entsprechen würde (aber s.u.);
- die Aufspaltung des Übersetzungsprozesses in zwei Phasen, nämlich Analyse und Synthese (im Gegensatz zur vorher vorherrschenden direkten Übersetzung ohne Zwischen-Repräsentation), legt den Grundstein zu einer weiteren Modularisierung im Sinne der Entwicklung von Transfer-Modellen mit drei Übersetzungsphasen (Analyse, Transfer, Synthese), wobei der Transfer die eigentliche Übersetzungsaufgabe, d.h. die Überwindung der spezifischen strukturellen Unterschiede zwischen Ausgangs- und Zielsprache übernimmt;
- kritisch ist anzumerken, daß in den CL-orientierten Projekten häufig angenommen wurde, daß Linguisten (ohne fundierte Informatikausbildung) sich ohne weiteres in die Programmierung der Systeme einarbeiten könnten (was sich bei der zunehmenden Komplexität der Werkzeuge immer mehr als ein Irrtum herausstellte und in den heutigen Projekten auch weitgehend als solcher erkannt worden ist);
- ein weiterer Kritikpunkt ist die Überschätzung der Syntax (und das heißt: Satz-Syntax), die mit der Orientierung an der im Grunde semantikfeindlichen Transformationsgrammatik zusammenhängt; in neueren Projekten (z.B. EUROTRA, vgl. Jahnson et al. 1985, und das in Rohrer 1986 beschriebene Projekt der EUROTRA-D-Begleitforschung) wird zwar versucht, auch semantische Bedingungen der Übersetzungs-Äquivalenz mit zu berücksichtigen; ob das aber letztlich zur Überwindung der bisher absoluten Beschränkung auf Einzelsatz-Übersetzungen führt, scheint mir zumindest fraglich.

Die Charakteristika des KI-orientierten MÜ-Ansatzes sind laut (Bátori 1986: 20ff) die folgenden:
- sprachliches und nichtsprachliches Wissen werden beim Problemlösen (hier beim Übersetzen) nicht separiert;
- Syntax und Semantik werden nicht abgegrenzt, sondern in der allgemeinen Verstehens-Komponente integriert;
- entsprechend dem Verstehensbegriff der KI, der sich auf ganze Texte bezieht, wird die Beschränkung auf Einzelsätze aufgehoben;
- mit der Entdeckung der Transferkomponente als des eigentlich übersetzungs-relevanten Aspekts der Problemlösung wird auch die Einbeziehung von Erkenntnissen aus der Übersetzungswissenschaft möglich;
- das Problem der Synthese wird - da es sich jetzt in der Form der Textgenerierung stellt - wesentlich ernster genommen als in den klassisch CL-orientierten Ansätzen;
- es findet eine deutliche Erweiterung des Modells in Richtung auf die Einbeziehung von fachspezifischem Hintergrundwissen statt (mit entsprechend en Inferenzmechanismen);

- durch die allgemeine Modellerweiterung kommt nun auch der Benutzer des MÜ-Systems, d.h. der menschliche Bearbeiter, ins Blickfeld: es werden Einbettungen in eine Textverarbeitungs-Umgebung oder interaktive Modelle mit unterschiedlich starker Unterstützung des Übersetzers durch das System (je nach Wahl) entwickelt.

Die ersten beiden Punkte ergeben sich aus dem ursprünglich holistischen Problemlösungs-Ansatz der KI; die weiteren Punkte betreffen echte Modellerweiterungen im Vergleich zum CL-orientierten Ansatz. (Bátori 1986) merkt zu den KI-orientierten Modellen der MÜ insbesondere kritisch an, daß hier der Verstehensbegiff der KI, der sich im wesentlichen auf eine extensionalisierte Semantik beziehe, möglicherweise ungerechtfertigterweise auf das für die Übersetzung notwendige Verstehen eines Textes angewandt werde. [3]

Wenn man nun versucht, die bestehenden Projekte zur MÜ im Hinblick auf die beiden erwähnten Paradigmen einzuordnen, stellt man fest, daß hier ein ähnlicher Effekt eingetreten ist, wie bei den MÜ-Systemen der ersten Generation: bei den CL-orientierten Projekten ist eine Beeinflussung durch die neu zur Verfügung gestellten Methoden in mehr oder weniger großem Umfang zu beobachten:
- in EUROTRA wird ein expliziter Transfer-Ansatz verfolgt, in den auch übersetzungstheoretische Erwägungen zu Äquivalenzklassen eingehen sollen;
- in dem in (Rohrer 1986) beschriebenen Projekt wird erwogen, die Einzelsatz-Analysen durch Anschluß einer Übersetzung in Diskursrepräsentationen im Sinne von (Kamp 1981) zu ergänzen, womit zumindest einige Aspekte von ganzen Texten repräsentiert und für die Lösung von Übersetzungsproblemen zugänglich gemacht werden könnten.
Es bleiben aber m.E. einige grundlegende Unterschiede im Hinblick darauf bestehen, was man eigentlich von einem MÜ-System erwartet und zu welchem Zweck man es entwickelt. Diese spezifischen Unterschiede sollen im folgenden Abschnitt anhand eines einfachen Beispiels erörtert werden.

2.2 Exemplarisch: Konsequenzen der beiden Ansätze

Obwohl also die Übergänge zwischen den beiden angesprochenen Paradigmen der MÜ fließend sind, wenn man sie auf konkrete Projekte anwendet, (das zeigt sich z.B. auch in den Ausführungen zu KI-orientierten MÜ-Projekten in Shann 1984 oder Tsujii 1986) gibt es doch m.E. einen grundlegenden Unterschied, der sich in der Behandlung des zu übersetzenden Textes manifestiert. Dieser Unterschied hängt offensichtlich genau damit zusammen, daß in den KI-orientierten Projekten in der einen oder anderen Weise versucht wird, die Leistungen des menschlichen Übersetzers - wie unvollkommen auch immer - nachzubilden oder zumindest dessen Resultate zum Maßstab zu nehmen.

----

[3] Diese Kritik wäre m.E. nur dann gerechtfertigt, wenn es in der Linguistik oder der Übersetzungstheorie einen klareren Verstehensbegriff gäbe als in der KI.

Hier scheint mir auch der tiefere Sinn des Begriffs der "fully automatic high quality translation" zu liegen, der inzwischen z.T. heftig in Frage gestellt wird (vgl. Slocum, 1985:2). Diesen Anspruch erheben die Projekte mit CL-Orientierung - soweit ich sehen kann - gerade nicht; sie streben eher einen von vornherein computer-spezifischen Übersetzungsstandard an.

Die deutlichste Manifestation findet dieser grundsätzliche Auffassungsunterschied darin, daß bezüglich eines lokal mehrdeutigen Textes (Satzes) im CL-Ansatz *alle zulässigen Lösungen* produziert werden (oder - was wesentlich schlimmer ist - irgendeine Lösung, die zufällig zuerst gefunden wird), während innerhalb des KI-Ansatzes versucht wird, *die im gegebenen Zusammenhang plausibelste Lösung* anzugeben (daß der Zusammenhang immer nur partiell gegeben ist, trifft übrigens auch für den menschlichen Übersetzer zu). Es kann natürlich im Einzelfall ganz unterschiedlich sein, was bei einem CL-Ansatz als zulässige Lösung gilt (hier werden z.T. auch einfache semantische Merkmale und die entsprechenden Selektionsrestriktionen benutzt); aber der weitere sprachliche und außersprachliche Kontext wird nicht mit einbezogen. Die Regel-Anwendung im CL-Ansatz führt jedenfalls immer zu einer eindeutigen Abgrenzung zwischen zulässigen und unzulässigen Lösungen, während es im KI-Ansatz möglich ist, Hypothesen aufgrund ihrer positiven oder negativen Evidenz zu bewerten und so verschiedene Alternativen gewichtet zu beurteilen.

Dieses Phänomen läßt sich am besten an einem kleinen Beispiel veranschaulichen. Angenommen, wir wollten den folgenden Text ins Englische übersetzen:

(1) Die Landwirtschaftsminister der EG haben verschiedene Lösungen für die Krise der Agrarpolitik vorgeschlagen. Einen Vorschlag werden die Staatschefs auf ihrem Gipfel verabschieden müssen.

Wir betrachten vorläufig nur den zweiten Teilsatz von (1). Ganz abgesehen davon, daß es in diesem kurzen Satz bereits mehrere systematisch mehrdeutige Wörter gibt [4] erhebt sich noch ein weiteres Übersetzungsproblem: wie ist die Nominalgruppe *einen Vorschlag* zu übersetzen? Die erste Schwierigkeit liegt in der Mehrdeutigkeit des deutschen unbestimmten Artikels, der im Englischen u.a. mit *a*, *one* oder *one of the* wiedergegeben werden kann. Zweitens erhebt sich die Frage, ob die Voranstellung des direkten Objekts relevant ist und deshalb bei der Übersetzung berücksichtigt werden muß. Das ergibt sich nicht automatisch, weil eine entsprechende Voranstellung im Englischen zwar nicht ganz unmöglich ist, aber erstens stilistisch stark markiert (und daher für sachbezogene Texte kaum angemessen) und überdies eigentlich nur auf

---

[4] Ich empfehle hier nur einen Blick in ein mittelgroßes deutsch-englisches Wörterbuch, um einen Eindruck vom Grad der potentiellen Mehrdeutigkeit von so harmlos aussehenden Wörtern wie *Vorschlag* oder *verabschieden* oder *Gipfel* zu gewinnen, ganz zu schweigen von den vielfältigen Übersetzungsmöglichkeiten für Funktionswörter wie *müssen* oder *auf*.

definite Nominalgruppen anwendbar ist. Um die Reihenfolge der Argumente des Verbs *verabschieden* also unverändert in den Zieltext übernehmen zu können, müßte z.B. Passivierung vorgenommen werden.

Allein aufgrund dieser Überlegungen ergeben sich schon sechs verschiedene Möglichkeiten der Übersetzung des zweiten Satzes von (1):

(Ü1) The Chiefs of State will have to adopt a proposal during their summit.

(Ü2) ... will have to adopt one proposal ...

(Ü3) ... will have to adopt one of the proposals ...

(Ü4) A proposal will have to be adopted by the Chiefs of State during ...

(Ü5) One proposal will have to be adopted ...

(Ü6) One of the proposals will have to be adopted ...

Ein MÜ-System, das auf die Produktion aller zulässigen Lösungen ausgelegt ist, müßte also mindestens diese sechs Varianten erzeugen (ganz abgesehen von den Kombinationen, die sich zusätzlich aus den verschiedenen Lesarten der mehrdeutigen Wörter ergeben); es sei denn, man stelle sich auf den Standpunkt, daß die Unterschiede ohnehin zu vernachlässigen sind.

Wenn wir die beiden (im CL-Ansatz einzeln zu übesetzenden) Sätze nun wieder zusammenfügen, ohne uns um eventuelle Übersetzungsprobleme beim ersten Satz zu kümmern, erhalten wir u.a. folgende englischen Texte (ich habe die beiden Extreme gewählt in dem Sinne, daß ich sie für die schlechteste vs. beste Übersetzung halte):

(TÜ1) The Ministers of Agriculture of the EC have suggested different solutions for the crisis of agrarian policy. The Chiefs of State will have to adopt a proposal during their summit.

(TÜ6) The Ministers of Agriculture of the EC have suggested different solutions for the crisis of agrarian policy. One of the proposals will have to be adopted by the Chiefs of State during their summit.

In der Variante (TÜ1) ist überhaupt nicht klar, daß die Staatschefs die Wahl zwischen einer begrenzten Menge von Vorschlägen haben - sie könnten irgendeinen beliebigen Vorschlag verabschieden. Der Text wirkt überdies nicht richtig kohärent. In der Variante (TÜ6) wird die m.E. naheliegendste Lesart des Ausgangstextes (daß die Staatschefs genau zwischen den im ersten Satz angedeuteten Vorschlägen zu wählen haben) klar zum Ausdruck gebracht. Der Text ist aufgrund der Voranstellung des Objekts (im semantischen Sinne) von *verabschieden* sofort als kohärent zu erkennen.

(TÜ1) ist nicht eklatant falsch; aber von menschlichen Übersetzern erwartet man Überlegungen der Art, wie wir sie zu dem Übersetzungsbeispiel angestellt haben. Wenn man für eine Lösung wie (TÜ6) plädiert, ist natürlich nun zu fragen, ob die notwendigen Informationen, die zu ihrer Wahl führen, in einem MÜ-System überhaupt zur Verfügung gestellt werden können. Folgende Voraussetzungen wären dafür notwendig:

- die englischen Übersetzungsalternativen für den deutschen unbestimmten Artikel müssen grundsätzlich verfügbar sein; die dazugehörigen Transfer-Regeln müssen die notwendigen Bedingungen enthalten – also für die Lösung *one of the* die Bedingung, daß ein anaphorischer Anschluß an etwas bereits Erwähntes möglich ist;
- der Ausgangstext muß als ganzes repräsentiert werden, so daß der verbale Ausdruck *vorschlagen* im ersten Satz mit dem nominalen Ausdruck *Vorschlag* im zweiten Satz in Verbindung gebracht werden kann, d.h. daß festgestellt werden kann, daß beide sich auf dasselbe Ereignis (genauer: dieselbe Menge von Ereignissen) beziehen;
- es muß eine Strategie vorhanden sein, die besagt, daß im Deutschen eine vorangestellte Nominalgruppe mit unbestimmtem Artikel i.a. als partiell anaphorisch (d.h. im Sinne von *eines der vorerwähnten Xe*) zu interpretieren ist, wenn es sich nicht um den ersten Satz eines Textes handelt und wenn kein Kontrast zu einer anderen indefiniten Nominalgruppe vorliegt (die Evidenz für partiell anaphorische Interpretation wird im vorliegenden Fall noch dadurch verstärkt, daß es sich um ein direktes Objekt handelt, das i.a. überhaupt nur vorangestellt wird, wenn es entweder thematisch (also z.B. als bekannt vorausgesetzt) oder kontrastiv fokussiert ist);
- es muß eine strukturelle Transfer-Regel geben, die besagt, daß deutsche Aktivsätze unter bestimmten strukturellen Bedingungen zu englischen Passivsätzen werden können, wenn die Reihenfolge der Argumente im Satz dadurch gewahrt werden kann (diese Regel ist vermutlich textsorten-spezifisch; zur Relevanz der Oberflächen-Reihenfolge vgl. auch Hauenschild 1982).

Alle diese Informationen, Strategien und Regeln sind zwar komplex, aber sie sind in KI-Systemen grundsätzlich verarbeitbar. Zusammengenommen würden sie im vorliegenden Beispielfall zur Lösung (TÜ6) führen, die m.E. im gegebenen Zusammenhang die optimale Übersetzung ist.

Um die Konsequenzen der beiden MÜ-Ansätze, die hier zur Debatte stehen, noch einmal zusammenzufassen:
- beim CL-orientierten Ansatz werden alle zulässigen Übersetzungslösungen oder schlimmstenfalls nur eine zufällig gefundene – das wäre im vorliegenden Beispiel vermutlich die erste und damit schlechteste – Lösung angegeben;
- im KI-Ansatz gibt es zumindest die Möglichkeit, nach der plausibelsten Lösung zu suchen, weil die entsprechenden Konzepte zur Repräsentation und Methoden zur Schlußfolgerung aufgrund verschiedenartiger Wissensquellen grundsätzlich zur Verfügung stehen.

2.3 Zu welchem Zweck wird MÜ betrieben ?

Im vorangehenden Abschnitt habe ich mit Bedacht ein Beispiel gewählt, das den computerlinguistischen Ansatz nicht diskreditiert (es kursieren ja bekanntlich eine ganze Menge Übersetzungsbeispiele, die die MÜ insgesamt lächerlich machen sollen). Es sollten lediglich die spezifischen Grenzen aufgezeigt und die potentiellen Lösungen aus dem Bereich der KI dagegengehalten werden (wieweit MÜ im Sinne von "fully automatic high quality tranlation" überhaupt möglich ist, halte ich persönlich nach wie vor für eine faszinierende, wenn auch völlig offene Frage).

Es könnte nun mit einem gewissen Recht darauf hingewiesen werden, daß der in Abschnitt 2.2 implizit erhobene Anspruch, die plausibelste Lösung zu finden, in der MÜ eigentlich nichts zu suchen hat. Hier sind m.E. zwei wesentliche Faktoren zu beachten:

1. die Frage, ob MÜ ausschließlich anwendungsorientiert betrieben wird, d.h. normalerweise ohne auch nur einen Gedanken an menschliches Übersetzen zu verschwenden (höchstens in rechtfertigenden Argumentationen, vgl. etwa Slocum 1985:2), oder ob u.a. auch etwas über menschliche Übersetzungsstrategien herausgefunden werden soll – eventuell sogar mit dem Hintergedanken, daß sich auf diese Weise langfristig auch die Performanz von MÜ-Systemen verbessern lassen könnte;

2. die Frage (die auch im reinen Anwendungsfall relevant ist), ob man das MÜ-System losgelöst von seiner Umgebung sieht oder ob der Zusammenhang zwischen MÜ-System und menschlichem Bearbeiter ins Blickfeld kommt; d.h. etwa, daß die Frage gestellt wird, welche Art von Output den Nachredakteur über kurz oder lang zur Verzweiflung bringt und welche er erträglich finden kann.

Daß KI-Methoden im Falle einer *theoretischen Orientierung am menschlichen Übersetzer* erfolgversprechend sein können, hoffe ich in Abschnitt 2.2 plausibel gemacht zu haben (wobei ich nicht behaupten will, daß die Lösung tatsächlich schon vorhanden sei); im Falle einer *praktischen Orientierung am menschlichen Übersetzer* als Systembenutzer kann man vorläufig nur auf die Ansätze zu interaktiven MÜ-Systemen hinweisen (vgl. z. B. Melby 1982); wieweit diese Ansätze wirklich tragen und ob sie die Arbeit des Nachredakteurs wirklich erleichtern, ist derzeit eine offene Frage. Hier kommt es natürlich auch nicht in erster Linie darauf an, ob man KI-Methoden oder CL-Methoden einsetzt, sondern ob man überhaupt darüber nachdenkt, wie die betroffenen Menschen mit dem System umgehen sollen und können. Allerdings glaube ich, daß auch hier KI-Methoden langfristig erfolgversprechender sind, genauer: daß man langfristig nicht ohne KI-Methoden auskommen wird. Letzten Endes ist m.E. eine Art integrierter KI- und CL-Ansatz anzustreben in dem Sinne, daß gewisse linguistische Annahmen (z.B. über die Modularisierung des Verstehensprozesses und die entsprechenden verschiedenen Typen von Repräsentationen) sich wieder gegen den ursprünglich in der KI vorherrschenden holistischen Ansatz durchsetzen. Diese Tendenz zeigt sich in verschiedenen neueren MÜ-Ansätzen (vgl. etwa Tsujii 1986 sowie den Sammelband Bátori & Weber 1986).

3 Was macht die Diskussion über KI-Methoden in der MÜ für die KI-Gemeinde interessant?

Es bleibt nun noch zu fragen, wieso diese relativ umfangreichen Ausführungen zu einem verhältnismäßig einfachen Übersetzungsbeispiel und die damit verknüpfte Methoden-Diskussion innerhalb der MÜ überhaupt auf einem KI-Workshop vorgetragen werden sollen. Wo soll das Interesse an einer Diskussion liegen, die zunächst einmal nur die MÜ-ler anzugehen scheint?

Mit diesem Beitrag mische ich mich implizit als Außenseiterin (genauer: als Grenz-bereichsbewohnerin) in eine KI-interne Debatte ein, die sich um Fragen dreht wie:

- Was sind die eigentlichen KI-Methoden?
- Wann ist ein System ein KI-System?

    usw.

Es scheint mir durchaus denkbar, daß diese Diskussion um einige (handfeste!) Aspekte bereichert werden kann, wenn sie im Hinblick auf spezifische Anwendungsbereiche und dabei insbesondere mit Bezug auf konkre. vorliegende Alternativen geführt wird. Dadurch tritt die Spezifik des KI-Ansatzes deutlicher zutage; andererseits könnte es sich auch herausstellen, daß einige Kriterien, die derzeit als konstitutiv für den KI-Ansatz angesehen werden, durchaus modifizierbar sind und durch anwendungsbereichspezifische Annahmen ergänzt oder ersetzt werden können.

LITERATUR

Bátori, Istvan (1986): "Paradigmen der maschinellen Sprachübersetzung". In. Bátori, Istvan; Weber, Heinz Josef (eds.): 3-27

Bátori, Istvan; Weber, Heinz Josef (eds.) (1986): Neue Ansätze in maschineller Sprachübersetzung: Wissensrepräsentation und Textbezug. Tübingen (Niemeyer)

Habel, Christopher (1986): Prinzipien der Referentialität. Berlin (Springer)

Hauenschild, Christa (1982): "Zur Rolle der Thema-Rhema-Gliederung in der automatischen Übersetzung". In: Stegentritt, Erwin (ed.): Maschinelle Sprachverarbeitung 1981. Vorträge auf der 12. Jahrestagung der GAL, Mainz 1981. Sektion "Maschinelle Sprachverarbeitung". Dudweiler (AQ-Verlag): 103 - 117

Hauenschild, Christa (1986): "KIT/NASEV oder das Problem des Transfers bei der maschinellen Übersetzung". In: Bátori, Istvan; Weber, Heinz Josef (eds.): 167 - 195

Johnson, Rod; King, Margaret; des Tombe, Louis (1985): "EUROTRA: A Multilingual System Under Development". In: Computational Linguistics, Vol. 11, No. 2-3: 155-169

Kamp, Hans (1981): "A Theory of Truth and Semantic Interpretation". In. Groenendijk, J; Janssen, T.M.V.; Stokhof, M (eds.) (1984): Truth, Interpretation and Information. Selected Papers from the Third Amsterdam Colloquium. Dordrecht-Holland (Foris): 1 - 41

Koller, Werner (1979): Einführung in die Übersetzungswissenschaft. Heidelberg (Quelle & Meyer)

Levý, Jiři (1967): "Übersetzen als Entscheidungsprozeß". In: Wilss, Wolfram (ed.) (1981): Übersetzungswissenschaft. Darmstadt (Wiss. Buchgesellschaft): 219 - 235

Melby, Alan K. (1982): "Multi-level Translation Aids in a Distributed System". In: Proceedings of COLING 82, Prag: 215 - 220

Rohrer, Christian (1986): "Maschinelle Übersetzung mit Unifikationsgrammatiken ". In: Bátori, Istvan; Weber, Heinz Josef (eds.): 75 - 99

Schefe, Peter (1986): Künstliche Intelligenz - Überblick und Grundlagen. Mannheim (BI Wissenschaftsverlag)

Shann, Patrick (1984): "Artificial Intelligence Approaches to Machine Translation". Paper presented for the Lugano Tutorial on Machine Translation, April 1984. To appear in: King, Margaret (ed.): Machine Tranlation Today. Cambridge-England (Cambridge Univ. Press)

Slocum, Jonathan (1985): "A Survey of Machine Translation: Its History, Current Status, and Future Prospects". In: Computational Linguistics, Vol. 11, No. 1: 1 - 17

Tsujii, Jun-ichi (1986): "Future Directions of Machine Translation". In: Proceedings of COLING 86, Bonn: 656 - 668

Generierung aus f-Strukturen als strukturgesteuerte Ableitung

Jochen Dörre, Stefan Momma

Institut für
Maschinelle Sprachverarbeitung
Universität Stuttgart

Zusammenfassung:

Das Papier beschreibt einen Algorithmus zur strukturgesteuerten Generierung aus f-Strukturen der LFG. Anhand von Beispielen werden Adäquatheitsbedingungen für den Generierungsprozeß formuliert, die zeigen, daß die Eingabe-f-Struktur als komplexes Constraint für die Ableitung einer Zeichenkette betrachtet werden muß. Es werden Methoden für eine effiziente Behandlung dieses Constraints entwickelt, die eine effiziente Methode zur Behandlung der bekannten constraining equations der LFG mit einschließen. Aus der Problemstellung der Generierung resultiert damit eine neue Motivation für die Verwendung von Constraints in einem unifikationsbasierten Formalismus.

1 Überblick

Das hier vorgestellte Generierungssystem ist Teil eines Projekts zur Maschinellen Übersetzung.[1] In diesem Projekt gehen wir von der Hypothese aus, daß für Analyse und Generierung in einem Übersetzungssystem derselbe Formalismus verwendet werden sollte. Der entscheidende Punkt dabei ist, daß die Generierung nicht mehr ad hoc abläuft, sondern von einer in einem deklarativen Grammatikformalismus spezifizierten Grammatik gesteuert wird. Aufbauend auf den bekannten Analysekonzepten für den Formalismus der LFG wurde ein formales Konzept für die Generierung in diesem Grammatikformalismus entwickelt. Das Generierungssystem wurde in C-Prolog auf einer MicroVAX implementiert.

---

[1] Diese Arbeit wurde im Rahmen der EUROTRA-D-Begleitforschung (BMFT-FKZ 1013207 0) und des ESPRIT-Projekts ACORD (P393) gefördert. Eine ausführlichere Beschreibung des Systems ist in (Momma 1986) zu finden.

2 Analyse mit LFG

Die Lexikalisch Funktionale Grammatik (Kaplan/Bresnan82) gehört zur Klasse der Unifikationsgrammatiken. Ihr wesentliches Merkmal ist die Verwendung kontextfreier Grammatikregeln, die mit funktionalen Gleichungen annotiert sind. Bei der Analyse eines Satzes wird durch den kontextfreien Teil der verwendeten Grammatikregeln zunächst eine Konstituentenstruktur aufgebaut. Die Knoten der Konstituentenstruktur werden anschliessend mit den funktionalen Annotationen versehen. Man erhält so ein Gleichungssystem, die sogenannte funktionale Beschreibung (f-description). Die minimale Lösung des Gleichungssystems beschreibt dann die funktionale Struktur des Satzes in Form einer Menge von Attribut-Wert-Paaren, bei der die Werte selbst wieder komplexe funktionale Beschreibungen sein können. Formal gesehen sind f-Strukturen markierte gerichtete azyklische Graphen (DAGs); daraus ergeben sich die im folgenden verwendeten Begriffe 'Knoten' und 'Pfade' für Teile einer f-Struktur.

Beispiel: Einem Satz wie "The cat tries to sleep" wird von der Grammatik G der annotierte Baum T zugeordnet (vgl. Abb. 1). Das angeführte System von funktionalen Gleichungen bildet die funktionale Beschreibung, die nach der Auflösung der Gleichungen dann die f-Struktur liefert. In der Beispielanalyse von Abb. 1 liegt ein Fall von funktionaler Kontrolle vor. Das Subjekt von 'try' kontrolliert das Subjekt des Verbkomplements. Die LFG behandelt dieses Phänomen in der Form, daß beiden Subjekten dieselbe Struktur zugewiesen wird, d.h. die Pfade <SUBJ> und <VCOMP SUBJ> führen zu ein und demselben Knoten im DAG. In der Matrixdarstellung der f-Struktur wird dies durch Koindizierung der betreffenden Teilstrukturen notiert.

3 Was bedeutet Generierung im Rahmen der LFG?

Basis für den Algorithmus zur Generierung aus f-Strukturen ist ein Ableitungsbegriff, bei dem Konstituenten- und funktionale Struktur parallel[2] aufgebaut werden. Er soll im folgenden kurz skizziert werden.

Eine angemessene Repräsentation der auftretenden Zwischenstrukturen ist ein 4-Tupel[3] aus:

---

[2]Dies steht im Gegensatz zur ursprünglichen Definition bei Kaplan u. Bresnan (Kaplan/Bresnan 1982), bei der die Lösung der f-Beschreibungen nach dem Aufbau aller möglichen c-Strukturen gültige Ableitungen ausfiltert.

[3]Eine Version dieses Ableitungsbegriffs, die nur eine Ebene der Repräsentation verwendet, beschreibt Wedekind (Wedekind 1986).

Grammatik G:

```
S  →    NP        VP                                    the: DET,(↑spec)=the
       (↑subj)=↓  ↑=↓
                                                        cat:  N,(↑pred)=cat
NP →  (DET)     N                                             (↑num)=sg

VP →  V  (NP       (NP))      PP*        (VP')          tries: V,(↑subj num)=sg
        (↑obj)=↓  (↑obj2)=↓  ↓∈(↑adj)  (↑vcomp)=↓              (↑pred)=try(subj,vcomp)
                                                               (↑vcomp subj)=(↑subj)
VP' →   (to)      VP                                           (↑vcomp infto)=c+
       (↑infto)=↓  ↑=↓
       (↑inf)=c+                                       sleep: V,(↑pred)=sleep(subj)
                                                              (↑inf)=+
```

Baum T:

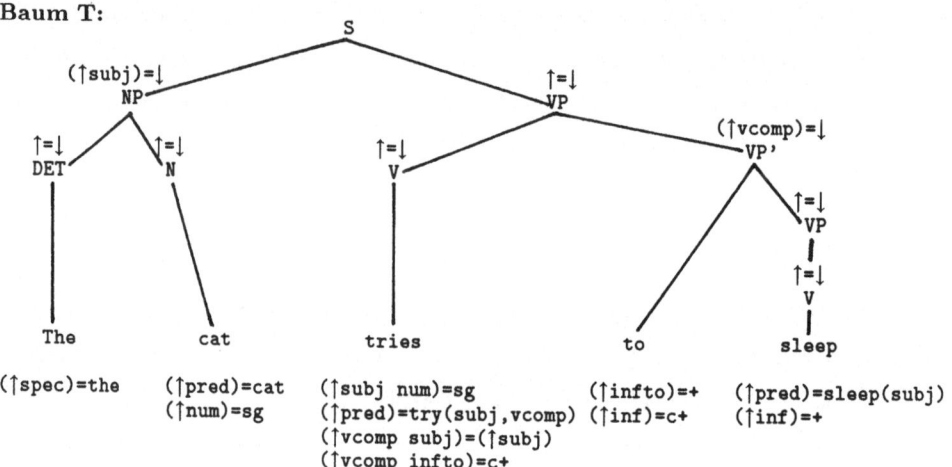

```
(↑spec)=the     (↑pred)=cat     (↑subj num)=sg            (↑infto)=+      (↑pred)=sleep(subj)
                (↑num)=sg       (↑pred)=try(subj,vcomp)   (↑inf)=c+       (↑inf)=+
                                (↑vcomp subj)=(↑subj)
                                (↑vcomp infto)=c+
```

Funktionale Beschreibung: f-Struktur F:

```
(f1 subj)=f2      (f6 pred)=try(subj,vcomp)
f1=f3             (f6 subj num)=sg
f4=f2             (f6 subj)=(f6 vcomp subj)
f5=f2             (f6 vcomp infto)=c+
(f4 spec)=the     (f7 infto)=+
(f5 pred)=cat     (f7 inf)=c+
(f5 num)=sg       f7=f8
f3=f6             f8=f9
(f3 vcomp)=f7     (f9 pred)=sleep(subj)
                  (f9 inf)=+
```

$$
\begin{bmatrix}
\text{subj} & {}_1\begin{bmatrix} \text{pred} & \text{cat} \\ \text{num} & \text{sg} \\ \text{spec} & \text{the} \end{bmatrix} \\[4pt]
\text{pred} & \text{try(subj,vcomp)} \\[4pt]
\text{vcomp} & \begin{bmatrix} \text{subj} & [1] \\ \text{pred} & \text{sleep(subj)} \\ \text{infto} & + \\ \text{inf} & + \end{bmatrix}
\end{bmatrix}
$$

Abbildung 1: LFG-Analyse des Satzes "The cat tries to sleep"

Diese Sätze lassen sich mit G erzeugen, und ihre jeweiligen f-Strukturen sind kompatibel mit der EFS. Offensichtlich müssen also zur Erfüllung unserer Adäquatheitsbedingung neben der Forderung nach Kompatibilität mit der EFS noch weitere Bedingungen erfüllt sein:

- die Bedingung der strukturellen *Vollständigkeit* [4], die fordert, daß alle Information, die in der EFS enthalten ist, während der Ableitung auch tatsächlich verwendet wird. Dies ist im Beispiel 1 dadurch verletzt, daß die Information über den Determinationstyp der Subjekts-NP vernachlässigt wurde.

- die Bedingung der strukturellen *Kohärenz*, die fordert, daß durch den (im Prinzip richtungsfreien) Unifikationsprozeß mit den Grammatikregeln nicht mehr Information in die abgeleitete Struktur aufgenommen werden darf, als in der EFS vorhanden war. Die abgeleitete Struktur muß also die minimale Struktur sein, die die Vollständigkeitsbedingung erfüllt. Dies ist in Beispiel 2 und 3 verletzt und kann auch nicht durch Überprüfung des Subkategorisierungsrahmens von 'try' sichergestellt werden, da die zusätzlich aufgenommenen Adjunkte eben nicht subkategorisiert sind und aufgrund der Regelstruktur auch nicht in ihrer Zahl eingeschränkt werden können.

5 Die Eingabe-Struktur als komplexes Constraint

Die oben formulierten Bedingungen führen zur Interpretation der EFS als *komplexes Constraint*, das analog zu den constraining equations, die in den Grammatikregeln enthalten sind, beachtet werden muß.

Analog zur Zweiteilung dieser zusätzlichen Wohlgeformtheitsbedingungen für die abgeleitete Struktur läßt sich nun wie folgt die EFS in zwei Klassen von atomaren Constraints zerlegen.

5.1 Completeness Constraints

Sie führen für jeden Pfad in der EFS eine entsprechende Existenzforderung für die abgeleitete Struktur ein. Um diese explizit zu machen, genügt es,

COMPa) den Wert eines terminalen Knotens der EFS jedem Pfad zuzuordnen, der von der Wurzel zu diesem Knoten führt, sowie

COMPb) alle Pfad–Äquivalenzen[5] (alle Pfade, die zu ein und demselben Knoten führen) anzugeben.

---

[4]nicht zu verwechseln mit der *funktionalen* Vollständigkeit (vgl. Kaplan/Bresnan82), die fordert, daß alle subkategorisierten Funktionen einer semantischen Form in der f-Struktur vorhanden sind.

[5]Diese Art von Constraints ist bisher noch nicht beschrieben worden, sie ist aber ebenso motiviert wie jede andere constraining equation.

1. der bisher abgeleiteten c-Struktur

2. der entsprechenden funktionalen Struktur

3. der Abbildungsfunktion von Knoten der c-Struktur auf solche der f-Struktur

4. der Menge der bis dahin gesammelten Constraints.

Ein einzelner Ableitungsschritt, d.h. die Anwendung einer Grammatikregel auf eine gegebene Zwischenstruktur, führt zu einer gleichzeitigen Erweiterung von Konstituenten- und funktionaler Struktur. Die Erweiterung der funktionalen Struktur geschieht durch Unifikation mit den Annotationen der Regel. Ein Fehlschlagen dieses Unifikationsschrittes schließt aus, daß die Regel angewendet werden kann und führt zum Rücksetzen der Ableitung. Die Ableitung beginnt mit dem Start-Symbol der Grammatik als Start-c-Struktur, der die leere f-Struktur zugeordnet ist, sowie mit einer leeren Menge von Constraints.

4   Adäquates Generieren mit LFG

Der eben skizzierte Ableitungsbegriff soll nun benutzt werden, um zu definieren, was unter Generierung im Rahmen der LFG zu verstehen ist. Dazu formulieren wir zunächst eine Adäquatheitsbedingung für den Generierungsalgorithmus: Durch die Ableitungsdefinition wird für jede Grammatik G eine Relation $R \subseteq S \times F$ zwischen Sätzen S und funktionalen Strukturen F definiert. Die Aufgabe eines adäquaten Generierungsalgorithmus ist es nun, zu einer gegebenen Instanz f von F alle diejenigen Elemente s von S zu finden, für die (s, f) Element von R ist. Effiziente Generierung setzt voraus, daß dabei der Ableitungsvorgang durch die Eingabe-f-Struktur (EFS) gesteuert wird.

Ein erster Ansatz könnte darin bestehen, anstelle der leeren FS die EFS in das Start-Tupel aufzunehmen. Damit läßt sich garantieren, daß nur solche Sätze abgeleitet werden, deren f-Struktur mit der EFS kompatibel (d.h. unifizierbar) sind. Im folgenden sei die Ableitungsstrategie in der Form festgelegt, daß der Aufbau der Konstituentenstruktur depth-first—left-to-right (mit Rücksetzen) vorangetrieben wird. Dieser Ansatz entspricht dem Algorithmus γ_3 in (Kindermann/Meier 1986). Daß dieser Ansatz u.U. problematisch sein kann, zeigen die folgenden Beispiele. Mit der Grammatik G und der f-Struktur aus Abb. 1 lassen sich u.a. Sätze ableiten wie:

1. Cat tries to sleep.

2. The cat tries to sleep in the garden.

3. The cat tries to sleep in the garden under the tree in a basket.

Nach dieser Unterteilung kann die Struktur aus Abb. 1 durch die folgende Menge von Completeness Constraints charakterisiert werden:

COMPa	COMPb
$(f_1$ subj pred$) =_c$ cat	$(f_1$ subj$) =_c (f_1$ vcomp subj$)$
$(f_1$ subj num$) =_c$ sg	
$(f_1$ subj spec$) =_c$ the	
$(f_1$ pred$) =_c$ try(subj,vcomp)	
$(f_1$ vcomp subj pred$) =_c$ cat	
$(f_1$ vcomp subj num$) =_c$ sg	
$(f_1$ vcomp subj spec$) =_c$ the	
$(f_1$ vcomp pred$) =_c$ sleep(subj)	
$(f_1$ vcomp infto$) =_c +$	
$(f_1$ vcomp inf$) =_c +$	

5.2 Coherence Constraints

Auch in dieser Constraint-Klasse muß man unterscheiden zwischen Informationen, die Pfadäquivalenzen betreffen und solchen, die Pfadexistenz beschreiben.

Kohärenz bezüglich *Pfadexistenz* bedeutet, daß außer den in der EFS vorhandenen Attributen keine weiteren abgeleitet werden dürfen.

Sind Pfade, die in der EFS zu verschiedenen Knoten führen, in der abgeleiteten Struktur äquivalent, so ist die Ableitung inkohärent bezüglich *Pfadäquivalenz* (vgl. Abb. 2).

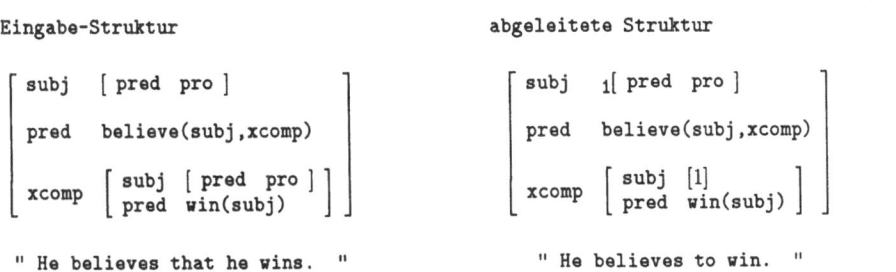

Abbildung 2: Beispiel für Inkohärenz bezüglich Pfadäquivalenz: die rechte Struktur enthält mehr Information als die linke, kann also nicht die minimale Lösung sein.

6 Generierung als strukturgesteuerte Ableitung

Um den Ableitungsprozeß angemessen zu steuern, muß die Verletzung von Constraints bei einem Ableitungsschritt möglichst frühzeitig erkannt werden. Dazu repräsentieren wir die verschiedenen Typen von Constraints wie folgt.[6]

Behandlung von COMPa: Jedem terminalen Knoten einer FS wird ein Flag zugeordnet, das dann und nur dann gesetzt wird, wenn auf diesen Knoten mit einer definierenden Gleichung zugegriffen wird.

Constraint-Gleichung: f-Struktur:

$(1\ SUBJ\ NUM) =_c SG$ [subj [num sg]]   [[-]]

Abbildung 3: Repräsentation eines COMPa-Constraints mit ungesetztem Flag

definierende Gleichung: f-Struktur:

$(1\ SUBJ\ NUM) = SG$ [subj [num sg]]   [[+]]

Abbildung 4: Repräsentation der entsprechenden definierenden Gleichung mit gesetztem Flag

---

In Abb. 3 ist eine Gleichung vom Typ COMPa zusammen mit ihrer korrespondierenden FS dargestellt. Diese wird zweigeteilt repräsentiert; der linke Teil ("Forderungsteil") enthält die geforderte Struktur, der rechte Teil ("Erfüllungsteil") trägt an den korrespondierenden Stellen die Flags, die gesetzt sind, wenn etwas bereits abgeleitet wurde.

Zum Vergleich ist in Abb. 4 die Repräsentation für die entsprechende definierende Gleichung zu sehen, in deren Erfüllungsteil das Flag gesetzt ist.

Eine Ableitung ist vollständig bezüglich COMPa, wenn am Ende der Ableitung alle Flags gesetzt sind.

Behandlung von COMPb: Jedem Pfad in einer f-Struktur, der nicht zu einem terminalen Knoten führt, wird zunächst eine eindeutige Variable zugeordnet. Das entspricht im Falle von Pfadäquivalenzen einem Auffalten der Struktur.

---

[6]Diese Methode, Constraints zu repräsentieren, wurde ursprünglich von Andreas Eisele entwickelt und in seinem LFG-Parser zur Behandlung der constraining equations eingesetzt.

Constraint-Gleichung: f-Struktur:

$$(1\ \mathrm{SUBJ}) =_c (1\ \mathrm{VCOMP\ SUBJ}) \qquad {}_{1}\begin{bmatrix} \texttt{subj} & 2[\ldots] \\ \texttt{vcomp} & 3\begin{bmatrix} \texttt{subj} & [2] \end{bmatrix} \end{bmatrix} \qquad {}_{X1}\begin{bmatrix} X2[\ldots] \\ X3\begin{bmatrix} X4[\ ] \end{bmatrix} \end{bmatrix}$$

Abbildung 5: Repräsentation eines COMPb-Constraints

definierende Gleichung: f-Struktur:

$$(1\ \mathrm{SUBJ}) = (1\ \mathrm{VCOMP\ SUBJ}) \qquad {}_{1}\begin{bmatrix} \texttt{subj} & 2[\ldots] \\ \texttt{vcomp} & 3\begin{bmatrix} \texttt{subj} & [2] \end{bmatrix} \end{bmatrix} \qquad {}_{X1}\begin{bmatrix} X2[\ldots] \\ X3\begin{bmatrix} X2[\ ] \end{bmatrix} \end{bmatrix}$$

Abbildung 6: Repräsentation der entsprechenden definierenden Gleichung

---

In Abb. 5 ist eine constraining equation vom Typ COMPb mit der zugehörigen FS dargestellt. Während im linken Teil die Pfade `<VCOMP SUBJ>` und `<SUBJ>` zur selben Struktur führen, tragen die korrespondierenden Stellen im rechten Teil unterschiedliche Variablen, die erst durch Anwendung der geforderten definierenden Gleichung (vgl. Abb. 6) unifiziert werden.

Ist am Ende der Ableitung der Erfüllungsteil der abgeleiteten Struktur isomorph zum Forderungsteil, so sind alle Constraints vom Typ COMPb erfüllt. Da die Beziehung zwischen Erfüllungsteil und Forderungsteil einen Epimorphismus darstellt (die Abbildung von Erfüllungsteil auf Forderungsteil ist ein surjektiver Homomorphismus) und da aufgrund der Kohärenzbedingung (s.u.) diese Eigenschaft bei der Unifikation erhalten bleibt, genügt es, jeweils die Anzahl der verschiedenen Teilstrukturen festzustellen, um Isomorphie zu überprüfen.

COHa: Kohärenz bzgl. Pfadexistenz wird erreicht, indem die internen Darstellungen der FSen als abgeschlossene PROLOG-Listen repräsentiert werden. Das Prädikat 'merge' (vgl. Eisele/Dörre86) kann dann keine neuen Attribute in eine FS mehr einbauen.

COHb: Um sicherzustellen, daß keine überzähligen Pfadäquivalenzen abgeleitet werden, werden die Teil-FS der EFS durch verschiedene Indizes markiert. Damit wird verhindert, daß Strukturen von Pfaden, die in der EFS nicht äquivalent sind, während des Ableitungsprozesses unifiziert werden.

Das komplexe Constraint, das aus der EFS konstruiert werden kann, stellt sich also als eine zweigeteilte f-Struktur dar. Ihr Forderungsteil ist die EFS selbst, wobei jeder Knoten mit einer eindeutigen Markierung versehen und "abgeschlossen" gegen die Aufnahme zusätzlicher Attribute sein muß. Der Erfüllungsteil ist ein Baum, der sich durch Auffaltung aller Pfadäquivalenzen konstruieren läßt. Er enthält zunächst an allen terminalen Knoten nur ungesetzte Flags (vgl. Abb. 7).

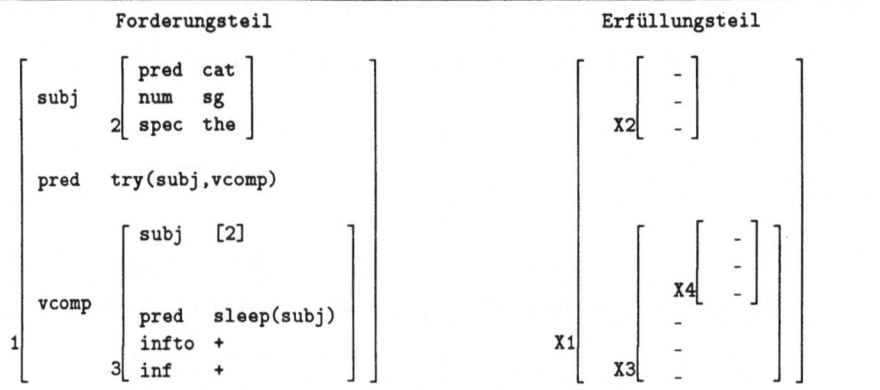

Abbildung 7: Repräsentation der EFS als komplexes Constraint

Beide Teile ergeben zusammen die Start-f-Struktur für die Ableitung bei der Generierung. Für die Zwischenstrukturen der Ableitung werden nunmehr nur noch 3-Tupel benötigt, da die Menge der angesammelten Constraints nun in der angereicherten f-Struktur selbst codiert wird. Eine Ableitung ist erfolgreich abgeschlossen, wenn alle Flags im Erfüllungsteil gesetzt sind und der Erfüllungsteil isomorph zum Forderungsteil ist.

7 Schlußbemerkung

Ähnlich wie eine gewöhnliche LFG-f-Struktur die Information aus definierenden Gleichungen in einer Weise repräsentiert, daß keine Inkonsistenzen auftreten können, werden also in unserem System Constraints in angereicherten f-Strukturen dargestellt, ebenfalls mit dem Ziel, Inkonsistenzen zwischen Constraints bzw. zwischen Constraints und verarbeiteten definierenden Gleichungen zu verhindern.

Die oben beschriebenen Verfahren sind nicht beschränkt auf den Formalismus der LFG, sondern können ebenso in anderen unifikationsbasierten Systemen Verwendung finden.

Das vorgestellte System wird am Institut für Maschinelle Sprachverarbeitung für die Generierung aus f-Strukturen eingesetzt. Es verfügt über einen Compiler, der in lesbarer Form notierte LFG-Grammatiken in eine interne Repräsentation überführt. Daraus ergibt sich auch, daß nicht von einem genau abgegrenzten Fragment gesprochen werden kann, das der Generator abdeckt. Seine Leistungsfähigkeit hängt vielmehr vom Umfang der jeweils eingesetzten Grammatik ab und ist nicht durch den Generator selbst beschränkt.

Das System wurde mit verschiedenen Grammatiken für Deutsch und Französisch getestet und in verschiedenen experimentellen Anwendungen bereits eingesetzt (als Front-End der Transferkomponente eines MÜ-Systems und als Generatorkomponente einer natürlich-sprachlichen Datenbank-Schnittstelle). Außerdem hat es sich als nützliches Werkzeug zum Testen von LFG-Grammatiken auf Übergenerierung erwiesen.

8 Literaturverzeichnis

Bresnan, J. (ed) (1982). *The Mental Representation of Grammatical Relations*. The MIT Press, Cambridge, MA.

Eisele, A. und J. Dörre (1986). A Lexical Functional Grammar System in Prolog. in: *Proc. COLING 86*, pp. 551 – 553. IKP, Bonn.

Kaplan, R. und Bresnan, J. (1982). Lexical Functional Grammar – A Formal System for Grammatical Representation. in: Bresnan, J. (ed.) (1982), pp. 173 – 281.

Momma, S. (1986). *Entwurf und Implementierung eines Generators für allgemeine LFG-Grammatiken*. Diplomarbeit, Institut für Informatik und Institut für Linguistik, Universität Stuttgart.

Kindermann, J. und J. Meier (1986). Generierung mit Lexical Functional Grammar. in: *Proc. of GWAI 1986*, Springer, Heidelberg.

Wedekind, J. (1986). A Concept of Derivation for LFG. in: *Proc. of COLING-86*, pp.486 – 489. IKP Bonn.

FREGE

Ein objektorientierter
FRont-End-GEnerator

Martin Emele

Projekt SEMSYN, Institut für Informatik
Universität Stuttgart, Herdweg 51
7000 Stuttgart 1

1 Einleitung

Für die Generierung natürlicher Sprache sind verschiedene Wissensquellen erforderlich, die auf den einzelnen Stufen linguistischer Beschreibungen angesiedelt werden können (Semantik, Syntax, Morphologie, ...). Objektorientierte Systeme unterstützen diese Trennung in einzelne Klassifikationsebenen sehr gut, da sie es erlauben, verschiedene Klassen zu definieren, die jeweils über separate Wissensquellen verfügen und untereinander über die Klassenhierarchie kommunizieren können. Die verschiedenen Ebenen stellen für sich genommen jeweils "Experten" für klar umrissene Teilbereiche dar, die bestimmte Aufgaben an andere "Experten" delegieren und selbst für die Erledigung von Teilaufgaben angefragt werden können.

Mit der Entwicklung von FREGE wurde das Ziel verfolgt, einen "Experten" für die Teilbereiche Syntax und Morphologie zu schaffen, der im Sinne einer "Black-box" als Front-End-Generator eingesetzt werden kann, um aus syntaktischen Strukturen geeignete Oberflächenketten zu generieren.

Den Ausgangspunkt für die Generierung von Deutsch bilden in SEMSYN semantische Repräsentationen in erweiterter Kasusrahmennotation, die entweder von einer Analysekomponente für die Ausgangssprache geliefert werden (z.B. ATLAS/II) oder die aus einer gebietsspezifischen Wissensbasis abgeleitet wurden, vgl. AMEX [Rösner 86] und GEOTEX [Kehl 86].

Die Entscheidung über die sprachliche Form einer Äußerung obliegt der Verantwortung des Generatorkerns (SEMGEN), der hierzu die entsprechende syntaktische Struktur der intendierten Äußerung erzeugen muß.

2 Die Notation der syntaktischen Eingabestrukturen

Die Form der syntaktischen Beschreibung — wir nennen sie *"Instantiiertes Realisierungsschema" (IRS)*, manchmal auch *IRS-Beschreibung* oder *IRS-Struktur* — legt das Generierungsergebnis vollständig fest: Zum einen geschieht dies durch die Wahl der syntaktischen Kategorie der Äußerung (Satz, Nominalgruppe, Präpositionalgruppe, ...), zum anderen durch die "Funktionale Struktur", mit der die syntaktische Funktion der einzelnen Konstituenten mit Attributen wie Subj, Obj und Obj2 gekennzeichnet wird. Zusätzlich enthält die syntaktische Eingabestruktur alle erforderlichen syntaktischen Merkmale und als terminale Elemente die Lexeme der im Text zu verwendenden deutschen Wörter.

In Abbildung 1 ist eine IRS-Struktur beschrieben, die als syntaktische Eingabestruktur zu FREGE dient.

IRS-Struktur:

```
(:CLAUSE (:HEAD "generier")
        (:Subj
          (:NG (:HEAD "Projekt")
               (:SPEC (:DET "d"))))
        (:Obj
          (:NG (:HEAD "Sprache")
               (:ATTRIBUTES (:AG (:HEAD "deutsch")))))
        (:Adjuncts
          (:PG (:HEAD "aus")
               (:FEATURES (:+source))
               (:Obj
                 (:NG (:HEAD "Netz")
                      (:FEATURES (:NUMBER pl))
                      (:Attributes (:AG (:HEAD "semantisch")))))))))
```

Generierungsergebnis:

"Das Projekt generiert deutsche Sprache aus semantischen Netzen."

Abbildung 1: Beispielhafte IRS-Struktur

Aus dieser IRS-Beschreibung wird vom morphologisch/syntaktischen "Front-End-Generator" die zugehörige Oberflächenstruktur in syntaktisch und morphologisch korrektem Deutsch erzeugt.

3 Überblick

Die objektorientierte Implementierung von FREGE spiegelt die Trennung der einzelnen Beschreibungsebenen in Form von unterschiedlichen Klassen innerhalb einer Vererbungsheterarchie wieder. Abbildung 2 zeigt einen Ausschnitt aus dieser Heterarchie.

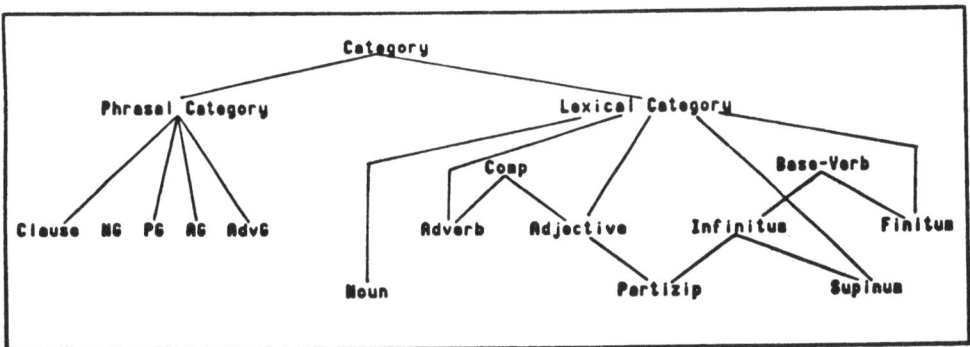

Abbildung 2: Ausschnitt aus der Heterarchie der Kategorien

Kategorien werden unterteilt in phrasale und lexikalische Kategorien, wobei phrasale Kategorien als Projektion von lexikalischen Kategorien im Sinne der $\bar{X}$ Theorie von Jackendoff [Jackendoff 77] anzusehen sind. Auf der Ebene der lexikalischen Kategorien sind die einzelnen morphologischen Prozesse (z.B. Deklination von Adjektiven und Substantiven) angesiedelt, während auf der Ebene der phrasalen Kategorien die einzelnen Merkmalstransportmechanismen durchzuführen sind:

Defaultbelegung: Die Belegung von Merkmalen erfolgt nach Defaultregeln, so daß nur für eine abweichende Belegung der Merkmalswert in der Eingabstruktur spezifiziert werden muß.

Kongruenz: Hierunter fallen alle Kongruenzphänomene (z.B. Subjekt-Verb-Kongruenz, Kongruenz des Reflexivpronomens mit dem Subjekt, Kongruenz zwischen Artikel, Adjektiv und Substantiv, usw.).

Kasuszuweisung: Kasuszuweisung für nominale Konstituenten. Denn gewisse grammatikalische Funktionen implizieren — falls nicht anders angegeben — gewisse morphologische Kasusmarkierungen, beispielsweise Subjekte den Nominativ, direkte Objekte den Akkusativ und indirekte Objekte den Dativ.

Ebenfalls dieser Ebene ist das Wissen zugeordnet, das zur Behandlung der Wortstellungsphänomene des Deutschen benötigt wird. In diesem Beitrag möchte ich mich im Folgenden auf diesen letztgenannten Aspekt von FREGE beschränken, während ich für die Beschreibung der anderen Teilaspekte auf meine Diplomarbeit [Emele 86] verweisen möchte.

4 LP-Regeln

IRS-Strukturen sind ordnungsfreie Strukturen. Das impliziert, daß die erforderliche Anordnung der einzelnen Konstituenten mit Hilfe einer separaten Wissensquelle durchgeführt werden muß.

Die hierarchische Struktur der IRS beschreibt dagegen die Dominanzbeziehungen, die zwischen den einzelnen Konstituenten bestehen. Betrachten wir die IRS-Struktur aus unserem Eingangsbeispiel, nachdem alle Merkmalstransportmechanismen durchgeführt und die Lexeme flektiert worden sind, so erhalten wir den in Abbildung 3 illustrierten ungeordneten und flektierten DAG (Directed Acyclic Graph).

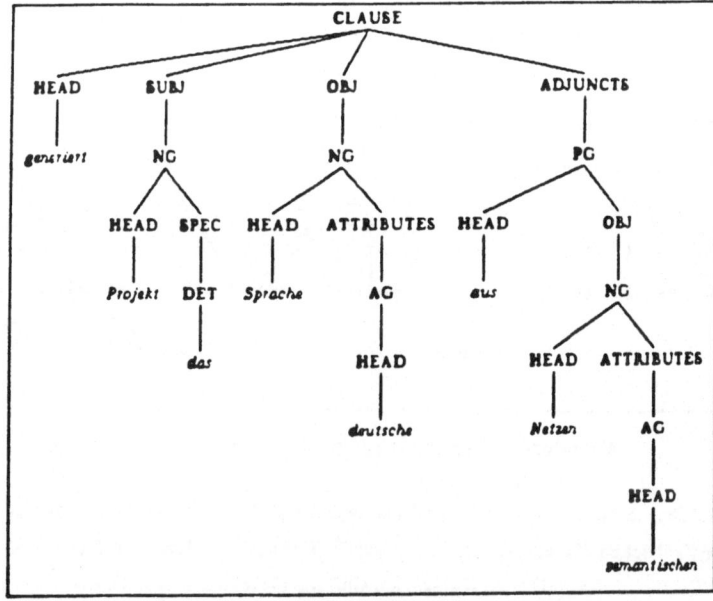

Abbildung 3: Ungeordneter, flektierter DAG

Die Wurzel des DAG bildet eine CLAUSE, die HEAD, SUBJ, OBJ und ADJUNCTS unmittelbar dominiert. Schneiden wir alle Teilstrukturen ab, die direkt unter den dominierten Bezeichnern liegen, so erhalten wir einen lokalen Graphen, der die unmittelbare Dominanzrelation zwischen dem Mutterknoten und seinen Töchtern beschreibt. Diese Beziehung läßt sich mit Hilfe einer kontextfreien Phrasenstrukturregel ausdrücken, wie sie z.B. im GPSG-Formalismus [Gazdar et al. 85] verwendet wird; sie wird dort ID-Regel genannt (ID steht für *"Immediate Dominance"*). Für unser Beispiel erhalten wir damit folgende ID-Regel:

$$CLAUSE \rightarrow HEAD, SUBJ, OBJ, ADJUNCTS$$

Die ID-Regel läßt alle Permutationen ihrer Tochterknoten als mögliche Linearisierungen zu. Somit erhalten wir 4! = 24 mögliche Linearisierungen. Davon bilden in der Regel aber nicht alle Anordnungen eine wohlgeformte Äußerung, so daß zusätzliche "Constraints" für die Vorgängerbeziehung zwischen den Töchtern formuliert werden müssen. Um dies zu tun, definieren wir eine lineare Vorgängerrelation '$\prec$': '$A \prec B$' ist genau dann erfüllt, wenn 'A' 'B' vorausgeht. Jeder Ausdruck der Form '$A \prec B$' wird LP-Regel genannt (LP steht für *"Linear Precedence"*). Die LP-Regeln, wie sie hier verwendet werden, bilden eine strikte Totalordnungsrelation mit folgenden Eigenschaften:

asymmetrisch:

$$\forall_{X,Y} : X \prec Y \Rightarrow \neg(Y \prec X)$$

transitiv:

$$\forall_{X,Y,Z} : X \prec Y \wedge Y \prec Z \Rightarrow X \prec Z$$

konnex:

$$\forall_{X,Y} : X \prec Y \vee Y \prec X$$

Die Eigenschaft der Konnexität wurde deshalb mit aufgenommen, um eine vollständige lineare Reihenfolge zu erzwingen. Diese Vorgehensweise kann für die Generierung insofern begründet werden, als im Grunde genommen jede Stellungsvariante, die überhaupt grammatikalisch zulässig ist, auf irgendeine Art und Weise stilistisch oder pragmatisch markiert sein muß. Liegt keine solche explizite Markierung in Form von speziellen Merkmalen wie beispielsweise TOPIC oder FOCUS vor, so wird eine unmarkierte Stellung produziert (vgl. hierzu die Definition der "unmarkierten Abfolge" in [Lenerz 77, S. 27]).

In unserem Beispiel müßten wir etwa folgende LP-Regeln formulieren, um die gewünschte Linearisierung zu erhalten:

$$SUBJ \prec HEAD \prec OBJ \prec ADJUNCTS$$
$$SPEC \prec ATTRIBUTES \prec HEAD$$

Stellen wir uns jetzt den DAG in Abbildung 3 als eine Art Mobile vor, dessen Kanten jeweils um den Mutterknoten herum verdrehbar sind. Arrangiert man nun das Mobile so, daß alle LP-Regeln erfüllt sind, so erhalten wir die gewünschte Reihenfolge der terminalen Elemente, indem wir von jedem Lexem eine senkrechte Projektionslinie auf eine hypothetisch gedachte Projektionsgerade nach unten ziehen. Die Projektionen der einzelnen Konstituenten ergeben jeweils einen Teilstring, der die Vorgängerrelation zwischen den verschiedenen grammatikalischen Funktionen wiederspiegelt. Wir erhalten somit die gewünschte Linearisierung: *"Das Projekt generiert deutsche Sprache aus semantischen Netzen."*

Im vorherigen Abschnitt wurden nur Beispiele für sehr einfache LP-Regeln betrachtet, bei denen jeweils eine eindeutige Vorgängerbeziehung zwischen grammatikalischen Funktionen formuliert wurde. Nun ist es aber eine bekannte Tatsache, daß in einer Sprache mit freierer Wortstellung, wie z.B. der deutschen Sprache, Ordnungsprinzipien vorherrschen, die sich gegenseitig widersprechen können. Greifen wir uns zwei LP-Regeln heraus, die unabhängig voneinander besehen korrekte Aussagen für die Anordnung ergeben:

$$\left\{ \begin{array}{ccc} SUBJ & \prec & OBJ \\ [+Pro] & \prec & [-Pro] \end{array} \right\}$$

1. *"Gestern sah   der Nachbar   ihn"*
   SUBJ $\prec$ OBJ
   [-Pro] $\succ$ [+Pro]

2. *"Gestern sah   ihn   der Nachbar*
   OBJ $\succ$ SUBJ
   [+Pro] $\prec$ [-Pro]

Sowohl (1) als auch (2) verletzen eine der beiden LP-Regeln, obwohl beide Varianten grammatikalisch sind. In der Tat entsteht der Konflikt dadurch, daß die LP-Regeln alle gleichzeitig erfüllt sein müssen. Dieses Problem läßt sich mit der Einführung komplexer LP-Regeln umgehen. Eine komplexe LP-Regel besteht aus einer Menge von atomaren LP-Regeln, die disjunktiv miteinander verknüpft werden. Eine komplexe LP-Regel ist genau dann wahr, wenn mindestens eine LP-Regel in der Menge erfüllt ist. Damit erhalten wir beide Sätze als korrekte Linearisierungen, da jeweils eine der beiden LP-Regeln erfüllt ist (für eine formale Definition der komplexen LP-Regeln siehe [Uszkoreit 85]). Uszkoreit begründet dort, daß eine Gewichtung der einzelnen LP-Regeln in Bezug auf die anderen Regeln innerhalb einer komplexen LP-Regel notwendig ist, ohne dies jedoch formal weiter auszuführen.

In obiger komplexer LP-Regel ist es offensichtlich, daß die Regel $[+Pro] \prec [-Pro]$ ein höheres Gewicht besitzt als die Regel $SUBJ \prec OBJ$, da im Deutschen, zumal wenn mehrere Pronomina vorkommen, eine obligatorische Reihenfolge für die pronominalen Satzglieder gilt.

Um die Gewichtung zwischen mehreren LP-Regeln ausdrücken zu können, wurden die komplexen LP-Regeln redefiniert:

$$\left\{ \begin{array}{ll} A \prec B & \text{falls } P(A,B) = true \\ A \succ B & \text{sonst} \end{array} \right.$$

$P(A, B)$ stellt ein komplexes Prädikat dar, das beliebige Bedingungen über die Merkmalsbündel der betreffenden Konstituenten A und B fordern kann, die jeweils durch aussagenlogische Operatoren wie *and*, *or* und *not* verknüpft werden können.

Das verwendete Format für die Deklaration derartige LP-Regeln kann abstrakt so beschrieben werden:

(LP (<A> <B>) <predicate>), <A> und <B> stehen jeweils für grammatikalische Funktionen, zwischen denen eine Reihenfolgebeziehung definiert werden soll. <predicate> bezeichnet eine Satzform der Aussagenlogik, deren Wahrheitswert sich aufgrund der aktuellen Merkmalsbelegung der betreffenden Konstituenten ergibt. Die einfachen LP-Regeln erhalten wir mit dieser Definition als Spezialfall der komplexen LP-Regeln, da die Bedingung unabhängig von der Merkmalsbelegung immer "wahr" ergibt. Für die Regel, daß die Artikelwörter immer vor dem Kopf der Phrase stehen ($SPEC \prec HEAD$), schreiben wir folgende Deklaration:

```
(lp (:Spec :Head) t)
```

Anhand der LP-Regel, die die Reihenfolge zwischen dem direkten und indirekten Objekt regelt, möchte ich die Funktionsweise der komplexen LP-Regeln illustrieren.

```
(lp (:Obj2 :Obj)
  (and (+dat obj2)
       (-pro obj)
       (or (+pro obj2)
           (+foc obj)
           (-def obj))))
```

Die unmarkierte Abfolge zwischen dem direkten und indirekten Objekt ist Obj2 $\prec$ Obj, da das direkte Objekt nur unter besonderen Bedingungen vorangestellt werden kann. Die erste dieser Bedingungen lässt sich für die fest vorgegebene Wortstellung der Personalpronomina im Deutschen angeben, und zwar falls das direkte Objekt pronominal ist, steht es immer vor dem direkten Objekt (vgl. [Helbig, Buscha 86, S. 571]).

"Peter schickt es {ihm/einem Kind/dem Kind}"

Im Rahmen einer Thema-Rhema Gliederung, wie sie in [Lenerz 77] mit Hilfe des Fragetests vorgestellt wird, ist Obj[+Foc] $\prec$ Obj2[-Foc] nicht möglich:

"Was hat Peter dem Kind geschenkt?"
* *"Peter hat   das Paket   dem Kind   geschenkt."*

       [+Foc]   [-Foc]

Die Tatsache, daß die Artikelwahl die Wortstellung beeinflußt, kann mit Hilfe der Definitheitsbedingung ausgedrückt werden. Die Reihenfolge Obj[-def] $\prec$ Obj2 ist nicht möglich, falls es sich bei Obj um eine indefinite Nominalphrase handelt (vgl. [Lenerz 77, S. 55]).

"Wem hat Peter ein Buch geschenkt?"
* *"Peter hat ein Buch {einem/dem} Kind geschenkt."*

Obj2 $\prec$ Obj mit Obj2 als Rhema ist in unmarkierter Abfolge nur durch Satzakzent auf Obj2 möglich. Für geschriebene Sprache wurde die komplexe Stellungsregel deshalb so formuliert, daß das indirekte Objekt im Sinne der Thema-Rhema Gliederung dem direkten Objekt nachgestellt wird, falls die dadurch bedingte Voranstellung des direkten Objekts nicht ausdrücklich durch eine der obigen Einschränkungen verhindert wird. Anstatt *"Peter hat dem Kínd das Buch geschenkt."* erhalten wir *"Peter hat das Buch dem Kind geschenkt."*.

4.1 Projektivität

Wir haben bereits im vorherigen Abschnitt angedeutet, wie der Zusammenhang zwischen der linearen Abfolge in der Oberflächenkette und der zweidimensionalen syntaktischen Struktur hergestellt werden kann: Man arrangiert die Knoten des Graphen so, daß eine Projektion möglich ist, die jedes Lexem mit einem Punkt auf der waagrechten Projektionsgeraden verbindet und durch senkrecht von oben nach unten verlaufende Projektionslinien darstellbar ist.

Sind alle Graphen in dieser Weise projektiv zu arrangieren? Ist also die Projektivitätsbedingung trivial? Nein, denn es gibt IRS-Strukturen, die nicht projektiv zu arrangieren sind.

Die Beantwortung dieser Frage hängt natürlich ganz wesentlich von der gewählten syntaktischen Struktur für die Oberflächenkette ab. Denn würden wir beispielsweise eine flache Struktur für einfache Aussagesätze des Deutschen annehmen, so wäre die Projektivitätsbedingung trivialerweise erfüllt, da alle Satzglieder dem Wurzelknoten *'Clause'* als zentralem Element direkt untergeordnet sind. Soll die syntaktische Struktur aber eher die Prädikat-Argument-Beziehungen in Form einer hierarchischen Struktur ausdrücken, so stellt sich die Ausgangsfrage in einer schwächeren Form: Welche syntaktischen Konstruktionen des Deutschen lassen sich nicht durch projektive Strukturen beschreiben, bei denen eine hierarchische Darstellung angesetzt wurde?

Es mag nun nicht verwunderlich erscheinen, daß gerade die "Long-Distance" Phänomene, die bekanntermaßen in den verschiedenen Grammatikformalismen als schwer zu beschreibende Konstruktionen gelten, diejenigen Konstruktionen sind, die die Projektivitätsbedingung verletzen können. Denn wie ihr Name schon sagt, beschreiben diese Phänomene Abhängigkeiten zwischen Elementen, die nicht in lokaler Nachbarschaft zueinander stehen müssen.

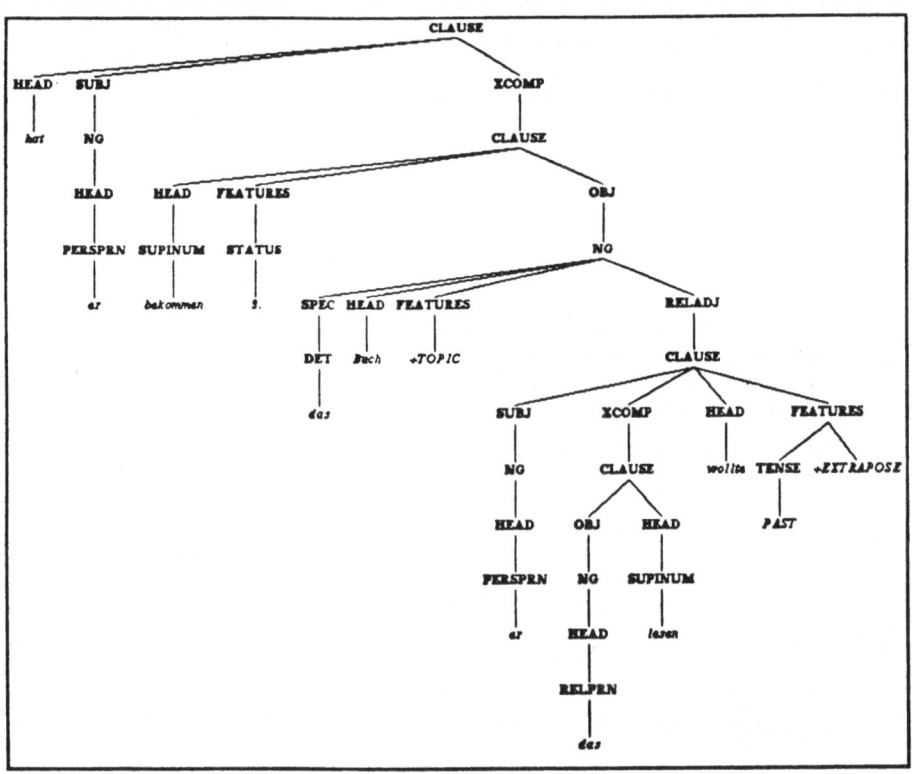

Abbildung 4: Nicht projektiver DAG

In Abbildung 4 haben wir mit der Struktur für den Satz *"Das Buch hat er bekommen, das er lesen wollte."* ein Beispiel für die mehrfache Verletzung der Projektivitätsbedingung, in der sowohl das Objekt des Satzes *"topikalisiert"*, der Relativsatz *"extraponiert"* als auch innerhalb des Relativsatzes das *Relativpronomen* in die Satzkomplementposition rückt, und somit ein projektives Arrangieren verhindert wird.

Da der Formalismus in seiner jetzigen Form ausschließlich aus projektiven Strukturen generieren kann, mußte ein geeigneter Mechanismus implementiert werden, der nichtprojektive Ausgangsstrukturen in flachere Strukturen umwandelt, die dann der Projektivitätsbedingung genügen. Daß dies in allen Fällen möglich ist, ergibt sich aus der Tatsache, daß eine genügend flache Struktur, bei der ein Knoten alle anderen Knoten direkt dominiert, die Projektivitätsbedingung trivialerweise erfüllt.

Für die Erzeugung solcher Strukturen eignen sich **Transformationen**, die auf Bäumen operieren. Der Graph, der als Eingabestruktur dient, wird durch eine Reihe von Tilgungs-, Ersetzungs- und Erweiterungsoperationen in einen Ausgabegraphen transformiert. Diese Operationen stellen in ihrer Allgemeinheit einen zu mächtigen Formalismus dar, als daß sich derartige Transformationen ohne die Formulierung geeigneter Restriktionen anwenden ließen. Folgende Einschränkungen für die Anwendung von Transformationen wurden aufgestellt:

- Es dürfen ausschließlich komplette Konstituenten transformiert werden, deren syntaktische Struktur dabei unverändert bleiben muß.

- Jede Transformation hinterläßt eine Spur an der Stelle, aus der die Konstituente bewegt wurde. Spuren sind abstrakte leere Kategorialknoten, die den gleichen Referenzindex besitzen wie die umgestellte Konstituente.

- Eine Transformation darf jeweils nur genau einmal auf dieselbe Struktur angewandt werden.

- Eine Transformation darf nicht über eine Satzgrenze hinausreichen, die ein Finitum enthält.

Die erste Einschränkung stellt sicher, daß nicht beliebig neue Konstituenten erzeugt werden, sondern ausschließlich Bewegungstransformation stattfindet. Denn das wahllose Hinzufügen neuer Konstituenten würde unter Umständen die rekursive Anwendung von Transformationsregeln erlauben, was zu einer unerwünscht mächtigen generativen Kapazität des Formalismus führen würde. Außerdem werden Transformationen nur bei der Instantiierung einer Konstituente, entweder durch spezielle Merkmale wie +TOPIC und +EXTRAPOSE oder durch die Zugehörigkeit zu einer bestimmten Wortklasse wie Relativpronomen (RELPRN) oder Fragepronomen (WH-PRN), angestoßen.

Wenden wir derartige Transformationen auf die Struktur in Abbildung 4 an, so erhalten wir die Ergebnisstruktur in Abbildung 5, die sich nun offensichtlich projektiv arrangieren läßt.

Das Objekt von *bekommen*, die NG *das Buch*, wird auf die Position TOPIC bewegt und hinterläßt eine Spur, die denselben Referenzindex *[2]* zugeordnet bekommt, wie das entsprechende Antezedens. In der Abbildung ist dies durch identische Indizierung der Konstituenten, mit in eckigen Klammern stehenden Zahlen, gekennzeichnet. *Das Buch* selber dominiert einen Relativsatz, der mit dem Merkmal +EXTRAPOSE versehen ist und auf die Position EXTRAPOSED transformiert wurde. Auch hier ist durch die Koindizierung nachvollziehbar, von welcher Stelle der Relativsatz wegbewegt wurde. Diese Information wird unter anderem dazu gebraucht, um Kongruenz hinsichtlich Numerus und Genus zwischen dem Relativpronomen und dem regierenden Substantiv herstellen zu können. Auch innerhalb des Relativsatzes muß eine Transformation angestoßen werden, die in diesem Fall nicht durch ein Merkmal sondern durch die Wortklasse **Relativpronomen** initiiert wird. Das Relativpronomen *das*, welches das Objekt von *lesen* bezeichnet, muß auf die nebensatzeinleitende Satzkomplementposition COMP transportiert werden, da ansonsten eine projektive Anordnung nicht möglich wäre.

Zusammenfassend lassen sich folgende Eigenschaften der komplexen LP-Regeln aufzählen:

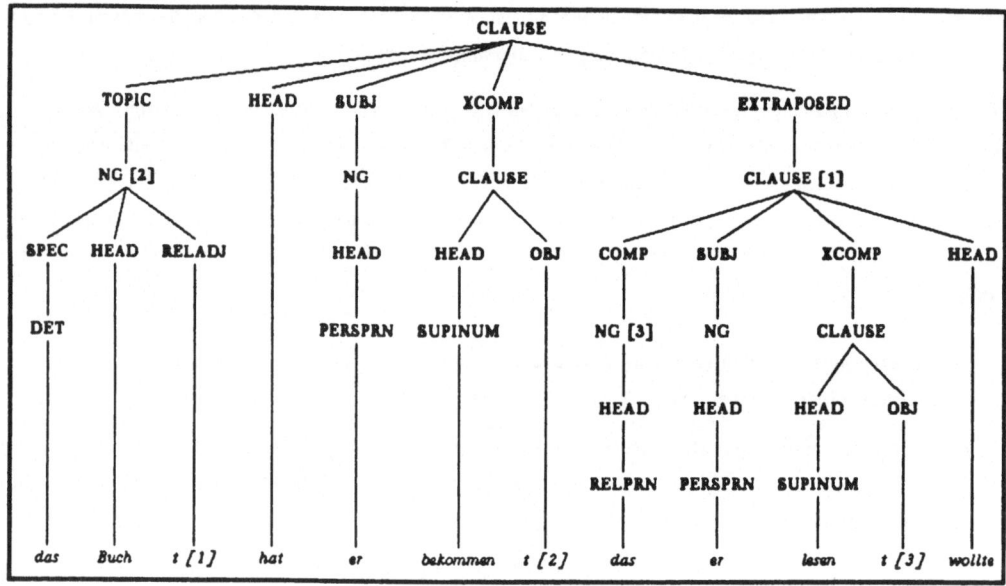

Abbildung 5: Projektiver DAG

- LP-Regeln werden deklarativ formuliert.

- Sie beschreiben Vorgängerbeziehungen, die zwischen grammatikalischen Funktionen bestehen und nicht zwischen syntaktischen Kategorien, wie dies im GPSG-Formalismus der Fall ist.

- Es handelt sich um komplexe LP-Regeln, die beliebige Bedingungen über die als Merkmalsbündel aufzufassenden Konstituenten fordern können.

- Die Linearisierung mit Hilfe solcher Regeln kann ausschließlich aus projektiven Graphen durchgeführt werden.

- Geeignete Transformationen sorgen für die Erzeugung projektiver Graphen, falls die Ausgangsstrukturen nichtprojektiv sind.

5 Ausblick

Die Trennung der linguistischen Beschreibungsebenen und die deklarative Formulierung der Beschreibungen erlaubt es, Teile des Systems auszutauschen, ohne daß die anderen Teile deswegen angepaßt werden müßten. Es liegt ein Entwurf vor für die Implementierung einer Version, die englische Sätze generieren kann, sowie einer Komponente, die französische Oberflächenformen erzeugen soll.

Der erste Schritt, der hierzu erforderlich ist, besteht im Austausch der morphologischen Komponente, die im Falle der englischen Version im wesentlichen auf den Umfang von einigen wenigen morphologischen Flexionsklassen zu reduzieren ist.

Die weiteren Schritte ergeben sich durch die Angabe geeigneter grammatikalischer Funktionen und die Formulierung neuer Stellungsregeln. Für das Englische ist zu erwarten, daß die Komplexität der erforderlichen

LP-Regeln im Vergleich zum Deutschen abnimmt, da es sich um eine konfigurationelle Sprache handelt im Gegensatz zur deutschen Sprache mit ihrer freieren Wortstellung.

Literatur

[Emele 86] Emele, M. (1986): *FREGE — Entwicklung und Implementierung eines objektorientierten FRont-End-GEnerators für das Deutsche*. Diplomarbeit Nr. 469, Institut für Informatik, Universität Stuttgart.

[Gazdar et al. 85] Gazdar, G., E. Klein, G. Pullum & I. Sag (1985): *Generalized Phrase Structure Grammar*. Cambridge: Harvard University Press.

[Helbig, Buscha 86] Helbig, G. & J. Buscha (1972): *Deutsche Grammatik: ein Handbuch für den Ausländerunterricht*. 9. Aufl., Leipzig: Enzyklopädie.

[Jackendoff 77] Jackendoff, R. (1977): *X̄ Syntax: A Study of Phrase Structure*. Cambridge (Mass.): MIT Press.

[Kehl 86] Kehl, W. (1986): *GEOTEX — Ein System zur Verbalisierung geometrischer Konstruktionen*. Diplomarbeit Nr. 458, Institut für Informatik, Universität Stuttgart.

[Lenerz 77] Lenerz, J. (1977): *Studien zur deutschen Grammatik. Bd. 5: Zur Abfolge nominaler Satzglieder im Deutschen*. Tübingen: TBL-Verlag Narr.

[Rösner 86] Rösner D. (1986): *Ein System zur Generierung von deutschen Texten aus semantischen Repräsentationen*. Dissertation, Universität Stuttgart.

[Uszkoreit 85] Uszkoreit, H. (1985): *Constraints on Order*. Stanford: CSLI.

Concretion Inferences in Natural Language Understanding

Dekai Wu

Computer Science Division
University of California, Berkeley
Berkeley, California 94720
U.S.A.
dekai@ucbvax.berkeley.edu

Institut für Informatik
Technische Universität München
Arcisstr. 21
D-8000 München 2
West Germany

Abstract This paper introduces the architecture of FRESCO, an integrated inference mechanism and knowledge representation suited to a cognitive model of natural language understanding processes. A particular type of disambiguation inference known as concretion which occurs in language interpretation is examined within this framework. I put forth some principles resolving several outstanding issues surrounding concretion inferences, and describe a technique called probabilistic map passing which is employed within FRESCO to implement these principles.

1. Introduction

The extent to which we can say that a natural language processing system has understood an utterance depends upon the level of specificity of its representation. Utterance interpretation becomes more refined with each stage of processing. To this end, a distinction has been suggested by Wilensky [1986] between the **primal** and **actual content** of an utterance.

The primal content of an utterance is that content which can be determined solely from its lexical and syntactic structures. Although related to what has traditionally been referred to as literal meaning, primal content usually captures a more abstract component of an utterance's meaning. While the literal meaning of "the cat on the mat" involves the sense of "on" that conveys its typical physical support relationship, the primal content of this utterance includes only the common abstract component of the various meanings of "on" relating their use. The "on" relationship is the same as that which holds for, say, the "writing on the wall" or "the file Nancy is printing on the printer".

The actual content of an utterance is the contextual interpretation of its primal content. The interpretation mechanism makes inferences about an utterance when it restructures a representation of its primal content into one containing the actual content, making use of knowledge about the world, specialized domains, the specific context, speaker intentions, and so forth.

A general type of inference that occurs during the interpretation process is the **concretion inference**. A concretion inference re-categorizes a concept as a more specific concept, based upon contextual clues. The desired result of a concretion inference is the most plausible interpretation possible. To satisfy the criteria of plausibility, the inference need not be logically sound. In the domain of language understanding, a concretion inference produces a more specific interpretation of an utterance than is justified from its linguistic content alone. This is done in order to explain the concepts that are present in the primal content in a plausible fashion, thereby producing a deeper understanding of the utterance. A simple example of a concretion inference occurs in interpreting two different but related senses of the word "delete". The general conception of "delete" has two more specific senses corresponding to "delete a file" and to "delete a word". Understanding "delete a file" invokes the idea of removing a word from a directory, whereas "delete a word" refers not to removing a word from a directory, but to a text editing operation. Although the two senses of delete have something in common, namely the sense captured by the abstract "delete" concept, full comprehension of the utterances requires concretion to one of the more specific concepts. A more sophisticated illustration of concretion processes is found in interpreting the italicized parts of

How do I *print on the laser printer*?

How do I *print on the roller coaster*?

as respectively meaning something akin to

How do I *cause the laser printer to produce a computer file printout*?

How do I *write block letters while unstably seated on a fast-moving thrill ride*?

Concretion inferences assist in solving many disambiguation problems that are traditionally treated independently, including homonym and word-sense diambiguation, adverbial and prepositional phrase attachment, noun-noun compounds, and anaphora. The theory generalizes KL-ONE classification [Schmolze and Lipkis 1983] and realization [Mark 1981] in the sense that a concretion inference categorizes the conceptual structures using partial feature descriptions, but may in addition over-step the logical inference bounds imposed by the definitional hierarchy in order to make plausible interpretations.

A prototype concretion mechanism based upon the KODIAK knowledge representation language was developed for the UNIX Consultant project [Wilensky et al. 1986] and was effective in reducing the number of specific patterns required for language analysis. Rather than rely upon specific parser patterns for each sense of "delete", a single pattern encoded the syntactic generalization ' "delete" object', producing the abstract "delete" concept. The concretion mechanism was then called to disambiguate among the senses by examining context information, in this case the type of object being deleted.

The previous approach did not adequately address the following issues:

1. Efficient retrieval of candidate structures representing contextually plausible interpretations.
2. Discrimination among multiple possible interpretations of the utterance, based upon their plausibilities relative to one another.
3. Determination of the appropriate level of specificity of interpretation.
4. Rigorous representation structure, without slot defaults, while permitting the system to maintain prototype and default *effects*.
5. Retraction of premature inferences.

Before discussing my proposal, I shall recall some previous approaches to several of these points. A technique that has frequently been employed in recent research as a solution to the first point is marker passing [Norvig 1987, Charniak 1986]. Commonly, in what are known as "smart" marker passing methods, markers are passed through various types of links as a retrieval heuristic. Two aspects of "smart" marker passing are that (1) the markers generally carry no structure, and consequently, (2) the usefulness of a collision must be determined by examining the semantics of the paths of the markers involved in the collision. Another marker passing method is exemplified by the work of Martin and Riesbeck [1986], in which a unified approach to parsing and inference depends upon an integrated marker passing algorithm employing structured markers. All of these systems propose to handle the combinatorial indexing process through a parallel network intersection search.

The fourth point deals with prototype and default effects, for which psychological evidence abounds [Rosch et al. 1976]. Slot defaults were invented to model these effects by attaching can-cellable default values to the slots of a frame in an inheritance hierarchy. For example, if one hears "print on the laser printer", one assumes that a computer file is being printed; this is reflected by a Computer Printing frame that holds a Print Object slot with a default value of Computer File. How-ever, Brachman [1985] has shown that such implementations fail to maintain rigorous representation structure.

Brachman's criticisms notwithstanding, slot defaults do not adequately maintain interdependencies. Consider the example that is typically proffered as justification for defaults: one aspect of a Bird is that it is a usually a Flying Creature. Another default for Bird might be Small Sized Creature. These values are not independent in that if the bird in question is extremely large, the likelyhood that it flies decreases dramatically. Roth and Shoben [1983] have observed significant differences in the prototype assumptions made by humans dealing with a single conceptual category, but in different contexts. Nonetheless, to use explicit rules giving default values for all possible combinations of known features would generate excessively combinatoric overhead. Rather, the knowledge representation used in FRESCO reflects the view that most kinds of default effects arise from multiple interacting pieces of knowledge about typical situations, and can be modelled with the aid of an appropriately structured base of typicality knowledge.

2. Knowledge representation and architecture

Network representations can be characterized as employing either **dispersed** or **schematic** representations. Figure 1 depicts a sample dispersed representation of knowledge about mineral water—that it has Carbonation, has a Mineral Taste, comes in a Glass Bottle, and has a Brand.

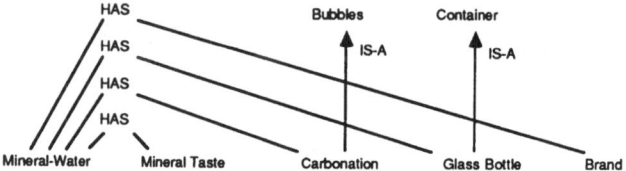

Figure 1. Dispersed representation.

This knowledge is encoded using separate relations stemming from the central concept Mineral Water. Each relation is a typically valid generalization about mineral water. However, suppose we wish to organize the knowledge such that it yields information about typical *combinations* of these properties. For instance, mineral water in a glass bottle is much more likely to be associated with a brand than mineral water in your glass at the dinner table. Likewise, the carbonation in mineral water is typically observed in conjunction with its mineral taste, while drinking; only infrequently is the carbonation associated with the glass bottle. A schematic representation such as that of Figure 2 is employed in order to accomodate such considerations. Concepts are enclosed within contexts provided by schemas.

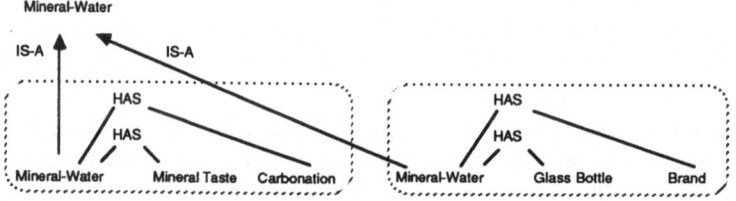

Figure 2. Schematic representation.

In FRESCO, all knowledge is structured schematically, and there are no dispersed representations. The schemas are called **situations**, and contain symbolic nodes called **concepts**. In Figure 3, Data and Computer File are concepts enclosed by one situation, depicted by dashed lines, and the concepts Contents and Container are within another situation.

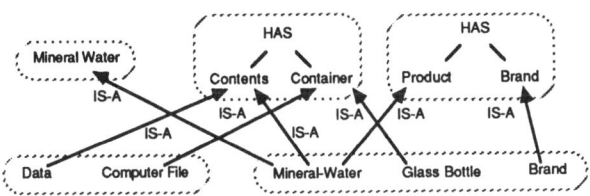

Figure 3. Inheritance of relations.

Figure 3 also demonstrates how relations can be inherited through an abstraction hierarchy or IS-A hierarchy. Containment is a useful abstract situation which is applicable in many situation, such as glass bottles containing mineral water, as well as computer files containing data. Implicitly inheriting relations through the hierarchy conserves space. In addition, the representation is modified one step further: the individual IS-A links are grouped in order to ensure that relations are properly inherited. A group of links is called a **compose map** because it establishes a mapping of concepts from one situation to another. Each link is known as a **role play**. Figure 4 shows these FRESCO primitives. All of the role plays of a compose map are joined by a dashed perpendicular crossbar.

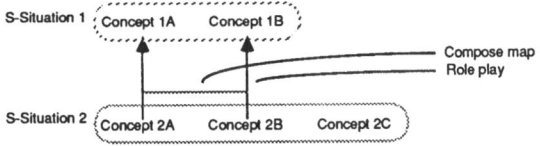

Figure 4. Some primitives.

The following is a summary of FRESCO primitives sufficient to describe concretion inferences:

1. **Concept**. A symbolic conceptual entity.
2. **Situation**. A schematic set of concepts with implicit inherited relationships between the concepts. Each concept belongs to exactly one situation.
3. **Compose map**. A structure map holding between two situations, with role play links identifying matching concepts. Compose maps point to abstract situations, capturing structural similarity generalizations between more specialized situations. It is possible for more than one compose map to hold between the same two situations, if they establish different concept mappings.

The compose maps build an abstraction hierarchy of situations called the **situation hierarchy**. Situations at the bottom of the hierarchy, which are the most specific situations, are called **instances**. Because of the schematic organization, the term "instance" refers to situations rather than concepts. A distinction from most knowledge taxonomies is that different concepts are required to represent the same object viewed in different situations, even though the object has only one real-world extension. For example, Nancy's Desk is a different concept in (1) Nancy Sitting At Nancy's Desk than in (2) Nancy's Wooden Desk. The fact that the desks in the example above are in reality the same desk is reflected by an abstract situation common to both (1) and (2), but containing only Nancy's Desk and its extensional concept.

Information about the degree of **typicality** is associated with every situation in the form of a numeric weight. The following terminology is sometimes helpful in characterizing a situation's typicality relative to that of its neighbors.

1. **Category**. A situation representing a cognitive category, that is, a cognitive abstraction of episodic instances with perceived commonalities. A situation is not necessarily a category; Small

Flying Creature With Two Wings, Two Feet includes birds and bats but is not a category in the cognitive sense. Categories are defined by their sub-ordinate types in the hierarchy.

2. **Type**. A situation which stands as a complete example of a cognitive category. A type of the Bird category might partially be described as a Small Flying Feathered Creature With Beak, Two Wings, Two Feet.

3. **Prototype**. A type that is the sole dominant examplar of its cognitive category is known as a prototype. Basic and most sub-ordinate categories have prototypes, like Bird; super-ordinate categories such as Vehicle include multiple competing types [Rosch et al. 1976].

The architecture is split into two main parts, the memory and the interpreter (Figure 5). The situation hierarchy implements the memory, which consists of **LTM** (long-term memory) and the **CP** (conscious process) unit. The CP unit acts as a focal point, representing the cognitive mechanism's current conception. It contains a single situation which is an instance; together, this situation and the set of compose maps connecting it to other situations in LTM are known as the **conceptualization**. Compose maps that are a part of the conceptualization are called **conceptualization maps**. A situation in LTM to which a conceptualization map points is used to interpret the CP situation. Such a situation is called an **interpreting situation**. The function of the interpreter can be seen as construal of a new situation by combining old situations in novel ways.

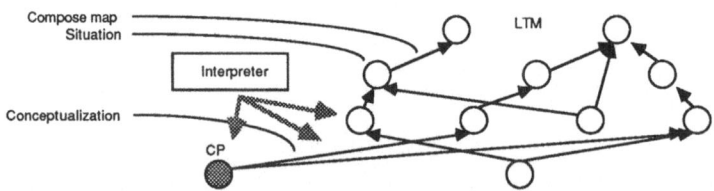

Figure 5. Architecture.

3. Interpretation principles

A set of principles used to guide the design of the interpreter is first presented, motivated with an eye to the issues listed in the introduction.* These "macro-semantics" use the definitions in the preceeding section, and are stated in a somewhat simplified form, sacrificing precision to bring out the intuitions more clearly. They assume that the interpreter begins with a **primal conceptualization**, presumably corresponding to the primal content of an utterance and produced by some hard-coded mechanism (a parser); and that the goal is to produce a **stable conceptualization** which better categorizes the concepts in CP. The process may involve inferring or deleting compose maps and concepts in CP.

1. **The exhaustion principle**. The stable conceptualization should cover the primal conceptualization. In order to avoid losing information, any conceptualization succeeding the primal conceptualization in CP should cover all composes of the primal conceptualization. The stable conceptualization will contain composes pointing to LTM situations that are usually more specific. The specific situations should include all of the situations of the primal conceptualization. Concreting Mineral Water to Glass Bottle Containing Mineral Water is legal with respect to this principle since the latter situation is a specialization of the former. On the other hand, to concrete Mineral

---

* Some similar principles are found in other models. Wilensky [1983] and Norvig [1983] formulated a precursor set of comprehension principles including least commitment, exhaustion, and parsimony. Marr [1977] defined an early least commitment principle, and Fillmore [1983] presented a general version of the parsimony principle.

Water to Glass Bottle Containing Water would lose information. Aspects of the primal conceptualization should only relatively infrequently be discarded, as when an unresolvable contradiction is detected.

2. **The type satisfaction principle.** Interpreting situations should satisfy types. The level of specificity of the LTM situation of a conceptualization map is not high enough if it does not fit a recognizable type. For example, Glass Object is unacceptable as part of a stable conceptualization, whereas Glass Bottle is permitted. While this principle is partially responsible for prototype effects, it also causes default effects: a default inference occurs when a concept not originally in CP must be created in order to fit an interpreting situation to a type. Inferring that a bird flies happens as follows: (1) the general concept of a bird (which need not fly) enters CP, possibly as a result of hearing the word "bird", (2) the concept is noticed to be a non-type, (3) concretion to a situation which *is* a type is required, (4) the Small Flying Feathered Creature mentioned above is chosen because it is the most dominant type.

3. **The parsimony principle.** Minimize the number of interpreting situations. This principle addresses both the issues of disambiguation among multiple interpretations and determination of the correct level of specificity. It aids disambiguation by preferring interpreting situations that construe CP with fewer separate situations that need to be connected. Given that all primal conceptualization maps are to be covered, to reduce the number of interpreting situations requires larger, more specific situations. The effect is to match CP as closely as possible to existing LTM situations, thus finding the best-fitting schemata. This principle draws the conceptualization towards situations that are as specific as possible; the following principles constrain this tendency.

4. **The least commitment principle.** Minimize the number of inferences. Assumptions, that is, inferred conceptualization maps and CP concepts, should not be made unless they serve to increase the schematicity of the conceptualization. Thus, if multiple plausible explanations exist, choose the conceptualization which requires fewest additional assumptions.

5. **The typicality principle.** Favor more dominant types over less dominant types. In the absence of evidence to the contrary, following this principle in determining the search order of the network aids in reducing the average retrieval time by traversing narrower search paths through the hierarchy. In addition, it provides for disambiguation between multiple plausible interpretations.

6. **The concurrence principle.** Maximize the overlap between interpreting situations. If more than one interpreting situation is required to cover the CP concepts, they should have as much in common as possible. Overlap between two interpreting situations is measured in terms of their common ancestral situations.

The principles in this model are prioritized. They are stated above roughly in order, from highest to lowest priority. For instructive purposes, suppose that the priority of principles were strictly followed. With a few other simplifying assumptions, the principles generate the following result: the stable conceptualization should use a single interpreting situation that is the least specific type in LTM covering every aspect of the primal conceptualization. (It must be assumed that such a single situation exists in LTM.)

However, in reality, the principles interact with one another. For example, if one of several possible interpretations of an utterance makes use of a highly dominant prototype, it may be preferred even if it generates more inferences than necessary. On the other hand, sometimes several interpreting situations are preferable to a single one if the single situation requires too many inferences. It is fairly complex to formalize application of the principles due to these interacting priorities. Consequently, the principles are not directly implemented by a straightforward concretion mechanism. The approach taken herein employs a derivative of marker passing, which effects these principles automatically, balancing their priorities.

Nonetheless, because of the parallel activation network approach, a grasp of the high-level principles is needed to motivate the interpreter's actual semantics. Moreover, the details of the solution are tentative and may be altered to better reflect the principles. The principles are central to concretion, while the implementation is incidental.

4. Probabilistic map passing

Concretion inference in FRESCO relies upon a mechanism called **probabilistic map passing**, which models the process of interpreting concepts in CP in terms of situations in LTM. Two networks are involved in probabilistic map passing. One network is the LTM situation hierarchy; the second is a network called the **closure hierarchy**. The LTM does not change during the interpretation process, and its nodes are not associated with any activation level. The closure hierarchy is a parallel activation network in which the activations of nodes are dynamically modified. In addition, the structure of the closure hierarchy is itself constantly updated.

This is accomplished with a special type of compose map internal to the interpreter, known as a **P-compose** (Probabilistic compose). A P-compose, like a conceptualization map, relates CP to an existing LTM situation, but is only a candidate to become a conceptualization map. Each P-compose corresponds to exactly one node of the closure hierarchy; the entire closure hierarchy represents every tentative conceptualization map under consideration. Each P-compose is also associated with the LTM situation to which it maps, but several P-composes may point to the same LTM situation when they establish different mappings from CP to the LTM situation. A P-compose has an activation representing the interpreter's estimate of the probability that the P-compose describes a part of a stable conceptualization. A **dominant** P-compose is estimated with greater than 0.5 probability differential to be correct, and always has a corresponding conceptualization map.

The closure hierarchy records parent-child relationships between P-composes, as well as mutual exclusion relations between P-composes. The closure hierarchy enforces two rules: (1) that a conceptualization does not include at once both an interpreting situation and an ancestor situation that it implies, and (2) that mutual exclusion conditions (which are implemented in LTM with a special kind of concept called an **exclusion concept**) are not violated. Case (1) is checked by restricting probabilities of any combination of P-composes in direct ancestry relationships to a sum not exceeding unity. Case (2) occurs, for example, in color concepts, since an object may not simultaneously be interpreted as being red as well as blue.*

The closure hierarchy is indirectly responsible for maintaining the parsimony principle. From all of the P-composes in the closure hierarchy, the parallel activation technique selects the combination of P-composes that best replaces the existing conceptualization maps. Two aspects of maintaining the closure hierarchy are pertinent: (1) how to structure the hierarchy appropriately, such that it contains all of the P-composes that might be relevant, and (2) how to weigh the different possible combinations of P-composes in the hierarchy against each other, and select the best combination.

To create the appropriate P-composes for the hierarchy structure, the interpreter maintains a "buffer zone" around the perimeter of the closure hierarchy, containing P-composes whose activation is below a threshold. Whenever the activation of a buffer P-compose rises above the threshold,

---

* Although space does not permit detailed discussion of this point, in order to check mutual exclusion constraints, the closure hierarchy actually keeps a complete hierarchy of P-composes mapping to interpreting situations which are ancestors of another P-compose's interpreting situation.

new buffer P-composes are created by traversing compose maps in LTM from the previous buffer P-compose's interpreting situation to immediately descendent LTM situations. Also, the weights upon the links between P-composes in the closure hierarchy must be calculated from the situation typicality weights recorded in LTM. The type satisfaction and least commitment principles are implemented by suitable weighting of closure hierarchy links.

Within the closure hierarchy, P-composes are weighed against each other by discrete simulation of activation redistribution. A potential function measures the fit of each P-compose's interpreting situation to the current conceptualization, using a weighted count of the inferred concepts and inherited relations that the P-compose would require. Activation is then redistributed among neighboring P-composes in the closure hierarchy subject to the potential function, as well as the link weights described above. The potential function ensures adherence to the exhaustion principle.

The method employed is designed to limit the overall number of P-composes in the system, and to search more likely activation paths first. An element of noise is introduced into the potential function in order to perturb the hill-climbing tendency of the activation network. The randomness is parameterized to allow experimentation with different noise levels; in general, the greater the noise permitted, the farther the stable conceptualization can range from the primal.

The interpreter checks for a **collision** whenever generating a new P-compose. Collisions occur in LTM, when newly created P-composes point to LTM situations which existing P-composes already point to. Because maps rather than simple activations are being "passed", and maps have structure, collisions between maps must also be checked for structure in order to determine whether the collision is useful. A P-compose is involved in an **intersection** if and only if another P-compose points to the same LTM situation such that the CP concepts structured by the P-composes also match. Intersecting P-composes are replaced by a single P-compose. There is an added complication: during the course of map passing, many P-composes are generated that have concepts that are not in CP because they may become inferred concepts. Such concepts are **unbound**, and necessitate the use of a concept binding mechanism similar to a simple pattern matching or unification algorithm. An unbound concept may thus be matched to an existing CP concept or to another unbound concept, increasing the overlap between interpreting situations in accordance with the concurrence principle.

When a P-compose becomes dominant, a matching conceptualization map is installed, along with any requisite inferred CP concepts. P-composes with probabilities below a parameterized threshold are pruned from the hierarchy.

Probabilistic map passing differs from most marker passing methods in several ways.

1. It does not rely upon any external algorithm to interpret the result of collisions; the result is in itself the interpretation. In so doing, it performs a number of types of inference usually relegated to separate mechanisms.

2. Maps retaining the semantic structure of situations, rather than markers on individual perceptions, are propagated. Maintaining the semantics drastically reduces the number of false collisions.

3. The use of probabilistic techniques enhances computational feasibility and improves the system's ability to make reasonable utterance interpretations.

5. Example

Consider the sentence, "Nancy is swimming to the bank." There are a number of concretion inferences required in understanding this simple sentence, including:

1. **Contextual assumption**. Nancy is swimming in a river.

2. **Prepositional attachment.** Swimming to a particular destination.

3. **Homonym disambiguation.** Riverbank, not financial institution.

The simplified diagram of the knowledge structures required to disambiguate this sentence is shown in Figure 6.

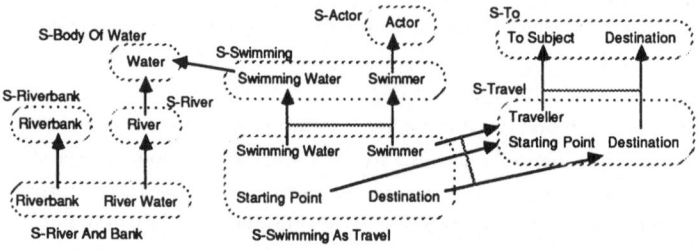

Figure 6. Partial knowledge base for disambiguation.

The syntactic analysis creates the primal conceptualization of Figure 7. This primal content involves no extra-syntactic inference. The primal conceptualization maps PC1, PC2, PC3, and PC4 are shown in their initial state. (Because the closure hierarchy which relates the corresponding P-Composes is not depicted, the mutual exclusion relationship between the two senses of "bank" is not visible.)

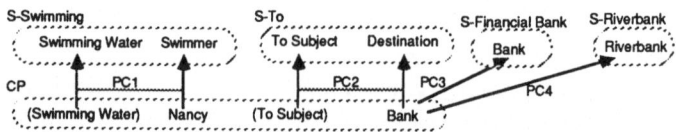

Figure 7. Primal conceptualization.

Upon commencing map passing, PC1 and PC2 will rapidly generate P-composes that intersect at S-Travel and S-Swimming As Travel. Likewise, PC4 and PC1 generate P-composes that collide at S-Body Of Water, S-River, and S-River And Bank. Then, concept binding produces a unified, inferred River Water concept, which is initially several unbound concepts. The stable conceptualization is shown in Figure 8.

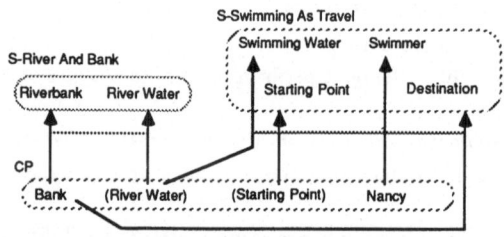

Figure 8. Stable conceptualization.

6. Future directions

A premature inference is detected when a change to the conceptualization is forced by the hard-coded syntactic mechanism in reaction to encountering subsequent text. The subsequent text may somehow conflict with the stable conceptualization already reached from a previous utterance, perhaps as a result of the speaker detecting the hearer's misinterpretation and saying something explicitly calculated to correct it. Alternatively, the system may simply decide that the best possible enforcement of the interpretation principles in light of the new changes to the conceptualization requires abandoning its dominant P-composes in favor of another re-categorization. However, if the semantic distance is too great, the system may not be able to discover a new suitable stable conceptualization. In this case, the entire text must be re-analyzed, but with the new concepts causing the system to be predisposed in a modified direction.

A number of other promising issues paper are being pursued, dealing with applications in parsing, generation, and analogical reasoning. We intend to fully integrate syntactic, semantic, and pragmatic processing in order to study interaction between these different knowledge sources. Although language analysis and production clearly involve different processes to some degree, knowledge that is common to both is structured as to be equally accessible. Another primitive known as a **vector** is being developed in connection with temporal and metaphoric models of knowledge. Another research direction involves modelling learning behavior. Remembering CP situations is done by adding conceptualizations to LTM; the system learns by readjusting the typicality weights of ancestral situations as a consequence of encountering new CP situations. Individual instances are forgotten as a function of relative typicality and time.

Probabilistic map passing systems show the potential to achieve disambiguation abilities close to that promised by neural networks in areas involving typicality and default reasoning, but at a higher conceptual level more amenable to study.

Acknowledgements   I am grateful to Robert Wilensky and the members of BAIR (Berkeley Artificial Intelligence Research) for many productive discussions. In addition, I appreciate the support of Wilfried Brauer, Christian Freksa and the PAKI group at TU Munich. This research was sponsored in part by DARPA (DoD), Arpa Order No. 4871, monitored by SPAWAR under Contract No. N00039-84-C-0089 and by ONR under contract N00014-80-C-0732.

References

Brachman, Ronald. 1985. "I lied about the trees: Or, defaults and definitions in knowledge representation." *AI Magazine*, Fall 1985, 80–93.

Charniak, Eugene. 1986. "A neat theory of marker passing." *Proc. AAAI-86*, 584–588.

Fillmore, Charles J. 1983. *Ideal Readers and Real Readers*. Report No. 5, Berkeley Cognitive Science Program.

Mark, William. 1982. "Realization." In J. G. Schmolze and R. J. Brachman (eds.), *Proc. of the 1981 KL-ONE Workshop*. Fairchild Laboratory for Artificial Intelligence Research, Tech. Rep. 4, Palo Alto, California, May 1982, 76–87.

Marr, D. 1977. "Artificial intelligence—A personal view." *Artificial Intelligence* 9: 37–48.

Martin, C. E., and C. K. Riesbeck. 1986. "Uniform parsing and inferencing for learning." *Proc. AAAI-86*, 257–261.

Norvig, Peter. 1983. "Frame activated inferences in a story understanding program." *Proc. IJCAI-83*.

Norvig, Peter. 1987. *A Unified Theory of Inference for Text Understanding*. C. S. Div., U. C. Berkeley, Report No. UCB/CSD 87/339.

Rosch, E., C. B. Mervis, W. D. Gray, D. M. Johnson, and P. Boyes-Braem. 1976. "Basic objects in natural categories." *Cognitive Psychology* 8: 382–439.

Roth, E. M., and E. J. Shoben. 1983. "The effect of context on the structure of categories." *Cognitive Psychology* 15: 346–378.

Schmolze, J. G., and T. A. Lipkis. 1983. "Classification in the KL-ONE knowledge representation system." *Proc. IJCAI-83*, 330–332.

Wilensky, Robert. 1983. *Planning and Understanding*. Massachusetts: Addison-Wesley.

Wilensky, R., J. Mayfield, A. Albert, D. Chin, C. Cox, M. Luria, J. Martin, and D. Wu. 1986. *UC: A progress report*. C. S. Div., U. C. Berkeley, Report No. UCB/CSD 87/303.

Modelling Heuristic Parsing Strategies

Hans Haugeneder

Manfred Gehrke

Siemens AG

München, W. Germany

Abstract

Besides a correct grammar, the strategy that applies the grammar rules to the input plays an important role in the performance of natural language parsers. In this paper a framework is presented offering comprehenensive facilities for defining and testing parsing strategies based on various heuristic criteria.

1. Introduction

Parsing natural language utterances can be considered a search problem, which is characterized by the application of grammatical descriptions (i.e. a set of grammar rules) to the input to be processed. In realistic applications in which one has to cope with grammars with a large coverage and a non-trivial complexity of the input (measured e.g. in sentence length and lexical ambiguity) one is confronted with difficulties that seem quite common to various search problems, namely

- the search space becomes extremely large, and
- there are several solutions, some or one of which are preferable to the others.

To these problems two quite opposite approaches have been proposed. On the one hand, the brute force of exhaustive search has been used, possibly augmented with some ranking scheme for the set of parses. On the other hand, the parsing of natural language utterances can be considered a deterministic process [13] , where a "wait and see" strategy makes the flavour of searching through the alternatives of application of different grammar rules disappear, at least for grammars with limited coverage. This approach, though being very attractive from its aim, at the present time suffers from the problem of not being able to parse all grammatical constructions (including the notoriously highly ambiguous ones).

The approach we are taking to this problem is to develop a best-first parsing strategy which enables the parser by means of heuristic criteria and information to achieve the most plausible analysis as the first one. Furthermore it should temporarily limit the overall search space as much as possible to arrive at the first parse at low costs. But we still want to maintain the ability of our mechanism to find further solutions, since we do not assume the order of the analyses to be correct all the time. This description of our aim contains vague specifications which should become more clear in the following discussion.

For the understanding of the following, one basic assumption should be very clear, however. What we propose is a practically oriented approach to the two types of problems mentioned; it is practical in the sense that our primary focus is not to model t h e human sentence processing mechanism, specify t h e human parsing strategy or even reopen the discussion on the psychological adequacy of ATNs [4], [10], which are used as the grammatical framework of our work. Our goals are not so far-reaching: We are aiming towards the development of parsing strategies, which are based on heuristic information enabling the parser to choose the right paths in the search space most of the time. Although psychological results on human sentence processing strategies may be incorporated in the heuristics to be developed - at least as far as they fit in our framework and do not assume special properties of the underlying processing scheme - we do not understand our work as contributing to the problem of characterizing inherent structures of the human sentence processor.

Thus our goal is not of an "all or nothing" character; we do not expect our parser to make the right choice all the time or to come up with the intended reading as the first one always. What we do want, however, is to develop a best-first strategy, which when applied to major samples of sentences, is able to give us the intended reading most of the time, at the same time excluding major parts of the overall search space.

At the moment, we are not able to give a founded quantitative characterization in terms of percentage of sentences with correct first reading or percentage of the search space traversed to come up with the first reading; but since working with rather simple-minded parsing strategies in our APE system [7] showed several promising results, we got the impression that giving the parser more guidance by increasing the information available at the choice points will pay by making parsing more efficient. Work in a similar direction on the MCC Lingo project [19] seems to give some indication for this, too.

Since the development of a suitable parsing strategy from the practical point of view we adopted is an empirical question of systematically "playing around" with the various factors influencing the overall strategy, the first steps towards our aim are to identify these factors, to make the corresponding information available during the parsing process and to allow for a facility for specifying the strategy that can be handled easily.

2.   Our Sense of Heuristics

The term "heuristics" is used quite often in the context of modelling some problem solving behaviour. Since it is thereby used in a few drastically different senses some clarification seems necessary.

One definition sees heuristics as affecting problem solving competence by not being foolproof, which means that the use of a heuristic of this type does not guarantee to be able to find the correct solution at all [15]. This is not true for our approach since we do not exclude the correct solution, which sometimes simply may not be the first analysis found, from our search space.

A second reading uses "heuristic" together with graph search algorithms [16], where heuristic evaluation functions diminish the search effort compared to uniform ones, still guaranteeing to reach the correct solution. This is not true either for our approach. We do not effectively reduce the overall search space as compared to uniform strategies like depth-first or breadth-first; we rather order the search steps in a way which allows us to get rid of parts of the search space in most of the cases.

In a third sense, the term "heuristics" is understood as describing means to improve the problem solving performance without affecting competence [14]. This exactly corresponds to our use of this term; we use heuristic information to improve the problem solving performance by coming up with the preferred analysis without traversing the whole search space. On the other hand, we do allow for getting more solutions, if the first one is not the "correct" one.

3. The Use and Need of Heuristic Information in Parsing

In a number of natural language parsers (especially in those with practical orientation and grammars with comprehensive coverage), the problem of dealing with alternative parses has been handled by some sort of scoring measures for sets of alternative parses already produced by breadth-first enumeration.

This is the case in the DIAGRAM parser, where arbitrary sub-procedures (so-called factors) assign likelihood scores to syntactic analyses [17]. In the EPISTLE system, a numerical metric is used for ranking multiple parses which is defined on the form of the phrase structure being built up [9]. And as a last example for that type, the METAL parser performs a scoring of the analyses found, which is based on both grammatical and lexical phenomena [18]. In all these examples, the criteria on which the scoring is based do not influence the parser's behaviour but acts as some sort of filter on the parser's results. If, however, the criteria used in these scoring methods express reasonable scoring intuitions, to us it seems more attractive to make use of this information (together with possibly other criteria) during the parsing process than to apply it after the parser has performed a blind all-paths analysis.

If one thinks of more ambitious and difficult applications, like speech understanding with the high degree of ambiguity in the input in the form of numerous word hypotheses, the application of such heuristic criteria during the parsing process seems even much more promising than the filter approach.

A further advantage of a best-first parser of the type proposed becomes clear if one thinks of the parser as part of a natural language understanding system with some processing modules which get their input from the parser. If one assumes that such subsequent processing (i.e. semantic interpretation) may be very expensive and that the parser and the semantic interpretation module interact on a phrasal level, one can save a lot of processing power if the parser does not deliver his constituents at random but instead delivers plausible phrases first.

4. A Framework for Modelling Heuristic Best-First Parsing
4.1 Active Chart Parsing

In order to be able to perform a heuristic best-first parsing strategy, one needs a suitable parsing mechanism which has enough flexibility for such a task. The most obvious mechanism for an approach like the one proposed is active chart parsing [11], [6] which is a highly general framework for constructing parsers. It combines the idea of an (active) chart as an extensive bookkeeping mechanism preventing the parser from performing two identical processing steps twice, with the idea of an agenda-driven control structure which enables a very elegant and highly modularized simulation of different control structures. A schematic description of the interaction of the major components is given in figure 1.

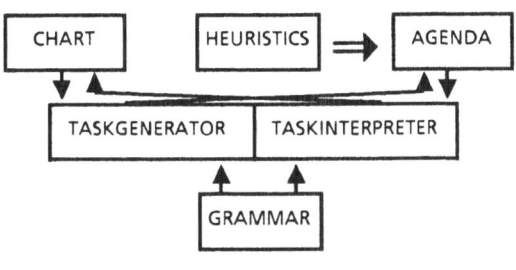

Figure 1

The core parser consists of two functions, the task generator and the task interpreter, which operate on the main data structures: the grammar, the chart, and the agenda. The agenda itself consists of a ordered list of tasks each of which specifies a possible step that can be performed given the current state of the parser. In somewhat more detail a task consists of an active edge (characterizing a partial analysis), an inactive edge (characterizing the next item to consume, i.e. a word or a phrase) and a grammatical rule which specifies the conditions under which the active edge may be continued. The operation of the algorithm thereby proceeds as specified in (CHP) (simplified for the sake of brevity):

```
(CHP)                    initialize chart and agenda
           loop      if  the agenda is not empty
                         then   apply task interpreter to the first task in the agenda
                         else   fail
                     if  the task can be performed successfully (i.e. the active edge can
                         be continued by the inactive under the conditions of the
                         grammatical rule)
                         then      put the newly created edge into the chart
                                   apply the task generator to this newly created edge
                                      to create the follow-up task(s)
                                   apply the heuristic function to the newly created
                                      task(s) and put them on to the agenda according
                                      to their heuristic score
                         else      go to loop
                     if  no complete analysis has been reached
                         then      go to loop
                         else      deliver result of analysis
```

This rough sketch of the basic mechanism shows that this framework offers maximal flexibility in using different control structures for processing the search space since it makes no demands on the nature of the heuristic function updating the agenda.

4.2   A Development Environment

Since we view the development of the heuristic function at the heart of the best-first parsing strategy as a result of going through a number of define-test-modify cycles to build up the final heuristics, it is necessary to have available an environment which enables the user to define and modify the heuristic function easily and supports him in seeing and checking immediately and without much effort the effects of a modification.

The APE system, in which this work is embedded, is an ATN programming environment based on an active chart parser. By means of a highly interactive, graphically oriented user interface it offers operational facilities that give the user a number of necessary possibilities for inspecting and debugging the parser's behaviour under a certain strategy, as for example an agenda editor, the possibility to change strategies during parsing, and a chart-based fully graphical parser stepper. Giving the details of this would go beyond the scope of this paper; they are described elsewhere [8].

Although the APE system is based on an ATN framework, the characteristics concerning heuristic information for scheduling are independent of the underlying ATN approach; the only critical point is the assumption of an active chart parsing processing scheme. Thus these considerations can be applied to a number of other grammar formalisms as well, especially to those belonging to the paradigms of (procedurally and descriptively) augmented phrase structure grammars.

5. The Specification of Heuristic Strategies

5.1 Factors Influencing Heuristic Strategies

When analyzing the two rather simple-minded strategies which we supplied our parser with - they did not do more than propagating the weights assigned to the grammar rules in either a global or a more local fashion - we identified the following types of information which, if available, can contribute to the definition of a more subtle and effective heuristic strategy:

- weight of the partial analyses, which is the value of the heuristic function associated with the active edge characterizing this partial analysis
  (By this weight the overall plausibility of a certain partial parse is characterized.)
- static characterization of the plausibilities of grammatical rules
  (This gives the possibility to scale the grammar with regard to the probability of the constructions; thus one can easily divide the grammar into a core and peripheral part.)
- different values assigned to the various homographic readings of words in the input
  (For a number of systematic but not equally distributed homographic ambiguities, as for examples the noun reading of certain verb forms, this offers an elegant way of supressing the "exotic" reading; there is also psychological evidence for such a treatment of homographic ambiguities [2].)
- span of an inactive edge as ratio of the edges' span and the total length of the input
  (With other factors being equal an inactive edge with a bigger span would be preferable, since this leads to a bigger overall span)
- number of input items left for processing, expressed as (I) with hv_{max} being the maximal heuristic value (i.e. 1), $whyp_{left}$ being the number of word hypotheses left in the remaining input and $whyp_{total}$ being the total number of word hypotheses

$$(I) \qquad hv_{max} \ - \ \frac{whyp_{left}}{whyp_{total}}$$

(This sort of information can be used to force the parser to behave in a resource-oriented manner if there are only a few items left to process.)
- complexity of the structure built so far, measured in terms of number of nodes depth and mode of embedding
  (Thus grammatical but hardly acceptable structures, like deep center embeddings for example, can be "postponed".)

All this information is fairly inexpensive to compute and making it available and accessible to the heuristic function during the parse can be accomplished very easily by attaching this information to the components of a task (i.e. the inactive edge, the active edge and the grammar arc).

Besides these more or less syntactic factors one can also think of integrating semantic criteria (as referential analysis of (noun) phrases or word sense disambiguation for example) directly as part of an heuristic strategy. Since the application of the strategy takes place at a very fine-grained level, where one reasonably may not expect semantic "feedback" in the form of a corresponding heursitic value hv_{sem} all the time, one has to cope with the problem of how to deal with an hv that is not defined. If one adopts the convention, that the effect of an hv which no value has been supplied for, is totally excluded from the overall heuristic function (as specified in (III*) below) one achieves a plausible and attractive style of syntax-semantics interaction. This offers a good deal of flexibility with the possibility of interaction at the word level (cf. [3]) as well as at the phrase level (cf. [1]) without committing to either.

5.2. The Heuristic Function

Assuming that the values for the various heuristic criteria are in the interval [0,1] resulting in an overall heuristic measure in the same interval, i.e. the heuristic function **hf** has the form specified in (II), there is still the question of how these criteria interact and how the values accumulate.

(II) **hf**: $[0,1]^n$ $\Rightarrow$ $[0,1]$ with n being the number of heuristic criteria

The interaction of these different heuristic values hv_j is handled by a weighting factor wf_j which is associated with each heuristic dimension (such as e.g. complexity of the structure). The weighting factor is intended to express the importance of the corresponding dimension and has a range from 0 to 5, with 0 meaning that the dimension does not play a role at all and 5 giving it maximal relevance.

Obviously, this weighting factor has no real qualitative interpretation; the only thing it expresses is the importance of a heuristic dimension relative to the other ones. Thus, for each heuristic criterion the actual value is computed by the product of the value of the heuristic dimension and the corresponding weighting factor, i.e. $wf_j * hv_j$. For the accumulation of the values of the heuristic criteria we have chosen the arithmetic mean, thus having the overall heuristic value being defined be the formula (III).

A simple example may illustrate the effects of changing the weighting factors. Assuming we have the three heuristic criteria hv_1 (grammar weight), hv_2 (active edge weight), and hv_3 (items left) and two tasks with the corresponding values (0.9, 0.8, 0.5) for $task_1$ and (0.7, 0.7, 0.8) for $task_2$. If we now assume the weighting factors $wf_1 = 3$, $wf_2 = 3$ and $wf_3 = 1$, (III) expands into (IV) for $task_1$ and into (V) for $task_2$, giving $task_1$ a higher priority.

(III)

$$\frac{\Sigma \ wf_j * hv_j}{\Sigma \ wf_j} \qquad \text{for all } hv_js \text{ and all } wf_js$$

(III*)

$$\frac{\Sigma \ wf_j * hv_j}{\Sigma \ wf_j} \qquad \begin{array}{l}\text{for all the } hv_js \text{ and corresponding } wf_js, \text{ such} \\ \text{that the value of } hv_j \text{ is defined}\end{array}$$

(IV)

$$\frac{3 * 0.9 + 3 * 0.8 + 1 * 0.5}{7} \qquad = 0.8$$

(V)

$$\frac{3 * 0.7 + 3 * 0.7 + 1 * 0.8}{7} \qquad = 0.71$$

If we put more emphasis on hv_3 which intuitively says if there is a partial analysis with very few alternatives in the remaining input, then continue this analysis with considerable emphasis (with wf_3 = 4 for example) then $task_1$ gets an overall heuristic value of 0.71 whereas that of $task_2$ climbs up to 0.74, now giving higher priority to $task_2$.

5.3   Implementation of the Heuristic Function and its Editor

The heuristics editor is integrated into APE's user interface in a straightforward way; in addition to the possibility of choosing between four predefined uniform and heuristic strategies, the user can define his own strategy. The specification of the intended heuristic function is performed by giving appropriate weighting factors wf_i to the various heuristic dimensions in a template-based manner (as shown in figure 2). By naming his strategies the user is also offered the possibility of defining a number of heuristic functions which then can be used and tested simultaneously.

After the specification of the values for the various wf_is, the user is presented the arithmetic expression associated with the corresponding heuristic function which he can modify

Figure 2

further (in standard infix notation) if he finds the system defined function unsatisfactory (as indicated in figure 3). This obviously can lead to modifications of hf's range definition, the consequences of which the user must be aware of when using this facility.

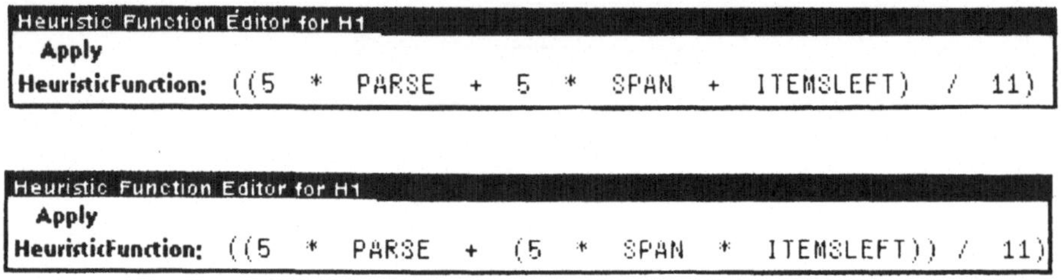

Figure 3

Thus, the user as tuner of the best-first strategy is equipped with a handy facility for defining and manipulating the parsing strategy.

The actual implementation of the APE system and the work described here has been performed in Interlisp-D on a Siemens EMS 5822 workstation.

6. Outlook

With the approach presented we feel that we are able to work in a conceptually flexible and powerful framework which enables us to explore the nature of a heuristic function that fulfills or comes near to our demands. Furthermore, the whole set-up is open to augmentations in the form of additional heuristic criteria and other (possibly more sophisticated) accumulation schemata. At the moment, however, it seems more important to actually get some experience with the facilities described and explore their strengths and weaknesses than to provide too many switches to play with.

Acknowledgements
We would like to thank Bob Frederking for helpful comments.

Literature

[1]   Bobrow, Robert J., Webber, Bonnie L., "PSI-KLONE - Parsing and Semantic Interpretation in the BBN Natural Language Understanding System". In: CSCSI/CSEIO Annual Conference. CSCSI/CSEIO 1980, 131-142

[2]   Carpenter, P.A., and Daneman, M., "Lexical Retrieval and Error Recovery in Reading: A Model Based on Eye Fixations". Journal of Verbal Learning and Verbal Behaviour Vol. 20 No. 2 (1981), 137-160

[3]   Charniak, E., "Passing Markers: A theory of contextual influence in language comprehension". In: Cogitive Science Vol. 7 (1983),171-190

[4]   Fodor, J. D., Frazier L.,, "Is the Human Sentence Parsing Mechanism an ATN?" In: Cognition Vol. 8 (1980), 417-459.

[5]   Gardner, A. v.d. L., "Search: An Overview". AI-Magazine Vol. 2 No. 1 (Winter 1980/81), 2-23.

[6]   Görz, G., "ATN und Kontrollstrukturen". In: Metzing, Dieter, Christaller, Thomas (eds), "ATN Grammatiken", Berlin, Einhorn Verlag 1979, 1-33.

[7]   Haugeneder, H., Gehrke, M., "A User Friendly ATN Programming Environment (APE)". In: Proc. COLING-86, 399-401.

[8]   Haugeneder, H., Gehrke, M., "APE User Manual". Siemens Report, to appear 1987.

[9]   Heidorn, G.E., "Experience with an Easily Computed Metric for Ranking Alternative Parses". In: Proc. ACL-82, 82-84.

[10]   Kaplan, R.M., "Augmented Transition Networks as Psychological Models of Sentence Comprehension". In: Artificial Intelligence, Vol. 3 (1972), 77-100

[11]   Kaplan, R.M., "A General Syntactic Processor". In: Rustin, R. (ed), "Natural Languange Processing", New York, Algorithmics Press 1973, 193-241.

[12]   Kay, M., "Algorithm Schemata and Data Structures in Syntactic Processing". Xerox PARC Tech. Report No. CSL-80-12, 1980.

[13]   Marcus, M., "A Theory of Syntactic Recognition for Natural Language". Cambridge/Mass., The MIT Press 1980.

[14]   Minsky, M., "Steps Towards Artificial Intelligence". In: Feigenbaum, E. A. and Feldman, J. (eds), "Computers and Thought", New York, McGraw-Hill 1963, 406-450.

[15]   Newell, A., Shaw, J. C., and Simon H.A., "Empirical Explorations with the Logic Theory Machine: A Case History in Heuristics". In: Feigenbaum, E. A. and Feldman, J. (eds), "Computers and Thought", New York, McGraw-Hill 1963, 109 - 133.

[16]   Nilson, N.J., "Principles of Artificial Intelligence". Palo Alto, Tioga 1980.

[17]   Robinson, J., "DIAGRAM: A Grammar for Dialogues". CACM Vol. 25 No. 1 (1982), 27-47.

[18]   Slocum, J., "A Status Report on thr LRC Machine Translation System". In: Proc. Conference on Applied Natural Language Processing 1983, 166-173.

[19]   Wittenburg, K., "A Parser for Portable NL Interfaces Using Graph-Unification--Based Grammars". In: Proc. AAAI-86, 1053-1058.

An Organization of Lexical Knowledge for Generation

Massimo Poesio
Project WISBER[§], University of Hamburg
PO BOX 302762, 2000 Hamburg 36, West Germany

Abstract

Recent work on generation focuses on the 'strategic' problem of producing a representation of what has to be said, assuming more or less implicitly that the 'tactical' problem of actually producing a sequence of words expressing that representation has been solved. This assumption is rather optimistic. Between the many problems which still remain, this paper focuses on the organization of lexical knowledge. The solutions adopted in a prototype tactical system called GEOGRAPH are presented. The representation language used by GEOGRAPH has been augmented to handle the problems raised by the organization of lexical knowledge; the epistemological affinities between lexical and domain knowledge have been evidentiated. Once lexical and domain knowledge are organized according to the same principles, some tools to ease their integration can be provided by the knowledge representation language itself. A first attempt in this direction is described.

1. Introduction

In recent years the focus of attention of generation research has shifted toward previously neglected problems, such as responding appropriately to the user's intentions, or organizing the text to be produced according to appropriate rhetorical structures ([1], [11], [13]). The resulting systems more or less share the assumption that the major problem in translating into words the representation of what has to be said is the development of an appropriate grammar. As pointed out by Marcus [12], however, this view is misleading, in that it underestimates the relevance of lexical knowledge and the problems connected with its organization and its association with domain knowledge. As a result, the dictionaries used are extremely ad hoc, and not usable by the analysis routines.

The GEOGRAPH (GEneratiOn from GRAPHs) system is the generation module of a speech question-answering system called SUSY (for Speech Understanding SYstem) ([15]). During the analysis SUSY produces a representation of the spoken question in form of a Conceptual Graph (CG) ([17]), which is evaluated to get the answer. GEOGRAPH receives a CG representing the content of the answer, and produces an Italian sentence from it . The sentences (1b) - (3b) are generated by GEOGRAPH to answer the questions (1a) - (3a).

[§]Part of this work was done while the author was at CSELT, Torino, Italy, under the EEC ESPRIT Project n.26 "Advanced Algorithms and Architectures for Signal Processing".

(1a)   In quale regione nasce il Po? (In which region originates the Po river?)

(1b)   Il Po nasce in Piemonte. (The Po river originates in Piemonte)

(2a)   Quali fiumi scorrono in Piemonte? (Which rivers flow through Piemonte?)

(2b)   Il Piemonte e`attraversato dalla Bormida, dalla Dora Baltea, dalla Dora Riparia, dal Po, dalla Stura, dal Tanaro, ... (Piemonte is crossed by ....)

(3a)   Quali sono i laghi della regione in cui nasce il fiume piu' lungo che scorre in Emilia? (What are the lakes of the region in which originates the longest river flowing through Emilia?)

(3b)   I laghi della regione in cui nasce il piu' lungo fiume che attraversi l'Emilia Romagna sono il lago di Candia, il lago Maggiore, il lago d'Orta ed il lago di Viverone. (The lakes of the region in which originates the longest river which crosses Emilia Romagna are the lake of Candia, the lake Maggiore, the lake of Orta and the lake of Viverone.)

GEOGRAPH is a *tactical* system: it must produce a correct 'linearization' of the information that SUSY has planned to give to the user. A non-trivial tactical system, however, must be able to generate sentences more complex than (1b) - whose production nevertheless requires at least some knowledge of syntax and some information about proper nouns. To generate a sentence like (2b), for instance, the system must be able to decide when the passive voice is more appropriate, and to choose between several alternative ways of expressing the same concept (in this case, the action concept corresponding to both "scorrere" and "attraversare"). The generation of a sentence like (3b) requires instead the ability to handle relative sentences; more generally, some handling of concept modifiers. This latter requirement imposes constraints on the kind of knowledge representation that is employed. All of these sentences, at last, include prepositions and articles, whose use in Italian is highly idiosyncratic ([10]).

In consequence of these requirements, in developing GEOGRAPH I have worked (between the themes proposed in [11]) on the development of a knowledge representation formalism and on the organization of lexical knowledge. The conceptual graph notation which has been adopted [17] is a formalism of general applicability, in the sense indicated in [16]: it can be, and in fact is, used in a reasoning system, and has a well-defined semantics. A knowledge representation language called CSL-0 has been developed on this basis; it provides the functionalities necessary to structure a knowledge base at the epistemological level. These functionalities have been used to organize both lexical and domain knowledge, with the twofold effect that i. CSL-0 has been enriched with new *system* links to represent appropriately some recurrent inter-lexemes relationships (e.g. similarity of use); ii. an attempt has been done of representing the interrelationships between the two knowledge sources in a principled way. These characteristics make it feasible to think that GEOGRAPH, while currently employed with fairly restricted purposes, could be used as a tactical component by a general purpose system including a strategic component as well.

2. Conceptual Graphs

Conceptual Graphs are a kind of semantic networks for which both a formal semantics and special composition rules are available. The semantics of CGs is based on the idea of using them to represent both the *model* and the *formulas* (of the object language) which have to be evaluated with respect to that model. A CG is evaluated by <u>projecting</u> it against the model formed by the previously asserted CGs: if the projection succeeds, the <u>denotation</u> of the graph is TRUE; otherwise it is FALSE (see [17], esp. par. 4.4 and par. 4.5., for more details). Conceptual Graphs can replace predicates in logic operations because of their formal semantics, but they are more useful than predicates to structure a knowledge base, since the constraints derived from the ontology are made more explicit ([14]). CGs are composed of <u>Concepts</u> and <u>Conceptual Relations</u> (CRs). Concepts can be either <u>Generic</u> (when the referent is a variable) or <u>Individual</u> (when the referent is a constant). The CG from which sentence (3b) is generated is shown in Fig.1. Rectangles represent concepts, and ovals CRs.

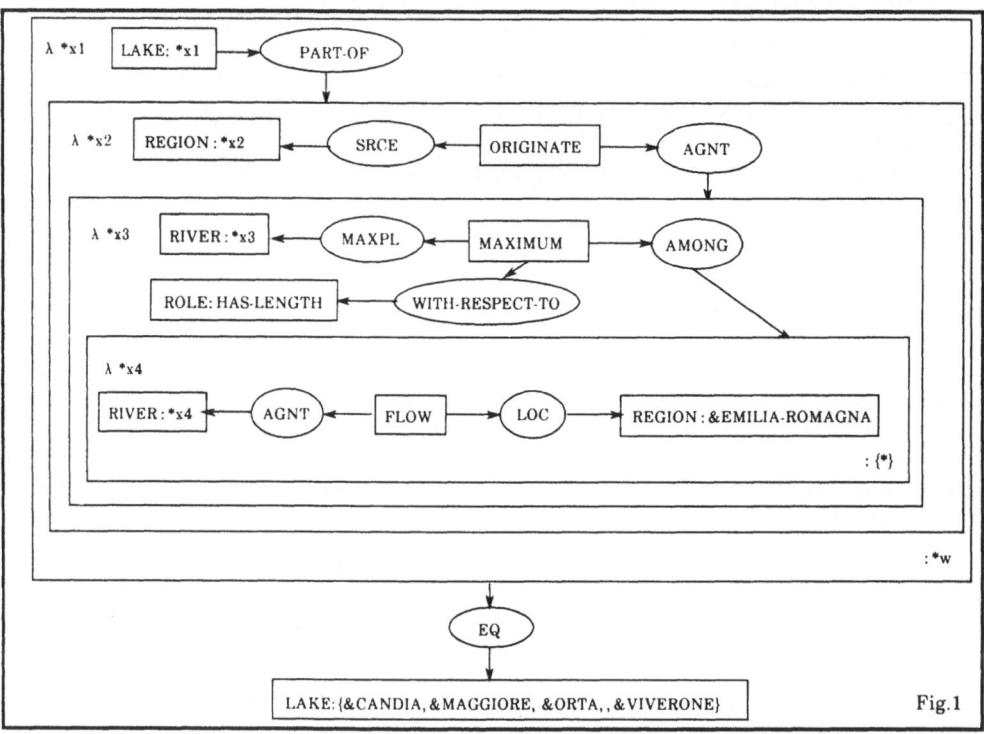

Fig.1

In Fig.1 <u>abstractions</u> are heavily used. They are parameterized conceptual graphs, whose semantic interpretation is similar to that of lambda expressions in lambda-calculus. They are used to define types, or directly in concepts instead of type labels. Using abstractions it is possible to deal with constructs used to specialize concepts, as relative sentences or adjectives, without introducing new types each time. The abstraction with formal parameter *x4, used in Fig.1 as type of a concept, defines for that concept an (unnamed) specialization of the type RIVER (type labels are always written capitalized), all of those instances partake in the role of AGNT to a FLOW-event whose LOC-role is filled by the individual &EMILIA-ROMAGNA (individuals of the domain are prefixed throughout by '&') of type REGION.

An epistemological level knowledge representation language based on CG theory, called CSL-0 [2], has been developed. CSL-0 is an object-centered language, including tools for the definition of a hierarchical KB (more or less in the spirit of KL-ONE [5]), and additional machinery for performing inferences and other operations on CGs. CSL-0 has been used in SUSY to represent both the lexical and the domain knowledge.

3. Lexical knowledge and its interaction with domain knowledge

To generate an utterance, GEOGRAPH needs i. the morphological knowledge necessary to generate the Italian words corresponding to the conceptual representation it has received; ii. the syntactic knowledge required to organize these words into an understandable sentence and iii. the links to the knowledge of type i. and ii. more closely related to the types and individuals included in the CG. One assumption underlying this work is that all this lexical knowledge (i.e., morphological knowledge, syntactic knowledge, and links) can be organized around units called lexemes. A further assumption is that lexical knowledge must be associated with domain knowledge. A simple example of this necessity is provided by the generation of proper nouns. As the final version of SUSY is expected to produce a spoken answer directed to a 'casual' user, the use of internal identifiers would not be considered acceptable. But the rules governing the generation of proper nouns are complex and highly idiosyncratic. The individual &TORINO-C of type TOWN, for instance, is described using the same word "Torino" used for &TORINO-P of type PROVINCE, but using different syntactic rules, therefore two different lexemes are required. While we can refer in Italian to the individual &MAGGIORE of type LAKE only using the expression "il lago Maggiore" (NOT by saying "il Maggiore"), we can refer to the individual &GARDA, again of type LAKE, *either* by using the expression "il lago di Garda" or "il Garda". As far as we can determine, there are not general rules applicable to every case - at least not for Italian. The lexemes encoding this knowledge must therefore be related somewhat to the entities of the KB to which they refer. The necessity of this connection is even more evident when considering the generation of prepositions or verbs: the choice of the appropriate lexeme here is crucially dependent on the kind of entities which are involved in the conceptual representation.

3.1. The organization of lexical knowledge

Every lexeme includes the vocabulary knowledge about gender, number and syntactic category; the rules for the use of articles, the generation of plurals, etc.; and links to other lexemes (e.g. synonyms), to the syntactic categories, and to domain knowledge. This knowledge is not epistemologically different from the knowledge about the domain: it can be organized in form of attributes, restrictions on the values of these attributes, etc.. Lexemes have therefore been represented using CSL-0, and stored in the same knowledge base which contains the domain knowledge. Every lexeme is represented as an individual whose type is a syntactic category, like e.g. COMMON-NOUN for "lago" ("lake"). This individual includes part of the knowledge necessary to generate the word corresponding to that lexeme, and points (directly or indirectly) to places where it is possible to get more information (e.g. phrase-level information). If some knowledge is associated with a type, it will be inherited by all individuals of that type: this way some useful generalizations can be captured. In Italian, for instance, all proper nouns of provinces have gender FEMALE, and take no article. We can therefore define a subtype of PROPER-NOUN (e.g. PROVINCE-NOUN), all of those instantiations have those characteristics, and restrict the LEXM link (see below) for instances of PROVINCE to instances of PROVINCE-NOUN.

The lexeme %GARDA (lexemes are indicated by the prefix '%') of type PROPER-NOUN, represented in Fig.2, is the lexeme which includes the information required by GEOGRAPH

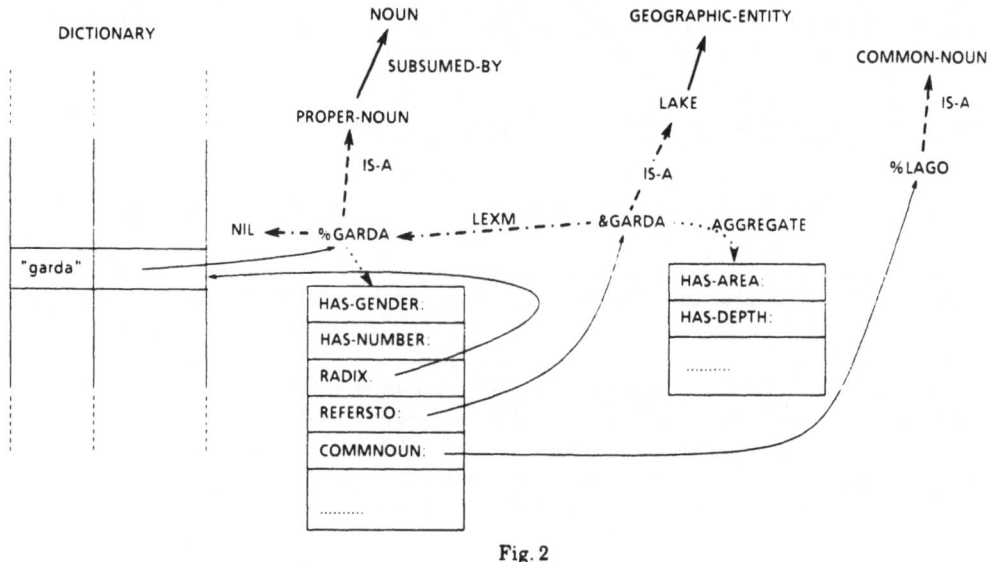

Fig. 2

to generate the proper noun "il lago di Garda". In Fig. 2 *system* links like IS-A or AGGRE-GATE are represented using different arrows; user-defined attributes as record slots. The attributes of &GARDA represent what is known about a particular LAKE (e.g. its depth), while the attributes of %GARDA represent the knowledge about a PROPER-NOUN.

Lexemes are shared between analysis and generation routines: they can be accessed either from the dictionary, to get morphological and semantic information, using the words of the language as pointers (e.g. "garda" in Fig.2); or from the conceptual representation, using conceptual entities (individuals, types, associations) as pointers. When accessing a lexeme from the dictionary, in addition to the morphologic and syntactic information, pointers to the semantic information (the REFERSTO link) can be obtained (typically, a single lexeme will refer to several conceptual entities). Following the REFERSTO link it is for instance possible to get the <u>canonical graph</u> (see [17] for details) which is used to build the semantic representation of the sentence. To provide the access from the conceptual entities, the lexical knowledge necessary to refer in natural language to an individual of the knowledge base can be associated in CSL-0 to that individual, using a *system* link named LEXM (see again Fig.3). LEXM is a pointer to the lexeme(s) containing this information. Since types themselves are stored as individuals of type METACLASS, they can be associated with lexemes as well. In Fig.3, for instance, the lexeme associated with the type WASH (used to represent those states in which an individual of type RIVER or SEA comes in contact with an individual of type TOWN, PROVINCE or REGION) is shown.

There are also inter-lexeme links, of course. The COMMNOUN association, for instance, relates a lexeme pn of type PROPER-NOUN to the lexeme of type COMMON-NOUN that can be used when generating an expression referring to pn. Still other associations are used by the process which looks for the lexeme appropriate in a particular context: for instance, a lexeme is connected by SYNONYM associations with all of its synonyms (i.e. those lexemes that *semantically* speaking can be used in the same way). The SIMILAR system link

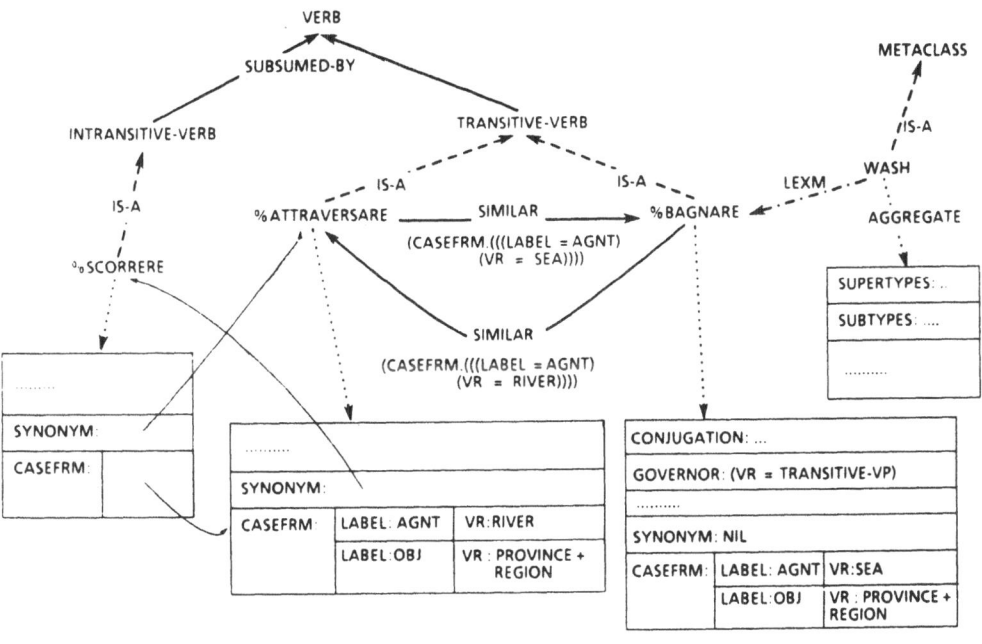

Fig. 3

is used to connect two lexemes *of the same type* which share some attributes, being (optionally) different in some respect (something more about this link will be said below).

In CSL-0 it is possible to define general <u>operations</u> and associate with types and individuals more specific procedures (<u>methods</u>) to specialize the operations when activated on individuals of a more specific type. In GEOGRAPH operations called <u>Morphologic Actors</u> (MAs) have been defined, which generate the terminals of the grammar using information about number, gender and tense, and deriving whenever possible the radix by following the RADIX association (see Fig.2). Methods handling MAs are associated with lexemes and their types.

Syntactic rules are represented as operations called <u>Syntactic Actors</u> (SAs). SAs are obtained from the syntactic rules used during the analysis, expressed in the formalism of Dependency Grammar [9]. SAs are associated with types corresponding to the syntactic categories (non-terminals) of the grammar. They are therefore inherited by lexemes whose type subsume the syntactic category of the GOVERNOR of that non-terminal. The SAs associated with the type VERB-PHRASE (VP), for example, are inherited by the lexemes whose type is a subtype of VERB, as individuals of type VERB can be GOVERNORs of VPs.

3.2 Retrieving an appropriate lexeme

A function called LOOKLEXICON receives a CG whose head is a concept or conceptual relation, and returns the list of semantically acceptable lexemes for that head. The operations that generate the sentence choose the syntactically more appropriate lexeme in this list.

If the head of the received graph is a *generic* concept, LOOKLEXICON searches from the individual associated with the *type*; otherwise, from the individual identified by the *referent*. A list of lexemes is associated with every individual via the LEXM link; one different lexeme for each different syntactic category. These first lexemes are those more often used to refer to that individual. Associated with each of them is an <u>activation context</u>, which is a specialization of the canonical graph associated with the conceptual entity that lexeme refers to (the reason for the specialization is that in generation a more precise form should be used than in analysis, as the system is expected to be more 'expert' than the user). The activation context is compared with the CG received by LOOKLEXICON; if the two match, LOOKLEXICON returns the lexemes pointed to by the SYNONYM attribute.

Not always the lexemes match, however. For instance, the parser (described in [15]) maps all of the verbs "bagnare" (to wash), "scorrere" (to flow through) and "attraversare" (to cross) onto the same concept WASH, with ValueRestriction of RIVER + SEA on the AGNT role. This happens because the number of canonical graphs used by the system is crucial to the efficiency of the parser. Therefore, when, as in this case, different verbs map on the same underlying association; and they can sometimes be used in the same way ("bagnare" can be used, in a colloquial way, as a synonym of "attraversare"), then a unique canonical graph is associated to all of them. But WASH is best expressed by the verbs "attraversare" or "scorrere" when the AGNT is of type RIVER, while when the AGNT is of type SEA the preference is for the form "bagnare". When LOOKLEXICON receives a conceptual graph whose head is of type WASH, but whose AGNT is not of type SEA, the %BAGNARE lexeme (see Fig. 3) cannot be used, and a lexeme which differs from it *in a known way* has to be found.

<u>Discrimination nets</u> ([6]) have traditionally been used for this purpose (for instance in BABEL [8]). The discrimination net mechanism, however, presents some problems (it is difficult for instance to walk through the net in a direction different from that originally planned) and doesn't fit well into an 'epistemologically appropriate' framework. Since the problem of finding an individual that differs in a known way from another is a recurring one, a new system link, the SIMILAR link, has been introduced, which can be used to connect two individuals A and B *of the same type*. Asserting that an individual A is SIMILAR to an individual B means that its attributes have the same description of those of B (i.e., same Value, same ValueRestriction, same NumberRestriction) except when a diference is 'carried' by the link. From an epistemological point of view, this link is a restriction of the 'horizontal' inheritance relation between individuals, included in languages like e.g. NETL [7] or KRL [3] but not in more recent, KL-ONE-like, epistemological languages (e.g. [4], [5]).

When the first lexeme (in the example, %BAGNARE) doesn't match, LOOKLEXICON follows the SIMILAR link (if any) which connects it to a lexeme which differs in the proper way; in this example, one such that the VR of a case (e.g. one element of the CASEFR attribute) having AGNT as a LABEL has a VR of type RIVER. As the lexeme %SCORRERE matches this description, it is returned (together with its synonyms).

An unfortunate situation is the one in which the LEXM link points to nothing, or, said otherwise, when no lexical knowledge has been associated with an individual which must be referred to. This happens either for those types which do not have a natural language correspondent, and must therefore be expressed using modifiers like relative clauses, adverbial clauses, etc.; or for those individuals which have been introduced by the system as a consequence of an indefinite description. Neither of these cases is currently handled by GEOGRAPH, but there are possible solutions in the present framework. In the first case, methods similar to those used for relative clauses could be used. In the second case, the generation of a definite description from the attributes of the individual would require (in principle, at least) no additional abilities from GEOGRAPH. As attributes of individuals are also represented as CGs, in fact, it would suffice to call GEOGRAPH recursively on this graph (caveat: it would be at least necessary to decide which attributes are more informative).

A second problem occurs when none of the lexemes produced by LOOKLEXICON satisfies the requirements of the syntactic actor; for instance, when a passive sentence has to be generated and no TRANSITIVE-VERB lexeme is found. In this case some form of backtracking is required. It should be noticed that at least one lexeme *must* match the semantic context, since the activation contexts are derived from the canonical graphs used in analysis (unless a system is assumed which is a more proficient listener than speaker).

CRs representing cases are usually expressed as prepositions. The choice of the preposition, is parameterized with respect to both the concepts attached to the CR and the direction from which the CR is entered (i.e., from 'in' or 'out' arrows: cf. Fig.1). For instance, one of the cases of ORIGINATE, SRCE (SouRCE) must be expressed using the preposition "da" (from) when the SRCE is of type MOUNTAIN ("il Po nasce DAL Monviso", "the Po originates from Monviso"); but using "in" when the SRCE is of type REGION ("il Po nasce IN Piemonte", "the Po originates in Piemonte").

4. Example Sentences

The function GENERATE is used to produce a sentence S from a canonical graph CG. It works by finding and activating appropriate SAs, which organize the walk through the CG during which S is produced. During this walk a sequence of concepts and CRs (<u>utterance path</u>) is traversed. At the beginning, the SA which can be retrieved from the head H of the CG is triggered. This SA determines the relative order in which concepts attached to H will be visited, by triggering SAs associated with these concepts. The segment of sentence associated to H itself is originated by triggering the appropriate MA (in Dependency Grammars each syntactic rule includes at least one terminal). Both the determination of the utterance path and generation of the sentence are accomplished *in a single step*.

4.1. Verb Phrases.

A simple example of the generation of verb phrases is provided by the generation of sentence (1b) from the conceptual graph of Fig.4. When GENERATE is called on that graph, it first

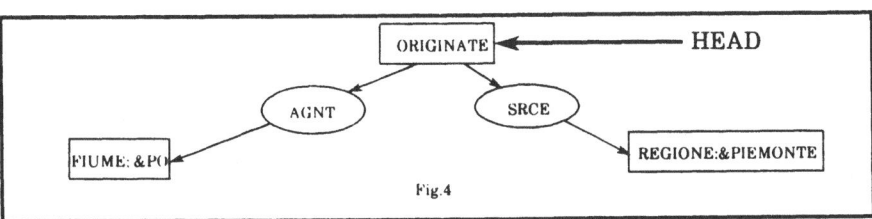

Fig.4

calls LOOKLEXICON, as described in section 3.3., to find a lexeme for the concept [ORIGINATE]. The lexeme %NASCERE of type INTRANSITIVE-VERB is returned. An individual of type INTRANSITIVE-VERB can only be GOVERNOR of a sentence of type ACTIVE-VP, so the SA associated to that category, ACTIVE-VERB-GOVERNOR-GENERATE, is activated. This SA has been obtained (by hand, currently) from the dependency rule (4) The meaning of (NUMBER ! ?N) and (NUMBER ? ?N) is that the NUMBER of the governor has to be obtained from the NUMBER of the first NP playing the role of subject. Each SA in

```
(4)  (VP = NP * NP
        (GOVERNOR (CATEGORY VERB)
                (MODE (IND))(TIME (PRES))
                (PERS 3) (NUMBER ??N))
        (NP1 (NUMBER !?N))
        (NP2 (COMPLEMENT (STAT-LOC))))
```

fact returns i. a tree whose leaves are strings, visiting which in preorder the sub-sentence is obtained and ii. the syntactic information that has been derived. ACTIVE-VERB-GOVERNOR-GENERATE, after having marked the conceptual relation AGNT as visited, calls recursively GENERATE on the concept [RIVER: &PO] passing it as additional parameter the lexeme which describes the preposition associated with AGNT in the caseframe of %NASCERE. The MA associated to %NASCERE is then activated to produce the string corresponding to the governor. This MA receives the NUMBER derived from the call of GENERATE just described, and the other information contained in (4). GENERATE is then called again, this time on the concept [REGIONE: &PIEMONTE], having marked SRCE as visited. The resulting tree corresponds to sentence (1b).

Passive VP are generated when the filler of the OBJ case is visited before the caseframe header: this is recognized by GEOGRAPH because the CR has already been marked (the decision about what must be the head is taken by the process which calls GENERATE, according to very simple criteria like e.g. that of emphasizing one concept by making it the subject of the sentence). In this case, none of the SAs associated to ACTIVE-VP can be activated: if therefore the lexeme considered is of type INTRANSITIVE-VERB, either a different lexeme must be considered or some backtracking must be attempted. This is not done by LOOKLEXICON, but by GENERATE itself (more precisely, by a sub-actor specialized for ACTs generation, called GENERATE-ACT). Consider for instance sentence (3b): if the first lexeme of the list returned by LOOKLEXICON was %SCORRERE (see Fig.3), it would not be usable, because it is of type INTRANSITIVE-VERB, and the operation GENERATE-PASSIVE-SENTENCE is undefined for governors of type INTRANSITIVE-VERB. GENERATE-ACT tries therefore to use %ATTRAVERSARE, with success. When no lexeme of type TRANSITIVE-VERB is found, GENERATE backtracks up to a state in which the OBJ case is unmarked, then shifts the head to the concept representing the verb and tries again.

4.2. Noun Phrases

The generation of noun phrases follows more or less the guidelines of generation of verb phrases, but some problems connected with the generation of proper nouns and of modifiers have to be taken into account.

Individual concepts are usually expressed using proper nouns. The generation of some proper noun requires the proper noun itself to follow a common noun (e.g. for the individual &MAGGIORE seen before). In other cases, this is not allowed (e.g. for &PO); in still other cases it depends on the context. In GEOGRAPH therefore three subtypes of the type PROPER-NOUN have been introduced, to separate the different kinds of proper nouns. The MA which provides for the generation of proper nouns requiring the presence of a common noun follows the COMMNOUN link to find the correct lexeme (there is not a standard one: individuals of type MOUNT, for instance, can be preceded by either the common nouns "punta", "vetta", or "monte") and calls the appropriate MA on that lexeme.

Generic concepts (nothing to do with Brachman's terminology) are expressed using either common nouns or more complex NP sentences (e.g. relative clauses), depending on whether the type is a label or an abstraction. In both cases an indefinite article is generated.

By using abstractions it is possible to isolate the modifiers of a concept, and it is therefore very easy to distinguish them from the proposition in which this concept participates (see Fig.1 for example). Depending on whether the modifier is another entity concept, or instead an action concept, a relative clause or an adjectival clause will be generated. In both cases our treatment do not differ substantially from that proposed by Sowa.

5. Conclusions

The version of GEOGRAPH described in this paper has been implemented and demonstrated during an ESPRIT meeting in October 1986. A longer version of this paper includes a detailed comparison of GEOGRAPH with other tactical systems. The main problem we are facing now is the representation of syntactic knowledge. An issue which we are also considering is the interaction between lexical and domain knowledge, which should be made much more strict. Last but not least, the study of the interaction between stylistic, syntactic, and semantic considerations can shed interesting lights on the kind of interaction that there should be between a tactical system like GEOGRAPH and a strategic system.

References

|1| D.E. Appelt: "Planning English Referring Expressions", Artificial Intelligence, v. 26, 1985, 1:33

|2| P. Baggia, M. Poesio: Using Conceptual Graphs in the Development of Knowledge Bases, CSELT Technical Report RD-86435, October 3, 1986

|3| D.G.Bobrow, T.Winograd:"An Overview of KRL, a Knowledge Representation Language", Cognitive Science, v.1, 1977, 3:46

|4| R. Brachman, V. Pigman Gilbert, H.J.Levesque: "An Essential Hybrid Reasoning System: Knowledge and Symbol Level Accounts of KRYPTON", Proc. IX IJCAI, Los Angeles,1985, 532:539

|5| R. Brachman,J.Schmolze: "An Overview of the KL-ONE Knowledge Representation System", Cognitive Science, v.9, 1985, 171:216

|6| E.Charniak, C.K.Riesbeck, D.McDermott: Artificial Intelligence Programming, Lawrence Erlbaum, Hillsdale,NJ, 1980

|7| S.Fahlman: A System for Representing and Using Real World Knowledge, Ph.D. thesis, MIT, Cambridge,MA, 1977

|8| N. M. Goldman: "Sentence Paraphrasing from a Conceptual Base", Communications ACM, v. 18, n.2, February 1975, 96:106

|9| D.G.Hays : Dependency theory: a formalism and some observations, Memorandum RM4087 PR, The Rand Corporation, 1964

|10| A.L.Lepschy, G.Lepschy: La lingua italiana, Bompiani, Milano, 1986 (3rd ed.)

|11| W. Mann (chairperson): "Text Generation", American Journal of Computational Linguistics, v.8, n.2, April-June 1982

|12| M.Marcus: "Generations Systems Should Choose Their Words", Proc. TINLAP-3, Las Cruces, NM, 1987, 211:214

|13| K. McKeown: "Discourse Strategies for Generating Natural Language Text", Artificial Intelligence, v.27, 1985, 1:41

|14| M.Poesio: "Interpretazione logica di una rappresentazione epistemologica", Proc. Secondo Convegno Nazionale Programmazione Logica, Torino, Italy, May 1987

|15| M.Poesio, C.Rullent:"Modified Caseframe Parsing for Speech Understanding SYstems", to appear in Proc. X IJCAI, Milano, Italy, 1987

|16| N.K.Sondheimer, B.Nebel, "A Logical-form and Knowledge-base design for natural language generation", Proc. AAAI-86, Philadelphia,Pa, 1986, 612-618

|17| J. F. Sowa: Conceptual Structures, Addison-Wesley, Reading (MA), 1984

A Knowledge-Based Framework for Effective Probabilistic Control Strategies in Signal Understanding

R. Gemello, E. Giachin, C. Rullent

CSELT - Centro Studi E Laboratori Telecomunicazioni
Via G. Reiss Romoli, 274 - 10148 Torino (Italy)
Tel. +3911-21691

ABSTRACT

We describe a problem solving framework for a knowledge based approach to signal understanding. The risk of erroneous analysis makes advisable the use of well-experimented probabilistic control methods. Such methods have been used in the past in task-specific applications, such as speech. Here they are generalized to the case of a deduction system, thus becoming applicable to a wider class of problems still maintaining their effectiveness. That results in a blackboard based framework where every knowledge source is abstracted as a set of operators, that allow integration of different deductive processes independently evolved, either forward or backward. Such framework allows the use of admissible control strategies proposed in the literature.

1 Introduction

Most signal understanding applications are characterized by noisy environments and uncertain data. In such cases two different requirements can be singled out:
- The use of well-experimented probabilistic methods to direct the search, especially when the application presents the risk of erroneous understanding;
- A flexible knowledge-based approach to the problem, avoiding application dependent problem solving frameworks.

Our research for a problem solving framework able to address these two aspects started from work in speech understanding. Past research in this area led to a number of systems of which HWIM [Wol80, Woo82] and Hearsay-II [Hay77, Erm80] are among the most significant ones. The HWIM system focused on the former requirement and proposed interesting strategies for combining word scores and methods for reaching admissibility. However the control strategy, based on the exploitation of the time adjacency constraint between words, is specific to the speech application. The Hearsay-II system was primarily involved on the latter requirement. The blackboard paradigm it proposed was adopted by many systems [Nii86] and appeared especially interesting when different pieces of knowledge had to be coordinated and multiple reasoning (such as forward and backward reasoning) had to be integrated [Cor82]. In this paper we describe a blackboard-based problem-solving framework that integrates the two requirements and aims at improving the trade-off between power and generality for a wide class of signal understanding applications.

This research has been partially supported by the EEC ESPRIT Project n.26 "Advanced Algorithms and Architecture for Signal Processing"

The framework addresses problems for which the knowledge embedded in the knowledge sources can constitute a deduction system able to run forward and backward; in other words, the KSs represent a set of bidirectional rules, as complex as needed. The possible interactions of each KS with the blackboard are formally described by a set of five operators. Operators are applied to a selected blackboard hypothesis generating new hypotheses. Some operators represent a forward deduction step, others a backward step, others allow to merge so-far independent deductive processes. Operators give the flexibility to organize control in a way suitable to reach admissibility as well as to use heuristics to move towards near-admissibility with improved efficiency.

The analysis starts with a set of scored low-level hypotheses (LLHs) that are directly obtained from the environment or from a lower level processing. Then, at each cycle, the best hypothesis generated so far is expanded either by adding a new low-level hypothesis or by merging it with other compatible hypotheses. This basic analysis principle shares some ideas with the HWIM system. One substantial difference is that the present framework does not commit control to application-specific constraints such as time-adjacency for speech [1] but uses more general constraints related to the tree-structured nature of the deduction activity. For this reason, hypotheses have a tree structure rather than being islands.

Control acts mainly in two respects: the strategy of applying operators on blackboard hypotheses and the way to assign them a priority. A control strategy is presented which is admissible for a set of priority-assigning methods, including those described in [Woo82].

The above framework has been implemented in an operational system named SUSY (from Speech Understanding SYstem) on a Symbolics 3600 Lisp Machine. SUSY performs understanding of speech at the syntactic/semantic level and works in conjunction with a continuous recognition system under development in CSELT [Laf87]. Work is in progress to implement a distributed version of the framework, aimed at reaching real-time performance, that will work on a highly parallel multiprocessor machine that is being developed by another CSELT staff. The present paper describes the general problem solving framework; an account on the architecture of the parallel system is given in [Bos87].

An overview of the framework is portrayed in Fig. 1. Next sections will successively deal with the blackboard, the operators and the control. An explanatory example and a discussion from the point of view of the speech application conclude the paper.

2 Deduction Instances and Blackboard

Blackboard elements are of three kinds: 1) low-level hypotheses (LLHs), obtained directly from environment or from processing at a lower level, 2) Deduction Instances (DIs), generated

---

[1] They can be introduced in the specific implementation as heuristics to improve efficiency.

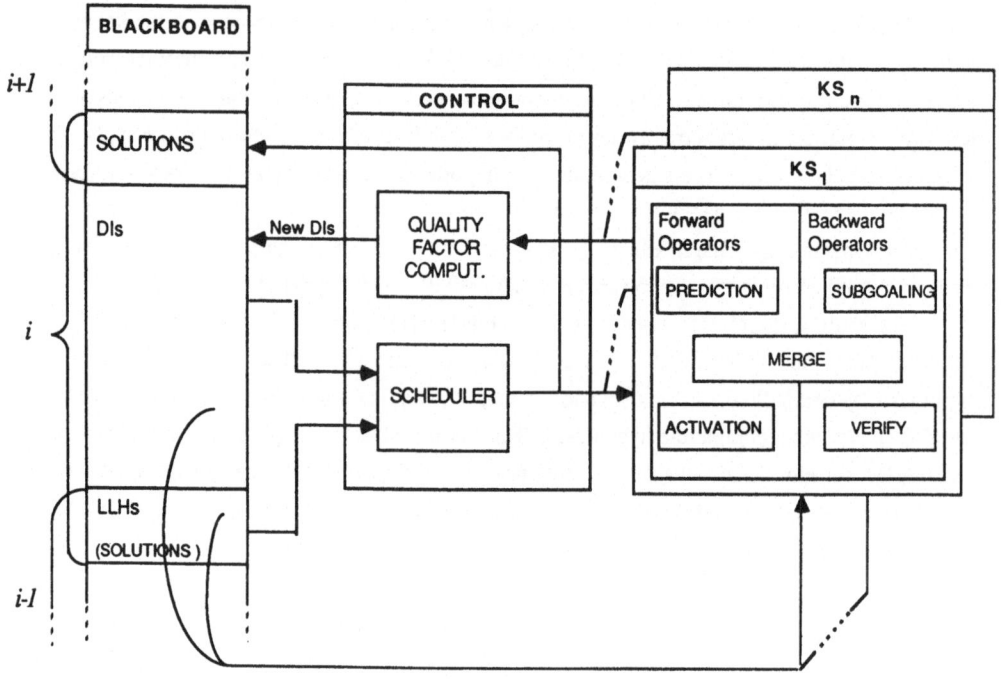

Fig. 1 - Overview of SUSY system organization

during the analysis and described below, and 3) solutions. Deduction Instances are a generalization of the "islands" of speech literature. Each DI is supported by a set of LLHs; thus a Quality Factor can be assigned to a DI on the basis of the scores of its supporting LLHs. In particular, methods like those described in [Woo82] can be used. During the analysis DIs are expanded either by adding them a LLH or by connecting them to compatible DIs. Since the knowledge embedded in the knowledge sources constitutes a deduction system, each DI has a tree structure. Such tree gives a trace of the deductive process that led to the generation of that DI, reason to which DIs owe their name. If each node of the tree corresponds to a LLH, the DI is said to be a fact; otherwise it is called a goal. Solutions are special cases of fact DIs.

According to the three types of elements, the blackboard is partitioned into three panels (see Fig. 1): the LLH panel, the DI panel and the solution panel (the rationale for distinguishing the LLH panel from the DI panel is similar to that of systems like Chrysalis [Ter83]). Roughly speaking, the system uses items from the LLH panel to create DIs in the DI panel and puts accepted solutions into the solution panel. The blackboard is incremental, that is nothing is ever deleted from it. The blackboard could be the i-th level of a greater blackboard; the KSs that operate at the other levels could be organized as the i-th level or not [2]. In the following, at any rate, we organize the discussion assuming that only the i-th level is present and all the KSs operate at this level.

3 The operators as a formalization of the knowledge source behaviour

It was assumed that the whole set of KSs constitutes a deduction system. The actions that a KS can perform when it is triggered can be described in terms of five operators. An operator represents a formal way, from the point of view of a KS, of interacting with the blackboard, that is of generating new hypotheses starting from others; the actual way knowledge is embedded in the KS is application-dependent and is not relevant here. Some operators behave in a forward fashion, others in a backward fashion, still others allow integration of different deduction processes. A KS can be triggered by a Deduction Instance or by a Low-level Hypothesis. The characteristics of such element define what operators are applicable. In the following the operators are described.

ACTIVATION
- Acts on a low level hypothesis (LLH).
- A DI having a terminal subgoal solved by the LLH is created and inserted into the blackboard.

SUBGOALING
- Acts on a goal DI whose Current Subgoal (the subgoal currently pursued) is a non-terminal one (i.e. it cannot be solved directly against the LLHs).
- The KS operates a subgoaling operation: the current subgoal is decomposed according to the problem reduction knowledge of the KS. A new goal DI is generated.

VERIFY
- Acts on a goal DI whose Current Subgoal is terminal.
- The terminal subgoal is solved by matching it against the LLHs. One or more fact or goal DIs are generated.

PREDICTION
- Acts on a fact DI.
- A goal DI having a non-terminal subgoal solved by the fact DI is generated. KS are able to make predictions given the bidirectional nature of a Deduction System.

---

[2] If levels i and i-1 follow the proposed organization, then the LLHs of level i can be considered as the solutions of level i-1.

MERGE

- Acts on a fact or goal DI.

- The DI is merged with other compatible DIs of the blackboard. From the merge of two DIs a new DI is generated. If the triggering DI is a goal, then the KS merges the current subgoal of such DI with compatible DIs. If the triggering DI is a fact, then the KS tries to merge such fact DI with compatible goal DIs having subgoals that can be satisfied by such fact.

Whenever a goal DI is created, a subgoal is selected as the current one. For this purpose application-dependent heuristics can be used.

The ACTIVATION operator corresponds to the "seed" generation activity in HWIM. The SUBGOALING, PREDICTION and VERIFY operators account for the principle of hypothesis expansion without the Island Collision feature: DIs can start from a LLH and gradually increase the number of supporting LLHs through the use of the VERIFY operator, together with the SUBGOALING and PREDICTION operators. They generalize the concept of expanding on the left and on the right of a HWIM's' Island to our general case ([3]). The MERGE operator gives the power of the Island Collision feature in the case of a Deduction System.

The ACTIVATION and PREDICTION operators correspond to a forward use of the KS, the VERIFY and SUBGOALING operators to a backward use. The MERGE operator can be applied in both senses and gives integration.

4 Control

There are three main aspects pertaining to control: 1) selecting an element (DI or LLH) on the blackboard to work on; 2) selecting the KS, given the selected element; and 3) selecting the operators to apply. In a flexible problem solving framework it is necessary to have ways to control all these aspects.

In Table I we present a control strategy, among the allowed ones, that was experimentally shown to be admissible for a set of priority assigning methods (a formal proof of admissibility is now in progress). Such methods include those in [Woo82]. This strategy is also used throughout the example in the next section.

Element selection is accomplished by assigning priorities to DIs and letting a Scheduler choose at each control cycle the highest-priority element (DI or LLH) on the blackboard. So the key point is how priorities are computed. If admissibility is required, the priority of a DI must result only from combination of the scores of the LLHs that support it and must satisfy the constraint in point 5. The priority of a LLH is simply given by its score. The best ways of combining

---

([3]) In the case of speech fact DIs are supported by adjacent lexical hypotheses while goal DIs in general are not. For fact DIs the sequence of supporting lexical hypotheses is both semantically and syntactically correct.

scores depend on the domain; some of them make admissibility difficult to reach ([4]). KS selection is accomplished simply by selecting all the KSs that can somehow operate on the selected element.

The proposed framework, in addition to the strategy outlined in Table I, also allows the use of application-dependent heuristics, acting on Quality Factor computation, operators application (for instance, limiting the applicability of MERGE, or similar) and KSs selection. Sometimes such heuristics are useful in that they improve efficiency while keeping near-admissibility; at any rate they require specific experimentation.

1. SELECT BLACKBOARD ELEMENT
   Choose the element, among DIs and LLHs, with the best quality factor or score.

2. TEST FOR SOLUTION
   If the element is an acceptable solution ,
       put it in the solution panel.

3. KS SELECTION
   Select all the KSs for which there is at least one operator applicable.

4. OPERATORS SELECTION
   If the element is a LLH,
       apply ACTIVATION.
   If the element is a goal DI and its current subgoal is terminal,
       apply VERIFY.
   If the element is a goal DI and its current subgoal is non-terminal,
       apply SUBGOALING and MERGE (in parallel).
   If the element is a fact DI,
       apply PREDICTION and MERGE (in parallel).

5. COMPUTE QUALITY FACTOR
   Apply a predefined score-combining function F to the LLHs of the new DIs.
   F must satisfy:
   $$\forall\ W \triangleq \{w_1, \dots, w_n\} \implies F(w_1, \dots, w_n) \leq \max_{W}(w_i)$$
   if the scores w_i represent quality, or
   $$\forall\ W \triangleq \{w_1, \dots, w_n\} \implies F(w_1, \dots, w_n) \geq \min_{W}(w_i)$$
   if scores represent cost.

Table I - Control strategy.

5 An example

This specialistic section intends to give a brief view of how DIs are represented with memory-saving structures and to illustrate how the control strategy of Table I operates on such

---

([4]) In the case of speech two interesting score-combining methods are density and shortfall density [Woo82]. Such methods require careful control. Simple score-guided forward strategies, for instance, should not be used because not only they are not admissible but also because they are inefficient: in fact bad (but correct) LLHs at the lowest level in the deduction tree delay the finding of the correct solution causing a lot of useless search. In HWIM density strategies required the special mechanism of Island Collision.

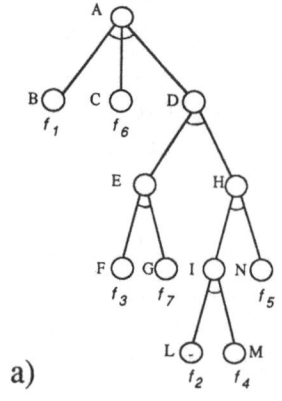

a)

Selected DI or LLH	Initial QF	Involved Operators	Generated DI	Involved LLHs	Component PHs	Final QF
f1	0.1	ACTIVATION	1	f1	1	0.1
1	0.1	VERIFY	2	f1, f6	2	0.4
f2	0.2	ACTIVATION	3	f2	3	0.2
3	0.2	VERIFY	4	f2, f4	4	0.35
f3	0.3	ACTIVATION	5	f3	5	0.3
5	0.3	VERIFY	6	f3, f7	6	0.6
4	0.35	PREDICTION	7	f2, f4	7, 4	0.35
7	0.35	VERIFY	8	f2, f4, f5	8, 4	0.45
2	0.4	SUBGOALING	9	f1, f6	9, 2	0.4
9 + 6	0.4	MERGE	10	f1, f3, f6, f7	10, 2, 6	0.5
8 + 10	0.45	MERGE	11	all	11, 12, 8, 4, 6	0.48

Table IV - Score guided generation
of Deduction Instances

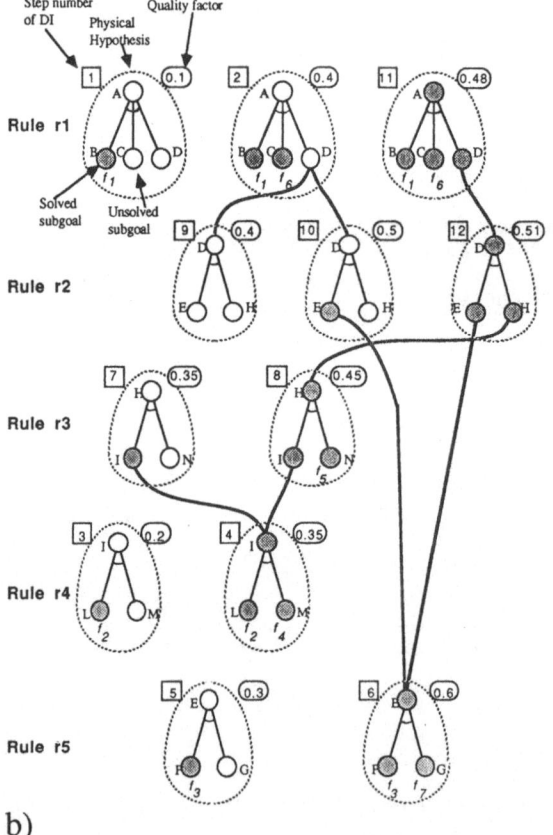

r1:	A	==>	B, C, D
r2:	D	==>	E, H
r3:	H	==>	I, N
r4:	I	==>	L, M
r5:	E	==>	F, G

Table II - Simplified
rules (KSs)

Low Level Hypotheses	Score	Type
f1 (best)	0.1	B
f2	0.2	L
f3	0.3	F
f4	0.5	M
f5	0.65	N
f6	0.7	C
f7 (worst)	0.9	G

Table III - Low Level
Hypotheses

b)

Fig. 2 - An example of an admissible control strategy: use of Physical Hypotheses
(PHs) to represent Deduction Instances (DIs)

structures. This is done through an example of analysis, from LLHs to the solution, in a very simple case. To make the example readable, only the DIs that were used for the solution are taken into consideration, and the KSs have been sketched as simple toy rules.

The example pivots upon Fig. 2. The KSs (toy rules on fact classes A-N) are given in Table II. Table III shows the low-level hypotheses (LLHs) f1 - f7 involved in the solution; the solution itself is given in Fig. 2a. Each LLH has a score proportional to -log(p), then high scores mean bad LLHs. Quality Factors are computed as the average value of the scores of the involved LLHs (a special case of a density method). DIs are composed of basic units called Physical Hypotheses (PHs). This allows DIs to share parts. DIs are implemented as AND-OR trees of Physical Hypotheses and each DI has a representative PH; similarly, when a new DI is generated, only one new PH is created.

Fig. 2b is a view of the DI panel of the blackboard at the end of the analysis process, ignoring DIs that did not lead to the solution. Each PH is characterized by a number (on the left), corresponding to the cycle in which it was generated, and by a Quality Factor (on the right). Shaded circles represent solved subgoals. Some PHs are entirely made up of solved subgoals; they are called complete PHs. The other ones, that contain unsolved subgoals, are called incomplete PHs. Complete PHs have a shaded root.
- A complete PH represents the DI obtained considering the PH itself and all its descendants.
- An incomplete PH represents the DI obtained considering the PH itself, all its complete descendants, all its ancestors and the complete descendants of these ancestors. For instance, PH10 represents DI10 which is made up of PH10, PH6 and PH2.

KSs are triggered directly on PHs and not on DIs; operators application is simplified, due to the fact that PHs are connected together to form the network. Every DI is represented by the PH having the same number.

Table IV aids the reading of Fig. 2b. The rows represent subsequent control cycles. Each row shows the selected element (DI or LLH), its Quality Factor, the applied operators, the generated DI together with the LLHs involved, the PHs that make it up and its Quality Factor.

Table IV shows that the Quality Factors of the selected DIs are becoming worse little by little as new LLHs are added, converging to 0.48, the Quality Factor of the solution. Admissibility is obtained: the deductive activity starts at the top (f1) and at the end (f2) of the solution tree and the solution can be found only by considering triggering DIs not worse than 0.48. Since f1 and f2 are at very different levels in the solution tree, the MERGE operator application is required. Note also that f7 is very bad (0.9) and in the middle of the solution tree.

6 Discussion from the speech understanding viewpoint

The above framework was implemented in SUSY, a system for understanding continuous speech. The LLHs are represented by a lattice of word hypotheses (Fig. 3) generated by a

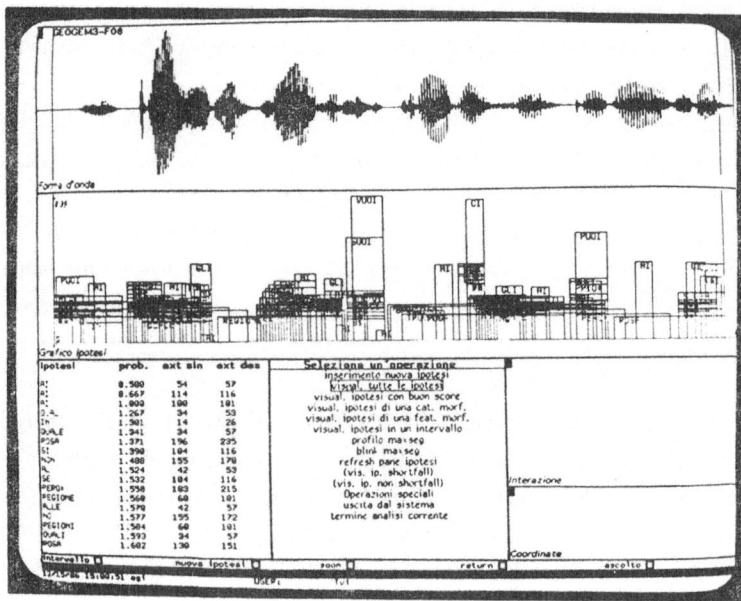

Fig. 3 - A LLH set in SUSY. LLHs are word hypotheses represented as rectangles in the middle pane, positioned against the waveform portion in which they were spotted. Height is proportional to the score (high scores mean bad hypotheses). The original utterance was "In quale regione si trova il monte Rosa?" ("In which region is mount Rosa located?"). About 200 LLHs are present.

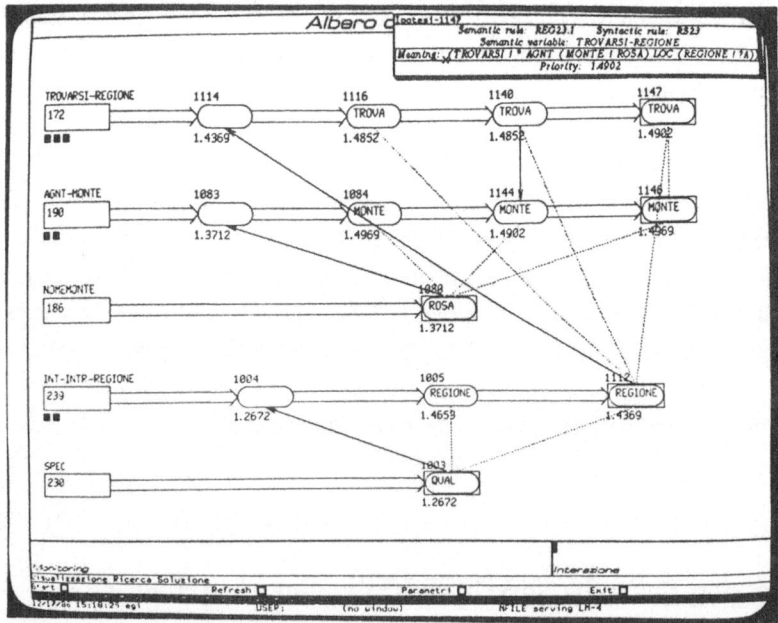

Fig. 4 - The Physical Hypotheses used to generate the solution for the LLH set of Fig. 3. The Physical Hypotheses that make up the solution are surrounded by a rectangle. To the solution a formal semantic representation is associated (shown in the upper right window).

recognition system. The solution (Fig. 4) contains a formal semantic representation of the most probable sequence of words, that is used as a query for retrieving information from a data base.

In many speech understanding systems, the knowledge at the syntactic/semantic level is partitioned into a small number of knowledge sources (for instance, in Hearsay-II there are six of them, not including those related to control problems), endowed with ad hoc procedures that generally pursue left-to-right or island-driven strategies. In our system, conversely, the knowledge is modeled as a Deductive System represented by a large number of KSs. This approach presents several advantages in terms of flexibility. For instance, it does not commit to semantic grammars, and thus allows the use of more appealing ways of expressing knowledge, preferred in more recent research ([Hay86], [Bri86]). In SUSY caseframes and dependency rules (augmented with morphologic agreement conditions) are compiled into complex rules that constitute the KSs. Also, the proposed approach makes feasible the partial understanding of a sentence when a relevant word was not recognized.

This approach requires to carefully control the cooperation among KSs, especially when a good trade-off between efficiency and admissibility has to be found. To summarize, the proposed framework reaches this goal by formalizing the behaviour of the KSs through a set of operators and making the KSs to cooperate in a way that allows admissible control methods even for density policies of combining scores.

References

[Bos87] P.Bosco, E.Giachin, G.Giandonato, G.Martinengo, C.Rullent, 1987. "A Parallel Architecture for Signal Understanding through Inference on Uncertain Data", *Proc. Parallel Architectures and Languages Europe*, Eindhoven, NL.

[Bri86] A.Brietzmann, U.Ehrlich, 1986. "The Role of Semantic Processing in an Automatic Speech Understanding System", *Proc. 11th Int. Conference on Computational Linguistics*, Bonn, WG, pp. 596-598.

[Cor82] D.D.Corkill, V.R.Lesser, E.Hudlicka, 1982. "Unifying data-directed and goal-directed control: an example and experiments", *Proc. 2nd National Conf. on Artificial Intelligence (AAAI '82)*, Pittsburgh, PA, pp. 143-147.

[Erm80] L.D.Erman, F.Hayes-Roth, V.R.Lesser, D.Raj Reddy, 1980. "The Hearsay-II Speech-Understanding System: Integrating Knowledge to Resolve Uncertainty", *ACM Computing Survey 12*, pp. 213-253.

[Hay77] F.Hayes-Roth, V.R.Lesser, 1977. "Focus of Attention in the Hearsay-II Speech Understanding System", *Proc. 5th Int. Joint Conf. on Artificial Intelligence,* Cambridge, Mass., pp. 27-35.

[Hay86] P.J.Hayes, A.G.Hauptmann, J.G.Carbonell, M.Tomita, 1986. "Parsing Spoken Language: a Semantic Caseframe Approach", *Proc. 11th Int. Conference on Computational Linguistics*, Bonn, WG, pp. 587-592.

[Laf87] P.Laface, G.Micca, R.Pieraccini, 1987. "Experimental results on a large lexicon access task", *Proc. ICASSP-87*, Dallas, Texas.

[Nii86] H.Penny Nii, 1986. "Blackboard Systems". Part one: "Blackboard Application Systems, Blackboard Systems from a Knowledge Engineering Perspective", *The AI Magazine*, August, 1986, pp.82-106. Part two: "The Blackboard Model of Problem Solving and the Evolution of Blackboard Architectures", *The AI Magazine,* Summer, 1986, pp. 38-53.

[Ter83] A.Terry, 1983. "The Chrysalis Project: Hierarchical Control of Production Systems", Tech. Rep. HPP-83-19, Stanford University, Heuristic Programming Project.

[Wol80] J.J.Wolf, W.A.Woods, 1980. "The HWIM Speech Understanding System", in W.Lea (Ed.), *Trends in Speech Recognition*, Prentice-Hall, Engelwood Cliffs, N.J.

[Woo82] W.A.Woods, 1982. "Optimal Search Strategies for Speech Understanding Control", *Artificial Intelligence 18*, pp. 295-326.

Issues of Integration and Balancing in Hybrid Knowledge Representation Systems*

Bernhard Nebel, Kai von Luck
Technische Universtät Berlin, CIS/KIT
Sekr. FR 5–8, Franklinstraße 28/29
D-1000 Berlin 10

Abstract

In the last several years the hybrid approach to Knowledge Representation has received much attention, because it was felt that one monolithic knowledge representation formalism cannot meet all representational demands. In this paper we will present one particular hybrid knowledge representation system, BACK, concentrating on matters of how to integrate different subformalisms and their interpretation. In particular, 'balancing the expressiveness' of the respective subformalisms and combining the reasoning of the subsystems in a sound way is discussed. This will lead to a new view on the realization inference, first described by Mark, as a process of constraint propagation.

1 Introduction

Aaron Sloman pointed out very clearly in [Sloman 85] the need for different knowledge representation formalisms for the adequate representation of a realistic portion of the world. This position contrasting the view that one uniform formalism is sufficient (e.g., [Kowalski 80]) is nowadays widely accepted. The most visible consequence of this is the emerging number of systems—so-called *hybrid systems*—supporting representation of knowledge by more than one formalism. The actual situation in research on hybrid systems is described in [Brachman et al 85, p. 532]:

> Many of the today's knowledge representation systems offer their users a choice of more than one language for expression of domain knowledge. While the idea has been important to the field for many years, 'multiple representations' seems to have recently become a popular catch phrase. Many of the modern expert system development environments wave the polyglot banner, and except perhaps for some stalwart first-order logicians, most everyone would probably agree that one uniform language will not serve all representational needs.
>
> It is sometimes difficult to discern the true value of multiple languages; some of the commercial development tools seem simply to appeal to the 'the more the merrier', without any clear idea of how merrier is better.

First of all, let's clarify some terms. If we talk about a *knowledge representation formalism*, we mean a formal language with given *syntax* and *semantics*[1]. This language can be analyzed

---

*This work was partially supported by the EEC and is part of the ESPRIT project 311, which involves the following participants: Nixdorf, Olivetti, Bull, Technische Universität Berlin, Universita di Bologna, Universität Hildesheim and Universita di Torino.

[1]In the sense of, e.g., [McDermott 78] or [Hayes 79].

for its expressivness, naturalness with respect to its intended purpose, decidability and inherent complexity of inference algorithms with respect to the formal semantics.

A *knowledge representation system* is a 'materialization' of a formalism supporting the *inter-pretation* of well-formed expressions of a knowledge representation language by means of infer-ence algorithms realizing the semantics to a certain extent. These inference algorithms should be *sound*—they should not lead to wrong propositions—and in the ideal case they should be *complete*—be able to deduce any true proposition. As it turns out, however, in the real world the latter goal can only be achieved if either the formalism is very simple or if we allow for arbitrary long computations. Therefore, often the solution is to provide only the obvious, easy to compute inferences and ignore the difficult ones.

Of course, a knowledge representation system is more than just a mechanized reasoner. Another task for such a system is the maintenance of represented knowledge, i.e., it has to account for *additions* to and *updates* of the represented knowledge. In fact, this is the main difference between a knowledge representation system and a static deductive calculus (or a programming language). Furthermore, any knowledge representation system claiming to be usable has to provide a friendly interface to the human user[2]. In the sequel, however, we will ignore the latter and focus on the former two points.

In the ideal case a hybrid knowledge representation system is an implementation of a hybrid knowledge representation formalism, consisting of two or more different subformalisms. However, the mere combination of formalisms does not necessarily result in a hybrid formalism. A kind of 'glue' is needed in order to constitute a hybrid formalism consisting of

- a *representational theory* (explaining what knowledge is to be represented by what formalism) and

- a *common semantics* for the overall formalism (explaining in a semantic sound manner the relationship between expressions of different subformalisms).

The representational theory should explain why there are different subformalism, what their benefits are, and how they relate to each other. An answer should at least refer to adequacy criteria such as (cf. [McCarthy, Hayes 69]):

- *epistemological adequacy*, i.e., that the subformalisms are necessary to represent epistemo-logical different kind of knowledge (e.g., analytic and contingent knowledge), or

- *heuristic adequacy*, i.e., that the different subformalisms permit representation of the same knowledge in different ways for reasons of efficiency.

A necessary precondition for gluing things together is that their shapes fit, a fact which might be violated in designing a hybrid formalism, at least in the case where the subformalisms are intended to represent epistemological different kinds of knowledge. For example, if one subformal-ism permitted definition of terms by using time relationships, but none of the other subformalisms referred to time at all, the subformalisms would be in some sense *unbalanced*. This, however, can be easily uncovered by inspecting the common semantics.

There is a more subtle sense of how two formalisms in such a hybrid system can be unbal-anced, which has to do with the fact that most knowledge representation systems are necessarily *incomplete* in their reasoning in order to provide answers in reasonable time. Because of this in-completeness there could be situations where one subformalism allows to express something which obviously should have some impact on another subformalism according to the common semantics, but the system does not realize this because it's reasoning is incomplete in this aspect. This 'black hole' might be there because the incompleteness has principal reasons or because the subformalism

---

[2] And usually, a large fraction of code in a knowledge representation system is devoted to the user interface.

is not heuristically adequate for this aspect. In any way, the subformalisms of the system appear to be unbalanced. Although the term *balancedness* is a little bit vague, it can be captured by the following *principle of balancedness in hybrid representation systems*:

> If a representation construct in a subformalism of a hybrid formalism suggests that its usage has some impact on knowledge represented with another subformalism (according to the common semantics), then this should be realized by the system.

An example for a system with unbalanced subformalisms is KL-TWO [Vilain 85]: While it is possible to define concepts with a very rich language, only a fraction of it is used for stating contingent propositions. In particular, the number restrictions used in the NIKL subformalism has only a very limited impact on the PENNI subformalism, because the latter is not heuristically adequate to deal with cardinalities.

In the last few years, much effort has been devoted to the development of hybrid systems. Besides systems favoring multiple representations for the sake of naturalness and efficiency of the represented knowledge, systems combining formalisms for the representation of knowledge according to the distinction Frege made between meaning (*Sinn*) and reference (*Bedeutung*) were developed. In particular, the connection of KL-ONE [Brachman, Schmolze 85] derivates as formalisms for representing terminological knowledge (*TBoxes*) with formalisms for representing assertions about the actual state of the world (*ABoxes*) has been investigated[3] (e.g., KRYPTON [Brachman et al 85], KL-TWO [Vilain 85], MESON [Edelmann, Owsnicki 86], BACK [Luck et al 87] and KANDOR [Patel-Schneider 84]). The main points in this research were the design of an appropriate ABox, sometimes requiring a restriction of the TBox (e.g., in KRYPTON), and developing means for connecting the reasoning of TBox and ABox.

In the sequel we will present one particular solution to these problems pursued in BACK[4]. The following design criteria have been taken into account in developing BACK:

- The subformalism of the BACK system should be balanced.

- The BACK formalism should permit tractable inference algorithms covering almost all possible inferences[5].

- The ABox formalism of BACK should be able to represent incomplete knowledge in a limited manner (cf. [Luck et al 86]).

- The BACK system should allow for extending the knowledge base incrementally (we do not consider retractions!).

- The BACK system should reject ABox entries which are inconsistent.

The rest of the paper is divided in four parts. The next section gives a very brief introduction to hybrid KL-ONE systems for those readers unfamiliar with this topic. Then the BACK ABox is discussed, and it is shown how we achieved the goals concerning the formalism stated above. Finally, we investigate what kind of inferences the combination of the ABox and the TBox permit, and how these inferences can be realized. This leads to a new view on the *realization* inference as discussed in [Mark 82], which can be characterized as a 'constraint propagation' process.

---

[3]A rough similarity of this distinction is known in the database area with the distinction of database schemata and database contents, but these approaches take the schema definition as a source of integrity constraints and not as a formalism for the intensional definitions of terms.

[4]The Berlin Advanced Computational Knowledge Representation System.

[5]Unfortunately, complete and tractable inference algorithms are possible only for very simple TBoxes (cf. [Nebel 87] and [Brachman, Levesque 84]).

2 A Short Characterization of Hybrid KL-ONE Systems

KL-ONE as described in [Brachman, Schmolze 85] is perfectly well suited for the introduction of a terminology. It allows to specify *concepts* by stating superconcepts and restrictions on relationships to other concepts, which are called *roles*. Concepts and roles correspond roughly to *generic frames* and *slots* in the frame terminology. Unlike frames, however, concepts are understood as purely *intensional*. Furthermore, concepts may be introduced as *primitive* or *defined*. In the former case, the concept description specifies only the *necessary* conditions, while in the latter case the concept description is *necessary* and *sufficient*.

The following is an (informal) example for the definition of the (slightly artificial) concept modern-small-team. Assuming that human, woman, and team are already introduced as concepts and that member is a role with leader as a *subrole*, the definition might look as follows:

> A modern-small-team is (defined as)
>> a team and
>> having at most 4 members and
>> all members are humans and
>> having exactly 1 leader and
>> all leaders are woman

This example shows some of the important *concept-forming operators* which may be used in order to create new concepts, namely *specialization, number restriction* and *value restriction* of a role. In KL-ONE, concepts and roles are usually presented by graphical means (cf. Fig. 1) which may be sometimes easier to comprehend. However, it does not make any difference whether a linear notation or a graphical network is used provided that a formal semantics can be given (cf. [Luck et al 87], [Luck, Owsnicki 87]).

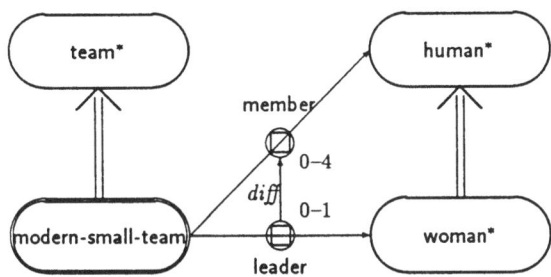

Figure 1: An example of a KL-ONE concept

While KL-ONE does very well in the area of defining concepts, it is weak in stating any contingent truth about the world, for example that "KIM is a woman, and that she is a member of some modern-small-team, but not the leader of that team". Another example would be that "there is at least one modern-small-team". In order to compensate for this, an ABox has to be employed, a topic we will discuss below.

3 The Design of the BACK ABox

The formalisms for representing terminological knowledge in the hybrid systems mentioned above differ only in what concept- and role-forming operators they provide—sometimes motivated by arguments concerning the computational complexity. The situation with ABoxes, however, is quite different. Here we meet a variety of approaches, e.g.:

KRYPTON Full first-order predicate logic.

KL-TWO Variable-free predicate logic with equality.

KANDOR Object-centered, frame-like schema.

MESON Object-centered, frame-like schema.

Using predicate logic (first-order or restricted) as the ABox has several advantages. One is that it gives a clear account to a *common semantics* for the entire formalism[6]. Another benefit of predicate logic is its *plasticity* as Hayes called it [Hayes 74]—the possibility to give *partial descriptions* and to extend a knowledge base *incrementally*. On the other hand, there are a lot of disadvantages. One obvious problem with unrestricted first-order predicate logic are the computional costs, a fact which exclude such systems from being used as a knowledge representation system in practical AI systems. Besides that, there are also problems with the expressiveness of predicate logic. For instance, there is no easy way to state that a given description is *exhaustive* or that different constants denote different objects. The latter two properties are responsible for the fact that *number restrictions* on roles are omitted from the KRYPTON TBox and that they are almost mere comments in the KL-TWO TBox.

For frame-like ABoxes as employed in KANDOR or MESON the situation is opposite. The *unique name hypothesis* and *closed world assumption* are taken for granted, very similar to conventional data bases. This forces the user of such a system to give a *complete* description of the state of affairs and prohibits incremental 'monotonic' additions. However, this kind of representation—called 'vivid' by Levesque in [Levesque 86]—allows for elegant and simple inference algorithms. In the case of hybrid KL-ONE systems it implies that number restrictions and value restrictions of the TBox can be fully utilized in the ABox. A short note about formal semantics might be in order here. While frame-like schemata are often viewed as some ad hoc data structure, it is nevertheless possible to specify a precise formal semantics for at least a subset (cf. [Hayes 79]).

In BACK we tried to combine the benefits of both approaches. An object-centered language was chosen to describe objects of the domain. However, instead of insisting that all role fillers for a given object have to be specified, the information can be *incomplete* and may be refined later. For this purpose the follwing operators are provided:

- stating the cardinality of a role-filler set, e.g., "MARY has at least 2 children";

- disjunctive information on role fillers, as e.g., "MARY is married to JOHN or TOM";

- stating the exhaustiveness of the provided information selectively (cf. [Hayes 74]), e.g., "MARY has as a friend TOM, and these are all friends MARY has".

In [Luck 86][7] it was shown that these operators are sufficient to achieve the goal of 'balanced expressiveness' at least with respect to number restrictions. This also applies to the other concept-forming operators introduced in section 2 as we will see below. Furthermore, the formalism permits the representation of *incomplete knowledge*, *incremental refinement* as well as the treatment of *complete information*. Finally, because of the careful selection of ABox operators, reasoning in the ABox appears to be *tractable* at least in a weak sense.

4 Combining the Reasoning of ABox and TBox

While it appears to be very obvious what kind of inferences are granted by the separate formalisms, the interesting problems stand up if we combine the reasoning of the TBox and the ABox.

---

[6]In these approaches concepts are viewed as 1-place predicates and roles as 2-place predicates.

[7]This article also gives a more formal account of the ABox semantics we ommited here because of lack of space.

The TBox alone is only good for *terminological inferences*, including detecting implicit specalization relationships between concepts, recognizing contradictory concepts and computing the properties inherited from superconcepts. The ABox alone, depending on its flavor, can draw the inferences sanctioned by first-order logic (in the KRYPTON case), by variable-free predicate logic with equality (in KL-TWO), or it can infer whether a domain object is related to other objects, and how many there are (in the case of object-centered ABoxes).

In order to demonstrate the interaction between ABox and TBox in BACK let us investigate a small (informal) example. Let us assume the following concept definitions:

> A man is a
>   human.
> A woman is a
>   human.
> man and woman are disjoint concepts.
> A team is (defined as) a
>   set with members which are all humans, and
>   any leaders are members as well.
> A male-team is (defined as) a
>   team with all members are men.
> A small-team is (defined as) a
>   team with at most 4 members.
> A modern-small-team is (defined as) a
>   small-team with at least 1 leader and
>   all leaders are women.

Now let us assume that the following object decriptions are given:

> TOM, DICK and HARRY are instances of
>   the concept man.
> JUNK is an instance of
>   modern-small-team with
>   TOM, DICK, HARRY and KIM
>   as members of the team.
> CHAUVIS is an instance of
>   male-team with
>   KIM
>   as one of its members.

After this sequence, nothing is wrong with the contents of the knowledge base at first sight. If, however, the situation is more thoroughly analyzed, it becomes obvious that

- after the JUNK team is introduced, KIM is known to be human, because of the value restriction on member;

- after the CHAUVIS team is introduced, it becomes clear that KIM is a man with the same argument;

- and because of that, nobody can become the leader of the JUNK team, because the leader subrole can only be filled with a woman.

Thus, the ABox contents is *contradictory*. The JUNK team cannot exist in this configuration and simultaneously be called a modern-small-team, or otherwise, KIM cannot a member of the male-team.

While the arguments above are only informal, it is, of course, possible to formalize the problem using the common semantics of the formalism [Luck et al 87] and deduce a contradiction as follows:

$$\forall x:\ man(x) \quad\Rightarrow\quad human(x) \tag{1}$$

$$\forall x:\ woman(x) \quad\Rightarrow\quad human(x) \tag{2}$$

$$\forall x:\ \neg man(x) \vee \neg woman(x) \tag{3}$$

$$\forall x:\ team(x) \quad\Leftrightarrow\quad set(x) \wedge (\forall y:\ member(x,y) \Rightarrow human(y)) \wedge$$
$$(\forall z:\ leader(x,z) \Rightarrow member(x,z)) \tag{4}$$

$$\forall x:\ male\text{-}team(x) \quad\Leftrightarrow\quad team(x) \wedge (\forall y:\ member(x,y) \Rightarrow man(y)) \tag{5}$$

$$\forall x:\ small\text{-}team(x) \quad\Leftrightarrow\quad team(x) \wedge$$
$$(\exists\, y_1, y_2, y_3, y_4:\ member(x,y_1) \wedge member(x,y_2) \wedge$$
$$member(x,y_3) \wedge member(x,y_4) \wedge$$
$$(\forall z:\ member(x,z) \Rightarrow z = y_1 \vee z = y_2 \vee z = y_3 \vee z = y4)) \tag{6}$$

$$\forall x:\ modern\text{-}small\text{-}team(x) \Leftrightarrow small\text{-}team(x) \wedge (\exists z:\ leader(x,z)) \wedge$$
$$(\forall y:\ leader(x,y) \Rightarrow woman(y)) \tag{7}$$

$$TOM{\neq}DICK \wedge TOM{\neq}HARRY \wedge TOM{\neq}KIM \wedge DICK{\neq}HARRY \wedge DICK{\neq}KIM \wedge HARRY{\neq}KIM[8] \tag{8}$$

$$man(TOM) \wedge man(DICK) \wedge man(HARRY) \tag{9}$$

$$modern\text{-}small\text{-}team(JUNK) \wedge member(JUNK,TOM) \wedge member(JUNK,DICK) \wedge$$
$$member(JUNK,HARRY) \wedge member(JUNK,KIM) \tag{10}$$

$$male\text{-}team(CHAUVIS) \wedge member(CHAUVIS,KIM) \tag{11}$$

by (5,11): $\quad man(KIM)$ \hfill (12)

by (3,9,12): $\quad \neg woman(KIM) \wedge \neg woman(TOM) \wedge \neg woman(DICK) \wedge \neg woman(HARRY)$ \hfill (13)

by (6,7,8): $\quad \forall z:\ member(JUNK,z) \Rightarrow z{=}TOM \vee z{=}DICK \vee z{=}HARRY \vee z{=}KIM$ \hfill (14)

by (4,7): $\quad \exists z:\ member(JUNK,z) \wedge woman(z)$ \hfill (15)

by (14,15): $\quad woman(KIM) \vee woman(TOM) \vee woman(DICK) \vee woman(HARRY)$ \hfill (16)

by (13,16): *contradiction*

5 Realization as Constraint Propagation

In order to find such contradictions and, more generally, to determine the concept which *most accurately describes* a given object a forward inference technique called *realization* [Mark 82] is usually employed. Realization is very similar to *classification*, an inference technique used to maintain the taxonomy of concepts in the TBox [Lipkis 82]. In fact, realization can be viewed as *abstraction*—generating a description in terms of the TBox—followed by *classification* of this description (cf. [Vilain 85]).[9]

A first approximation to the implementation of this inference could be realized as follows. After a new assertion about an indivdual enters the ABox (either a new concept or a new role filler) the following has to be done:

- Propagate all role fillers of subroles to the corresponding superrole.

- Determine the cardinality of the role filler sets for each role (this can be a range in the case of incomplete information). This cardinality information is used as the actual number restriction for the role in the abstraction process.

- If a role-filler set is closed, i.e., all potential candidates are known, then the *generalization*[10] of the descriptions of all potential role fillers can serve as the actual value restriction in the abstraction process.

---

[8]This statement expresses the *unique name hypothesis*.

[9]Another view on realization, pursued in [Mark 82], can be described as *recognition* and *retrieval*.

[10]Generalization is not a concept-forming operator and there seems to be no easy way to assign a compositional semantics to it. However, it is easy to build such a concept structurally, which is the most specialized one subsuming a given set of concepts.

- Now, the generated number and value restrictions, the old description of the individual as well as the new one can be used to construct a concept definition which can be classified and after that serve as the new *most general specialization* (MSG) of the individual under investigation.

This algorithm does take into account all information which is supplied *locally* to an individual, but ignores any non-local consequences. In the example of the last section, we would at least require that after the abstraction process the role fillers are to be specialized according to the value restriction of the male-team. Additionally, we note that in order to detect the contradiction in the example we also have to account for the case that the specialization of an individual (KIM from human to man) can lead to the specialization of another individual (JUNK from modern-small-team to the empty concept) the first one is a role filler of.

If we analyze this algorithm more thoroughly, we may note that this process can trigger other specializations which in turn may propagate restrictions. Because this sounds very expensive from a computational point of view, one could argue that because the system reasoning process is incomplete anyway, it is legitimate to restrict the resources allocated for the realization process and leave such situations alone. And this was indeed the first approximation to a solution we chose. However, this is not a general incompleteness of the inference algorithm, but it depends on the order of input! If, in our example, the order of input between the JUNK and the CHAUVI would have been reversed the contradiction would be easily detected. In general, this order dependence appears not only in the special case of contradiction detection, but, of course, in the general process of determining MSGs as well.

That is certainly not the kind of behaviour we expect from a knowledge representation system. Although it is clear that we have to live with incomplete reasoners, this incompleteness should be systematic, perhaps even describable by a systematic, model-theoretic approach (cf. [Patel-Schneider 86]). In conclusion, if we claim to *integrate* the reasoning of two formalisms, a minimal requirement is that the inferences are independent of the order of input.

The only solution to this problem is to employ some sort of 'constraint propagation'[11]. After a new MSG is determined for some individual I,

- all role fillers at I have to be specialized to the corresponding value restriction (forward propagation);

- additionally, all individuals, which mention I as a role filler have to be checked whether it is possible to specalize them (backward propagation); this can only happen if the corresponding role-filler set is closed;

- finally, these steps have to be performed for all individuals which get new MSGs during this process.

For the example above, this suffices to detect the contradiction. The JUNK team will be specialized to the following concept:

    a modern-small-team and
    all of its members are men

In classifying this concept, the value restriction of the member role is propagated to the subrole leader (a subrole has to adhere to the value restriction of its superrole) resulting in a value restriction of (AND man woman) which apparently is contradictory.

Altogether, this process assures that incompleteness depending on the order of input cannot appear. However, it also sounds very costly from a computational point of view. At first sight, it

---

[11] While we first thought that BACK is the only system using this technique, because the literature does not give any hints in this direction, latter on we learned from Marc Vilain that KL-TWO works in a similar way.

does not even seem very clear whether this process always terminates. Fortunately, the process of propagating MSG is not a general constraint propagation process. A first fact about this process, we may note, is that backtracking cannot occur. That means if we encounter a contradiction there is no way to resolve it, but to reject the input which led to the contradiction.[12] This tells us that we will not get a combinatorial explosion because of reasoning by case. There are more facts which constrain the propagation space:

- An individual which gets a new MSG by backward propagation cannot trigger new forward propagations. This is because the new MSG does reflect the current role fillers as necessary and sufficient conditions, i.e., there cannot be any new restrictions on role fillers.

- Backward propagation leads to a new MSG, if the role-filler set is closed and all other role fillers are already more specialized than the value restriction, a situation which does not occur very often.

- Forward propagation has a significant non-local effect only if the chain of individuals the value restrictions are propagated along corresponds to a line of concepts which are specialized in parallel, which is not very likely.

- In the worst case, the number of recomputations of an MSG during forward and backward propagation is bounded by the product of the number of individuals and the number of concepts in the TBox (before the entire process starts). This, however, would result in MSGs which cannot be specialized further, i.e., the upper bound can be divided by the number of input operations.

Finally, we should discuss where incompleteness might arise in in the integrated reasoning process. First, realization cannot be more complete than classification. This means that some very weird cases of contradictions cannot be recognized (cf. [Nebel 87]). Furthermore, the abstraction process is a source of incompleteness as well. In our example, we could prove that KIM is necessarily a woman after the first two inputs; however, the abstraction failed to recognize this. The reason is, that this would require some kind of reasoning by case we strictly avoided because of the computional costs.

6 Conclusion

We have argued that a hybrid knowledge representation system should be balanced in its expressiveness and integrate the reasoning of its subformalisms in a sound manner based on a common semantics. Furthermore, we made plausible that the BACK system does very well in these respects. By giving a thorough description of an inference technique known as 'realization', we demonstrated that this inference can only be realized as a constraint propagation process, a very special and limited one, though.

Acknowledgement

Many of the ideas presented here are the result of the work in the KIT-BACK project. The other members of this project, Christof Peltason and Albrecht Schmiedel, deserve much of the credit for these ideas. Additionally, the discussions with Marc Vilain and Bob MacGregor

---

[12]This is due to the fact that we do not handle reason maintenance.

were very helpful in shedding more light on the realization process. The presentation of our results in section 4 and the analysis of the algorithm in section 5 profited heavily from these discussions.

References

[Brachman, Levesque 84] Ronald J. Brachman, Hector J. Levesque, The tractability of subsumption in frame-based description languages, in: *Proc. AAAI-84*, Austin (Tex.), August 1984, 34–37.

[Brachman, Schmolze 85] Ronald J. Brachman, James G. Schmolze, An overview of the KL-ONE knowledge representation system, in: *Cognitive Science*, 9(2), April–June 1985, 171–216.

[Brachman et al 85] Ronald J. Brachman, Victoria Pigman Gilbert, Hector J. Levesque, An Essential Hybrid Reasoning System: Knowledge and Symbol Level Accounts in KRYPTON, in: *Proc. 9th IJCAI*, Los Angeles (Cal.), 1985, 532–539.

[Edelmann, Owsnicki 86] Jürgen Edelmann, Bernd Owsnicki, Data Models in Knowledge Representation Systems: A Case Study, in: C.-R. Rollinger, W. Horn (eds.), *GWAI-86 und 2. Österreichische Artificial-Intelligence-Tagung*, Springer, Berlin (Germany), 1986, 69–74.

[Hayes 74] Patrick J. Hayes, Some Problems and Non-Problems in Representation Theory, *Proc. AISB Summer Conference*, University of Sussex, 1974, 63–79.

[Hayes 79] Patrick J. Hayes, The Logic of Frames, in: D. Metzing (ed.), *Frame Conceptions and Text Understanding*, deGruyter, Berlin (Germany), 1979, 46–61.

[Kowalski 80] Robert A. Kowalski, Contribution to the SIGART Special Issue on Knowledge Representation, in: *SIGART Newsletter*, No70, February 1980.

[Levesque 86] Hector J. Levesque, Making Believers out of Computers, Computers and Thougth Lecture at IJCAI-85, Los Angeles (Cal.), published in: *Artificial Intelligence*, 30(1), 1986, 81–108.

[Lipkis 82] Tom Lipkis, A KL-ONE Classifier, in: J. G. Schmolze, R. J. Brachman (eds.), *Proc. 1981 KL-ONE Workshop*, BBN Technical Report 4842, Bolt, Berank and Newman, Inc., Cambridge (Mass.), 1982, 128–145.

[Luck 86] Kai von Luck, Semantic Networks with Number Restricted Roles or Another Story about Clyde, in: C.-R. Rollinger, W. Horn (eds.), *GWAI-86 und 2. Österreichische Artificial-Intelligence-Tagung*, Springer, Berlin (Germany), 1986, 58–68.

[Luck, Owsnicki-Klewe 87] Kai von Luck, Bernd Owsnicki-Klewe, Neuere KI-Formalismen zur Repräsentation von Wissen, to appear in: T. Christaller (ed.), *Künstliche Intelligenz*, Springer, Berlin (Germany), 1987.

[Luck et al 86] Kai von Luck, Bernhard Nebel, Christof Peltason, Albrecht Schmiedel, BACK to Consistency and Incompleteness, in: H. Stoyan (ed.), *GWAI-85*, Springer, Berlin (Germany), 1986, 245–257.

[Luck et al 87] Kai von Luck, Bernhard Nebel, Christof Peltason, Albrecht Schmiedel, The Anatomy of the BACK System, KIT Report 41, Technische Universität Berlin, Berlin (Germany), January 1987.

[Mark 82] William Mark, Realization, in:J. G. Schmolze, R. J. Brachman (eds.), *Proc. 1981 KL-ONE Workshop*, BBN Technical Report 4842, Bolt, Berank and Newman, Inc., Cambridge (Mass.), 1982, 78–89.

[McCarthy, Hayes 69] John McCarthy, Pat Hayes, Some Philosophical Problems from the Standpoint of Artificial Intelligence, in: B. Meltzer, D. Michie (eds.), *Machine Intelligence* 4, Edinburgh University Press, Edinburgh (Great Britain), 1969, 463–502.

[McDermott 78] Drew McDermott, Tarskian semantics, or no notation without denotation!, in: *Cognitive Science*, 2(3), July–September 1978, 277–282.

[Nebel 87] Bernhard Nebel, Computational Complexity of Terminological Reasoning in BACK, to appear in: *Artificial Intelligence*, 1987.

[Patel-Schneider 84] Peter F. Patel-Schneider, Small can be Beautiful in Knowledge Representation, in: *Proc. IEEE Workshop on Principles of Knowledge-Based Systems*, Denver (Colo.), 1984, 11–16.

[Patel-Schneider 86] Peter F. Patel-Schneider, A Four-Valued Semantics for Frame-Based Description Languages, in: *Proc. AAAI-86*, Philadelphia (Pa.), August 1986, 344–348.

[Sloman 85] Aaron Sloman, Why We Need Many Knowledge Representation Formalisms, in: M. Bramer (ed.), *Research and Development in Expert Systems*, Cambridge University Press, Cambridge (Great Britain), 1985.

[Vilain 85] Marc B. Vilain, The Restricted Language Architecture of a Hybrid Representation System, in: *Proc. 9th IJCAI*, Los Angeles (Cal.), 1985, 547–551.

Der Aspekt der Zeitstruktur in zeitlogischen Formalisierungen in der KI

Klaus Groth

Danet GmbH

Otto-Röhm-Str. 71

D-6100 Darmstadt

Abstract

Es werden die Zeitstrukturen der zeitlogischen Formalisierungen von McDermott und Allen näher betrachtet. Für die Formalisierung von Allen wird gezeigt, daß sich aus der Intervallstruktur ein Mangel an Eigenschaften bzgl. des Konzepts eines *Ereignisses* ergibt. Auch die Definition eines *Faktes* wird durch die Betrachtung der Zeitstruktur und von Arbeiten zu modalen Zeitlogiken verständlicher. Sie ist, entgegen einer Aussage von Shoham, nicht durch die fehlende Atomarität der Zeitstruktur bestimmt. Abschließend wird die Beziehung der Zeitstruktur und der bzgl. ihr definierten Konzepte in einer Formalisierung des Autors diskutiert[1].

Einleitung

Innerhalb der letzten Jahre ist in der KI verstärkt die Notwendigkeit zur Repräsentation von Zeit erkannt und die Möglichkeit ihrer Repräsentation durch Logik untersucht worden. Als Beispiele seien hier die Arbeiten von McDermott /8/, Allen /1/, Kowalski und Sergot /7/ und Shoham /9/ genannt.

McDermott geht dabei von einer Menge von *Situationen* aus, die durch eine *Vorgänger-/Nachfolgerrelation* strukturiert ist. Kowalski und Sergot hingegen betrachten *Ereignisse* als grundlegend, während Allen von einer Menge von *Zeitintervallen* ausgeht, die durch dreizehn Relationen /1/ oder eine Relation /2/ strukturiert ist. Allgemein kann man sagen, daß die Grundlage der Formalisierungen jeweils eine Menge O von Basisobjekten ist, die, entsprechend der Interpretation der Objekte, durch eine Anzahl von Relationen R_i strukturiert ist. Für die Interpretation der Basisobjekte als Intervalle ist z. B. die Annahme einer *Enthaltenseinrelation* '$\subseteq$' naheliegend.

Bezüglich der Basisstruktur $S = (O, R_1, \ldots, R_n)$, oder einer aus ihr abgeleiteten Struktur, z. B. der Menge der konvexen Teilmengen (Intervalle, s. /8/, /9/), werden dann verschiedene Konzepte, wie *Ereignis*, *Fakt* und *Prozeß* formalisiert. Diese lassen sich (semantisch) durch eine Bedingung an die mit dem jeweiligen Konzept identifizierbare Menge von Basisobjekten charakterisieren. So versteht Allen das Stattfinden des *Ereignisses* e im Intervall x als die Tatsache, daß e in keinem Teilintervall y von x stattfindet. Dies läßt sich für die Menge M der Intervalle in denen das Ereignis e stattfindet durch die folgende Bedingung beschreiben:

$$x \in M \Rightarrow \forall y(y \subset x \Rightarrow y \notin M)^2. \qquad (A)$$

---

[1] Dieser Aufsatz ist ein Ergebnis der Beschäftigung des Autors mit zeitlogischen Formalisierungen in der KI im Rahmen seiner Diplomarbeit /4/ bei Prof. Dr. Gerd Veenker, Universität Bonn.

[2] '$y \subset x$' drücke aus, daß das Intervall y *echt* in x enthalten ist

Nachfolgend soll nun die Beschreibung (Formalisierung) der Basisstrukturen in den Arbeiten von McDermott /8/ und Allen /1/, bzw. /2/, sowie die Auswirkung der Basisstrukturen auf die jeweiligen Konzepte näher betrachtet werden.

Über die Vorliebe für die reellen Zahlen

Einige der Autoren in der KI verwenden für die von ihnen beschriebene Zeitstruktur das Modell der (Intervallstruktur über den) reellen Zahlen bzw. ordnen der Basisstruktur die Kontinuitätseigenschaft der reellen Zahlen zu. Am Beispiel der Formalisierungen von McDermott und Allen soll gezeigt werden, daß dies nur bedingt zulässig ist.

Um ausgehend von einer Menge von Situationen auch von Zeitpunkten in einem intuitiven Sinne reden zu können, macht McDermott die Annahme der Existenz der Menge R der reellen Zahlen als *Zeitpunkte*. Jede maximale linear geordnete Teilmenge von Situationen (*Chronik*) soll isomorph zu R sein. Für die Struktur der Menge R gibt er dabei keine Axiomatisierung an. Die Kontinuitätseigenschaft der reellen Zahlen ist jedoch nur in einer Formel 2. Ordnung formalisierbar (s. /3/ S. 29). So wird bei McDermott gar nicht deutlich, daß er, auf Grund der sich selbst auferlegten Formalisierungsbeschränkung der alleinigen Verwendung einer Sprache erster Ordnung (S. 104), die Basisstruktur gar nicht in dem gewünschten Maß spezifizieren kann.

Allen /1/ beschreibt unter der Annahme von 13 transitiven Intervallrelationen seine Zeitstruktur durch eine Formalisierung in der für jedes Intervall x ein Intervall y existiert, so daß $(x, y) \in R_i$, $i = 1, \ldots, 13$, und für zwei Intervalle x und y genau eine der 13 Relationen gilt. Darüber hinaus spezifiziert er 169 Axiome der Form $(x R_i y \wedge y R_j z) \Rightarrow x R_{i_1} z \vee \ldots \vee x R_{i_k} z$, die die *transitive Hülle* der 13 Relationen beschreiben. In /4/ wird gezeigt, daß sich aus diesen Annahmen die folgenden Bedingungen *a)* und *b)* nicht ableiten lassen:

a) Zu zwei beliebigen Intervallen existiert ein Intervall, das beide enthält.

b) Zwei sich überlappende Intervalle besitzen ein maximales gemeinsames Teilintervall.

Diese Bedingungen wird man jedoch intuitiv für eine Intervallstruktur als gültig annehmen und für die Menge der (offenen/abgeschlossenen) Intervalle über R sind sie natürlich auch erfüllt. Allen's Formalisierung zeitlogischer Axiome erlaubt also wesentlich mehr Modelle, als das von ihm angegebene Modell der offenen Intervalle über R. Die hier aufgezeigten *Mängel* der Zeitstruktur machen auch verständlich, wieso der Autor in /2/ eine vollständig neue Axiomatisierung einer Intervallstruktur angibt, die diese Mängel nicht aufweist. Eine entsprechende Begründung für seine neue Formalisierung gibt Allen selbst jedoch nicht.

Die Betrachtung hat also gezeigt, daß die von den Autoren verwendeten Modelle z. T. gar nicht vollständig beschrieben werden können (McDermott) oder nicht beschrieben sind (Allen).

Die Auswirkung der Zeitstruktur auf die definierten Konzepte

In *(A)* ist eine semantische Charakterisierung des Konzepts eines *Ereignisses* nach dem Verständnis von Allen angegeben worden. Aus dem Stattfinden der Ereignisse e_1 und e_2 in zwei sich überlappenden Intervallen x und y, d. h. x und y besitzen mindestens ein gemeinsames Teilintervall, wird man intuitiv auf das Stattfinden von e_3, '*der Überlappung von e_1 und e_2*', schließen wollen. Das

Intervall z, in dem e_3 stattfindet muß sich auf Grund von *(A)* durch eine in Bezug auf '$\subseteq$' eindeutige Eigenschaft auszeichnen. Für die Menge M aller gemeinsamen Teilintervall von x und y ist dies naheliegenderweise die Maximalität des Intervalls. Auf Grund der fehlenden Bedingung *b)* muß jedoch das maximale gemeinsame Teilintervall von x und y nicht existieren. Daher kann aus dem Stattfinden von e_1 und e_2 auch nicht auf das Stattfinden von e_3 geschlossen werden. In Analogie dazu erlaubt das Fehlen der Bedingung *a)* keine eindeutige Identifikation eines Intervalls z, das als das Intervall des Stattfindens von e_4, *'dem Stattfinden der Ereignisse e_1 und e_2'*, angesehen werden kann. An diesen beiden Beispielen wird der Einfluß der Eigenschaften der Basisstruktur auf die Eigenschaften der Konzepte der Formalisierung deutlich.

Wie sich am Beispiel des Konzepts eines Faktes zeigen läßt, beeinflußt die Zeitstruktur jedoch auch die Definition der Konzepte selbst. So versteht Allen die Gültigkeit eines Faktes in einem Intervall x als die Gültigkeit des Faktes in allen Teilintervallen y von x. Das heißt, daß die Menge M der Zeitintervalle, für die ein Fakt gilt, die folgende Bedingung *(B)* erfüllt:

$$x \in M \iff \forall y (y \subset x \implies y \in M). \tag{B}$$

Daß Allen statt dessen die folgende Bedingung *(C)* zugrunde legt, begründet er lediglich mit bestimmten Ableitungsmöglichkeiten innerhalb seines Axiomensystems (/1/ S. 130).

$$x \in M \iff \forall y (y \subset x \implies \exists z (z \subset y \land z \in M)). \tag{C}$$

Eine explizite (semantische) Begründung für die Annahme von *(C)* an Stelle von *(B)* gibt er nicht. Einen Versuch der Begründung dieser Entscheidung unternimmt Shoham, der behauptet (/9/ S. 392), daß diese Entscheidung durch die fehlende Atomarität der Intervallstruktur bedingt ist. Die Bedingung *(C)* drücke bzgl. einer atomaren Intervallstruktur aus, daß ein Fakt in einem Intervall gilt, genau dann wenn er in jedem atomaren Teilintervall gilt. So definiert Shoham auf einer (abgeleiteten) atomaren Intervallstruktur das Konzept eines *liquiden Aussagetyps*, durch die folgende Bedingung *(D)* an die Intervallmenge M, für die der Aussagetyp gilt:

$$(x \in M \implies \forall y (y \subseteq x \implies y \in M)) \land (\forall y (y \subset x \implies y \in M) \implies x \in M) \tag{D}$$

Seine Behauptung, auf diese Weise Allen's Konzept eines Faktes äquivalent beschrieben zu haben (S. 396) ist jedoch falsch. Ein Gegenbeispiel ist die Struktur S der abgeschlossenen Teilintervalle über den rationalen Zahlen Q. Ist M die Menge der atomaren Intervalle $[r,r], r \in Q$, so erfüllt M die Bedingung *(D)*, nicht jedoch die Bedingung *(C)*, da jedes nicht-atomare Intervall x ($x \notin M$) mindestens ein (atomares) Teilintervall z ($z \in M$) enthält. Die Menge M kann also als Intervallmenge eines liquiden Aussagetyps in Shoham's Formalisierung, aber nicht als die Intervallmenge eines Faktes in Allen's Formalisierung verstanden werden. Für eine atomare Intervallstruktur haben alle drei Bedingungen zudem die Konsequenz, daß jeder Fakt fuer jedes atomare Intervall x gilt. Dies dürfte jedoch nicht im Sinne von Allen sein.

Auf der Suche nach einer Begründung der Annahme von *(C)* wird man im Bereich modaler Zeit-logiken fündig. Dort werden für modale Zeitintervallogiken verschiedene Gültigkeitsverständnisse, d. h. Bedingungen an die Intervallmenge M für die eine Formel ϕ gilt, und ihre Konsequenzen bzgl. einer Logik diskutiert. So untersucht Humberstone in /6/ unter Annahme der Bedingung

$$x \in M \;\Rightarrow\; \forall y(y \subset x \;\Rightarrow\; y \in M) \tag{E}$$

die Konsequenz der Bedingung *(F)*:

$$x \notin M \;\Rightarrow\; \exists y(y \subseteq x \land \forall z(z \subseteq y \;\Rightarrow\; z \notin M)). \tag{F}$$

Er zitiert dabei eine Aussage von Hamblin /5/, derzufolge die Annahme von *(F)* für ein Intervall y, in der eine Formel ϕ nicht gilt, die Existenz einer unendlichen Folge (z_i) von ineinander enthaltenen Teilintervallen von y ausschließt, so daß ϕ nicht für die z_i mindestens jedoch für je ein Teilintervall der z_i gilt.

Die Ungültigkeit einer Formel wird also auf die *eindeutige* Ungültigkeit in einem Teilintervall y, d. h. für alle Teilintervalle des Intervalls y, zurückgeführt. Für eine nicht atomare Intervallstruktur sind die Bedingungen *(E)* und *(F)* jedoch äquivalent zu *(C)*. Die Wahl von *(C)* an Stelle von *(B)* ist also bedingt durch die Absicht, in einer bzgl. '$\subset$' unendlichen Intervallstruktur die Gültigkeit bzw. Ungültigkeit eines Faktes auf die eindeutige Gültigkeit bzw. Ungültigkeit für alle Teilintervalle bzw. ein Teilintervall zurückzuführen. Wesentlich ist also an dieser Stelle die Existenz unendlicher Folgen von ineinander enthaltenen Intervallen.

Eine wohldefinierte Zeitstruktur

Abschließend soll eine in /4/ verwendete Zeitstruktur und deren Konsequenz auf die bzgl. ihr definierten Konzepte untersucht werden. Dies wird zeigen, daß die Atomarität der Zeitstruktur keine direkte Übertragung des Konzepts eines *Prozesses* von Allen erlaubt.

Ausgangspunkt ist dabei eine Menge T von Zeitpunkten, die durch eine transitive, irreflexive und lineare *Vorgänger-/Nachfolgerrelation* '$\prec$' strukturiert ist, so daß jedes Element einen Vorgänger und Nachfolger besitzt und jeweils ein *direkter* Vorgänger bzw. Nachfolger existiert. Wie van Benthem /3/ zeigt (S. 21), besitzt die Theorie **DI**, die die Menge der Axiome enthält, die diese Bedingungen formalisieren, wesentlich mehr Modelle als das naheliegende Modell $(Z, \prec)$ der Menge der ganzen Zahlen mit der arithmetische *kleiner-Relation* '$\prec$'. Auch die Struktur $Z + Z = (\{(z, i) \mid z \in Z, i = 1, 2\}, \prec')$, mit $(x, i) \prec' (y, j) \Leftrightarrow x \prec y \lor i \prec j$, ist ein Modell dieser Theorie. $Z + Z$ kann als eine Struktur der Wiederholung von Z angesehen werden.

Die Menge I der konvexen Teilmengen von T mit mindestens zwei Elementen aus T kann daher neben den durch zwei Zeitpunkte t_1 und t_2 eindeutig bestimmten *Intervall* $[t_1, t_2]$ auch *unendliche* Intervalle enthalten, wie z. B. das Intervall $[0, \infty] = \{x \mid x \in Z, 0 \preceq x\}$ in Bezug auf $(Z, \prec)$, oder das Intervall $[\langle 0, 1 \rangle, \langle \infty, 1 \rangle]$ in Bezug auf das Modell $Z + Z$.

In /4/ wird das Konzept einer *Beobachtung* durch eine beliebige Menge M von Intervallen charakterisiert. Die Konzepte Ereignis und Prozeß in Allen's Formalisierung lassen sich dann als Spezialisierung des Konzeptes Beobachtung folgendermaßen definieren:

Ereignis $\quad x \in M \;\Rightarrow\; \forall y(y \subset x \;\Rightarrow\; y \notin M),$ $\tag{A}$

Prozeß $\quad x \in M \;\Rightarrow\; \exists y(y \subset x \land y \in M).$

Diese Definition würde jedoch auf Grund der Intervallstruktur bedeuten, daß für ein atomares Intervall keine Beobachtung eines Prozesses möglich ist. Dies ist eine unerwünschte Konsequenz der Atomarität der Intervallstruktur. Daher wird in /4/ das Konzept eines Prozesses durch die folgende Bedingung charakterisiert:

$$x \in M \Rightarrow (\forall y(y \subseteq x \Rightarrow y \in M) \land \exists y(y \in M \land (y \subset x \lor x \subset y))). \qquad (G)$$

Diese Beziehung drückt das Verständnis eines Prozesses als *kontinuierliche* Beobachtung aus, d. h. der Ablauf eines Prozesses in x bedeutet den Ablauf des Prozesses in jedem Teilintervall von x. Zudem ist durch $\exists y(y \in M \land (y \subset x \lor x \subset y))$ sichergestellt, daß Prozesse stets länger andauern als ein atomarer Beobachtungszeitraum. Da sich die Bedingungen *(A)* und *(G)* wechselseitig ausschließen, läßt sich für eine beliebige Intervallmenge eindeutig bestimmen, ob sie ein Ereignis, ein Prozeß oder keines der beiden Konzepte repräsentiert (man vergleiche dagegen /1/).

Zusammenfassung

An zwei grundlegenden Arbeiten zur Formalisierung von Zeit durch Logik in der KI wurde gezeigt, daß in ihnen die Charakterisierung der zugrundeliegenden Basisstrukturen nur unzureichend durchgeführt ist. Es ist deutlich worden, daß eine konkrete Charakterisierung der Basisstruktur wesentlich ist zur Bestimmung der Eigenschaften der bzgl. ihr definierten Konzepte. Wie die Arbeit von Shoham zeigt, ist die Bedeutung der Eigenschaften der Basisstruktur auch in neueren Arbeiten noch nicht voll erkannt worden. Es ist eine Erfahrung des Autors, daß dazu die Beachtung von Arbeiten zu modalen Zeitlogiken eine Hilfe sein kann. Die abschließend vorgestellte Zeitstruktur und die bzgl. ihr definierten Konzepte als eine adäquate Übertragung der jeweiligen Konzepte von Allen auf die obige Zeitstruktur betrachtet werden können.

Literatur

/1/ Allen, J. F.: "Towards a General Theory of Action and Time", *Artifcial Intelligence, Vol. 22*, (1984), pp 123-154.

/2/ Allen, J. F. und P. J. Hayes: "A Common-Sense Theory of Time", *Proc. of IJCAI 8*, (1985), pp 528-531.

/3/ van Benthem, J. F. A. K.: "The Logic of Time", *Reidel Publishing Comp., Dordrecht*, 1982.

/4/ Groth, K.: "Temporale Logik und die logische Repräsentation von Zeitwissen in der KI", *Universität Bonn, Institut für Informatik, Diplomarbeit*, Bonn, 1987.

/5/ Hamblin, C. L.: "Instants and Intervals", *Stadium Generale, Vol. 27*, (1971), pp127-134.

/6/ Humberstone, I. L.: "Interval Semantics for Tense Logic: Some Remarks", *Journal of Philosophical Logic, Vol. 8*, (1979), pp 171-196.

/7/ Kowalski, R. und M. Sergot: "A Logic-Based Calculus of Events", *New Generation Computing 4*, (1986), pp 67-95.

/8/ McDermott, D.: "A Temporal Logic for Reasoning about Processes and Plans", *Cognitive Science, Vol. 6, (2)*, (1982), pp 101-155.

/9/ Shoham, Y.: "Reified Temporal Logic: Semantical and Ontological considerations", *Proceedings of the ECAI-86*, Brighton, pp 390-397, 1986.

Higher-order Concepts in a Tractable
Knowledge Representation

Stefan Wrobel

Techn. Univ. Berlin, FR 5-8,
Franklinstr. 28/29, 1000 Berlin 10
West Germany

Abstract

Due to the intractability of providing the full set of higher-order logical inferences, the introduction of higher-order concepts into knowledge representation formalisms is usually avoided. In fact, this needn't be so. We present the knowledge representation of the knowledge acquisition system BLIP, and describe how higher-order concepts are represented by using *metapredicates*. We then show that metapredicates have the necessary properties to qualify for inclusion in a knowledge representation: they can be given a precise semantics, and allow a natural set of inferences to be provided effectively. We specify the inference rules for the representation, and prove they are *fact-complete* and tractable.

1. Introduction

Despite their apparent power, the introduction of higher-order concepts into a knowledge representation formalism is usually strictly avoided. Almost all representation formalisms are restricted to first-order concepts, i.e., expressions about properties of base-level objects in the world. Higher-order concepts, by contrast, treat those properties in turn as objects that can be described, i.e., they talk about properties of properties. It is one of the important features of any natural language that first-order and higher-order concepts can be expressed with the same ease. We can say "Sugar is sweet." just as well as we can say "Sweet is the opposite of salty." The unrestricted inclusion of such expressions into a formal system, however, requires the use of a typed, higher-order logic to avoid Russell's famous paradox.

Unfortunately, higher order logic has very undesirable computational properties (it is not even semi-decidable) that make it unsuitable as the basis for a knowledge representation formalism. Furthermore, it is not even powerful enough to represent all the interesting concepts one needs in an all encompassing knowledge representation: as Perlis [Perlis 85] points out, certain very natural statements about truth and beliefs of an agent cannot be expressed at all in a typed system. As a result, higher-order logic is rightfully not considered a good basis for a knowledge representation, and there have been several attempts to "flatten" the concepts one needs into a first-order logic (e.g., [McCarthy 79], [Perlis 85], [Hobbs 86]).

As a consequence, this has unfortunately also brought about the exclusion of higher-order concepts from knowledge representations. In this paper, we will show that this needn't be so. There are certain higher-order concepts which are very useful for knowledge representation and which can naturally be introduced into a knowledge representation without needing to provide the full set of higher-order logical inferences.

In particular, our position (similar to [Levesque, Brachman 85]) is that a knowledge representation system should
- (a) have a well-defined semantics (truth theory),
- (b) provide a well-defined and natural set of inferences, and
- (c) do that effectively.

Point (a) requires that the user of a knowledge representation formalism can tell which worlds can be models of a particular knowledge base, thus making clear the "meaning" of a statement in the knowledge base. Point (b) is of particular importance: it does not require the set of inferences to be complete, but it does require that the set of inferences be describable naturally without reference to the particular inference strategy used, which excludes, for example, inference sets describable only by using depth or time limits. The effectiveness requirement (c) is a direct consequence of a functional view on knowledge representations: it requires that all inferences be providable in finite time (decidability), ideally with an upper bound that is polynomial in the size of the knowledge base.

In the rest of this paper, we will present how higher-order concepts have been introduced into the knowledge representation used in the knowledge acquisition system BLIP ([Emde, Morik 86]) that we have been developing in the KIT-LERNER[1] project. We will formalize this knowledge representation by setting up an axiomatic theory ("MF"), and then address each of the three points above. In particular, we will specify what it means for an MF statement to be true by defining an appropriate interpretation, give a set of inference rules for MF and examine the set of inferences they define (they are fact-complete), and finally examine whether those inferences can be provided effectively. We conclude with a brief discussion of some possible extensions of the representation presented.

2. Higher-order concepts in BLIP

2.1. Overview

For the purposes of this paper, we will use a sorted horn-clause logic without function symbols as the base representation into which higher-order concepts are introduced[2]. The elementary unit of knowledge is a *fact*, i.e., a statement about the world such as

contains(aspirin,asa) [3]

which we could interpret as the statement that "Aspirin contains Acetyl Salicyl Acid." The arguments to such facts must be constants, which can be interpreted as denoting objects in the world. Composed terms (with functions), such as **price(aspirin)**, are not allowed as arguments. The set of constants is structured into different sorts forming a sort hierarchy. Each predicate is required to have a definition specifying its *argument sort mask* (ASM) to which the arguments of a fact must conform. **contains**, for example, might have the following ASM:

contains(<drug>,<substance>),

implying that **aspirin** must be an element of the sort **drug**, and **asa** must be an element of the sort **substance**.

----

[1] The KIT-LERNER project is partially supported by the Bundesministerium für Forschung und Technologie (BMFT) under contract ITW8501B1. Industrial partners are Nixdorf Computer AG and Stollmann GmbH.

[2] The base representation in BLIP also includes negation and a set of computed arithmetic predicates. Since our goal here is to examine the representational properties of metapredicates, which are independent of those two features, we have not included them in the following discussion. See section 3.4. for some remarks about the consequences of introducing those two features.

[3] All examples are taken from an experimental application of BLIP to the domain of side-effects of pain-killers.

Finally, *rules* express general inferential relations that hold between different facts, such as
    contains(X,Y) & cure_1(Y,Z) --> cure_2(X,Z)[4] ,
which can be interpreted as "If a drug X contains a substance Y, and Y cures a disease Z, then X cures Z as well." Each rule may consist of one or more premises ("facts" with variables) connected by **&**, and a single conclusion which must not contain variables not bound in the premises. Rules are implicitly all-quantified on all their variables.

The difficulty in introducing higher-order concepts is in choosing the right restrictions to what can be stated in the representation and what can't. The included features should be such that they are interesting for knowledge representation while at the same time allowing a natural set of inferences to be provided effectively. In BLIP, we use a form of higher-order concepts which first originated in the context of the natural language system BACON (e.g., [Habel/Rollinger 81]). There, a set of innate higher cognitive concepts like "transitive" was assumed, each of which was to be defined by a meaning postulate in the form of a *rule schema*. Since in BLIP, we are interested in a knowledge representation system for knowledge acquisition, we do not regard those higher concepts as innate and predefined: instead, they are fully accessible to a user as a representational construct in the form of *metapredicates*.

A metapredicate definition associates a rule schema with the metapredicate to be defined, such as
    transitive(p): p(x,y) & p(y,z) --> p(x,z),
where **p** is a predicate variable. Such a definition is to be interpreted as implicitly all-quantified on its predicate variables and states that whenever we assert a *metafact* such as
    transitive(taller),
the rule that results from instantiating the rule schema with the actual predicates used as arguments to the metafact is to hold as well. Here, we would get
    taller(x,y) & taller(y,z) --> taller(x,z).
Besides predicate variables, it is also possible to use argument variables as arguments to the metapredicate (such as shown below for the metapredicate **factoring**.) Just as metapredicates describe properties of predicates, *metametapredicates* (actually, *metametafacts*), are used to describe properties of metapredicates; metametapredicates are defined exactly like metapredicates.

Besides the basic metapredicates such as transitive, opposite, symmetrical, inverse, etc., there is a large variety of several other things expressible with metapredicates, such as a metapredicate defining general inheritance relationships:
    inherits(p,q): p(x,y) & q(x,z) --> q(y,z)
which states that the value of the "q"-property of an object is inherited down a "p"-link, such as in
    inherits(isa,color),
where the color of an object (class) is inherited down an isa-hierarchy, or
    inherits(sibling,parent),
which states that siblings have the same parents. Metapredicates can also be used to explicitly represent relationships such as
    factoring(p, val,q): p(x,val) --> q(x) ,
where the one-argument predicate **q** is "factored" into the two-argument predicate **p**, such as in
    factoring(diagnosis,flu,has_flu).

----
[4] The different numbers appended to "cure" are necessary because the two predicates have different ASMs.

The BLIP system fully supports the representation above plus some extensions discussed at the end of the paper. Facts, rules, and predicate definitions at the domain, meta, and metameta levels are stored in and manipulated by BLIP's inference engine [Emde forthcoming], which also carries out the necessary inference and reason maintenance operations. A windowing interface provides convenient access and manipulation operations on a BLIP knowledge base. For information on BLIP as a knowledge acquisition system, its *sloppy modeling* philosophy and its learning algorithms, see [Morik86].

2.2. Formal definition

Let us now make the informal description above more precise by developing a formal theory ("MF") whose well-formed formulae correspond to the statements that are possible in the above representation (albeit in a slightly more explicit syntax).

Let $\Sigma = M \cup C \cup P \cup V$ be the *alphabet* of MF, with $M = \{(,), ,, \forall, \&, \longrightarrow, :\}$ a set of punctuation and connective symbols, $C = \{ c_i \}$ $_{i \in I_C}$ a set of constants, $P = \{ p_i^{t,a} \}$ $_{i \in I_P}$ a set of predicate symbols (type t and arity a), and finally $V = \{ v_i^t \}$ $_{i \in I_V}$ a set of variable symbols (type t). The set of *terms* consists of the constant, predicate, and variable symbols.

Then define a *type function* τ such that $\tau(c_i) = 0$ $\forall i \in I_C$, $\tau(p_i^{t,a}) = t$ $\forall i \in I_P$, and $\tau(v_i^t) = t$ $\forall i \in I_V$. The *sort hierarchy* of MF is a set $S \subset \mathfrak{P}(C)$ such that for any two non-disjoint sorts $s_1 \in S$ and $s_2 \in S$, either $s_1 \subset s_2$, or $s_2 \subset s_1$. Then define a mapping α that assigns each $p_i^{t,a} \in P$ a tuple $\alpha(p_i^{t,a}) \in S^a$ called its *argument sort mask*.

Now we can define the atomic formulae of MF: If $p_i^{t,a} \in P$, and $A_1, ..., A_a$ are terms, then
$$F = p_i^{t,a} (A_1, ..., A_a)$$
is an *atomic formula* iff
$$\tau(A_k) < t, \, k=1..a, \, \text{and, if } t=1, \, A_k \in s_k, \, k=1..a, \, \text{for } \alpha(p_i^{t,a}) = (s_1, ..., s_a).$$
$p_i^{t,a}$ is said to be in *functor position* in F. If there is no k such that $A_k \in V$, F is called *ground*, and *variable* otherwise. We define $\tau(F) = t$. If $t=1$, F is called a *fact*, if $t=2$, a *metafact*, if $t=3$, a *metametafact*.

If $F_1, ..., F_n, F_{n+1}$ are variable atomic formulae, and $V_1, ..., V_m$ is the set of variables in $F_1, ..., F_n$, then
$$R = \forall V_1 , ..., V_m : F_1 \& ... \& F_n \longrightarrow F_{n+1}$$
is a *regular rule* iff all variables in F_{n+1} occur in at least one of $F_1, ..., F_n$, and $\tau(F_1) = ... = \tau(F_{n+1}) = t$. Iff $t = 1$, R is called a *domain level rule*, if $t = 2$, a *metarule*.

Finally, we need MF expressions corresponding to metapredicate definitions: A *rule schema* of type t is a regular rule of type t-1 in which all predicate symbols in functor position have been replaced by variables of type t. If RS is a rule schema of type t with the set of variables $V_{RS} = \{V_1, ..., V_m\}$, and $F = p_i^{t,a} (A_1, ..., A_a)$, is a variable atomic formula, then
$$G = \forall A_1, ..., A_a : F \longrightarrow RS$$
is a *rule-generating rule* iff $A_k \in V_{RS}$, $k=1..a$, and for each variable $V \in V_{RS}$ in functor position in RS, there is a k such that $V = A_k$. In other words, the arguments of F must be all variables in functor position in RS, plus possibly other variables from RS (as in the **factoring** example above).

The set of *well-formed formulae* of MF consists of all ground atomic formulae, all regular rules, and all rule-generating rules.

3. The properties of MF

Now that we have a precise definition of MF, let us see how well it rates on the three criteria mentioned above.

3.1. Semantics

What does it mean to enter a certain statement into MF, a fact, rule, or rule-generating rule? One way to answer that question is by defining which "worlds" could be possible models of an MF knowledge base, or, to put it differently, by specifying which properties the statements in the knowledge base necessarily require from the domain they describe. For MF, this can be done fairly straightforwardly with a Tarskian semantics ([Mendelson 64]) as follows:

We will first define what we mean by an interpretation for MF. Let D be a non-empty set, the set of individual domain objects. Then recursively define D^t and D^* as follows:

$$D^0 = D, \quad D^t = \bigcup_a \mathfrak{P}((D^{t-1})^a), \text{ and } D^* = \bigcup_t D^t,$$

i.e., D^t is the set of all relations (of any arity) over D^{t-1}, and D^* is the union of all those sets. An interpretation is a mapping $I: C \cup P \to D^*$ with the following properties:

$I(C) \in D$ for all $C \in C$, and $I(p_i^{t,a}) \in \mathfrak{P}((D^{t-1})^a)$ for all $p_i^{t,a} \in P$.

We define a domain substitution δ as a mapping
$$\delta: C \cup P \cup V \to D^*, \text{ such that } \delta(V) \in D^t \text{ if } \tau(V) = t, \forall V \in V, \text{ and } \delta(S) = I(S) \forall S \quad V.$$
Intuitively, δ "instantiates" all variables in an MF formula with domain elements (if they are of type 0) or with relations of the appropriate level (if they are predicate variables).

A ground atomic wff $F = p_i^{t,a} (A_1, ..., A_a)$ is *true* under an interpretation I iff for all domain substitutions δ,

$(\delta(A_1), ..., \delta(A_a)) \in I(p_i^{t,a})$.

A regular rule $R = \forall V_1, ..., V_m : F_1 \& ... \& F_n \dashrightarrow F_{n+1}$, where $F_i = P_i(A_{1,i}, ..., A_{a_i,i})$, i=1..n+1, is *true* iff for all domain substitutions δ, either

$\exists i: (\delta(A_{1,i}), ..., \delta(A_{a_i,i})) \quad I(P_i)$, or $(\delta(A_{1,n+1}), ..., \delta(A'_{a_{n+1},n+1})) \in I(P_{n+1})$.

This defines the meaning of $\&$ and $\dashrightarrow$.

Consequently, a rule-generating rule $G = \forall V_1, ..., V_m: F_0 \dashrightarrow \forall V'_1, ..., V'_{m'} : F_1 \& ... \& F_n \dashrightarrow F_{n+1}$, where $F_i = P_i(A_{1,i}, ..., A_{a_i,i})$, i=1..n+1, is *true* iff for all domain substitutions δ for which $(\delta(A_{1,0}), ..., \delta(A_{a_0,0})) \in I(P_0)$, either

$\exists i: (\delta(A_{1,i}), ..., \delta(A_{a_i,i})) \quad \delta(P_i)$, or $(\delta(A_{1,n+1}), ..., \delta(A'_{a_{n+1},n+1})) \in \delta(P_{n+1})$.

Since all formulae in MF are closed (contain no free variables), whenever a formula is not true (in I), it is *false* (in I).

An interpretation I is called a *model* of a set of sentences Γ if all sentences in Γ are true under I. Γ *logically implies* a formula F (Γ F) iff F is true in all models of Γ.

The above makes explicit our intuitive understanding of when an MF statement is true: A fact is true iff the relation denoted by its predicate holds of the objects denoted by its arguments; a rule is true iff whenever its antecedents are true, its consequent is true as well. Finally, a rule-generating rule is true iff whenever its antecedent fact is true, the resulting rule is true as well.

Given the above semantics, we now have to define the syntactical notion of derivability in MF ($\vdash$) in such a way that it either mirrors $\vDash$ or at least produces a reasonable subset of the logically implied inferences, i.e., $\vdash$ must be *sound*, and *complete* at least with respect to a naturally describable subset of inferences.

3.2. Inference rules

The purpose of specifying a set of inference rules for a representation is to make explicit what inferences the user (be it a human or a computer system) of a knowledge representation subsystem can expect to be provided. Ideally, this set of (syntactically derivable) inferences provided by the representation system should correspond exactly to those inferences that are logically implied (as defined by $\vDash$, see 3.1.) by the given knowledge base. Since computing this set of inferences would be too expensive in MF (due to the higher order concepts), we provide only a subset of it, namely all inferences on the fact level. Thus, given the following knowledge base:

intoxicating(x) $\longrightarrow$ addictive(x), addictive(x) $\longrightarrow$ dangerous(x), intoxicating(methodan)

the query **dangerous(methodan)?** would be answered affirmatively, but the rule intoxicating(x) $\longrightarrow$ dangerous(x) would not be inferred explicitly (even though it is implicitly present on the factual level, of course).

The key point is that, as required by criterion (b) in the introduction, even though all inferences are not provided, the subset that is provided is describable in a natural form ("all facts"), and a simple syntactical check suffices to tell whether a given statement belongs to the class of inferences that are completely provided.

The inference rules we use are defined as follows:

A *symbol substitution* is a (possibly partial) mapping $\sigma : V \rightarrow C \cup P$. The application $A(\sigma,F)$ of a substitution σ to an MF formula F is defined as the formula F_σ that is generated by replacing V with $\sigma(V)$ for all V in F for which σ is defined. (Substitution corresponds to unification: F unifies with $A(\sigma,F)$.) The two inference rules for MF are the following:

(I) If $R = \mathbf{V} V_1, ..., V_m : F_1 \& ... \& F_n \longrightarrow F_{n+1}$ is a regular rule, and $F'_1, ..., F'_{n+1}$ are ground atomic formulae, then

$R, F'_1, ..., F'_n \vdash F'_{n+1}$ iff $\exists \sigma : A(\sigma,F_i) = F'_i$, i=1..n+1.

(II) If $G = \mathbf{V} V_1, ..., V_a : F \dashrightarrow RS$ is a rule-generating rule, F' is a ground atomic formula, and R is a regular rule, then

$G, F' \vdash R$ iff $\exists \sigma$ defined on $V_1, ..., V_a$ only, such that: $A(\sigma,RS) = R$, and $A(\sigma,F) = F'$.

3.3. Fact-completeness of $\vdash$

How well does $\vdash$ correspond to $\vDash$? Ideally, $\vdash$ should be sound and complete for MF, i.e. $\Gamma \vdash F$ iff $\Gamma \vDash F$, for any $F \in MF$. It should be obvious from 3.2. that $\vdash$ won't derive incorrect theorems:

P1: MF, $\vdash$ is sound.
As we already know from 3.2., MF is not complete:
P2: MF, $\vdash$ is incomplete.
Proof: Let $\Gamma = \{ \mathbf{V} v_1^0 : p_1^{1,1} (v_1^0) \longrightarrow p_2^{1,1}(v_1^0), \mathbf{V} v_1^0 : p_2^{1,1} (v_1^0) \longrightarrow p_3^{1,1}(v_1^0) \}$, and
$F = \mathbf{V} v_1^0 : p_1^{1,1} (v_1^0) \longrightarrow p_3^{1,1}(v_1^0)$. $\Gamma \vDash F$, but not $\Gamma \vdash F$.

However, as described there, ⊢ does derive all facts that are logically implied in a given knowledge base:

P3: MF, ⊢ is *fact-complete*, i.e., for all ground atomic formulae $F \in MF$, and any finite set of sentences Γ in MF, $\Gamma \vdash F$ iff $\Gamma \models F$.

Proof: The first direction follows from P1. We prove the second direction by constructing a "minimal" model of Γ, i.e., a model in which only the sentences of Γ and their ⊢-implications are true. In other words, this model will correspond to a *closed-world assumption* on the knowledge base: anything not stated (explicitly or implicitly via ⊢) in the knowledge base will be false in the model. We can then show that for any fact that is not an ⊢-implication of Γ, there is a model in which that fact is false, so it cannot logically follow from Γ either. (In other words, we show not($\Gamma \vdash F$)⇒not($\Gamma \models F$).)

Let Γ^* be the closure of Γ under ⊢, and let $F_1, .., F_f$ be a fixed enumeration of the facts in Γ^* such that

$$\forall i,j: 1 < i < j < f \Leftrightarrow \tau(F_i) \le \tau(F_j).$$

Then define the sequence of interpretations I_j, $j = 0..f$, as follows:

$$I_j(C) = C \ \forall C \in \mathbf{C}, \ \forall j \in J$$

$$I_0(p_i^{t,a}) = \{(p_i^{t,a}, ..., p_i^{t,a})\} \ \underset{< \ \text{a times} \ >}{} \ \forall \ p_i^{t,a} \in P.$$

and for $F_j = P(A_1, ..., A_a)$, $1 \le j \le f$,

$$I_j(p_i^{t,a}) = \begin{cases} I_{j-1}(p_i^{t,a}) & \text{if } p_i^{t,a} \ne P \\ I_{j-1}(p_i^{t,a}) \cup \{(I_{j-1}(A_1), ..., I_{j-1}(A_a))\} & \text{if } p_i^{t,a} = P. \end{cases}$$

(Note that because of the ordering of the F_j, the $I_{j-1}(A_k)$ are used only after they don't change any more.) Let $I = I_f$. An important property of I is that it is invertible: $I(S_1) = I(S_2) \Rightarrow S_1 = S_2$.

L1: $I = I_f$ is a model of Γ.

Proof: By the construction of I, all facts in $\Gamma \subseteq \Gamma^*$ must be true under I. So, let

$$R = \forall V_1, ..., V_m : F_1 \ \& ... \& F_n \longrightarrow F_{n+1} \ , \ F_i = P_i(A_{1,i}, ..., A_{a_i,i}) \ i=1..n+1,$$

be a regular rule in Γ. Thus, all $A_{k,i}$ must be either constants or one of $V_1, ..., V_m$:

(1) $\forall i \forall 1 \le k \le a_i: A_{k,i} \in \mathbf{C} \cup P$ or $A_{k,i} = V_{jk,i}$

Let δ be a domain substitution such that

$$(\delta(A_{1,i}), ..., \delta(A_{a_i,i})) \in I(P_i) \text{ for } i=1..n.$$

Then, again by the construction of the model, there must be facts $F'_i = P_i(A'_{1,i}, ..., A'_{a_i,i}) \in \Gamma^*$, $i=1..n$, such that

$$\forall i=1..n \ \forall k=1..a_i : I(A'_{k,i}) = \delta(A_{k,i}).$$

Then define a substitution σ such that

(2) $\sigma(V) = I^{-1}(\delta(V))$.

By using inference rule (I) with σ, we obtain a fact $F'_{n+1} = P_{n+1}(A'_{1,n+1}, ..., A'_{a_{n+1},n+1})$ such that

(3) $\forall 1 \le k \le a_{n+1} \exists j: A'_{k,n+1} = \sigma(V_{j k,n+1})$

Now we can show that

$$\forall 1 \le k \le a_i \ \exists 1 \le j \le m: I(A'_{k,n+1}) = \delta(A_{k,n+1})$$

Case 1: $A'_{k,n+1} \in V$:

$$I(A'_{k,n+1}) =_{(3)} I(\sigma(V_{jk,n+1})) =_{(2)} I(I^{-1}(\delta(V_{jk,n+1}))) = \delta(V_{jk,n+1}) =_{(1)} \delta(A_{k,n+1}).$$

Case 2: $A'_{k,n+1} \in \mathbf{C} \cup V$. Then, $A'_{k,n+1} = A_{k,n+1}$, and, by definition of δ, $\delta(A_{k,n+1}) = I(A'_{k,n+1})$.

Thus, by the construction of I, $(\delta(A_{1,n+1}), ..., \delta(A_{a_{n+1},n+1})) = (I(A'_{1,n+1}), ..., I(A'_{a_{n+1},n+1})) \in I(P_{n+1})$, and so R is true. The proof for rule-generating rules is more complicated, but follows along the same lines. We thus showed that all facts, rules, and rule-generating rules in Γ are true under I, so I is a model of Γ.

L2: If F is true under I, then $F \in \Gamma^*$.
Proof: From the construction of I.

We can now conclude the proof of **P3**: Let F be a fact such that not $\Gamma \vdash F$. Then by **L1** and **L2**, I is a model in which F is not true, so not $\Gamma \models F$. Thus, MF, $\vdash$ is fact complete, q.e.d.

3.4. Complexity

We now know that the two inference rules we have specified provide a natural and interesting set of inferences, namely, all facts following from a given knowledge base. This alone, however, is not quite enough if we take a functional view on a knowledge representation system: what good is an inference that is in principle provided, but not effectively? A reasoner (e.g., a robot) depending on the knowledge representation system as a subsystem surely cannot wait infinitely long for an answer! The least one must require is thus the *decidability* of the representation, i.e., that all queries can be answered in finite time. In practice, this is usually not enough, so one also requires a polynomial upper bound on the time it takes to answer a query.

Our goal in this section, then, is to show that such an upper bound exists for MF. We will not be interested in proving a particularly good upper bound and will just try to show it is polynomial. To that end, consider the following proof procedure for MF, which is not very clever, but sufficient to prove a polynomial upper bound:

In order to answer a query about a fact $F = p_i^{t,a} (A_1, ..., A_a)$, first check to see whether there exist any rule-generating rules which would generate rules whose consequent matches F. If so, instantiate the rule-generating rule's antecedent, and try to prove the resulting facts (using this proof procedure recursively). If that succeeds, add the rule it generates to set of rules at level t. Using the existing rules and the newly generated rules, try to prove F by standard goal-directed backchaining (within level t).

P4: The above proof procedure correctly implements $\vdash$. (Without proof.)

If we assume there is a level/type T above which there are no facts any more, and also assume a fixed maximal arity A and maximal branching factor B for all rules, and let N stand for the number of statements in the knowledge base, G for the number of rule-generating rules, we obtain the following result for the complexity of the above decision procedure:

P5: MF is decidable in $O(N^{T(A+1)})$.
Proof: The bound we derive here is extremely generous: Let $K = |P| + |C|$ be the number of constant and predicate symbols used in the knowledge base, The backwards match on rule-generating rules introduces at most G facts to be proved at the next higher level, which can be instantiated in at most K^{A-1} ways. Since there are T levels, this amounts to at most $T*(G*K^{A-1})^T$ proofs by backchaining within a level (we are very generous again). Each of those proofs can take at most K^{A+1} steps, because from K constant symbols, one cannot form more than K^{A+1} different facts. The total cost of any proof attempt is thus: $C = K^{A+1}*T*G^T*K^{T(A-1)}$. Now, since every statement in

the knowledge base can introduce no more than $(B+1)*(A+1)$ new constant or predicate symbols, $K=N*(B+1)*(A+1)$, which, by moving out the constants, proves the proposition.

The above bound is very generous indeed, but it is sufficient to show that MF inferences can be computed in a polynomially bounded time. In practice, the large majority of predicates can be kept unary or binary, and there are hardly ever more than two levels. Nonetheless, it would be an interesting topic for further research to examine how much the above bound can be improved by basing it on a more clever proof procedure and being a little less generous in computing the bound. The inference strategy actually used in BLIP exploits the fact that there are usually significantly fewer metapredicates than predicates (i.e., $G \ll K$) by forward-inferring all rules, thus reducing the "query-time" cost of reasoning to the cost of reasoning in the base representation.

3.5 Extensions to MF

The representation actually used in BLIP includes two features not present in MF, namely the possibility to use *negation* in facts and rules, and several predefined computed arithmetic predicates, such as **add**, **prod**, etc. Those additional features are independent of whether metapredicates are present in the representation or not; this is why we have not included them in MF, the purpose of which was to demonstrate the properties of metapredicates. The following negative results hold with or without metapredicates:

P6 : With negation, MF, ⊢ is no longer fact-complete.
Proof: Given a rule $p(x) \dashrightarrow q(x)$, and $not(q(x))$, $not(p(x))$ is logically implied, but not derived.

The reason for this incompleteness is that introducing negation in facts and rules leaves the Horn-clause restriction we had assumed for our base representation.

P7: With computed predicates, the proof procedures of MF are no longer guaranteed to terminate.

Proof: Given just the rule $p(x)$ & **add**$(y,x,1) \longrightarrow p(y)$, the query $p(1)$, when answered with the backchaining strategy discussed above, will not terminate. (In BLIP, computed predicates are not applied "backwards", which prevents the non-termination problem, but makes a precise statement of which inferences will be provided difficult.)

4. Conclusion

The results obtained in this paper have interesting consequences for the design of knowledge representations. Despite the unacceptable computational properties of higher-order logic, there is no need to give up completely on higher-order concepts and the representational power they provide. The key element is to find a suitable restriction on the higher-order statements that are allowed in the representation. Above, we saw that *metapredicates*, i.e., higher-order predicates defined by a lower-order rule schema, have the necessary properties that qualify them for inclusion in a knowledge representation: we showed that their semantics can be made clear by referring back to higher-order logic in a straightforward way, and that they permit a natural set of inferences to be provided effectively. We proved that the two inference rules we specified are *fact-complete*, i.e., they derive all facts that are logically implied in a given knowledge base. Furthermore, we have seen a proof procedure (an extension of goal-directed backchaining) that answers any query within a time that is polynomial in the size of the knowledge base.

What we have seen here is typical of a basic problem faced by people working on knowledge representations: for sufficiently powerful representations, providing the complete set of inferences is intractable, as has been shown in the KL-ONE [Brachman, Schmolze 85] paradigm by [Nebel forthcoming]. Even though one can sometimes formally restore completeness by using a different semantics [Patel-Schneider 85], the key issue is always whether it is easy to tell where the representation will do what we expect (from a "standard" semantics), and where it won't. In our case, that question has been answered by showing the fact-completeness, in the KL-ONE paradigm, it seems to be still open.

Acknowledgements

I am grateful to the other members of the KIT-LERNER project, Werner Emde, Katharina Morik, and Sabine Thieme for their comments, suggestions and criticism, which made this paper possible. Many thanks also to Kai von Luck and Bernhard Nebel, who provided valuable hints, and the rest of the KIT group, for their questions and comments about our system in various KIT colloquia.

References

Brachman, Ronald J., and Schmolze, J. G., "An Overview of the KL-ONE Knowledge Representation System," in *Cognitive Science*, Vol., 9, 1985.

Emde, Werner, "IM 2.0 - Eine Inferenzmaschine für ein lernendes System," forthcoming.

Emde, Werner, and Morik, Katharina, "The BLIP system," KIT-REPORT 32, Techn. Univ. Berlin, February 1986.

Habel, Christopher, and Rollinger, Claus-Rainer, "Aspekte der rechnergestützten Generierung von Inferenzregeln durch Regelschemata," in *Proc. GWAI-81*, ed. J. Siekmann, Springer-Verlag, Berlin, 1981.

Hobbs, Jerry R., *Discourse and Inference*, chapter 2, Draft, Stanford University, June, 1986.

McCarthy, John, "First-order Theories of Individual Concepts and Propositions," in *Machine Intelligence 9*, ed. J. Hayes, D. Michie, and L. Mikulich, pp. 129-147, reprinted in *Readings in Knowledge Representation*, ed. R. Brachman and H. Levesque, pp. 523-533, Morgan Kaufman, Los Altos, CA, 1985.

Mendelson, Elliot, *Introduction to MATHEMATICAL LOGIC*, pp. 49ff, Van Nostrand, New York, 1964.

Morik, Katharina, "Acquiring Domain Models," in *Proc. of the Knowledge Acquisition for Knowledge-Based Systems Workshop*, pp. 32-0 - 32-15, Banff, Canada, Nov. 1986. (Also to appear in *Int. Journal of Man-Machine Studies*)

Levesque, Hector J., and Brachman, Ronald. J., "A Fundamental Tradeoff in Knowledge Representation and Reasoning (Revised Version)," in *Readings in Knowledge Representation*, ed. R. Brachman and H. Levesque, pp. 41-70, Morgan Kaufman, Los Altos, CA, 1985.

Nebel, Bernhard, "Computational Complexity of Terminological Reasoning in BACK," forthcoming.

Patel-Schneider, Peter F., "A Four-Valued Semantics for Frame-Based Description Languages ," in *Proc. AAAI-86*, pp. 344-348, Morgan Kaufman, Los Altos, CA, 1986.

Perlis, Donald, "Languages with Self-Reference I: Foundations (or: We Can Have Everything in First-Order Logic!)", *Artificial Intelligence 25*, pp. 301-322, 1985.

Using Logic Programming for
Fault Diagnosis in Digital Circuits

H.Simonis, M.Dincbas

European Computer-Industry Research Centre (E.C.R.C)

Arabellastr. 17

8000 Muenchen 81

West-Germany

Abstract

In this paper we show how a Prolog-like logic programming language can be efficiently used for fault diagnosis in digital circuits. We take the approach of *diagnosis from first principles*, i.e., reasoning from circuit description and behavior. With the single-fault assumption a program written in CHIP, an extended Prolog, locates the faulty gate from a hierarchical description of a circuit and faulty input/output patterns. The fault finding process is modeled in terms of *constraint relaxation*. We show how the introduction of the *demon* concept in logic programming can improve the consistency checking mechanism and thus makes possible the diagnosis of big circuits. The program was successfully tested on circuits with more than 17000 gates.

1. Introduction

In this paper we show the use of an extended Prolog for fault diagnosis in digital circuits. Circuits can be described in a natural, hierarchical form. We use reasoning from first principles to find the fault from the circuit description and its faulty behavior. The fault finding process is modeled in terms of constraint relaxation with a single fault assumption. We introduce data driven demons to improve the efficiency of the consistency checking. With these techniques large circuits can be diagnosed in a few minutes. The program has been successfully tested on circuits with more than 17000 gates.

This work is part of our CHIP (Constraint Handling in Prolog) project aiming at the integration of constraint solving techniques into logic programming (demon driven computation, consistency checking, extended unification,...) [Dinc 86] [Vanh 86] [Butt

87] [Vanh 87] [Dinc 87] [Simo 87].

The paper is structured as follows. In chapter 2 we describe different methods of fault diagnosis. We then show how circuits can be described in Prolog. In chapter 4 we explain the constraint relaxation procedure on which our fault-finder is based. The demon concept to improve the search strategy of Prolog is introduced in chapter 5. An example of the operation is shown in chapter 6. Some experimental results on large circuits are given in chapter 7. We conclude with a comparison of other approaches to fault finding from first principles.

2. Fault Diagnosis in Digital Circuits

Fault diagnosis is a reasoning process which, from the observations of some behavior which is recognized as a deviation from the expected one, tries to find some hypotheses that can explain this misbehavior. In the case of digital systems, the problem is to determine the components whose malfunctioning can cause the discrepancy between the observed (faulty) and the expected (correct) system behavior.

There are two main approaches in diagnostic reasoning :

- diagnosis from experience
- diagnosis from first principles

The *diagnosis from experience* is the traditional approach taken in expert systems. In this approach, a knowledge base containing "symptoms --> faults" or "observations --> diagnostic" rules, is compared with the observed symptoms. The most famous of such a system is MYCIN [Shor 76] where human expertise about medical diagnosis on human pathophysiology is encoded in a knowledge base in the form of rules associating symptoms with possible diseases. One can say that in this approach the diagnosis is based on "shallow" knowledge.

On the other hand, the *diagnosis from first principles* is based on "deep" knowledge, i.e, on the structure and the behavior of the system to be analyzed. This approach is also called "model-based" because it reasons directly on the model of the system in order to explain the misbehavior of the system from its structural defects. No heuristic information ("symptoms --> faults" rules, etc...) is needed for this approach. A general theory of "diagnosis from first principles" is given in [Reit 85].

This paper deals with the application of this second approach to fault finding in digital circuits. Recently, some authors like Davis [Davi 84] Genesereth [Gene 84], deKleer [DeKl 86] advocated the use of this approach (rather than the first one) for fault diagnosis in digital circuits. Our purpose here is twofold : first, to show the use of an (extended) Prolog language to solve this problem, rather than to devise a specialized inference engine, and second, to diagnose big circuits (having thousands of gates) efficiently by introducing the demon concept into Prolog.

In this paper we solve the following problem. Suppose a complex digital circuit is not working correctly, i.e. there is an input/output pattern which is not consistent. We want to locate the cause of the error (i.e. the faulty component) without probing inside the circuit, only by experimenting with (faulty) input/output patterns and a description of the circuit. We make the following assumptions :

- Single fault assumption : there is only one faulty component in the circuit

- No bridge fault : there are no bridges between two lines

We restrict ourselves to diagnosis of single faults for three reasons: Since reliability of components is high, the probability of independant failure of multiple parts is very low. The inherent computational complexity of diagnosing multiple faults prevents application to large circuits. The combination of hierarchical description with multiple faults is unclear.

In the following we assume that the basic components of the circuits are gates, but it is also possible to use more complex parts as basic components (eg full adder, multiplexer, TTL devices). In this case multiple gate-errors in these devices will be correctly recognized.

Note that the error model is not restricted to "stuck-at" errors or an other explicit fault model. Failure of the device means any (even intermittend) deviation from its model.

3. Using Prolog for Digital Circuit Design

Prolog is a high-level language which is very convenient for a natural description of circuits. It supports in a natural way top-down development and mixing of various hierarchical levels of circuit description. In Prolog, a circuit can be specified by means of *clauses* which describe the basic components and interaction between modules. Suppose we want to describe a full-adder (see figure 1). A Prolog description is the following:

Figure 1 : full-adder circuit diagram

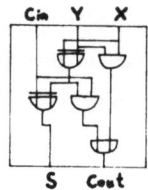

```
f_adder(N,X,Y,Cin,S,Cout) :-
        and([1|N],X,Y,C1),
        xor([2|N],X,Y,S1),
        and([3|N],Cin,S1,C2),
        xor([4|N],Cin,S1,S),
        or([5|N],C1,C2,Cout).
```

the definition of the basic elements "and", "xor" and "or" can be given, for example, by a set of ground clauses (the truth-table definition) :

```
and(N,0,0,0).
and(N,0,1,0).
and(N,1,0,0).
and(N,1,1,1).
```

and the like for the others.

In this description, the first argument of a predicate is used to assign a unique label for each part (module or basic component) of the circuit. Thus a hierarchical naming convention can be easily implemented in Prolog. The other arguments represent the inputs and the outputs of the components. Connections (wires) between components are represented by shared logical variables. This specification can now be used for the definition of a four-bit-adder (see figure 2) :

Figure 2 : four-bit-adder

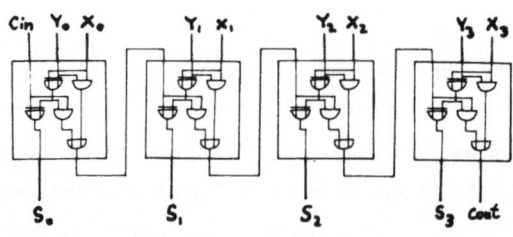

```
four_bit_adder(N,X3,X2,X1,X0,Y3,Y2,Y1,Y0,Cin,
               S3,S2,S1,S0,Cout):-
        f_adder([1|N],X0,Y0,Cin,S0,C1),
        f_adder([2|N],X1,Y1,C1,S1,C2),
        f_adder([3|N],X2,Y2,C2,S2,C3),
        f_adder([4|N],X3,Y3,C3,S3,Cout).
```

This kind of hierarchical description of circuits follows the style of Prolog in a top-down development. One can replace the description of a lower-level component without affecting the higher-level circuit definition (see section 5).

Furthermore, due to the *unification* (a powerful pattern-matching process) and the automatic *backtracking* mechanism of its interpreter, Prolog provides an automatic circuit simulator, i.e. the specification of a circuit can be directly used for its simulation.

4. Constraint Relaxation Method for Fault Diagnosis

The fault finding process in digital circuits can be best described in terms of *constraint relaxation*. Indeed, a circuit can be viewed as a *network of constraints* [Suss 80]. Each component forces some constraint between its input and output lines. If the circuit works correctly, all constraints are satisfied. If some subcomponent is faulty, then it does not satisfy its constraints, i.e. the values on the connections are *inconsistent* with the constraints. Finding the faulty component is equivalent to finding which constraints must be *relaxed* (removed) such that the remaining constraints are consistent with the faulty input/output pattern. This leads to the following (sketch of the) algorithm to find the faulty component in a circuit.

> *Initialisation : Set candidate-set = all components of the circuit*
> *Take a faulty input/output pattern*
> > *For each component in the candidate-set*
> > > *Remove it from the circuit description (i.e. relax its constraints)*
> > > *Check whether the rest of the circuit is consistent with*
> > > *the faulty I/O pattern*
> > > *If YES then this component is a candidate (i.e. keep it in the*
> > > > *candidate-set) and look at its subparts to find*
> > > > *those which are also candidates*
> > > *If NO then no error in this component or any of its parts could*
> > > > *explain the misbehavior, remove the component and*
> > > > *all its parts from the candidate-set*

After this loop, the candidate-set will contain a list of possible faulty components which are identified by their label. If this set contains only one gate, then this gate is the faulty one. If it contains more than one gate, the algorithm is repeated with a new faulty input/output pattern in order to reduce the candidate-set. This process continues until there is only one candidate gate left.

The algorithm uses the *hierarchical description* to prune the search space. As soon as the relaxation of some component does not explain the error, all its subcomponents can be excluded as well.

The constraint relaxation procedure is written as a *meta program* which takes the circuit description (itself a PROLOG program) and a faulty I/O pattern and searches for possible candidates.

5. Improving the Search Strategy of PROLOG

We did not specify how to make the consistency check in the fault finding algorithm. A naive approach uses the truth table definition of the logic gates (as given in section 3) to check the constraints. We can use this definition together with a *'generate and test'* approach to check all constraints on the internal lines of the circuit. While this method is sufficient for small examples, it is too inefficient to use for large circuits. We therefore need another mechanism to solve the consistency check.

In our program we use a *demon* [Davi 84] concept. Each gate is represented by a demon which propagates values as soon as possible from an input to the output or from the output to the inputs. The demons use rules like (for an "and" gate)

- If one input is 0, the output is also 0.

- If the output is 1, both inputs are 1.

- If the inputs are equal, they are equal to the output.

- If one input is 1, the output is equal to the other input.

- If the output is 0, at least one input is 0.

These demons can be simulated in PROLOG using the logical variable feature and a delay mechanism (like wait declarations [Nais 84]). But this is not very efficient. In CHIP these demons are implemented at the interpreter level.

Note that the last three demon rules, which express symbolic constraint propagation, cannot be handled in the constraint propagation mechanism of Davis [Davi 84].

6. Example

We will now explain on a small example the operation of the above algorithm. We use the four-bit-adder described in section 3. Suppose we have observed the faulty I/O pattern

```
Cin X0 Y0 X1 Y1 X2 Y2 X3 Y3  |   S0 S1 S2 S3 Cout  |
─────────────────────────────────────────────────────────
 1   1  1  1  1  1  1  1  1   |    1  1  1  1   1    |  <-- correct
                             |    1  1  0  1   1    |  <-- faulty
```

We show the relaxation procedure of module [2]. Propagating values from the inputs and the outputs we reach a consistent labeling (values underlined). All constraints (except for adder [2], which is removed) are satisfied. Therefore an error in adder [2] would explain the fault.

We then look at the subcomponents of module [2]. If we relax and-gate [1,2], we just need to propagate values through the remaining parts of module [2], we need not reconsider the labeling of the rest of the circuit. This leads to another consistent labeling(values marked '). Therefore part [1,2] is a possible candidate. Removing instead for example part [3,2] will lead to an inconsistency. This part is not a candidate.

Figure 3: relaxation example

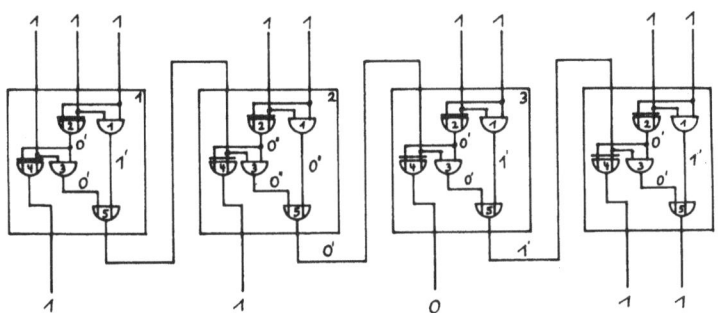

If we continue the procedure, we find as candidates the modules [2], [1,2], [5,2], [3], [2,3], [4,3]. Using additional pattern will lead to detection of the fault.

Since we do not use a labeling procedure [Vanh 86] together with our constraint propagation, not all internal lines will necessarily receive values. The advantage of our approach is that we avoid the expensive backtracking inside the labeling procedure, where we would need to try every possible combination of values to detect an inconsistency.

7. Some Results

In this chapter we show the results from running our procedure on some bigger circuits. Examples described in the literature have only a small number of components. No execution times are given.

All circuits are specified at the logic level (boolean values) in several hierarchical levels. The programs were executed on VAX 785 running our Prolog interpreter CHIP incorporating a delay mechanism and demons.

circuit	number of gates	execution time	number of test pattern
naive approach Standard Prolog			
8bit multiplier	320	15313 sec (4h 15min)	4
CHIP			
8 bit multiplier	320	30 sec	4
d74 (8/16 bits)	1120	43 sec	4
fft-butterfly (8/16 bits)	3720	146 sec	3
fft-butterfly (16/32 bits)	17680	648 sec	3

While the *naive approach* is sufficient for very small examples, it is obviously infeasible for bigger circuits because of the combinatorial explosion. The program with the builtin demon runs about *500 times faster* than the naive program. This ratio increases with circuit size.

The demon program can be used for larger circuits, if these are described in a hierarchical way. The examples show that both the execution time and the number of test pattern only increase slowly with the number of gates in the circuits (contrarily to the exponential growth expected in the literature).

The 8 bit multiplier is a parallel multiplier with 8 bit input and 16 bit result. The d74 consists of 2 multiplier and 3 adder. The fft-butterfly circuit performs the "butterfly" operation of the Fast-Fourier-Transform using addition and multiplication on complex numbers. It is not possible to execute this program with a naive (standard) Prolog approach (it should take more than 4 days of CPU time !).

8. Related Works and Conclusion

Diagnosis from first principles is a powerful paradigm for fault diagnosis in digital circuits. Probably, De Kleer was the first to advocate this approach [DeKl 76]. Using this ideas, Davis used a domain-specific language which incorporates the concepts and vocabulary for circuits [Davi 84]. Two kinds of rules are used for behavioral description : simulation rules (for modeling causality) and inference rules (for making conclusions about the device). This entails the handling of two slots for each input and output of a component. Furthermore, the constraint propagation mechanism is limited to local propagation of ground values and cannot handle symbolic value or expression propagation as in our case.

In [Reit 85], Reiter gives a general theory for diagnosis from first principles (not only for digital circuits). This is a theoretical work emphasizing the logical foundations of the approach. The basic idea for faulty candidates generation is as in our approach: remove one component and check the consistency of the remaining part of the system. In the formalism of Reiter circuits and faults are described in terms of non-Horn clauses and therefore require the availability of a sound and complete theorem prover for consistency checking of arbitrary first order formulae. Genesereth uses a first order logic language for describing circuits [Gene 84]. In his approach a circuit is represented in an extensional way: connections between components are represented in explicit ground clauses using constants to indicate wires. This kind of representation complicates the description of circuits (in comparison to our more natural representation). His system uses an inference mechanism which is a variation of resolution called "resolution residue". It is a theorem prover for full first order logic, therefore involving some inefficiency.

Finally, in [Eshg 85], fault diagnosis is viewed as a special case of induction. The representation of the circuits and the naming process, although done in Prolog, are more complicated than in our case. It seems that the program has been applied only for very small circuits (< 20 gates). Furthermore Eshghi deals only with "stuck-at" errors.

De Kleer and Williams [DeKl 86] describe the use of ATMS to diagnosis of multiple faults. Their system does not incorporate a hierarchical description and is not shown to work on reasonably sized problems.

Our approach has two advantages in comparison to the above-mentioned ones. The first one is the use of the Prolog language to describe circuits in a natural way and to write the fault diagnosis program. The second one is the introduction of a demon concept in Prolog in order to achieve efficiency in the execution of the constraint relaxation procedure. Thus we can find single faults in large circuits (thousands of gates) within a few minutes. It seems that with our approach we can solve much larger problems than the ones cited in the literature.

9. Acknowledgement

We would like to thank P. Van Hentenryck and H. Gallaire for many fruitful discussions.

References

[Butt 87]   Buttner, W. and Simonis, H.
              Embedding Boolean Expressions into Logic Programming.
              Journal of Symbolic Computation , (to appear), 1987.

[Davi 84]   Davis, R.
              Diagnostic Reasoning Based on Structure and Behavior.
              Artificial Intelligence 24():347-410, 1984.

[DeKl 76]   de Kleer, J.
              Local Methods of Localizing Faults in Electronic Circuits.
              Technical Report AIM-394, Artificial Intelligence Laboratory, MIT, Cambridge, USA , 1976.

[DeKl 86]·   de Kleer, J. and Williams, B.C.
              Reasoning about Multiple Faults.
              In *Proceedings of the National Conference on Artificial Intelligence (AAAI-86)*, pages 132-139.
                  Philadelphia, USA, August, 1986.

[Dinc 86]   Dincbas, M.
              Constraints, Logic Programming and Deductive Databases.
              In *Proceedings of France-Japan Artificial Intelligence and Computer Science Symposium*,
                  pages 1-27. ICOT, Tokyo, Japan, October, 1986.

[Dinc 87]   Dincbas, M., Simonis, H. and Van Hentenryck, P.
              Extending Equation Solving and Constraint Handling in Logic Programming.
              In *Proceedings of Colloquium on The Resolution of Equations in Algebraic Structures
                  (CREAS)*. MCC, Austin, Texas, USA, May, 1987.

[Eshg 85]   Eshghi, K.
              Application of Meta-Level Programming to Fault Finding in Logic Circuits.
              Logic Programming and its Applications.
              Ablex Publishing Corporation, 1985, pages 208-219.

[Gene 84]   Genesereth, M.R.
              The Use of Design Descriptions in Automated Diagnosis.
              Artificial Intelligence 24():411-436, 1984.

[Nais 84]   Naish, L.
              Mu-Prolog 3.1db Reference Manual
              Melbourne University edition, 1984.

[Reit 85]   Reiter, R.
              A Theory of Diagnosis from First Principles.
              Technical Report, University of Toronto, December, 1985.

[Shor 76]   Shortliffe, E.
              MYCIN : Computer-Based Medical Consultation.
              American Elsevier, New York, 1976.

[Simo 87]   Simonis, H. and Dincbas, M.
              Using an Extended Prolog for Digital Circuit Design.
              In *IEEE-International Workshop on AI-Applications to CAD-Systems for Electronics.* Munich,
                  W.Germany, October, 1987.

[Suss 80]   Sussman, G.J. and Steele, G.L.
              CONSTRAINTS-A Language for Expressing Almost-Hierarchical Descriptions.
              Artificial Intelligence 14(1):1-39, 1980.

[Vanh 86]   Van Hentenryck, P.. and Dincbas, M.
              Domains in Logic Programming.
              In *Proceedings of the National Conference on Artificial Intelligence (AAAI-86)*, pages 759-765.
                  Philadelphia, USA, August, 1986.

Specifying Meta-Level Architectures for Rule-Based Systems

Michael Beetz
Basisentwicklung (EVX)
TA Triumph-Adler AG
Fuerther Str. 212
8500 Nuernberg 80

Abstract

Explicit and declarative representation of control knowledge and well-structured rule bases are crucial requirements for efficiently developing and maintaining rule-based systems. The CATWEAZLE rule interpreter allows the knowledge engineer to partition rule bases and specify meta-level architectures for control.

Among others the following questions arise immediately when one wants to provide tools for specifying meta-level architectures for control:

1. What is a suitable language to specify meta-level architectures for control?

2. How can general and declarative languages for meta-level architectures be interpreted efficiently?

This paper outlines solutions to both research questions provided by the CATWEAZLE rule interpreter:

1. CATWEAZLE provides a small set of concepts based on a separation of control knowledge in control strategies and control tactics and a further categorization of control strategies.

2. For rule-based systems it is efficient to extend the RETE pattern matching algorithm such that it can process control knowledge as well.

1. Introduction

Problems tackled using knowledge-based systems often require complex systems. For that reason tools are needed that facilitate time-efficient design, implementation and testing of special purpose problem solvers for different problem domains. The most promising approach to build knowledge-based systems being adequate problem-solving models is to structure domain knowledge and to represent expert problem-solving methods explicitly. The goal to build adequate problem-solving models has major impact on the structure, inference techniques, strategies of knowledge-based systems and on requirements for tools supporting their efficient construction:

1. **Application systems require problem-dependent control strategies that are often not known at the beginning of system design:**
   Therefore, formalisms are needed that allow us to easily describe, modify and incrementally refine control strategies.
2. **Application systems contain large amounts of knowledge:**
   In order to be maintainable and explainable, knowledge-based systems should be well-structured and modular and control knowledge should be represented in an explicit and declarative way. Intermixing different kinds of knowledge in rules yields badly structured systems which are hard to maintain and validate and have reduced explainability [Neches,Swartout,Moore-85].

Thus, it is necessary to design and implement

a tool that provides a framework to build structured knowledge bases and to describe control strategies in an explicit and declarative way.

This paper deals with problems of meta-level architectures for control and tries to give some solutions that allow to provide tools for specifying them. In a companion paper [Beetz-87a] we focussed on problems when intermixing different kinds of reasoning knowledge and how the CATWEAZLE language tries to overcome these problems. Here we proceed as follows: We argue to apply meta-level architectures to avoid problems when using existing tool systems. Problems in providing tools for specifying meta-level architectures are identified. We discuss features of a suitable language for specifying control and briefly describe the concepts of the CATWEAZLE language to address them. In the last part of the paper it is discussed how such a general mechanism for rule-based systems can be interpreted efficiently.

2. Problems with Current Tool Systems

Gary Martins [Martins-84] summarizes some problems he had with existing tool systems:

"For applications of even modest complexity, most expert systems code is generally hard to understand, debug and maintain."

"The virtues of suppressing explicit control statements in expert systems is certainly debatable. In practice, they tend to be replaced by hidden control variables, or artificial database elements that are created to secretly track program states. Invariably, these complicate both the database and the rules themselves.

"The lack of explicit control makes it painful to identify the causes of misbehaviour in rule-based programs. As rule sets grow large, the collection as a whole takes on the character of a mysterious black box. It has behaviours, but we don't know why."

3. The Proposed Solution: Meta-Level Architectures

A main cause for these problems is the lack of structure and explicit representation of control. Representing control explicitly requires an interpreter for control knowledge guiding the search for problem solutions and an explicit model of the problem solving process and the knowledge available. Meta-level architectures provide these features. For that reason many researchers argue to structure complex knowledge-based systems as meta-level architectures ([Bundy,Welham-81], [Aiello,Levi-84], [Clancey-83], [Genesereth-83]).

The main characteristic of meta-level architectures is the existence of meta-level knowledge. In [Davis,Buchanan-77] Randall Davis and Bruce Buchanan emphasize:

> "*In the most general terms, meta-level knowledge is knowledge about knowledge. Its primary use here is to enable a program to "know what it knows", and to make multiple uses of its knowledge. That is, the program is not only able to use its knowledge directly, but may examine it, or direct its application.*"

Production rule systems are the most widespread approach for expert systems [Hayes-Roth-85]. Arguments, like those stressed in [Martin-84], caused us to implement a tool for building meta-level architectures to control problem-solving in rule-based systems. We argue that the concept of meta-level architectures forces users to design well-structured systems that will be easy to maintain.

Three problems arise immediately when one wants to provide tools for specifying meta-level architectures for control:

I. What is a suitable language to specify meta-level architectures for control?

Several researchers argue to use a logical language for specifying control [Hayes-77]. While there is no doubt that other computational models can be simulated in logic ([Hayes-73], [Hayes-79]) the following limitations of predicate logic reduce its applicability for our purposes:

(1) No explicit structuring of the knowledge base is supported.

(2) No built-in concepts are provided to describe the control flow in the system. Everything has to be done by deduction and this enlarges the overhead for meta-level computation.

II. How can a general and declarative language for meta-level architectures be interpreted efficiently?

Declarative and explicit representations of the object-level and the control knowledge are required for meta-level architectures. On the other hand, the interpretation of explicit and declarative knowledge is very time-consuming. Thus, when providing such languages it has to be guaranteed that they are interpreted in an efficient way.

III. What is the meaning of such a language?

A major advantage of using logic to control search is its well-defined semantics. When providing another kind of language it has to be defined what it means to specify a control strategy for an object-level knowledge base.

Contributions to the solution of each of these problems are outlined in the following sections.

4. The CATWEAZLE Approach

4.1. Features of a Language to Represent Control Knowledge

To be able to build *adequate* problem-solving models, a language has to provide different concepts to represent different types of control knowledge and different kinds of problem-solving methods. I.e. knowledge about which rules are relevant for which problems or in which situations they are useful. As argued in [Beetz-87a] intermixing different types leads to unstructured rule bases. However, to offer a set of unrelated commands without providing guidelines how to use them does not help very much either.

To avoid the problems pointed out above, one can provide a set of different concepts to describe control and classify them in order to get guidelines how to use them. Such a classification of control knowledge has to fulfill at least two requirements:

1. To be expressive it must be possible to represent a wide range of expert system architectures using concepts in the classification.
2. To be adequate different concepts have to characterize different methods of problem-solving.

CATWEAZLE is based on such a categorization of reasoning knowledge and distinguishes between **control strategies** and **control tactics**. **Control strategies** specify in which order problems should be solved in a problem solving process. Three types of control strategies are distinguished depending on how much the order of tackling subproblems can be constrained by the knowledge engineer.

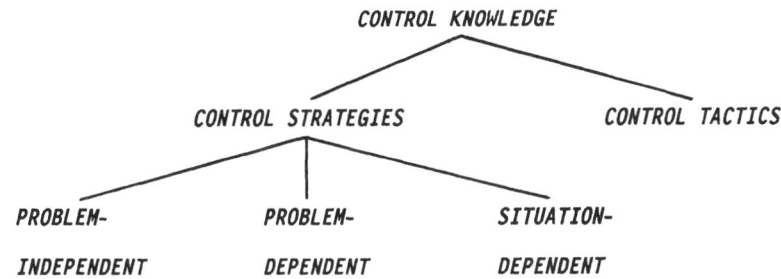

Figure 1: A classification of control knowledge in rule-based systems

Firstly, the sequence for tackling subproblems is known and independent of individual problems, e.g. as in models of medical consultations [Puppe-83]. Then, application systems behave deterministically at the strategic level. This can be represented in CATWEAZLE using **phase sequences** (see section 4.2).

Secondly, sometimes the problem domain is too broad to be controlled by a single phase sequence. But knowing the particular problem one can often plan a phase sequence which is likely to solve the problem. For instance, proving a particular theorem in mathematics has these characteristics. Planning phase sequences is not yet incorporated in the CATWEAZLE system.

In a third class of problems even knowing the problem does not really help us to determine a suitable phase sequence in advance. The reason is that too many variations in data can occur when applying a phase sequence. For such problems it seems to be more adequate to determine situation-dependently which subproblems to tackle next. This can be represented in CATWEAZLE using **rules about structured rule sets** (a particular kind of meta-rules, see below).

Categorizing control strategies and separating them from the rule base has important advantages: One can determine the appropriate type depending on how much is known about the strategy and how flexible it must be. The more knowledge engineers constrain the search the less search needs to be done by the control component and the more efficient is the problem solving process. Thus, it is important to represent the control strategy in the most appropriate type. If more knowledge is acquired to constrain the search the strategy can be reformulated in another type without changing the rest of the rule base.

Control tactics on the other side specify how to behave in a single problem solving state. They determine which rule to apply if several rules are applicable. Control tactics can be represented as rules about object rules. Separating control strategies and control tactics drastically improves the modularity and explainability of rule bases.

The above paragraphs presented arguments for the adequacy of the classification. The expressive power of the classification is measured in [Beetz-87b] using the well-known classification of expert system architectures in [Stefik,etal.-82].

4.2. A Brief Overview on the CATWEAZLE Language for Control Knowledge

In this section we briefly introduce the CATWEAZLE language to see how concepts in the classification are represented in CATWEAZLE and to understand how features of the language can be used to increase the efficiency of interpretation (section 4.3). To keep this paper concise we do not describe the system architecture at all or give a more complex example. Both can be found in [Beetz-87b].

The CATWEAZLE rule language provides the concept of **structured rule sets** to partition the rule base into small rule sets. Structured rule sets have an abstract description and contain two sets of rules. The abstract description consists of a pre-, a postcondition and their name. The postcondition can be used to represent the subproblems a rule set is intended to solve. Partial solutions required as a condition for the successful application of the rule set can be formalized as preconditions. Structured rule sets can be activated by the control component of the interpreter. When a structured rule set is activated and its precondition is satisfied, its rules are interpreted on the working memory until its postcondition holds. The control component then regains control and activates another rule set. In each state of interpretation only one structured rule set is active.

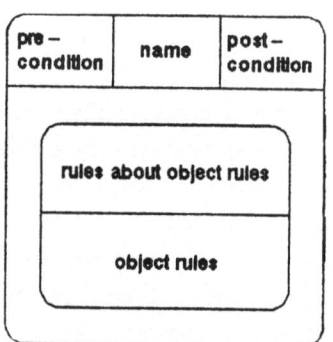

Figure 2: structured rule set

Structured rule sets contain two sets of rules: firstly, **object rules** (like rules in OPS5 [Forgy-81]) and secondly, **rules about object rules**, which are another kind of control knowledge (see [Davis-80]). The latter describe tactics to resolve conflicts when more than one object rule is applicable to a state, and thus, they can activate

or suspend applicable instances of object rules. An example for such a rule is shown
by figure 3.

```
(metarule mr1*
    (objectrule ?or1
        (with-actions
            (add (under ?b12 ?b11 ?state)))))
    (under ?b12 ?b11 ?state)
    -->
    (suspend ?or1))
```

Figure 3: rule suspending an object rule from activation

The rule describes the following conflict resolution tactic: "*If the result of a
rule application is explicitly contained in the current working memory, it is not
useful to apply this rule and therefore it is suspended.*" Condition parts of rules
about object rules contain descriptions of object rules that must be handled by a
pattern matcher for the rule language.

```
control-strategy HYPOTHESIZE-AND-TEST
    INITIAL-QUESTIONS
    loop
        GENERATE-HYPOTHESIS
        TEST-HYPOTHESIS
    until {HYPOTHESIS(?PAT,?NAME-OF-ILLNESS,?,EVIDENT)}
    end-loop
    DIAGNOSIS-AND-THERAPY
end-control-strategy
```

Figure 4: phase sequence modelling the "Hypothesize-and-Test" control strategy

Control strategies are specified in this formalism by describing how rule sets
should interact to build an efficient problem-solving process. This is done by a
sequence of structured rule set names specifying the order in which rule sets should
be interpreted in a problem solving process. This concept is called **phase sequence.**
A LOOP-UNTIL and a IF construct are provided in order to allow more sophisticated
phase sequences (see figure 4).

```
(metarule mr1*
    (applicable-ruleset ?ruleset
        (with-postconditions
            (subgoal ?name-of-subgoal satisfied)))
    (subgoal ?name-of-subgoal satisfied)
    -->
    (suspend ?ruleset))
```

Figure 5: rule suspending a structured rule set from activation

Another method to formalize control strategies is to specify a set of **rules about
structured rule sets.** In this case structured rule sets are interpreted in a
different way. They are applicable to a given state whenever their precondition is

satisfied in this state. Conflicts may arise if more than one rule set is applicable to a state. Rules about structured rule sets describe similarily to rules about object rules tactics to resolve these conflicts. An example for a rule about structured rule sets is given by figure 5.

4.3. Extending the RETE Algorithm to Process Meta-Level Architectures for Control

This section deals with the second research question, the efficient interpretation of meta-level architectures.

Meta-level architectures for control interpret declarative and explicit representations of control strategies, control tactics, and an explicit model of the object-level computation. Such representations of control strategies result in explainable systems that are easy to modify and maintain. To provide a general framework for specifying meta-level architectures we need a suitable language, and a general interpreter for it. Since such interpreters are highly pattern-directed and pattern matching is the most time-consuming task within the interpretation of rule bases this would yield inefficient systems. Efficiency, however, is crucial for interactive systems.

To implement the CATWEAZLE interpreter the RETE algorithm is chosen to be the basic pattern matching algorithm. The reasons for this decision are twofold: Firstly, it is one of the most efficient algorithm for production rule systems. Secondly, it can be extended to process the control concepts of the CATWEAZLE language. The basic idea of the RETE algorithm is to compile patterns in the condition parts of rules into a network of test nodes, which allows to exploit structural similarities between condition parts and temporal redundancy during the interpretation process.

To keep this paper concise we do not describe the algorithm at all. We rather give some highlights on how characteristics of the language can be exploited to increase the efficiency. A description of the algorithm and a comparison with other approaches for increasing the efficiency of meta-level architectures can be found in [Beetz-87b].

Firstly, partitioning of rule bases can be used to speed up the matching process. There are at least two characteristics of the interpretation of control knowledge that can be exploited for this purpose:

I. Rule sets that cannot be activated anymore

After a rule set has been activated the last time within a problem solving process any further matching against working memory elements is a waste of time. The basic idea to exploit this is to ignore subnets of phases when their interpretation is completed.

II. Rules about structured rule sets

When interpreting rule sets such that they are applicable to a problem solving state whenever their precondition is satisfied it cannot be foreseen whether a rule set is activated in a process or not. What we want is something like "*lazy evaluation*": rules should only be matched when they are relevant. This is, matching of rules is delayed until the rules become active.

The solution to these problems is rather obvious. We have to match only the active rule set against the working memory. Test nodes of rules in rule sets that are not active need to recognize only modifications in the working memory in order to restore their memories when they are activated. In [Beetz-87b] extensions of the RETE algorithm are described that allow to implement this idea.

Secondly, not every rule description within a rule about object rules needs to be matched against every rule instance in the rule set. Rules that have no instance satisfying an rule description (see figure 1) are filtered out at compile time and are not matched at run time.

Rules about structured rule sets are handled in a similar way.

4.4. On the Semantics of Controlled Rule-Based Systems

Partial results are provided for the third research question. In [Beetz-87b] a declarative and procedural semantics for phase sequences is given. It is formalized how phase sequences affect the shape of the search space. The procedural semantics, an abstract description of the implemented interpreter, is defined as a set of PROLOG clauses and proved correct but incomplete with respect to the declarative semantics.

5. Conclusions

The paper describes the implementation of the CATWEAZLE system done in the context of a diploma thesis. The most important results are that the concept of meta-level architectures can be successfully applied to rule-based systems to improve their maintainability. And, equally important, that extending the RETE pattern matching algorithm to process the control concepts of the CATWEAZLE language yields computationally tractable systems. However, compiling rule bases into the RETE net formalism reduces explainability. To avoid this drawback we additionally keep the uncompiled rule base at run time.

The most important extensions of the prototype will be:
- a more expressive pattern language,
- an extension of the concept of structured rule sets. Thus, a structured rule set itself may contain other structured rule sets which allows hierarchically structured rule bases and
- coupling rules and objects. This means, to add features that allow processing objects within rules adequately and efficiently.

6. References

[Aiello,Levi-84]
   L. Aiello and G. Levi:
   The Uses of Metaknowledge in AI Systems,
   Proc. of Sixth European Conference on Artificial Intelligence, ECAI-84,
   Pisa, September 1984, pp. 707-717.

[Beetz-87a]
   M. Beetz:
   A Knowledge Representation Language for Control Knowledge in Rule-Based Systems
   Proc. of Expert Systems'87, Concepts and Tools,
   Nuremberg, April 1987.

[Beetz-87b]
   M. Beetz:
   Specifying Meta-Level Architectures for Rule-Based Systems,
   Diploma Thesis,
   University of Kaiserslautern, 1987,
   also: SEKI-REPORT (forthcoming)
   University of Kaiserslautern, 1987.

[Bundy,Welham-81]
   A. Bundy, B. Welham:
   Using Meta-Level Inference for Selective Application of Multiple Rewrite Rules
   in Algebraic Manipulation,
   Artificial Intelligence, Vol. 16, No. 2, pp. 189-212, 1981.

[Clancey-83a]
   W. Clancey:
   The Advantages of Abstract Control Knowledge in Expert System Design,
   Proc. of the National Conference on Artificial Intelligence, AAAI-83,
   pp. 74-78

[Davis-80]
   R. Davis:
   Meta-Rules: Reasoning about Control,
   Artificial Intelligence, Vol. 15(1980), pp. 179-222

[Forgy-79]
   C. Forgy:
   On the Efficient Implementation of Production Systems,
   Ph.D. Dissertation,
   Computer Science Department, Carnegie Mellon University,
   Pittsburgh, 1979

[Forgy-81]
C. Forgy:
OPS5 User Manual,
CMU-CS-81-135,
Computer Science Department, Carnegie Mellon University,
Pittsburgh, 1981

[Genesereth-83a]
M. Genesereth:
An Overview of Meta-Level Architecture,
Proc. of the National Conference on Artificial Intelligence, AAAI-83, pp. 119-124.

[Hayes-73]
P. Hayes:
Computation and Deduction,
Proceedings of Mathematical Foundations of Computer Science (MFCS) Symposium,
Czechoslovakian Academy of Sciences.

[Hayes-77]
P. Hayes:
In Defence of Logic,
Proceedings of the Fifth International Joint Conference on Artificial
Intelligence, IJCAI-77,
Cambridge, Mass., pp. 559-565.

[Hayes-79]
P. Hayes:
The Logic of Frames,
in: Frame Conceptions and Text Understanding,
Walter de Gruyter and Co., pp. 46-61.

[Hayes-Roth-85]
F.Hayes-Roth:
Rule-Based Systems,
Communications of ACM,
Vol. 28(1985), No. 9, pp. 921-932

[Martins-84]
G. Martins:
The Overselling of Expert Systems,
DATAMATION, Vol. 30 No. 18, 1984, pp. 76-80

[Neches,Swartout,Moore-85]
R. Neches, W.R. Swartout, J. Moore:
Explainable (and Maintainable) Expert Systems,
Proceedings of the Ninth ernational Joint Conference on Artificial
Intelligence, IJCAI-85,
pg. 383-389.

[Puppe-83]
F. Puppe:
MED1 - Ein heuristisches Diagnosesystem mit effizienter Kontrollstruktur,
MEMO SEKI-83-04,
Universitaet Kaiserslautern, 1983.

[Stefik,etal.-82]
M. Stefik, J. Aikins, J. Benoit, L. Birnbaum, F. Hayes-Roth, E. Sacerdoti:
The Organization of Expert Systems - A Tutorial,
Artificial Intelligence 18(1982), pp. 135-173.

Guiding the Maintenance of
a Model-Based Advisory System
by Explanation-based Learning

Werner Konrad[*], Andreas Jaeschke[#]
Helmut Orth[#], Ono Tjandra[*]

abstract:

For a nuclear recycling process an analysis management system (CAA) is described that generates analysis plans in accordance to analysis task, process phase, operational mode, lab organization, and available analysis operators.

These process and analysis properties are represented as explicit and orthogonal models.
An explanation-based generalization mechanism, residing on some qualitative knowledge about chemistry and · chemical analysis in particular, allows for the semi-automatical incorporation of generalized versions of an expert's corrections of CAA's analysis plans.

keywords:

model-based expert systems, knowledge base maintenance, explanation-based generalization, chemical analysis models

authors' affiliations:
[#] Kernforschungszentrum, IDT, D-7500 Karlsruhe 1, Tel.: +49.7247-82.57.02
[*] SYNERGTECH Gesellschaft für die Technologie Cooperativer Software mbH,
Sendlinger Str. 57, D-8000 München, Tel.: 089 260.70.02

0   Introduction

Analyzing samples from a nuclear recycling process w. r. to the amount of acid, uran, etc, they contain, is an inherently complex task due to the amount of decisions to be made in order to select appropriate analysis procedures matching the particular origin and type of a sample.

Any solution approach has to take into account parsimony criteria for solving the analysis task: since any nuclear waste deserves special treatment (ranging from evaporation for samples of low radioactivity to sealing in glass and concrete for highly radioactive ones) the volume of any sample taken from the recycling process (especially from the 'hot' phases) has to be minimized.

Having a sample returning from a lab station to one that it already has passed during an analysis procedure is both time-consuming and wasting analysis material; therefore an analysis of a sample that includes the application of different analysis operators which are available at distinct lab stations only has to be planned thoroughly in order to avoid the reentering of lab stations after the sample has left them before. Such a `linearzation´ of analysis operators, however, often is precluded by the causal interdependecy of the operators (eg., one might prepare the sample in order to make another one applicable).

Fig. 0 shows how the analysis is integrated into the recycling process. The supervising personel has to check the recycling process during particular phases in order to determine its progress. Thus an analysis task is issued, stating the very analytical subject as well as the process environment the sample is taken from. The Chemical Analysis Assistant system accepts this task, plans an appropriate analysis procedure and calculates the volume of the sample needed to carry out this procedure. Now the according sample quantity is taken from the process and sent to the lab. Here the analysis is performed according to the analytical procedure as prescribed by the Chemical Analysis Assistant and its results are transmitted to the process surveillance personel. According to the analysis results parameters of the recycling process (like the amount of solvent to be added during a process phase) are adjusted, and the process continuation is controlled (eg., some phase has to be repeated because of bad seperation of radioactive substances).

Due to the dynamics of the recycling process as well as the improving analytical procedures updates and corrections of the program are rather frequent.

Obviously, in order to solve this dilemma the knowledge about the analysis itself and the factors that determine it need to be represented **explicitly** in the program. Therefore our analysis program must not capture surface knowledge only, but rather has to incorporate a deep model of the task domain (i.e., an understanding of the anaysis process is mandatory,and has to be brought to bear in the program). In the sequel we key the analysis system that conforms to our deliberations as Chemical Analysis Assistant (CAA for short).

Such a model-based domain knowledge base will state the expert's deliberations concerning the analysis for the sake of correction and updating explicitly, recording the constraints, expectations, and other criteria that led to a certain organization of the analysis process and the selection of particular procedures.

Capitalizing upon the deep domain model sound explanation of what is going on in CAA is feasible, giving a handle not only to understanding CAA's actions, but also to the updating of its knowledge base. Such high-quality explanations allow for the control and check of the analysis process and are especially valuable for proving CAA's correct operation to surveillance institutions.

The understanding of CAA's operations also serves as a correction and updating guidance focusing on suspicious chunks of knowledge that are supposed to be revised. Departing from wrong analysis decisions corrections are suggested to the expert (exploiting the general knowledge about principles of analysis and some qualitative chemistry) in order to focus attention to potential culprits among the decisions, procedures, initial sample descriptions, etc.

When innovative analysis methods (eg., as improved instrumentation) become available, the expert who checks the analysis procedure as proposed by CAA will correct it accordingly. Capitalizing upon knowledge about chemical analysis a generalization-based generalization can integrate the expert's correction in a general manner into the knowledge base.

The paper is organized as follows: first of all we treat the models that constitute the CAA knowledge base in some detail (chapt. 1). Maintenance support for these models employing an explanation-based learning approach is described in chapt. 2. A first sketch of the issues an appropriate qualitative chemistry should encompass and a discussion of **CAA**'s possible extensions as well as its applicability to non-nuclear chemical processes conclude the paper.

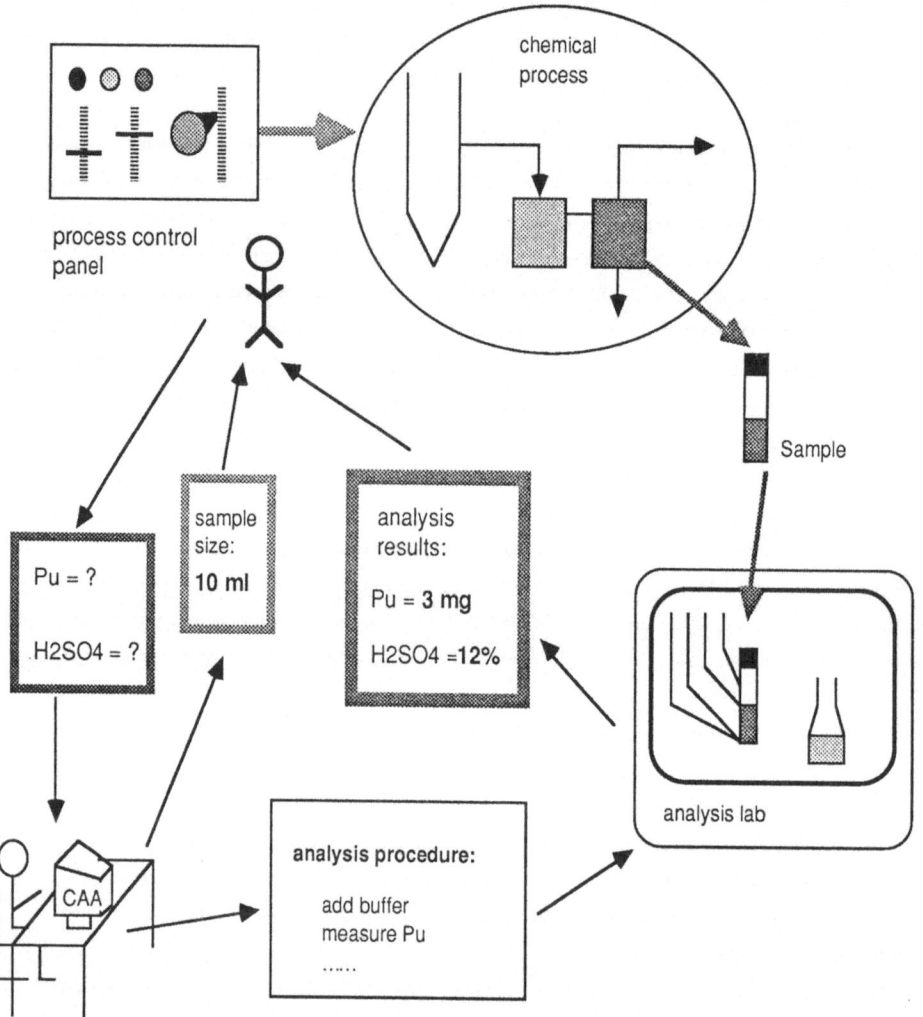

Fig. 0   The Role of Analysis in the Recycling Process

1   The Chemical Analysis Assistant

The importance of deep domain models for generating sound explanation and for knowledge base portability and maintenance support is consensus in the Artificial Intelligence community and is heavily emphasized as a feature of advanced expert systems (cf. Neches et al. 85, Davis 84, and Swartout 83, for instance).

1.1   Models in the Chemical Analysis Assistant

CAA's knowledge about the analysis of recycling samples is mainly composed of the following models:

- **process model:** process phase - radioactivity level, expected sample contents

(The actual representation of this process model can be done via relations describing the structure of the process as well as the attributes of single subprocesses in a frame-like manner); the process model also includes a description of the **operational modes:** as 'normal', 'start up', 'test', and 'failure' with associated analysis constraints like accuracy, response time, etc., and process data)

- **lab organization:** spatial layout, instrumentation, radioactivity protection level
- **analysis operators:** preconditions and effects of elementary analytical operations
  (see below for a more thorough description).
- some rudimentary **qualitative chemistry**: substance taxonomics, etc. (cf. below for more detail).

The partitioning of the knowledge base as sketched above conforms to functional differences of the domain aspects described in the single models: the process model is completely independent of the lab organization, the analysis operators, and the chemical knowledge. The analysis lab and the methods that can be realized in it depend on the various compounds occurring in recycling, but have nothing in common with the process´ organization. As an operationalization of analytical chemistry the analysis operators at least ideally could be derived from the chemical knowledge and a description of analysis technology (like instrumentation capabilities and the like). The sheer amount of knowledge from analytical and technical chemistry such a representation would require currently prohibts this approach (obviously such an on-line deduction of analysis operations would be attractive both for explanation and maintenance purposes). Rather the chemical knowledge is employed for guiding the correction of the analysis operators in case of knowledge base maintenance (see below for some more detail of this approach). Keeping these remarks in mind, we refer to the location of functionally different kinds of domain knowledge in distinct parts of the knowledge base as an orthogonalization of the knowledge base

The models mentioned above are employed for task processing, knowledge base maintenance (and for the construction of similar systems due to the orthogonality and explicitness of the models), and explanation purposes (see also Fig. 1). A more detailed description of these roles can be found in the sequel.

Imagine an analysis task for measuring the concentration of Pu (Plutonium) in a certain phase of the recycling process. Obviously the applicable analysis procedure heavily depends on the chemical composition of the sample (eg., some substances may have to be masked before the amount of a particular element can be determined). In the context of the nuclear recycling process the radioactivity of the sample puts additional constraints on the selection of the analysis procedure: some procedure may be well suited to measure the Pu concentration in samples of low radioactivity (the analysis personel can handle the sample with no special precautions), but the same procedure may be too difficult and risky for dealing with samples that emmit strong radiation (and thus can be handled by using telecontrol behind thick shields of protective glass only).

Information concerning the radioactivity of a sample can be derived from the model of the chemical process; this model additionally provides us with coarse hints about the expected composition of the sample, too.

Taking into account these requirements a specification for an analysis task AT may look like:

Analytical_Task : <Analytical Subject> <Process Phase> <Operational Mode>

where <Analytical Subject> describes the goal of the analysis like 'determine the concentration of Pu', <Process Phase> denotes the phase of the chemical process the sample is taken from, and <Operational Mode> specifies the accuracy and responce time for the analysis w. r. t. to the very operational mode of the process.

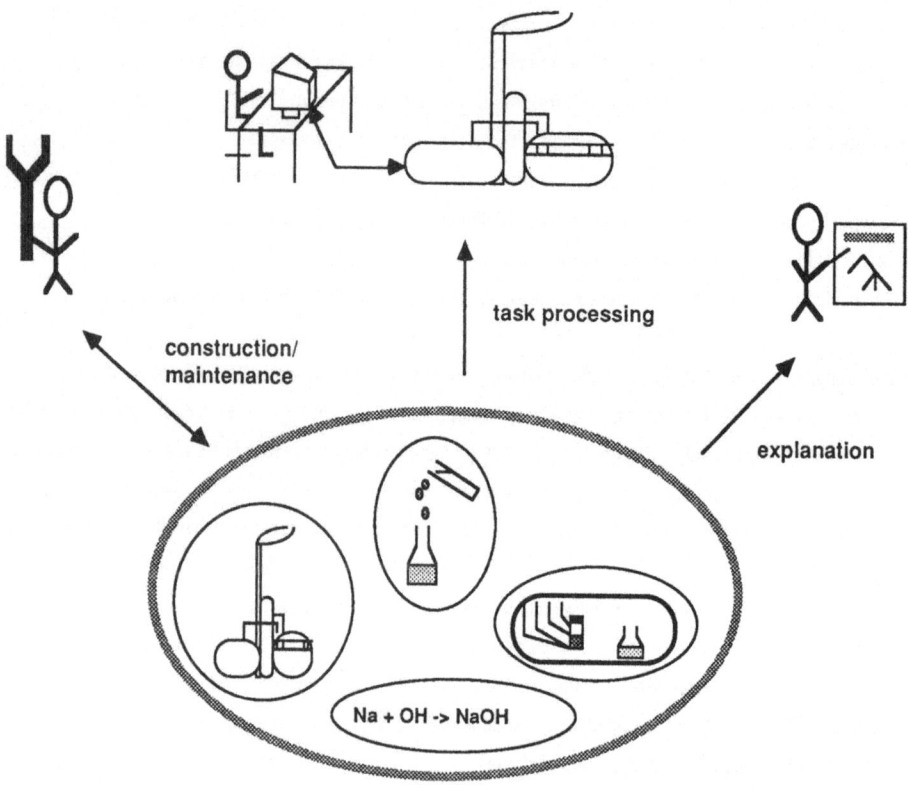

constituents of the KB:

- **process model**
- **operator description**
- **lab model**
- **qualitative chemistry**

Fig. 1 Roles of CAA's Knowledge Base

Structure of Analysis Operators

    Analysis operators AOs are genetical elementary analytical processes that are available at some lab station, like:

- add buffer B, titrate acid A, mask substance S, and the like.

An analytical operation AO in turn is characterized by

- its preconditions for applicability, as
  - ◊   constraints (i.e, the prerequisits the actual state of the sample must fulfill in order to make AO applicable like 'medium radioactivity of sample')
  - ◊   purpose (i.e., the characterizing reaction AO can induce like eg. 'calculation of sulfur acid concentration') •
- description of the genetical analytical operation AO (which might be instantiated by parameters like the specific substance to be treated by AO)

◊   characteristics like response time and accuracy

◊   instrumentation required

- its outcomes, as

◊   results ('the concentration calculation ')

◊   expectations (i.e., assumptions for the ongoing analysis)

◊   side-effects (like masking of some substances).

2   Maintenance Support System

The data and knowledge that describe the recycling process are neither complete nor absolutely correct. In general, data about the contents of some aggregates involved in the process partly relies on estimations. Due to advances in technological and chemical sciences, new and improved analysis methods become available, and have to be integrated into the knowledge base where they either replace some other methods or restrict their applicability. Suppose a new method for measuring the concentration of some compound is more accurarty than the old one, but unfortunately can be applied to a subset of sample compositions of the old method. Thus the new method will replace the old one only partly.

Since the knowledge base has to be updated very often, a dedicated facility is provided that supports the expert in accomplishing this task. In principle, the maintainability of an expert system depends on the quality of support the system provides for the expert in:

- diagnosing model faults
- formulating a correction or modification of a model
- control of correction/modification effects.

Controlling the effects of some correction/modification means the systematical investigation and checking of possible side-effects in order to keep the knowledge consistent. Due to the partitioning of the knowledge base into orthogonal models which are coupled by the planning operator corrections and updates can not only be localized to certain models but even are isolated on single chunks of knowledge. Support for the diagnosis of errors is provided by the explanation facility which allows for the abstract tracing of the planning process,.

Any model modification has to be based upon answers to the following questions:

◊   what has to be modified ?

◊   where ?

◊   in which manner ?

◊   in which manner should the modification change the results of the reasoning process ?

Model modifications can be guided by means of meta-descriptions of the knowledge representations (update schemes as conceptual data indexing as 'which concepts are described where and how ?', (cf. Davis' schema-schemes in Theiresias, Davis 82). An error diagnosis, however, should rely on a `misconception analysis´ which takes into account cognitive errors of an expert as overgeneralization of analysis operators, forgetting about constraints, etc. Of course an operator for measuring the concentration of nitric acid is less likely to be confused with one suited for sulphuric acid than with one for identifying uran. Those discriminations can be suggested by some elementary chemical knowledge (see below). Misconception analysis is the subject for future research on this topic with respect to knowledge acquisition.

Semi-Automatical Generalization of Model Corrections

Modifications of the process and lab models operate on simple structured representations and are guided by the update schemes mentioned above.

Entering a new analysis operator instead might become difficult. In a typical updating scenario the lab personel while using the Chemical Analysis Assistant will be confronted with an analysis procedure that contains some analysis operator AO (or sequence of operators) which could be substituted by a more efficient one AO* (w. r. t. accuracy, response time, etc.). Obviously, a simple substitution of AO by AO* in this concrete analysis procedure would provide tentative success only. Rather than such an ad hoc substitution an automatic generalization of AO* and its integration in the model containing the analytical operators would guarantee the future application of AO* when it is superior to AO.

An example (used for illustrating the following considerations also) may clarify this situation:
In order to measure the concentration of sulphuric acid during some process phase **CAA** *recommends titration. For exactly this analysis the expert now has got a pH-meter for the electrochemical measurement of concentration (the pH-meter operates faster and with greater accurancy than titration).*

Of course we would like to have the pH-meter applied whenever it economically could replace titration. The general applicability of the pH-meter is determined along deliberations like:

- can it principially substitute titration ?
- is it applicable for certain classes of acid only ?
- is it applicable for certain sample compositions only ?

For system that incorporate some domain knowledge (a 'domain theory') we can capitalize upon generalization methods developed in machine learning. Mitchell et al. 86, 85, Mahadevan 85 and others have devised the 'explanation-based generalization' technique which enables a system to derive new knowledge from the expert's correction of its solution. The system 'explains to itself (sc. in terms of the underlying domain theory)' why some correction is valid, regards this correction now as a positive training instance and generalizes it. A remarkable feature of 'explanation-based generalization' is its capability to 'learn' from single positive training instances only, in opposit to generalization techniques (like version spaces, cf. Mitchell 79) that require sets of both positive and negative instances.

Returning to our example, explanation-based generalization operates as follows (see also Fig. 2):

◊ **explanation phase:**
proofing the validity of the expert's correction (training instance C) by reasoning about the domain theory, i.e., generating an explanation why the pH-meter can reasonably substitute titration by infering the functional equivalence of both operations: *'the pH-meter measures the concentration of hydrogen ions which is a proportion of the pH-value'.*

◊ **generalization of the preconditions for applying C:**
regressing C through the proof of its correctness (this goal regression approach will produce sufficient preconditions, but not always the weakest ones. Thus the generalization of C's applicability might be too restrictive). In our example a generalization could look like: *'the amount of hydrogen ions is proportional to the pH-value exactly when no metal ions are present'.*

◊ **generalization of C w. r. to its operational part:**
C becomes generalized in its description of the analysis operation in accordance to the generalized preconditions for its applicability: *'the pH-meter can measure the pH-value in cases when metal ions are absent'.*

Since currently no domain theory for chemical analysis is avaliable **CAA** is not able to generate the explanations for the validity of the corrections itself - rather we use some rudimentary chemical knowledge (see below) to guide **CAA**'s interrogation of the expert for providing the jusitification for his criticism. Sample question schemes are:

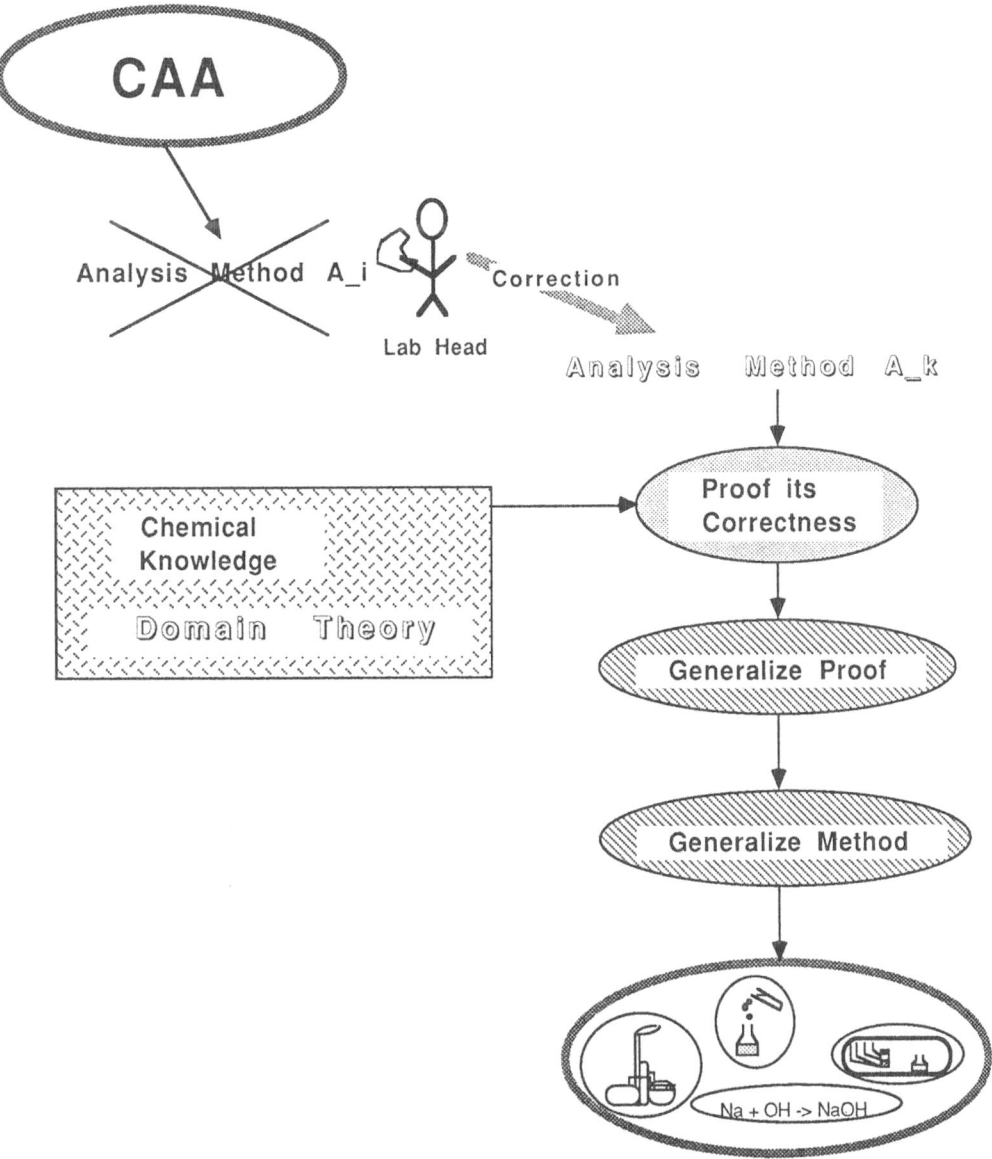

Fig. 2   Explanation-Based Learning for Knowledge-Base Maintenance

◊   'does the pH-meter substitute titration for all inorganic acids ?'
    - derived from a compound taxonomy
◊   'which sample characteristics are required ?'

- from the description of the analysis operator representation, etc.

Comparing a direct update of the analysis operator descriptions in the knowledge base with the semi-automatical generalization of corrections as outlined above shows the advantages of the latter method:

◊   the update is performed during normal operation of the system by the expert himself

◊   the update is articulated in the expert's concepts rather than in some knowledge representation syntax

◊   the expert is asked by the system for explicitly justifying his correction in terms of the domain theory, thus rendering implausible knowledge base modifications less likely.

A Draft of Chemical Analysis Knowledge

In order to verify the expert's corrections the system puts questions to him that are derived from a still rather rudimentary knowledge of chemical analysis and knowledge about the contents of model descriptions (like the 'precondition' property of analysis operators as mentioned above). The subset of chemical analysis knowledge we incorporated so far was chosen w. r. to the explanation derivation we use in the update guidance. In principle, the theory has to incorporate the descriptive and prescriptive knowledge of the domain (in terms of Swartout 83 the 'domain model' and 'domain principles'). By no means pretending to be a sufficient base for reasoning about chemical analysis, the model of the analysis domain encompasses:

•   elements and compound classifications

  elements are organized as periodic system with simple correlations concerning period/group position and reactivity, stability of compounds, etc.

  ◊   for elements and a set of compounds a collection of chemical characteristics is already available in a database

•   list of chemical properties that might be of any interest as radioactivity, solvability, pH-value, light absorption, realtive mass in mass spectroscopy, etc.

•   principles of chemistry like

  ◊   correlation of relative weight in the mass spectroscope and formular

  ◊   stoichiometry that establish a quantitative relation among reacting substances

  ◊   neutralization, etc.

•   principles of analytics as

  ◊   qualitative methods like substance indication by reactions involving some colouring, sedimentation, shape discriminations for cristalls, etc.

  ◊   quantitative methods including mass spectroscopy, refraction of light, etc.

An improvement of the chemical analysis domain knowledge is one of the main scientific objectives of the future work in this project.

Conclusion

We have described the Chemical Analysis Assistant CAA, a system for managing sample analysis for a nuclear recycling process. CAA's knowledge base consists of orthogonal models of the recycling process, the lab organization, analytical operators, and a rudimentary theory of chemical analysis. Relying on knowledge about the analysis domain, expert corrections of CAA's analysis plans can be generalized and integrated into the knowledge base in a semi-automatical manner.

Obvioulsy, the gappiness of the chemical knowledge model precludes a realization of the theoretical potential of explanation-based learning as automatically operationalizing parts of the domain theory by generalizing (or spezializing) single positive training instances (the expert's corrections in our case). Nevertheless, the capability of this machine learning approach for guiding and controlling the maintenance of knowledge bases will clearly foster the research in building domain models appropriate to automatically 'understand' an expert's corrections of its reaasoning results and intergrating the correction rationals into its knowledge base.

A prototype of **CAA** is implemented in a Prolog shell based on semantical networks and frames. Capitalizing upon a still tiny model of chemical knowledge, a first implementation of explanation-based learning is operational, too. The application of the **CAA** approach to 'standard' (viz., non-nuclear) chemical processes seems to be feasible because one has not to cope with the constraints put upon the generation of analysis plans by a radioactive environment . Readers who are interested in more technical detail of the Chemical Analysis Assistant are referred to Jaeschke et al. 87, and CAA 86.

Acknowledgements

We owe thanks to Günther Gerl, Bernd Radig, and Rainer Weidemann for a lot of valuable suggestions. Rita Konrad, Wolfgang Katzer, Jürgen Kesper, Walter Klar, and Klaus-R. Müller have been helpful in establishing and maintaining the technical environment for **CAA**. Thanks are also due to the referees of the paper for their claryfying criticism. With all these people having contributed to the project, the responsibility for the paper is solely ours.

References

CAA (1986). Model-Based Chemical Analysis Assistant and Interactive Learner. SYNERGTECH Technical Report SY-TR-2/86, Munich , FRG

Davis R. (1982). Teiresias: Application of Meta-Level Knowledge. in: Davis R., & Lenat D. B. (1982). Knowledge-Based Systems in Artificial Intelligence. McGraw-Hill, New York et al.

Davis R. (1982). Reasoning from First Principles in Electronic Troubleshooting. in: Coombs M. J. (ed.) (1984). Developments in Expertsystems. Academic Press, London et al., pp. 1

Jaeschke A., Konrad W., Orth H., Tjandra O., Uhlik C. (1987). CAA - a Model-Based Advisory System for Analysis Management in Chemical Processes. 7th Intl. Workshop on Expertsystems & their Applications, Avignon, France, May 13 - 15, pp. 353-369

Mahadevan S. (1985). Verification-Based Learning: A Generalization Strategy for Inferring Problem-Reduction Methods; IJCAI '85, pp. 616

Mitchell T. M. (1979). Version Spaces: An Approach to Concept Learning. Ph. D. dissertation, Stanford University, Stanford CS report STAN-CS-78-711, HPP-79-2

Mitchell T. M., Mahadevan, S., & Steinberg L. I. (1985). LEAP: A Learning Apprentice for VLSI Design, IJCAI '85, pp. 573

Mitchell T. M., Keller R. M., & Kedar-Cabelli S. T. (1986). Explanation-Based Generalization: A Unifying View. Machine Learning, vol. 1, no. 1, pp. 47

Neches R., Swartout W. R., & Moore J. (1985). Explainable (and Maintainable) Expert Systems. IJCAI '85, pp. 382

Swartout W. R. (1983). XPLAIN: a System for Creating and Explaining Expert Consulting Programs. Artificial Intelligence, vol. 21, pp. 285

Thompson C. W., Kolts J., & Ross K., M. (1985). A Toolkit for Building 'Menu-Based Natural Language' Interfaces. ACM Ann. Conf., Denver, Colorado, pp. 318

Woods D. D. (1986).Paradigms for Intelligent Decision Support. in: Hollnagel E., Mancini G., & Woods D. D. (eds) (1986). Intelligent Decision Support in Process Environments, Berlin et al.

An Efficient Interpreter for a Rule-Based Non-Monotonic Deduction System

Hartmut Freitag
ZT ZTI INF 312
SIEMENS AG
Otto-Hahn-Ring 6
8000 München 83
Bundesrepublik Deutschland

Michael Reinfrank*
Department of Computer and
Information Science
University of Linköping
58183 Linköping
Sweden

Abstract: We present an efficient interpreter for CAPRI, a non-monotonic deduction system using rules of the form if ... unless ... then ... . The interpreter is built on top of a reason maintenance system maintaining its current database and includes a fast pattern matcher combining both ideas from RETE and from non-monotonic dependency network update algorithms.

1. Introduction

Determining the set of rule instances that apply to a current state of a database is often the most time-consuming task to be performed by a rule-based deduction system. Non-monotonic deduction systems usually suffer from a couple of additional complexity problems that arise from fundamental properties of non-monotonicity. Therefore, an efficient pattern matcher is an essential part of any rule-based non-monotonic deduction system.

In the present paper we discuss an interpreter for CAPRI [Reinfrank|Freitag-87], a deduction system using rules of the form if ... unless ... then ..., which is built on top of a Goodwin-style reason maintenance system (RMS) [Goodwin-82]. This interpreter uses a pattern matching algorithm which combines methods from RETE [Forgy-82] and RMS-techniques to compute and continuously update the set of applicable rule instances.

The paper is organized as follows: First of all, we briefly introduce the concept of admissible extensions which provides a framework to describe theories of non-monotonic reasoning (NMR). We then sketch the overall structure of an NMR-system and identify its major tasks. In chapter 4 we discuss the basic concepts of an interpreter of a concrete NMR-system, and finally we give a little example in chapter 5.

2. Admissible Extensions

To characterize the set of conclusions which can be reasonably drawn from a given set of premises using a set of non-monotonic rules, we introduce the idea of admissible extensions of a given premise set.

We define a **non-monotonic formal system** by a pair (F, R) where

- F is the set of formulae of an arbitrary language L, and
- R is a set of inference rules of the form if $p_1, ..., p_m$ unless $q_1, ..., q_n$ then r
    where all p_i's, q_i's and r are formulae

---

* The author's work is kindly supported by the SIEMENS AG, ZTI INF 3, Muenchen

Given F,R and a set of premises $P \subseteq F$, an admissible set of beliefs should only contain beliefs for which we can find some valid, non-circular arguments using the premises and rules available.

We define a **derivation** for a formula p from P as a sequence $(a_1, a_2, ..., a_n = p)$ where:

$\forall i \in \{1, 2, ..., n\}$ $a_i \in P$ or $\exists j_1, ..., j_k < i$ s.t. there is a rule
$\underline{if}\ a_{j1}, ..., a_{jk}\ \underline{unless}\ q_1, ..., q_n\ \underline{then}\ a_i$ in R.

Derivations generalize the notion of proof to non-monotonic calculi.
Let T be a set of beliefs held by a problem solver. A derivation is **valid in T** if and only if

$\forall i \in \{1, 2, ..., n\}$ $a_i \in T$ and if $a_i \notin P$, but has been established by a rule
$\underline{if}\ a_{j1}, ..., a_{jk}\ \underline{unless}\ q_1, ..., q_n\ \underline{then}\ a_i$
then $q_1, ..., q_n \notin T$

An admissible extension of a given premise set should also contain every belief for which a valid derivation can be found. Therefore we define an admissible extension of a set P of premises to be a superset E of P which is both

- **grounded** in P, i.e. every q in E has a derivation from P that is also valid in E.
- **closed**, i.e. for every rule $\underline{if}\ p_1, ..., p_m\ \underline{unless}\ q_1, ..., q_n\ \underline{then}\ r$ we have:
     if $\{p_1, ..., p_m\} \subseteq E$ and $\{q_1, ..., q_n\} \cap E = \emptyset$ then $r \in E$

In the literature on NMR, this static definition is often replaced by an equivalent fixed point characterization (see e.g. [Doyle-83]).

While monotonic formal systems always induce exactly one admissible extension (cf. deductive closure) for a given premise set, this is not the case for non-monotonic formal systems. As one can easily verify, the empty premise set has the two admissible extensions {p}, {q} with repsect to the rules {$\underline{unless}$ p $\underline{then}$ q, $\underline{unless}$ q $\underline{then}$ p}, whereas there is no admissible extension at all for the rule set {$\underline{unless}$ p $\underline{then}$ p}.

In the terminology of reason maintenance systems [Reinfrank-87], the latter case corresponds to an odd non-monotonic loop. Unfortunately, there are only weak results available on the existence and uniqueness of admissible extensions, e.g. the absence of odd loops is a sufficient (but not necessary) condition for the existence of at least one admissible extension.

3. Rule-Based NMR-Systems

After a conclusion is drawn using a non-monotonic rule it can be invalidated by further inferences and additional premises. Therefore an NMR-system has to continously revise its current set of beliefs. Consequently such systems usually consist of two components: an interpreter which decides upon which rule to fire next and a reason maintenance system which maintains an admissible extension of the current premises with respect to the rules fired so far. The reason maintenance component represents the system's current state by means of a dependency network composed of *nodes* standing for beliefs and *justifications* for these beliefs in terms of belief and/or disbelief in other nodes. The dependency network is incrementally generated by the deduction rules: The application of a rule results in asserting its conclusion and an explicit justification for the conclusion using the rule's antecedents. This explicit network is a subnetwork of the complete, only implicit network which is induced by all rules. By assigning labels IN and OUT to the nodes according to their current status of belief, the reason maintenance system does some kind of propositional deduction in the explicit network. The labelling algorithm reasons only from the structural dependencies and does not access the contents of nodes.

A concrete realization of such an abstract NMR-system is CAPRI, a non-monotonic deduction system with rules of the form if ... unless ... then ... built on top of a Goodwin-style reason maintenance system. CAPRI-rules use variables to provide finite representations of their sets of ground instances. A CAPRI-rule applies to the current state if all of its monotonic antecedents are IN and none of its non-monotonic antecedents either. The CAPRI-Interpreter follows the usual recognize-act cycle of deduction systems: First of all the set of all applicable rule instances is determined. The conflict resolution component then selects one of these rule instances to be fired. The interpreter applies the selected rule by integrating the conclusion and a corresponding justification into the network and calling the reason maintenance component to update the system's current set of beliefs. The remainder of this paper focuses on the task of determining and updating the set of applicable rules.

4. A Fast Pattern Matcher for CAPRI

Determining the set of rules that apply to a current state has often a crucial impact on the performance of a deduction system. So some systems have been observed to spend more than ninety percent of their total run time performing pattern matching. This forced the development of fast pattern matching algorithms like RETE [Forgy-82]. A simle approach would be to iterate after each execution cycle over the whole database and the whole rule set to compute the conflict set. The RETE-algorithm avoids iteration over the current database by storing information about previous match results and computing only changes of the conflict set caused by changes of the database. The compilation of the rules into an augmented discrimination network prevents RETE from iterating over the set of rules. This idea relies heavily on the fact that only a small fraction of the database changes during each cycle.

The use of a dependency network as database for CAPRI leads to additional problems for the interpreter: Changes of the set of applicable rules are not only caused by the addition of new elements to the database (dependency net nodes are never deleted) but also by changes of the network's labelling. If an assertion changes its label from IN to OUT it
- can make a rule applicable, if it is matched by one of the rule's non-monotonic antecedents and/or
- can block the applicability of a rule, if it is matched by one of the rule's monotonic antecedents.
Similar cases arise if an assertion changes its label from OUT to IN.

Let a first trial to use RETE as pattern matcher for CAPRI be the following: Interpret the set of current beliefs as current database. Additions to this database are new IN-labelled assertions or assertions changing their label from OUT to IN. Assertions changing their label from IN to OUT are treated as deletions. However, this approach has several drawbacks: Changes of the current set of beliefs do not necessarily affect only a small fraction of the database. And even if we could minimize the work that has to be done for each database change often a lot of work has to be redone if an assertion changes its belief status twice.

Therefore our pattern matcher uses a two-step method to treat changes of the dependency structure and changes of the current belief status differently. First of all we determine the set of *potentially applicable* rule ground instances which consists of all rule ground instances whose monotonic antecedents are represented as dependency net nodes. We call this set *extended conflict set*. This extended conflict set is a superset of all applicable rule ground instances and can only be changed by the addition of nodes to the dependency network. The compilation of the current rule set into an augmented discrimination network provides a basis for the efficient computation of changes of the extended conflict set caused by structural changes of the dependency network. Added assertions are passed to this discrimination network which in turn determines all rule ground instances which become potentially applicable by the new assertions. The actual conflict set can be computed by filtering the set of potentially applicable rule ground instances using the current labelling. To facilitate this filtering we extend our current dependency network by those justifications which would be generated by firing all rule ground instances of the extended conflict set. The applicability of such a potentially applicable rule ground instance is then represented by the label of its corresponding justification which can be determined by just propagating labels of its supporting nodes. To separate justifications representing potentially applicable rule ground instances from justifications representing already fired rules the pattern matcher uses *virtual justifications*. These are special justifications which are only visible to the pattern matcher. Assertions of the non-monotonic antecedents of a potentially applicable rule ground instance which are not yet represented by dependency net nodes are added to the dependency network by using *virtual nodes*, whose assertions are not elements of the represented database and which are always OUT. This means: By utilizing the main principles of RETE we extend our explicit dependency network by all justifications of the complete network whose monotonic antecedents are nodes of the explicit network and which are not themselves part of the explicit network. The use of virtual nodes and justifications gives us the possibility to determine changes of the conflict set caused by changes of the current labelling by means of the dependency net update algorithm of the reason maintenance component. Furthermore, it reduces the application of a rule ground instance to the transformation of the corresponding virtual justification into a "normal" one. The decision which justification should be transformed is a matter of the conflict resolution component which is not discussed in this paper.

5. An Example

To illustrate the above described approach for efficient pattern matching within CAPRI consider the following set of rules:

ρ_1:   if (Bird ?x) (Cat ?y) <u>unless</u> (ExceptionalBird ?x) <u>then</u> (InterestedIn ?y ?x)
ρ_2:   if (Bird ?x) (Cat ?y) (InterestedIn ?y ?x) <u>then</u> (InDanger ?x)
ρ_3:   if (Bird ?x) <u>unless</u> (InDanger ?x) <u>then</u> (Singing ?x)

These rules are compiled into an augmented discrimination network whose task is to compute changes of the extended conflict set caused by new assertions. Furthermore, suppose that there are two initial premises (Bird Tweety) and (Cat Sylvester). These premises are passed to the augmented discrimination network which computes two potentially applicable rule instances:

   if (Bird Tweety) (Cat Sylvester) <u>unless</u> (ExceptionalBird Tweety)
      <u>then</u> (InterestedIn Sylvester Tweety)
   if (Bird Tweety) <u>unless</u> (InDanger Tweety) <u>then</u> (Singing Tweety)

The system inserts the corresponding virtual justifications into the dependency network and calls the dependency net update algorithm. Both rule instances are applicable because their monotonic antecedents are IN and none of their non-monotonic antecedents either. Assume that the control component decided to fire the instance of ρ_1. The virtual justification is transformed into a "normal" one and nodes for (ExceptionalBird Tweety) and (InterestedIn Sylvester Tweety) are added to the dependency net. The augmented discrimination network computes a new potentially applicable rule instance

<u>if</u> (Bird Tweety) (Cat Sylvester) (InterestedIn Sylvester Tweety)
<u>then</u> (InDanger Tweety)

which is marked by the dependency network update algorithm as applicable. This continues until the conflict set is empty.

6. Conclusions

Since pattern matching is a major source of inefficiency in rule-based systems, an efficient solution to the problem of determining and maintaining the set of applicable rule instances is crucial for the performance of any such system. In particular this is true for NMR-systems which have to cope with some additional complexities.

We have sketched a fast interpreter for a rule-based non-monotonic deduction system, built on ideas of RETE and of reason maintenance mechanisms. Although we cannot offer formal estimates on the algorithmic complexity (so far, there are no such results available for the original RETE-algorithm), experimental results with a first prototype [Freitag-87] are quite encouraging.

One challenging issue for future research will be the development of elaborate control strategies to guide CAPRI's line of reasoning.

Acknowledgements

We would like to thank Gerd Brewka, Rainer Decker, Oskar Dressler, Alex Herold, Peter Struß and Hans Voss for commenting on earlier draft versions of this paper. Claudia Johnson was so kind to reduce the number of linguistic bugs.

References

[Doyle-83]   Doyle, Jon: Some Theories of Reasoned Assumptions. CMU-CS-83-125, CMU (Pittsburgh, May 1983)

[Freitag-87] Freitag, Hartmut: An Admissible Extension Theory Based Non-Monotonic Deduction System. Diplomarbeit, Fachbereich Informatik, Universität Kaiserslautern (forthcoming).

[Forgy-82]   Forgy, Charles L.: RETE: A Fast Algorithm for the Many Pattern/Many Object Match Problem. Artificial Intelligence 19, pp.17-38 (1982)

[Goodwin-82] Goodwin, James: An Improved Algorithm for Non-Monotonic Dependency Net Update. LITH-MAT-R-82-23, Linkoeping University (Linkoeping, August 1982)

[Reinfrank-85] Reinfrank, Michael: An Introduction to Non-Monotonic Reasoning. MEMO SEKI-85-02, Univ. Kaiserslautern (Kaiserslautern, 1985)

[Reinfrank-87] Reinfrank, Michael: Reason Maintenance Systems. In: Stoyan, H. (ed.): Proc. Workshop on Truth Maintenance Systems (Berlin, Oct. 1986). Springer Verlag (to appear)

[Reinfrank|Freitag-87] Reinfrank, Michael; Freitag, Hartmut: An Integrated Non-Monotonic Deduction and Reason Maintenance System. In: Stoyan, H. (ed.): Proc. Workshop on Truth Maintenance Systems (Berlin, Oct. 1986). Springer Verlag (to appear)

Belief Revision in Diagnosis

Frank Puppe
Universität Karlsruhe, FB Informatik

Abstract: The efficiency of general belief revision techniques like the TMS or the ATMS decreases rapidly with the size and connectivity of the knowledge base and they are not designed for integrating non-monotonic and probabilistic evidence. Our belief revision algorithm ITMS overcomes these shortcomings by exploiting peculiarities of diagnostic reasoning. It is implemented in the diagnostic shell MED2 with good results.

For each conclusion, a well-founded categorical or probabilistic indicator of its strength is continuously updated. Upon retractation of a justification, the ITMS immediately decides the new state (established, unknown or excluded) of the affected conclusion by checking its remaining strength. The correctness depends on avoiding circular justifications. They can easily be blocked if circular inference paths are precomputed in the knowledge base and the blockage does not manipulate the inference process. Both requirements can be fulfilled in diagnosis.

1. Introduction

Diagnostic problem solving is the art of drawing certain conclusions from uncertain knowledge and incomplete data. While uncertainty can only be represented probabilistically, incompleteness should be treated in a more structured way. The two major techniques are hierarchical and default reasoning. Hierarchies allow representing the knowledge, that a disease category (e.g. liver disease) is established, but nothing is known about its successors (type of liver disease). Default reasoning enables the reasoner to draw conclusions in the absence of precise data: A -> B II- C meaning   A yields evidence for B if the exceptions in C are unknown or false [Doyle 83]. Default reasoning is necessary in diagnosis because it is rarely cost-effective or may not even be possible to wait until all data are available. Instead actions must often be taken with partial data about the case. However, if additional data show a conclusion to be wrong, it must be retracted with all its consequences. Therefore, a good diagnostic shell should allow the combination of probabilistic, hierarchical and default reasoning [Puppe 86].

In section 2, we discuss problems of current belief revision procedures with diagnosis. In the next section, we motivate the basic ideas of the ITMS and extend them in section 4 to probabilistic reasoning. The ITMS is described and illustrated by an example in section 5. Some remarks about its implementation in MED2 and a discussion are given respect. in sections 6 and 7.

2.   General Belief Revision Techniques

The two major belief revision techniques are justification based and assumption based systems. Both have serious disadvantages for diagnosis. The ATMS (Assumption-Based Truth Maintenance System, [de Kleer 84, 86]) stores along with each conclusion the basic assumptions under which the conclusion holds. To use the ATMS, "it must be possible to attribute all conclusions to a small set of antecedents it depends on, *otherwise no TMS can do much good* " [de Kleer 84, p 79]. In diagnosis, the typical situation is just the opposite: a small number of conclusions (diagnoses) depends on a large number of basic facts (symptoms). Additionally, the qualification of diagnostic rules with probabilities and exceptions is very difficult to handle in the ATMS.

The justification based approach stores for each conclusion its justifications only. The basic belief revision procedure is simple and efficient (Fig. 1).

---

(1) If a fact or conclusion changes, check all justifications connected to it.
(2) If a justification becomes invalid, see if the conclusion has other justifications.
(3) If a conclusion has no valid justifications, then retract it and call recursively this procedure with the retracted conclusion.

Fig. 1:   A simple belief revision procedure

The main problem is the treatment of circular justifications preventing the retraction of the conclusions involved in the loop (Fig. 2).

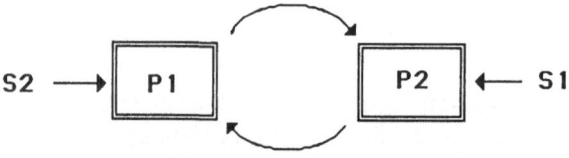

Fig. 2: Once P1 and P2 are established, they cannot be retracted with the simpe belief revision procedure in Fig. 1.

One may ask, whether such loops can be avoided altogether in diagnosis. This is indeed possible by restricting the knowledge represention to a strict diagnostic hierarchy as e.g. in MDX [Chandrasekaran 83]. However, diagnostic networks with inference loops are more flexible, because they avoid restrictions, that one pathoconcept must be established first to infer other pathoconcepts (Fig. 3).

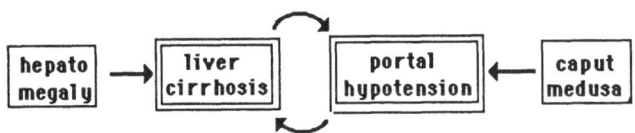

Fig. 3: If the diagnostician can infer liver cirrhosis, then portal hypotension is very probable and vice versa. Which pathoconcept is established first depends on the symptoms given and can vary from case to case.

The major mechanisms to avoid the possible distortions caused by circular justifications are:

(1) The "current support"-strategy of the TMS (Truth Maintenance System, [Doyle 79, Mc Allester 80, Goodwin 82]) marks the first derived justification of a conclusion as its "current support", because it must be a non-circular, well-founded justification. If upon a change the current support of a conclusion remains unaffected, no update is necessary, otherwise a major procedure is initiated. Since the other justifications of the conclusions may be circular, the conclusion is temporarily unlabeled, this change is propagated to all the justifications it is involved in and this procedure is repeated for all conclusions having as their current support an unlabeled justification. After this "deforestation", all conclusions which still have a valid justification are relabeled and the results are propagated until the network is "afforested" again. It is clear that this procedure may unlabel and relabel actually unaffected conclusions (Fig. 4), and depending on the connectivity of the network, it may waste much time.

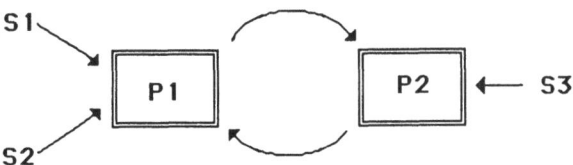

Fig. 4: If P1 has S1 as its current support and S1 is retracted, the TMS cannot distinguish between the non-circular support from S2 and the circular support from P2. Therefore it must temporally unlabel P1 with all its consequences.

(2) A very similar problem must be solved in automatic storage management systems based on reference counting [Bobrow 80]. Such systems keep track of the number of references to any cell and deallocate a cell, when the number of its references drops to zero. If a cell A references B which (more or less directly) references A, then the counter of A remains at least 1

(from B) even with no external references to A or B. The basic idea of Bobrow is to divide the references to any cell of such reentrant structures into internal references from cells inside the group and external references from outside the group. If a reentrant structure has no external references, it is deallocated. The main problem is recognizing reentrant structures. This is the programmer's responsibility.

3.   Basic Ideas of the ITMS

The key idea of our belief revision procedure is a justification counter which does not count circular justifications. This is reasonable for diagnosis because circular evidence generally leads to overestimating the strength of a hypothesis. Whether a conclusion must be retracted can now immediately be decided from the current score of its justification counter. Therefore, we call this procedure "Immediate-Check TMS" (ITMS). For recognizing loops we take advantage of the fact, that a rich diagnostic network makes the use of variables in rules unneccessary. For example, a rule "for all x (x is element of {x1, x2, x3}) x => y" can be reformulated by several rules and by naming X as an intermediate pathoconcept "x1 => X, x2 => X, x3 => X, X => y". This is a common method in many diagnostic domains. Hence, for blocking circular justifications efficiently, all circular inference paths of the knowledge base are precomputed, which is possible with rules without variables. All rules belonging to a loop are marked as "circular" and noted on an attribute CIRCRULES of the conclusion they support. As a side effect, odd non-monotonic circularities (i.e. where establishing a conclusion may result in its retraction) are also detected during the precomputation of loops and the user is urged to eliminate them.

If a conclusion is established during the problem solving process, all its CIRCRULES which did not participate in its deduction are blocked (CIRCRULES, which were already fired, must have a non-circular support and need not be considered). If the conclusion is retracted, the consequences are propagated first and then the blockage of the CIRCRULES is lifted. The run-time cost for performing these operations is very cheap, since only a precomputed list of rules has to be marked.

These mechanisms allow us to use the simple belief revision procedure from Fig. 1 for retracting conclusions. To avoid inefficiency by retracting and establishing a conclusion several times if several of its rules are revised, we extend the procedure by using a priority list called AGENDA. If the support of a conclusion has changed, this conclusion is registered on the AGENDA and will be checked only if its justification depends on no other conclusions in the AGENDA. Thereby, the revision test of a conclusion is delayed until all effects concerning it have been propagated.

4. Probabilistic Reasoning within the ITMS

Probabilistic Reasoning can easily be integrated into the ITMS, because the justification counter can represent categorical integers as well as probabilistic real numbers. The main problem is the interpretation of probabilistic circularities in the diagnostic network (Fig. 5).

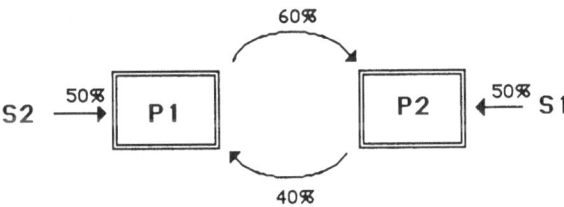

Fig. 5: If S2 is known, P1 gets a probability of 50% and P2 of 30%. If S1 becomes known later, how much evidence should be given to P2 and be propagated from P2 to P1?

Our solution is to avoid such propagations of partial evidence altogether by converting the probability of a hypothesis in one of three states: "excluded", "unknown", or "established". If a hypothesis is unknown, no consequences can be drawn, and if it is established or excluded, further evidence from circular rules can be ignored, since it confirms what is already known (provided that non-monotonic circularities do not exist). Accordingly, rules relate in their conditions only to the state of a hypothesis and not to its detailed probability, e.g. if (P1 is established) then (conclude X with certainty Y), where Y is independent from the probability of P1. The reduction of the uncertainty space to these three states is performed by the differential diagnosis method (Fig. 6), which is basic for diagnostic problem solving [Pople 82].

P1 (70%) ------>		-----> P1 excluded
P2 (90%) ------>	**Differential**	-----> P2 established
P3 (10%) ------>	**Diagnosis**	-----> P3 excluded
P4 (40%) ------>		-----> P4 excluded

Fig. 6: Differential diagnosis means to select the best alternative from a list of competitors.

The ITMS is tailored to differential diagnosis, where its advantages over the TMS are especially clear: deciding the state of a hypothesis by comparison with competitors increases the connectivity of the network and thus makes the "deforestation" of the TMS even more inefficient, while in the ITMS small changes may not cause any revisions since differential diagnosis decisions are usually quite stable (except in borderline cases).

5. Description of the ITMS

The ITMS is applicable to inference systems where conclusions are drawn with probabilistic or categorical rules from facts and previously made conclusions. Non-monotonic circularities are forbidden. If monotonic circularities exist, the rules and conclusions contained in them must fulfill the following requirements:

* A conclusion may not have more than three states: unknown, established, and excluded.
* For all rules in the loops the following data structures are precomputed: Circular rules yielding positive or negative evidence for a conclusion are listed as its positive or negative CIRCRULES respectively.

Treatment of Circularities:

If a conclusion is established / excluded, all its positive / negative CIRCRULES are blocked respectively (if they were not already fired). If a conclusion is retracted (i.e. its state is set back to unknown), the consequences are propagated and then the blocked CIRCRULES are released.

The ITMS-Algorithm:

INPUT: Fact, interpretation or rule to be revised.
OUTPUT: Correction of all affected conclusions with the result, that the knowledge base is in the same state as if the revision would have been considered from the beginning.
SPECIAL DATA STRUCTURES: Storage of the STRENGTH of the conclusions (in a categorical reasoning system: number of justifications; and in a probabilistic reasoning system: degree of belief).

1. All rules directly affected by the INPUT are updated (if a fact or a conclusion has changed, all rules based on the old value are retracted and all rules enabled by the new value are fired).
   The retraction of a rule is carried out as executing its inverse action.
2. All conclusions directly affected by the update in STEP 1 are gathered on a global list AGENDA.
3. If AGENDA is empty, then STOP,
   else select a basic object X from AGENDA (an object is basic, if its justification depends on no other object in AGENDA).
4. Delete X from AGENDA.
5. Check the new STRENGTH of X: if its state has not changed, then GOTO 3, else GOTO 1.

To illustrate the treatment of circularities we present an example of a simple, categorical knowledge base:

R1: P1 => P2
R2: P2 => P3
R3: P3 => P1
R4: S1 => P1 II- S4
R5: S2 => P1 II- S5
R6: S3 => P2

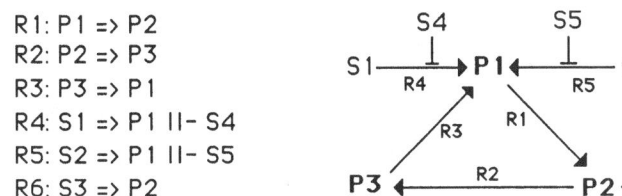

During knowledge base construction, the following data structures are precomputed:

P1: FORWARDRULES: (R1)   CIRCRULES: (R3)
P2: FORWARDRULES: (R2)   CIRCRULES: (R1)
P3: FORWARDRULES: (R3)   CIRCRULES: (R2)
S1: FORWARDRULES: (R4)
S2: FORWARDRULES: (R5)
S3: FORWARDRULES: (R6)
S4: FORWARDRULES: (R4)
S5: FORWARDRULES: (R5)

An example of a possible reasoning chain is: (in the following, we omit the AGENDA since always only one retraction is enabled; "-R1" = retraction of R1; [comments are in square brackets]):

Start: (Unknown P1, P2, P3, S1, S2, S3, S4, S5)
1.   Userprovided (S1)
2.   STRENGTH (P1) := 1 => Established (P1)   by R4
3.   Blockage of CIRCRULES (P1) => Blocked (R3)
4.   STRENGTH (P2) := 1 => Established (P2)   by R1
5.   Blockage of CIRCRULES (P2); but since R1 has already
       fired, it is not blocked.
6.   STRENGTH (P3) := 1 => Established (P3)   by R2
____   STOP [R3 is blocked; current state S1 -> P1 -> P2 -> P3]
7.   Userprovided (S2)
8.   STRENGTH (P1) := 2   by R5
____   STOP
9.   Userprovided (S3)
10.   STRENGTH (P2) := 2   by R6
____   STOP
11.   Userprovided (S4)
12.   STRENGTH (P1) := 1 [an exception of R4 became known]   by -R4
____   STOP [the ITMS recognizes immediately, that P1 still
       has a non-circular justification. The TMS would have
       temporarily unlabeled P1 (because R4 was its current
       support) with all its consequences (P2 and P3). Only
       then, it would discover the well-foundedness of R5.]

13.   Userprovided (S5)

14.   STRENGTH (P1) := 0 => Unknown (P1)   by -R5

15.   STRENGTH (P2) := 1 [again the TMS would have some trouble recognizing that P2 has another wellfounded support]   by -R1

16.   Blocked (R1) [because R1 is a CIRCRULE, which did not fire]

17.   Released (R3) [the blocked CIRCRULES of P1 are released, after all other inferences have been derived]

18.   STRENGTH (P1) := 1 => Established (P1)   by R3

_____   STOP [final state: S3 -> P2 -> P3 -> P1]

Probabilistic rules would only change the domain of STRENGTH (to real numbers) and the decision criteria for establishing a conclusion (to differential diagnosis). We omit an example because an insightful knowledge base would be too complex.

The correctness and termination of the algorithm is straightforward, because circular justifications are blocked and non-monotonic circularities do not exist.

The efficiency of the ITMS depends on how well the algorithm approximates the best case, where all conclusions affected by a revision are checked only once. There are two problems:

1. The given method of blocking circular justifications may block justifications containing a non-circular part leading to multiple checking of a conclusion. In the example, it was not necessary to block the rule R3 (P3 => P1) because it had a non-circular support (via S3), which was detected only after retracting P1. The problem could be avoided if the strategy to block circular rules were to be better informed. However, the costs to recognize such derivations are quite high and may not be worth their benefits.

2. The selection of a basic object from the AGENDA in STEP 3 of the ITMS is only possible if for all conclusions the transitive closure of all their dependant objects is computed. If this costly procedure is avoided and only one-step dependencies are checked, then a multiple revision of one object may happen.

    Example: Given are the rules P1 => P2, P2 => P3, S1 => P1, S2 => P3;
            P1, P2, P3 are established.

    If S1 and S2 change their states, then P1 should be checked before P3, since P3 depends on P1 by a two-step relation. However this cannot be recognized by checking one-step relations only.

An optimal overall implementation of the ITMS depends on the domain dependant compromise between the costs for avoiding multiple checking of conclusions in both cases and the costs of doing so occasionally. Our experience is that such situations occur very rarely.

6.   Implementation of the ITMS in MED2

MED2 [Puppe 87a, 87b] is a commercial expert system shell for associative (heuristic) diagnostic problem solving. It provides special mechanisms for typical diagnostic requirements like data-base reasoning, cost-effective data gathering, evaluation of therapies and changing data in follow-up sessions, and hybrid diagnosis evaluation based on categorical and probabilistic rules with exceptions, predisposition, and an explanation value. A need for belief revision arises in the following situations:

* Facts are corrected by the user or change in follow-up sessions. All rules based on the old facts must be retracted.
* An exception of a rule becomes known.
* New facts yield opposite evidence for an established or excluded diagnosis. Whether the state of the diagnosis changes depends on two criteria: A diagnosis is established, if its absolute STRENGTH and the difference to the STRENGTH of the best competitor exceeds a threshold. Competitors of diagnoses are retrieved from the knowledge base.

MED2 then interrupts its normal reasoning process and enters the belief revision mode. All conclusions affected by any change are registered on the AGENDA for checking their states in an efficient order. The first ordering criteria is the type of the conclusion, e.g. data abstractions are always updated before diagnoses. Secondly, MED2 computes "basic objects" of one type by considering one-step relations only. In our current knowledge bases, this rarely leads to any multiple revisions.

The runtime performance of the ITMS in MED2 is similiar to that of the ordinary reasoning process, since the retraction of a rule is treated as the execution of its inverse action. The overhead costs for blocking and releasing circular rules and for the management of the AGENDA are negligible.

7.   Discussion

The ITMS differs from the TMS in maintaining a more informed indicator in the belief of a hypothesis than the current support, and in using numbers instead of justifications as the indicator (similiar to a reference counter in a garbage collection algorithm). The additional information permits the use of the simple basic belief revision procedure (fig. 1) instead of the "cumbersome and very inefficient TMS-machinery" [de Kleer 84]. The key idea is the precomputation of reasoning loops in the knowledge base for efficiently recognizing circular justifications. The first requirement is, that rules inside the circularities contain no variables (of course, other rules may contain variables). This condition typically holds in diagnosis, because the rich terminology of intermediate diagnoses makes the use of variables unnecessary.

The second requirement is that conclusions are not drawn from partial confirmation of other conclusions. Otherwise, the treatment of circularities would require a clear distinction between the circular and the non-circular part of evidence which is very expensive to maintain. Avoiding partial confirmation is achieved by differential diagnosis. However, this may be unsatisfactory in borderline cases, because the decision in favor of the best hypothesis of the competitor set would neglect the uncertainty and no decision would prevent further diagnostic or therapeutic progress. A good solution to this problem (but not yet implemented in MED2) would be to proceed along the most promising alternatives seperately, either in order to compare the results later or to present with the user the alternative solutions. For realizing this idea, the ATMS-technique is suitable, where the differential diagnosis alternatives are treated as "basic assumptions".

An informal comparison with human belief revision techniques served as guideline for developing the ITMS. Humans tend to check first the importance of a new piece of evidence before revising anything, since there is considerable redundancy in many justifications. The main problem are circularities which may be related to prejudice in humans. The best remedy for their detection seems to be a simple inference system (e.g. avoiding variables). The reduction of the uncertainty space to the three states `excluded`, `unknown`, and `established`, decision by differential diagnosis and pursuing multiple lines of reasoning in difficult cases seem to be much more common for humans than the alternative of propagating partial evidence through a diagnostic hierarchy.

Acknowledgements: Thanks to Michael Reinfrank for reading earlier drafts of this paper and making many helpful comments.

8.   References

[Bobrow 80] Bobrow, D.: Managing Reentrant Structures Using Reference Counts, ACM Transactions on Programming Languages and Systems, Vol 2, No. 3, 269-273, 1980.

[Chandrasekaran 83] Chandrasekaran, B.: Towards a Taxonomy of Problem Solving Types, AI-Magazine 4, No. 1, 9-17, 1983.

[de Kleer 84] de Kleer, J.: Choices without Backtracking, AAAI-84, 79-86, 1984.

[de Kleer 86] de Kleer, J.: An Assumption Based Truth Maintenance System, AI-Journal 28, No. 2, 1986.

[Doyle 79] Doyle, J.: A Truth Maintenance System, AI-Journal 12, 231- 272, 1979.

[Doyle 83] Doyle, J.: Methodology Simplicity in Expert System Construction: the Case of Reasoned Assumptions, AI-Magazine 4, No. 2, 39-44, 1983.

[Goodwin 82] Goodwin, J.: An Improved Algorithm for Non-Monotonic Dependency Net Update, LITH-MATH-R-82-23, Linjoeping University, 1982.

[McAllester 80] McAllester, D.: An Outlook on Truth Maintenance, MEMO 551, MIT Ai-Lab, 1980.

[Pople 82] Pople, H.: Heuristic Methods for Imposing Structure on Ill-structured Problems, in Szolovits, P., (ed.): Artificial Intelligence in Medicine, AAAS Selected Symposium 51, 1982.

[Puppe 86] Puppe, F.: Hybride Diagnosebewertung, GWAI-86, Informatik Fachberichte 124, Springer, 332-342, 1986.

[Puppe 87a] Puppe, F.: Diagnostisches Problemlösen mit Expertensystemen, Informatik Fachberichte, Springer, 1987.

[Puppe 87b] Puppe, F.: Übersicht über das Diagnostik-Expertensystem-Shell MED2, ACM-Tagung "Expertensysteme 87", Berichte des German Chapter of the ACM 28, Teubner Verlag, 356-375, 1987.

Erweiterungen des Basic ATMS

Oskar Dressler
ZT ZTI INF 3
Siemens
Otto-Hahn-Ring 6
8 München 83
dressler@ztivax.uucp

Zusammenfassung

Truth Maintenance Systeme halten zu jeder Zeit eine konsistente Datenbasis und verarbeiten nicht-monotone Justifications. De Kleers ATMS [de Kleer 86a] berechnet multiple Kontexte simultan, verarbeitet aber nur monotone Justifications. Erst auf höheren Ebenen lassen sich nicht-monotone Justifications und die darauf aufbauenden normal- und non-normal Defaults sowie Negation einführen [de Kleer 86b].
Wir schlagen eine zusätzliche Art von ATMS-Knoten vor und codieren damit nicht-monotone Justifications, normal- und non-normal Defaults sowie Negation schon auf der Ebene des Basic ATMS. Unsere Behandlung von nicht-monotonen Justifications vermeidet einige Probleme, die in Truth Maintenance Systemen vom Doyle'schen Typ auftreten.

1. Einleitung

Bei der Suche in kombinatorischen Räumen wird ein Problemsolver ständig mit Alternativen konfrontiert, die sich ganz oder teilweise ausschließen können. Um weiter arbeiten zu können, muß er sich für eine entscheiden. Das weitere Vorgehen und die dabei erzielten Ergebnisse basieren dann auf dieser Entscheidung. Truth Maintenance Systeme unterstützen solche Prozesse, in dem sie dem Problemsolver anbieten, Abhängigkeiten zwischen den für die Berechnung eines Datums benötigten Daten (Antezedenten) und dem berechneten Datum (Konsequenz) zu verwalten. Der Problemsolver wird z.B. aufgrund von Einträgen a und b in der Datenbasis auf c schließen. Dies kann dem Truth Maintenance System in Form einer sogenannten (monotonen) Justification c ← a,b mitgeteilt werden. Wenn der Problemsolver später eine grundlegende Entscheidung revidiert, kann anhand der eingetragenen Justifications festgestellt werden, welche Einträge in der Datenbasis davon betroffen sind. Führt der Problemsolver z.B. den Schluß

Wenn Peter die 10 Uhr Maschine genommen hat (A) und
der Flug zwei Stunden dauert (b),
dann wird er um 14 Uhr hier sein (c).

aus, dann kann er dem Truth Maintenance System eine Justification c ← A,b übergeben. Dabei ist A eine Annahme, die der Problemsolver einführt, um weiter arbeiten zu können, während b aus anderen Daten hergeleitet sein kann. Ein Problemsolver, der mit der Möglichkeit von Flugzeugentführungen und Streiks rechnet, wird das bei seinem Schluß berücksichtigen.

Wenn Peter die 10 Uhr Maschine genommen hat (A),
der Flug zwei Stunden dauert (b),
das Flugzeug nicht entführt wird (D) und
der Flug nicht von einem Streik betroffen ist (E),
dann wird Peter um 14 Uhr hier sein (c).

Oft basieren Berechnungen eines Problemsolvers also auch auf der Abwesenheit eines Datums. In [de Kleer 77] wird das z.B. auf den ableitenden Prozeß selbst angewendet. Weil ein bestimmtes Datum nicht vorhanden ist, wird versucht, es abzuleiten. Damit auch solche Fälle unterstützt werden, gibt es nicht-monotone Justifications. c ← (A,b) (D,E) vermerkt, daß c nicht nur von der Anwesenheit von A,b in der Datenbasis sondern auch von der gleichzeitigen Abwesenheit von D,E abhängt. (A,b) heißt IN-List, (D,E) OUT-List.
Truth Maintenance Systeme sind in zwei Gruppen einzuteilen, Truth Maintenance Systeme vom Doyle'schen Typ (TMS) und de Kleers Assumption-based Truth Maintenance System (ATMS). Ein TMS versucht, zu jeder Zeit <u>eine</u> konsistente Menge von Daten aus der Menge der überhaupt im System vorhandenen Daten auszuzeichnen (current set of beliefs) und dem Problemsolver zugänglich zu machen. ATMS berechnet <u>alle</u> konsistenten Mengen von Daten im System (multiple Kontexte) simultan. Weiter ist festzustellen, daß TMS nicht-monotone Justifications erlaubt, wogegen ATMS nur monotone Justifications zuläßt. Die wesentliche Idee des ATMS ist das simultane Berechnen multipler Kontexte. Sie sollte sich im Prinzip auch mit nicht-monotonen Justifications realisieren lassen. Es scheint jedoch zunächst so, daß nicht-monotone Justifications multiple Kontexte unmöglich machen, weil sie eine wichtige Eigenschaft (Monotonie der Ableitbarkeit) des Basic ATMS [de Kleer 86a] zerstören. Das Interesse an nicht-monotonen Justifications ist groß, weil es damit möglich wird, Negation sowie normal und non-normal Defaults zu codieren. Deshalb zeigt [de Kleer 86b] eine Möglichkeit auf, wie nicht-monotone Justifications auf höheren Schichten des Systems doch noch eingeführt werden können. Aus Platzgründen kann in diesem Papier nicht auf diese Codierung eingegangen werden.

Im Gegensatz dazu schlagen wir eine Integration nicht-monotoner Justifications schon auf der Ebene des Basic ATMS vor. Dazu wird ein neuer Knotentyp eingeführt (Teil 3.), der dann unmittelbar die Codierung nicht-monotoner Justifications (Teil 4.) sowie die Codierung von Negation, normal und non-normal Defaults (Teil 5.) erlaubt. In Teil 4. wird außerdem dargestellt, daß unsere Codierung einige in TMS auftretende Probleme vermeidet. Zuvor fassen wir in (Teil 2.) die für uns wesentlichen Aspekte des Basic ATMS zusammen.

2. Basic ATMS

Dem Basic ATMS werden vom Problemsolver wie im Falle konventioneller Truth Maintenance Systeme Justifications übergeben, die jeweils festhalten, daß der Problemsolver aufgrund gewisser Antezedenten auf eine Konsequenz geschlossen hat.

$$c \quad \leftarrow \quad a_1,......, a_n$$

Dabei werden den Problemsolver-Daten $(c, a_1,......, a_n)$ sogenannte **ATMS-Knoten** zugeordnet, auf denen das ATMS ausschließlich operiert. Drei Ideen sind nun grundlegend:

- Jeder Knoten wird mit all den Kontexten markiert, in denen der betreffende Knoten gilt. Diese Markierung heißt **Label**.

- Kontexte können durch Mengen von gewissen, ausgezeichneten Knoten, sogenannten Assumptions, eindeutig charakterisiert werden.

Assumptions sind vom Problemsolver bestimmte Knoten, die er anläßlich von Entscheidungen zugunsten einer von mehreren Möglichkeiten einführt. Sie begründen von einer solchen Entscheidung abhängige Knoten und treten selbst nicht als Konsequenz auf. Sie sind deshalb terminale Knoten im Netzwerk der Justifications. Eine Menge von Assumptions heißt **Environment**. Ein Knoten n ist unter einer Menge von Justifications J aus einem Environment E **ableitbar** (E,J ⊢ n), wenn eine Sequenz von Mengen $S_1,...., S_m$ gefunden werden kann, sodaß $E = S_1$, n $\in S_m$ und $\forall i \in \{1,...,m-1\}$: $S_{i+1} = S_i \cup \{Konsequenz(j_k)\}$ gilt, wobei Konsequenz(j_k) die Konsequenz einer Justification $j_k \in J$ ist, deren Antezedenten in S_i liegen [Dressler 86].

Ein Environment wird dann als **inkonsistent** bezeichnet, wenn ein spezieller Knoten, **False**, aus ihm ableitbar ist. Andernfalls ist es **konsistent**. Ein inkonsistentes Environment heißt **Nogood**. Die Menge der aus einem konsistenten Environment ableitbaren Knoten (einschließlich der im Environment enthaltenen !) heißt **Kontext**.

Fassen wir diese drei Ideen zusammen, dann hat jeder Knoten ein Label, das aus einer Menge von (konsistenten) Environments besteht, die jeweils einen Kontext charakterisieren, in dem der betreffende Knoten gilt.
Wird vom Problemsolver eine neue Justification übergeben, dann kann durch Kombination der Label der Antezedenten und Vergleich mit dem bereits existierenden Label des Konsequenz-Knotens sein neues Label berechnet werden. Dabei wird durch eine Schnittoperation die Menge der Kontexte bestimmt, in denen alle Antezedenten gelten, und mit der Menge der Kontexte vereinigt, in denen der Konsequenz-Knoten aufgrund anderer Justifications schon gilt.
Die Effizienz des ATMS gründet nun auf der Monotonie der Ableitbarkeit: wenn ein Environment E einen Knoten ableitet, dann leitet auch jede Obermenge von E diesen Knoten ab. Deshalb braucht das Label eines ATMS-Knotens nur minimale Environments zu enthalten. Aus dem gleichen Grund sind Obermengen von Nogoods ebenfalls Nogoods.

3. OUT-Assumptions

Wenn man den oben definierten Begriff der Ableitbarkeit auf nicht-monotone Justifications erweitert (kein Element der OUT-List einer der beteiligten Justifications darf in S_m liegen), dann wird die Monotonie der Ableitbarkeit zerstört. Weil nicht-monotone Justifications Abhängigkeiten formulieren, die auf der Abwesenheit von Knoten in Kontexten beruhen, können durch Hinzufügen weiterer Assumptions zu einem Environment nun gerade solche Knoten ableitbar werden, auf deren Abwesenheit man gebaut hat. D.h. nicht jede konsistente Obermenge eines konsistenten Environments, das einen bestimmten Knoten ableiten kann, kann ebenfalls diesen Knoten ableiten. Wenn wir im anfangs benutzten Beispiel lediglich annehmen, daß *Peter die 10 Uhr Maschine genommen hat*, dann können wir ableiten, daß *er um 14 Uhr hier sein wird*. Wenn wir zusätzlich annehmen, daß *das Flugzeug entführt wird*, dann können wir dessen nicht mehr sicher sein. Die Annahmen, daß *Peter die 10 Uhr Maschine genommen hat*, und daß *das Flugzeug entführt wird*, sind zwar durchaus miteinander verträglich (wir könnten daraus evtl. ableiten, daß er auf dem Weg nach Sydney ist; es besteht also kein Anlaß, sie zusammen zum Nogood zu machen). Aber obwohl wir eine konsistente Obermenge haben, ist die Konsequenz nicht mehr ableitbar.

Zusätzlich zum in [de Kleer 86a] beschriebenen Sprachumfang führen wir eine schwache Form von Negation ein. Wenn ein Knoten ¬a eingetragen wird, so wird - sobald a vom Problemsolver eingeführt wird oder schon war - eine Justification False ← a,¬a eingetragen.
Bei der Gültigkeit eines Knotens a bezüglich eines Kontextes C unterscheiden wir drei Fälle:

1.   a   ∈ C   dann gilt   ¬a   ∉ C

2.   ¬a ∈ C   dann gilt   a   ∉ C

3.   weder a noch ¬a gelten im Kontext C

Damit beachtet das System zwar ¬ (a ∧ ¬a) jedoch nicht a ∨ ¬a .

Definieren wir nun zwei (Meta-) Prädikate. Bezüglich eines Kontextes C gilt:

IN(a)   ⇔   a   ∈ C

OUT(a)   ⇔   ¬a ∈ C <u>oder</u> weder a noch ¬a gelten in C

Die Aussage OUT(a) können wir dann mit einem ATMS-Knoten unterlegen. Dieser Knoten wäre sinnvollerweise mit einem Label auszustatten, das alle Kontexte charakterisiert, in denen a <u>nicht</u> gilt. Wir werden das Label von OUT(a) nie tatsächlich berechnen. Denn wir haben eine sehr einfache Möglichkeit festzustellen, ob OUT(a) in einem bestimmten Kontext gilt: Dazu brauchen wir nur das Label von a (soweit überhaupt vorhanden) zu untersuchen.

Wenn wir OUT(a) nun wie einen gewöhnlichen ATMS-Knoten (mit einem Label) behandeln, treten Schwierigkeiten auf. Zum einen wollen wir das Label von OUT(a) gar nicht explizit berechnen. Zum anderen ändert sich das Label von OUT(a) nicht nur durch Hinzufügen neuer Kontexte und bei Entdeckung relevanter Nogoods, sondern auch bei jeder Änderung des Labels von a. Würden wir also das Label von OUT(a) bei der Berechnung des Labels der Konjunktion von Antezedenten einer Justification benutzen, so würden in das Label des Konsequenz-Knoten möglicherweise Environments aufgenommen werden, von denen wir erst später erfahren, daß sie nicht für OUT(a) gelten. Wären z.B. in die Berechnung eines Labels für einen Knoten c Environments eingegangen, die von einem Knoten OUT(a) herstammen, dann kann durch Hinzufügen weiterer Assumptions zu einem dieser Environments a ableitbar werden. Dann gilt OUT(a) nicht in dem neuentstandenen Environment und damit auch c nicht. Ebenso wie bei der naiven Einführung nicht-monotoner Justifications ginge die für die Effizienz so wesentliche Monotonie der Ableitbarkeit verloren.

Die Alternative, nun alle Environments in die Label aufzunehmen, die Kontexte charakterisieren, in denen der betreffende Knoten gilt, kommt nicht in Betracht. Schon für kleine Anzahlen von Assumptions wäre die Anzahl der relevanten Environments zu groß. Allein um die Label von a und OUT(a) darzustellen, bräuchte man $2^{\text{Anzahl Assumptions}}$ Environments.

Wenden wir uns nun unserer Lösung zu. Statt OUT(a) wie einen ganz normalen Knoten zu behandeln, interpretieren wir OUT(a) als eine (Meta-) Assumption. Wir machen damit die Annahme, daß a nicht ableitbar ist. Das mag je nach Kontext wahr oder falsch sein. Wir wissen es nicht, deswegen ist es eine Annahme, die später ungültig werden kann. OUT(..) nennen wir **OUT-Assumption**. Eine OUT-Assumption verhält sich bei der Berechnung von Labels wie eine Assumption. Insbesondere ist sie nicht Konsequenz einer Justification.

Mit den Mechanismen des Basic ATMS sind wir in der Lage, die Kontexte, in denen OUT(a) gilt, von denen zu trennen, in denen IN(a) (oder kürzer a) gilt:

$$\text{False} \quad \leftarrow \quad a \, , \, \text{OUT}\,(a)$$

Jedes Environment im Label von a ergibt vereinigt mit der Assumption OUT(a) einen Nogood.

Es sind bisher keine schwerwiegenden Eingriffe in das ATMS erfolgt; der Ableitbarkeitsbegriff wird in naheliegender Weise erweitert (aus ¬a kann OUT(a) abgeleitet werden). Deshalb treten auch keine Probleme auf, die nicht auch im Basic ATMS auftreten würden. Daß durch unsere Interpretation einige Assumptions als OUT-Assumptions angesehen werden, führt jedoch eine neue Qualität von Abhängigkeit ein. Darauf geht der folgende Abschnitt ein.

Logische Unabhängigkeit von Assumptions

Assumptions im Sinne des Basic ATMS sind *logisch voneinander unabhängig*. Aus dem Vorhanden- oder Nicht-Vorhandensein der einen kann nicht auf das Vorhandensein der anderen geschlossen werden. Assumptions sind terminale Knoten im Netzwerk der Justifications. Wären sie logisch voneinander abhängig, dann könnte ihre Abhängigkeit analysiert und als eine Menge von Justifications eingetragen werden. Die logisch abhängigen sind damit ganz normale Knoten. Eine Menge von logisch unabhängigen Assumptions charakterisiert eine Welt (= Kontext).

Komplikationen mit OUT-Assumptions

Die Einführung von OUT-Assumptions verletzt die Auffassung von den Assumptions als logisch voneinander unabhängigen Aussagen.

OUT-Assumptions können auf verschiedene Weisen von den anderen Assumptions in einem Environment abhängen.

Sei $E = \{A,B,...,OUT(b_i),....\}$ ein Environment. Wir unterscheiden die Fälle:

1. $E \setminus \{OUT(b_i)\}$ kann b_i ableiten. Wegen $b_i, OUT(b_i) \rightarrow$ False ist E dann ein Nogood.

2. $E \setminus \{OUT(b_i)\}$ kann $\neg b_i$ und damit $OUT(b_i)$ ableiten. Das Environment E beschreibt dann den gleichen Kontext wie $E \setminus \{OUT(b_i)\}$ und kann deshalb durch dieses ersetzt werden (Minimalisierung).

3. $E \setminus \{OUT(b_i)\}$ kann weder b_i noch $\neg b_i$ ableiten. $E \setminus \{OUT(b_i)\}$ leitet $OUT(b_i)$ in einem anderen Sinne ab. Wir schreiben dafür $|\sim$. Ein Environment leitet einen Knoten $OUT(b_i)$ in diesem Sinn ab, wenn es nicht möglich ist, b_i im herkömmlichen Sinne abzuleiten. Wir könnten das mit *Negation as failure* vergleichen. E darf nicht durch $E \setminus \{OUT(b_i)\}$ ersetzt werden, weil durch Hinzufügen von Justifications b_i ableitbar werden könnte. Dann ist E ein Nogood, während $E \setminus \{OUT(b_i)\}$ durchaus noch konsistent sein kann.

Anhand der Label von b_i bzw. $\neg b_i$ lassen sich alle drei Fälle unterscheiden.

Nogoods

Wenden wir nun unser Wissen über mögliche logische Abhängigkeiten bei Vorhandensein von OUT-Assumptions auf Nogoods an. Generell unterscheiden wir folgende Fälle.

1. Wie im Basic ATMS gilt, daß alle Obermengen von Nogoods selbst wieder Nogoods sind. Das gilt auch, wenn logisch abhängige Assumptions zu einem Nogood hinzugefügt werden.

2. Durch logisch abhängige Assumptions gibt es zusätzlich die Möglichkeit, daß Untermengen eines Nogoods auch als Nogoods identifiziert werden können. Entsprechend der drei verschiedenen Arten von logischer Abhängigkeit sind folgende Fälle zu unterscheiden.

    Sei $E = \{A_1,....,A_n, OUT(b_1),..., OUT(b_n)\}$ ein Nogood.

    2.1 Wenn $E \setminus \{OUT(b_i)\}$ b_j ableitet $(i \neq j)$,
    dann ist $E \setminus \{OUT(b_i)\}$ ein Nogood wegen False $\leftarrow OUT(b_j), b_j$.

    2.2 Wenn $E \setminus \{OUT(b_i)\}$ $\neg b_i$ ableitet,
    dann ist $E \setminus \{OUT(b_i)\}$ ein Nogood, weil $OUT(b_i)$ logisch abhängig ist. $E \setminus \{OUT(b_i)\}$ leitet zunächst $OUT(b_i)$ und dann (nach Voraussetzung) False ab.

    2.3 Wenn $E \setminus \{OUT(b_i)\}$ weder b_i noch $\neg b_i$ ableitet, d.h. $OUT(b_i)$ wird im zweiten Sinne $(|\sim)$ abgeleitet,
    dann führt die gleiche Überlegung wie bei 2.2 dazu, daß $E \setminus \{OUT(b_i)\}$ ein Nogood ist.

Wenn OUT-Assumptions an einem Nogood beteiligt sind, können wir also unter bestimmten Umständen auf kleinere Nogoods schließen. Der Fall 2.3 ist jedoch mit Vorsicht zu behandeln, wogegen 2.1 schon vom bisherigen Basic ATMS erkannt wird und 2.2 durch eine geringfügige Erweiterung realisiert werden kann. Wenn nämlich $E \setminus \{OUT(b_i)\}$ im Fall 2.1 b_j ableitet, dann gibt es im Label von b_j ein Environment, das $E \setminus \{OUT(b_i)\}$ subsumiert. Bei Kombination mit $OUT(b_j)$ anläßlich der Einführung der

Justification False ← OUT(b_i), b_i entsteht ein Nogood, der Teilmenge von E \ {OUT(b_i)} ist. Damit wird E \ {OUT(b_i)} schon gemäß Fall 1. als Nogood erkannt. Im Fall 2.2 beschreiben die Environments E und E \ {OUT(b_i)} den gleichen Kontext, weil OUT(b_i) logisch abhängig ist. Dies kann bei der Minimalisierung der Label berücksichtigt werden. Während wir in allen anderen Fällen wissen, daß die erschlossenen Nogoods durch Hinzufügen von Justifications stets Nogoods bleiben werden, ist dies bei 2.3 nicht der Fall. Durch Hinzufügen einer Justification kann aus E \ {OUT(b_i)} b_i ableitbar werden, womit dann OUT(b_i) nicht mehr ableitbar ($\nvdash$) wäre. Eine Implementierung wird dieser Überlegung durch eine separate Nogood Database Rechnung tragen. Für alle Obermengen von Nogoods in der bisherigen Nogood Database gilt weiterhin, daß sie Nogoods sind und stets bleiben werden. Für die Elemente in der separaten Nogood Database gilt, daß sie nur im augenblicklichen Zustand des Systems mit Sicherheit Nogoods darstellen.

Gültigkeit eines Knotens in einem Kontext

Die Frage, ob ein Knoten a in einem Kontext gilt, der durch ein Environment E charakterisiert ist, wird im Basic ATMS dadurch entschieden, daß im Label von a nach einem Environment E' gesucht wird, für das E' ⊆ E gilt. Durch die mögliche logische Abhängigkeit von OUT-Assumptions können, wie oben dargestellt, unterschiedliche Environments gleiche Kontexte beschreiben. Dabei war je nach Art der Ableitung ($\vdash$ bzw. $\nvdash$) zu unterscheiden, ob minimalisiert werden darf oder nicht. Wir müssen deshalb in Betracht ziehen, daß im Label von a Environments enthalten sein können, die zum Zeitpunkt der Anfrage die gleichen Kontexte charakterisieren wie Environments, die weniger OUT-Assumptions enthalten. Um zu entscheiden, ob der Knoten im fraglichen Kontext gilt, muß man im Label von a ein Environment E' finden (d.h. E' $\vdash$ a), aus dem man schließen kann, daß a aus E ableitbar ist. Im folgenden sollen die Indizes i und o an Environment-Namen die Mengen der IN- bzw. OUT-Assumptions bezeichnen, z.B. E = E_i ∪ E_o und E' = E_i' ∪ E_o'. Es muß E_i' ⊆ E_i gelten, denn IN-Assumptions können nicht abgeleitet werden. Die fehlenden OUT-Assumptions E_o' \ E_o müssen aus E ableitbar sein. Das ist, wie der folgende Satz zeigt, genau dann der Fall, wenn E ∪ (E_o' \ E_o) konsistent ist. Wenden wir dieses Kriterium auf alle Environments im Label des Knotens a an, so können wir in einfacher Weise feststellen, ob a im durch E charakterisierten Kontext enthalten ist.

Satz: Sei E = E_i ∪ E_{o_1} ∪ E_{o_2}, E_i die Menge der IN-Assumptions in E , E_{o_1} ∪ E_{o_2} die Menge der OUT-Assumptions in E, E_{o_1} ∩ E_{o_2} = ∅, E_{o_2} = {OUT(b_1), ... , OUT(b_m)} die fehlenden OUT-Assumptions und E_i ∪ E_{o_1} konsistent. Es gilt: E_i ∪ E_{o_1} und E_i ∪ E_{o_1} ∪ E_{o_2} charakterisieren genau dann den gleichen Kontext, wenn E_i ∪ E_{o_1} ∪ E_{o_2} konsistent ist.

Beweis: (=>) Wenn E_i ∪ E_{o_1} und E_i ∪ E_{o_1} ∪ E_{o_2} den gleichen Kontext charakterisieren, dann können die Elemente von E_{o_2} aus E_i ∪ E_{o_1} abgeleitet werden. Könnte E_i ∪ E_{o_1} ∪ E_{o_2} False ableiten, dann auch E_i ∪ E_{o_1}, was ein Widerspruch zur Voraussetzung wäre. Also ist E_i ∪ E_{o_1} ∪ E_{o_2} konsistent.
(<=) Wenn E_i ∪ E_{o_1} ∪ E_{o_2} konsistent ist, ist keines der b_i aus E_i ∪ E_{o_1} ∪ E_{o_2} ableitbar, insbesondere auch nicht aus E_i ∪ E_{o_1}. Also sind die OUT(b_i) aus E_i ∪ E_{o_1} ableitbar. Damit charakterisieren E_i ∪ E_{o_1} und E_i ∪ E_{o_1} ∪ E_{o_2} die gleichen Kontexte.

Wir können nun dazu übergehen, die Codierungen für non-monotonic Justifications, normal und non-normal Defaults sowie Negation anzugeben. Bei den folgenden Darstellungen nehmen wir an, daß das System die Justification False ← OUT(a),a ohne explizite Aufforderung einträgt. Eine Implementierung wird diese Justification ebenso wie False ← ¬a,a gesondert behandeln. Es entstehen nämlich Nogoods, deren vorrangige Behandlung aus Effizienzgründen geboten ist.

4.   Non-monotonic Justifications

Eine nicht-monotone Justification enthält eine aus zwei Teilen bestehende Antezedentenliste, IN-List und OUT-List.

$$c \quad \leftarrow SL \quad (a_1,.....,a_n)(b_1,.....,b_m)$$

..the support-list justification ... is valid if and only if each node in its inlist is IN, and each node in its OUT-list is OUT [Doyle 79]. Bezogen auf die ATMS-Terminologie heißt das, daß der Knoten c in all den Kontexten gilt, in denen $a_1,....,a_n$ ableitbar (IN) und $b_1,....,b_m$ nicht ableitbar (OUT) sind.

Wenn wir die obige SL-Justification in die folgende Menge von Justifications transformieren, erreichen wir genau diesen Effekt.

$$(1.1) \quad b \leftarrow b_1$$
$$....$$
$$(1.m) \quad b \leftarrow b_m$$
$$(2.) \quad c \leftarrow a_1,....,a_n,OUT(b)$$

Der neu erzeugte Knoten b gilt in all den Kontexten, in denen mindestens einer der Knoten $b_1,....,b_m$ gilt. Der Knoten OUT(b) gilt dann in all den Kontexten, in denen b nicht gilt. Durch die Konjunktion dieses Knotens mit den Knoten der IN-List erreichen wir, daß c in all den Kontexten gilt, in denen $a_1,....,a_n$ gelten und außerdem OUT(b) gilt.

Diese Codierung von non-monotonic Justifications ist simpler als die in [de Kleer 86b] angegebene. Sie hat darüberhinaus den Vorteil, daß sie unmittelbar in das Basic ATMS integriert werden kann.

Sehen wir uns nun einige Beispiele an. Aus [Goodwin 82] übernehmen wir die folgende graphische Notation.

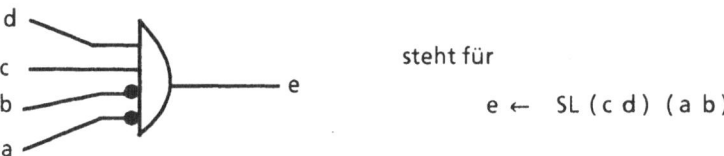

steht für

$$e \leftarrow SL(c\ d)(a\ b)$$

Odd Loops

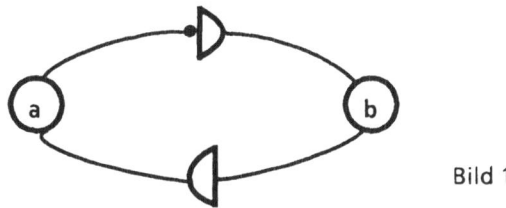

Bild 1

Odd Loops sind Schleifen von Justifications, bei denen eine ungerade Anzahl von nicht-monotonen Justifications durchlaufen werden muß, um wieder am Startpunkt anzukommen. Doyles TMS [Doyle 79] reagiert auf odd Loops mit einer nicht terminierenden Programmschleife. [Goodwin 82] vermeidet diesen Effekt.

Odd Loops stellen jedoch logischen Unsinn dar [Charniak 80], wenn die Gültigkeit der beteiligten Justifications verlangt wird. Im obigen Beispiel ist a aus b (im Sinne von TMS) ableitbar, was wiederum dazu führt, daß b nicht ableitbar ist. Umgekehrt ist b ableitbar, weil a nicht ableitbar ist, was dazu führt, daß a nun doch ableitbar ist.

Ein Kontext, in dem diese Odd Loop gilt, müßte sowohl a,b als auch OUT(a),OUT(b) enthalten. Durch False ← a,OUT(a) und False ← b,OUT(b) schließen wir das aus. Es verwundert daher nicht, wenn jeder Kontext, der eine Odd Loop mit gültigen Justifications enthält, inkonsistent wird:

Die SL-Justifications

$$
\begin{array}{lll}
\text{(a)} & a \leftarrow SL \ (\,b\,) \ (\,) \\
\text{(b)} & b \leftarrow SL \ (\,) \quad (\,a\,)
\end{array}
$$

werden nach

$$
\begin{array}{ll}
\text{(a.1)} & a \leftarrow b \\
\text{(b.1)} & a' \leftarrow a \\
\text{(b.2)} & b \leftarrow OUT(a') \quad \text{transformiert.}
\end{array}
$$

Zu Anfang gilt: Label(a) = Label(b) = ∅. Die endgültigen Label von a und b erhalten wir in folgenden Schritten:

$$
\begin{array}{lll}
\text{(a.1)} & \text{Label(a)} = \varnothing & \text{wegen Label(b)} = \varnothing \\
\text{(b.1)} & \text{Label(a')} = \varnothing \\
\text{(b.2)} & \text{Label(b)} = \{\{OUT(a')\}\} \\
\text{(a.1)} & \text{Label(a)} = \{\{OUT(a')\}\} \\
\text{(b.1)} & \text{Label(a')} = \{\{OUT(a')\}\}
\end{array}
$$

Wegen   False ← a',OUT (a')

ist   {OUT(a')}   ein Nogood.

OUT(a') muß deshalb aus Label(a), Label(a') und Label(b) entfernt werden.

Even Loops

Even Loops führen in konventionellen TMS zwar nicht zu Endlosschleifen. Es gibt jedoch einen anderen unerwünschten Effekt. Wenn Netze auf unterschiedliche Weise konsistent markiert werden können, so wird zwar eine konsistente Markierung gefunden, welche Markierung gewählt wird, bleibt aber dem Zufall überlassen [Doyle 79]. Bestenfalls [Goodwin 82] erkennt das System die Möglichkeit mehrfacher konsistenter Belegungen und wirft dann den Groschen.

Diese Systeme schaffen keine Basis, um über multiple Extensionen einer innerhalb einer nicht-monotonen Logik gegebenen Menge von Axiomen zu reden, und sind nicht in der Lage, diese zu identifizieren [Doyle 79] und kontrolliert zu selektieren [Goodwin 82].

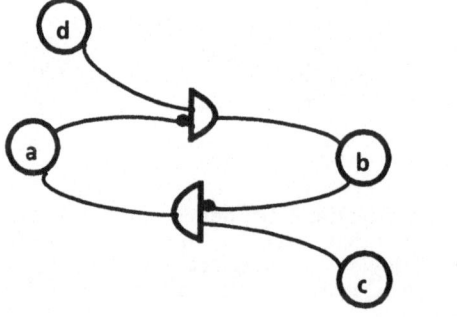

Bild 2

Das Beispiel in Bild 2 wird verdeutlichen. wie unsere Codierung von non-monotonic Justifications dazu führt, daß multiple Extensionen (d.h. maximale Kontexte) auseinander gehalten werden. Nehmen wir an, daß c und d in einem gemeinsamen Kontext, der durch {X,Y} charakterisiert sei, gelten.

Die beiden SL-Justifications

$$b \leftarrow \quad SL \quad (d) \quad (a)$$
$$a \leftarrow \quad SL \quad (c) \quad (b)$$

werden nach

$$a' \leftarrow \quad a$$
$$b \leftarrow \quad d, OUT(a')$$
$$b' \leftarrow \quad b$$
$$a \leftarrow \quad c, OUT(b') \qquad \text{transformiert.}$$

Ausgehend von Label(c) = Label(d) = {X,Y} erhalten wir für das Label von a {{X,Y,OUT(b')}}, für b das Label {{X,Y,OUT(a')}}. Damit sind die beiden möglichen Markierungen als verschiedene Kontexte erkannt worden. Dem Problemsolver sind deshalb anders als bei konventionellen TMS beide Kontexte zugänglich.

5.   Negation, normal und non-normal Default

Negation

Wenn wir wollen, daß a $\vee$ $\neg$a in unserem System beachtet wird, so können wir den anfangs unterschiedenen Fall, daß weder a noch $\neg$a in einem (maximalen) Kontext gelten, durch

$$\neg a \leftarrow OUT(a) \qquad \text{und}$$
$$a \leftarrow OUT(\neg a)$$

eliminieren .

$$a \quad \leftarrow \quad SL \quad () \quad (\neg a)$$
$$\neg a \quad \leftarrow \quad SL \quad () \quad (a)$$

erzielt das gleiche Ergebnis.

Normal- und non-normal Defaults

De Kleer codiert Reiters normal Default [Reiter 80] $\dfrac{a : Mn}{n}$

durch $n \quad \leftarrow \quad a, N'$

wobei N' die Aussage "Es ist konsistent, n anzunehmen" darstellt.

Der non-normal Default $\dfrac{a : Mb}{c}$

ist dann in Analogie zur Codierung von SL-Justifications schon wesentlich aufwendiger.

Wir codieren die beiden Default-Typen durch

$$n \quad \leftarrow \quad a, OUT(\neg n)$$
$$c \quad \leftarrow \quad a, OUT(\neg b)$$

OUT($\neg$n) drückt aus, daß entweder n gilt oder weder n noch $\neg$n gelten.

Zusammenfassung

Wir haben gezeigt, daß in das Basic ATMS ein neuer Knotentyp (OUT-Assumption) eingeführt werden kann, der die Codierung von nicht-monotonen Justifications auf der Ebene des Basic ATMS erlaubt. Mit dem gleichen Knoten-Typ lassen sich auch Negation, normal und non-normal Defaults realisieren.

Dank

Ich danke Jutta Estenfeld, Hartmut Freitag, Michael Reinfrank und besonders Peter Struß für Diskussionen sowie zahlreiche Korrekturen und inhaltliche Verbesserungen früherer Versionen dieses Papiers.

Literatur

[Charniak 80]   Charniak, E.; McDermott, D.; Riesbeck, C
                Artificial Intelligence Programming Chapter 16
                Lawrence Earlbaum Ass., New Jersey, 1980

[de Kleer 77]   de Kleer,J.; Doyle,J.; Sussman,G.
                AMORD: Explicit Control of Reasoning
                SIGART Newsletter, No. 64 August 1977, 116-125

[de Kleer 86a] de Kleer,J.   An Assumption-based TMS
                Artificial Intelligence 28(1986) 127-162

[de Kleer 86b] de Kleer,J.   Extending the TMS
                Artificial Intelligence 28(1986) 163-196

[Doyle 79]   Doyle,J.   A Truth Maintenance System
                Artificial Intelligence 12 (1979) 231-272

[Dressler 86]   Dressler, O. Assumption-based Truth Maintenance
                Siemens Labor-Bericht, erscheint in
                Stoyan,H. Proceedings TMS-Workshop Berlin Okt. 1986

[Goodwin 82]   Goodwin,J. An Improved Algorithm for Non-Monotonic Dependency Net
                Update
                LITH-MAT-R-82-23, Linjoeping University Aug. 1982

[Reiter 80]   Reiter,R. A Logic for Default Reasoning
                Artificial Intelligence 13 (1980) Special Issue on Non-Monotonic Reasoning
                81-132

OLDY BUT GOODY
PARAMODULATION REVISITED

Ulrich Furbach

Universität der Bundeswehr München

INTRODUCTION

This short note is aiming at a justification of a statement which seems to be a folklore theorem: Almost everyone asked about "the completeness of input resolution and paramodulation for Horn clauses" is spontaneously affirming, however, wihout beeing able to give a proof or at least a reference.

This is amazing because of the tremendeous interest in Horn clause logic and input resolution, set up by the success of the logic programming idea since the middle of the 70th. Of course there is a lot of interest in this area in handling equality, and there do exist numereous formalisms for the treatment of equational theories within logic programming, e.g. narrowing, superposition or surreduction (c.f. Bellia, Levi 86 or Jaffar et al. 84). However the paramodulation rule, although a well known mechanism in resolution-like theorem proving, has been discarded in logic programming. This is obviously because of efficiency reasons, but we see at least a theoretical interest in completeness results concerning paramodulation.

Another reason for this work is to provide a basis for a convenient semantic description for an interface between logic and functional programming languages. Elsewhere we proved that equality can be used in an elegant way to model the combination of logic and functional programming languages (c.f. Furbach, Hölldobler 86); however being not aware of a completeness result of input resolution and paramodulation for Horn clauses we had to use resolution together with the axioms of equality, instead of the paramodulation rule. With the result of this paper it will be possible to redefine the semantics of such a combined language being much more closer at an operational level, without narrowing the class of models (which is the case with narrowing and many other approaches).

In the following section some known results from the literature are discussed. It will become obvious that a completeness theorem for paramodulation does exist, however in a form, where factoring is necessary. In the originate section of this paper we prove that factoring can be omitted without loosing completeness.

The reader is assumed to be familiar with the basic notations and definitions of theorem proving (c.f. Chang and Lee 73). Readers interested in logic programming are refered to Furbach et al. 87, where the results of this paper are presented within the framework of the theory of logic programming.

COMPLETENESS WITH FACTORING

In this paper resolution is assumed to be binary, i.e. factoring is treated as an extra inference rule: If two or more literals (with the same sign) of a clause C have a most general unifier σ, then $C\sigma$ is a <u>factor of</u> C.

Besides resolution and factoring we need paramodulation as a third inference rule: Let C_1 and C_2 be two clauses with no variables in common, such that C_1 is $L[t] \vee C_1'$ and C_2 is $r=s \vee C_2'$, where $L[t]$ denotes a literal containing t at a particular position. If t and r have a mgu σ then infer

$$L\sigma[s\sigma] \cup C_1'\sigma \cup C_2'\sigma$$

where $L\sigma[s\sigma]$ denotes the result obtained by replacing the occurrence of $t\sigma$ in $L\sigma$ by $s\sigma$. The above infered clause is called <u>a (binary) paramodulant</u>.

<u>An input deduction</u> of a clause A with respect to a set S of clauses and a set of inference rules Ω is a deduction $D_1,..., D_n=A$, such that if D_i is obtained by application of a rule from Ω different from factoring, then at least one of the parents of D_i is a member of S or , if factoring is contained in Ω, a factor of a member of S .

In the above defintion we implicitly assumed binary inference rules with the only exception of factoring. We depict input deductions as usual in the form $D_0, \dots , D_n$ where D_i is from S or it is obtained either from D_{i-1} by factoring or from D_{i-1} and D_{i-2} by application of a binary rule from Ω. In the latter case we will assume without loss of generality, that D_{i-1} is the input (resp. a factor of the input) clause. Note that in the above definition factoring of an input clause as well as factoring of "center clauses" is allowed. In (Henschen, Wos 74) this defintion is formulated, such that one is not sure weather factoring on center clauses is possible. To make things explicit we include it in the definition and will prove later that it can be eliminated without loosing completeness in the case of resolution and paramodulation. (By the way in (Noll 76) there is an interpretation of Henschen and Wos which does not allow factoring on center clauses.)

In the following we explicitly denote the inference system in writing curly brackets and the obvious abbreviations R, P and F for resolution, paramodulation and factoring.

If paramodulation is not employed, Henschen and Wos have shown that the completeness result of input resolution for Horn clauses holds without factoring.

THEOREM 1 (Theorem 2 in (Henschen, Wos 74)) : *If S is an unsatisfiable set of Horn clauses, then there exists an input refutation with respect to {R}.*

A similar theorem for resolution and paramodulation is given by Henschen and Wos only for the case where factoring is present:

THEOREM 2(Theorem 3 in (Henschen, Wos 74)) : *If S is an E-unsatisfiable set of Horn clauses containing x=x and its functional reflexive axioms, then there exists an input refutation D_1 and a unit refutation D_2 with respect to $\{R,P,F\}$.*

For the proof of this theorem, as given by Henschen and Wos the presence of factoring is essential. This is because they first show that a T-supported refutation D_1 exists, where T is the set of negative literals from S. From this they conclude that D_1 is an input deduction and hence the first part of the theorem is proven. To show the second half they use a theorem from (Chang, Slagle 71), which ensures the existence of a unit refutation. This theorem, however, is only applicable if factoring is present.

The above theorems are primarily aiming at conditions for the existence of unit refutations, which are decidable by inspection (obviously this is the case with the property of being Horn in the case of finite sets of clauses). In the field of theorem proving unit deductions are of interest , because unit resolution provides a means for progressing rapidly towards shorter clauses. In logic programming, however, we usually assume Horn clauses and hence always can use an input strategy for processing Horn clause logic programs (in Yamasaki et al. 84 this aspect is discussed further, together with an inference strategie which combines input and unit resolution). For obvious efficiency reasons we are interested in completeness results where factoring is not involved. In the following we therefore prove that factoring is unnecessary, even if we use paramodulation.

ELIMINATION OF FACTORING

In the following lemma we show, that factoring of center clauses as well as factoring of input clauses can be eliminated. This is, with respect to paramodulation, an extension of lemma 2 given in (Henschen, Wos 74).

LEMMA 3: *If S is a set of Horn clauses and D an input deduction of a clause A with respect to $\{R,P,F\}$, then there exists an input deduction E of a clause B with respect to $\{R,P\}$, such that B subsumes A.*

Proof : The proof of the lemma proceeds in two steps: First we give a transformation of the input deduction D into a deduction E, where factoring is not used. In parallel we construct for each literal in a clause from D a set of corresponding literals in the respective clause from E. In a second step we prove the conclusion by an induction on the length of D.

Transformation : Let $D = D_0, D_1, ..., D_{i-1}, A (=D_i)$ be an input deduction. We now construct a deduction E of B where factoring is not used, by giving an induction on the length of D.

If $i = 0$ then $D_0 = A$; set $E_0 = D_0 = B$. The corresponding literal in E_0 of a literal M in D_0 is the literal M.

If $i > 0$ and D_i is obtained by factoring from D_{i-1}: Set $E_i = E_{i-1}$ and let the set of literals in E_i corresponding to a literal L in D_i be the set $M = M_1 \cup ... \cup M_m$ of literals in E_{i-1} such that M_j is the set of literals in E_{i-1} corresponding to a literal L_i in D_{i-1} and L_i is mapped onto L by factorisation. Note that from this step there result consecutive identical clauses E_i and E_{i-1}. This is necessary for the construction of corresponding sets of literals. At the end of the proof these superfluous clauses will be removed to yield an input deduction.

If $i > 0$ and D_i is obtained by an inference rule different from factoring we distinguish two cases: If D_{i-1} is an unfactored input clause set $E_{i-1} = D_{i-1}$ and let the set of literals in E_{i-1} corresponding to a literal M in D_{i-1} be the singelton M. If factoring is present, E_{i-1} is the input clause of which D_{i-1} is a factor of. The set of literals in E_{i-1} corresponding to a Literal L in D_{i-1} is the set $M = \{M_1,...,M_l\}$ of literals in E_{i-1} such that $M_j \theta = L$, where θ is the mgu used for the factoring of the input clause.

Let M be the literal in D_{i-2} which is manipulated in this deduction step (resolution or paramodulation). The corresponding set of literals in E_{i-2} is $M' = \{M_1,...M_l\}$. Let K be the positive literal in D_{i-1} and K' the corresponding literal in E_{i-1} (note that there is only one, since with Hornclauses factoring with positive Literals cannot occur). Let F_1 be a resolvent (paramodulant) of E_{i-2} and E_{i-1} where the literal M_1 is manipulated using K', F_2 a resolvent (paramodulant) of F_1 and E_{i-1} where the descendant of M_2 is manipulated using K', ... , F_p a resolvent (paramodulant) of F_{p-1} and E_{i-1}, where the descendant of M_l is manipulated using K'. Set E_i to F_p and let the set of literals in E_i corresponding to a literal L in D_i be $L_0 \cup ... \cup L_p$, where L_0 is the set of literals in E_{i-2} corresponding to L' in D_{i-2} and L' is mapped onto L in the deduction step. We have p new deduction steps and therefore p sets L_q ($1 \leqslant q \leqslant p$), where L_q is the set of literals in E_{i-1} corresponding to a literal L'' in D_{i-1} and L'' is mapped onto L in the appropriate new deduction step. This completes the first part of the proof.

Subsumption: It remains to show that B subsumes A, i.e. $\exists \lambda : B\lambda \subseteq A$. Again we give an induction on the length of D.

For $i=0$ we see immediately that $D_0 = A$ and $E_0 = B$ and hence the conclusion holds. If $i>0$ and if D_i was obtained by factoring the result is trivial. For the remaining cases assume M to be the negative literal manipulated in D_{i-2} and K to be the positive literal in D_{i-1} and θ the mgu of this deduction step. From the induction assumption we conclude:

$$\exists \alpha_{i-1} \exists \alpha_{i-2} : \quad E_{i-1}\alpha_{i-1} \subseteq D_{i-1}$$
$$E_{i-2} \alpha_{i-2} \subseteq D_{i-2} \quad , \text{ such that } \alpha_{i-1} \text{ and } \alpha_{i-2} \text{ are most general}$$

Let $E_{i-1}(1), ..., E_{i-1}(p)$ be the p copies of E_{i-1}, which were used in the p extra deduction steps in E and $K'_{(j)}$ the copy of K' in $E_{i-1(j)}$ for $1 \leq j \leq p$. Obviously there exist substitutions $\alpha_{i-1(j)}$, such that

$$E_{i-1(j)} \; \alpha_{i-1(j)} \subseteq D_{i-1}$$

then $\quad \beta = \alpha_{i-2} \cup (\underset{j}{\cup} \alpha_{i-1(j)})$ is a most general substitution, such that

$$E_{i-2}\beta \subseteq D_{i-2} \quad \text{and}$$
$$E_{i-1(j)}\beta \subseteq D_{i-1} \quad \text{for all } 1 \leq j \leq p.$$

Let $M' = \{M_1,...,M_p\}$ be the set of literals in E_{i-2} which correspond to M in D_{i-2}. We now consider two cases:

a) The deduction step is a resolution step. Then D_i has the following form:

$$D_i = (\; (D_{i-2} - M) \; \cup (D_{i-1} - K) \;) \; \theta$$

and hence $\beta\theta$ is a unifier of M' and $\{ K'_{(j)} \mid 1 \leq j \leq p \}$. If δ is a mgu of these two sets, we get with $\beta\theta = \delta\lambda$:

$$E_i \subseteq (\; (E_{i-2} - M') \cup \underset{j}{(}\cup(E_{i-1(j)} - K'_{(j)})\;) \;) \; \delta$$

$$E_i\lambda \subseteq (\; (E_{i-2} - M') \cup \underset{j}{(}\cup(E_{i-1(j)} - K'_{(j)})\;) \;) \; \delta\lambda$$

$$= (\; (E_{i-2} - M')_j\cup (\cup(E_{i-1(j)} - K'_{(j)})\;) \;)\beta\theta$$

$$\subseteq (\; (D_{i-2} - M) \cup (D_{i-1} - K) \;) \; \theta$$

$$= D_i.$$

b) The deduction step is a paramodulation step. Assume K has the form $s=t$ and the literal M has an occurrence of r, such that $r\theta = s\theta$. Then D_i has the following form:

$$D_i = (\; (D_{i-2} - M) \cup M[t] \cup (D_{i-1} - K) \;)\theta$$

Let r_l be the term in M_l, $1 \leq l \leq p$, corresponding to r in M. Then $\beta\theta$ is a unifier of $\{r_1,...,r_p\}\cup\{s'_{(j)} \mid 1 \leq j \leq p \}$ where $s'_{(j)}$ corresponds to s in the jth copy of E_{i-1} .
E_{i-2} can be written as

$$E_{i-2} = F_{i-2} \cup M_1[r_1] \cup ... \cup M_p[r_p]$$

and so $\beta\theta$ is a unifier of $M_1[r_1] \cup ... \cup M_p[r_p]$. If δ is a mgu we get with $\beta\theta = \delta\lambda$:

$$E_i \subseteq (\; (E_{i-2} - M') \cup M_1[r_1] \cup ... \cup M_p[r_p]_j\cup (\cup(E_{i-1(j)} - K'_{(j)})\;) \;)\delta$$

$$E_i\lambda \subseteq (\; (E_{i-2} - M') \cup M_1[r_1] \cup ... \cup M_p[r_p]_j\cup (\cup(E_{i-1(j)} - K'_{(j)})\;) \;)\delta\lambda$$

$$= (\; (E_{i-2} - M') \cup M_1[r_1] \cup ... \cup M_p[r_p]_j\cup (\cup(E_{i-1(j)} - K'_{(j)})\;) \;)\beta\theta$$

$$\subseteq (\; (D_{i-2} - M) \cup M[t] \cup (D_{i-1} - K) \;) \; \theta$$

$$= D_i.$$

The remaining case , where

$$D_i = (D_{i-2} - M) \cup (D_{i-1} - K) \cup K[t]$$

is a variation of the theme and omitted.

In a last step we have to eliminate a clause E_i from the deduction E, whenever it is identical to E_{i-1}, which results in the input deduction .

□

As an immediate consequence from this lemma we get the desired result, if we look at deductions of the empty clause:

THEOREM 4: *If S is an E-unsatisfiable set of Horn clauses containing x=x and its functional reflexive axioms, then there exists an input refutation with respect to {R,P}.*

CONCLUSION

We have restated a known result from the theorem proving literature concerning completeness of resolution and paramodulation for input deductions of Horn clauses. We shortly compared the motivation of work in theorem proving with that of work in logic programming. We concluded that in logic programming one needs a completeness theorem for paramodulation without factoring. We finally gave such a theorem.

ACKNOWLEDGEMENTS: It is a pleasure to acknowledge a lot of fruitful discussions with my colleagues Steffen Hölldobler and Joachim Schreiber.

REFERENCES

Bellia, Levi 86 : M.Bellia, G. Levi. The Relation Between Logic and Functional Languages: A Survey. J. Logic Programming, 3, 1986

Chang, Lee 73 : C.L.Chang, R.C.T.Lee. Symbolic Logic and Mechanical Theorem Proving. Academic Press. 1973

Chang, Slagle 71: C.L.Chang, J.R.Slagle. Completeness of Linear Refutation for Theories with Equality. J. ACM, Vol.18, 1, 1971

Furbach, Hölldobler 86: U.Furbach, S.Hölldobler. Modelling the Combination of Functional and Logic Programming Languages. J. Symb. Comp., 2, 1986

Furbach et al. 87: U.Furbach, S.Hölldobler, J.Schreiber. SLD-Resolution with Para-modulation. In preparation.

Henschen, Wos 74: L.Henschen, L.Wos. Unit Refutations and Horn Sets, J. ACM, Vol. 21, 4, 1974

Jaffar et al. 84: J.Jaffar, J.H.Lassez, M.J.Maher: A Theory of Complete Logic Programs with Equality. Proc. Int. Conf. 5TH Gen. Comp. Sys., 1984

Noll 76: H.Noll. A Note on Resolution: How to Get Rid of Factoring without Loosing Completeness. Report TU Berlin, 1976

Yamasaki et al. 83: S.Yamasaki, M.Yoshida, Doshita S. A new combination of input and unit deductions for Horn Sentences. IPL 1984

Program Verification by
Symbolic Execution and Induction

M. Heisel, W. Reif, W.Stephan

Universität Karlsruhe

Institut für Logik, Komplexität und Deduktionssysteme

Postfach 6980, D-7500 Karlsruhe

Abstract
BURSTALL´s verification method which is based on symbolic execution and mathematical induction is extended and formalized within the framework of dynamic logic. An example is presented. An implementation using the metalanguage of the Karlsruhe Interactive Verifier is described.

1 Introduction

1.1 BURSTALL´s Method

More than ten years ago BURSTALL [Bu 74] presented a verification method for proving total correctness assertions by symbolic execution and mathematical induction. A similar idea is incorporated in the BOYER and MOORE system [BM 79] for proving properties of LISP functions. As is pointed out in BURSTALL´s paper, the method, we call it the SI method (Simulation and Induction), works well on many verification problems which are very hard to tackle when using other approaches (e.g. invariant method). From the viewpoint of a working programmer the method is intuitively appealing: It is very like checking out a program by doing a step-by-step hand simulation. The reader is referred to section 2 for a typical example.

In this paper we present a formalization of the SI method within the framework of dynamic logic. BURSTALL´s original method is extended in that pre- and postconditions are allowed to contain assertions about programs, i. e. are not limited to predicate logic formulas. This feature is used in the example presented in section 2. We give an implementation of the SI method in PPL (Proof Programming Language) which is the metalanguage of the Karlsruhe Interactive Verifier (KIV) [HHRS 86].

In this section we give a brief overview over the system. In the next section we describe the strategy and give a detailed example of its application. Section 3 is concerned with the automatization of the strategy in the system.

1.2 The Logic Underlying the KIV System

KIV is an interactive program verification system based on dynamic logic. Dynamic logic (DL) extends first-order logic by formulas $[\alpha]\varphi$, where α is a program and φ again is a formula. $[\alpha]\varphi$ has to be read "if α terminates, φ holds". $\langle\alpha\rangle\varphi$ is an abbreviation for $\neg\,[\alpha]\neg\varphi$ and has to be read " α terminates, **and** φ holds". The SI method is a strategy for proving assertions of the form $\varphi \to \langle\alpha\rangle\psi$. For a survey of dynamic logic see [Har 84]. The programming language considered is made up of assignments $x := \tau$, compositions $\alpha;\beta$, conditionals **if** ε **then** α **else** β **fi**, while-loops **while** ε **do** α **od** and iterations α^i.

The KIV system is based on **a sequent calculus** [Re 84], [Ri 78]. We write $\Gamma \Rightarrow \psi$ for sequents where Γ, a list of formulas, is called the antecedent and ψ the succedent. A sequent is true, if the conjunction of the formulas in Γ implies ψ.

The rule base includes **basic rule schemes** as well as **user-defined rule schemes** (macros) which comprise several proof steps (steps of the basic calculus or again macro steps). Some basic rule-schemes have associated **variable conditions** which impose syntactical restrictions on the set of sound instances of that scheme. To guarantee soundness the user has to supply a **validation** for each macro step. A validation is a PPL-function that takes the premisses and the conclusion of the macro step as its arguments and produces a proof tree having the conclusion as root and the premisses as leaves. I. e. the validation function describes uniformly how to prove the conclusion from the premisses for all instantiations of the metavariables of the scheme.

1.3 Proof Trees

Proofs can be regarded as tree-like objects: The proven formula is the root of the tree, the axioms are its leaves, and $f_1,\ldots,f_n$ are sons of node f iff f can be derived from $f_1,\ldots,f_n$ by application of one rule of the calculus. For a sequent calculus the nodes are sequents instead of formulas. We generalize the notion of proof tree in the following way: We do not always begin (or end up) with axioms. Instead we admit arbitrary sequents (hypotheses) as leaves of a proof tree. These are called **premisses**. Moreover, sequents may contain metavariables which may become instantiated later on in the proof.

Rule schemes are elementary proof-trees. New proof trees can be generated by operations called **infer** and **refine**. The infer operation performs a forward proof step by using the conclusions of n proof trees $\tau_1,\ldots,\tau_n$ as premisses of a proof tree τ yielding a new conclusion. The refine operation performs a backward proof step by replacing one premise of a proof tree σ_1 by a proof tree σ_2 yielding the premisses of σ_2 as new subgoals. Both operations use matching: The proof trees τ and σ_2 can be considered as generalized inference rules and thus be instantiated by applying a matcher Θ to some of the metavariables. Θ satisfies the following conditions: the i-th premise of $\Theta\,(\tau)$ is equal to the conclusion of τ_i for i=1,...,n (infer) or the conclusion of $\Theta\,(\sigma_2)$ is equal to the i-th premise of σ_1 (refine).

1.4 The metalanguage PPL

In order to express proof ideas without getting lost in details, and to implement various proof-searching strategies we developed a functional programming language for constructing proofs, called Proof Programming Language (PPL)[HRS 86]. The language allows an arbitrary combination of forward and backward proof steps, i.e. the derivation of theorems and goals can be interleaved. It is also the language in which validation functions (see 1.2) are written. Via indeterminism the language supports a depth-first-search with controlled backtracking as search strategy.

Besides operations on data strucures (e.g. infer and refine) the language offers various control structures, such as conditionals, recursion , and indeterministic branch. The last one will be used extensively in section 3. e_1 or e_2 is evaluated as follows: If e_1 is evaluated without failure this is the value of the whole expression. If a failure occurred, e.g. because of a mismatch during a refine operation, the state before the execution of e_1 is restored, and the value of the or-expression is the value of e_2.

2 The SI Strategy

2.1 A DL Account of Burstall's Method

SI is a goal-directed proof strategy for total correctness assertions $\Gamma \Rightarrow \langle \alpha \rangle \psi$. It is an extension of the first-order version presented in [Bur 74] to dynamic logic.

Like every proof strategy, SI has two characteristic aspects: Firstly it uses besides some general logical reduction rules a collection of basic reduction steps that are typical for the intended application. These are **tactics** in the sense of ML [GMW 79]. Secondly it provides some heuristics how to combine tactics to find proofs. The central idea of SI is to use **symbolic execution** of programs. Therefore the proof search is guided by the syntactical structure of the given program α.

A goal $\Gamma \Rightarrow \langle \alpha \rangle \psi$ is tranformed to a normalized version $\Gamma \Rightarrow \langle \alpha_1 \rangle \langle \beta \rangle \psi$ where α_1 is the first instruction of α and β the rest of α. The tactic for symbolic execution of an assignment considers Γ as the current "state" and computes a successor "state" Γ_1 which is used as the new precondition of the the subgoal $\Gamma_1 \Rightarrow \langle \beta \rangle \psi$. Formally:

ASSIGNT: $\Gamma \Rightarrow \langle x := \tau \rangle \langle \beta \rangle \psi$ is reduced to $\Gamma', x = \tau \Rightarrow \langle \beta \rangle \psi$

　　　　　　　where Γ' is the $(x := \tau)$-invariant part of Γ.

With a goal of the form $\Gamma \Rightarrow \langle \alpha_1 \rangle \langle \beta \rangle \psi$ SI roughly does the following case analysis of α_1: **skip** and ($x := \tau$) can always be executed. At a conditional the strategy may be able to decide the test and to apply the corresponding execution tactics, or it may have to pursue both branches. If α_1 is a while instruction the strategy needs user interaction, since in general Γ does not determine the number of iterations to be executed. The user can choose between two tactics. The first one should be applied if the loop can actually be simulated by a definite number of iterations. The second and more important one expects the user to supply two "states" φ and ψ_1 (and an induction variable) such that for some number i of iterations ψ_1 can be reached from φ. The strategy proves this proposition through induction (subgoal 1), and extracts from it by specialization (subgoal 2) and unravelling (subgoal 3) a successor state for Γ with respect to α_1:

WHILET$_2$:   The user has to supply φ, ψ_1 and the induction variable u which usually occurs free in

　　　　　　　φ and ψ_1 and which is assumed not to occur in programs.

　　　　　　　$\Gamma \Rightarrow \langle$ while ε do α_2 od $\rangle \langle \beta \rangle \psi$ is reduced to

(1) $\varphi(u)$, $IND(u) \Rightarrow \exists i \langle (if\ \varepsilon\ then\ \alpha_2\ fi)^i \rangle \psi_1(u)$

(2) $\Gamma \Rightarrow \Theta(\varphi)$

(3) $\Gamma', \Theta(\psi_1) \Rightarrow \exists i \langle (if\ \varepsilon\ then\ \alpha_2\ fi)^i \rangle (\neg\varepsilon \wedge \langle \beta \rangle \psi)$

$IND(u)$ is the induction hypothesis:

$IND(u) \equiv \forall u', \underline{x}\ [(u' << u \wedge \varphi(u') \rightarrow \exists i \langle (if\ \varepsilon\ then\ \alpha_2\ fi)^i \rangle \psi_1(u')]$

and $\underline{x}$ is the vector of the remaining variables that occur in φ, ψ_1, ε and α_2. The induction ordering $<<$ is given via (non-logical) axioms. Θ is a substitution of metavariables for $\underline{x}$ and u and Γ' is the α_2-invariant part of Γ.

The strategy uses the following tactics to unravel loops:

EXITT : $\qquad \Gamma \Rightarrow \exists i \langle \alpha^i \rangle \psi$ is reduced to $\Gamma \Rightarrow \psi$

ITT : $\qquad \Gamma \Rightarrow \exists i \langle \alpha^i \rangle \psi$ is reduced to $\Gamma \Rightarrow \langle \alpha \rangle \exists i \langle \alpha^i \rangle \psi$

All of the above execution tactics have one common property: They are associated with a single instruction enabling a step-by-step simulation. Many proofs, however, become easier and more elegant if we consider complex programs (including inner loops etc.) as executable units. This is a special advantage of dynamic logic, since the current "state" of a goal given by the antecedent may already contain the information for a complex execution step. For this purpose the SI strategy makes use of the tactic:

ANTT : $\qquad \Gamma, \forall \underline{x}\ [\varphi \rightarrow [1]\ \psi_1] \Rightarrow [2]\ [3]\ \psi$ is reduced to

(1) $\Gamma, [1]\Theta(\psi_1) \Rightarrow [2]\Theta(\psi_1)$

(2) $\Gamma \Rightarrow \Theta(\varphi)$

(3) $\Gamma', \Theta(\psi_1) \Rightarrow [3]\psi$

where $[1], [2], [3] \in \{\langle \alpha \rangle, \exists i \langle \alpha^i \rangle\}$, and Θ is a substitution of metavariables for those variables in $\underline{x}$ that are not changed by $[1]$. Γ' is that part of Γ which is invariant under the program in $[2]$.

Before we talk about the automatization of SI in PPL, we illustrate the topics presented so far with a nontrivial example.

2.2 Example

The following program *postfix* which is taken from [HS 87] converts an arithmetic expression to postfix form. For example $e = A * B + C ** (D + E)$ is converted to $A\ B * C\ D\ E+ ** +$. Taking into account the usual priority rules every infix expression e is uniquely composed of a left part $lt(e)$, a main operator $op(e)$, and a right part $rt(e)$. In our example we have $lt(e) = A*B$, $op(e) = +$ and $rt(e) = C ** (D + E)$. For infix expressions e the function postfix is defined recursively as postfix$(e) =$ postfix$(lt(e)) \circ$ postfix$(rt(e)) \circ$ str$(op(e))$, where str converts tokens to strings and $\circ$ is the concatenation. Although *postfix* is an **iterative** program the correctness proof given below follows the **recursive** definition of the function postfix.

postfix:

stack:= <u>empty</u> ; output := <u>null</u>;

while input ≠ <u>null</u>

do   x := first (input); input := rest (input);

      if isoperand (x)

      then output := output ∘ str (x)

      else **if**   x =)

      then **while** stack ≠ <u>empty</u> **do**

                  output := output ∘ str (top (stack));   } pop_2

                  stack := pop (stack)

          od;

          stack := pop(stack)

      else **while** isp (top (stack)) > icp(x) **do**

                  output := output ∘ str (top (stack));   } pop_1

                  stack := pop(stack)

          od;

          stack := push (x, stack)

          fi

      fi

od

while stack ≠ <u>empty</u> **do**

      output := output ∘ str (top (stack));   } pop_2

      stack := pop (stack)

od;

body   loop

Symbol	isp	icp
)	-	-
**	3	3
*, /	2	2
binary +, -	1	1
(	0	4

We prove the following correctness assertion:

(1) input = e, Isexpr (e) ⇒ ⟨*postfix*⟩ output = postfix (e)

By executing the first two assignments we get

(2) Γ_1 ⇒ ⟨*loop*; pop_2 ⟩ output = postfix (e)

    where Γ_1 ≡ input = e , Isexpr (e) , stack = <u>empty</u> , output = <u>null</u>

The application of *WHILET_2* yields three new subgoals, respectively sets of subgoals, because the system automatically breaks up conjunctions in the succedent of a sequent:

(3) input = u • v, output = w, stack = s, Isexp (u), P (u,s), IND(u) ⇒ ∃ i ⟨*loop* ↓i⟩ POST(u)

where $POST(u) \equiv (\text{input} = v \wedge (\text{Isinfexp}(u) \to \langle x := \text{op}(u) \rangle \langle pop_1 \rangle (\text{stack} = s \wedge \text{output} = w \cdot$
$\text{postfix}(u))) \wedge (\neg \text{Isinfexp}(u) \to \text{stack} = s \wedge \text{output} = w \cdot \text{postfix}(u))$

$IND(u) \equiv \forall u', \text{input}, v, \text{output}, w, \text{stack}, s \ [u' << u \wedge (\text{input} = u' \cdot v \wedge \text{output} = w \wedge \text{stack} = s \wedge$
$\text{Isexp}(u) \wedge P(u',s)) \to \exists i \langle loop{\downarrow}i \rangle POST(u')]$

$loop {\downarrow} i$ is $(\textbf{if } \text{input} \neq \underline{\text{null}} \textbf{ then } body \textbf{ fi })^i$

(4) $\Gamma_1 \Rightarrow \text{input} = \tau_0 \cdot \tau_1 \qquad \Gamma_1 \Rightarrow \text{output} = \tau_2 \qquad \Gamma_1 \Rightarrow \text{stack} = \tau_3 \qquad \Gamma_1 \Rightarrow \text{Isexp}(\tau_0)$
$\Gamma_1 \Rightarrow P(\tau_0, \tau_3)$, where $P(u,s) \equiv (\text{Isinfexp}(u) \to \text{isp}(\text{top}(s)) < \text{icp}(\text{op}(u)))$

(5) $\Gamma_2 \Rightarrow \exists i \langle loop {\downarrow}i \rangle (\text{input} = \underline{\text{null}} \wedge \langle pop_2 \rangle \text{output} = \text{postfix}(u))$, where Γ_2 contains
$\text{input} = \tau_1$, $(\text{Isinfexp}(\tau_0) \to \langle x := \text{op}(u) \rangle \langle pop_1 \rangle (\text{stack} = \tau_3 \wedge \text{output} = \tau_2 \cdot \text{postfix}(\tau_0)))$,
$(\neg \text{Isinfexp}(\tau_0) \to \text{stack} = \tau_3 \wedge \text{output} = \tau_2 \cdot \text{postfix}(\tau_0))$
(τ_i are metavariables that are instantiated during the proof of (4))

We continue with (3). The following cases are possible: u ist an infix expression, or a parenthesized expression, or an operand. We only pursue the first subgoal

(6) $\Gamma_3 \Rightarrow \exists i <loop{\downarrow}i> POST$
where Γ_3 contains $\text{input} = u \cdot v$, $\text{output} = w$, $\text{stack} = s$, $\text{Isinfexp}(u)$, $P(u,s)$, IND

which is reduced to

(7) $\Gamma_3 \Rightarrow \exists i \langle loop{\downarrow}i \rangle \exists i \langle loop{\downarrow}i \rangle POST$.

Now we can apply *ANTT* to make use of the induction hypothesis and get two (sets of) subgoals:
(The first subgoal of the tactic is a tautology since [2] = [1]

(8) $\Gamma_3 \Rightarrow \text{input} = \tau_0 \cdot \tau_1 \qquad \Gamma_3 \Rightarrow \text{output} = \tau_2 \qquad \Gamma_3 \Rightarrow \text{stack} = \tau_3 \qquad \Gamma_3 \Rightarrow \text{Isexp}(\tau_0)$
$\Gamma_3 \Rightarrow P(\tau_0, \tau_3) \qquad \Gamma_3 \Rightarrow \tau_0 << u$

(9) $\text{input} = \tau_1$,
$(\text{Isinfexp}(\tau_0) \to \langle x := \text{op}(\tau_0) \rangle \langle pop_1 \rangle (\text{stack} = \tau_3 \wedge \text{output} = \tau_2 \cdot \text{postfix}(\tau_0)))$,
$(\neg \text{Isinfexp}(\tau_0) \to \text{stack} = \tau_3 \wedge \text{output} = \tau_2 \cdot \text{postfix}(\tau_0))$, $\text{Isinfexp}(u)$, IND, ...
$\Rightarrow \exists i . \langle loop{\downarrow}i \rangle POST$

The proof of (8) instantiates the metavariables as follows: $\tau_0 \leftarrow \text{lt}(u)$, $\tau_1 \leftarrow \text{str}(\text{op}(u)) \cdot \text{rt}(u)$,
$\tau_2 \leftarrow w$, $\tau_3 \leftarrow s$. With this our goal for the case $\text{Isinfexp}(\text{lt}(u))$ becomes

(10) $\Gamma_4 \Rightarrow \exists i \langle loop{\downarrow}i \rangle POST$, where Γ_4 contains
$\text{input} = \text{str}(\text{op}(u)) \cdot \text{rt}(u) \cdot v$, $\text{Isinfexp}(\text{lt}(u))$, $\langle x := \text{op}(\text{lt}(u)) \rangle \langle pop_1 \rangle (\text{stack} = s \wedge$
$\text{output} = w \cdot \text{postfix}(\text{lt}(u)))$, $\text{Isinfexp}(u)$, $P(u,s)$, IND

By *ITT* we get

(11) $\Gamma_4 \Rightarrow \langle \textbf{if } \text{input} \neq \underline{\text{null}} \textbf{ then } body \textbf{ fi } \rangle \exists i \langle loop {\downarrow}i \rangle POST$
After executing the tests and the first two assignments of *body* we get

(12) $\Gamma_5 \Rightarrow \langle pop_1 \rangle \langle$stack := push (op (u), stack)$\rangle \exists$ i $\langle loop\downarrow$i$\rangle$ POST

   where Γ_5 = input = rt (u) • v , x = op (u) , Isinfexp (lt (u)) , $\langle$x := op (lt (u))$\rangle \langle pop_1 \rangle$

   (stack = s $\wedge$ output = w • postfix (lt (u))) , Isinfexp (u) , P (u,s) , IND

An application of *ANTT* yields (13) as a lemma

(13) Γ_5 , $\langle$x := op (lt (u))$\rangle \langle pop_1 \rangle$ Q $\Rightarrow \langle pop_1 \rangle$ Q

   where Q $\equiv$ stack = s $\wedge$ output = w • postfix (lt (u))

and

(14) stack = s , output = w • postfix (lt (u)) , input = rt (u) • v , x = op (u), Isinfexp (u) ,

   P (u,s) , IND, ... $\Rightarrow \langle$stack := push (x , stack)$\rangle \exists$ i $\langle loop\downarrow$i$\rangle$ POST

Executing the assignment and applying *EX* (see section 3) yields

(15) $\Gamma_6 \Rightarrow \exists$ i $\langle loop\downarrow$i$\rangle \exists$ i $\langle loop\downarrow$i$\rangle$ POST , where Γ_6 contains

   input = rt (u) • v , stack = push (x , s) , x = op(u) , output = w • postfix (lt (u)) , Isinfexp (u),

   P(u,s) , IND

To use the induction hypothesis we apply *ANTT* again and get (again the first subgoal is a tautology)

(16) $\Gamma_6 \Rightarrow$ input = τ_0 • τ_1 $\Gamma_6 \Rightarrow$ output = τ_2 $\Gamma_6 \Rightarrow$ stack = τ_3 $\Gamma_6 \Rightarrow$ Isexp (τ_0)

   $\Gamma_6 \Rightarrow$ P(τ_0,τ_3) $\Gamma_6 \Rightarrow \tau_0 << $u

(17) input = τ_1 , (Isinfexp (τ_0) $\rightarrow \langle$x := op (τ_0)$\rangle \langle pop_1 \rangle$ (stack = τ_3 $\wedge$

   output = τ_2 • postfix (τ_0))) , ($\neg$ Isinfexp (τ_0) $\rightarrow$ stack = τ_3 $\wedge$ output = τ_2 • postfix (τ_0)) ,

   Isinfexp (u) , P(u,s), ... $\Rightarrow \exists$ i $\langle loop\downarrow$i$\rangle$ POST

The proof of (16) instantiates the metavariables as follows: $\tau_0 \leftarrow$ rt (u) , $\tau_1 \leftarrow$ v ,

$\tau_2 \leftarrow$ w • postfix (lt (u)), $\tau_3 \leftarrow$ push (x , s). Finally, we apply *EXITT* , do some simplifications
and execute the assignment x := op (u). What remains is lemma (18)

(18) $\langle$x := op (rt (u))$\rangle \langle pop_1 \rangle$ (stack = push (op (u), s) $\wedge$

   output = w • postfix (lt (u)) • postfix (rt (u))) , Isinfexp (u) , x =op(u) , ...

   $\Rightarrow \langle$x := op (u)$\rangle \langle pop_1 \rangle$ (stack = s $\wedge$ output = w • postfix (u)

3   Implementing the Strategy in PPL

   As a first step to implement the SI method one has to define appropriate derived rules. For example
the rule scheme

$$\Gamma \Rightarrow \exists\, i \, \langle\, (\, \textbf{if}\, \varepsilon\, \textbf{then}\, \alpha\, \textbf{fi}\,)^{\,i}\, \rangle\, (\neg\, \varepsilon\, \wedge\, \varphi\,)$$

$$\Gamma \Rightarrow \langle \textbf{while}\, \varepsilon\, \textbf{do}\, \alpha\, \textbf{od} \rangle\, \varphi$$

is used to deal with while-loops.

Using these derived rules it is not too difficult to program the tactics mentioned above as PPL functions. These functions take a goal (logically a sequent) as an argument and produce a proof tree the premisses of which correspond to the newly generated subgoals. Subgoals of the form $\Gamma \Rightarrow \exists i \langle \alpha^i \rangle \varphi$ or $\Gamma \Rightarrow \langle \alpha \rangle \varphi$ are again reduced by tactics. The remaining subgoals are treated as verification conditions. Some of them are easily proven by simplification rules while others represent nontrivial properties of the underlying data structure(s). These subgoals are left open. That is, we have in mind some sort of verification condition generator based on the SI method.

So far the SI strategy has been formalized within the framework of dynamic logic, and the basic building blocks have been isolated and then implemented as PPL functions which we called tactics. Using the KIV system as a proof-checker the user may now generate **formal** proofs in a way that is very close to the short informal proofs which are carried out by hand. For example the user does not need to use the axiom scheme for induction in an explicit way because all these intermediate steps are incorporated in the tactic which deals with while-loops.

Although this seems to be a valuable result, see [CBK 85] for a discussion of formal versus informal proofs, we would like to go further. We are looking for a PPL- strategy which generates nontrivial verification-conditions (if there are any) when supplied with pre -and postconditions for the inductive proof of while-loops. Without user interaction the sytem has now to decide which tactic has to be applied. If NORMALIZET (the normalize-tactic) generates a goal of the form $\Gamma \Rightarrow \langle\, x{:}{=}\tau\, \rangle$ $\langle \beta \rangle \varphi$ clearly only ASSIGNT (the assign-tactic) may be applied successfully (without failure). However for $\Gamma \Rightarrow \langle\, \textbf{if}\, \varepsilon\, \textbf{then}\, \alpha_0\, \textbf{else}\, \alpha_1\, \textbf{fi}\, \rangle \langle \beta \rangle \varphi$ there are three possibilities: We may try to prove $\Gamma \Rightarrow \varepsilon$ or $\Gamma \Rightarrow \neg\, \varepsilon$ yielding $\Gamma \Rightarrow \langle \alpha_0 \rangle \langle \beta \rangle\, \varphi$ or $\Gamma \Rightarrow \langle \alpha_1 \rangle \langle \beta \rangle\, \varphi$ as remaining subgoals, or we my decide to take $\Gamma, \varepsilon \Rightarrow \langle \alpha_0 \rangle \langle \beta \rangle \varphi$ and $\Gamma, \neg\, \varepsilon \Rightarrow \langle \alpha_1 \rangle \langle \beta \rangle \varphi$ as new subgoals. There are three tactics COND1T, COND2T and COND3T corresponding to these cases. For goals of the form $\Gamma \Rightarrow \exists\, i \langle \alpha^i \rangle\, \varphi$ things get even worse. We may try to finish the induction proof using EXITT (the exit-tactic) or we may try to execute α using ITT (the iteration-tactic) or we may apply the rule

$$\Gamma \Rightarrow \exists\, i \, \langle \alpha^i \rangle\, \exists\, i \langle \alpha^i \rangle\, \varphi$$

$$\Gamma \Rightarrow \exists\, i \langle \alpha^i \rangle\, \varphi \qquad \text{(EX)}$$

and then ANTT (the antecedent-tactic) to use the induction hypothesis. In the last case we have to test whether the premise of the hypothesis is provable in the "state" we have reached so far.

Before we are going to discuss our solution in some detail let us have a look at the overall structure of the §imulation and İnduction §trategy (SIS) . Like tactics it is applied to goals of the form $\Gamma \Rightarrow \langle \alpha \rangle \varphi$ or $\Gamma \Rightarrow \exists\, i \langle \alpha^i \rangle\, \varphi$. It tries to generate a proof tree which has no open subgoals of this form.

SIS(g) = **let** pt0 = NORMALIZET(g) **in**
        let g0 = PREM(1, pt0)) (* selects first premise *) **in**
           let pt1 = ASSIGNS(g0) **or** SKIPS(g0) **or** CONDS(g0) **or**
                    WHILES(g0) **or** EXITS(g0) **or** HYPS(g0) **or** SIMS(g0) **or**
                    ITS(g0) **or** ANTS(g0) **in**
              REFINE(pt0, 1 , pt1)

The substrategies ASSIGNS, SKIPS, ... call SIS recursively on certain subgoals. For example CONDS (the conditional-strategy) looks like

CONDS(g) = **let** pt0 = COND1T(g) **or** COND2T(g) **in**
           let pt1 = TESTS(PREM(1, pt0) **in**
                REFINE(REFINE(pt0, 2 , SIS(PREM(2, pt0))), 1, pt1)
        or
           let pt0 = COND3T(g) **in**
                REFINE(REFINE(pt0 , 2 , SIS(PREM(2 , pt0))) , SIS(PREM(1 , pt0)))

TESTS (the test-strategy) uses a fixed set of rules to establish that the test or its negation follows from the information given by the antecedent. If it fails both arms of the conditional are pursued by the SIS strategy.

If more than one tactic is applicable to a given goal we resolve the conflict by proving **some** of the potential subgoals which could be generated. But what subgoals should be attacked by our strategy and what subgoals should be left open as verification conditions? The basic idea of this method is to execute a program on symbolic data. Hence it seems to be reasonable to restrict the evaluation and simplification strategies in a way that they use only **structural** information. That is, our strategies will have knowledge only about symbols concerning the representation of data objects. Technically this is done by grouping the relevant rules and axioms into one or more lists which are accessed by these strategies. But what do we excactly mean by structural information? First of all there are the axioms for our basic datatypes. In the case of strings we have the well known axioms like u ∘ null = u. In addition to that we need structural information from our problem specification. In our example we have in the specification of expressions Isexp (u) ↔ Isinfexp (u) ∨ Isoperandexp (u) ∨ Isparexp (u) as well as Isinfexp (u) ↔ u = lt (u) ∘ str (op (u)) ∘ rt (u) ∧ Isexp (lt (u)) ∧ Isexp (rt (u)) ∧ Isoperand (op (u)) . To be able to use the inductive hypothesis the system must have knowledge about the << predicate. From u = lt (u) ∘ str (op (u)) ∘ rt (u) we must be able to infer lt (u) << u.

The most important substrategy is HYPS (the hypothesis-strategy) which tries to use the induction hypothesis on goals of the form $\Gamma \Rightarrow \exists\, i \langle \alpha^i \rangle \varphi$.

HYPS(g) = **let** pt0 = REFINE(MKSTREE(g) , 1 , EX) (* the rule EX is applied to the tree
           in   consisting only of the sequent g *)
          let g0 = PREM(1 , pto) **in**
              let pt1 = MATCHS(REPANTT(g0 , LENGTH(ANTOF(g0)))) **in**
                REFINE(pt1, 2, SIS(PREM(2, pt0)))

REPANTT(g , k) = [k = 0 → **fail**

true → TAUTT(PREM(1, ANTT(g)) **or**

REPANTT(PREM(1 , PERMUTET(g)) , k-1)]

After using EX (see above) HYPS repeatedly tries ANTT and checks whether the first subgoal is a tautology. If this is the case, i.e. there is an induction hypothesis which can be used, MATCHS tries to solve all subgoals where the succedent is of the form ...=... , ...<<... or Q(...) where Q is a structure predicate like Isexp. During this process the metavariables which have been introduced by ANTT become instantiated. SIS is then applied to the second subgoal (premise) of the tree generated by ANTT.

4 Conclusion

It has been demonstrated that in a system that allowes sound extensions of a basic logic (by derived rules, tactics and strategies) various verification strategies can easily be implemented. It should be noted that different strategies may be combined freely. It remains open to what extent user interaction can be replaced by automatic decision making. This will be the subject of further research. However, formal proofs can be as short as informal ones which seems to be a great advantage. So far (our variant of) DL has turned out as an adequate formalism for practical program verification.

References

[BM 79]   Boyer, R.S./ Moore, J.S. A Computational Logic. Academic Press, New York 1979

[Bu 74]   Burstall, R.M. Program Proving as Hand Simulation with a little Induction. Information Processing 74, North-Holland Publishing Company (1974)

[CKB 85] Constable,R./Knoblock,T./Bates,J. Writing Programs That Construct Proofs. Journal of Automated Reasoning, Vol.1, No.3, pp 285 - 326 (1985)

[GMW 79] Gordon,M/Milner,R./Wadsworth,C. Edinburgh LCF. Springer LNCS 78 (1979)

[Har 84] Harel, D. Dynamic Logic. Handbook of Philosophical Logic, D. Gabbay and F. Guenther (eds.), Reidel (1984), Vol. 2, 496-604

[HHRS 86] Hähnle, R./Heisel, M./Reif, W./Stephan, W. An Interactive Verification System Based on Dynamic Logic. Proc. 8-th International Conference on Automated Deduction, J.Siekmann (ed), Springer LNCS 230 (1986), 306-315

[HRS 86] Heisel,M./.Reif, W./Stephan, W. A Functional Language to Construct Proofs. Interner Bericht 1/86, Fakultät für Informatik, Universität Karlsruhe (1986)

[HS 87]   Horowitz,E./Sahni,S. Data Structures in Pascal. Computer Science Press (1987)

[Re 84]   Reif, W., Vollständigkeit einer modifizierten Goldblatt-Logik und Approximation der Omegaregel durch Induktion. Diplomarbeit, Fakultät für Informatik, Universität Karlsruhe (1984)

[Ri 78]   Richter, M.M. Logikkalküle, Teubner (1978)

RESOLUTION ON FORMULA-TREES

Ulf R. Schmerl

Mathematisches Institut der Universität München

Theresienstraße 39, 8000 München 2

Abstract. We introduce a nonclausal resolution calculus on formula-trees
which comprises classical resolution as a special case. The resolvents
produced in this calculus are more structure preserving than in nonclausal
resolution by Murray and Manna and Waldinger and simpler than in nested
resolution by Traugott. Proofs of correctness and completeness are sketched.
In some examples, first experiences made when implementing the calculus
are discussed.

0. Introduction. In Robinson's classical resolution calculus [8], the process of
logical inference takes place exclusively at the level of atomic formulae; in addition, all formulae have to be normalized to clause form. This is in sharp contrast
to typical man-made deductions where proof steps can involve formulae of arbitrary
shape and complexity. In this paper, we develop a calculus which, due to its data
structure, systematically tries to resolve on subformulae of highest possible complexity. The formulae need not to be in any normal form (although here, for the sake
of simlicity, we use trees which correspond to the negated normal form of formulae).

The idea to improve resolution by allowing more complex proof steps is not new:
Hyperresolution or nonclausal resolution rules as in Murray [6], Manna and Waldinger
[5], or Traugott [9] can be cited as examples. Macro-steps have also been considered
in other calculi of automated theorem proving, e.g. in Bibel [1].

1. Resolution on formula-trees. A natural form to represent problems in predicate
logic are Gentzen-sequents [4] (also see [3])

$$(*) \qquad A_1,..,A_m \vdash B_1,..,B_n,$$

where $A_1,..,A_m$ and $B_1,..,B_n$ are (possibly empty) lists of first-order formulae. The
intended meaning of $(*)$ is $A_1 \wedge .. \wedge A_m \rightarrow B_1 \vee .. \vee B_n$, i.e. a disjunction of conclusions has to
be deduced from a list $A_1,..,A_m$ of axioms or assumptions. - So we start with a given
input sequent $A_1,..,A_m \vdash B_1,..,B_n$. Throughout the following, the sequent

$$r(t) \wedge (p(t) \vee q(t)), \forall x[(p(x) \vee q(x)) \rightarrow (r(x) \wedge s(x))] \vdash \exists y[r(y) \wedge s(y)]$$

will be taken as an example. In order to prove an input sequent $A_1,..,A_m \vdash B_1,..,B_n$, it
is first transformed into a list $F_1,..,F_{m+n}$ of formula-trees. As in the classical resolution calculus, this list is then continued by production of resolvents and factors

until the goal tree "T" is found. In that case, the provability of the input sequent is established. Therefore, our calculus will be a proving one where the validity of sequents is tried to be shown rather than unsatisfiability as in the classical case.

The given input sequent is first split into a list of formulae with positive or negative polarity:

Definition: Polarity of formula occurrences

(i) If A is an occurrence of a first-order formula, then ⊢A indicates that this occurrence has positive polarity and A⊢ indicates negative polarity.

(ii) A sequent $A_1,..,A_m \vdash B_1,..,B_n$ is assigned the following list of formulae with polarity: $A_1\vdash,..,A_m\vdash,\vdash B_1,..,\vdash B_n$.

For our example sequent, we obtain the following list of formulae with polarity:

$$r(t) \land (p(t) \lor q(t)) \vdash, \forall x[(p(x) \lor q(x)) \rightarrow (r(x) \land s(x))] \vdash, \vdash \exists y[r(y) \land s(y)]$$

From a formula with polarity we construct a labelled formula-tree. The construction proceeds in a recursive way according to the outermost logical symbol of the formula written at the root of the tree. We use A for conjunctive and $\land$ for disjunctive branching as in Nilsson [7].

Definition: Labelled formula-tree of a formula with polarity

0. If A is a prime formula, then ⊢A and A⊢ are leaves.

1.
```
        ⊢¬A                    ¬A⊢
         |                      |
        A⊢                     ⊢A
```

2.
```
       ⊢A∧B                   A∧B⊢
         A                      ∧
      ⊢A  ⊢B                 A⊢  B⊢
```

3.
```
       ⊢A∨B                   A∨B⊢
         ∧                      A
      ⊢A  ⊢B                 A⊢  B⊢
```

4.
```
       ⊢A→B                   A→B⊢
         ∧                      A
      A⊢ ⊢B                  ⊢A  B⊢
```

5.
```
     ⊢∀xA(a,x)               ∀xA(x)⊢
         |                      |
    ⊢A(a,f(a)) (*)           A(a)⊢ (**),
```

   (*) here f(a) is a Skolem function depending on the free variables in ∀xA(a,x); if a is empty, then f is a constant
   (**) here a is a new free variable

6.
```
      ⊢∃xA(x)              ∃xA(a,x)⊢
         |                      |
       ⊢A(a)              A(a,f(a))⊢

      see (**)                see(*)
```

Example: The second formula with polarity of the example sequent has the labelled formula-tree

$$\forall x[(p(x)\lor q(x))\rightarrow(r(x)\land s(x))]\vdash$$
$$(p(a)\lor q(a))\rightarrow(r(a)\land s(a))\vdash$$
$$\vdash p(a)\lor q(a) \qquad r(a)\land s(a)\vdash$$
$$\vdash p(a) \quad \vdash q(a) \qquad r(a)\vdash \quad s(a)\vdash$$

We could now directly introduce resolution on labelled formula-trees; this would indeed best preserve the structure of the given input problem. For the sake of simplicity, however, we shall define resolution on unlabelled formula-trees which are easily obtained from labelled trees and obviously simpler than the latter.

Definition: (Unlabelled) tree of a formula with polarity

It is obtained from a labelled tree by

1. deleting all formulae with polarity written at nodes which are not leaves, **and**

2. contracting nodes with unary branching with their unique descendant.

Note that unlabelled trees are pure AND-OR-trees.

Example: From the sequent example, we obtain the following list of formula-trees:

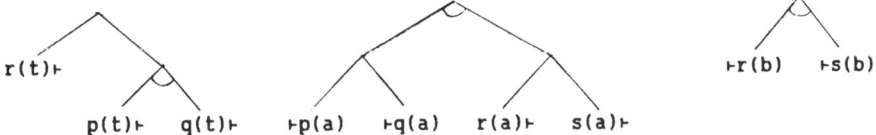

$$r(t)\vdash \qquad p(t)\vdash \quad q(t)\vdash \qquad \vdash p(a) \quad \vdash q(a) \quad r(a)\vdash \quad s(a)\vdash \qquad \vdash r(b) \quad \vdash s(b)$$

In the following we shall use $C,D,E,F,G,..,C_i,..$ etc. to designate unlabelled formula-trees. Special formula-trees are the trivial trees "T" and "$\perp$" standing for "truth" and "falsity". If T or $\perp$ occurs in a tree, this tree can be simplified according to the following obvious rules:

Definition: Reduction of formula-trees

1. $\underset{T\ \ F}{\overset{\land}{}} \Rightarrow F,$ $\qquad\qquad$ $\underset{F\ \ T}{\overset{\land}{}} \Rightarrow F$

2. $\underset{T\ \ F}{\overset{\land}{}} \Rightarrow T,$ $\qquad\qquad$ $\underset{F\ \ T}{\overset{\land}{}} \Rightarrow T$

3. $\underset{\perp\ \ F}{\overset{\land}{}} \Rightarrow \perp,$ $\qquad\qquad$ $\underset{F\ \ \perp}{\overset{\land}{}} \Rightarrow \perp$

4. $\underset{\perp\ \ F}{\overset{\land}{}} \Rightarrow F,$ $\qquad\qquad$ $\underset{F\ \ \perp}{\overset{\land}{}} \Rightarrow F$

We can now explain how resolvents and factors are constructed from formula-trees. First some notation: $F(C_1,..,C_n)$ denotes that there are specified occurrences of sub-trees $C_1,..,C_n$ in F. $F\theta$ stands for the tree obtained if the free variables in F are replaced by terms according to the substitution θ.

Definiton: Two formula-trees C and D are complementary,
denoted by C⊥D, if D can be obtained from C by

1. changing each branching in C into its dual, i.e. ∆ is replaced by ∧ and ∧ is
replaced by ∆,   and

2. inverting the polarity of the leaves, i.e. occurrences of ⊢A are replaced by A⊢
and occurrences of B⊢ by ⊢B.

Definition: Resolution on formula-trees

$$F(C)$$

$$G(D) \quad C_6 \perp D_6$$

$$F_6(G_6(T))$$

i.e. given two formula-trees F(C) and G(D) and a most general unifier 6 unifying C
and D up to complementarity, the resolvent $F_6(G_6(T))$ of F(C) and G(D) is obtained
in the following way:

1. Replace the specified occurrence of D_6 in G_6 by T to obtain the tree $G_6(T)$, then
2. substitute this tree for the specified occurrence of C_6 in F_6 to obtain
$F_6(G_6(T))$, and
3. reduce $F_6(G_6(T))$ according to the reduction rules stated above.

Example: From the first two trees in the list of formula-trees shown above,
a resolvent is obtained in the following way (taking tree 1 as G and tree 2 as F):
1. The right subtree of G is complementary to the left subtree of F with MGU t/u,
hence $G_6(T)$ is obtained as

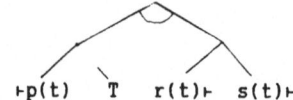

            r(t)⊢   T

2. Substituting this tree for the left subtree in F(t/a), we obtain

            ⊢p(t)   T   r(t)⊢   s(t)⊢

3. Reduction yields the resolvent

                r(t)⊢ s(t)⊢

We are of course interested in obtaining resolvents which are as simple as possible.
In the classical resolution calculus, a shorter resolvent is obtained by unit resolution. We have a similar situation in resolution on formula-trees if the tree $G_6(T)$
reduces to T: In this case, the resolvent $F_6(T)$ is always shorter than F. Now $G_6(T)$
reduces to T if all the branchings in $G_6(T)$ above the occurrence of T are disjunctive.
More precisely, we define:

<u>Definition:</u> disjunctive parts of a formula-tree

1. F is a disjunctive part of F.

2. If A is a disjunctive part of F and if the first branching in A is disjunctive, then the direct subtrees of A are disjunctive parts of F.

We write $F^\vee(C_1,..,C_n)$ to indicate that there are specified occurrences of subtrees $C_1,..,C_n$ in F which are disjunctive parts of F.

Hence, in order to obtain a simplified resolvent, it suffices to assume that the specified occurrence of D in G is a disjunctive part of G, i.e. that we have G (D). Simplifying resolution can be carried out with several subtrees simultaneously. This provides a very powerful inference rule which we call strong resolution.

<u>Definition:</u> strong resolution

$$F(C_1,..,C_n)$$
$$G_1^\vee(D_1)$$
$$.$$
$$\dot{G}_n^\vee(D_n) \quad C_1 6 1 D_1 6,..,C_n 6 1 D_n 6$$
$$F6(T,..,T),$$

where again F6(T,..,T) is supposed to be reduced according to the reduction rules.

<u>Example:</u> In the case of our example sequent, strong resolution can be applied to tree 2 as F, taking the right subtree of tree 1 as G_1 and tree 3 as G_2. The strong resolvent produced in this case is "T" (hence our example sequent is proved).

The second inference principle of our calculus is the construction of factors - in a way which is similar to classical resolution.

<u>Definition:</u> construction of factors

$$F(_A{}^A{}_{B(C)}) \ A6=C6$$
$$F6(_{A6}{}^A{}_{B6(T)})$$

$$F(_{B(C)}{}^A{}_{A}) \ A6=C6$$
$$F6(_{B6(T)}{}^A{}_{A6})$$

$$F(_A{}^\wedge{}_{B(C)}) \ A6=C6$$
$$F6(_{A6}{}^\wedge{}_{B6(\bot)})$$

$$F(_{B(C)}{}^\wedge{}_{A}) \ A6=C6$$
$$F6(_{B6(\bot)}{}^\wedge{}_{A6})$$

<u>Remark 1:</u>   Robinson's resolution as a special case of resolution on formula-trees

In Robinson's resolution calculus a given set of clauses $C_1,..,C_n$ is tried to be refuted by the construction of resolvents and factors. In terms of our calculus this means that the sequent $C_1,..,C_n \vdash$ has to be proved valid. A formula with polarity $C\vdash$, where $C = l_1 \vee .. \vee l_n$ and the l_i's are literals, has the following formula-tree:

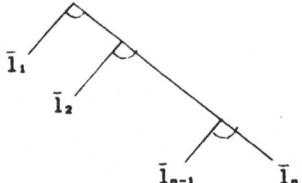

Here $\bar{l}_i$ is $p_i \vdash$ if $l_i = p_i$ and $\bar{l}_i$ is $\vdash p_i$ if $l_i = \neg p_i$. Now suppose given two clauses C_1, C_2 and literals $l_1 \in C_1$, $l_2 \in C_2$ which are unifiable up to complementarity by a MGU σ. We consider the tree-resolvent of C_1 and C_2 in l_1, l_2: First we have to replace $l_2\sigma$ in $C_2\sigma$ by T. Since C_2 is a pure AND-tree, the result after reduction is a pure AND-tree made up by the literals of $C_2\sigma - \{l_2\sigma\}$. When this tree is substituted for $l_1\sigma$ in $C_1\sigma \vdash$, again a pure AND-tree is obtained; it is made up by the literals of $(C_1\sigma - \{l_1\sigma\}) \cup (C_2\sigma - \{l_2\sigma\})$, which corresponds exactly to the classical resolvent of C_1 and C_2. In the same way, it is possible to compare the construction of factors in both calculi.

Remark 2:   Nonclausal resolution by Murray and Manna and Waldinger

Murray [6] and Manna and Waldinger [5] proposed an inference rule on quantifier-free formulae without normal form. In the propositional case, this rule reads as follows:

$$F[C]$$
$$\underline{G[C]}$$
$$F[T] \vee G[\bot] \quad .$$

Here $F[C]$ and $G[C]$ indicate occurrences of a subformula C in F and G. In $F[T] \vee G[\bot]$, **all** occurrences of C in F have been replaced by T and those in G by $\bot$. A polarity strategy for the occurrences of C has to be added in order to prevent the rule from producing unnecessary resolvents (see [6]). Note that this rule is correct for a refuting calculus. There is no similarity with resolution on formula-trees. An advantage of this rule is the fact that it allows to resolve on complex subformulae and that the resolvent $F[T] \vee G[\bot]$ can be simplified by reduction. A disadvantage seems to be the introduction of the disjunction; in iterated applications, this tends to produce resolvents in clause form.

Remark 3:   Nested resolution by Traugott

Traugott [9] proposed another nonclausal resolution rule. In the propositional case, it has the following form:

$$F[P^+, P^-]$$
$$\underline{G[P]}$$
$$F[G[T], \neg G[\bot]] \quad .$$

Notation is the same as in remark 2, P⁺ indicates positive and P⁻ negative occurrences
of P in F. Traugott's rule is sound for refuting calculi. Since there is no polarity
distinction of the occurrences of P in G, the rule cannot directly be compared to
resolution on formula-trees. In the special case, however, where only negative occurrences of P in G and only positive occurrences of P in F are considered, Traugott's
rule becomes similar to a special case of our resolution rule. Traugott's rule offers
some advantages in comparison to nonclausal resolution by Murray and Manna and
Waldinger: It better preserves the structure of given formulae, since - as in resolution on formula-trees - no new logical symbols are introduced. Moreover, Traugott's
resolvent is stronger than the conventional nonclausal resolvent. A disadvantage
might be the fact that the complexity of resolvents can easily increase due to several
substitutions of G[T] and ¬G[⊥] for P in F. In addition, the missing polarity
distinction of P in G allows the production of unnecessary resolvents: Taking
F[P⁺,P⁻]:=P and G[P]:=P, the resolvent produced is T. This can of course easiliy
be overcome by introducing a polarity strategy as in Murray [6].

2.Correctness and completeness. Resolution on formula-trees is correct and complete:
A sequent of first-order formulae is provable in the calculus iff it is provable in
Gentzen's sequent calculus LK (which is known to be correct and complete). Here we
only sketch the proofs of correctness and completeness; the complete proofs can be
found in a forth-coming paper by the author.

In order to be able to compare sequents and formula-trees, we assign a canonical
formula to each formula-tree.

Definition: the canonical formula (F) of a formula-tree F

0. (T):=T, (⊥):=⊥

1. If ⊢A and A⊢ are leaves, then (⊢A):=A, (A⊢):=¬A

2. $(\underset{A\ B}{\overset{\wedge}{}})$:= (A)∧(B)

3. $(\underset{A\ B}{\overset{\wedge}{}})$:= (A)∨(B)

Variable convention: Free variables occurring in (F) are considered to be
existentially quantified.

If A⊢ or ⊢B is a first-order formula with polarity, then (A⊢) or (⊢B) is the
canonical formula of the formula-tree of A⊢ or ⊢B.

Lemma 1: A sequent A₁,..,Aₘ⊢B₁,...,Bₙ is provable in LK iff the sequent
⊢(A₁⊢),..,(Aₘ⊢),(⊢B₁),..,(⊢Bₙ) is provable in LK.

Proof: by propositional logic and a theorem on Skolem normal forms of formulae.

Correctness is based on the following simple lemma:

Lemma 2: (i) If R is a resolvent of the formula-trees F and G, then (R) $\rightarrow$ (F)v(G).
(ii) If F is a factor of G, then (F) $\rightarrow$ (G).
Proof: by induction on the number of branchings in F and G.

Theorem (Correctness): Each sequent of first-order formulae which is provable by resolution on formula-trees is also provable in the sequent calculus and is hence valid.
Proof: If the sequent $A_1,..,A_m \vdash B_1,..,B_n$ is derivable in our calculus, then by definition the list of formula-trees belonging to $A_1\vdash,..,A_m\vdash,\vdash B_1,..,\vdash B_n$ is derivable, i.e. there exists a list $F_0,..,F_N$ of formula-trees with F_N = T and such that for each i<N, F_i is either one of the input trees or a resolvent or factor of trees F_j, F_k with j,k<i. Since F_N = T, the sequent $\vdash(F_0),..,(F_N)$ is trivially derivable in the sequent calculus. By lemma 2 it follows that $\vdash(A_1\vdash),..,(A_m\vdash),(\vdash B_1),..,(\vdash B_n)$ is derivable, and by lemma 1 we obtain the derivability of the given input sequent in LK.

The completeness proof is very similar to one of classical resolution. First we distinguish ground case and general case.

Lemma 3: If $F_1,..,F_n$ are ground formula-trees and $\vdash(F_1),..,(F_n)$ is provable in LK, then $F_1,..,F_n$ is provable by resolution.
Proof: By induction on the height of cut-free LK-derivations of $\vdash(F_1),..,(F_n)$.

Lemma 4 (Lifting): (i) Let F_1' and F_2' be substitution instances of formula-trees F_1 and F_2, R' a resolvent of F'_1 and F'_2. Then there exists a resolvent R of F_1 and F_2 such that R' is an instance of R.
(ii) If F' is an instance of a formula-tree F and if G' is a factor of F', then there is a factor G of F such that G' is an instance of G.
Proof: this is completely similar to the classical case.

Theorem (Completeness): Each valid sequent of first-order formulae is provable by resolution on formula-trees.
Proof: The ground case is covered by lemma 3; the general case follows by Herbrand's theorem and the lifting lemma.

3. Implementation. Our calculus has been implemented by F. Schmalhofer in doing his graduation thesis in computer science at the Technical University of Munich; he was supervised by Dr. W. Meixner. The programm is written in Pascal and runs on a Siemens 6850 computer. The proof search is organized in the following way: A complexity-preference-strategy makes sure that only trees of lowest-possible complexity are produced. For each complexity bound, the inference rules are applied in the following priority: First strong resolution, then factoring, and last normal resolution. The search for resolvents and factors proceeds according to the ordering of the given list of trees. For each single tree, the search starts at the root and proceeds through the tree to its leaves. In order to keep the search space as small as possible, a subsumption strategy was added.

Numerous examples have been tested. As expected, it turned out that the program spends the greater part of time for the search of strong resolvents of low complexity. Due to complexity preference and subsumption, in all test problems the total number of trees produced was moderate. In the following, we present only four examples.

Example 1: This is the example sequent introduced in the beginning. As shown above, it can be proved in one step by strong resolution; CPU time is about .01 sec.

Example 2: Find a derivation of $A(t) \rightarrow \exists x A(x)$ where A is the formula $(p(x) \vee q(x)) \wedge (r(x) \vee s(x))$. In classical resolution, the translation of $A(t) \rightarrow \exists x A(x)$ into clause notation produces 6 clauses which no longer reflect the structure of the problem; its refutation needs 18 more resolvents (applying level saturation with unit preference). Since the formula-trees of $A(t) \vdash$ and $\vdash \exists x A(x)$ are complementary up to a substitution, in tree resolution the trivial tree T is produced at the first step; CPU time is .007 sec.

Example 3: McCarthy's Monkey-Banana-problem (as stated in [2])

Here only 4 strong resolvents are produced, the last one being T; CPU time is .60 sec.

Example 4: Schubert's Steamroller as stated in [10]
The derivation produces 45 resolvents. Again only strong resolution is needed. CPU time is 70.12 sec.

References.

[1] Bibel, W., Automated Theorem Proving, Vieweg, Braunschweig 1982

[2] Chang, C.-L. and Lee, R.C.-T., Symbolic Logic and Mechanical Theorem Proving, Academic Press, New York 1973

[3] Gallier, J., Logic for Computer Science, Harper&Row, New York 1986

[4] Gentzen, G., Untersuchungen über das logische Schließen, Math. Z. 39 (1934) 176-210, 405-431

[5] Manna, Z. and Waldinger, R., Special relations in automated deduction, Journal of the ACM 33 (1986) No.1,1-59

[6] Murray, N.V., Completely non-clausal theorem proving, Artificial Intelligence 18 (1982) 67-85

[7] Nilsson, N.J., Principles of Artificial Intelligence, Tioga Publ. Co. 1980

[8] Robinson, J.A., A machine-oriented logic based on the resolution principle,
     Journal of the ACM 12,1 (1965) 23-41

[9] Traugott, J., Nested Resolution, Proc. 8th Conf. on Autom. Deduct., 1986,
     SLNCS 230, 394-402

[10] Walther, C., A mechanical solution of Schubert's Steamroller by many-sorted
     resolution, Artificial Intelligence 26,2 (1985) 217-224

A HYPERRESOLUTION-BASED PROOF PROCEDURE
AND ITS IMPLEMENTATION IN PROLOG

Rainer Manthey and Francois Bry

ECRC

Arabellastr. 17

D-8000 Muenchen 81

1. Introduction

Our work on automated deduction has been motivated by database problems. The set of deduction rules and integrity constraints of a logic database can be considered as axioms of a first-order theory while the actual sets of facts constitute (finite) models of this theory. Satisfiability of the underlying axioms is a necessary prerequisite for any logic database. The procedure described in this paper is the basis of a program called SATCHMO (SATisfiability CHecking by MOdel generation) that has been implemented at ECRC as part of a prototype schema design system for logic databases.

Although SATCHMO has initially not been intended as a proof procedure, it turned out that a considerable amount of examples discussed in the theorem proving literature could be solved by model generation with remarkable efficiency. We have successfully tested our approach, e.g., on most of the 75 problems in [PEL86] as well as on a large collection of problems that we received from Argonne National Laboratory. Besides many encouraging results - Schubert's Steamroller has been solved in little more than a second, e.g. - we know about examples that lead to unacceptable results and that will probably never be solved by "pure" model generation.

SATCHMO's approach is based on hyperresolution. This inference rule allows to make benefit of the range-restrictedness of clauses. Range-restrictedness - introduced in [NIC82] - is a necessary condition for an efficient evaluation of queries against a database. Every variable in a range-restricted clause occurs at least once inside a negative literal in that clause. This property can be naturally expected for problems with a structured domain.

If applied to range-restricted clauses, hyperresolution always produces clauses that are ground. This allows to simulate exhaustive application of hyperresolution by means of unit hyperresolution and clause splitting. Unit hyperresolution fits particularly well to PROLOG. In addition, a depth-first implementation of clause splitting is well supported by PROLOG backtracking. The resulting PROLOG program for automatic model generation is stunningly short and simple. As nowadays PROLOG interpreters are offered for a huge variety of computers, theorem proving technology might become available to a wider audience if it could be based on standard PROLOG features instead of requiring special machines and languages.

The paper consists of six sections. After this introduction we give some basic definitions around hyperresolution and introduce notations. In section 3 we elaborate on range-restricted clauses and show that every set of clauses can be transformed into a range-restricted set while preserving satisfiability. Model trees are introduced in section 4 and the correspondence between model tree search and hyperresolution saturation is shown. A PROLOG implementation of model tree generation is described in section 5 and its application to the Steamroller problem is discussed. In section 6 we give an improved procedure that is a decision procedure for a syntactically definable class of problems. Section 7 contains concluding remarks and hints to possible extensions. We don't give proofs within this paper.

2. Basic definitions and notation

Throughout the paper, Boolean connectives and/or/not/implies, resp., will be denoted by $,/;/~/$--->, resp. Clauses will be represented in implicational form

$$A_1,...,A_m \text{ ---> } C_1;...;C_n$$

where $~A_1$ to $~A_m$ are the negative, C_1 to C_n the positive literals in the clause. Completely positive clauses are written as true ---> $C_1;...;C_n$, while completely negative clauses are implicationally represented in the form $A_1,...,A_m$ ---> false. Thus negation never occurs explicitly. We call the left-hand side of an implication *antecedent* and the right-hand side *consequent*. Clauses with antecedent 'true' will be called *statements*, all other clauses will be called *rules*.

The hyperresolution inference principle allows to derive a new statement - the *hyperresolvent* - from a single rule - the *nucleus* - and as many other statements - the *satellites* - as there are literals in the antecedent of the nucleus. Each of the antecedent literals has to be unifiable with a literal in one of the satellites. The respective unifiers must be compatible, i.e., a most-general unifier has to exist that allows to unify antecedent and satellite literals simultaneously. This mgu is applied to nucleus and satellites before the hyperresolvent is constructed by disjunctively conjoining the consequent of the nucleus with those satellite literals that do not occur in the antecedent of the nucleus. If all satellites consist of a single literal we speak of *unit hyperresolution*.

For any set P of statements and any set N of rules, hyp(N,P) denotes the set of all hyperresolvents that can be derived from a nucleus in N and satellites in P.

Let S denote a finite set of clauses, $S^+(S^-)$ the subset of statements(rules) in S. The *hyperresolution levels* of S can be inductively defined as $Hyp^0(S)=S^+$ and $Hyp^i(S)=Hyp^{i-1}(S)$ *Union* $hyp(S^-,Hyp^{(i-1)}(S))$ for $i>0$. The *hyperresolution saturation* of S is the union over all hyperresolution levels and is denoted by Hyp(S).

In [ROB65] hyperresolution has been shown to be sound and complete for refutation, i.e., S is unsatisfiable iff Hyp(S) contains 'false'. In case of satisfiability, models of S can be extracted from Hyp(S) rather straightforwardly. For this purpose the ground instances of Hyp(S) over the ground terms in S (if any - a single artificial' constant else) have to be considered. Every subset M of the Herbrand base of S that covers each of these instances induces a model of S in which exactly the atoms in M are true and every other atom is false. A set of ground literals is a *cover* of a set of ground clauses iff each of the clauses is subsumed by one of the literals. We call a model that is induced by a cover of the instance set of Hyp(S) a *h-model* of S.

3. Hyperresolution for range-restricted clauses

Many satisfiability problems are dealing with a non-uniform domain of interpretation, i.e., variables range over well-distinguished subdomains. This is in particular the case if problems are inherently many-sorted. Range-restrictedness requires that for every variable in a clause the subset of the domain over which the variable ranges is explicitly specified inside the clause. A clause is *range-restricted* if every variable in the consequent of the clause occurs in its antecedent as well. Range-restricted statements are necessarily ground. The class of range-restricted formulas consists mainly of those first-order formulas that can be equivalently expressed by means of restricted quantification.

For problems dealing with a single unstructured domain, range-restrictedness of clauses cannot be naturally expected. Examples of this kind can be found mainly among algebraic or set-theoretic problems. Especially non-ground statements have to be expected in this case. If a set S contains clauses that are not range-restricted, it nevertheless may be transformed into a set S^* that is range-restricted and that is satisfiable iff S is satisfiable. For this purpose an auxiliary predicate 'dom' has to be introduced and the following transformations and additions to be performed:

- Every statement   true ---> C   containing variables X_1 to X_n is transformed into a rule $dom(X_1),...,dom(X_n)$ ---> C.

- Every rule   A ---> C   such that C contains variables X_1 to X_n that don't occur in A is transformed into a rule $A,dom(X_1),...,dom(X_n)$ ---> C.

- For every ground term t that occurs in S, the unit clause   true ---> dom(t)   is added to S. If S is free of ground terms, a single unit   true ---> dom(a)   is added where 'a' is an artificial constant.

- For every n-ary predicate p and Skolem term t occurring as the i-th parameter of a p-atom in the consequent of a clause in S, a rule $p(X_1,..,X_i,..,X_n)$ ---> $dom(X_i)$ is added to S.

The predicate 'dom' makes explicit the domain of interpretation. The 'dom' literals added to non-range-restricted clauses provide an implicit instantiation of the respective variables over the whole domain. The additional clauses are necessary for guaranteeing that the relation 'dom' contains an entry for every ground term that occurs in Hyp(S). Although the transformation is not preserving equivalence in the strict sense, a kind of weak equivalence between S and S^* exists: if the relation assigned to the new auxiliary predicate 'dom' is removed from any model of S^*, a model of S is obtained. There is a one-to-one correspondence between models of S and models of S^* up to the 'dom' relation. Therefore the transformation described preserves satisfiability as well.

Every set of clauses may be transformed into a range-restricted set in this way, but it has to be mentioned that the transformation may have the same effect as a partial instantiation.

One can easily prove that Hyp(S) consists of ground clauses only iff all clauses in S are range-restricted. Hyperresolution saturation can be implemented very efficiently in this case. We will show that a combination of unit hyperresolution and clause splitting is sufficient in place of full hyperresolution. In addition, h-models can be determined particularly easily, as a ground Hyp(S) coincides with its instance set. The method we describe may therefore be interpreted as an implementation of a systematic search for covers of Hyp(S).

4. Model trees

In this section we investigate how to make benefit of the particularities of hyperresolution in the range-restricted case. As an introductory example let us consider the following range-restricted set S_1:

$$
\begin{array}{ll}
\text{true} \dashrightarrow p(a) \; ; \; q(b) & r(X,Y) \, , \, u(Y) \dashrightarrow t(Y) \\
p(X) \dashrightarrow r(X,f(X)) & q(X) \dashrightarrow t(X) \\
r(X,Y) \dashrightarrow t(Y) \; ; \; s(X) & p(X) \, , \, t(f(X)) \dashrightarrow \text{false} \\
s(X) \dashrightarrow u(f(X)) & q(X) \, , \, t(X) \dashrightarrow \text{false}
\end{array}
$$

Instead of starting hyperresolution from p(a) ; q(b), one can analyse the case where p(a) is true independently from the case where q(b) is true. Such a splitting into two independent subproblems is sound because the clause p(a) ; q(b) is a ground disjunction. In each subcase unit hyperresolution is now applicable. Whenever non-unit hyperresolvents are obtained they are immediately split as well, i.e., new sub-subproblems are created. For each of the subproblems we finally will be able to derive 'false' by means of unit hyperresolution, which indicates that S_1 is unsatisfiable. Fig. 1 illustrates the different splitting and unit hyperresolution steps in form of a tree.

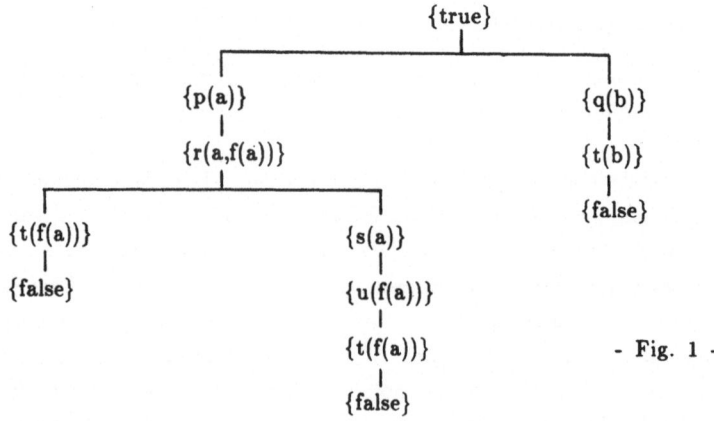

- Fig. 1 -

If the rule $p(X),t(f(X)) \longrightarrow false$ would be missing in S_1, the two leftmost branches in this tree could be cut one step earlier - indicating the existence of two different h-models. The respective models - $\{p(a), r(a,f(a)), s(a), u(f(a)), t(f(a))\}$ and $\{p(a), r(a,f(a)), t(f(a))\}$ - can be directly extracted from the tree by collecting all literals along a branch not ending with 'false'. Because of this property we would like to call such a tree a *model tree*. Every tree T_S that satisfies the following conditions is a model tree for S:

1. The nodes of T_S are finite sets consisting of truth values or of ground literals from the Herbrand base of S.

2. The root of T_S is the set $\{true\}$.

3. Let N be any node of T_S and let anc(N) denote the union of N and all its ancestor nodes.

   a. N is a leaf iff either N contains 'false', or hyp(S^-,anc(N)) is empty.

   b. N has a direct descendant N' iff N' is a non-empty cover of hyp(S^-,anc(N))

We call leaves containing 'false' *failure nodes* and branches ending in a failure node *closed*. A leaf that does not contain 'false' is a *model node*. A model tree is closed if all its branches are closed.

Two important properties of model trees can be easily proved:

(*) If any model tree for S contains a model node N, then S is satisfiable with h-model anc(N).

(**) If any closed model tree for S exists, then S is unsatisfiable.

Thus model tree generation provides the basis for a sound and complete proof procedure for the class of clause sets with a hyperresolution saturation that is ground. As soon as a model node has been found, satisfiability has been proved due to (*). In case of unsatisfiability, however, the whole model tree has to be generated for being sure that all its branches are closed (**).

There are two cases in which satisfiability can be reported immediately: In case S consists of rules only, hyperresolution is not applicable and S is trivially satisfiable with empty h-model. If on the other hand no rule in S has the consequent 'false' no branch will ever be closed.

Model trees are related to special analytic tableaux in the sense of [Smu68]. The strategy by which this kind of tableaux can be constructed is such that a branch is expanded by splitting a clause C iff all negative literals in C are simultaneously unifiable with positive literals along the branch. This particular strategy could be expressed in terms of hyperresolution as well. Removing all negative literals from such a tableau leads directly to the corresponding model tree.

In general there are many different ways how a model tree may be constructed. Choices have to be made in which order to try the different possible covers of a partial saturation hyp(S⁻,anc(N)). In the next section we will present an implementation of a pure depth-first strategy for model tree generation. In general, Hyp(S) and therefore any model tree for S can be infinite. In case Hyp(S) is finite, however, all model trees for S are finite as well and model tree generation will always terminate. Therefore satisfiability is decidable for such sets of clauses. In section 6 we will further characterize this decidable class and give a more efficient procedure for deciding satisfiability of clause sets from this class.

5. A PROLOG-implementation of model tree generation

Unit hyperresolution can be implemented in PROLOG extremely easily and efficiently. After having defined '--->' as a PROLOG binary operator, problem clauses can be directly asserted as PROLOG facts. Solving the PROLOG goal '(A ---> C), A, not C' implements the search for a hyperresolvent C that is derivable with all satellites being units in the current database and C being "new", i.e., not subsumed by any of these units. (Note that all non-unit statements will be "derived" this way as well, because 'true' is a PROLOG goal that always succeeds). PROLOG's search through the '--->'-relation corresponds to the search for a nucleus of the next derivation step. Regarding antecedent and consequent of a clause as PROLOG goals (with Boolean connectives represented like in PROLOG) permits to implement the search for suitable satellites as well as the subsumption test via PROLOG goal interpretation. Unit hyperresolution saturation relative to a fixed set of satellites - as required in the definition of a model tree - can be achieved by means of a 'setof' procedure which is available as a system predicate in most PROLOG interpreters.

The following three predicates determine all covers of a given set of hyperresolvents - represented as a PROLOG list - successively on backtracking. The elements of the cover are asserted as facts into the PROLOG database and are automatically retracted on back-tracking:

```
cover([ ]).                        component(L, (L; _)).
cover([H|T]) :-                    component(L, (_; D)) :- !, component(L, D).
    H, !, cover(T).                component(L, L).
cover([H|T]) :-
    component(L, H),
    assume(L),                     assume(X) :- assert(X).
    cover(T).                      assume(X) :- retract(X), !, fail.
```

Immediately after a cover has been computed we can already determine whether any of the descendants of this cover in the model tree under construction will contain 'false'. For this purpose we have made the choice not to treat completely negative clauses in the same way as the remaining clauses, but to represent every rule A ---> false as a PROLOG derivation rule 'false :- A'. This allows to cut branches of a model tree that lead to con-tradictions already one level before 'false' would be explicitly derived. If the PROLOG goal 'false' succeeds after the computation of any cover, backtracking is initiated and a different choice for reaching a cover is made.

The whole proof procedure can now be programmed in form of two simple mutually recursive predicates:

satisfiable :-
    setof(C, ((A ---> C), A, not C), S),
    satisfiable(S).

satisfiable([ ]) :- !, not false.
satisfiable(S) :-
    cover(S),
    not false,
    satisfiable.

If 'satisfiable' succeeds, the database contains a h-model of the set of clauses in the 'rule' relation. Failure of 'satisfiable' indicates that no h-model can be found.

Despite of its simplicity this program appears to be surprisingly efficient if applied to problems that are naturally range-restricted. Schubert's Steamroller - introduced in [WAL84] - is an excellent example of this kind of problems. Our PROLOG representation of it corresponds to the 'standard' unsorted formulation of the problem given in [STI86]:

wolf(X) ---> animal(X)
fox(X) ---> animal(X)
bird(X) ---> animal(X)
snail(X) ---> animal(X)
caterpillar(X) ---> animal(X)
grain(X) ---> plant(X)
fox(X),wolf(Y) ---> smaller(X,Y)
bird(X),fox(Y)--> smaller(X,Y)
snail(X),bird(Y) ---> smaller(X,Y)
caterpillar(X),bird(Y) ---> smaller(X,Y)
bird(X),caterpillar(Y) ---> likes(X,Y)
animal(X),animal(Y),smaller(Y,X),plant(W),likes(Y,W),plant(Z) --->
    likes(X,Y) ; likes(X,Z).

true ---> wolf(w)
true ---> fox(f)
true ---> bird(b)
true ---> snail(s)
true ---> caterpillar(c)
true ---> grain(g)
snail(X) ---> plant(i(X))
snail(X) ---> likes(X,i(X))
caterpillar(X) ---> plant(h(X))
caterpillar(X) ---> likes(X,h(X))

false :- likes(X,Y), wolf(X), fox(Y).
false :- likes(X,Y), bird(X), snail(Y).
false :- animal(X), animal(Y), likes(X,Y), grain(Z), likes(Y,Z).
false :- likes(X,Y), wolf(X), grain(Y).

The best cputime Stickel has reported for the solution of this problem is 6 secs. Meanwhile [ENG87] has achieved 1 sec. We have applied the above program to the given formulation of the Steamroller (using a simplified 'setof' procedure for sets of ground elements) in interpreted C-Prolog (Vers. 1.5) on a VAX 11/785. Using the built-in predicate 'cputime' we have measured 1.35 secs. The model tree constructed by the program consists of 14 nodes and has 10 closed branches. If the theorem is omitted, we reach a h-model of 25 literals after 0.83 secs.

On the other hand there are cases where the implicit instantiation introduced through the transformation into range-restricted form makes model tree search impracticable because of the immense size of the tree. Problems 66 to 69 in [PEL86] - difficult function-problems suggested by Ch. Morgan - belong to this kind of examples.

6. An improved procedure for a syntactically defined class

As mentioned before model tree generation is a decision procedure for satisfiability for clause sets with a finite hyperresolution saturation. If we would know in advance that a given set belongs to this class we could use an even simpler (and in general more efficient) PROLOG implementation of model tree generation:

```
satisfiable_fin :-
        (A ---> C), A, not C, !,
            component(L,C),
            assume(L),
            not false,
            satisfiable_fin.
    satisfiable_fin.
```

This predicate does no longer determine sets of hyperresolvents before trying to cover them. Instead it generates hyperresolvents as they come and covers them immediately. If the set of all possible hyperresolvents is finite, the program is guaranteed to exhaust this set and thus to reach 'false' whenever possible. In case Hyp(S) is infinite, 'satisfiable_fin' may work correctly as well, but there are cases where refutation-completeness is lost. The following clause set S_2 is an example for this:

$$\text{true} ---> p(a) \qquad\qquad p(Y) ---> p(f(Y))$$
$$p(X) , q(X) ---> \text{false} \qquad p(Z) ---> q(f(Z))$$

S_2 has infinitely many hyperresolution levels. The nodes of the model tree for S_2 are the sets $\{p(a)\}$, $\{p(f(a)),q(f(a))\}$ and $\{p(f(f(a))),q(f(f(a))),\text{false}\}$, respectively. Thus model tree generation with the predicate 'satisfiable' will terminate as opposed to 'satisfiable_fin': this procedure reaches only the p-atoms in each level but never derives 'false'. Every atom is asserted immediately after its generation and thus leads to a new application of the same rule. The search function of 'satisfiable_fin' is simple, but inherently "unfair". Thus its simplicity can be exploited only for refuting sets with finite hyperresolution saturation.

The infinite generation of hyperresolvents is due to the presence of a special recursive rule in S_2: $p(Y) ---> p(f(Y))$ is recursive and in addition leads to the generation of infinitely many nested terms via hyperresolution. The Steamroller contains a recursive rule as well, namely

$$\text{animal}(X),\text{animal}(Y),\text{smaller}(Y,X),\text{plant}(W),\text{likes}(Y,W),\text{plant}(Z) --->$$
$$(\text{likes}(X,Y);\text{likes}(X,Z))$$

However, no new nested terms can be generated through this rule, as no Skolem term is involved in the recursion.

There is another phenomenon that influences a potential infinite generation of hyperresolvents. Consider the following set S_3:

$$\text{true} ---> p(a) \qquad\qquad p(X) , s(Y,Z) ---> r(Z,f(X))$$
$$r(X,f(X)) ---> \text{false} \qquad r(X,Y) ---> s(Y,f(X))$$

This set contains a cycle of recursion between the two rules on the right column that involves Skolem terms as well. Despite this similarity with S_2, $\text{Hyp}(S_3)$ is finite and both procedures, 'satisfiable' as well as 'satisfiable_fin' terminate. This happens because the respective rules do not participate in any hyperresolution step.

A syntactical characterization of clause sets that contain a cycle of recursion leading to infinite term-generation when entered during hyperresolution can be given in terms of the connection graph of the set. Certain cycles in this graph can be distinguished by means of compatible unifiers, recursive substitutions and a reachability relation between atoms. The presence of these special cycles characterizes a solvable class of clause sets. This class properly contains two well-known solvable classes, namely the Bernays-Schoenfinkel class (clauses without non-constant Skolem terms) and the class of compact clause sets [LEW75] (sets without recursive rules). The formal definition of this class and a proof of its solvability will be given in a forthcoming paper.

7. Conclusion

In this paper a proof procedure for sets of range-restricted clauses has been proposed which is based on model generation via hyperresolution. The method exploits that hyperresolvents derivable from range-restricted clauses are ground. The procedure can be interpreted as generating a model tree in a depth-first manner. A PROLOG implementation of the approach has been described that is simple but allows to solve many problems with considerable efficiency. As a satisfiability preserving transformation into a range-restricted problem is always possible, the procedure is general purpose.

Two possible extensions are under investigation at the moment. First, one can use PROLOG derivation rules for representing other Horn clauses than only completely negative ones. Moreover, a careful use of non-ground PROLOG facts for representation of unit clauses can help to avoid many of those cases where a combinatorial explosion of generated facts due to implicit instantiation via 'dom' would otherwise occur. As long as it is guaranteed that non-Horn statements are always grounded before splitting, these deviations from a purely generative approach are acceptable and often very useful. However, it should be noted that PROLOG-specific problems due to recursion or missing occurs check may arise, that do not exist for the method described in this paper.

Second, we are going to make the method sound and complete for finite satisfiability as well. Most theorem provers do not terminate in many cases where a finite model exists. For applying the procedure in a database context, existence of finite models has to be detected. The price to be paid for being able to terminate more often in case of satisfiability will be a decrease in efficiency for refutation, however. In [BM86] we have investigated which additional features are required for achieving completeness for both, unsatisfiability as well as finite satisfiability. An extension of our method with these additional features appears to be straightforward.

Apart from the two points mentioned, further increase in efficiency may be obtained by means of more sophisticated strategies for model tree generation.

Acknowledgement:

We would like to thank L. Wos, R. Overbeek and the other members of the Argonne team for their hospitality and the stimulating discussions during the visit of one of the authors at Argonne. Furthermore we would like to acknowledge the many useful remarks made by the anonymous referees.

References:

[BM86]   F. Bry and R. Manthey, *Proving finite satisfiability of first-order theories*, Internal Report KB-27, ECRC, 1986

[ENG87] D. Engelhardt, *Model elimination - Grundlagen und Implementation*, Diplomarbeit, Tech. Hochschule Darmstadt, Fachbereich Informatik, 1987

[LEW75] H. Lewis, *Cycles of unifiability and decidability by resolution*, Techn. Report, Aiken Comp. Lab., Harvard Univ., 1975

[NIC82] J.M. Nicolas, *Logic for improving integrity checking in relational databases*, Acta Informatica 18, 1982, 227-253

[PEL86] F.J. Pelletier, *Seventy-five Problems for Testing Automatic Theorem provers*, J. of Autom. Reasoning 2, 1986, 191-216

[ROB65] J.A. Robinson, *Automated Deduction with Hyper-Resolution*, Intern. Journ. of Computer Math. 1, 1965, 227-234

[SMU68] R. Smullyan, *First-order logic*, 1968

[STI86] M. Stickel, *Schubert's steamroller problem: formulations and solutions* J. of Autom. Reasoning 2, 1986, 89-101

[WAL84] C. Walther, *A mechanical solution to Schubert's steamroller by many-sorted resolution*, Proc. AAAI 1984, Austin(Tex.), 330-334
         (rev. version: Artificial Intelligence 26, 1985, 217-224)

Narrowing Techniques
Applied to Idempotent Unification

Alexander Herold

European Computer-Industry Research Centre (ECRC)

Arabellastr. 17, D-8000 Muenchen 81, West-Germany

net-address: ...!mcvax!unido!ecrcvax!herold

Abstract: A complete unification algorithm for idempotent functions is presented. This algorithm is derived from the universal unification algorithm, which is based on the narrowing process. First an improvement of the universal algorithm is shown. These results are applied to the special case of idempotence resulting in an idempotence unification algorithm.

Several refinements for this algorithm are proposed: the clash criterium and the occur-check of ordinary Robinson unification are extended to the case of idempotence. Finally certain conditions are investigated, which prohibit the generation of redundant unifiers.

1. Introduction

Unification of terms modulo an equational theories is a basic operation in many applications of Artificial Intelligence and Computer Science. It is of particular use in Automated Deduction Systems and in the design of programming languages for Artificial Intelligence, in particular in Logic Programming [MV 87].

Unification theory is concerned with problems of the following kind: given two terms built from function symbols, constants and variables, do there exist terms that can be substituted for the variables such that the two terms thus obtained become equal? Robinson [Ro 65] was the first to give an algorithm to find such a substitution with the additional property that the returned 'unifier' is most general (or is an mgu for short), i.e. all other substitutions 'unifying' the two terms can be computed from that substitution. From an algebraic point of view unification is solving equations and an mgu is a 'basis' of the whole set of unifiers.

Equational unification extends the classical unification problem to solving equations in equationally defined theories. But then there may not exist one single mgu. Depending on the equational theory there are finite or infinite sets of mgu's and in some cases a set of mgu's does not even exist. Equational theories can therefore be classified into unitary (a single mgu exists), finitary (there is a finite set of mgu's) and infinitary (the set of mgus is infinite) theories and the class of nullary theories (i.e. a set of most general unifiers may not exist). For a detailed bibliography we refer to the state-of-the-art survey of J. Siekmann [Si 86].

Since every equational theory T requires a special purpose T-unification algorithm, there are recent attempts to combine these special unification algorithms [He 86, He 87, Ki 85, Ti 86 and Ye 85]. But all these combination algorithms do not work for collapse theories. Collapse theories are those theories which contain an axiom t = x, e.g. idempotence f(x x) = x. On the other hand there is a very powerful tool for unification in canonical theories: the universal unification algorithm [Fy 79, Hl 80, SS 81, Sz 82]. Given a canonical term rewriting system for an equational theory we at once have a unification algorithm for that theory. This algorithm is based on narrowing using rewrite rules, which is essentially oriented paramodulation [RW 69] and it can be extended to equational rewrite systems [He 82, Hl 80, JK 83]. A similar algorithm has been recently proposed in [MM 87]. These extensions are one possibility to avoid the restriction in the combination algorithms for collapse free theories. Theories, which are only defined by one collapse axiom, mostly have a canonical rewrite system and by a result of Hullot the universal unification algorithm terminates for those theories [Hl 80]. Moreover the universal unification algorithm can trivially be combined with uninterpreted function symbols, since these symbols do not change the term rewriting system.

As a prototype we study the theory of idempotence. Since one problem with the universal unification algorithm is its inefficiency we try to improve the obvious solution given by the universal unification algorithm by pruning the search space. After an introduction into the notions and notations of unification theory we present the universal unification algorithm based on narrowing. We then give a method to improve this universal algorithm. These results are applied to idempotent functions resulting in a first version of an unification algorithm for idempotence. Exploiting the fact that we only have idempotent and uninterpreted function symbols we present special results improving this first version for an idempotent unification algorithm. For space limitations we have omitted all proofs and some of the exact definitions. They are carried out in [He 87].

2. Definitions and Notations

Given a family of operators F with their arities and a denumerable set of variables V, we define T, the set of *first order terms*, over F and V, as the least set with (i) $V \subseteq T$, and if arity(f) = 0 for $f \in F$ then $f \in T$ and (ii) if $t_1, ..., t_n \in T$ and arity(f) = n then $f(t_1 ... t_n) \in T$. The algebra with carrier T and with operators, namely the term constructors corresponding to each operator of F, i.e. it just gives an algebraic structure to T. Let $V(s)$ be the set of variables occurring in a term s.

Terms can be also viewed as labelled trees [JK 83]: A term is a partial function of N^* into $F \cup V$ such that its domain $D(t)$ satisfies the following condition:

(i) the empty word Λ is in $D(t)$ and (ii) $\pi.i$ is in $D(t)$ iff π is in $D(t)$ and $i \in [1, arity(t(\pi))]$,

where . denotes the concatenation of strings. $D(t)$ is the set of *occurrences* and $O(t)$ denotes the set of non-variable occurrences, t/π the subterm of t at the occurrence π of t and $t[\pi \leftarrow t']$ the term obtained by replacing t/π by t' in t. We say that two occurrences π_1 and π_2 are independent iff one selected term is not a subterm of the other selected term (i.e. there exists an occurrence π such that $\pi_1 = \pi.i.\pi'_1$, $\pi_2 = \pi.j.\pi'_2$ and $i \neq j$).

A *substitution* $\sigma: T \to T$ is an endomorphism on the term algebra, which can be represented as a finite set of pairs: $\sigma = \{x_1 \leftarrow t_1 ... x_n \leftarrow t_n\}$. The restriction $\sigma|_V$ of a substitution σ to a set of variables V is defined as $\sigma|_V x = \sigma x$ if $x \in V$ and $\sigma|_V x = x$ else. The set of substitutions is denoted by Σ and the identity by ε. Let $DOM\sigma = \{x \in V \mid \sigma x \neq x\}$ be the domain of σ, $COD\sigma = \{\sigma x \mid x \in DOM\sigma\}$ the codomain of σ and $VCOD\sigma = V(COD\sigma)$ be the variables introduced by σ.

An *equation* s = t is a pair of terms. For a set of equations T, the equational theory presented by T (in short: the equational theory T) is defined as the finest congruence $=_T$ containing all pairs $\sigma s = \sigma t$ for s = t in T and σ in Σ (i.e., the Σ-invariant congruence relation generated by T). We extend T-equality in T to the set of substitutions Σ by:

$$\sigma =_T \tau \qquad iff \qquad \forall x \in V \qquad \sigma x =_T \tau x .$$

If T-equality of substitutions is restricted to a set of variables W we write

$$\sigma =_T \tau [W] \qquad iff \qquad \forall x \in W \qquad \sigma x =_T \tau x$$

and say σ and τ are *T-equal on W*. A substitution τ is *more general* than σ on W (or σ is a *T-instance* of τ on W):

$$\sigma \geq_T \tau [W] \qquad iff \qquad \exists \lambda \in \Sigma \qquad \sigma =_T \lambda\tau [W].$$

Two substitutions σ, τ are called *T-equivalent* on W

$$\sigma \equiv_T \tau [W] \qquad iff \qquad \sigma \leq_T \tau [W] \text{ and } \tau \leq_T \sigma [W].$$

Given two terms s, t and an equational theory T, a unification problem for T is denoted as $\langle s = t \rangle_T$. We say $\sigma \in \Sigma$ is a solution of $\langle s = t \rangle_T$ (or σ is a T-unifier of s and t) iff $\sigma s =_T \sigma t$. For the set of all T-unifiers of s and t we write $U_T(s, t)$. For a given unification problem $\langle s = t \rangle_T$, it is not necessary to compute the whole set of unifiers $U_T\langle s, t\rangle$, but instead a smaller set useful in representing U_T. Therefore we define $cU_T\langle s, t\rangle$, a *complete set of unifiers* of s and t on $W = V(s, t)$ as [Pl 72]:

(i) $cU_T\langle s, t\rangle \subseteq U_T\langle s, t\rangle$ (correctness)

(ii) $\forall \delta \in U_T\langle s, t\rangle \ \exists \ \sigma \in cU_T\langle s, t\rangle: \delta \geq_T \sigma \ [W]$ (completeness)

A *set of most general unifiers* $\mu U_T\langle s, t\rangle$ is a complete set with

(iii) $\forall \ \sigma, \tau \in \mu U_T\langle s, t\rangle: \sigma \leq_T \tau \ [W]$ implies $\sigma = \tau$ (minimality).

The set μU_T does not always exist [FH 86, Ba 86, Sc 86]; if it does then it is unique up to the equivalence $\equiv_T [W]$ (see [Hu 76, FH 86]).

A unification algorithm is called *complete* (and *minimal*) if it returns a correct and complete (and minimal) set of unifiers for every pair of terms.

A *term rewriting system* $R = \{ l_1 \Rightarrow r_1 ,..., l_n \Rightarrow r_n \}$ is a directed set of pairs of terms $l_i, r_i \in T$ with $V(r_i) \subseteq V(l_i)$ for $1 \leq i \leq n$. We say that a term $s \rightarrow_R$-reduces to a term t at occurrence π with $l_i \Rightarrow r_i$ and we write $s \rightarrow_R t$ or $s \rightarrow_{[\pi,i]} t$ iff:

$\exists \ l_i \Rightarrow r_i \in R, \ \sigma \in \Sigma, \ \pi \in O(s)$ such that $s/\pi = \sigma l_i$ and $t = s[\pi \leftarrow \sigma r_i]$.

In order to aviod conflicts a new variant of the rule $l_i \Rightarrow r_i$ is used in each step. The indices of $\rightarrow_R$ are omitted if they are understood from the context. A term t is said to be *reducible* if $t \rightarrow_R t'$ for some t', else t is said to be *irreducible* or in $\rightarrow_R$-*normal form*. The reflexive and transitive closure of $\rightarrow_R$ is denoted by $\xrightarrow{*}_R$. A term rewriting system is said to be a *complete* set of reductions or a *canonical* term rewriting system iff:

$\rightarrow_R$ is *noetherian* , i.e. there does not exist an infinite reduction $t_1 \rightarrow_R t_2 \rightarrow_R t_3 \cdots$

$\rightarrow_R$ is *confluent* , i.e. for s, s_1, s_2 with $s \xrightarrow{*}_R s_1$ and $s \xrightarrow{*}_R s_2$
there exists t such that $s_1 \xrightarrow{*}_R t$ and $s_2 \xrightarrow{*}_R t$.

For an equational theory T there are techniques to obtain a term rewriting system R_T such that this system has the Church-Rosser property, i.e. $s =_T t$ iff there exists $r \in T$ with $s \xrightarrow{*} r$ and $t \xrightarrow{*} r$; moreover it is sometimes possible to obtain a canonical term rewriting system [KB 70, HO 84, Bu 85]. Canonical systems are an important basis for computations in equational logics, since they yield a decision procedure for T-equality: $s =_T t$ iff $\|s\| = \|t\|$ where $\|s\|$ denotes the unique normal form of s. A substitution σ is called in normal form or *normalized* iff all terms in the codomain are in normal form.

The following relation is the basis for a universal unification algorithm. We say s is *narrowable* to t at occurrence π with the substitution σ and the rule $l_i \Rightarrow r_i$ and write $s \rightarrowtail_{[\pi,i,\sigma]} t$ or shortly $s \rightarrowtail t$ iff

$\exists \ l_i \Rightarrow r_i \in R, \ \sigma \in \Sigma, \ \pi \in O(s)$ such that σ is mgu of s/π and l_i and $t = \sigma(s[\pi \leftarrow r_i])$.

Again the new variants of the rules are used. The substitution σ is called a narrower or narrowing substitution. Narrowing is the same as oriented paramodulation [RW 69]. In [Hl 80] the relationship between narrowing and reduction is established:

Theorem 1:   Let s be a term and η be a normalized substitution with $DOM\eta \subseteq V(s)$. For every $\rightarrow$ - derivation issuing from ηs

$(1) \ \eta s = t_0 \rightarrow_{[\pi_1,k_1]} t_1 \rightarrow_{[\pi_2,k_2]} t_2 \rightarrow \cdots \rightarrow_{[\pi_n,k_n]} t_n$

there exists a $\rightarrowtail$ - derivation issuing from s

$(2) \ s = s_0 \rightarrowtail_{[\pi_1,k_1,\sigma_1]} s_1 \rightarrowtail_{[\pi_2,k_2,\sigma_2]} s_2 \cdots \rightarrowtail_{[\pi_n,k_n,\sigma_n]} s_n$

for each i, $1 \leq i \leq n$, a normalized substitution η_i such that $\eta_i(s_i) = t_i$ and $\eta = \eta_i \theta_i \ [V(s)]$, where $\theta_i = \sigma_i \ldots \sigma_1$. Conversely, to each $\rightarrowtail$ - derivation (2) and every η such that $\eta \leq \theta_n \ [V(s)]$ we can associate a $\rightarrow$ - derivation (1).

This result can be depicted in a diagram as:

$$\eta s = \quad t_0 \quad \to_{[\pi 1, k1]} \quad t_1 \quad \to_{[\pi 2, k2]} \quad t_2 \to \quad \cdots \quad \to_{[\pi n, kn]} \quad t_n$$

$$\uparrow \qquad\qquad \uparrow \qquad\qquad \uparrow \qquad\qquad\qquad \uparrow$$

$$|\ \eta_0 \qquad\quad |\ \eta_1 \qquad\quad |\ \eta_2 \qquad\qquad\quad |\ \eta_n$$

$$|\qquad\qquad\quad |\qquad\qquad\quad |\qquad\qquad\qquad\quad |$$

$$s = s_0 \rightarrowtail_{[\pi 1, k1, \sigma 1]} \quad s_1 \rightarrowtail_{[\pi 2, k2, \sigma 2]} \quad s_2 \rightarrowtail \cdots \rightarrowtail_{[\pi n, kn, \sigma n]} \ s_n$$

Diagram 1

This close relationship leads to a universal unification algorithm, which is essentially an enumerating process of the narrowing tree: Let t be a term then $\mathcal{N}_R(t)$ is the narrowing tree with

- t is the root of $\mathcal{N}_R(t)$
- if t' is a node in $\mathcal{N}_R(t)$ and $t' \rightarrowtail_{[\pi, k, \sigma]} t''$ then t'' is a successor node of t' in $\mathcal{N}_R(t)$.

Given a T-unification problem $\langle s = t \rangle_T$ the following theorem yields that enumerating the narrowing tree $\mathcal{N}_R \langle s = t \rangle$ combined with standard Robinson unification defines a complete unification algorithm. The sequence $\langle . = . \rangle$ is considered as a binary function symbol, we perform the narrowing steps on the term $\langle s = t \rangle$.

Theorem 2: Let T be an equational theory that admits a canonical term rewriting system R. Let s, t be two terms and let $N_R \langle s = t \rangle$ be the set of all substitutions τ such that there exists a $\rightarrowtail$ – derivation:

$$\langle s = t \rangle \rightarrowtail_{[\sigma 1]} \langle s_1 = t_1 \rangle \rightarrowtail_{[\sigma 2]} \cdots \rightarrowtail_{[\sigma n]} \langle s_n = t_n \rangle,$$

where $\theta_n = \sigma_n \ldots \sigma_1$ is normalized, s_n and t_n are unifiable with the most general unifier β and $\tau = \beta \theta_n$. Then $N_R \langle s = t \rangle$ is a complete set of unifiers of s and t.

Since for every substitution produced by a narrowing sequence there is a corresponding reduction sequence, from which we can show that the substitution is indeed a unifier for the given two terms, correctness is obvious. On the other hand to every unifier η' there exists a normalized unifier η such that $\eta' =_T \eta$. Hence there exists a derivation $\eta \langle s = t \rangle \xrightarrow{*} \langle r = r \rangle$ and by Theorem 1 a corresponding $\rightarrowtail$ –derivation $\langle s = t \rangle \rightarrowtail^{*} \langle s_n = t_n \rangle$ with $\eta \leq \sigma \theta_n [\mathbb{V}(s, t)]$, where σ is a most general Robinson unifier of s_n and t_n. This establishes the completeness of the narrowing technique. A detailed proof of the above theorem can be found in [Hu 80]. So by enumeration of the narrowing tree $\mathcal{N}_R \langle s = t \rangle$ and ordinary unification at each node we can construct a complete unification algorithm. Since this algorithm is very inefficient, it is important to find criteria for pruning subtrees out of the narrowing tree.

3. Pruning the Narrowing Tree

A first improvement of the above universal unification algorithm was given by Hullot [Hl 80]. He proposed to use only **basic** $\rightarrowtail$ - derivations. Roughly speaking basic narrowing suggests an inside-outside strategy and additionally is not allowed to narrow at the occurrences introduced by the narrowing substitutions. Hullot showed this method to be complete using the correspondance stated in the diagram after Theorem 1 and the fact that there always exists an innermost-outermost reduction of a term to its normal form. Moreover the method of basic derivation gives a sufficient condition for the termination of the narrowing process [Hl 80]. We shall illustrate the idea of basic narrowing by an example: Let $\{f(x\ x) \Rightarrow x\}$ be the rewriting system then $f(f(x\ y)\ f(a\ z)) \rightarrowtail_{[\Lambda]} f(a\ y) \rightarrowtail_{[\Lambda]} a$ is not a basic derivation, but $f(f(x\ y)\ f(a\ z)) \rightarrowtail_{[2]} f(f(x\ y)\ a) \rightarrowtail_{[1]} f(x\ a) \rightarrowtail_{[\Lambda]} a$ is basic.

Another well-known reduction strategy is the leftmost strategy. We define a narrowing strategy corresponding to a leftmost reduction sequence. The idea is to follow a left-to-right strategy, in other words, if we have performed a narrowing step at an occurrence then we do not allow to narrow on those occurrences that are to the left and independent of the current occurrence. Exactly, for a term t, a prefix-closed set of occurrences $O_0 \subseteq O(t)$ and a normalized substitution η a $\rightarrow$ - derivation issuing from ηt

$$\eta t = s_0 \rightarrow_{[\pi 1, k1]} s_1 \rightarrow_{[\pi 2, k2]} s_2 \rightarrow \cdots \rightarrow_{[\pi n, kn]} s_n$$

or a $\rightarrowtail\rightarrow$ – derivation issuing from t

$$t = t_0 \rightarrowtail\rightarrow_{[\pi 1, k1, \sigma 1]} t_1 \rightarrowtail\rightarrow_{[\pi 2, k1, \sigma 2]} t_2 \rightarrowtail\rightarrow \cdots \rightarrowtail\rightarrow_{[\pi n, kn, \sigma n]} t_n$$

is **left-to-right** in O_0 iff $\pi_i \in O_i$ for $1 \le i \le n$ with

$$O_i = O_{i-1} \setminus \{\pi \in O_{i-1} \mid \pi = \pi'.i'.\pi'', \pi_i = \pi'.i.\pi'' \text{ and } i' \le i\} \cup \{\pi_i.\pi'' \mid \pi'' \in O(r_{ki})\}$$

If we consider the above example then $f(f(x\ y)\ f(a,\ z)) \rightarrowtail\rightarrow_{[1]} f(x\ f(a\ z)) \rightarrowtail\rightarrow_{[2]} f(x\ a)$ is a left-to-right derivation whereas $f(f(x\ y)\ f(a\ z)) \rightarrowtail\rightarrow_{[2]} f(f(x\ y)\ a) \rightarrowtail\rightarrow_{[1]} f(x\ a)$ is not (note that the occurrence 1 is left and independent of the occurrence 2).

A derivation of t is said to be **left-to-right** iff it is left-to-right in $O_0 = O(t)$. Completeness is preserved when only left-to-right derivations are used. Moveover left-to-right and basic derivations can be combined. The idea of the proof is again to exploit the correspondence between narrowing and reduction stated in diagram 1 and the fact that a leftmost-innermost reduction to the normal form always exists. Additionally we can restrict the enumeration process of the narrowing tree to consider only those nodes such that the narrowing unifier is normalized. We summmarize these results in the following proposition:

Proposition 3: Given two terms s and t and a normalized T-unifier η then there exists a left-to-right basic $\rightarrowtail\rightarrow$ – derivation $\langle s = t \rangle = \langle s_0 = t_0 \rangle \rightarrowtail\rightarrow \langle s_1 = t_1 \rangle \ldots \rightarrowtail\rightarrow \langle s_n = t_n \rangle$ such that s_n and t_n are unifiable with the most general Robinson unifier β and $\eta \le \beta\theta_n [V(s, t)]$. The narrower θ_n can always be assumed to be normalized.

Another way to show this proposition is to establish a restricted local confluence of the narrowing relation depicted in the following commuting diagram where $\sigma*\tau$ denotes the most general instance of σ and τ:

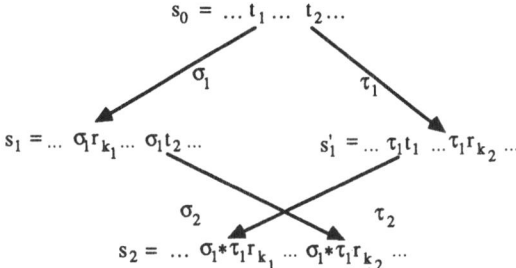

Diagram 2

This restricted confluence can also be used in a negative direction: non-unifiability (i.e., the fact that certain rules are not applicable at certain occurrences) can be inherited during the narrowing process, a fact that can be used in an implementation of the universal unification algorithm. We shall now apply these results to the equational theory of idempotence.

4. An Algorithm for Idempotent Unification

The first paper on unification under idempotence was published by P. Raulefs and J. Siekmann [RS 78]. Since the idempotence law $I = \{f(x\ x) = x\}$ can be directed into a canonical term rewriting system $R_I = \{f(x\ x) \Rightarrow x\}$, we can apply the results of the universal unification procedure. Moreover using the termination criterion of Hullot [Hl 80] we already have a complete unification algorithm for idempotence.

Since this algorithm is not minimal we tried to find a minimal algorithm.

Of course the results of [SS 81, Sz 82] could be used, but testing the minimality at each node of the narrowing tree as required in the algorithm of [SS 81, Sz 82] would be more expensive than minimizing the returned set of redundant unifiers. Before we will improve the universal algorithm for the special theory of idempotence we shall discuss the algorithm presented by Raulefs and Siekmann since their work was a starting point for our algorithm.

The algorithm they suggested was designed for only one idempotent function symbol f, constants and variables. It is split up into two interlocking parts: the collapsing phase and the R-unification phase. The collapsing phase is the same as narrowing with the idempotence rule on the original terms. The R-unification process unifying the collapsed terms differs from standard Robinson unification in unifying compound terms with constants and variables. In the case of unifying a term with a constant b all variables in the term are replaced by b. If as a result the term contains only constants b, the R-unification process terminates with success, otherwise with failure. In case of unifying a term t with a variable x they distinguish two cases: if the variable x does not occur in the term t then $\{x \leftarrow t\}$ is returned, in the other case a subterm q is searched where the variable x does not occur but the 'brother' of this subterm is an occurrence of the variable x. If $\{x \leftarrow q\} t =_I q$ the returned unifier is $\{x \leftarrow q\}$ else both terms are not R-unifiable. As the universal unification algorithm shows it is superfluous to consider these additional subcases and the returned unifiers are redundant. Siekmann and Raulefs then observed that their algorithm is not minimal. To come closer to minimality they proposed to collapse only on 'hot' nodes, i.e., on those nodes in the tree representation of the original terms such that the node of the opposite term is also not a leaf node. But then the modified algorithm is no longer complete: Consider $s = x$ and $t = f(f(f(a\ b)\ x)\ f(f(a\ y)\ x))$ then there are no hot nodes and s and t would not be R-unifiable since neither $\{x \leftarrow f(a\ b)\}$ nor $\{x \leftarrow f(a\ y)\}$ unify s and t; but s and t are in fact I-unifiable with $\{x \leftarrow f(a\ b), y \leftarrow b\}$.

We now want to refine the universal unification algorithm for idempotent functions. We consider a family of function symbols consisting of denumerable many constants C, of a finite set of binary idempotent function symbols F_I and a finite set of arbitrary free function symbols $F_\emptyset$. Then the equational theory I is presented by

$$I = \langle \{f(x\ x) = x \mid f \in F_I\}, F_\emptyset \cup F_I \cup C \rangle$$

and the corresponding canonical term rewriting system is

$$R_I = \{f(x\ x) \Rightarrow x \mid f \in F_I\}.$$

If there is only one idempotent function symbol in the following examples, we sometimes omit that function symbol and write (s t) for f(s t). Since the rewrite system R_I is fixed in the following we omit the index I in $\mathcal{N}\langle s = t \rangle$. Moreover we always restrict the domain of the narrowers to the variables in the term to which the rule is applied, i.e., the new variable x of f(x x) is always omitted. Hence the narrower is the most general unifier of the right and left subtree of the corresponding subterm.

We are now looking for special criteria to confine the narrowing tree in the case of idempotence. A sufficient condition for stopping the enumeration process at a node $\langle s' = t' \rangle$ is non-unifiability under I, i.e., stop if $U_I\langle s' = t' \rangle = \emptyset$. A quick test for non-unifiability under idempotence is to check whether the two terms start or end with different constants, i.e., in the tree representation of s' the first or last leaf is a constant and different from that of t'. This condition can be generalized to an 'extended clash criterium' for idempotence. As a point of reference we define a first stopping criterion:

(S_1) $\langle s' = t' \rangle \in \mathcal{N}\langle s = t \rangle$ and s' and t' start or end with different constants.

As we have seen in Proposition 3 we can always restrict ourselves to normalized narrowers and hence as soon as the collected narrower is no longer normalized we can stop the enumeration process at that node:

(S_2) $\langle s' = t' \rangle \in \mathcal{N}\langle s = t \rangle$ and $\langle s = t \rangle \rightarrowtail^*_\theta \langle s' = t' \rangle$ and θ not normalized.

If a node $\langle s' = t' \rangle \in \mathcal{N}\langle s = t \rangle$ is reached where s' is a variable and $s' \notin V(t')$ then the only most general unifier is $\{s' \leftarrow t'\}$. Hence we can formulate a third stopping criterion

(S_3) $\langle x = t' \rangle$ or $\langle t' = x \rangle \in \mathcal{N}\langle s = t \rangle$ and $x \notin V(t')$

Another method to diminish the costs of enumerating the tree is to find nodes $\langle s' = t' \rangle \in \mathcal{N}\langle s = t \rangle$ where we need not perform Robinson unification for s' and t', i.e., we are sure that the unifier generated at that node is redundant. But we are not allowed to stop the enumeration process at the node $\langle s' = t' \rangle$ since non-redundant unifiers may be generated in the subtree starting at $\langle s' = t' \rangle$. Consider the following example $\langle (x\ y) = (u\ (v\ w)) \rangle_I$.

We show a part of the narrowing tree, which generates a complete set of unifiers.

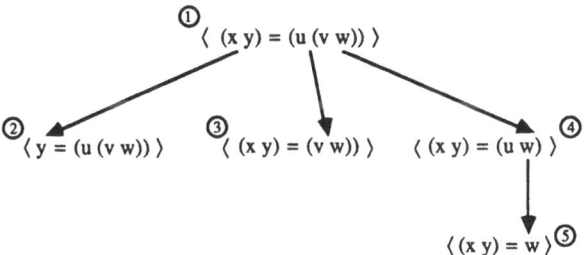

Node	narrower	Robinson unifier	I-unifier
1: $\langle (x\ y) = (u\ (v\ w)) \rangle$	ε	$\{x \leftarrow u,\ y \leftarrow (v\ w)\}$	$\sigma_1 = \{x \leftarrow u, y \leftarrow (v\ w)\}$
2: $\langle y = (u\ (v\ w)) \rangle$	$\{x \leftarrow y\}$	$\{y \leftarrow (u\ (v\ w))\}$	$\sigma_2 = \{x \leftarrow (u\ (v\ w)),\ y \leftarrow (u\ (v\ w))\}$
3: $\langle (x\ y) = (v\ w) \rangle$	$\{u \leftarrow (v\ w)\}$	$\{x \leftarrow v,\ y \leftarrow w\}$	$\sigma_3 = \{u \leftarrow (v\ w),\ x \leftarrow v,\ y \leftarrow w\}$
4: $\langle (x\ y) = (u\ w) \rangle$	$\{v \leftarrow w\}$	$\{x \leftarrow u,\ y \leftarrow w\}$	$\sigma_4 = \{v \leftarrow w,\ x \leftarrow u,\ y \leftarrow w\}$
5: $\langle (x\ y) = w \rangle$	$\{v \leftarrow w,\ u \leftarrow w\}$	$\{w \leftarrow (x\ y)\}$	$\sigma_5 = \{u \leftarrow (x\ y),\ v \leftarrow (x\ y),\ w \leftarrow (x\ y)\}$

Diagram 3.

We applied the third stop criterion (S_3) to node 2. Observe that $\sigma_4 =_I \{v \leftarrow w\}\sigma_1$. Hence we have $\mu U_I\langle s = t \rangle = \{\sigma_1, \sigma_2, \sigma_3, \sigma_5\}$. We will now generalize the situation at node 4. If we look at the subterm in $(x\ y)$, which is opposite to the subterm we have narrowed upon, we see that this subterm is the variable y occurring only once in both terms.

Exactly, if $\langle s' = t' \rangle \in \mathcal{N}\langle s = t \rangle$ and there exist occurrences $1.\pi, 2.\pi \in D(\langle s' = t' \rangle)$ with $s'/\pi = z$ (resp. $t'/\pi = z$), and z occurs only once in $\langle s' = t' \rangle$, and $\langle s' = t' \rangle \rightarrowtail_{[2.\pi']} \langle s'' = t'' \rangle$ (resp. $\langle s' = t' \rangle \rightarrowtail_{[1.\pi']} \langle s'' = t'' \rangle$), and $\pi' = \pi.\pi''$, i.e., we narrow in a subtree, which is opposite to a variable occurring only once in both terms, then the unifier generated at the node $\langle s'' = t'' \rangle$ is an I-instance of the unifier generated at the node $\langle s' = t' \rangle$ provided that s'' and t'' are Robinson unifiable. Hence we need not perform the Robinson unification of s'' and t''. We call such a criterion a non-evaluation condition.

(NE_1) $\langle s = t \rangle \rightarrowtail_{[2.\pi']} \langle s' = t' \rangle$ (resp. $\langle s = t \rangle \rightarrowtail_{[1.\pi']} \langle s' = t' \rangle$) and $\pi' = \pi.\pi''$ with $1.\pi, 2.\pi \in D(\langle s' = t' \rangle)$ and $s/\pi = z$ (resp. $t/\pi = z$), z occurs only once in s, t.

Given the narrowing sequence $\langle s = t \rangle \rightarrowtail_{[1.\pi]} \langle s_1 = t_1 \rangle \rightarrowtail_{[2.\pi]} \langle s_2 = t_2 \rangle$ it can be shown that the I-unifier generated at $\langle s_2 = t_2 \rangle$ is an I-instance of the Robinson unifier of s and t. We can generalize this lemma to a non-evaluation criterion, which we call the parallel path condition:

(NE_2) Given a left-to-right derivation

$$\langle s = t \rangle \rightarrowtail_{[\pi 1]} \langle s_1 = t_1 \rangle \rightarrowtail_{[\pi 2]} \cdots \rightarrowtail_{[\pi n]} \langle s_n = t_n \rangle$$

where $n = 2m$ and $\pi_i = 1.\pi'_i$ and $\pi_{m+i} = 2.\pi'_i$ for $1 \le i \le m$

The proof of the parallel path condition uses an induction argument. Both non-evaluation criteria can be applied simultaneously during the enumeration process.

Before giving a final version of the idempotent unification algorithm we will discuss the strategy running through the derivation tree. Of course there are the two possiblities for a complete enumeration: depth–first and breadth–first. Consider the example: $\langle\,((x\ a)\ b) = ((y\ b)\ (z\ w))\,\rangle_I$.

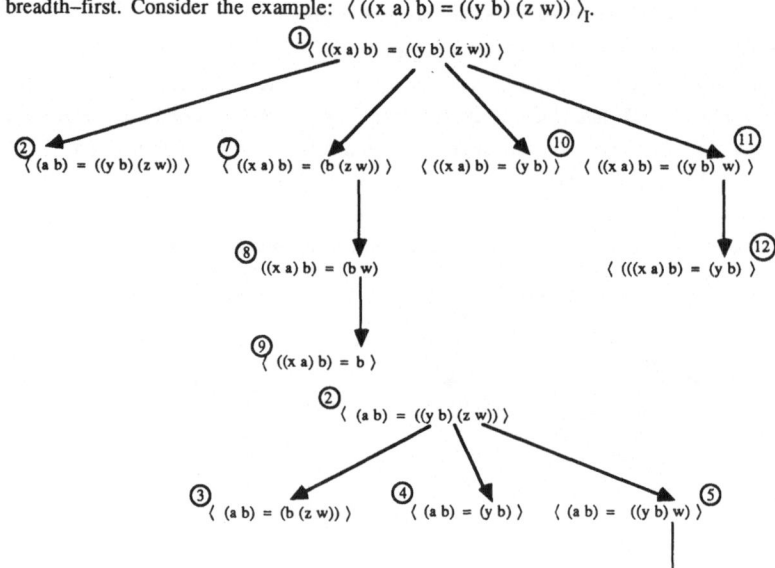

Node	narrower	Robinson unifier	I-unifier
4 $\langle(a\ b)=(y\ b)\rangle$	$\{x \leftarrow a, z \leftarrow y, w \leftarrow b\}$	$\{y \leftarrow a\}$	$\{x \leftarrow a, z \leftarrow a, w \leftarrow b, y \leftarrow a\}$
6 $\langle(a\ b)=(y\ b)\rangle$	$\{x \leftarrow a, z \leftarrow (y\ b), w \leftarrow (y\ b)\}$	$\{y \leftarrow a\}$	$\{x \leftarrow a, z \leftarrow (a\ b), w \leftarrow (a\ b), y \leftarrow a\}$
10 $\langle((x\ a)\ b)=(y\ b)\rangle$	$\{z \leftarrow y, w \leftarrow b\}$	$\{y \leftarrow (x\ a)\}$	$\{z \leftarrow (x\ a), w \leftarrow b, y \leftarrow (x\ a)\}$
12 $\langle((x\ a)\ b)=(y\ b)\rangle$	$\{z \leftarrow (y\ b), w \leftarrow (y\ b)\}$	$\{y \leftarrow (x\ a)\}$	$\{z \leftarrow ((x\ a)\ b), w \leftarrow ((x\ a)\ b), y \leftarrow (x\ a)\}$

Diagram 4.

To ease the notation we write t_k for the term at node k, θ_k for the narrower collected so far, β_k for the Robinson-unifier and σ_k for the I-unifier generated at node k. At the nodes 1, 2, 3, 5, 7, 8, 9 and 11 we do not obtain unifiers since s_k and t_k are not unifiable. At node 3 we can apply the stop criterion (S_1), by which two unnecessary narrowing steps can be avoided.

If we choose a depth-first strategy the unifiers σ_4 and σ_6 are generated first. But to obtain a minimal set of unifiers we have to reject them after generating σ_{10} and σ_{12} since σ_4 is an I-instance of σ_{10} and σ_6 is an I-instance of σ_{12}. Using a right-to-left strategy we would find the instances without an instance test since for the derivations $\langle\,s_{10}=t_{10}\,\rangle \rightarrowtail\!\!\rightarrow_{[1.1]} \langle\,s_4=t_4\,\rangle$ and $\langle\,s_{12}=t_{12}\,\rangle \rightarrowtail\!\!\rightarrow_{[1.1]} \langle s_6 = t_6\,\rangle$ the non evaluation criterion (NE_1) is applicable. But of course there are examples, for which a right-to-left strategy will not work (take the above example reversed $\langle\,((y\ b)\ (z\ w)) = ((x\ a)\ b)\,\rangle_I$). We did not find a criterion to decide, which strategy works best for which terms.

But if we look at the derivation length of the unifiers in the above example we see that the length of instances is larger than the length of more general unifiers. We did not find either a proof or a counterexample for this phenomenon, so we state it as an open conjecture:

If $\sigma_i \leq_I \sigma_j$ then the derivation length of σ_j is smaller than that of σ_i.

But this is the key idea of the minimal universal unification algorithm of Siekmann and Szabó [SS 81, Sz 82] who give a decision algorithm to test at any point in the narrowing tree, whether a more general unifier than the just generated will be found later in the unification process. Hence a proof of the above conjecture would make this decision procedure obsolete in the case of idempotence and a minimal unification algorithm were found. This observation and the possibility to find a reordering of the narrowing steps such that we can apply the conditions (NE_1) and (NE_2) motivated the use of a breadth-first search in the narrowing tree.

We will state an algorithm which is not minimal but incorporates the results collected so far:

FUNCTION   I-UNIFY
    INPUT: Two arbitrary terms s and t in normal form
        Enumerate the narrowing tree $\mathcal{N}\langle\, s = t\,\rangle$ with basic, left-to-right and breadth-first
        strategy. At every node try
            (i) to apply the stop criteria (S_1) to (S_3)
            (ii) to find a reorder of the narrowing steps such that
                the non-evaluation criteria (NE_1) and (NE_2) are applicable
    OUTPUT: The set $A_I\langle\, s = t\,\rangle$ of unifiers of s and t away from $Z \supseteq V(s, t)$
ENDOF   I-UNIFY

5. Conclusion and Comparison with Related Work

We have presented a complete unification algorithm for idempotent functions. The algorithm is based on the universal unification algorithm as described by Hullot [Hl 80] and Kirchner [Ki 85]. It uses narrowing with rewrite rules as its central computation rule. We have improved on ordinary narrowing by using special derivation strategies and by giving some conditions where the enumeration of the narrowing tree can be stopped.

We did not succeed in finding a minimal unification algorithm for idempotent function symbols. Using the results of Siekmann and Szabo [SS 81, Sz 82] the universal unification algorithm can be extended to be minimal. However, this extension involves at each node of the narrowing tree the computation of a complete set of solutions for a matching problem, which is a very expensive operation. But since the narrowing tree is always finite the theory of idempotence is finitary unifying and hence the redundant unifiers can be eliminated by minimizing the returned set of unifiers. This minimizing step only involves a decision test for a matching problem, which is less expensive.

We have shown conditions, which prevent the generation of redundant unifiers. We called them non-evaluation conditions since we were able to show that on certain nodes of the narrowing tree only redundant unifiers were generated. These conditions only depend on information that is locally known. Another possibility to reduce the minimizing costs after the enumeration of the narrowing tree is to prevent the generation of I-equal unifiers, i.e., not normalized unifiers. Since the narrowers are always normalized (confer stop condition (S_2)) there remain two possibilities. First the Robinson unifier β may not be in normal form and hence the I-unifier $\beta\theta$ is not. But excluding such unifiers results in an incompatibility with the non-evaluation condition (NE_1). Consider the following example $\langle\, ((x\ a)\ b) = (((y\ b)\ a)\ y)\,\rangle_I$ then the Robinson unifier $\beta = \{x \leftarrow (b\ b), y \leftarrow b\}$ is not normalized. The only successful narrowing derivation

$$\langle\, ((x\ a)\ b) = (((y\ b)\ a)\ y)\ \,\rangle \rightsquigarrow_{[2.1.1,\ \sigma\,=\,\{y\,\leftarrow\,b\}]} \langle\, ((x\ a)\ b) = ((b\ a)\ y)\ \rangle$$

yields the I-unifier $\beta'\sigma = \{x \leftarrow b, y \leftarrow b\}$. But the non-evaluation condition can be applied to this derivation eliminating the generation of β's. Hence combining both ideas results in incompleteness since both terms from the example are I-unifiable but no unifier is returned. With the elimination of not normalized I-unifiers $\beta\eta$ where both β and η are normalized we have similar difficulties.

The original version of the universal unification algorithm was not based on ordinary narrowing but on superreduction, i.e., after each narrowing step the newly generated terms are normalized as described in [La 75, Fy 79, RK 85 and Ki 85]. But there are several compatibility problems with superreduction. First superreduction does not fit into the concept of non-evaluation conditions: Consider the example $\langle\, ((a\ x)\ (x\ a)) = (u\ a)\ \rangle_I$ then the superreduction derivation $\langle\, ((a\ x)\ (x\ a)) = (u\ a)\ \,\rangle \rightsquigarrow_{[1]}$

$\langle$ a = (u a) $\rangle \mapsto \mapsto \mapsto_{[2]} \langle$ a = a $\rangle$ is possible, where the first problem $\langle$ ((a x) (x a)) = (u a) $\rangle$ is not Robinson unifiable but the second $\langle$ a = a $\rangle$. This contradicts the parallel path condition. The same problem arises with the given strategies: basic and left-to-right derivations are not compatible with superreduction, because the reduction steps are performed at occurrences that are not in the subsets U_i of occurrences defined by the strategies. So we have to perform superfluous reductions using the concept of superreduction. Besides that if the terms at the nodes of the narrowing tree are always normalized we loose the pruning effect of the given strategies.

Recently a new universal unification algorithm for canonical theories has been developed in [MM 86]. This approach is not based on narrowing, but on an outermost term rewriting strategy. This strategy is contrary to basic narrowing, which implements an innermost procedure. However, the left-to-right strategy can be also successfully exploited in this new algorithm. Specializing it to idempotence a new idempotent unification algorithm is obtained which proposes an outermost strategy. This algorithm can be improved by applying the stop criteria (S_1) and (S_3) and the non-evaluation criterium (NE_2), whereas (S_2) and (NE_1) are not applicable because of the built-in strategy. Because of the different features, it is difficult to compare the two algorithms.

6. References:

[Ba 86] Baader,F., 'The Theory of Idempotent Semigroups is if Unification Type Zero', Journal of Automated Reasoning, Vol. 2, No. 3, 283-286, (1986)

[Bu 85] Buchberger, B., 'Basic Features and Developments of the Critical-Pair/Completion Procedure', Proc. of 'Rewriting Techiques and Applications' (ed J.-P. Jouannaud), Springer-Verlag, LNCS 202, 1-45, (1985)

[DV 87] Dincabs, M. and Van Hentenryck, P., 'Extended Unification Algorithms for the Integration of Functional Programming into Logic Programming', Journal of Logic Programming, (to appear), (1987)

[FH 86] Fages, F. and Huet, G., 'Unification and Matching in Equational Theories', Journal of Theoretical Computer Science 43,189-200, (1986)

[Fy 79] Fay, M., 'First Order Unification in an Equational Theory', Proc.of 4th Workshop on Automated Deduction', 161-167, Texas, (1979)

[He 82] Herold, A., 'Universal Unification and a Class of Equational Theories', Proc. of GWAI-82 (ed. W.Wahlster), Springer-Verlag, IFB-82, 177-190, (1982)

[He 86] Herold, A., 'A Combination of Unification Algorithms', Proc. of 8th CADE (ed. J. Siekmann), Springer-Verlag, LNCS 230, 450-469, (1986)

[He 87] Herold, A., 'Combination of Unification Algorithms in Equational Theories', Thesis, Universität Kaiserslautern, (1987)

[Hl 80] Hullot,J.M.,'Canonical Forms and Unification', Proc. of 5th CADE (eds. W.Bibel and R.Kowalski), Springer-Verlag, LNCS 87, 318-334, (1985)

[HO 80] Huet, G. and Oppen, D. C., 'Equations and Rewrite Rules: A Survey', in 'Formal Languages: Perspectives and Open Problems (ed R. Book), Academic Press, (1980)

[Hu 76] Huet, G., 'Résolution d'équations dans des langages d'ordre 1,2...ω', Thèse de doctorat d'état, Université Paris VII, (1976)

[JK 83] Jouannaud,J.-P., Kirchner, C. and Kirchner, H., 'Incremental Construction Of Unifcation Algorithms In Equational Theories', Proc. of 10th ICALP (ed J.Diaz),LNCS 154,361-373 (1983)

[KB 70] Knuth, D.E. and Bendix, P.B., 'Simple Word Problems in Universal Algebras', in 'Computational Problems In Abstract Algebras' (ed. J. Leech), Pergamon Press, 263-297, (1970)

[Ki 85] Kirchner, C., 'Methodes et Outils de Conception Systematique d'Algorithmes d'Unification dans les Théories Equationelles', Thèse de doctorat d'état, (in French) Université de Nancy 1, (1985)

[La 75] Lankford, D.S., 'Canonical Inference', Report ATP-32, University of Texas, Austin, (1975)

[MM 86] Martelli,A., Moiso, C. and Rossi, G.F., 'An Algorithm for Unification in Equational Theories', Proc. of Symposium on Logic Programming 1986, 180-186, (1986)

[Pl 72] Plotkin, G., 'Building in Equational Theories', Machine Intelligence 7, 73-90, (1972)

[RK 85] Réty,P., Kirchner, C., Kirchner, H. and Lescanne, P. 'Narrower: A New Algorithm For Unifcation And Its Application To Logic Programming', Proc. of 'Rewriting Techiques and Applications' (ed J.-P. Jouannaud), Springer-Verlag, LNCS 202, 141-157, (1985)

[Ro 65] Robinson, J. A., 'A Machine-Oriented Logic Based on the Resolution Principle', JACM 12, Nº. 1, 23-41, (1965)

[RS 78] Raulefs,P. and Siekmann, J., 'Unifcation of Idempotent Functions', MEMO SEKI-78-II-KL, Universität Karlsruhe, (1978)

[RW 69] Robinson, G. and Wos, L.,'Paramodulation and Theorem-Proving in First-Order Theories with Equality', Machine Intelligence 4 (eds. B.Meltzer and D.Michie),135-151, (1969)

[Sc 86] Schmidt-Schauß, M., 'Unification under Associativity and Idempotence is of Type Nullary', Journal of Automated Reasoning, Vol. 2, No. 3, 277-282, (1986)

[Si 86] Siekmann, J., 'Unification Theory', in Proc. of 8th ECAI'86, Brighton (1986)

[SS 81] Siekmann, J,. and Szabó, P.,'Universal Unification and Regular ACFM Theories', Proc.of IJCAI-81,Vancouver, (1981)

[Sz 82] Szabó, P., Unifikationstheorie Erster Ordnung, Dissertation (in German), Universität Karlsruhe, (1982)

[Ti 86] Tidén, E., 'Unification in Combinations of Equational Theories', Thesis, Stockholm, Sweden

[Ye 85] Yelick, K., 'Combining Unification Algorithms for Confined Regular Equational Theories', Proc. of 'Rewriting Techiques and Applications' (ed J.-P. Jouannaud), Springer-Verlag, LNCS 202, 365-380, (1985)

THEOPOGLES - A THEOREM PROVER BASED ON FIRST-ORDER POLYNOMIALS AND A SPECIAL KNUTH-BENDIX PROCEDURE

JUERGEN MUELLER

COMP. SC. DEP.

UNIVERSITY OF KAISERSLAUTERN (FRG)

Tel.:049/631/2052555

UUCP:...!mcvax!unido!uklirb!mueller

Abstract

THEOPOGLES is a complete theorem prover for First-Order Predicate Logic. It is based on a special Knuth-Bendix completion procedure working on First-Order Polynomials. The method does not need special AC-unification, as the N-Strategie of Hsiang, nor special overlaps with the idempotency- and nilpotence-rule, as the equational approach of Kapur and Narendran. The algorithm supports structure sharing and also linking of literals which is used for example in the Connection Graph Procedure.

1. Introduction

In recent years there were a lot of approaches in theorem proving by completion [H82] [HD83] [F85] [H85] [KN85] [Pe85]. Most of them were initiated by the method of Hsiang which is based on a special Knuth-Bendix procedure [KB70] [Hu81]. The idea is the following: Given a formula F in First-Order Logic which is to be proved valid. Transform F into a set of polynomials $\{f_1,...,f_n\}$, e.g. quantifierfree formulae with * (AND) and + (XOR) as the only connectives, s.th. F is valid iff the equational system $\{f_1=0,...,f_n=0\}$ has no solution. Build rewrite rules from the equations and run a specialized Knuth-Bendix algorithm until the rule 1->0 is created. Thus, since the inferences are sound and the final equational system contains 1=0 , the system has no solution and hence F is valid.

Hsiang [H82] builds rules from the equational system in just replacing the = by -> and creates superpositions between rules of the form m->0 (N-rules), where m is a monomial, and all other rules in all monomials with all possible combinations of literals. The superposition is made by using a special AC-unification algorithm, called BN-unification. Further for the reduction only rules of the form m->0 and m->1, where m is a monomial, are used (cf. [H85]). Thus there are three major disadvantages: First, the complicated and expensive unification, second, the weak reduction relation and third, that there are a lot of unnecessary superpositions created and processed.

In the approach of Kapur and Narendran (KN-method for short) [KN85] the rule defined by an equation f=0 is hd(f)->tl(f), where hd(f) (the head-polynomial) is the polynomial defined by the biggest monomials in f according to a well-founded partial ordering on monomials, and where tl(f)=f-hd(f). The superpositions are build on all head-polynomials of the rules essentially with the same unification algorithm as in Hsiang's approach and moreover with the idempotency rule of $*$ (x*x->x) and, since the head-polynomials may consist of several monomials in the First-Order case, with the nilpotence rule of + (x+x->0). Thus the reduction relation is much stronger than Hsiang's, but there must be used a strong (and expensive) ordering and there are new kinds of superpositions to handle.

The stategy of THEOPOGLES overcomes all these difficulties. First of all not the whole equational system is transformed into a rule system. Only those equations become rules which are "easy" to handle. This is, a very simple ordering is used to create rules of the form m_1->0, m_1->1 and m_1->m_2, where the m_i's are monomials. Second the superpositions are restricted to N-rules as in Hsiang's case, but only superposition at one atom of the corresponding polynomial is performed and in addition not all monomials have to be considered. This decreases the search space for critical pairs drastically. Third, the current system is always kept in a "minimal" form by normalisation. This does not hurt the completeness of the procedure and this fact is not considered in Hsiang's completeness proof nor guaranteed in the general case by the KN-method. Thus THEOPOGLES is easy to understand and the approach is closer to the computation with equational systems over the ring of First-Order polynomials, because it does not use any complicated unification procedures nor special superposition mechanisms.

2. The THEOPOGLES Approach

It is supposed that the reader is familiar with First-Order Logic (FOL) , resolution theorem proving and Knuth-Bendix completion algorithms (cf.[CL73] [L78] [WOLB84] [Hu81] [B85]).

2.1 The Objects

Different from other theorem proving procedures, the completion approach deals with polynomials over the First-Order-Ring, i.e. terms over the Boolean Algebra (B,+,*,0,1) where + (XOR) is nilpotent and * (AND) is idempotent, 0,1 stand for false and true resp. and B is the set of positive literals (atoms) in FOL. Such a representation results in a unique normal form (up to commutativity of + and *) for all skolemized formulae in FOL (cf. [H82]).

Def.: A **monomial** m is the product (conjunction) of distinct atoms $m = L_1*L_2*...*L_n$ or m = 1. A **polynomial** is any term over (B,+,*,0,1) and a polynomial f is a **normal polynomial**, if f is the sum of distinct monomials or f=0.

For example, the normal polynomial of Px*(Qy+1)+Rxy*1+Px*0+1 is PxQy+Px+Rxy+1, with the connective * ignored to improve readability. The normal polynomial **NF(f)** of a polynomial f is computed by transforming f with the rules of the Boolean Ring together with the rules x*x->x and x+x->0 until no rule is applicable.

2.2 The Initial System

Given a First-Order formula F, which is to be proved valid, the set S_F of clauses equivalent to the negation of F is computed. For each clause C in S_F compute the normal polynomial f_C equivalent to ¬C and equate $f_C=0$. Set $E_F = \{f_C=0 \ / \ C \text{ in } S_F\}$. A **set of equations** $E=\{f_i=0\}_{i=1..n}$ is **solvable** iff there is an (Herbrand-) interpretation I, s.th. $I(f_i)$=FALSE for all i $(1 \leq i \leq n)$. If E is solvable then I is a **solution** of E.

Theorem: A formula F in FOL is valid iff the corresponding equational system E_F has no solution.

Proof: (sketch) F is valid iff ¬F is unsatisfiable iff $S_F = \{C_1,...,C_n\}$ is unsatisfiable iff $I(C_1 * ... * C_n)$=FALSE for all interpretations I iff there is no interpretation I, s.th. $I(C_i)$=TRUE for all i $(1 \leq i \leq n)$ iff there is no interpretation I, s.th. $I(\neg C_i)$=FALSE for all i $(1 \leq i \leq n)$ iff $\{f_{C_i}=0\}_{i=1..n} = E_F$ has no solution.

Now the problem to prove F to be valid is reduced to prove E_F to be unsolvable. Suppose $E'=\{f_i=0\}_{i=1..n}$ is the equational system to be proved to have no solution. The initial system is generated from E' by separating E' into a set R of rewrite rules and a set E of equations.

<u>Def.:</u> a) The rule hd(f)->tl(f) is a **rewrite rule w.r.t. f=0** iff

        1) f is a monomial and hd(f)=f and tl(f)=0 or

        2) f is of the form m+1, where m is a monomial $\neq 1$ and hd(f)=m and tl(f)=1 or

        3) f is of the form m_1+m_2, where m_1,m_2 are monomials $\neq 1$ with all literals in m_1 also occur in m_2 and hd(f)=m_2 and tl(f)=m_1.

b) The **initial system** l=(R,E) w.r.t. E' is defined by R={r / r is a rewrite rule w.r.t. an equation f=0 in E'} and E={f=0 / f=0 is in E' and there is no rewrite rule w.r.t. f=0}.

<u>Example1:</u> Let S={Qa v Rx, ¬Qx v Rx, ¬Ra v ¬Sa, Sx} be a set of clauses. The corresponding equational system is E_S={QaRx+Qa+Rx+1=0, QxRx+Qx=0, RaSa=0, Sx+1=0} and the initial system l w.r.t. E_S is ({QxRx->Qx, RaSa->0, Sx->1} , {QaRx+Qa+Rx+1=0}).

Notice that we have split E' into a set R of rewrite rules and a set E of equations, such that for the rewrite system the following holds: 1) The left hand side of a rule is a single polynomial. This simplifies the test whether a rule is applicable. 2) A reduction step consist of a deletion of literals only, so there is no need to apply the distributivity law after a reduction.

For example consider in the case of propositional calculus the polynomial pq+p+q+1 and the rule pq->p. Then by definition (see below) f= pq+p+q+1 is reduced to q+1. In Hsiang´s approach the representation of the rule is pq+p->0 and thus it is not applicable (by definition) to f. On the other side p->r+s might be a rule in the KN-method and the polynomial f is reduced to (r+s)q+(r+s)+q+1 which is rq+sq+r+s+q+1. Thus f is replaced by a polynomial which is smaller w.r.t. the KN-ordering, but intuitively more complex than the original one and harder to handle.

Further , since the KN-ordering is a partial ordering in the First-Order case, it is possible to have rules like Rax + Rxa->1. This means that + has to be considered in the matching algorithm.

2.3 The Inference Mechanism

From now on we deal with systems (R,E), where R is a rewrite rule system with rules of the form m_1->0, L->1 and m_1->m_2 (m_i monomials, L positive literal) and E is a equational system of equations f=0 that do not correspond to rules. We are looking for an algorithm which decides whether a system (R,E) is solvable or not.

a) The Reduction Relation =>$_R$ on Polynomials

Let R={hd $_i$ -> tl $_i$}$_{i=1..n}$ be a set of rewrite rules of the form given above. Further let m be a monomial. The rewrite relation =>$_R$ on monomials is defined as follows:

<u>Def.:</u> a) **m=>$_R$m´** iff there is a rewrite rule hd->tl in R and a substitution μ and a monomial u, s.th. u•μ(hd)=m (up to commutativity of •) and m´=NF(u•μ(tl)).

b) **m=>m´ with rule hd->tl and substitution** μ iff there is a monomial u, s.th. u•μ(hd)=m and m´=NF(u•μ(tl)).

The relation =>$_R$ is extended to normal polynomials.

c) Let f= m_1+m_2+...+m_n be a polynomial with monomials m_1,...,m_n. **f=>>$_R$f´** iff there is a rewrite rule hd->tl and a substitution μ, s.th. M={m_i / m_i is in f and m_i=>m_i´ with hd->tl and μ} is not empty and f´=NF(m"$_1$+...+m"$_n$), where m"$_i$=m_i if m_i is not in M and m"$_i$=m_i´ if m_i is in M.

Intuitively the definition c) means that whenever a rule is applicable to a monomial of a polynomial f, then it has to be applied to all possible monomials in f in parallel.

For sake of simplicity we write => for =>$_R$ and =>>$_R$ if the context is clear. Further let =$^+$> be the transitive and =*> be the transitive and reflexive closure of =>.

If f=>f´ holds we say that **f reduces to f´**. f " is a <u>normal form</u> (w.r.t. R) of a polynomial f iff f=*>f " and there is no f´, s.th. f "=>f´.

<u>Example:</u> The normal polynomial QaRaSb+QaSb+RaSb+Sb reduces to its normal form Ra+1 in two steps by the rewrite rules from example1.

The reason for defining a "parallel" reduction is twofold. First, the number of possible normal forms of a polynomial is reduced and hence if one normal form of a polynomial is 0 the probability of generating the 0 is higher. For example consider the rules pq->p and qr->0. Reducing the polynomial pqrs+pqr with pq->p gives prs+pr. Using qr->0 the result is 0 and if first pq->p will be applied at the first monomial and then qr->0 will be applied to the second one, the nonparallel reduction step yields in prs. Second, if a matching substitution is computed it should be used as often as possible to avoid multiple computations. Further the datastructure (see chap.3) supports the parallel reduction. This is, if one monomial where a rule can be applied is found in a polynomial, the other monomials are implicitly given.

The following lemma guarantees that every reduction sequence eventually terminates and is easy to proof.
Lemma: $=^*>$ is noetherian.

b) Generating new Equations by Critical-Pair Computation

<u>Def.:</u> Let L,L' be positive literals, $m=L*u$ be a monomial and let $f=L'*(f')+f''$ be a polynomial with f',f'' L'-free polynomials.. The polynomial $\mu(u)*\mu(L*(f')+f'')$ is the **L,L'-superposition** of m and f iff μ is the mgu of L and L'.

<u>Def.:</u> a) Let L,L' be positive literals and $L*m->0$ and $L'*m_1->m_2$, where $m_2 \neq 0$ and L' is not in m_2 be two rewrite rules .
$<c,0>$ is an **R-critical pair** of $L*m->0$ and $L'*m_1->m_2$ iff $\mu(m*L*m_1)$ is the L,L'-superposition of $L*m$ and $L'*m_1$ and $\mu(m*L*m_1)=>c$ with $L*m->0$ and μ.

b) Let L,L' be positive literals and $L*m->0$ be a rewrite rule and $f=0$ be an equation with a positive literal L' that does not occur in all monomials of f (e.g. $f=0$ can be written as $L'*f_1+f_2=0$ where f_1,f_2 are L'-free).
$<c,0>$ is an **E-critical pair** of $L*m->0$ and $f=0$ iff $\mu(m)*\mu(L*(f_1)+f_2)$ is the L,L'-superposition $L*m$ and f and $\mu(m)*\mu(L*(f_1)+f_2)=>c$ with $L*m->0$ and μ.

<u>Example:</u> Consider the initial system from example1. The left hand sides of the rules RaSa->0 and QxRx->Qx define the Ra,Rx-superposition QaRaSa with the mgu {x<-a} of Ra and Rx. The R-critical pair is <QaSa,0>. Overlapping RaSa->0 with the polynomial in the equation QaRx+Qa+Rx+1=0 at Ra results in the Ra,Rx-superposition QaRaSa+Sa*(Qa+Ra+1) which is equivalent to QaRaSa+SaQa+SaRa+Sa and the E-critical pair is <SaQa+Sa,0>.

In contrast to Hsiang only overlapps on one literal have to be considered and if a literal L occurs more than once but not in all monomials in a polynomial then only one superposition at L is computed. For example the only superposition of the rule pqr->0 and the equation pqs+ps+pq+p=0 is prpqs+prps+prpq+prp. Hsiang has to compute the overlapps at p (which results in the trivial critical pair),q <u>and</u> pq in <u>all</u> monomials; that are qrpqs+qr(ps+pq+p), qrps+qr(pqs+pq+p),......, prpqs+pr(ps+pq+p), prpq+pr(pqs+ps+p) and rpqs+r(ps+pq+p). In the KN-method the equation becomes pqs->ps+pq+p and there are three overlapps (at p,q and pq) and in addition the superpositions with the idempotency rule (x*x->x), that are ppqs, pqqs,pqss for pqs->ps+pq+p and ppqr,pqqr and pqrr for the rule pqr->0.

c) Completing a System (R,E)

The next step towards the algorithm is the transformation of the Initial System $I=(R_0,E_0)$ into systems $(R_1,E_1),(R_2,E_2),\ldots$ until it is obvious whether or not (R_0,E_0) has a solution. According to the Knuth-Bendix algorithm, there are two possibilities to generate new equations and rules.

<u>Def.:</u> Given a system (R,E), a **successor system** (R´,E´) of (R,E) is defined as follows:

(1) **Normalizing Equations**

there is an equation f=0 in E, s.th. $f={}^+>_R f´$ and f´ is a normal form of f:

if f´=0 then E´:=E-{f=0}

else if there is a rewrite rule w.r.t. f´=0 then R´:=RU{hd(f´)->tl(f´)}; E´:=E-{f=0}

else E´:=E-{f=0}U{f´=0}; R´:=R

(2) **Interreducing Rules**

there is a rewrite rule $m_1->m_2$ in R, s.th. $m_1+m_2={}^+>_{R-\{m1->m2\}} f´$ and f´ is a normal form of m_1+m_2:

if f´=0 then R´:=R-{$m_1->m_2$}

else if there is a rewrite rule w.r.t. f´=0 then R´:=R-{$m_1->m_2$}U{hd(f´)->tl(f´)}; E´:=E

else E´:=EU{f´=0}; R´:=R-{$m_1->m_2$}

(3) **Critical-Pair Handling**

there is an R- (E-) critical pair <c,0> of two rules in R (a rule and an equation):

let c" be a normal form of c w.r.t. R.

if there is a rewrite rule w.r.t. c" and c"≠0 then R´:=RU{hd(c")->tl(c")}; E´:=E

else E´:=EU{c"=0}; R´:=R.

Case (1) and (2) are called **interreduction steps** and a system (R,E) is **interreduced** if there is no interreduction step possible. Case (3) is called an **R- (E-) completion step.**

Lemma: Let (R,E) be a system.
Every sequence of interreduction steps starting with (R,E) terminates.

Corollary: For each system (R,E) there exists a interreduced system (R",E").

2.4 The Control Mechanism

The control of the prover is performed by a special Knuth-Bendix procedure, where special means that only the R-critical pairs between rewrite rules are considered and in contrast to usual Completion Procedures superpositions between rules and equations (E-critical pairs) are generated too. Further the algorithm stops as soon as the rule 1->0 is found. The whole algorithm is now as follows:

THEOPOGLES:
Generate the Initial System (R,E) from a formula F;
Interreduce (R,E);
If 1->0 is in R then stop("proved");
repeat
                 while possible but fairly and finitely often do
                      perform an R-completion step and interreduce
                         if 1->0 is in R then stop("proved")
                   perform an E-completion step and interreduce
                       if 1->0 is in R then stop("proved")
until all possible critical pairs are considered
stop("f is not valid").

Notice that the while-loop without the additional condition "finitely often" always terminates in the propositional case, but may not terminate in the full First-Order case. But nevertheless the algorithm may loop forever because it is possible that infinitely many rules can be created.

Theorem: Let F be a formula in First-Order Predicat Calculus.
F is valid iff the rule 1->0 is generated by THEOPOGLES.

Proof: (Since the proof is rather long and technical, we will just give a sketch of it). Consider the equational system $E(S_i)$ of the i-th system $S_i=(R_i,E_i)$ generated by the algorithm.

if: Let 1->0 be generated by THEOPOGLES. Then there is a sequence $E_F=E(S_0)$, $E(S_1)$,...,$E(S_n)$, s.th. 1=0 is in $E(S_n)$. By inspection of the interreduction steps and the completion steps it follows that if $E(S_{i+1})$ has no solution then $E(S_i)$ has no solution. Since that is true for all i ($1 \leq i \leq n$), $E(S_0)$ has no solution and by the first theorem F must be valid.

only if: Since F is valid and S is the set of clauses corresponding to ¬F, S is unsatisfiable and hence by the Herbrand theorem every complete semantic tree of S has a finite closed subtree. Thus there is a closed complete E-semantic tree T_0 (cf. [H82]) of E_F where the rightmost leaf has the form m->0. Starting with T_0 we associate a closed E-semantic tree T_i to each S_i. If S_{i+1} is computed from S_i by an interreduction step and the polynomial equation f=0 to be reduced is a leaf of the corresponding tree T_i, then replace f=0 by the resulting polynomial equation f'=0 and create the minimal tree T_{i+1}. If S_{i+1} is computed from S_i by a completion step w.r.t. the rightmost leaf m->0 and a polynomial equation f=0 in T_i, then replace f=0 by the resulting polynomial and create the minimal tree T_{i+1}. The invariant for the equational systems $E(S_i)$ is, that for all leafs f=0 in the tree there is a normal polynomial f_c corresponding to a clause C, s.th. $f_c =>_{R_i} f$. By the invariant it is guaranteed that if the equation f=0 is deleted through interreduction it can be replaced by an other equation from the current equational system $E(S_i)$. And moreover that the rightmost leaf in the tree is of the form m->0 where m is a monomial. Thus for all T_i there is a T_k, s.th. i<k and T_k has fewer nodes than T_i. And from that we get that the tree with root 1->0 eventually has to be generated.

248

2.5 Some Remarks to the Algorithm

There are two refutational strategies which are implicitely in the algorithm. The first is that at the beginning and after each inferece step interreduction is activated. This means that always some kind of minimal representation of the current system is generated. This mechanism is closely related to the subsumption-, merging- and tautology-elimination steps used in resolution theorem provers. To eliminate redundant information keeps the search space for possible inference steps down and increases efficency. In fact there are a lot of examples, where the rule 1->0 is generated during the first interreduction (for instance try example1). The second strategy is, that R-critical pairs are to be created first. The reason is that having a interreduced system, the rule 1->0 has to be computed by a superposition of a rule L->0 and L´->1. Thus it is prefered to generate such rules and to infer with those rules which are potentially "near the solution". The reader might have noticed that the last step is equivalent to the unit resolution step to generate the empty clause.

3. The Implementation

There were two major problems in the implementation of THEOPOGLES. The first is to find a good representation for the polynomials and the second point is to minimize the time complexity for the search of possible interreduction- and completion-steps. Further, it should be easy to incorporate modifications of the inference mechanisms and to adopt heuristics in the future. The solutions were a structure sharing approach and a graph concept in analogy of Kowalskis Connection-Graph-Procedure. Notice that the use of these concepts are strongly supported by the form of the normal polynomials and the definition of the reduction relation and the superposition. The data structure of a polynomial is given in the following diagram, where the stoned squares represent terms:

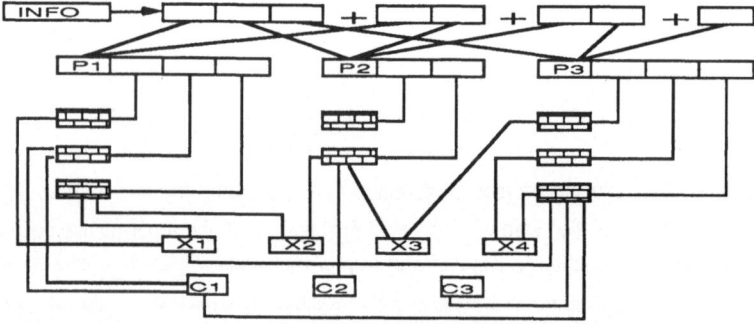

Each literal in the polynomial is represented in a literal-list only once and there are pointers from each literal to the occurences in the polynomial. A literal contains the name of the predicate and pointers to the arguments. The terms in the arguments were not completely shared, but only the common variables and constants are represented only once and pointers show where they are from. This idea is taken from the improved Robinson unification algorithm descibed in [CB83] which is used in the implementation. Further there is a block with specific information about the polynomials, e.g. whether the polynomial is treated as an equation or as a rewrite rule, and if it is a rule, where the left hand side is etc.

To find possible occurences for the reduction steps and the superpositions, the literal-lists of the left hand sides of the rewrite rules are linked with two kinds of links as shown by the example below. The rewrite rules and equations corresponding to the literal-lists are given in parenthesis.

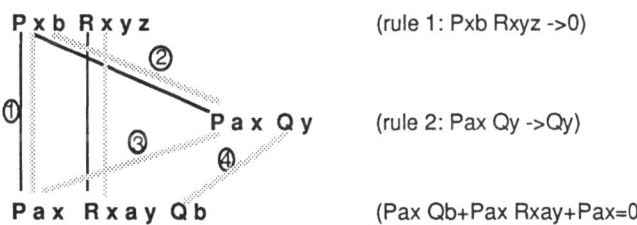

(rule 1: Pxb Rxyz ->0)

(rule 2: Pax Qy ->Qy)

(Pax Qb+Pax Rxay+Pax=0)

The unbroken links characterise potential superpositions (unification positions) and the dotted links mark potential reductions (match positions). The evaluation whether a unification or a match is possible, is done in a lazy manner. If the equation should be reduced by rule 2, the matchers of link 3 and 4 are computed and then proved to be compatible. After the reduction is done the links are deactivated. Link 2 is deactivated during the computation, because no match is possible. The links are not deleted, because for example rule 2 might be reduced by a rule Qx->1 and after the reduction the links have to be activated again. Also link 1 is passive, because Pxb and Pax are unifiable, but before unification is tried it is checked that Pax occurs in all monomials in the equation. It will be only passiv, because if the equation is reduced for instance by a rule PxyRyaz->Ryaz it must be active again. Links may also be deleted if the match or unification fails because of different function symbols.

If a new polynomial is generated by a completion step, the links of the parents can be used to incorporate the polynomial into the graph structure. Further the links will aid the design and implementation of new strategies and heuristics.

4. Conclusion

The theorem prover THEOPOGLES was introduced. It was shown that THEOPOGLES is a complete theorem prover based on First-Order polynomials and a special Knuth-Bendix algorithm. It overcomes the major problems of other completion theorem proving approaches. That is, no special unification nor complicated orderings are needed. The number of critical pairs is drastically reduced by the simple overlap mechanism at just one literal and not considering superpositions with the idempotency and nilpotence rules (which is not necessary in this approach). Further a structure is developed to represent the polynomials in a efficent way. From the completion algorithm a minimal representation of the system is guaranteed in a natural way, e.g. without introducing special inference mechanisms like in resolution procedures. Moreover the completeness of THEOPOGLES is stated with the interreduction, which is in general not shown in the approach of Kapur and Narendran [KN85]. To improve another "quasi" reduction of the search space, the preference is given to the R-completion steps, because they are the potential inferences for the last step. THEOPOGLES is implemented in LISP on APOLLO -Workstation and runs fairly good on most examples in the literature, even in problems declared to be difficult in [Pe86].

ACKNOWLEDGEMENT: I would like to thank Prof. Dr. J. Avenhaus for many helpful discussions and Jörg Denzinger for the careful implementation of THEOPOGLES.

References:

[B85]   Buchberger, B.: Basic Features and Development of the
             Critical-Pair/Completion Procedure, 1. Int. Conf. on Rewriting Techniques
             and Applications (RTA), Dijon, May 1985, Springer LNCS 202 , 1-45.

[CL73]   Chang, C.L. and Lee, R.C.T.: Symbolic Logic and Mechanical Theorem
             Proving, Academic Press, N.Y. 1973.

[CB83]   Corbin, J., Bidoit, M. : A Rehabilitation of Robinson's Unification Algorithm,
             in Information Processing 83, R.E.A. Mason (ed.), Elevier Sc. Pub.
             (North Holland), 909-914

[F85]   Fribourg, L.: A Superposition Oriented Theorem Prover, TCS35 (1985),
             124-164.

[H82]   Hsiang, J.: Topics in Automated Theorem Proving and Program Generation
             Ph.D. Thesis, Dec. 1982, University of Illinois at Urbana-Champaign,
             UIUCDCS-R-82-1113 .

[H85]   Hsiang, J.: Two Results in Term Rewriting Theorem Proving, Proc. RTA,
             Dijon, May1985, Springer LNCS 202, 301-324

[HD83]   Hsiang, J. and Dershowitz, N.: Rewrite Methods for Clausal and Non-
             Clausal Theorem Proving, Proc. of the 10. EATCS Int. Colloq. on Automata,
             Languages and Programming (ICALP), Spain 1983.

[Hu81]   Huet, G.: A Complete Proof of Correctness of the Knuth-Bendix Completion
             Algorithm, Journal of Computer and System Sciences 23 (1981), 11-21.

[KB70]   Knuth, D.E. and Bendix, P.B.: Simple Word Problems in Universal Algebras
             in Computational Problems in Abstract Algebras (Ed. J. Leech),
             Pergammon Press, 1970, 263-297.

[KN85]   Kapur, D. and Narendran, P.: An Equational Approach to Theorem Proving
             in First-Order Predicat Calculus, 84CRD322, General Electric Corporate
             Research and Development Report, Schenectady, N.Y., Sept.1985.
             see also (short version) Proc. of the IJCAI-85, Los Angeles, CA, Aug.1985.

[L78]   Loveland, B.W.: Automated Theorem Proving: a logical basis, North
             Holland, Amsterdam 1978.

[Pa85]   Paul, E.: On Solving the Equality Problem in Theories defined by Horn
             Clauses, Poc. Eurocal-85, Linz, Austria.

[Pe86]   Seventy-Five Problems for Testing Automatic Theorem Provers, JAR 2
             (1986), 191-216.

[WOLB84]   Wos, L. et al., Automated Reasoning, Prentice-Hall, 1984.

COMPUTATIONAL REFLECTION

Pattie Maes

AI-LAB
Vrije Universiteit Brussel
Pleinlaan 2
B-1050 Brussels
pattie@arti.vub.uucp

ABSTRACT. This paper brings some perspective to various concepts in computational reflection. A definition of computational reflection is presented, the importance of computational reflection is discussed and the architecture of languages that support reflection is studied. Further, this paper gives a survey of some experiments in reflection which have been performed. Examples of existing procedural, logic-based and rule-based languages with an architecture for reflection are presented. The final part of the paper describes an original experiment to introduce a reflective architecture in an object-oriented language. The examples show that a lot of programming problems that were previously handled on an ad hoc basis, can in a reflective architecture be solved more elegantly.

1. Introduction

Computational reflection is the activity performed by a computational system when doing computation about (and by that possibly affecting) its own computation. Although "computational reflection" (further on called reflection) is a popular term these days, the issues related to it are very complex and at the moment still badly understood. The first part of the paper (sections 2 to 5) attempts to elucidate some of these issues. It gives a definition of reflection and presents examples of its use. It further introduces the concept of a language with a reflective architecture, which is a language designed to support reflection.

Section 5 presents a survey of the reflective architectures that have already been realised for procedure-based, logic-based and rule-based languages. Section 6 discusses our experiment to introduce a reflective architecture in an object-oriented language (further on called OOL). This experiment shows that it is possible to realise a reflective architecture in an OOL and that there are specific advantages as well to object-oriented reflection. The paper ends with some conclusions.

2. What is Reflection

This section presents a definition of computational reflection applicable to any model of computation, whether it be procedural, deductive, imperative, message-passing or other. We define **computational reflection** to be the behavior exhibited by a reflective system, where a **reflective system** is a computational system which is about itself in a causally connected way. In order to substantiate this definition, we next discuss relevant concepts such as computational system, about-ness and causal connection.

A **computational system** (further on called system) is a computer-based system whose purpose is to answer questions about and/or support actions in some domain. We say that the system **is about** its

---

This research was supported by ESPRIT project number 440: "Message Passing Architectures and Description Systems" and COST-13 project number 7: "Advanced Issues in Knowledge Representation". The author is a senior research assistant of the Belgian National Fund for Scientific Research.

domain. It incorporates internal structures representing the domain. These structures include data representing entities and relations in the domain and a program prescribing how these data may be manipulated. Computation actually results when a processor (interpreter or CPU) is executing (part of) this program[1]. Any program that is running is an example of a computational system.

A system is said to be **causally connected** to its domain if the internal structures and the domain they represent are linked in such a way that if one of them changes, this leads to a corresponding effect upon the other. A system steering a robot-arm, for example, incorporates structures representing the position of the arm. These structures may be causally connected to the position of the robot's arm in such a way that (i) if the robot-arm is moved by some external force, the structures change accordingly and (ii) if some of the structures are changed (by computation), the robot-arm moves to the corresponding position. So a causally connected system always has an accurate representation of its domain and it may actually cause changes in this domain as mere effect of its computation.

A reflective system is a system which incorporates structures representing (aspects of) itself. We call the sum of these structures the **self-representation** of the system. This self-representation makes it possible for the system to answer questions about itself and support actions on itself. Because the self-representation is causally-connected to the aspects of the system it represents, we can say that:

(i) The system always has an accurate representation of itself.

(ii) The status and computation of the system are always in compliance with this representation. This means that a reflective system can actually bring modifications to itself by virtue of its own computation.

3. The Use of Reflection

At first sight the concept of reflection may seem a little far-fetched. Until now it has mostly been put forward as a fascinating and mysterious issue albeit without technical importance. We claim however that there is a substantial practical value to reflection. A lot of functionalities in computation require reflection. Most every-day systems exhibit besides **object-computation**, i.e. computation about their external problem domain, also many instances of **reflective computation**, i.e. computation about themselves. Examples of reflective computation are: to keep performance statistics, to keep information for debugging purposes, stepping and tracing facilities, interfacing (e.g. graphical output, mouse input), computation about which computation to pursue next (also called reasoning about control), self-optimisation, self-modification (e.g. in learning systems) and self-activation (e.g. through monitors or deamons).

Reflective computation does not directly contribute to solving problems in the external domain of the system. Instead, it contributes to the internal organisation of the system or to its interface to the external world. Its purpose is to guarantee the effective and smooth functioning of the object-computation.

Programming languages today do not fully recognise the importance of reflective computation[2]. They do not provide adequate support for its modular implementation. For example, if the programmer wants to follow temporarily the computation, e.g. during debugging, he often changes his program by adding extra statements. When finished debugging, these statements have to be removed again from the source code, often resulting in new errors. Reflective computation is so inherent in every-day

---

[1] In some languages the distinction between data and program is opaque. This however does not affect the understandability of the definition of reflection presented here. Also, it would be more appropriate to substitute the term "computation" by "deduction" for some languages.

[2] Note that more advanced programming environments might provide facilities for handling some of the problems dis-

computational systems, especially in knowledge-based systems, that it should be supported as a funda-mental tool in programming languages. The next section discusses how languages might do so.

4. What is a Reflective Architecture

A programming language is said to have a **reflective architecture** if it recognises reflection as a funda-mental programming concept and thus provides tools for handling reflective computation explicitly. Concretely, this means that:

(i) The interpreter of such a language has to give any system that is running access to data representing (aspects of) the system itself. Systems implemented in such a language then have the possibility to perform reflective computation by including code that prescribes how these data may be manipulated.

(ii) The interpreter also has to guarantee that the causal connection between these data and the aspects of the system they represent is fulfilled. Consequently, the modifications these systems make to their self-representation are reflected in their own status and computation.

Reflective architectures provide a fundamentally new paradigm for thinking about computational sys-tems. In a reflective architecture, a computational system is viewed as incorporating an object part and a reflective part. The task of the object computation is to solve problems and return information about an external domain, while the task of the reflective level is to solve problems and return infor-mation about the object computation.

In a reflective architecture one can temporarily associate reflective computation with a program such that during the interpretation of this program some tracing is performed. Suppose that a session with a rule-based system has to be traced such that the sequence of rules that is applied is printed. This can be achieved in a language with a reflective architecture by stating a reflective rule such as

```
IF a rule has the highest priority in a situation,
THEN print the rule and the data which match its conditions
```

In a rule-based language that does not incorporate a reflective architecture, the same result can only be achieved either by modifying the interpreter code (such that it prints information about the rules it applies), or by rewriting all the rules such that they print information whenever they are applied.

So clearly reflective architectures provide a means to implement reflective computation in a more modular way. As is generally known, enhanced modularity makes systems more manageable, more readable and easier to understand and modify. But these are not the only advantages of the decompo-sition. What is even more important is that it becomes possible to introduce abstractions which facili-tate the programming of reflective computation the same way abstract control-structures such as DO and WHILE facilitate the programming of control flow.

5. Existing Reflective Architectures

---

cussed here. However, typically, programming environments are not built in an "open-ended" way, which means that they only support a fixed number of those functionalities. Further, they often only support computation about computation in a static way, i.e. not at run-time.

5.1. Procedure-Based Example

Procedure-based, logic-based and rule-based languages incorporating a reflective architecture can be identified. 3-LISP (Smith, 1982) and BROWN (Friedman and Wand, 1984) are two such procedural examples (variants of LISP). They introduce the concept of a **reflective function**, which is just like any other function, except that it specifies computation about the currently ongoing computation. Reflective functions should be viewed as local (temporary) functions running at the level of the interpreter: they manipulate data representing the current object-level computation.

Reflective functions take a number of quoted arguments. They have access to two extra variables, called "env" and "cont", which by default represent the environment (a list of bindings) and the continuation at the time the reflect function is called. A reflective function is able to inspect these (e.g. checking variable bindings) and to modify these (e.g. changing the continuation or changing variable bindings). The env and cont variables are causally connected to the real environment and continuation of the system, such that the results of this reflective computation are reflected in the system's future object-level computation. Figure 1 shows a very simple reflective program[3]. The code represented is conform with the Common-LISP conventions.

```
(define-REFLECT boundp-else-bind-to-one (symbol &optional env cont)
       (let ((value (binding symbol env)))
          (funcall cont
                   (if value
                       value
                       (rebind symbol 1 env)))))
```

Fig. 1. A reflective procedural program.

When the above function is called, for example in

```
(let ((x 36))
   (/ x (boundp-else-bind-to-one y)))
```

The evaluation returns 36 after reflection (because the symbol y is not bound in this environment). On the other hand, the evaluation of

```
(let ((x 36)
      (y 12))
   (/ x (boundp-else-bind-to-one y)))
```

returns 3.

This example illustrates the architecture for reflection incorporated in languages like 3-LISP and BROWN: any program can specify reflective computation by means of an application of a reflective function. The evaluation of this sub-expression brings the interpretation of the program one level up, being the level where the interpretation of the program was run until that moment. This level reasons about and acts upon the environment and continuation of the level below.

The interpreter takes care of the causal connection between the system and the representation it has of itself. Whenever the program specifies reflective computation (by calling a reflective function), the interpreter constructs variables denoting the environment and the continuation at that moment of

---

[3] Note that the purpose of this example is to present the idea behind the design of a procedure-based language with a reflective architecture. It is thus not written to serve as an example of a programming problem for which a reflective architecture should be used.

interpretation. The reflective computation can manipulate these variables. When the reflective computation reactivates the object-computation, the interpreter continues the computation at the level below, after reflecting the bindings of these variables in the actual environment and continuation.

5.2. Logic-Based Example

FOL (Weyhrauch, 1980) and META-PROLOG (Bowen, 1986) are two examples of logic-based languages with a reflective architecture. These languages adopt the concept of a **meta-theory**. A meta-theory again differs from other theories (or logic programs) in that it is about the deduction of another theory, instead of about the external problem domain. Examples of predicates used in a meta-theory are "provable(Theory,Goal)", "clause(Left-hand,Right-hand)", etc.

Figure 2 presents a small example. The syntactical conventions adopted are that capitalised symbols represent variables, and commas should be read as "and". The theory called my-theory contains some facts and inference rules that I believe in. The theory called john's-theory contains facts and inference rules John believes in. Meta-t is a meta-theory for john's-theory (or any other theory which models the beliefs of somebody other than myself). The data (or variables) of meta-t are representations of the theorems and clauses of another theory T. This means that the predicates of meta-t range over predicates and clauses of T. Note particularly the final rule of meta-t which states that a clause from my theory may be used to prove a theorem F in a theory T. If this happens,

```
theorem(T,F)
```

is asserted in meta-t.

```
my-theory: mortal(X) :- human(X).

john's-theory: human(X) :- greek(X).
               greek(socrates).
               P :- reflect(meta-t,P).

meta-t: provable(T,F) :- theorem(T,F).
        provable(T,and(F,G)) :- provable(T,F), provable(T,G).
        provable(T,F) :- clause(T,F,G), provable(T,G).
        provable(T,F) :- clause(my-theory,F,G), provable(T,G), assert(theorem(T,F)).
```

Fig. 2. A reflective logic program.

This implements the autoepistemic rule that I may assume that somebody else uses the same inference rules (but not the same facts) as I do, complemented by inference rules specific to him. An attempt to prove in john's-theory

```
mortal(socrates)
```

results, when the other clauses have failed to prove the goal, in the exploration of the last clause of john's-theory. This means that the interpreter proceeds with an attempt to prove

```
reflect(meta-t,mortal(socrates))
```

Reflect is a special predicate that attempts to prove a theorem in a meta-theory. If the meta-theory succeeds in proving the theorem, this result is reflected in the theory. For the above example, it means that the fact

```
mortal(socrates)
```

will be asserted in john's-theory, if the theory meta-t succeeded in proving the theorem

```
provable(john's-theory,mortal(socrates))
```

This example illustrates an architecture for reflection in a logic-based language. Programs are represented by means of theories. A theory may have one or more meta-theories which specify deduction about the theory. The language interpreter has mechanisms that are responsible for the causal connection between a theory and a meta-theory. These mechanisms guarantee the communication of results between the two levels, i.e they specify how to reflect the results of meta-theory computation in object-theory computation (and vice versa) and are therefore called reflection principles (Weyhrauch, 1980).

5.3. Rule-Based Example

TEIRESIAS (Davis, 1982) and SOAR (Laird, Rosenbloom and Newell, 1986) are examples of rule-based languages with a reflective architecture. They incorporate the notion of **meta-rules**, which are just like normal rules, except that they specify computation about the ongoing computation. The data-memory these rules operate represents the object-level computation. It contains elements such as "there-is-an-impasse-in-the-inference-process", "there-exists-a-rule-about-the-current-goal", "all-rules-mentioning-the-current-goal-have-been-fired", etc.

Meta-rules are often used to handle the problem of control (i.e. the problem of which rule should be applied next). When an "impasse" in the inference process occurs, the interpreter activates the meta-rules which will try to resolve the impasse. A typical example of an impasse is when there is more than one rule which matches with data in the current working-memory. Figure 3 presents an example.

```
WORKING-MEMORY: ((o1.True)(o2.True)(o3.True)(p1.)(p3.)(p2.)...)

GOAL: ((p1.True) (p3.True))

RULE MEMORY:    (1) IF o1 and o2
                     THEN set(p1,True) and set(p2,False)
                (2) IF o3
                     THEN set(p2,True) and set(p1,False)
                ...

META-RULE MEMORY: (3) IF error-flag-1
                       THEN set(data-elm(o2),False) and set(rule-to-be-fired(2),True)
                  (4) IF satisfied(1) and satisfied(2)
                       THEN set(error-flag-1,True)
```

Fig. 3. A reflective production rule program.

The computation is in an impasse, because both rule (1) and rule (2) match the current working-memory. The system will try to solve this impasse by initiating a reflective production rule program. The goal of this reflective program is

```
rule-to-be-fired(?rule) = True
```

The program in figure 3 incorporates meta-rules which might help to solve this impasse. For example the meta-rule

```
IF satisfied(1) and satisfied(2)
THEN set(error-flag-1,True)
```

says that, when both rule 1 and rule 2 can be fired, this is a special event in the object-level inference process (note that rule 1 and 2 propose contradictory actions). Consequently, the data-element error-flag-1 has to be set true. This will enable rule 3 to fire, which modifies the status of the object-level inference process (think of rule 3 as an error-handling procedure).

When the meta-rules have succeeded in solving the "reflective subgoal" of the above example, the reflective computation will have affected the object computation by determining which of the two competing rules will be applied and by modifying the status of the working-memory. This example illustrated the reflective architecture incorporated in systems like SOAR or TEIRESIAS. Note that in this example reflection is controlled (activated) implicitly as opposed to being programmed explicitly in the procedural and logic-based example.

5.4. Discussion of the Existing Architectures for Reflection

If we study the reflective architectures discussed above, many common issues can be identified. One such issue is that almost all of these languages operate by means of a **meta-circular interpreter** (F.O.L. presents an exception which will be discussed later). A meta-circular interpreter is a representation of the interpretation in the language, which is also actually used to run the language[4]. Virtually, the interpretation of such a language consists of an infinite tower of circular interpreters interpreting the circular interpreter below. Technically, this infinity is realised by the presence of a second interpreter (written in another language), which is able to interpret the circular interpreter (and which should be guaranteed to generate the same behavior as the circular one).

The reason why all these architectures are this way is because a meta-circular interpreter presents an easy way to fulfill the causal connection requirement. The self-representation that is given to a system is exactly the meta-circular interpretation-process that is running the system. Since this is a procedural representation of the system, i.e. a representation of the system in terms of the program that implements the system, we say these architectures support **procedural reflection**.

The consistency between the self-representation and the system itself is automatically guaranteed because the self-representation is actually used to implement the system. So there is not really a causal connection problem. There only exists one representation which is both used to implement the system and to reason about the system. Note that a necessary condition for a meta-circular interpreter is that the language provides one common format for programs in the language and data, or more precisely, that programs can be viewed as data-structures of the language.

One problem with procedural reflection is that a self-representation has to serve two purposes. Since it serves as the data for reflective computation, it has to be designed in such a way that it provides a good basis to reason about the system. But at the same time it is used to implement the system, which means that it has to be effective and efficient. These are often contradicting requirements.

Consequently, people have been trying to develop a different type of reflective architecture in which the self-representation of the system would not be the implementation of the system. This type of architecture is said to support **declarative reflection** because it makes it possible to develop self-representations merely consisting of statements about the system. These statements could for example say that the computation of the system has to fulfill some time or space criteria. The self-representation does not have to be a complete procedural representation of the system, it is more a collection of constraints that the status and behavior of the system have to fulfill.

---

[4] This representation minimally consists of a name for the interpreter-program (such as "eval" in LISP) plus some reified interpreter-data (such as the list-of-bindings and the continuation). It might also be richer (for example by making more explicit about the interpreter-program).

The causal connection requirement is more difficult to realise here: it has to be guaranteed that the explicit representation of the system and its implicitly obtained behavior are consistent with each-other. This means that in this case, the interpreter itself has do decide how the system can comply with its self-representation. So, in some sense the interpreter has to be more intelligent. It has to find ways to translate the declarative representations about the system into the interpretation-process (the procedural representation) that is implementing the system.

Such an architecture can be viewed as incorporating representations in two different formalisms of one and the same system. During computation the most appropriate representation is chosen. The implicit (procedural) representation serves the implementation of the system, while the explicit (declarative) representation serves the computation about the system. Although in architectures for declarative reflection more interesting self-representations can be developed, it is still is an open question in how far such architectures are actually technically realisable. GOLUX (Hayes, 1974) and Partial Programs (Genesereth, 1987) are two attempts which are worth mentioning.

Actually the distinction between declarative reflection and procedural reflection should more be viewed as a continuum. A language like F.O.L. (Weyhrauch, 1980) is situated somewere in the middle: F.O.L. guarantees the accuracy of the self-representation by a technique called **semantic attachment**. The force of the self-representation is guaranteed by **reflection principles**. It is far less trivial to prove that the combination of these two techniques actually also succeeds in maintaining the consistency between the self-representation and the system.

6. Reflection in an Object-Oriented Language

6.1. Introduction

The previous section discussed examples of existing reflective architectures in procedure-based, logic-based and rule-based languages. We are particularly interested in object-oriented languages. Although the first OOLs, such as SIMULA (Dahl and Nygaard, 1966) or SMALLTALK-72 (Goldberg and Kay, 1976), did not yet incorporate facilities for reflective computation, it must be said that the concept of reflection fits most naturally in the spirit of object-oriented programming. An important issue in OOL is abstraction: an object is free to realise its role in the overall system in whatever way it wants to. Thus, it is natural to think that an object not only performs computation about its domain, but also about how it can realise this (object-) computation.

Designers of OOLs have actually felt the need to provide such facilities. Two strong motivations exist. A first motivation is the design of specialised interpreters. It has become clear that a specific design for an OOL suits some applications, but is inappropriate for others. Reflective facilities present a solution to this problem. A language with reflective facilities is **open-ended**: reflection makes it possible to make (local) specialised interpreters of the language, from within the language itself. For example, objects could be given an explicit, modifiable representation of how they are printed, or of the way they create instances. If these explicit self-representations are causally connected (i.e. if the behavior of the object is always in compliance with them) it becomes possible for an object to modify these aspects of its behavior. One object could modify the way it is printed, another object could adopt a different procedure for making instances, etc.

A second motivation is inspired by the development of **frame-based languages**, which introduced the idea to encapsulate domain-data with all sorts of reflective data and procedures (Roberts and Goldstein, 1977) (Minsky, 1974). An object would thus not only represent information about the thing in the domain it represents, but also about (the implementation and interpretation of) the object itself:

when is it created? by whom is it created? what constraints does it have to fulfill? etc. This reflective information seems to be useful for a range of purposes:

- it helps the user cope with the complexity of a large system by providing documentation, history, and explanation facilities,
- it keeps track of relations among representations, such as consistencies, dependencies and constraints,
- it encapsulates the value of the data-item with a default-value, a form to compute it, etc,
- it guards the status and behavior of the data-item and activates procedures when specific events happen (e.g. the value becomes instantiated or changed).

OOLs have responded to this need by providing reflection in ad hoc ways. Reflective facilities were mixed in the object-level structures. In languages such as SMALLTALK-72 (Goldberg and Kay, 1976) and FLAVORS (Weinreb and Moon, 1981), an object not only contains information about the entity that is represented by the object, but also about the representation itself, i.e. about the object and its behavior. For example, in SMALLTALK, the class Person may contain a method to compute the age of a person as well as a method telling how a Person object should be printed. Also in FLAVORS, every flavor is given a set of methods which represent the reflective facilities a flavor can make usage of (cfr. figure 4).

```
:DESCRIBE (message): ()
GET-HANDLER-FOR: (OBJECT OPERATION)
MAKE-INSTANCE: (FLAVOR-NAME &REST INIT-OPTIONS)
:OPERATION-HANDLED-P (message): (OPERATION)
SYS:PRINT-SELF (message :PRINT-SELF): (OBJECT STREAM PRINT-DEPTH SLASHIFY-P)
:SEND-IF-HANDLES (message): (MESSAGE &REST ARGS)
:WHICH-OPERATIONS (message): ()
```

Fig. 4. The structure of the vanilla-flavor.

There are two problems with this way of providing reflective facilities. One is that these languages always support only a fixed set of reflective facilities. Adding a new facility means changing the interpreter itself. For example, if we want to add a reflective facility which makes it possible to specify how an object should be edited, we have to modify the language-interpreter such that it actually uses this explicit edit-method whenever the object has to be edited. A second problem is that they mix object-level and reflective level, which may possibly lead to obscurities. For example, if we represent the concept of a book by means of an object, it may no longer be clear wether the slot with name "Author" represents the author of the book (i.e. domain data) or the author of the object (i.e. reflective data).

Several steps towards a cleaner handling of reflective facilities have been taken, for example by the introduction of meta-classes in SMALLTALK-80 (Goldberg and Robson, 1983). Another example is the development of OOLs such as PLASMA (Smith and Hewitt, 1975), ACTORS (Lieberman, 1981), RLL (Greiner, 1980) and OBJVLISP (Briot and Cointe, 1986). These languages contribute to the uniformity of the different notions existing in OOLs by representing everything in terms of objects: class, instance, meta-class, instance-variable, method, message, environment and continuation of a message. This increased uniformity makes it possible to treat more aspects of object-oriented systems as data for reflective computation.

In general, it can be said that the evolution of OOLs tends towards a broader use of reflective facilities. However none of the existing languages has ever actually recognised reflection as the primary programming concept developers of OOL are (unconsciously) looking for. The languages mentioned above only support a finite set of reflective facilities, often designed and implemented in an ad hoc way. The next section discusses in what ways an OOL with a reflective architecture differs from these languages. It highlights the issues that were missing in the existing languages.

6.2. The 3-KRS Experiment

This section discusses an OOL with an architecture for procedural reflection. The discussion is based on a concrete experiment that was performed to introduce a reflective architecture in the language KRS (Steels, 1986). The resulting language is called 3-KRS (Maes, 1987). The important innovation of 3-KRS is that it fulfills the following crucial properties of an object-oriented reflective architecture[5]:

1. A first property is that it presents the first OOL adopting a **disciplined split** between object-level and reflective level. Every object in the language is given a **meta-object**. A meta-object also has a pointer to its object. The structures contained in an object exclusively represent information about the domain entity that is represented by the object. The structures contained in the meta-object of the object hold all the reflective information that is available about the object. The meta-object holds information about the implementation and interpretation of the object (cfr. figure 5). It incorporates for example methods specifying how the object inherits information, how the object is printed, how a new instance of the object is made, etc.

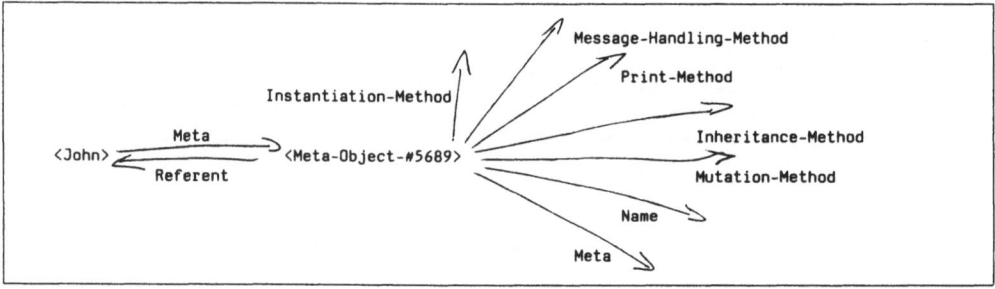

Fig. 5. An object and its meta-object.

Note that the meta-relation is not collapsed with the instance-relation (as it is in SMALLTALK-80 or LOOPS). The object John has a type-link to the Person object and a meta-link to its meta-object (named "Meta-Object-#5689").[6]

Note also that although there is a one-to-one relation between objects and meta-objects (which might suggest to combine them into one object), it is important that object and meta-object are also physically separated (which is again not true for the meta-classes of SMALLTALK). This way a standard message protocol can be developed between an object and its meta-object. This protocol makes it possible to create abstractions of the behavior of an object (i.e. ready-made meta-objects), and to temporarily attach such a special behavior to an object.

---

[5] None of the languages discussed above fulfills the entire list, although they might fulfill one or more of the properties.

[6] However, the "meta" slot of an object is also inherited. When the object John does not override the "meta" slot, it will when needed make a copy of the meta-object of Person.

2. A second property is that the self-representation of an object-oriented system is **uniform**. Every entity in a 3-KRS system is an object: instances, classes, slots, methods, meta-objects, messages, etc. Consequently every aspect of a 3-KRS system can be reflected upon. All these objects have meta-objects which represent the self-representation corresponding to that object. Note that since meta-objects are again objects, meta-objects have to be created in a lazy way. KRS incorporates a lazy-construction mechanism which takes care of this (Van Marcke, 1986): meta-objects are only con-structed when they are actually needed.

3. A third property is that 3-KRS provides a **complete self-representation**. The meta-objects contain all the information about objects that is available in the 3-KRS language. Actually, the contents of meta-objects was designed on the basis of the interpreter. The code of the interpreter was divided in blocks which represent how a specific aspect of a certain type of object is implemented. All of these blocks were afterwards reified (i.e. made explicit) under the form of objects (fillers of slots in the meta-objects). 3-KRS incorporates a set of primitive meta-objects which together represent the com-plete 3-KRS interpreter (cfr. figure 6). When a specific object is created in some application, it will automatically inherit one of these meta-objects from its type.

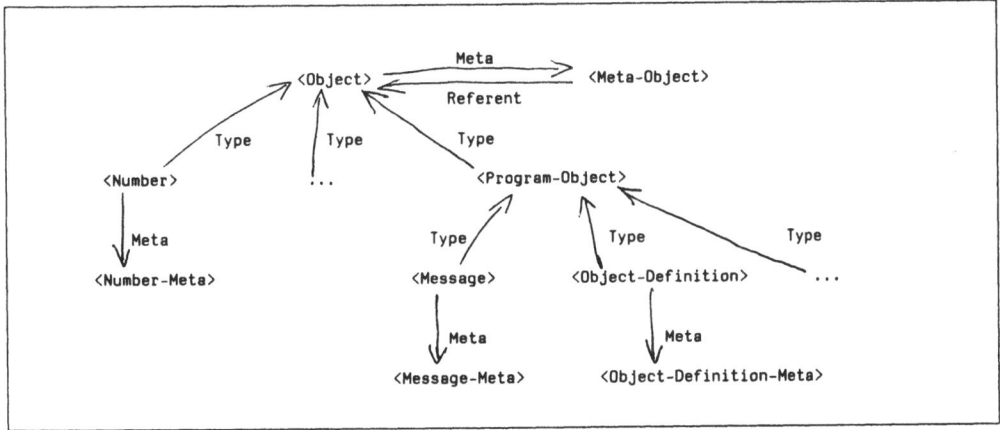

Fig. 6. The primitive meta-objects of 3-KRS, or the theory the language 3-KRS incorporates about the implementation of its objects and the interpretation of its programs.

"Meta-Object" is the most general meta-object. It roughly contains what was illustrated in figure 2. The other meta-objects in the figure above add to or specialise the information in Meta-Object. For example, Message-Meta represents the information that is available about message-objects. It adds to Meta-Object slots representing the method to be used to evaluate the message and the continuation and environment of the evaluation.

4. A fourth property is that the self-representation of a 3-KRS system is **consistent**. The self-representation is actually used to implement the system. The explicit representation of the interpreter that is embedded in the meta-objects is used to implement the system. Whenever some operation has to be performed on an object, e.g. an instance of the object has to be created or the object has to answer a message, or a message-object has to be evaluated, the meta-object of the object is requested to perform the action. The technique that is used in order to avoid an infinite loop is that there is a second, implicit interpreter which is used to implement the default (or standard) behavior[7].

---

[7] The real (i.e. implicit) interpreter of the 3-KRS language tests for every operation that it has to perform on an object

5. A final property is that the self-representation can also at run-time be modified, and these modifications actually have an **impact on the run-time computation**. The self-representation of the system is explicit, i.e. it consists of objects. Thus, any computation may access this self-representation and make modifications to it. These modifications will result in actual modifications of the behavior of the system.

The 3-KRS experiment is extensively described in (Maes, 1987). It shows that it is feasible to build a reflective architecture in an object-oriented language and that there are even specific advantages to object-oriented reflection. These advantages are a result of the encapsulation and abstraction facilities provided by object-oriented languages. The next section illustrates these advantages. It presents two examples of programming in an object-oriented reflective architecture.

6.3. A New Programming Style

Although the implementation of 3-KRS is far from trivial, from the programmer's point of view the language has a simple and elegant design. The basic unit of information in the system is the object. An object groups information about the entity in the domain it represents. Every object in 3-KRS has a meta-object. The meta-object of an object groups information about the implementation and interpretation of the object. An object may at any point interrupt its object-computation, reflect on itself (as represented in its meta-object) and modify its future behavior.

Reflective computation may be guided by the object itself or by the interpreter. An object may cause reflective computation by specifying reflective code, i.e. code that mentions its meta-object. The interpreter causes reflective computation for an object whenever the interpreter has to perform an operation on the object and the object has a special meta-object. At that moment the interpretation of the object is delegated to this special meta-object.

This reflective architecture supports the modular construction of reflective programs. The abstraction and encapsulation facilities inherent to OOLs make it possible to program object-computation (objects) and reflective computation (meta-objects) independently of each other. There is a standard message protocol between an object and its meta-object which guarantees that the two modules will also be able to work with each other[8]. This makes it possible to temporarily associate a certain reflective computation with an object without having to change the object itself. Another advantage is that libraries of reflective computation can be constructed.

This section (schematically) illustrates what programming in a reflective OOL is like. It demonstrates the particular style of modular programming that is supported by reflective architectures. More (operational code) examples of programming in 3-KRS can be found in (Maes, 1987).

A first example illustrates the object-oriented equivalent of the tracing example presented in section 4. The reflective architecture of 3-KRS provides a modular solution for implementing reflective computation such as stepping and tracing of programs. One can temporarily associate a meta-object with a program (-object) such that during its evaluation various tracing or stepping utilities are performed.

---

whether the meta-object of this object specifies a deviating method for this operation. "Deviating" meaning here: different from (overriding) the methods of the primitive meta-objects listed in figure 3. If so, the interpreter will apply the explicit method (3-KRS program). If not, it handles this operation implicitly. This implicit handling guarantees the same results as the explicit methods described in the primitive meta-objects.

[8] More specifically, the meta-object has to specify values for a predefined set of slots (variables and methods), which for the 3-KRS experiment roughly correspond to the names listed in figure 2. Actually this set varies according to the type of object at hand. E.g. the meta-object of a program-object in addition has to specify an evaluation-method.

Note that the object itself remains unchanged, only its meta-object is temporarily specialised to a meta-object adapted to stepping or tracing.

Figure 7 illustrates the idea. Message-#3456 is an object representing some message. It has a meta-object, called Message-Meta-#2342 which may be a copy of the default meta-object for a message or a user-defined specialisation of this. The Tracer-Meta object is designed to be temporarily attached to any program-object. The meta-link from the program-object to the old meta-object is temporarily replaced by a meta-link to (a copy of) the Tracer-Meta. Tracer-Meta-#8765 inherits from this old meta-object and overrides the Eval-Method: it adds some actions before and after the eval-method of the old meta-object (such that the evaluation itself is still handled by Message-Meta-#2342). These actions will take care that when Message-#3456 is evaluated, some information is printed before and after the evaluation.

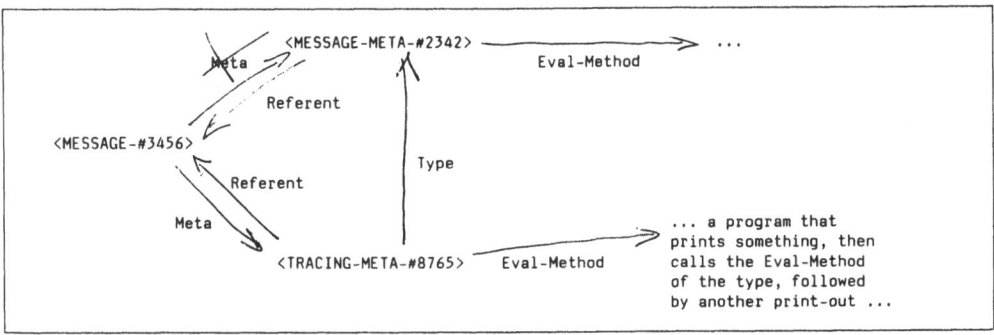

Fig. 7. Associating a tracing behavior temporarily.

Notice that it is not only possible to add before or after methods. The eval-method itself could also be overridden or specialised (it is again an object that can be manipulated).

A second example illustrates how a local deviating interpreter may be realised. A major advantage of a language with a reflective architecture is that it is open-ended, i.e. that it can be adapted to user-specific needs. But even more, a reflective architecture makes it possible to dynamically build and change interpreters from within the language itself. It allows for example to extend the language with meaningful constructs without stepping outside the interpreter. Note that this way the language itself can be made more concise (and thus more efficient). The extra structure and computation necessary to provide objects with special features such as documentation, constraints or attachment do not have to be supported for all objects in the system but can be provided on a local basis.

Figure 8 illustrates a very simple example. The 3-KRS language does not support multiple-inheritance. However, if a multiple-inheritance behavior is needed for some object (or class of objects), it can be realised by a specialised meta-object. The object Mickey-Mouse has a deviating interpreter which takes care of the multiple-sources inheritance behavior of this object. The specific strategy for the search of inherited information is implemented explicitly in the language itself by overriding the inheritance-method of the default meta-object.

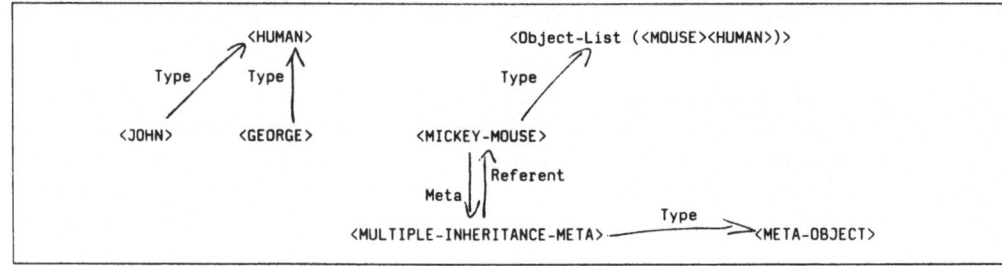

Fig. 8. Implementing a local variation on the language.

For frequently used variations on the language, abstractions may be provided. The 3-KRS system currently provides an initial library of reflective behaviors including meta-objects for pretty-printing, tracing and stepping, several variations on the language (multiple-inheritance, frames, monitors, streams, defaults, etc). The programmer can simply pick such a special behavior and attach it to an object in his application. Very few slots of such a meta-object remain to be filled.

Note finally that the architecture of object-oriented reflection provides a sophisticated control of the granularity of reflective computation. Local reflective computation can be obtained by making reflective individual instances. E.g. a reflective object John, or a reflective particular message. More general reflective computation can be obtained by making reflective abstract objects (which serve as the type of other objects). E.g. one can make all person objects reflective, by making the class person object reflective. Or one can make a class of messages in the system behave in a special way, by making their class message object reflective.

6.4. Discussion of the Experiment

We can conclude that the experiment of 3-KRS does for the object-oriented paradigm what languages like 3-LISP, F.O.L. and TEIRESIAS did for the procedure, logic and rule-based paradigm respectively. Just like these languages, 3-KRS introduced a new concept (or programming-construct) being the notion of a meta-object. Meta-objects are just like the other objects of the language, except that they represent information about the computation performed by other objects and that they are also taken into account by the interpreter of the language when running a system.

Another common issue is the way the causal connection requirement is handled. Just like the main part of the languages discussed in section 5, 3-KRS represents an architecture for procedural reflection. 3-KRS is run by a meta-circular interpreter: the self-representation that is given to a system is an explicit representation of the implementation of the system. Consequently this self-representation also represents the system in terms of the concepts inherent in the interpretation of an object-oriented language: handling messages, creating instances, etc.

7. Overal Conclusion

This paper briefly introduced some of the concepts and experiments in computational reflection. The conclusions that can be made are that

- reflection can be defined in a clear and technical way,
- reflection occurs frequently in real-world programming, particularly in knowledge-based systems,
- a reflective architecture provides better support for programming reflective computation,

- a reflective architecture can be realised by very similar techniques for procedural, logic-based, rule-based and object-oriented languages.

Many aspects of reflection, reflective architectures and particularly of object-oriented reflection (its implementation and use) have not been discussed in this paper. The interested reader may consult (Maes, 1987).

8. Bibliography

Bobrow D. and Stefik M. (1981) "The LOOPS manual". Tech. Rep. KB-VLSI-81-13. Knowledge Systems Area. Xerox Palo Alto Research Center. Palo Alto, California.

Borning A. and O'Shea T. (1987) "Deltatalk: An Empirically and Aesthetically Motivated Simplification of the Smalltak-80 Language". In: *Proceedings of the ECOOP Conference*. Paris, France.

Bowen K. (1986) "Meta-level Techniques in Logic Programming". In: *Proceedings of the International Conference on Artificial Intelligence and its Applications*. Singapore.

Briot J.P. and Cointe P. (1986) "The OBJVLISP Model: Definition of a Uniform Reflexive and Extensible Object-Oriented Language". In: *Proceedings of the European Conference on Artificial Intelligence - 1986*.

Dahl O. and Nygaard K. (1966) "SIMULA - An Algol-Based Simulation-Language". *Communications of the ACM*. 9: 671-678.

Davis R. (1982) In: "Knowledge-Based Systems in Artificial Intelligence". Davis R. and Lenat D. Mc Graw-Hill, New York.

Friedman D. and Wand M. (1984) "Reification: Reflection without meta-physics". *Communications of the ACM*. Vol 8.

Genesereth M. (1987) "Prescriptive Introspection". In: *Meta-Level Architectures and Reflection*. Eds: P. Maes and D. Nardi. North-Holland, Amsterdam, June 1987.

Goldberg A. and Kay A. (1976) "SMALLTALK-72 Instruction Manual". Technical Report SSL-76-6, Xerox Palo Alto Research Center. Palo Alto, California.

Goldberg A. and Robson D. (1983) "Smalltalk-80: The Language and its Implementation". Addison-Wesley. Reading, Massachusetts.

Greiner R. (1980) "RLL-1: A Representation Language Language". Stanford Heuristic Programming Project. HPP-80-9. Stanford, California.

Hayes P. (1974) "The Language GOLUX". University of Essex Report. Essex, United Kingdom.

Laird J., Rosenbloom P. and Newell A. (1986) "Chunking in SOAR: The Anatomy of a General Learning Mechanism". In: *Machine Intelligence*. Vol 1. Nr 1. Kluwer Academic Publishers.

Lieberman H. (1981) "A Preview of ACT1". Massachusetts Institute of Technology, Artificial Intelligence Laboratory. MIT AI-MEMO 625. Cambridge, Massachusetts.

Maes P. (1987) "Computational Reflection". PhD. Thesis. Laboratory for Artificial Intelligence, Vrije Universiteit Brussel. Brussels, Belgium. January 1987.

Minsky M. (1974) "A Framework for Representing Knowledge". Massachusetts Institute of Technology, Artificial Intelligence Laboratory. MIT AI-MEMO 306. Cambridge, Massachusetts.

Roberts R. and Goldstein I. (1977) "The FRL Primer". Massachusetts Institute of Technology, Artificial Intelligence Laboratory. MIT AI-MEMO 408. Cambridge, Massachusetts.

Smith B. (1982) "Reflection and Semantics in a Procedural Language". Massachusetts Institute of Technology. Laboratory for Computer Science. Technical Report 272. Cambridge, Massachusetts.

Smith B. and Hewitt C. (1975) "A PLASMA Primer (draft)". Massachusetts Institute of Technology. Artificial Intelligence Laboratory. Cambridge, Massachusetts.

Steels L. (1986) "The KRS Concept System". Vrije Universiteit Brussel. Artificial Intelligence Laboratory. Technical Report 86-1. Brussels, Belgium.

Van Marcke K. (1986) "A Parallel Algorithm for Consistency Maintenance in Knowledge Representation". In: *Proceedings of the European Conference on Artificial Intelligence, 1986*. Brighton, England.

Weinreb D. and Moon D. (1981) "Lisp Machine Manual". Symbolics Inc. Cambridge, Massachusetts.

Weyhrauch R. (1980) "Prolegomena to a Theory of Mechanized Formal Reasoning". In: *Artificial Intelligence* Vol. 13 No. 1,2. North Holland. Amsterdam. The Netherlands.

COGNITIVE MODELLING AND EDUCATION

A. de Haan

Department of education (IDOK)

State University

Groningen - The Netherlands

In the design of computational systems to coach pupils in the acquisition of an ability it can be profitable to consider errors in the performance of the pupil. In such a situation the coaching system should be able to make a diagnosis of erroneous performance. For the diagnosis of errors in the execution of certain tasks, one should gain insight in the processes that are involved in the execution of these tasks. A way to acquire this insight is to construct a computational model of the processes and to run it on a computer in a so-called simulation.

We implemented a simulation model of the beginning speller in order to better understand the cognitive processes involved in the development of spelling. We shall describe the way the behaviour of the model gave us indications about the computational principles that guide the development of the spelling ability.

The research that is the basis for this paper took place within the wider setting of a computercoach project (COSPAR) for arithmetic and spelling in primary classes (1st and 2nd) of primary school.

Man and machine, learning and teaching

"A key operation in an instructible system is that of explaining how the system has arrived at some behaviour, whether correct or wrong. In the case of wrong behaviour, the instructible system must reveal enough of its processing to allow the more intelligent instructor to determine what behaviour is missing, incorrect, or improperly represented" (Rychener, page 439, 1983).

In this quotation the instructible system is not a human being but an IPS, an Instructible Production System. An IPS is a computer program designed to learn through instruction, by "being told". The construction of these kinds of learning programs takes place in a branch of artificial intelligence called machine learning (Michalski et. al., 1983).

The purport of the above quotation seems, however, to relate to human as well as machine learning. In particular this is true with respect to the information about the processing responsible for the behaviour of the system that is revealed to the observing instructor.

In order to explain how an instructible system, mechanical or human, has arrived at some behaviour, the observing instructor should be able to effectively interpret the revealed information. The way in which the information is interpreted depends on the knowledge of the instructor about the instructible system.

When the observing instructor is mechanical, as is e.g. the case in an Intelligent Tutoring System (ITS, Sleeman et. al., 1982), the knowledge that makes it possible to interpret the information provided by the observer, instructed system should be embodied in computer procedures.

In general, an ITS is not constructed to instruct mechanical systems, such as Instructible Production Systems, but human learners. This has consequences for the kind of knowledge that has to be implemented in the system. The knowledge we have about the processes that guide human performance is of a different nature than the knowledge we have about mechanical intelligent systems. While the latter knowledge is more or less knowledge about explicit rules and representations, of which the nature is in principle directly accessible, the former knowledge is knowledge about hypothetical rules and representations, about theoretical constructs, meant to explain human performance (Chomsky, 1980). The theoretical character of the observed entities implies that in explaining human behaviour, observations are theory laden.

Machine teaching

In an ITS (Sleeman & Brown, 1982), the interaction of the system with the pupil is guided by a diagnostic explanation of the pupils performance. This explanation can consist of a set of possible procedural explanations of a set of observations. The set of explanations can be constructed using the inferential knowledge of the tutoring system. Every possible explanation of a set of observations can be seen as a hypothsesis about the cognitive behaviour that supported the observed behaviour. The correct explanation is selected by a heuristic process of testing and weeding out alternative explanations.

When a systematic error is suspected, erroneous behaviour can be provoked by the construction of relevant conditions for the potential erroneous behaviour. In this way the hypotheses about the erroneous behaviour can be tested and verified.

For a structural description of the pupil's knowledge only systematic behaviour is important. Systematic behaviour is behaviour that can be explained by the observing system. The more the system knows, the more systematics it perceives in the behaviour, the more similarities and dissimilarities between errors are discerned. We shall illustrate this in the next section with some examples from the spelling domain.

The sound to spelling strategy

"In spelling, application of sound-to-spelling rules to irregular words could result in the generation of a spelling for an item which would not correspond to a visual-orthographic entry in the lexicon; "debt" might be spelled as "det", "yacht" as "yot" and "sword" as "sord"." (Barron, 1980).

The emergence of diagnostic expertise changes the way the observer carves up a set of observed errors. The professional observer is likely to interpret "det" as a phonemic error. According to this interpretation, the child first constructed a phonemic representation of the word, (d e t), and accordingly used sound to letter regularities to discover the proper graphemic sequence.

"Debt" is an irregular word because the employment of a phonemic strategy can lead to an error. According to this professional diagnostic perspective, all other irregular words are similar to "debt" with respect to specific missspellings. Similar errors would be faults like "yacht" as "yot", "sword" as "sord" (Barron, 1980), "freeze" as "freez" or "freas" and "cough" as "coff" or "cof" (Frith, 1980).

The characterisation of a fault as a phonemic error is still rather general and operationally inadequate. "Yot" and "det" are both phonemic errors, and thus similar, but the processes that led to the errors can be assumed to be different. The generality involved prevents one from knowing the exact structural properties of the knowledge state that explains the erroneous performance.

Because of this one cannot expect this explanation to be comprehensive enough to provide a structure for research on the processes responsible for specific performance of the speller.

The more sensitive the inferential knowledge of the diagnostic system is, the more refined its hypothesis about the cognitive sources of the behaviour can be. But the inferential knowledge can be too specific, too sensitive and its consequential hypotheses too specific to be of any use.

The construction of a simulation model for the beginning speller can give an indication of the relevant structural characteristics involved in the development of the spelling ability. This construction should be based on whatever knowledge is available about the development of this ability.

The structure of the knowledge

On entering primary school by the age of six, children can in general be seen as rather mature language users (Schaerlakens, 1977). By mastering the fonological and morphological system of their native language they have learned how to segment spoken sound into meaningfull units. They have learned how to relate spoken language and reality. In learning how to spell they must use this maturity to master a functional relation between temporal soundstructures and, in most cases lineair, sign structures.

In the literature it is generally agreed that the beginning speller uses a fonemic strategy (Verhoeven, 1983). A transformation is being accomplished from in the spelling process segmented phonemes to graphemes that are accessible to the pupil. This transformation is accomplished by means of a phoneme-grapheme correspondency (Frith, 1980; Verhoeven, 1983). The spelling of a sounded out word can be modelled as the steps in a transition network.

In the fonological reconstruction of the spelling process three consecutive phases can be distinguished (Frith, 1980). First, there is a correct or incorrect analysis of the speech sounds. A correct analysis indicates that the "approximate" phonemes have been derived. We assume that in principle the child can manage this decomposition on entering primary school because most children of that age seem to have mastered the phonemic system (Schaerlakens, 1977).

The second phase in the spelling process consists in the establishment by the pupil of a relation between perceived phonemes and graphemes, that is, a relation between a well-known structure and a relatively unknown structure. The established relation consists in knowledge with respect to the regularities that govern the relation. An essential aspect of this second phase is the fact that for the beginning speller the relation is unequivocal. Every phoneme is related to one and only one grapheme. In this phase the transition network that models the spelling is deterministic.

The third phase in the spelling process is a consequence of the fact that the advanced speller has to manage equivocal relation. Some phonemes are, conditionally, related to more than one grapheme and vice versa. In this third phase the conventionally correct graphemes have to be selected out of all the phonetically plausible graphemes (figure 1).

Owing to the arising equivocal non deterministic relations between phonemes and graphemes, the child has to increasingly employ considerations with respect to conditional features that hinge on the position of the phonemes in the word, the phonological and morphological context and semantic characteristics in order to solve these ambiguities.

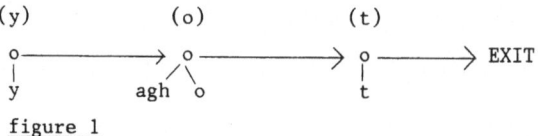

figure 1

As a consequence in a later development phase the speller seems to use a more advanced strategy (Verhoeven, 1983). The speller manages larger orthographic units in relation to the phonemic sequences in the word that has to be spelled (figure 2). The development in the spelling ability can thus be characterised as an orientation towards larger phonological-orthographic units (Kruidenier, 1985).

```
    (y,o)          (t)
    o────────────→ o ──────→ EXIT
    |              |
    yagh           t
```

figure 2

In the next section the structure of the model that simulates the development of spelling ability is discussed.

The representation of the knowledge

The knowledge needed to provide a fine-grained diagnosis can be acquired through a procedural description of the behaviour involved (e.g. Sleeman, 1983) and a description of the generic development of the procedures as the ability matures (e.g. Goldstein, 1982).

We implemented a rule based system that was expected to model the development of spelling performance in Dutch spellers. The basic structure of the model is simple. Following the assumption that the beginning speller uses a phonemic strategy, we implemented development of the different phases of the spelling process that are concomitant with the strategy. The rules that govern the behaviour of the simulation are hierarchical. Rules that are characteristics of a more developed stage screene out rules characteristics of a less developed stage and rules that consider conditions implicit in the conditions of other rules are screened out when the latter rules are active. Whether this screening out takes place depends on what developmental stage the simulated pupil is supposed to function.

The level of abstraction was kept as low as possible, that is, we did not generalise about phonemes or graphemes when this was not necessary. The consequence is that concepts like phoneme, consonant or grapheme are not explicitly represented in the system. Only the members of sets designated by the concepts are present.

The structure of the simulation

In the description of the results of this implementation we shall try to give equivalent English cases where possible. Herewith it should be borne in mind that the empirical facts that are the basis for some of the research come from Dutch subjects and imply thus no observation pertaining to English spelling strategies. In the construction of the simulation we used the available knowledge in our department and elsewhere about spelling and spelling development with beginning spellers.

The available literature only supports the assumption that the development concerns a development of a three phase process. This development can be seen as a development from a deterministic, context free automaton, via a non deterministic automaton to a deterministic context sensitive automaton. The development of the first phase, the structuring of sound sequences into phonemic sequences was not explicitly considered in the simulation on the assumption that children have in general mastered the phonemic system when they enter primary school. It is needless to say that we do not consider the occurrence of errors in this phase unimportant. On the contrary, as research shows that spellers that have difficulty in the acquisition of the ability to perform a correct phonological analysis, seem to be language disordered and probably prone to developmental dyslexia (Snowling, cited in Frith, 1980).

The development in the second phase, the conversion of phonemes into graphemes, was explicitly considered and became a main subject of our simulation. The conversion depends on the knowledge the spelling child has with respect to the regularities that govern the mapping. Our starting point in the spelling process was the unequivocal relation of sound to sign that characterises the beginning speller in the second phase. This unequivocal relation is responsible for the correct spelling of regular words like "drum" and "dump". If words are irregular this strategy leads to predictable errors in words like "debt" and "freeze".

A second stage in the second phase is the occurrence of ambiguous sound to sign relations (figure 1). In Dutch, (t) can be transcribed as both "d" and "t", a (ü), pronounced like the "a" in "ago", can be transcribed as "ij", "u" and "e" (Kruidenier, 1985). The development from unequivocal to ambiguous relations is generally ahead of the development of the knowledge required to correctly solve the ambiguities. It can be seen as a process of diversification of transcription without mastering the conditions that guide the correct transcription. The child knows, that some sounds can be spelled in a number of ways, but does not yet have the knowledge to use the conditions with respect to the correct conversion.

It is probable that the emergence of the ambiguities in the second stage is not completely unconditional (Koster & Kruidenier, 1986). When a phoneme (x) has two or more orthographic candidates, and is thus ambiguous, the ambiguities do, in most cases, seem to arise with specific occurrences of the phoneme. The second stage in the conversion phase can be seen as being responsible for the emergence of the third phase in the spelling process. In this third phase the ambiguities that arose in the second phase are resolved (figure 2). The selection of the correct correspondence from among a set of plausible alternatives is guided by considerations with respect to the position of an ambiguous phoneme in the word or part of the word, with respect to the phonemes that surround the phoneme, with respect to lexical and semantic similarities and with respect to conjuncts and disjuncts of more than one of these categories.

Reconsidering the simulation

After comparing the system with actual spelling errors made by second grade pupils we concluded that the first prototype seemed to be on the right track but was too incomplete to sketch the development of pupils in general (Terwisscha van Scheltinga and Zijlstra, 1987).

The overlap of the behaviour of our model with the errors that were relatively frequent was evident. We draw the conclusion that many errors that are made by children at the end of the second grade can be explained as arising from a phonemic strategy. But there were a number of deviations in the spelling performance of the pupil from the way this strategy was modelled in our first prototype.

The first deviation concerned errors due to the first phase in the spelling process, i.e. errors that could be explained as errors due to an incorrect analysis of the phonemes involved. We did not simulate the first part of the process on the assumption that a child should be able to correctly analyse a word into phonemes. In general this assumption seemed to be correct. However, in some cases this assumption proved to be inadequate. These cases can be traced back to structural relations between phonemes. It seems that, for instance, whenever in Dutch phonology in a consonant cluster at the beginning of a syllabe a more sonoric phoneme is followed by a less sonoric phoneme, as in "psalm", this syllabic order is erroneously maintained when it is reversed at the end of a syllabe, as in "wasp". A word like "wasp" can be analysed as (w o: p s) and lead to "waps".

A second exception concerned errors that could be traced to assimilation, the influence of neighbouring phonemes on one another. The (eu) drifts to the (u) in front of a (r). A special case is so-called palatalisation in a word like "warm", a Dutch word that has the same meaning as its orthographic, English equivalent but that is commonly vocalised as (w a: r u m). A common error in beginning spellers is accordingly "warum".

The remaining errors that were made by the pupils and that did not occur in the simulation were not frequently made. They concerned word ruins, "diwah" for "tower", the change of letter sequences that could not be accounted for by a phonemic strategy, "otwer" for "tower", or replacements of motoric spelling procedures, "senn" as "seen".

Besides errors that were made by the pupils in our research sample and that were generated by our system a vast group of generated errors remained that were not found in the research sample. Our system seems to explain too much. It explains errors due to ambiguities that never arise. The principles on which the system is built are not restrictive enough and do not seem to reflect the core development of spelling ability. When, for instance, "attendance" is commonly missspelled as "attendence" and "attandance" and never as "attentence" this implies that some erroneous applications of sound to spelling rules do not occur simultaneously in real life.

Two general trends could be distilled from the empirical material (Terwisscha van Scheltinga and Zijlstra, 1987). Firstly, the development with respect to different phonemes was not parallel in time and there seemed to be a gradual development for phonemes with multiple conditions. Ambiguities with respect to definite morphemes were resolved relatively early. Then, ambiguities with respect to closed or open syllables, long and short vowels and the doubling of consonants were resolved while some errors that had to do with lexical access seemed to be last. Secondly, as stated before, some ambiguities do not seem to occur at all. This corroborated our

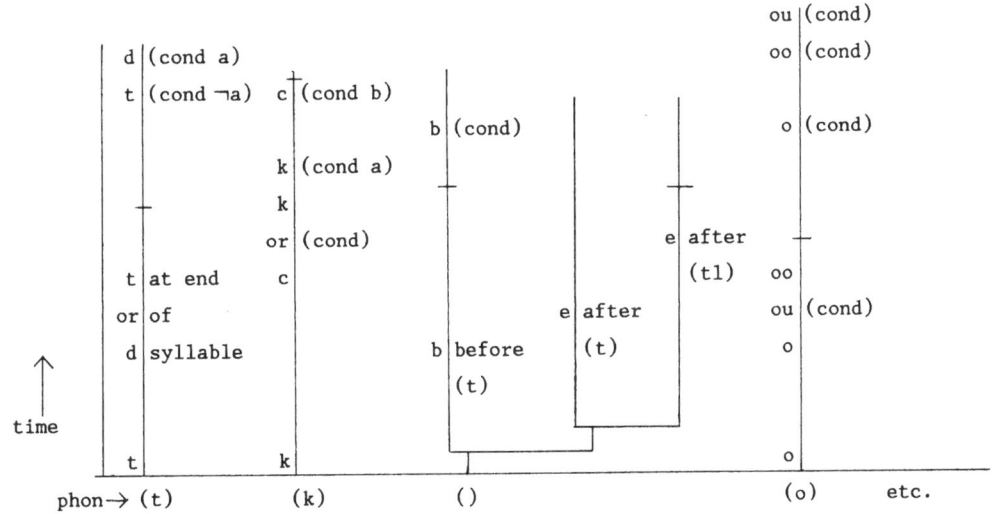

figure 3

earlier assumption that the overgeneralisation with respect to introduced ambiguities would be conditional. A (t) is not ambiguous in general but only at places where it could be a "d" in the orthography of the word. Thus "top" (Dutch for "top") is not systematically written as "dop" while "fort" (Dutch for "fort") is systematically written as "ford", and, by the way, as "foord" because of the influence of the (r) on the (o).

A representation of the structure of the system following the assimilation of the above-mentioned research is depicted in figure 3.

Application of the simulation model

In an applicative context, however, an employable and valid simulation model can also be used as the backbone of an ITS (Goldstein, 1982). The procedural knowledge, used to generate spelling examples in the simulation model is then used to search for a procedural model for the spelling ability of a specific pupil. The procedural knowledge should then be amplified by procedures for the heuristic search for the best structural hypothesis as mentioned above. Essentially, this heuristic search consists of the progressive collection of constraints on the procedural models that simulate the spelling.

Furthermore, information about the development of procedural knowledge involved in beginning spelling can be used in teaching as it shows how knowledge in a later developmental stage is dependent upon knowledge in earlier stages. The teaching activity ties in to the existing procedural model of the pupil and tries to enhance the pupil's performance by e.g. a learning by being told approach.

Concluding remarks

"One should not multiply explanations and causes without an urgent necessity" (Umberto Eco, The name of the Rose).

This paraphrase of Ockham's razor is significant for our activities. We have shown how inferential knowledge with respect to cognitive processing determines the way we can explain performance. We should, however, try to be as sparse as possible in our explanations of certain phenomena and not multiply the mental universe beyond necessity. The employment of the phonemic perspective is an exercise in the employment of this adagium. Try to explain as much erroneous behaviour as possible from within a single perspective with the help of a limited set of principles.

According to arbitrary associations between sounds and signs through existing words, a phonemic explanation can be given for any error, when conditions are relaxed enough. So, the burden of validating evidence cannot be put on the construction of a simulation model alone. The simulation should be placed in a wider context of knowledge to avoid the danger of methodological solipsism. It seems for instance that more proficient spellers do not only use larger phono-orthographic units but do not, in general, use the phonological entries in the lexicon at all when they spell familiar words. For a simulation of the expert speller this means that no mapping from sound to sign takes place but a mapping from meaning to the whole orthographic structure of the word.

But even when we can be reasonably sure about the phonemic character of a spelling error, it is often very difficult to decide what the right representational format is for the mapping procedures and how these formats can change in time. In our model we adopted a minimal approach. Regularities on a higher level of description are not explicitly represented but are a consequence of low level regularities.

Current research in the COSPAR project is being undertaken in order to address the representational question. The main problem is whether the procedures underlying beginning spelling performance should be reconstructed as general, abstract rules or as relatively simple, low level associations where no knowledge about consonants, vowels etc. is explicitly represented.

Literature

Barron, R.W., Visual and phonological strategies in spelling. In: Cognitive processes in spelling, U. Frith (Ed.), Academic Press, 1980.

Chomsky, N., Rules and Representations, Columbia University Press, New York, 1980.

Ecco, U., In the name of the Rose, Picador, Pan Books Ltd., London, 1984.

Frith, U., Unexpected spelling problems, In: Cognitive processes in spelling, U. Frith (Ed.), Academic Press, 1980.

Goldstein, I.P., The Gemetic Graph, in: Intelligent Tutoring Systems, D. Sleeman & J.S. Brown (Eds.), Academic Press Inc., London, 1982.

Koster, K.B. & Kruidenier, J., Cognitieve conflicten bij het leren spellen door eerste klassers, Tijdschrift voor taalbeheersing 8 (1986), 4, 268-277.

Kruidenier, J., Classificatie van spelfouten nader geanalyseerd, Tijdschrift voor taalbeheersing, 7, 56-64, 1985.

Michalski, R.S., Carbonell, J.G. & Mitchell, T.M., An overview of machine learning, in: Machine Learning, an Artificial Intelligent Approach, R.S. Michalski, J.G. Carbonell & T.M. Mitchell (Eds.), Tioga Publishing Company, Palo Alto, California, 1983.

Rychener, M.D., The instructible Production System: A retrospective Analysis, in: Machine Learning, an Artificial Intelligent Approach, R.S. Michalski, J.G. Carbonell & T.M. Mitchell (Eds.), Tioga Publishing Company, Palo Alto, California, 1983.

Schaerlaekens, A.M., De taalontwikkeling van het kind, Wolters-Noordhoff B.V., Groningen, 1977.

Sleeman, D., Inferring student models for intelligent computer-aided instruction, in: Machine Learning, R.S. Michalski, J.G. Carbonell & T.M. Mitchell (Eds.), Tioga Publishing Company, Palo Alto, California, 1983.

Sleeman, D. & Brown, J.S., Introduction: Intelligent Tutoring Systems, in: Intelligent Tutoring Systems, D. Sleeman & J.S. Brown (Eds.), Academic Press Inc., London, 1982.

Terwisscha van Scheltinga, A. & Zijlstra, H., Spellingdiagnose geautomatiseerd?, stageverslag, RUG, Groningen, 1987.

Venezky, R.L., The structure of english orthography, Mouton, The Hague, 1970.

Verhoeven, L.Th., Foutenclassificatie bij beginnende spellers, in: Tijdschrift voor Taalbeheersing, 5 (1983), p. 131-138.

Spezielle Sektion: Kognition
– Wissensstrukturen beim Aufgabenloesen

Christian Freksa
Technische Universität München

Die Suche nach geeigneten Wissensrepräsentationsformen für Fragestellungen in der
Kognitionsforschung – oder spezifischer: für Aufgabenstellungen an wissensbasierte
Systeme – ist untrennbar verbunden mit der Entlarvung von Wissensstrukturen, die den
kognitiven Prozessen zugrundeliegen.   Die Wissensrepräsentationsansätze in der KI
erstrecken sich von der Wahl einer einheitlichen Repräsentationsform, auf die alle
Wissensstrukturen abgebildet werden sollen, bis hin zur Bereitstellung einer
Vielzahl von Repräsentationsformen für unterschiedliche Wissensstrukturen und für
unterschiedliche Aufgabenstellungen.

Wenig Ansätze gibt es bisher zu einer Theorie, die eine einheitliche Beurteilung von
Wissensrepräsentationsformen in bezug auf die darzustellenden Wissensstrukturen und
die zu lösenden Aufgaben ermöglicht.   Ein Fernziel bleibt es vorläufig, aus einer
gegebenen Wissensstruktur und einer Aufgabenstellung eine geeignete Repräsentationsform automatisch zu generieren.

Ziel dieser Sektion ist es,   einen Einblick in Wissensstrukturen aus einem
interdisziplinären   Blickwinkel   zu   vermitteln   sowie   Anforderungen   an
Repräsentationsansätze für   unterschiedliche Wissensformen   und Fragestellungen
aufzuzeigen.   Der Begriff "Aufgabenlösen" im Thema der Sektion wurde anstelle des
häufiger verwendeten Begriffes "Problemlösen" gewählt, um für den Fall Rechnung zu
tragen,   daß   das   Problem   in   der   aufgabenspezifischen   Auswahl   einer
Repräsentationsform liegt und nicht in der Durchführung des Lösungsprozesses auf
einer gegebenen Repräsentationsform; nach erfolgter Abbildung des Problems auf eine
geeignete Repräsentationsform reduziert sich das Problem idealerweise auf den Fall
einer Aufgabe, die nach einem gegebenen Schema gelöst werden kann.   Eine "Aufgabe"
schließt also den Fall mit ein, bei dem ein Lösungsweg für eine gegebene
Wissensstruktur bereits vorhanden ist.

Der erste Beitrag, von Klaus Rehkämper, gibt einen Einblick in die "Imagery Debate",
die in der Cognitive Science in den vergangenen zehn Jahren eine wichtige Rolle
spielte.   Die Grundfrage dieser Auseinandersetzung war, ob die Bewältigung von
bestimmter kognitiver Aufgaben nur durch bildartige bzw. nur durch sprachartige
(propositionale) Darstellungsformen erkl@t werden könnten. Diese beiden
Darstellungsweisen wurden als sich wechselseitig ausschließend angesehen.   Die
Debatte hat viel zu der inzwischen verbreiteten Ansicht beigetragen, daß die
Hauptschwierigkeit bei der Bewältigung von Aufgaben oft nicht in der Durchführung
von Inferenzprozessen auf gegebenen Wissensstrukturen liegt,   sondern in der
Transformation von einer gegebenen Wissensform in eine für ein Lösungsverfahren
geeignete andere Wissensform.

Gerhard Strube erläutert in seinem Beitrag anhand einiger Thesen den Erkenntnisstand
der kognitiven Psychologie über die Repräsentation von Wissen beim Menschen.   Er
zeigt auf, welche Anforderungen sich für die Modellierung menschlichen Wissens in
der KI ergeben und wo Grenzen fuer die Nachbildbarkeit zu erwarten sind.   Er macht
aber auch deutlich, daß es unterschiedliche Wege geben kann, Aufgaben effizient zu
lösen und daß das menschliche Vorbild für eine Nachbildung kognitiver Fähigkeiten
nicht unbedingt verbindlich ist.

Barbara Becker beleuchtet die Vorgehensweise in der KI aus philosophischer und
soziologischer Sicht. Sie stellt die Beschreibbarkeit von Wissen bzw. Expertise zur
Bewältigung von Aufgaben grundsätzlich in Frage.   Sie weist auf menschliche
Fähigkeiten hin,   die sich nicht ohne Weiteres durch symbolische
Repräsentationsformen nachbilden lassen.   Der Beitrag enthält Anregungen für Fragestellungen, die für die Wissensrepräsentationsproblematik wichtig sind, bisher in
der KI jedoch wenig Berücksichtigung fanden.

Wissen und Können

Anmerkungen zur Wissensrepräsentation beim Aufgabenlösen

Barbara Becker

Fachbereich Gesellschaftswissenschaften,
Philosophie und Theologie
Universität Dortmund
Postfach 500 500
4600 Dortmund 50

ABSTRACT

Ziel des Beitrags ist die Infragestellung der grundlegenden Annahme innerhalb der KI-Forschung, daß Wissen beim Menschen in strukturierter Form repräsentiert ist und daß Menschen beim Aufgabenlösen auf dieses Wissen zugreifen. Unter Bezug auf Ryle wird eine Unterscheidung von beschreibbarem Wissen und nichtrepräsentiertem Können vorgenommen, um die Bereiche menschlichen Wissens zu berücksichtigen, die gerade für die Kompetenz von Experten charakteristisch zu sein scheinen. Soziologische Konsequenzen der Auffassung einer grundsätzlichen Beschreibbarkeit von Wissen werden im Hinblick auf die zunehmende Verbreitung von Expertensystemen thematisiert und anhand konkreter Beispiele (medizinische Diagnostik, VLSI-Design) erläutert.

I Einleitende Bemerkungen

Der Titel des Workshops: "Wissensstrukturen beim Aufgabenlösen" impliziert eine grundlegende Annahme, die für die KI-Forschung insgesamt charakteristisch ist: sie lautet: wenn Menschen Aufgaben lösen, greifen sie auf Wissen zu, daß entweder bereits in strukturierter Form im Bewußtsein repräsentiert ist oder aber im Zuge einer Aufgabenlösung in strukturierte Form gebracht wird. Damit sind zwei Hypothesen verknüpft:

1. Menschliches Wissen ist im Bewußtsein repräsentiert,

2. kognitive Fähigkeiten setzen strukturiertes, grundsätzlich
   beschreibbares Wissen voraus.

Ziel meines Beitrages ist die Problematisierung dieser Annahmen; ich
möchte die Frage aufwerfen, ob alles menschliche Wissen überhaupt in
strukturierter Form repräsentiert ist und ob sich gerade jenes Wissen, das
für Aufgabenlösungen relevant ist, vollständig auf explizite Repräsentationen zurückführen läßt. Diese Fragen lassen sich – betrachtet man den
gegenwärtigen Stand der Forschung – nicht klären, dies ist auch nicht
Ziel meines Beitrags; vielmehr liegt mir daran, durch das Aufwerfen dieser
Fragen und die Kritik an gängigen Konzepten zur Wissensrepräsentation
beim Problemlösen Anregungen für weitere Diskussionen zu geben (1).

Die Mannigfaltigkeit der Probleme, die sich aus der Behandlung einer
derart komplexen Thematik ergeben, macht eine Einschränkung der
Fragestellung notwendig: ich werde mich hier vorwiegend auf die Kompetenz von Experten beziehen , d.h. Aufgabenlösungen betrachten, die
gekennzeichnet sind durch nichtdeterminiertes und nichtdeterministisches
Vorgehen (2), einen offenen Problemraum sowie einen nicht vollständig
berechenbaren Ablauf.

II Kritik gängiger Problemlösungskonzepte in der KI-Forschung

---

Betrachtet man die Ansätze zur Wissensrepräsentation beim Problemlösen
in der KI-Forschung, so lassen sich generell drei Richtungen unterscheiden:

1. das Problemkonzept von Newell und Simon – die Gleichsetzung von
   Problemlösung mit Suchprozessen;
2. der Logik-Ansatz – Problemlösung wird als logisches Schließen oder
   Beweisen begriffen;
3. der Repräsentationsansatz – Problemlösen als Transformation von
   Repräsentationen.

Überprüft werden soll am Beispiel der medizinischen Diagnostik und des
VLSI-Design, inwieweit mit diesen Konzepten Expertise repräsentiert
werden kann und wo die Grenzen dieser Ansätze liegen.

III Konträre philosophische Positionen zum Repräsentationsansatz

Unabhängig von ihrem unterschiedlichen Vorgehen eint alle oben vorgestellten Konzepte die Vorstellung, daß Wissen in strukturierter Form
repräsentiert wird, Menschen also Repräsentationen bilden bzw. auf mental
repräsentiertes Wissen zugreifen, wenn sie Aufgaben lösen. Gegen diese
Annahme richten sich philosophische Positionen, die grundsätzlich davon
ausgehen, daß der Mensch, wenn er eine ihm gestellte Aufgabe zu lösen
hat, durchaus nicht auf mentale Repräsentationen zugreift. Es sei ihm
möglich, auf der Grundlage seines praktischen Verstehens intelligent zu
operieren, ohne daß er zuvor theoretische Überlegungen anstellt und auf
explizites Wissen zurückgreift, d.h. genau begründen kann, warum er dies
oder jenes genau macht. Die grundlegende These lautet, daß Menschen
keine mentalen Repräsentationen benötigen, um mit der Welt zu interagieren, weil sie ein intuitives Verständnis besitzen alleine dadurch, daß sie
stets eingebettet sind in die Welt und ihre Tradition. Während hier also
die Repräsentationsidee völlig abgelehnt wird, differenzieren Philosophen
wie Ryle zwischen dem Wissen im strengen Sinne, d.h. begrifflichem,
inhaltlichem Wissen, das in Propositionen repräsentiert wird, und dem
Können, daß sich der direkten Repräsentation entzieht. Er nennt als
entscheidendes Kriterium für intelligentes Operieren, daß "der Handelnde
etwas kann und von diesem Können bei seiner Handlung Gebrauch macht"
(3). Ryle argumentiert, daß derjenige, der über Können verfügt, dieses
nicht letztlich begründen geschweige denn auf Kriterien oder Regeln
zurückführen kann. Der Mensch vollziehe Handlungen auf der Basis von
durch konkrete Praxis erworbenen Dispositionen, ohne daß er eine Theorie
darüber hat, wie er sie vollzieht (4).

Diese Einsicht führt zu maßgeblichen Konsequenzen, betrachten wir die
Ausgangsproblemstellung; sie stellt in Frage, ob der Mensch überhaupt auf
konkrete Wissensstrukturen zugreift, wenn er eine Aufgabe löst. Zwar ist
nach Ryle Wissen im strengen Sinne mental repräsentiert, doch gilt dies
nicht in der unmittelbaren Form für das Können; dieses wird nur offenbar
in der Leistung, im Tun, seine explizite Repräsentation bleibt unklar. Das
theoretische Wissen um eine Fähigkeit hat niemals zwingend dessen
praktische Umsetzung durch den Wissenden zur Folge; es wäre also
zunächst eine Erklärung erforderlich, wie begriffliches Wissen mit dem
Können zusammenhängt und ob überhaupt Können direkt erklärbar ist
durch Wissen im obigen Sinne.

Die Vermittlung von Wissen und Können erfolgt durch das Subjekt im konkreten Prozeß der Problemlösung. Stellt hier das Wissen primär die Abbildung des Faktischen dar, impliziert das Können einen schöpferischen Akt, der das je Gegebene stets neu schafft und damit über das repräsentierbare Wissen hinausgeht. Dabei geht einerseits die Praxis, die konkrete Erfahrung also, dem Räsonnieren und Theoretisieren voraus und ist damit die Voraussetzung aller Abstraktion und Verallgemeinerung; andererseits birgt das Tun im Sinne der Fertigkeit bzw. Kunst immer ein MEHR gegenüber dem Theoretischen in sich – es geht also über das Theoretische hinaus: Theorie und Praxis, Reflexion und Erfahrung lassen sich niemals umkehrbar eindeutig aufeinander beziehen, das Können ist also niemals vollständig auf das theoretische Wissen zurückzuführen.

Weitere Probleme bleiben offen, die entscheidend sind für den Versuch, die der Aufgabenlösung zugrundeliegenden Wissensstrukturen zu ermitteln, ich möchte sie hier nur kurz anschneiden, wobei ich im Folgenden unter dem globalen Begriff Wissen sowohl Wissen im strengen Sinne als auch Können subsumiere – die begriffliche Unklarheit von "Wissen" legt dies nahe.

1. Es stellt sich die Frage, inwieweit die menschliche Expertise von der jeweiligen Situation abhängt, in der sie wirksam wird. Der Mensch steht der Situation nicht gegenüber, sondern er ist stets in ihr, gestaltet und verändert sie durch sein eigenes Sein und Werden. Gleichzeitig wird sein Handeln, seine Kompetenz von der Situation beeinflußt, diese prägt also das Wissen eines Experten ebenso. Expertise ist damit das Ergebnis der Wechselwirkung von Person und Situation, ist also eine ganz besondere Kompetenz in einer ganz besonderen Anwendungssituation.

2. Wissen ist immer auch Interpretation, setzt Verstehen voraus, ist gebunden an die existentiellen Erfahrungen eines Menschen und von diesem nicht zu trennen; bedingt der Versuch, Wissensstrukturen für bestimmte Aufgabenbereiche zu ermitteln, nicht eine unzulässige Abkoppelung der Expertise vom allgemeinen Wissen und Können eines Menschen, unzulässig deshalb, weil sich Expertise ohne jenes existentielle Wissen gar nicht denken läßt? Zeigt nicht gerade das Beispiel der medizinischen Diagnostik, bei der es neben dem fachspezifischen Wissen und Können ganz maßgeblich auch auf die Sinnerfahrung und kommunikative Erlebnisfähigkeit (verstanden hier als Erfahrung, die unmittelbar gekoppelt ist an die menschliche Existenz) ankommt, wie unabdingbar notwendig wahre

Könnerschaft mit existentiellem Wissen verknüpft ist? Der für die KI-Forschung insgesamt charakteristische atomistische Konzeption von Wissen ist damit ein holistisches Verständnis von Wissen entgegenzusetzen.

3. Kompetente Aufgabenlösung hängt ganz wesentlich von subjektiver Erfahrung ab, die geprägt ist durch Unmittelbarkeit und Prozessuralität. Es erscheint fraglich, ob sich jene individualspezifische Erfahrung auf beschreibbare Repräsentationen zurückführen läßt, ist sie doch ganz unmittelbar gekoppelt an langjährig erworbene Fertigkeiten, womit sie dem Können im Ryleschen Sinne weitgehend gleichzusetzen wäre.

Betrachten wir beispielsweise das Tätigkeitsfeld eines Wissenschaftlers: ein Wissenschaftler erwirbt die für sein Gebiet notwenigen Fertigkeiten, wie beispielsweise das Hypostasieren, Argumentieren, Experimentieren,... . Dabei bedient sich der Experte nicht nur der Fachbücher, sondern er hat auch in seiner konkreten Praxis gelernt, wie Forschung zu betreiben ist. Zwar greift er bei der Bewältigung von Aufgaben aus seinem Fachgebiet auf anerkannte Problemlösungsstrategien und Paradigmen zurück, aber seine subjektive Erfahrung läßt seine Kompetenz über diese hinauswachsen, sie wird zu einer Fähigkeit, die sich nicht ausschließlich auf sein theoretisches Wissen reduzieren läßt. Es stellt sich damit die Frage, ob nicht im Versuch, jenen individuellen Erfahrungshorizont in Wissensstrukturen zu fassen, genau dieses MEHR an Kompetenz negiert wird, da man sich auf beschreibbares Wissen beschränken muß?

IV Soziologische Anmerkungen

An die oben getroffene Unterscheidung zwischen Wissen und Können lassen sich - zumindest bezogen auf das Wissen und Können von Experten - soziologische Überlegungen anknüpfen. Innerhalb jeder Wissenschaftlergemeinde existieren eine Reihe von Experten, die eine Kollektion normativer Basissätze formulieren (5), d.h. als gültig begriffenen "Denkgesetze", die als Paradigma eines Wissenschaftszweiges dienen. Dazu zählen auch bestimmte Problemlösungsmuster, die als Standards des jeweiligen Faches gelten und vom Anfänger im Zuge des Erwerbs von Fertigkeiten übernommen werden. Experten eines Faches bilden ein "Denkkollektiv"(6), das den Denkstil eines Fachgebietes maßgeblich prägt und vorgibt, auf welche Weise Aufgaben im jeweiligen Fachgebiet gelöst werden (7). Dieses Wissen ist theoretisches Wissen, es wird zumeist explizit gemacht und ist der

Beschreibung und Begründung zugänglich. Davon zu unterscheiden ist jedoch das individuelle Können, jene Fähigkeit also, die subjektgebunden sich vom fachspezifischen Procedere abhebt und eine individualtypische Ausprägung des allgemeinen Standards darstellt.genau dies scheint mir der Bereich von menschlichem Know-How zu sein, der mit dem Terminus "Expertise" gemeint ist; nicht nämlich die allgemein zugänglichen, beschreibbaren Verfahren, die als Standard eines Faches gelten, sondern die individuelle Fähigkeit, das sich vom Gängigen abhebende Können, das auf der individuellen Auseinandersetzung mit einem gegebenen Problem beruht und sich der begrifflichen Beschreibung entzieht. Betrachten wir nun aber den Vorgang der Wissensakquisition, wie er beispielsweise bei der Konzeption einer Wissensbasis in Expertensystemen vollzogen wird, so wird rasch deutlich, daß sich die eruierte Expertise auf das beschreibbare Wissen beschränkt, nämlich auf die Explikation des standardisierten Procedere. Nicht dagegen ermittelbar, weil der direkten Beschreibung nicht zugänglich, bleibt das individualtypische Können, jener kognitive Bereich also, der ja gerade die Expertise im Sinne ihrer individuellen Besonderheit ausmacht. Dies impliziert potentielle Konsequenzen, von denen ich lediglich drei benennen möchte:

1. Da nur das Wissen, das dem Denkstil einer Fachgruppe entspricht, ermittelt wird, besteht die Gefahr, daß dieses Wissen zunehmend zum Standard von Expertise insgesamt wird (8). So wird ein Denkkollektiv zum "knowledge czar"(9), d.h., das begriffliche Wissen einer Forscher-gemeinde, das diese eint und sie spezifiziert, wird zum allgemeingültigen Maßstab, nach dem sich individuelles Tun zu richten hat.

2. Durch die Abkoppelung des Wissens vom Subjekt erfolgt eine Verob-jektivierung und Verdinglichung von Wissen, die schon deshalb zu einer Reduktion der Expertise führt, weil weder der Bereich des subjektiven Könnens noch situationsspezifische und durch die Situation stimulierte Fähigkeiten ermittelt und repräsentiert werden können.

3. Dies führt langfristig zu einem Verlust von Wissen, sofern nicht deutlich gemacht wird, wo die Grenzen der Repräsentierbarkeit liegen, da es Bereiche menschlicher Kompetenz gibt, die sich erst in der Praxis, im konkreten Handeln offenbaren.

Da zudem Wissen und Können nicht nur individualspezifische, sondern immer auch soziale Größen sind, ist die Beschränkung auf einzelne Subjekte bei der Ermittlung von Wissensstrukturen schon deshalb mit einem Fehler behaftet, weil die je spezifischen Bedeutungen in der

sozialen Interaktion immer neu gebildet werden und sich niemals als fixe
unabänderliche Momente begreifen lassen.

Die weit verbreitete Auffassung in der KI, Problemlösungen basierten auf
der Manipulation symbolischer Repräsentationen, trifft also scheinbar nur
einen Teil dessen, was unter menschlichem Wissen gemeinhin subsumiert
wird. Verkannt wird, daß Menschen bei weitem nicht immer auf der Basis
von Repräsentationen agieren, wenn sie sich intelligent verhalten.
Vielmehr interagieren sie in einem Geflecht aus sozialen Beziehungen, die
über kulturelle Konventionen, vor allem aber konkrete Praxis aufrechter-
halten werden und die ihr Wissen und Können maßgeblich beeinflussen.

Die hier vorgenommene Differenzierung zwischen Wissen und Können legt
Überlegungen nahe, die den praktischen Einsatz von wissensbasierten
Systemen betreffen. Geht man von der Annahme aus, daß sich menschliche
Expertise nicht vollständig auf Repräsentationen zurückführen läßt, gibt es
Bereiche menschlichen Wissens, die gegenwärtig nicht an eine Maschine
delegiert werden können. Dies impliziert, daß wissensbasierte Systeme in
den Entscheidungsprozeß des Menschen miteinbezogen werden können,
jedoch nicht isoliert zu Expertenentscheidungen in der Lage sind.

V Konkretisierung: Menschliche Expertise und ihre Darstellung

Die obigen Überlegungen muten recht abstrakt an, sind möglicherweise für
die Implementation nur insofern interessant, als sie die Annahme, alles
menschliche Wissen basiere auf Repräsentationen, in Frage stellen. Ich
möchte aber zum Abschluß noch konkreter werden und zwei Bereiche, die
medizinische Diagnostik und das VLSI-Design beispielhaft anführen, um
meine Überlegungen zu illustrieren, und Konsequenzen meiner Ausführungen für den direkten Einsatz von wissensbasierten Systemen darzulegen.

Unter der Prämisse, daß nicht alle Expertise der Beschreibung zugänglich
ist, beschränke ich mich auf die Betrachtung jenes Wissens, das verbali-
sierbar ist und von dem man annehmen kann, daß es in mentalen Repräsentationen vorliegt. Meidzinische Diagnostik und VLSI-Design haben
gemeinsam, daß es sich hier typischerweise um offene Problemsituationen
handelt, um nicht determinierte Aufgaben, die zwar die Anwendung von

Regeln zulassen (diagnostische Regeln; Design-Regeln), jedoch nicht alleine dadurch zu lösen sind.

Folgende Fragen scheinen mir hier diskussionswürdig:

1. Ist die Annahme, daß der Mensch eine mentale Repräsentation des Problemraums bildet, zulässig? Wenn ja, wie ist sie gestaltet?

2. Geht man von der Vorstellung einer mentalen Problemrepräsentation aus, erscheint es plausibel, eine Modifikation dieser Repräsentation im Verlauf einer Aufgabenlösung anzunehmen. Handelt es sich bei den Veränderungen dieser Ausgangsrepräsentation lediglich um Transformationen (d.h. geringfügige Modifikationen, die nur Funktionen der Ausgangsrepräsentation sind) oder um qualitativ andere Repräsentationsformen (z.B. andere Klassen wie propositionale vs. analoge)?

3. Alternieren Experten zwischen verschiedenen Abstraktions- und Komplexitätsgraden bei einer Aufgabenlösung oder gehen sie eher gradlinig vor (TopDown oder BottomUp)?

4. Wie relevant ist das sogenannte "Randbewußtsein"(10) für eine Aufgabenlösung und inwieweit läßt es sich bei der Ermittlung von Wissensstrukturen berücksichtigen (z.B. durch ein Konzept von aktiver und semiaktiven Hypothesen)?

Diese Fragen tangieren nur das Problemfeld, gleiches gilt für die generellen Betrachtungen am Anfang dieses Beitrags; angesichts der Fülle an offenen Fragen kann dieser Beitrag wohl kaum mehr leisten, als Anregungen für weiterführende Diskussionen zu geben – wenn dies gelingen würde, wäre mein Anliegen schon erfüllt.

Anmerkungen

---

(1) Erste Ansätze in diese Richtung wurden ja bereits von Winograd und Flores entwickelt; siehe hierzu:
Winograd, T., Flores, F., "Understanding Computers and Cognition", Norwood, New Jersey 1986

(2) Schefe, P., "Künstliche Intelligenz – Überblick und Grundlagen", Zürich 1986

(3) Kemmerling, A., "Gilbert Ryle: Können und Wissen", in: Philosophie der
    Gegenwart III, Göttingen 1984; sowie
    Ryle, G., "The Concept of Mind", Harmondsworth 1986

(4) Als typisches Beispiel für das Können wird gemeinhin die Fähigkeit
    des Menschen herangeführt, seine Muttersprache zu beherrschen, ohne
    daß er alle Regeln dieser Sprache kennt; siehe hierzu: Kemmerling,
    A., Philosophischer Kognitivismus und die Repräsentation sprachlichen
    Wissens", München 1987 (bislang unveröffentl. Manuskript)

(5) Kuhn bezeichnet Experten als die Kristallisationskerne einer Wissen-
    schaftlergemeinde; siehe Kuhn, Th.S., "Die Struktur wissenschaftlicher
    Revolutionen", Frankfurt 1979

(6) Fleck schuf diesen Begriff und zeigte auf, wie sehr die geistigen
    Strömungen in einem Fach durch diesen Denkstil geprägt werden;
    siehe: Fleck, L., "Die Entstehung und Entwicklung einer wissenschaft-
    lichen Tatsache", Frankfurt 1980

(7) Auf Firmen übertragen wäre dies das sogenannte Firmenwissen, d.h.
    bestimmte Standards der Programmierung oder des Entwurfs, in der
    Medizin beispielsweise eine bestimmte Schule des Operierens.

(8) wie z.B. in der Medizin, wo der Denkstil einer Schule bestimmt,
    welches Procedere als richtig gilt und alle anderen Vorgehensweisen
    der potentiellen forensischen Bestrafung unterliegen, da sie nicht
    der Meinung des jeweiligen Denkkollektivs entsprechen.

(9) siehe hierzu: Brachman, R.J., Amarel, S. et al., "What are Expert
    systems", in: Hayes-Roth, F. et al (eds), "Building Expert Systems",
    Reading, Mass. 1983

(10)siehe hierzu Dreyfus, H., "Die Grenzen künstlicher Intelligenz",
    Königsstein 1985 ; sowie
    Dreyfus, H., Dreyfus, S., "Mind over Machine", New York 1986

Repräsentationsformen
beim menschlichen Problemlösen

Gerhard Strube

Die Befundlage in der kognitiven Psychologie erlaubt m.E. gegenwärtig folgende Aussagen, die hier in Gestalt einiger Thesen dargestellt und kurz erläutert werden sollen:

(1) Wir Menschen verfügen über ganz unterschiedliche Repräsentationsformen. Neben abstrakt-"semantische", wie sie z.B. in Propositionen modellierbar sind, treten konkret-sinnliche Repräsentationen, vor allem bildhafte Vorstellungen.

Angesichts der ausgiebigen Debatte, die in den späten siebziger Jahren über "imagery" und speziell über den Status visueller Vorstellungen als eigenständiger Repräsentationsform geführt worden ist, braucht die obige These eigentlich kaum weiter begründet zu werden (vgl. Anderson, 1982, 1983, Kosslyn, 1980, und Pylyshyn, 1973, 1981, die Protagonisten der Imagery-Debatte).

Für die Funktion des Erinnerns ist mehrfach nachgewiesen worden, daß die Konkretheit und Vorstellbarkeit von Begriffen das Behalten erleichtert (z.B. Paivio, 1971). Ebenso ist - wenn man's genau nimmt, seit den alten Griechen bekannt, daß die absichtsvolle Verknüpfung von Dingen, die man sich merken will, zu einem Vorstellungsbild hilft, sich an die einzelnen Dinge besser zu erinnern (z.B. Bower, 1972). Weniger bekannt ist die Rolle bewegter Vorstellungsbilder (Zimmer, 1982) und motorischer Enkodierungen, wie sie von Engelkamp und Zimmer (1984) in mehreren Untersuchungen nachgewiesen wurden.

Für kognitive Operationen, die über das Erinnern hinausgehen, haben z.B. Shepard und Metzler (1971) gezeigt, daß dem Vergleich zweier vorgegebener dreidimensionaler Muster offenbar Prozesse der Manipulation, speziell Rotation, von Vorstellungsbildern zugrundeliegen; jedenfalls ist die Reaktionszeit bei solchen Aufgaben eine fast lineare Funktion des Winkels, um den das eine Muster gedreht werden muß, um in seiner Orientierung mit dem anderen übereinzustimmen.

Schließlich ein Beispiel aus dem engeren Bereich des Problemlösens, das Herb Simon gerne berichtet, in der Version von Glass und Holyoak (1986): *Ein buddhistischer Mönch steigt eines Morgens auf einem langen, spiralig gewundenen Weg auf den Gipfel eines Berges - mal langsamer, mal schneller, mal macht er eine Rast. Abends kommt er oben an und betet. Er übernachtet auf dem Gipfel und beginnt am andern Morgen den Abstieg. Schnell steigt er denselben Weg hinab und ist mittags wieder unten. Man beweise nun, daß es einen Punkt auf dem Weg gibt, wo der Mönch beim Aufstieg wie beim Abstieg zur gleichen Tageszeit am gleichen Ort gewesen ist.* Bei dieser Denksportaufgabe ist sofort einsichtig, daß analoge Repräsentationen bei der Lösung helfen. Dies kann z.B. eine diagrammartige Vorstellung sein:

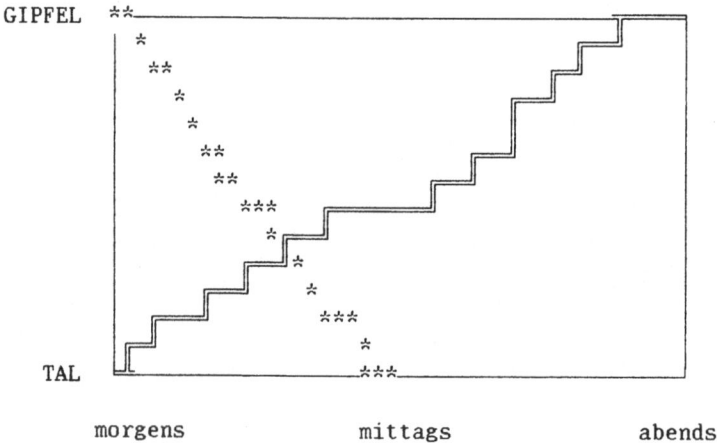

Wir können aber auch (und vielleicht noch besser) eine konkrete Alltagssituation imaginieren, indem wir - wie schon im obigen Diagramm) die Tage des Auf- und des Abstiegs ineinanderschieben und den Mönch als doppelten, einmal aufsteigend, einmal hinabgehend, sich selbst entgegengehen lassen, wobei dieser dann natürlich notwendig - zur gleichen Zeit, am selben Ort - sich selber treffen muß.

Versuchspersonen berichten jedenfalls, daß die eine oder andere Vorstellung ihnen bei dieser Aufgabe hilft. Auch über den berühmten Pendelversuch von Maier (1931: Zwei von der Decke hängende Kordeln sollen zusammengebunden werden, sind aber so weit auseinander, daß man sie nicht zugleich ergreifen kann) berichtet der Autor, daß ein "zufälliges" Vorbeistreifen an einer der Kordeln, das sie in leichte Schwingung versetzte, seinen Versuchspersonen bei der Lösung half.

Eine frappierende Vorstellungsleistung hat Stigler (1984) untersucht. Chinesische Rechenmeister haben den Umgang mit der Rechenmaschine, dem Abakus, so perfektioniert, daß die mechanische Bewegung der Holzperlen ihnen zu langsam geworden ist. Als Konsequenz verzichten sie ganz auf das Gerät und arbeiten mit einem bloß vorgestellten Abakus, dessen Perlen sie in der Vorstellung blitzschnell bewegen und von dem sie das Ergebnis "ablesen". Stigler hat diese Selbstaussagen der Abakusrechner untersucht und durch Reaktionszeit- und Fehleranalysen bestätigen können.

(2) Die Möglichkeit des Menschen, zugleich mehrere verschiedenartige Repräsentationen aufzubauen und flexibel zwischen diesen zu wechseln, ist eine der Grundlagen für seine gelungene Anpassung an die Anforderungen der Umwelt. Daneben gibt es auch Indizien für individuell stabile Bevorzugungen.

Die bisherigen Beispiele sollen nicht zu der Annahme verleiten, daß visuelle Vorstellungen für jede Art von Problem eine hilfreiche Repräsentationsform sind. Es darf aber davon ausgegangen werden, daß in vielen Fällen sozusagen spontan auf Vorstellungen zurückgegriffen wird. Allen umfassenden neueren Modellen menschlicher Kognition und menschlichen Verstehens von Texten und Ereignissen ist gemeinsam, daß sie ein Nebeneinander von unterschiedlichen Repräsentationsformen postulieren (Anderson, 1983, Johnson-Laird, 1983, van Dijk & Kintsch, 1983).

Empirisch ist keinesfalls geklärt, welche Repräsentationsformen sogenannten mentalen Modellen oder Situationsmodellen zugrundeliegen; ob diese eine einheitliche und eher "analoge" (Johnson-Laird legt das nahe, ohne sich darauf festzulegen), oder eine hybride Vielgestalt von Mechanismen darstellt, oder ob sie doch einheitlich propositional gefaßt werden könnten (Rips, in press). Meines Erachtens müssen wir aber für die menschliche Kognition mit einer Vielzahl von Repräsentationen und insbesondere zahlreichen nur unzureichend kohärenten Teilbeständen repräsentierten Wissens rechnen. Dies führt zu den bekannten Mängeln menschlichen Räsonnierens, wie sie beispielsweise von der Forschergruppe um Tversky in Bezug auf Wahrscheinlichkeitsurteile beschrieben worden sind (vgl. Kahneman, Slovic & Tversky, 1982).

Das wichtigste Merkmal von Wissensrepräsentation beim Menschen ist aber die Mühelosigkeit, mit der Bezüge hergestellt, Perspektiven gewechselt und Beschreibungs- wie Handlungsebenen gewechselt werden. Der Rückgriff auf

Abstraktionen (Schemata oder Regeln) ist selten pur, wird vielmehr spontan vermischt mit Erinnerungen an Beispiele und mit Vorstellungen. Wie könnten wir sonst so selbstverständlich Metaphern und Analogien verstehen? (Vgl. dazu Lakoff, 1982) Weshalb so schwer uns tun mit Logik, und so anfällig sein für die Einkleidungen von Aufgaben? (Kintsch & Greeno, 1985, Wason & Johnson-Laird, 1972). Das hessesche Glasperlenspiel stellt sich so als Idealisierung alltäglich-menschlicher Flexibilität dar. Multiple inheritance und Perspektiven, wie sie in der traditionellen KI Verwendung finden, bleiben dahinter weit zurück.

Man könnte vermuten (und hat es lange getan), daß es indiviuell charakteristische Bevorzugung bestimmter Repräsentationsformen gibt: Menschen, die "mehr visuelle Typen" sind oder solche, die "besser abstrakt denken können". Eine empirisch haltbare Typologie ist dabei sowenig herausgekommen wie bei der im Gefolge der Befunde zur Spezialisierung der Großhirnhemisphären geführten Diskussion um Intuition (Bastick, 1982).

Individuell spezifische Verarbeitungsstile sind jedoch vielfach beobachtet worden (vgl. etwa Foard & Kemler-Nelson, 1984, Jacoby & Brooks, 1984, über nicht-analytische bzw. holistische Verarbeitung). Die entsprechenden Befunde sind allerdings immer auf bestimmte Aufgabenstellungen bezogen. Dem steht die intraindividuelle Variation durch Wechsel der Aufgabenstellung oder auch durch bloße Übung gegenüber (z.B. durch Automatisierung im Sinne von Schneider & Shiffrin, 1977).

Dazu noch ein Beispiel für das Nebeneinander unterschiedlicher Wissensorganisationen: Wenn die Ähnlichkeit von Tieren (deren Namen man den Versuchspersonen paarweise vorgibt) von Experten, nämlich Zoologen, beurteilt wird, so findet man, daß sie nicht nur wie wir Laien Ordnungsdimensionen wie *Größe* oder *Wildheit* verwenden, sondern auch *Ernährungsweise* und *Reproduktionsrate*. Bei veränderter Aufgabenstellung (z.B. freies Aufzählen von Tiernamen oder freies Assoziieren) finden sich aber solche Experten-Besonderheiten nicht (Hejj & Strube, in press, Storm, 1980). Derartige Flexibilität läßt sich unter Zugrundelegung ein und derselben Wissensstruktur (konzipiert als Speicherung von Merkmalsmengen) modellieren per Selektion von Merkmalsgruppen (Strube, 1984).

(4) Wesentliche individuelle Unterschiede gehen auf Instruktion und Übung zurück. Es sind Organisations- und Repräsentationsformen bereichsspezifischen Wissens, die für menschliche Expertise charakteristisch sind.

Die inzwischen an Zahl schnell zunehmenden psychologischen Untersuchungen über menschliche Expertise und ihre Genese haben deutlich gemacht, daß "Intelligenz" als allgemeines oder zumindest auf einen breiten Bereich unterschiedlicher Aufgabenstellungen bezogenes Konstrukt lediglich eine der Grundlagen geistiger Leistungen darstellt. Gerade die KI hat erfahren müssen, wie stark dem die sozusagen selbstverständlichen Leistungen menschlicher Kognition vorausgehen: Objekte erkennen, sprachlich kommunizieren, kontrollierte Bewegungen ausführen usw. (Wer würde das im Alltag *intelligent* nennen?) Expertise schließlich ergänzt das Bedingungsgefüge kognitiver Leistungen um bereichsspezifisches Wissen und bereichsspezifische Lösungsmuster bzw. Strategien.

Offenbar ist für Leistungsunterschiede zwischen verschiedenen Menschen entscheidend, wie lange sie in einem bestimmten Bereich Erfahrung erworben haben. Erfahrung und langjährige Übung (man unterstellt, daß der Weg zum Experten mindestens acht bis zehn Jahre dauert) bewirken für das Wissen zweierlei: die wachsende Ansammlung von Wissensbeständen und deren immer bessere Organisation. Anfänger im Physikstudium neigen beispielsweise dazu, oberflächliche Charakteristika von Aufgaben zur Einschätzung der Aufgabenähnlichkeit heranzuziehen (und bilden Kategorien wie "Aufgaben zur schiefen Ebene", "Aufgaben zur Rotationsbewegung" usf.); Experten hingegen kategorisieren nach den physikalischen Prinzipien, die der Lösung zugrundeliegen ("Aufgaben zum Energieerhaltungssatz" etc.), unabhängig vom augenfälligen Phänomen (Chi, Glaser & Rees, 1982).

Wachsende Übung führt aber auch dazu, daß handlungsrelevante Wissensbestände, wie Anderson (1982) es ausdrückt, "kompiliert" werden (*knowledge compilation*). Was der Anfänger sich noch Schritt für Schritt zusammensucht, führt der Experte sozusagen als ein einziges Programm aus - die einzelnen Teilschritte sind routinisiert, automatisiert. Unter Umständen fällt es dann schwer, auf die ursprünglichen Bestandteile solch schematisch integrierten Handlungswissens einzeln noch zuzugreifen. (Könnten Sie als geübte Autofahrer einem Anfänger gut erklären, wie er seine Bewegungen zu koordinieren hat, um effizient und getriebeschonend zu schalten?)

Ein oft besonders wichtiger Bereich des Expertenwissens - und hier tangieren wir erneut die Frage der Repräsentationsform - ist die Fähigkeit, buchstäblich tausende kompliziertester Muster exakt zu diskriminieren, wiederzuerkennen und bei Bedarf zu reproduzieren. Wir alle können dies da, wo wir alle Experten sind: in der Kenntnis vieler unserer Mitmenschen, die wir an ihren Gesichtszügen (oder auch nur an ihrem Gang) erkennen. Das menschliche Bildgedächtnis ist frappierend gut: 91 % Treffer beim Wiedererkennenstest nach Darbietung von 2500 Dias (Standing, Conezio & Haber, 1970), immerhin noch 73 % Treffer nach Darbietung von zehntausend Dias (Standing, 1973; Zufallsquote jeweils 50 %).

Experten haben gelernt, bestimmte Muster sehr gut zu erkennen. Das haben Untersuchungen an Röntgenärzten (Lesgold, 1984) ebenso gezeigt wie Tests mit Schachspielern (Chase & Simon, 1973). Simon und Gilmartin (1973) schätzen, daß Spitzenspieler an die fünfzigtausend Stellungsmuster "parat" haben. Daß solche im Gedächtnis von Schachexperten gespeicherten Muster unter strategischen Gesichtspunkten analysiert und organisiert sind, haben unsere eigenen Untersuchungen im Vergleich von Partiespielern und Problemschachexperten gezeigt (Gruber & Strube, in press).

(5) Unter dem Aspekt der möglichen Übertragbarkeit der am Menschen gewonnenen Erkenntnisse auf Systeme künstlicher Intelligenz ist zu beachten, daß die Vielfalt menschlicher Repräsentationsformen aufbaut auf einem differenzierten und phylogenetisch alten System sensorischer Analyse, wie es in der Künstlichen Intelligenz nirgendwo verfügbar ist.

Expertensysteme als die bislang am Markt erfolgreichste Art von KI-Software haben sich mit Erfolg an die Erkenntnis gehalten, daß bereichsspezifisches Wissen eine wesentliche und in Grenzen auch andere Mängel kompensierende Grundlage intelligenter Leistungen ist. Eine auf diesem Gebiet vieldiskutierte Frage ist dementsprechend, welches Wissen einzubeziehen ist und wie man es am besten modelliert, d.h. welche Formen der Repräsentation dieses Wissens seinen optimalen Gebrauch garantieren. Der starke Gebrauch, den Menschen insbesondere von visuellen Mustern und Vorstellungen machen, läßt derzeit den Gedanken einer subsymbolischen Wissensrepräsentation attraktiv erscheinen (insbesondere im Zusammenhang mit Parallelverarbeitung, vgl. Rumelhart & McClelland, 1986).

Warum macht menschliches Problemlösen so stark von "analoger" Repräsentation Gebrauch? Mir scheint, daß damit lediglich das bereits Vorhandene genutzt wird. Im Laufe der Phylogenese ist sind diverse leistungsfähige Systeme sensorischer Analyse entstanden (Lettvin, Maturana, Pitts & McCulloch, 1959, ist eine der ersten Untersuchungen dazu), und zwar lange vor der Ausbildung neocortikaler Strukturen. Die im Laufe der Phylogenese sich ausbildenden "höheren" kortikalen Funktionen, Sprachfähigkeit und schlußfolgerndes Denken, konnten auf wohlfunktionierenden Systemen sensumotorischer Koordination aufbauen. Aus dem, daß dies naturgeschichtlich so gewachsen und somit Natur des heutigen Menschen ist, folgt allerdings nicht, daß die in Frage stehenden Funktionen nur so und nicht anders realisiert werden könnten.

Betrachten wir noch einmal die Aufgabe von Shepard & Metzler (1971), in der jeweils zwei identische oder bloß ähnliche aus Würfeln zusammengesetzte Objekte, die aus verschiedener räumlicher Perspektive dargestellt sind, miteinander verglichen werden müssen. Es ist festgestellt worden, daß die Reaktionszeiten der Versuchspersonen gut durch eine lineare Funktion des Winkels zwischen den räumlichen Perspektiven der Abbildungen dargestellt werden können. Dies läßt darauf schließen, daß Menschen zur Lösung solcher Aufgaben eine "mentale Rotation" vornehmen, also die Objekte in der Vorstellung räumlich so drehen, daß wichtige Teile in dieselbe Lage kommen. Dann "sieht" man leicht, ob die beiden Objekte von gleicher Gestalt sind oder nicht.

Ein Computerprogramm zur Lösung derartiger Aufgaben - beispielsweise ein mit Optosensoren ausgestatteter Fertigungsautomat, der spiegelbildlich gleiche Teile zu Paaren zusammenstellen muß - könnte weit einfacher gestaltet sein. Ein Programm wie das von Waltz (1975) ist durchaus zu solchen Leistungen in der Lage, obwohl es lediglich die Winkel zwischen angrenzenden Kanten an Scheitelpunkten analysiert. Möglicherweise könnte man eine derartige Strategie auch einem Menschen beibringen, aber man müßte ihm dazu den ihm selbstverständlichen, natürlichen Weg der mentalen Rotation verstellen. Umgekehrt ist das Feld der Bildwahrnehmung in der KI gegenüber den existierenden biologischen Wahrnehmungsapparaten noch so in den Anfängen, daß mentale Rotation keine realisierbare Strategie darstellt - ja in Abwesenheit eines billigen aber hoch leistungsfähigen künstlichen Wahrnehmungssystems nicht einmal eine wünschbare.

Ich rede also nicht der möglichst vollständigen Übertragung der am Menschen beobachtbaren Verhältnisse das Wort, wenngleich ich hoffe, daß die Wechselbeziehungen zwischen KI und Psychologie so fruchtbar bleiben wie sie in den letzten Jahren waren. Die schiere Menge von Wissen (und der höchst effiziente Zugriff darauf), die für menschliches Problemlösen charakteristisch ist, kann und muß gar nicht nachgebildet werden, und Ähnliches gilt für die Vielfalt gerade der sensorischen Repräsentationen. Schließlich kann maschinelle Intelligenz aufbauen auf logiknahen Repräsentationen wie z.B. Horn-Klauseln, oder auf Listenstrukturen beliebiger Komplexität - alles Repräsentationsformen, deren Handhabung die Architektur der menschlichen Kognition nicht eben entgegenkommt. Intelligenz ist nicht nur auf einem Weg erreichbar. Das Studium der bislang fortgeschrittensten Implementierung – der menschlichen Kognition – kann dennoch dem Fortschritt der KI nur nützen.

Literatur

Anderson, J. R. (1982). Acquisition of cognitive skill. *Psychological Review, 89*, 369–406.

Anderson, J. R. (1983). *The architecture of cognition.* Cambridge MA: Harvard Univ. Press.

Bastick, T. (1982). *Intuition: How we think and act.* New York: Wiley.

Bower, G. H. (1972). Mental imagery and associative learning. In L. W. Gregg (Ed.), *Cognition in Learning and Memory* (Vol. 5, pp. 51–88). New York: J. Wiley & Sons.

Chase, W. G., & Simon, H. A. (1973). The mind's eye in chess. In W. G. Chase (Ed.), *Visual information processing* (pp. 215–281). New York: Academic Press.

Chi, M. T. H., Glaser, R., & Rees, E. (1982). Expertise in problem solving. In R. J. Sternberg (Ed.), *Advances in the psychology of human intelligence* (Vol. 1, pp. 7–75). Hillsdale, NJ: Erlbaum.

Engelkamp, J., & Zimmer, H. D. (1984). Motor programme information as a separable memory unit. *Psychological Research, 46*, 283–299.

Foard, C. F., & Kemler-Nelson, D. G. (1984). Holistic and analytic modes of processing: The multiple determinants of perceptual analysis. *Journal of Experimental Psychology: General, 113*, 94–111.

Glass, A. L., & Holyoak, K. J. (1986). *Cognition* (2nd ed.). New York: Random House.

Gruber, H., & Strube, G. (in press). *Zweierlei Experten. Problemisten, Partiespieler und Novizen beim Lösen von Schachproblemen.*

Hejj, A., & Strube, G. (in press). Wortfeld im Wandel: Entwicklung und Expertise als strukturierende Faktoren des semantischen Bereichs "Säugetiere". In W. Marx (Ed.), *Allgemeine Psychologie. Forschungsbericht 1.* Göttingen: Hogrefe (Münchener Universitätsschriften Psychologie & Pädagogik).

Jacoby, L. L., & Brooks, L. R. (1984). Nonanalytic cognition: Memory, perception, and concept learning. In G. R. Bower (Ed.), *The Psychology of Learning and Motivation* (Vol. 18, pp. 1–47). New York: Academic Press.

Johnson-Laird, P. N. (1983). *Mental models. Towards a cognitive science of language, inference, and consciousness.* Cambridge, MA: Harvard University Press.

Kahneman, D., Slovic, P., & Tversky, A. (1982). *Judgment under uncertainty: Heuristics and biases.* Cambridge: Cambridge University Press.

Kintsch, W., & Greeno, J. L. (1985). *Psychological Review, 92*, 1–.

Kosslyn, S. M. (1980). *Image and mind.* Cambridge, MA: Harvard University Press.

Lakoff, G. (1982). *Categories and mental models* (Berkeley Cognitive Science Report No. 2). Berkeley: University of California Cognitive Science Program.

Lesgold, A. M., (1984). Human skill in a computerized society: Complex skills and their acquisition. *Behavior Research Methods, Instruments, & Computers, 16*, 79–87.

Lettvin, J. Y., Maturana, H. R., Pitts, W. H., & McCulloch, W. S. (1959). What the frog's eye tells the frog's brain. *Proceedings of the IRE, 47*, 1940–1951.

Maier, N. R. F. (1931). Reasoning in humans. II. The solution of a problem and its appearance in consciousness. *Journal of Comparative Psychology, 12*, 181–194.

Paivio, A. (1971). *Imagery and verbal processes.* New York: Holt, Rinehart & Winston.

Pylyshyn, Z. (1973). What the mind's eye tells the mind's brain: A critique of mental imagery. *Psychological Bulletin, 80*, 1–24.

Pylyshyn, Z. W. (1981). The imagery debate: Analogue media versus tacit knowledge. *Psychological Review, 88,* 16–45.

Rips, L. J. (in press). Mental Muddles. In M. Brand & R. M. Harnish (Eds.), *Problems in the Representation of Knowledge and Belief.* Tucson, AZ: University of Arizona Press.

Rumelhart, D. E., & McClelland, J. L. (1986). *Parallel distributed processing: Explorations in the microstructure of cognition.* Çambridge, MA: MIT Press.

Schneider, W., & Shiffrin, R. M. (1977). Controlled and automatic human information processing: I. Detection, search, and attention. *Psychological Review, 84,* 1–66.

Shepard, R. N., & Metzler, J. (1971). Mental rotation of three-dimensional objects. *Science, 171,* 701–703.

Simon, H., & Gilmartin, K. (1973). A simulation of memory for chess positions. *Cognitive Psychology, 5,* 29–46.

Standing, L. (1973). Learning 10,000 pictures. *Quarterly Journal of Experimental Psychology, 25,* 207–222.

Standing, L., Conezio, J., & Haber, R. N. (1970). Perception and memory for pictures: Single-trial learning of 2560 visual stimuli. *Psychonomic Science, 19,* 73–74.

Stigler, J. W. (1984). "Mental abacus": The effect of abacus training on chinese children's mental calculation. *Cognitive Psychology, 16,* 145–175.

Storm, C. (1980). The semantic structure of animal terms: A developmental study. *International Journal of Behavioral Development, 3,* 381–407.

Strube, G. (1984). *Assoziation. Der Prozeß des Erinnerns und die Struktur des Gedächtnisses.* Berlin: Springer.

van Dijk, T. A., & Kintsch, W. (1983). *Strategies of discourse comprehension.* New York: Academic Press.

Waltz, D. L. (1975). Understanding line drawings of scenes with shadows. In P. H. Winston (Ed.), *The psychology of computer vision* (pp. 19–91). New York: McGraw-Hill.

Wason, P. C., & Johnson-Laird, P. N. (1972). *The psychology of reasoning.* Cambridge, MA: Harvard University Press.

Zimmer, H. D. (1982). Rezeption und Produktion komplexer Temporalsätze. *Sprache & Kognition, 1,* 90–103.

Klaus Rehkämper
Universität Hamburg
FB Informatik Projekt LILOG
Bodenstedtstr. 16
2000 Hamburg 50

Mentale Bilder und Wegbedeutungen[1]

Abstract

Mental images are of great importance in the text comprehension of human beings. Text understanding computer systems which intend to meet the demands of cognitive adequacy must take this fact into account. Human beings use these images to represent knowledge. Thus, images are - in addition to propositions - another way of gaining and representing knowledge. In this paper I want to show some of the new possibilities opened up by this second form of representation as well as the restrictions connected with it. Route descriptions form a class of texts which obviously require mental images for their generation and comprehension. During the generation of a route description the informant uses a cognitive map of a quasi-pictorial format, on which he locates his position, the destination and the route between them. To understand the following description the hearer must re-transform the verbal information into an appropriate format - presumably a combination of propositional and quasi-pictorial representation.

Vorbemerkungen

Das Problem, das hier behandeln werden soll, ist nicht das einer beliebigen, formalen Beschreibung der Produktion bzw. des Verstehens einer Weg-beschreibung, sondern es geht mehr um den Aspekt der kognitiven Adäquatheit einer solchen Beschreibung, also um die Frage, was Menschen tun, wenn sie eine Wegbeschreibung verstehen. Dies ist eng verbunden mit der generelleren Frage-stellung, was gegeben sein muß, damit Menschen eine zutreffende mentale Re-präsentation ihrer Umwelt aufbauen können. Es gibt Gebiete innerhalb der Künstlichen-Intelligenz-Forschung, bei denen die Frage nach der Ähnlichkeit in bezug auf die beim Menschen vermuteten Prozesse keine oder doch nur eine untergeordnete Rolle spielen; dort mögen Fragen nach der effektiven Performanz eines Systems im Vordergrund stehen und dadurch die Kriterien vorgeben, an denen diese Systeme gemessen werden. Im weiteren geht es aber um Text-verstehensprozesse, um Prozesse also, deren Daten (Material) von Menschen ge-schaffen wurden und deren Ergebnisse wiederum von Menschen verstanden werden sollen. Hierbei kann es m.E. nur förderlich sein, wenn man die dem menschlichen Textverstehen zugrundeliegenden Vorgänge kennenlernt und dadurch ihrer formalen Erfassung - d.h. aber auch ihrer Programmierbarkeit - näher kommt.

So gehört es scheinbar unabdingbar zum menschlichen Textverstehen, daß der Leser eines Textes zur Illustration Bilder in seiner Vorstellung verwendet. So schreibt z.B. Dahlgren (1986: 1 ff.): "A person reading a text ... actively constructs a mental picture from prior knowledge (and generalization) about the objects and events mentioned there ... As the reader reads "John is a miner", words and pictures of the typical miner are formed in his mind." Sie führt weiter aus, daß der Leser natürlich kein Bild des wirklichen John vor seinem inneren

---

[1] Dieser Artikel entstand im Rahmen des IBM-Projekts LILOG an der Universität Hamburg. Ich danke meinen Kolleg(inn)en - insbesondere Christopher Habel - für die zahlreichen Anmerkungen und Hinweise.

Auge hat, es sei denn, er kennt zufällig die Person, um die es in der Geschichte geht, sondern daß er einen typischen Stellvertreter wählt. (Die Frage, wann ein Stellvertreter typisch ist und welche Eigenschaften er dann erfüllt, ist äußerst interessant, kann aber leider an dieser Stelle nicht ausführlich behandelt werden. Zu berücksichtigen sind hierbei jedoch die Ergebnisse und Überlegungen, die E. Rosch in ihren Arbeiten zur Prototypentheorie (z.B. Rosch 1978) angeführt hat.) Das mentale Modell, das der Leser von John hat, ist nun zwei Stufen von dem wirklichen John entfernt (Stufe 1 ist die schriftliche oder mündliche Fixierung des Sachverhaltes, also der Satz "John is a miner"), und ein Computermodell, das versucht, die Eigenschaften dieses mentalen Modells des Lesers widerzuspiegeln, ist somit drei Stufen von der Wirklichkeit entfernt. In den meisten bisherigen Textverstehenssystemen ist das Computermodell zwar nur zwei Stufen von der Wirklichkeit entfernt, aber, und das ist für das Problem der mentalen Bilder von entscheidender Bedeutung, "the computer model is not only removed, but it radically abstracts away from the reader's experience." (Dahlgren 1986: 3) Bei dieser Art von Modellierungen wird also kein Wert darauf gelegt, menschliches Textverstehen nachzuempfinden. Daher erfüllt diese Vorgehensweise nicht das von mir oben angeführte Kriterium der kognitiven Adäquatheit, und aus den Äußerungen Dahlgrens ergibt sich somit als eine Schlußfolgerung, daß der Versuch unternommen werden sollte, das mentale Modell des Menschen computerisierbar zu machen. M.a.W. man muß dem Phänomen der mentalen Bilder nachgehen.

Der Begriff des mentalen Bildes und seine Eigenschaften

Beschäftigt man sich mit dem Problem der mentalen Bilder, so beschäftigt man sich automatisch mit der Frage nach der Repräsentation von Wissen, genauer gesagt, mit der Frage nach der geeigneten Repräsentation von Wissen. Daß Wissen propositional dargestellt werden kann - und in den meisten Fällen propositional dargestellt wird - ist bekannt. Bekannt ist weiterhin, daß man Wissen auch in einer anderen als einer sprachähnlichen Form erfassen kann. Es gibt also mindestens zwei Arten der Repräsentation von Wissen: propositionale, d.h. sprach-ähnliche und nicht-propositionale. Eine Art der nicht-propositionalen Repräsentation sind mentale Bilder.

Um zu verdeutlichen, was unter einem mentalen Bild - oder auch kurz "image" genannt- zu verstehen ist, möchte ich einige Beispiele von John Haugeland (1985: 221) übernehmen:

1) Gegeben sei folgendes Problem: Bei einem Würfel von 3cm Kantenlänge seien zwei gegenüberliegende Seiten rot und eine Seite blau bemalt. Nun wird dieser Würfel durch zwei horizontale und vier vertikale Schnitte in 1cm große Würfel zerlegt. Die Frage ist nun, wie viele dieser kleinen Würfel haben genau eine rote und eine blaue Seite?

(An dieser Stelle sollte der geneigte Leser eine kleine Pause machen und das Problem lösen.)

2) Man stelle sich vor, daß man mitten in der Wüste auf einer Giraffe sitzt und gemütlich vor sich hin reitet; mit einem Mal, vielleicht weil das arme Tier

eine Schlange gesehen hat, bricht die Giraffe aus und stürmt in wildem Galopp davon. Wo befinden sich in diesem Moment Ihre Arme?

Bei Problem 1) lautet die richtige Antwort – wie jeder herausgefunden hat –, daß sechs Würfel genau eine rote und eine blaue Seite haben. Es geht hierbei natürlich nicht um die jeweils vorhandenen Rechenkünste, sondern um den Weg, den wohl die meisten beschritten haben, um zu diesem Ergebnis zu kommen. Dieser Weg bestand wahrscheinlich darin, sich zuerst einen (farblosen oder durchsichtigen) Würfel vorzustellen, imaginativ zwei Seiten rot und eine Seite blau anzumalen, diesen rot-blauen Würfel in kleine Würfel zu zerschneiden und das Ergebnis nun einfach abzuzählen. M.a.W. es wurde eine bildliche Vorstellung benutzt, um dieses Problem zu lösen; und diese Vorstellung wurde nicht benutzt, weil dies in der Aufgabenstellung angeraten worden wäre, sondern sie wurde von allein als das dem Problem adäquate Medium zur Repräsentation des Wissens ausgewählt. Ein unabtrennbarer Seiteneffekt, der sich bei der bildlichen Darstellung des Problems automatisch einstellt, ist die Einsicht, daß die blaue Seite die beiden roten Seiten verbindet. Dies ergibt sich unmittelbar bei der Inspektion des Bildes; würde das Problem auf propositionaler Basis gelöst, müßte man diese Erkenntnis erst mittels eines Inferenzprozesses herbeiführen. Vergleicht man nun dieses Problem mit Problemen der Art "Aus wievielen Buchstaben besteht das Wort 'Cicero'?" oder "Gibt es eine gerade Primzahl, die größer als 5 ist?", dann sieht man sofort, daß bei verschiedenen Problemen verschiedene Medien adäquat sein können. Sogar bei der Frage "In wieviele kleine Würfel wurde der große Würfel eigentlich zerteilt?" wird man voraussichtlich nicht eine bildliche, sondern eine propositionale Lösung wählen – man überlegt sich, daß der Würfel eine Kantenlänge von 3cm hat, diese Kante gedrittelt wird und 3x3x3 = 27 ist. Obwohl man eine dazu passende bildliche Vorstellung griffbereit hat – sie wurde ja erst vor wenigen Augenblicken generiert –, wird also bei diesem Problem ein anderer Weg eingeschlagen. Allerdings ist es möglich, daß die bildliche Repräsentation das Auffinden eines geeigneten propositionalen Lösungsweges unterstützt, indem sie durch das Zerlegen des Würfels einen Ansatzpunkt für die Rechnung aufzeigt. Beide Repräsentationsformen interagieren miteinander, und es könnte sogar sein, daß bei einigen Aufgabenstellungen – es müssen ja nicht immer Probleme sein, wie 2) deutlich zeigt – einige Probanden eine bildliche Verdeutlichung bevorzugen, während andere eine propositionale Repräsentation für geeigneter halten. Als momentanes Fazit möge hierbei genügen, daß zumindest zwei unterschiedliche Repräsentationsformen – propositional und bildlich – nebeneinander existieren – dies ist sehr kurz gefaßt die sogenannte *dual-coding*-Hypothese (Paivio 1971).[2]

Außerdem muß angemerkt werden, daß das Format der Repräsentation Einfluß auf das Problemlösungsverfahren haben kann. So gibt es Probleme, die auf den ersten Blick sehr kompliziert erscheinen, sich aber, wählt man nur eine geeignete Repräsentation, scheinbar von selbst lösen (vgl. Abb. 1, ein Hinweis auf die Lösung findet sich am Ende des Artikels). Aufgabenstellung 2) soll dazu

---

[2] Allerdings sollte nicht der Eindruck enstehen, daß es nur um die Frage bildlich vs. propositional geht, da die Fragestellung allgemeiner ist und unter das Problem propositional vs. analog (siehe unten) subsumiert werden muß, denn eine bildliche Repräsentation ist analog, aber nicht jede analoge Repräsentation ist bildlich.

dienen zu zeigen, bei welchen verschiedenen Gelegenheiten man bildliche Vorstellungen benutzen kann und welche Voraussetzungen dabei erfüllt bzw. nicht
erfüllt sein müssen. Sind bei 1) die Ingredienzien bekannt, d.h. jeder hat schon
einmal einen Würfel gesehen, ganz zu schweigen von den Farben, ist es bei 2)
etwas ganz anderes. Manche mögen schon einmal eine Giraffe gesehen haben, aber
nur sehr wenige werden schon einmal den Versuch unternommen haben, auf solch
einem Tier zu reiten. Daher ist die Anzahl der Menschen, die in der Lage sind,
diese Frage - "Wo halte ich mich auf einer ausbrechenden Giraffe fest?" - aus
ihrer Erfahrung heraus zu beantworten, voraussichtlich ziemlich klein, aber dennoch dürften die Antworten der meisten Befragten sehr ähnlich ausfallen: Die
Arme sind während des ungestümen Galopps um den Hals der Giraffe geschlungen.
Dieses Bild kann man nicht bzw. nicht nur mittels schon früher Wahrgenommenem
erklären. Hier kommen neue Komponenten ins Spiel, so daß wir vorläufig
festhalten dürfen, daß man sich auch noch nicht Erlebtes bildlich vorstellen kann.

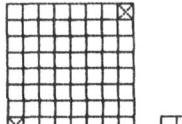

Dieses Quadrat aus 8*8=64 Feldern läßt sich
mit 32 Dominosteinen abdecken. Gilt dies
auch, wenn man die mit X gekennzeichneten
Felder entfernt und nur 31 Steine benutzt?

Abb. 1 (vgl. Raphael 1976: 31ff.)

Hauptvertreter und -verfechter einer Theorie der bildlichen Repräsentation
ist Stephen Kosslyn, der zusammen mit seinen Mitarbeitern etliche Untersuchungen zum Imagery-Problem gemacht und dabei systematisch die Eigenschaften dieser inneren Bilder erforscht hat.
Eigenschaften dieser mentalen Bilder sind u.a. (vgl. Haugeland 1985: 224),
daß

- die einzelnen Teile des Bildes zu einzelnen Teilen des Originals
  korrespondieren
- beide - Original und Repräsentation - die gleiche Struktur der Beziehungen
  aufweisen.

Auch die Manipulationen, die man an mentalen Bildern vornehmen kann, wurden
von Kosslyn et al. erforscht. Typische Operationen mit Images sind:

- Zooming (Vergrößern des Bildes)
- Wiedererkennen hervorstechender Eigenschaften oder Merkmale
- Rotation (Drehung um eine oder mehrere Achsen)
- Änderung einzelner Teile
- Übereinanderlegen zweier Bilder zum Vergleich

Die Kognitionswissenschaftler Shepard und Metzler legten bei einem ihrer
Experimente Versuchspersonen Bilder vor, wie sie hier in Abb. 2 dargestellt sind.
Die Vpn sollten entscheiden, ob es sich um verschiedene Ansichten eines Gegen-
standes handelt oder nicht. Bei der Überführung zweier Bilder ineinander (Abb. 2)

fällt ein Phänomen auf, das Rückschlüsse auf die Dimensionalität mentaler Bilder zuläßt. Es spielt augenscheinlich keine Rolle, ob nur in einer Ebene rotiert werden muß (Abb. 2a), oder ob alle drei Dimensionen beteiligt sind (Abb. 2b), die Rotationsdauer ist dieselbe - 60°s^{-1}. Nur wenn die Bilder sich nicht ineinander überführen lassen (Abb. 2c), benötigen die Probanden mehr Zeit, um dies herauszufinden.

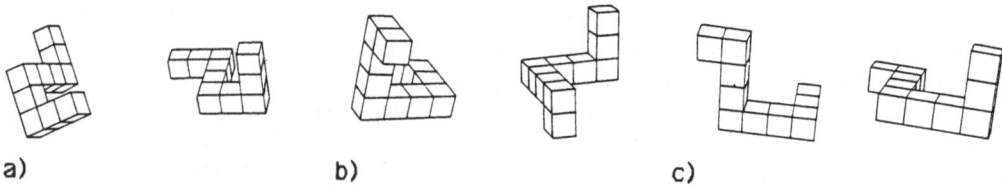

a)   b)   c)

Abb.2 (vgl. Shepard/Metzler 1971)

Die Fähigkeit der imaginären Rotation kann bei der Erkennung von Gegenständen von äußerster Wichtigkeit sein. So behaupten Miller/Johnson-Laird (1976), daß zum Erkennen eines Tisches u.a. die Tatsache, daß er eine Oberfläche hat, sehr wichtig ist. Nun ist es jedoch möglich, daß der Tisch verkehrt herum liegt, und daher in diesem Moment die Oberfläche nicht oben ist. Damit hört der Tisch allerdings nicht auf ein Tisch zu sein, und eine Möglichkeit, ihn zu erkennen, ist, das momentane Perzept in der mentalen Vorstellung zu drehen, bis eine Übereinstimmung mit dem normalen Bild eines Tisches erzielt wird. "We could imagine some perceptual mechanism that on failure to recognize an object tried rotating it various ways in imagination." (Miller/Johnson-Laird 1976: 228) Eine andere Möglichkeit wäre allerdings, daß im Konzept "Tisch" sehr viele perspektivische Ansichten abgelegt sind, so daß ein Tisch auch in außergewöhnlichen Situationen erkannt werden kann, ohne daß ein Transformationsprozeß, der mentale Bilder manipuliert, benötigt wird. Diese Möglichkeit erscheint mir aber (1) nicht sehr ökonomisch in Hinsicht auf möglichen Speicherplatzbedarf und (2) ist mir nicht klar, welche und wieviele Ansichten eines Tisches man ablegen sollte, damit kein Prozeß mehr eine mögliche Ansicht des Tisches errechnen muß.

Ich möchte nun - sehr kurz und skizzenhaft - propositonale und quasi-piktorielle Repräsentation nebeneinander stellen, um die Unterschiede deutlicher hervortreten zu lassen. Dabei orientiere ich mich an Kosslyn (1980: 31 Abb.3.1) (vgl. Abb. 3). [Detailliertere Beschreibungen der Experimente, die die folgenden Ergebnisse stützen, finden sich u.a. in Kosslyn (1980).]

Der Ball liegt auf der Kiste.
On (Ball, Box)

Abb.3

Für eine propositionale Darstellung gilt, daß

- mindestens eine Relation angegeben werden muß
- die Anzahl der Argumentstellen der Relation(en) festliegt

- diese Darstellung eine Syntax verlangt
- sie wahrheitswertfähig ist
- sie abstrakt ist
- sie kein räumliches Medium verlangt
- es keinen abstrakten, räumlichen Isomorphismus gibt
- keine Angaben über Größe und Orientierung der Gegenstände gemacht wird.
- die Bezeichnungen für die Gegenstände und die Relation kontingent sind

Für eine quasi-piktorielle Darstellung hingegen gilt, daß

- keine Relation explizit erwähnt wird
- die Anzahl der 'Argumente' beliebig ist
- diese Darstellung keine eigene Syntax erfordert
- der Wahrheitswert durch einen Vergleich gewonnen wird, d.h. er gilt nur für eine bestimmte Interpretation
- sie konkret ist
- sie ein räumliches Medium benötigt
- ein abstrakter räumlicher Isomorphismus vorliegt und daher jedem Ausschnitt des Bildes ein Ausschnitt der Welt entspricht
- die Gegenstände eine Größe und eine Orientierung haben müssen
- die Einheiten, die die Gegenstände repräsentieren, nicht beliebig gewählt werden können.

Für den Moment soll darauf verzichtet werden, die einzelnen Punkte zu diskutieren, aber zwei Probleme, die mit den verschiedenen Repräsentationsformen verbunden sind, sollen doch erwähnt werden. Problem (1) betrifft die Detaillierung der bildlichen Darstellung; wie man in Abb. 3 sieht, ist es hierbei - im Gegensatz zur propositionalen Darstellung - nicht möglich, sich eine Kiste ohne Form, einen Ball ohne Größe und ohne Muster vorzustellen, außerdem muß der Ball irgendwo auf der Kiste plaziert werden. Diese Angaben werden durch die Art der Repräsentation gefordert, aber alle diese Angaben sind kontingent, d.h. sie sind zufällig gewählt, ohne durch den Text verlangt oder festgelegt zu sein. Erforderlich werden diese Angaben durch die Wahl des Repräsentationsmediums. Die Werte, die wir diesen Angaben zuordnen, werden durch unsere Konzeptualisierung der verschiedenen Gegenstände beeinflußt. Wir werden Werte aussuchen, die wir für typisch halten. Zufällig sind diese Angaben also nur unter dem Gesichtspunkt, daß ihre Werte durch neu hinzukommende Information geändert werden können. So ist in Abb. 3 allein die Tatsache, daß der Ball auf der Kiste liegt, unabänderlich. M.a.W., in einem Bild gibt es Information, die wörtlich genommen werden muß, und Information, die allein durch die Wahl des Repräsentationsmediums und unsere individuelle Konzeptualisierung der Gegenstände ins Spiel gebracht wird. Allerdings ist eine quasi-piktorielle Repräsentation nicht in dem Maße zur Detaillierung verpflichtet, wie dies bei einem Photo der Fall ist. Sie gleicht eher einer Skizze oder einem Piktogramm, bei dem auch die Möglichkeit der "unausgesprochenen Unverbindlichkeit" (Block 1981: 12f) existiert. So wird niemand von einem Piktogramm, das ein weibliches Wesen darstellt, verlangen, daß man erkennen kann, ob die dort Abgebildete eine Bluse, einen Pullover oder ein T-Shirt trägt.

Problem (2) betrifft die prinzipiellen Unterschiede der verschiedenen Darstellungsarten, die trotz der Gegenüberstellung von propositionaler und quasi-piktorieller Form vielleicht noch nicht ganz klar hervorgetreten sind. Dazu muß ich aber erst noch darauf hinweisen, daß die bildhafte Repräsentation eventuell nur eine Alternative zur propositionalen ist. Alle diese Alternativen fallen aber unter den Oberbegriff der analogen Repräsentation, deren allgemeine Eigenschaften - die natürlich auch die bildhafte Repräsentation beschreiben - zumindest teilweise schon erwähnt wurden. Eine analoge Repräsentation ist dem Original in einer noch genauer zu bestimmenden Weise ähnlich; so korrespondieren Teile des Bildes (das Bild steht im weiteren stellvertretend für jede analoge Repräsentation) zu den entsprechenden Teilen des Originales. Dies gilt für eine propositionale Darstellung nicht. Habe ich eine Vorstellung von meinem Auto, so kann ich Teilen dieser Vorstellung - z.B. der Türe - Teile in der Realität zuweisen. Bei einem Teil des Wortes "Auto" kann ich diese Zuweisung nicht durchführen. Für die analoge Form gibt es einen Isomorphismus zweiter Ordnung (Shepard & Shipman 1970). Diese Beziehung besteht nicht zwischen den externen und internen Gegenständen - dies wäre ein Isomorphismus erster Ordnung, der behaupten würde, daß ich irgendwo ein kleines Auto im Kopf haben müßte -, sondern eine Isomorphie besteht zwischen den externen und internen Relationen, die für die jeweiligen Objekte zutreffen. Dabei möchte ich noch darauf hinweisen, daß Images nicht immer statisch sein müssen, sondern sehr wohl Vorgänge oder Handlungen wiedergeben können (vgl. Freyd 1983).

Zuerst erhebt sich die Frage, wie sich Kosslyn et al. eine geeignete mentale Repräsentation von Bildern vorstellen. Hierbei ist die leitende Idee die Vorstellung eines Computer- oder Fernsehbildschirmes (englisch: cathod-ray tube, daher der Name CRT-Metapher), auf dem ein Bild generiert wird, das von einer interpretierenden Funktion (a mind's eye) ausgewertet wird. Kosslyn (1980: viii) beschreibt die Analogie, die auch in Habel (1987) in bezug auf die topologische Struktur Verwendung findet, folgendermaßen:

> The catalyst that truly launched the present project was the idea that images are like displays a computer can generate on a cathod-ray tube. On this view, images are 'surface representations' that are generated from more abstract underlying representations.

Somit müßte ein Modell bzw. eine Theorie der mentalen Bilder ein bildschirmartiges Medium beinhalten, außerdem Techniken zur Generierung und Interpretation von Bildern in diesem Medium. Es muß erklärt werden, wie Information aus dem Langzeitgedächtnis zur Generierung eines Images beiträgt und wie ein Image, ist es erst einmal generiert, bei verschiedenen, kognitiven Aufgaben eingesetzt werden kann (vgl. Kosslyn et. al 1979: 150). Hier wird m.E. deutlich, daß eine enge Verbindung zwischen der konzeptuellen Feinstruktur, d.h. dem Inhalt einzelner Konzepte, und dem bildlichen Verarbeitungsmechanismus besteht (vgl. auch Miller/Johnson-Laird 1976: 221), denn die Konzepte sind im Langzeitgedächtnis abgelegt und enthalten die Teile, aus denen mentale Bilder generiert werden können. Erinnert man sich an das Tisch-Identifikationsproblem von Miller/Johnson-Laird, sieht man, daß zuerst das Image eines Tisches geschaffen werden muß, um es dann mit dem Image des Perzeptes vergleichen zu können.

Bei diesem Generierungs- und Interpretationsprozeß spielen auch Gestaltgesetze (siehe Abb. 4) eine Rolle, denn durch sie ist es möglich, Teile eines

Musters auf dem geistigen Bildschirm als zusammengehörig zu verstehen. Wie das genaue Zusammenspiel von Image, konzeptueller Struktur und Gestalteigenschaften ist, wird man in nächster Zeit erarbeiten müssen.

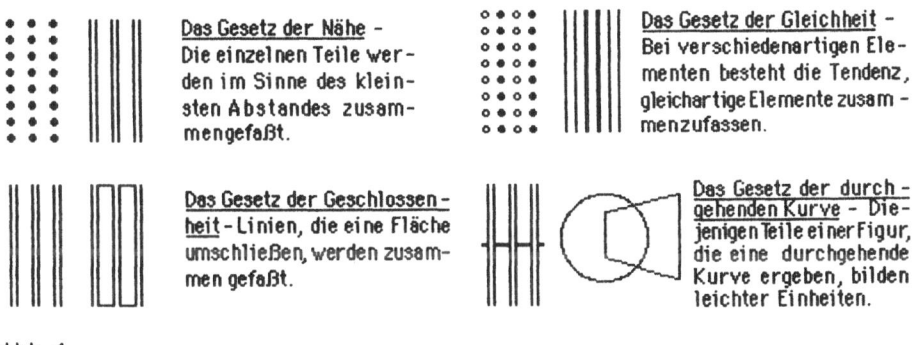

Abb.4

Mentale Bilder und ihre Verwendung zur Repräsentation des Raumes

Nun soll auf die Verwendung mentaler Bilder zur Repräsentation räumlichen Wissens etwas genauer eingegangen werden. Images spielen hierbei zweifellos eine wesentliche Rolle, aber dennoch soll dies mit zwei Zitaten belegt werden. So schreiben Downs/Stea in ihrem Buch über kognitive Karten: "Durch zwei Medien – durch Bilder oder durch Worte – haben wir die Möglichkeit, unser räumliches Wissen auszudrücken." (Downs/Stea 1982: 120) Und Wolfgang Klein (1979: 18) beschreibt die Planungsphase bei einer Wegauskunft als eine "imaginäre Wanderung vom Standpunkt zum Ziel". Auch hier spielt also, wie wahrscheinlich jeder schon einmal bei sich selbst erfahren hat, die bildhafte, kognitive Karte eine wesentliche Rolle.

Mentale Bilder als Wegbedeutungen

Grundlegend für die mit dem Phänomen der Wegbeschreibung verbundenen Probleme ist offenbar der Begriff der 'imaginären Wanderung', die der Auskunftgebende A unternimmt, bevor er den Rezipienten R dieser Auskunft auf den – hoffentlich richtigen – Weg schickt (vgl. Klein 1979, Wunderlich 1982). Ich werde im weiteren im Anschluß an Klein (1979) und Wunderlich/Reinelt (1982) bzw. Sichelschmidt (1981) eine Wegbeschreibung als eine Folge von Teilwegbeschreibungen verstehen, deren Teile auf einer kognitiven Karte lokalisiert werden. Wegbeschreibungen enthalten mindestens drei Elemente (vgl. Klein 1979: 10f): (1) Fixpunkte, an denen die deiktischen Ausdrücke (2) festgemacht werden, und an denen neue Handlungsanweisungen (3) Berücksichtigung finden können. Hierbei dienen Nominalphrasen zur Benennung dieser Fixpunkte. Als Fixpunkte dienen entweder Landmarken – also allgemein auffällige Gebilde wie etwa Kirchen, Kaufhäuser, Plätze u.ä. – oder aber nur in diesem Zusammenhang wichtige Referenzpunkte, wie etwa "der kleine Schuhladen" oder "die Ecke, wo der Zigarettenautomat hängt". Die in diesem Zusammenhang verwendeten Bewegungsverben beschreiben die auszuführenden Handlungen. Zusätzlich gibt es noch Richtungsangaben und Hinweise darauf, ob ein Teilstück beendet ist und ein neues beginnt (vgl. dazu auch Wunderlich/Reinelt 1982: 190). Ein Weg ist in diesem Sinne eine Folge von Wegabschnitten (vgl. Habel 1987: 9), und ihre Beschreibung setzt sich Einheit um Einheit fort (vgl. Klein 1976: 10).

Wir haben damit folgende Situation: Der Auskunftgebende A muß den Weg, den er auf einer imaginären Karte als den zu vermittelnden erkannt hat - dies geschieht in der von Klein (1979: 10) beschriebenen Planungsphase -, aus dieser kognitiven in eine sprachliche, d.h. sequentiell, linear ablaufende Form überführen. Dem Rezipienten R fällt wiederum die Aufgabe zu, diese verbale Information, die er von A erhält, in eine geeignete, wahrscheinlich nicht-propositionale, topologische Repräsentation zurückzuübersetzen. Da R den Weg zumindest teilweise nicht kennt - sonst hätte er ja nicht gefragt -, muß er geeignete Stellvertreter bei der Konstruktion seiner Repräsentation verwenden. Diese Stellvertreter müssen ihm von den Konzepten, die mit den zur Beschreibung verwendeten Worten verbunden sind, zur Verfügung gestellt werden. Schon Karl Bühler (1934: 137) stellt fest, daß R in einem solchen Fall mitwandert, die Dinge aus seiner Erinnerung sieht und, falls er noch niemals dort war, einen Ersatz wählt, den er kennt. Sichelschmidt (1981: 18f) plädiert nun dafür, daß die geeignete Repräsentationsform für diesen kognitiven Prozeß eine Mischung aus propositionaler und analoger Darstellung ist, da das "'imagery'-Modell zur Beschreibung raumzeitlicher dynamischer Prozesse bzw. zur Beschreibung kontinuierlicher Dimensionen insofern adäquater ist, als es mit weniger Zusatzannahmen auskommt als ein rein propositionaler Ansatz. ... Aufgrund dieser Überlegungen wird davon ausgegangen, daß rezeptive Sprachverarbeitung sich sowohl eines digitalen wie auch eines analogen Repräsentationsformats bedienen kann." Dabei scheint nicht von vorne herein festzuliegen, welche Teile in welchem Format abgelegt werden. Eine Annahme besteht darin, daß der grundlegende Verlauf der Beschreibung analog, spezifische Einzelheiten dagegen eher propositional (bzw. in Sichelschmidts Terminologie: digital) dargestellt werden. Inwieweit dies zutrifft und welche Rolle eventuell aus Konzepten gewonnene bildhafte Vorstellungen bei der Memorierung von Einzelheiten spielen, kann nur durch empirische Untersuchungen genauer belegt werden. Die Annahme, daß Menschen zum Verstehen einer Wegbeschreibung nicht-propositionale Repräsentationsformate verwenden, steht auch nicht im Gegensatz zur Erkenntnis, daß nicht syntaktische Strukturen, sondern der durch sie ausgedrückte semantische Inhalt im Gedächtnis bleibt; man weiß noch was gesagt, nicht mehr unbedingt wie es gesagt wurde. Allerdings glaube ich - anders als Wessells (1984: 336) - daß zur Erklärung dieses Phänomens nicht nur eine propositionale Wissensrepräsentation ausreicht, denn sie allein wäre zu eingeschränkt und würde einige Erscheinungen aus dem Bereich der Generierung und des Verstehens einer Wegbeschreibung, so z.B. die Verwendung deiktischer Ausdrücke wie *hier* und *jetzt* , nicht hinreichend erklären.

Man kann im weiteren davon ausgehen, daß "mehr verstanden als gesagt wird" (Engelkamp 1976: 44). Verstehen ist in diesem Fall ein integrativer Prozeß, bei dem das durch die Sprache vermittelte Wissen in einen größeren Zusammenhang eingebettet wird. Einen Satz zu verstehen, heißt also nicht einfach zu wissen, was der Fall ist, wenn er wahr ist, sondern Verstehen bedeutet, Aktivierung vorhandenen Wissens und seine Verbindung mit der neuen Information. Die Aktivierung des alten Wissens umfaßt hierbei auch die Spezialisierung dieses Wissens auf den gerade vorliegenden Fall. Dieser Verstehensprozeß stellt also in gewisser Weise das Pendant zu der von Klein beschriebenen Wegplanungsphase bei einer Wegauskunft dar und auch Sichelschmidt (1981: 23) geht in seinem Resumee von der Auffassung aus, daß Verstehen ein integrativer, konstruktiver Prozeß ist. In ihm dokumentiert sich der Versuch des Hörers, anhand der verbalen Wegbeschreibung und der ihr zugrundeliegenden linearen Struktur "ein kognitives Netzwerk ... räumlicher Relationen zu konstruieren und zu repräsentieren". Sprecher und Hörer unterscheiden sich jedoch prinzipiell, während nämlich A Start und Ziel auf seiner kognitiven Karte lokalisieren kann und dadurch auch der sie verbindende Weg "auf einen Blick" gegeben ist, muß R seine Karte erst Schritt für Schritt aufbauen. A besitzt eine kognitive Repräsentation bestehend aus visueller Erinnerung und "Bewegungserinnerung" (vgl. Klein 1976: 24f.), R muß diese kognitive Repräsentation allein durch verbale Vermittlung (er-)schaffen.

Literatur

Bühler, K. (1934) *Sprachtheorie: Die Darstellungsfunktion der Sprache.* Stuttgart, New York: Fischer, (pb.) 1982

Dahlgren, K. (1986) Naive Semantics for Natural Language Understanding. Unv. Man. (Los Angeles)

Downs, R.M./Stea, D. (1982) *Kognitive Karten: Die Welt in unseren Köpfen.* New York: Harper & Row

Engelkamp, J. (1976) *Satz und Bedeutung.* Stuttgart: Kohlhammer

Freyd, J. (1983) The Representation of Action. *The Behavioral and Brain Sciences* (1)

Habel, Ch. (1987) Prozedurale Aspekte der Wegplanung und Wegbeschreibung. Lilog-Report 17

Haugeland, J. (1985) *Artificial Intelligence - The very idea.* Cambridge/Mass.: MIT-Press

Katz, D. (1943) *Gestaltpsychologie.* Basel: Schwabe & Co 1969[4]

Klein, W. (1979) Wegauskünfte. *Zeitschrift für Literaturwissenschaft und Linguistik* (9), 9-57

Kosslyn, S. M.(1980) *Image and Mind.* Cambridge/Mass.: Harvard UP

Kosslyn, S.M. et al. (1979) On the Demystification of Mental Imagery. In: Block, N. (Hrsg.) (1981) *Imagery.* Cambridge/Mass.: MIT-Press 1982[2]

Miller, G./Johnson-Laird, P. (1976) *Language and Perception.* Cambridge/Mass.: Cambridge UP

Paivio, A. (1971) *Imagery and verbal processes.* New York: Holt, Rinehart & Winston

Raphael, B. (1976) *The Thinking Computer - Mind Inside Matter.* San Francisco: W.H.Freeman & Co

Rosch, E. (1978) Principles of categorization. In: Rosch, E./LLoyd, B. (Hrsg.) (1978) *Cognition and categorization.* Hillsdale, N.J.: Erlbaum, 27-48

Shepard, R.N. /Shipman, S. (1970) Second-Order Isomorphism of Internal Representations: Shapes of States. *Cogn. Psychology* (1), 1-17

Shepard, R.N./Metzler, J. (1971) Mental Rotation of Three-dimensional Objects. *Science* (171), 701-703

Sichelschmidt, L. (1981) Wegbedeutungen. Unv. Man. (Bochum)

Wessells, M. G. (1984) *Kognitive Psychologie.* New York: Harper & Row

Wunderlich, D. (1978) Wie analysiert man Gespräche? Beispiel Wegauskünfte. *Ling. Ber.* (58), 41-76

Wunderlich, D. (1982) Sprache und Raum. *Studium Linguistik* (12/13), 1-19/37-59

Wunderlich, D./Reinelt, R. (1982) How to get there from here. In: Jarvella, R./Klein, W. (Hrsg.) (1982) *Speech, place and action. Studies on deixis and related topics.* Chichester: Wiley, 183-201

Ein Tip zum Problem des Abdeckens des Quadrates: Man stelle sich die 8*8-2 Felder schachbrettartig eingefärbt vor; nun wird deutlich, daß jeder Dominostein immer ein schwarzes und ein weißes Feld belegt. Es wurden aber zwei gleichfarbige Eckfelder entfernt.

GENERIERUNG IN NATÜRLICHSPRACHLICHEN SYSTEMEN:
Beziehungen zwischen der Erzeugung von Inhalt und Form
Spezielle Sektion - GWAI-87

Wolfgang Hoeppner

EWH Rheinland-Pfalz, Abt. Koblenz
Angewandte Informatik,
Schwerpunkt Linguistik
Rheinau 3-4, 5400 Koblenz

Universität Hamburg
Fachbereich Informatik
Projektgruppe WISBER
Postfach 30 27 62, 2000 Hamburg 36

Ein Charakteristikum für die Anfangsphase sprachorientierter KI-Forschung ist, daß implementierte Systeme aus dieser Zeit vor allem die Abbildung natürlichsprachlicher Eingabeäußerungen in eine interne Repräsentation leisteten, die dann als Grundlage für Auswertungsprozesse verwendet wurde. Der systematischen Erzeugung sprachlicher Äußerungen widmeten sich in dieser Phase vergleichsweise wenige Wissenschaftler. Seit Anfang der achziger Jahre hat sich dieses Bild gewandelt: zahlreiche Forschungsarbeiten haben die Erzeugung von sprachlichen Äußerungen thematisiert, so daß heute die Zeit reif erscheint, sich mit prinzipiellen Fragen der Sprachgenerierung auseinanderzusetzen.

Traditionell wird Generierung als ein Prozeß angesehen, der zwei Teilaufgaben zu lösen hat: die Bestimmung des Inhalts von Sprachäußerungen und die Formulierung dieses Inhalts in natürlicher Sprache (WAS soll gesagt werden und WIE soll es gesagt werden, sind die üblicherweise verwendeten Schlagwörter). Mit dieser Unterscheidung ist allerdings noch keine Aussage über die spezifischen Beziehungen zwischen den beiden elementaren Prozessen impliziert. Die spezielle Sektion dient dazu, diese Beziehungen aus theoretischer und praktischer Sicht näher zu beleuchten und sie in einem größeren Rahmen zu diskutieren.

Zwei extreme Standpunklte bezüglich Inhalt und Form lassen sich wie folgt skizzieren:

- die Bestimmung des Inhalts von Sprachäußerungen und die Produktion der sprachlichen Form sind vollständig getrennte Prozesse, zwischen denen eine Schnittstelle definiert werden kann.

- Inhalt und Form von Sprachäußerungen bedingen sich gegenseitig. Der Erzeugungsprozeß für die Inhaltsauswahl antizipiert die sprachliche Realisierbarkeit, und die sprachliche Formulierung kann Modifikationen bzw. Ergänzungen des Inhalts notwendig machen.

Argumente für diese Extremstandpunkte oder für eine dazwischenliegende Position lassen sich auf verschiedenen Ebenen finden. Modularisierungsgesichtspunkte für die Architektur eines natürlichsprachlichen Systems spielen hier ebenso eine Rolle wie beobachtbare Performanzphänomene der menschlichen Sprachproduktion. Denkbar wäre darüberhinaus ein Modell, das die Beziehungen zwischen Inhalt und Form an spezifische Spracherzeugungssituationen bindet, das also keine einheitliche Lösung anbietet.

In den folgenden vier Beiträgen wird zu den hier aufgeworfenen Fragen Stellung bezogen. Eine endgültige Klärung des Verhältnisses zwischen Inhalt und Form kann damit nicht vorliegen und war auch nicht intendiert. Das primäre Ziel dieser Sektion liegt vielmehr darin, eine Diskussionsgrundlage für eines der zentralen Probleme bei der Generierung natürlicher Sprache zu schaffen.

Generation of content vs. generation of form:
A review of recent work in the SEMSYN project

Dietmar Rösner

c/o Projekt SEMSYN

Institut für Informatik, Universität Stuttgart

Herdweg 51, D-7000 Stuttgart 1, West Germany

e-mail: semsyn@ifistg.uucp

1 Introduction and overview

The focal point of this workshop on natural language generation will be the traditional distinction between *What to say* and *How to say it*. Under this perspective we will review and discuss the experiences from recent work in text generation done in the framework of the SEMSYN project. [1] We will both illustrate the relative merits of this work [2] and work out its current limitations. We will argue that further progress is only to be expected when future research concentrates on questions related to the generation of content. Remarks on other work in nl generation in the final section of the paper shall provide additional material for the discussion at the workshop.

2 A reference model of the generation process

As a basis for the discussion to follow we will use a model of natural language generation that has been adopted from McDonald's proposal at the Nijmegen workshop on Natural Language Generation (McDonald et al. 87). This model basically distinguishes between

- the "situation" where the need for natural language generation arises from,
- the conceptual specification or "message" that encodes the meaning to be expressed,
- the "more linguistic specification" that determines the grammatical properties of the intended utterance,
- and finally the generated utterance.

A "situation" in this model may be seen as some state of the world *plus* the intention to communicate about it. We may think of "real life" situations involving humans as well as those involving machines: an operating system in an error state where the user should be informed with an adequate error message, an expert system that has been prompted to justify the results of its deductions, a data base that is interrogated about its content.

The primary task during the transition from "situation" to "message" is the generation of content: Deciding what to say and - even more important in complex situations - deciding what *not* to say.

---

[1] SEMSYN is an acronym for *SEMantic SYNthesis*. The SEMSYN project is funded by the West German Ministry for Research and Technology (BMFT).

[2] The SEMSYN generator and its applications as described in this paper are fully implemented and run in ZetaLISP and FLAVORS on SYMBOLICS lisp machines.

The "message" will - ideally - represent the content in a format that is not dependent on a particular natural language. The step from a "message" to a linguistic representation of the utterance is often called "realization" (of the message) (e.g. McDonald 1983). Realization involves decisions on linguistic form, e.g.:

- What is the adequate syntactic form for the utterance as a whole?
- How should the subparts of the conceptual representation be realized and integrated into the utterance?
- What are appropriate lexicalizations - as lexemes or whole phrasal structures of the target language - for the elements of the message?

The need for an explicit linguistic representation of the intended utterance and a separate final processing step performing linearization and morpho-syntactic transformations - often called a front end generator (Emele 86) - is especially obvious for highly inflectional languages with a rich repertoire of agreement phenomena (e.g. French, German).

3 Case study 1: Generation of German news stories

Within the framework of Japanese/German machine translation efforts the project SEMSYN has implemented a system for the generation of German noun groups and clauses from semantic representations (Rösner 86a). Extended versions of this system have been used for the generation of multisentential texts:

- SEMTEX: generation of German news stories (Rösner 86b, 87),
- GEOTEX: generation of descriptive texts related to geometric constructions (Kehl 86).

3.1 From situations to text plans

Starting point for the generation of newspaper stories is a real situation: the state of the labor market as represented by the data from the oficial monthly labor market statistics (numbers of unemployed, open jobs, ...).

A rudimentary "text planner" - best seen as an implementation of a kind of "text grammar" for the class of texts under investigation - takes these data and those of relevant previous months, checks for changes and significant developments, simulates possible argumentations of various political speakers on these developments and finally creates - by filling templates - a representation of the intended text as an ordered list of frame descriptions. SEMTEX then converts this list into a newspaper story in German.

A typical text plan produced is given in Figure 1, a corresponding generated text is given in 3.2.[3]

3.2 Context sensitive generation

The main concern in implementing SEMTEX has been to provide the SEMSYN generator with mechanisms that keep track of previous generation decisions thus creating a representation of the textual context built up by the already uttered sentences. When deciding on the linguistic form for elements of the text plan the context is used:

---

[3] Natural numbers in the text plan are printed in octal.

```
.((INCREASE :QUANTITY (NR-UNEMPLOYED :GROUP *GLOBAL* :AREA FRG)
.          :MANNER REMARKABLE
.          :TIME-PERIOD (DURING :TIME DEZ-85))
. (INCREASE :QUANTITY (NR-UNEMPLOYED :GROUP *GLOBAL*)
.          :FROM 10335614
.          :TO 10750134
.          :TIME-PERIOD (DURING :TIME DEZ-85))
. (HAVE-VALUE :QUANTITY (UNEMPLOYMENT-RATE :GROUP *GLOBAL*)
.            :VALUE (PERCENTAGE :VALUE 9.4)
.            :TIME-POINT (END-OF :TIME-PERIOD DEZ-85))
. (HAVE-VALUE :QUANTITY (UNEMPLOYMENT-RATE :GROUP *GLOBAL*)
.            :VALUE (PERCENTAGE :VALUE 9.3)
.            :TIME-POINT (END-OF :TIME-PERIOD DEZ-84))
.(*COMMENT*
.    :SPEAKER *DGB
.    :COMMENT (EVALUATE-NEGATIVE
.                :SPEAKER *DGB
.                :FACT
.                 (INCREASE
.                  :QUANTITY (NR-UNEMPLOYED :GROUP *GLOBAL*)))))
```

Figure 1: A text plan for SEMTEX

- to avoid repetition in wording,

- to deliberately elide information still valid (e.g. about the time period concerned),

- to decide on pronominalisation and other types of reference.

In addition a representation of the temporal context is used

- to dynamically determine grammatical tense and

- to produce appropriate natural language descriptions for time units (Rösner 86b).

Based on its context handling mechanisms SEMTEX converted the text plan from Fig. 1 into the following text:

> "Die Zahl der Arbeitslosen in der Bundesrepublik Deutschland ist im Dezember spürbar angestiegen. Sie hat von 2210700 auf 2347100 zugenommen. Die Arbeitslosenquote betrug Ende Dezember 9.4 Prozent. Sie hatte sich Ende Dezember des letzten Jahres auf 9.3 Prozent belaufen. Der DGB hat erklärt, er sehe in der Vergrößerung der Arbeitslosenzahl ein negatives Zeichen."

3.3 Simulating political comments

The simulation of political comments on labor market developments takes advantage of the observed predictability of those reactions: speakers of the government or their supporting parties try to see positive aspects in the current situation, whereas speakers of the opposition are expected to underline whatever negative aspects are available.

3.3.1 Rhetorical schemata

For the representation of political statements in text plans we use abstract rhetorical schemata.[4] For each rhetorical schema, the generator kernel has been enriched with knowledge about the various ways how these schemata may be realized in the texts. One may look at these schemata as operating on the conceptual structures from their slots. The generator needs to know how the slot fillers may be realized (e.g. as noun group or as clause) and how the corresponding realization results may be combined. Depending on the type of the partial realizations this combination may demand for appropriate connectives or phrasal patterns (Becker 75).

3.3.2 An example: EMPHASIZE-NEGATIVE and EMPHASIZE-POSITIVE

EMPHASIZE-NEGATIVE and EMPHASIZE-POSITIVE may be used in rhetorics in order to combine two statements that have different evaluations (:POS-FACT resp. :NEG-FACT). The rhetorical effect is achieved by a kind of "non-commutativity" of arguments. Given the same two facts one can present them to the hearer in a way that puts the stress on the negative aspect (EMPHASIZE-NEGATIVE) or just the other way round such that the positive fact becomes more prominent (Rösner 85).

Among the implemented variants for realizing an EMPHASIZE-NEGATIVE rhetorics in German are the following possibilities:[5]

> "**Trotz** $<: NG : POS - FACT ><: CLAUSE : NEG - FACT >$"
> "**Zwar** $<: CLAUSE : POS - FACT >$, **aber** $<: CLAUSE : NEG - FACT >$"
> "$<: NG : POS - FACT >$ **darf nicht darüber hinwegtäuschen,**
> **daß** $<: CLAUSE : NEG - FACT >$"

This allows the generation of comments like the following:

> "Der DGB erklärt, ...
> ... daß **trotz** der Verringerung der Arbeitslosenzahl sie jetzt noch immer einen Wert von 2148800 habe."
> ... sie habe sich **zwar** vermindert, die Zahl der Arbeitslosen habe jetzt **aber** noch immer einen Wert von 2148800."
> ... daß die Reduzierung der Zahl der Arbeitslosen **nicht darüber hinwegtäuschen dürfe, daß** sie jetzt noch immer einen Wert von 2148800 habe."

3.3.3 Content vs. form in rhetorics

Rhetorical schemata allow a fairly clear distinction between choosing the content of the related propositions and choosing the form to express this relation in natural language:

---

[4] The use of such schemata in text understanding has been discussed in (Rösner, Laubsch 82),(Rösner 85); for other work on rhetorical structures in generation cf. e.g. (Mann 84).

[5] Read $<:NG :POS-FACT >$ as: "realization of the filler of slot :POS-FACT as noun group"

- In order to build up an EMPHASIZE-NEGATIVE structure and to decide what statements could be combined in such a way, one has to know about the evaluation of facts and their relations within the domain under discussion.

- The generator on the other hand only needs to know in what ways such a structure might be expressed. He has not to check (at least in our implementation) if the combination of the conceptual structures in such a rhetoric makes sense. In this respect the generator should rely on the text planner's work.

4 Case study 2: Verbalizing objects and operations

In the GEOTEX application SEMTEX is combined with a tool for interactively creating geometric constructions (Kehl 86). The latter offers formal commands for manipulating (i.e. creating, naming and - deliberately - deleting) basic objects of Euclidean geometry. The generator is used to produce descriptive texts related to the geometric construction:

- descriptions of the geometric objects involved,
- descriptions of the sequence of steps done during a construction.

4.1 Describing formal objects

During the course of a construction all geometric objects are represented as instances of their respective FLAVOR class (point, line, circle etc.). These instances keep track of:

- by means of which operation the object came into existence and
- how the object is related to other objects within the drawing (e.g. a point being the center of a circle or the intersection of two lines).

This information is used when GEOTEX is asked to render descriptive texts about the objects in the drawing. An example:

"Der Punkt $a hat die X-Koordinate 8 und die Y-Koordinate 8. Er ist der Mittelpunkt des Kreises $km, ist der Endpunkt der Strecke $ma und ist der Anfangspunkt der Strecke $ab. Außerdem liegt der Punkt $a auf dem Kreis $k."

4.2 Verbalizing the course of the construction

In GEOTEX' other mode - describing the course of a construction in a concise and coherent text - the "situation" is given by the sequence of commands of the geometry language. Let us look at an example:

(PUN $A 15 10) (PUN $B 20 7)(KRE $K $B $A)

Each of these commands in turn causes GEOTEX

- to update the associated FLAVOR representation for the domain,

- to display (if possible) the objects on the screen (in this case: point $A with coordinates (15, 10), point $B with coordinates (20, 7), circle $K with center $B and through $A),

- to create a message from the operation and give it as input to SEMTEX.

SEMTEX renders this information in the order given. For the example this resulted in the following text:

. "Ich zeichne den Punkt $a (15/10) ein."
. "Und den Punkt $b (20/7)."
. "Um ihn schlage ich den Kreis $k durch $a."

To achieve this result SEMTEX' context-handling mechanisms have been enriched:

- Elision is no longer restricted to adjuncts. For repetitive operations verb and subject will be elided in subsequent sentences (cf. the sentences 1 and 2).

- The distinction between known information (i.e. known geometric objects) and new one (i.e. new objects created from known ones) is exploited to decide on constituent ordering: the constituent referring to the known object is "topicalized", i.e. put in front of the sentence (cf. sentence 3).

In addition the system allows for more ways to refer to objects introduced in the text: pronouns, textual deixis using demonstrative pronouns ("dieser Punkt"), names. The choice is done deliberately: Pronouns are avoided if their use might create an ambiguity; reference by name is used when an object has not constantly been in focus and therefore has to be re-introduced.

5   The need for sophisticated text planning

The primary concern in implementing both SEMTEX and GEOTEX has been to provide the SEMSYN generator with context handling mechanisms. The weakest aspect of both applications is how the text plans are currently being produced:

In SEMTEX the content of the newspaper story is determined through the interaction of options chosen by the user ("Include information from preceding year", "Include political comments", etc.), the availability of the necessary data and some random elements in the templates. The templates are already ordered according to a kind of "text grammar".

A satisfactory solution would involve real text planning: Text plans should be created on the basis of domain knowledge that allows to determine the relative importance of information that is available within the representation of the "situation". In addition text specific knowledge should explicitly be taken into account: How is relevance of information reflected in the text structure for the class of text under consideration?

For news stories the default ordering is based on the general principle to present the most relevant information first; for longer stories - with several subtopics - this may be combined with a kind of breadth first strategy: Give the most prominent information of each subtopic first (e.g. in the "lead" paragraph), then elaborate on the details of each subtopic in separate paragraphs.

GEOTEX' expressibility is limited by poor content generation as well: Simply reporting on the sequence of drawing actions is not sufficient. More interesting texts could only be produced if information about goal/subgoal relations were available. This would allow to give motivations or to report on whole sequences of simple steps as single higher level actions.

6 Content vs. form: remarks and theses

Thesis: None of the currently available generation systems is equally well developed with respect to all steps of the generation process (from situation to surface text).

- Some work is primarily oriented towards the creation of powerful domain independent "tactical generators" that provide sufficient linguistic coverage of the target language. These systems are intended to be interfaced with domain specific message generators. This category includes e.g. generators like MUMBLE (McDonald et al. 87), PHRED (Jacobs 84), IPG (Hoenkamp 83; Kempen, deSmedt 87) or SEMSYN (Rösner 86b).

- On the other hand there is research that has fully concentrated on the problems of generation of content thereby - more or less - neglecting linguistic aspects. The XPLAIN system may be taken as extreme representative for this category: Concentrating on sophisticated strategies for producing explanations and justifications for the reasoning of a digitalis advisor XPLAIN runs into problems even with the correct placement of determiners within a noun group (Swartout 81, p.84).

Thesis: There are still no systems available with general techniques for global text organization. Current systems heavily rely on starting from strongly structured domains:

- Gabriel's YH produces a documentation text for a *well written* program (Gabriel 81)
- McKeown's TEXT delivers informative texts on the content of a *hierarchically structured* data base (McKeown 83)

Thesis: Interesting contributions - to the field as a whole as well as to the content vs. form discussion - may be expected from recent work in "multilingual generation":

- RAREAS, a system synthesizing weather forecasts from data provided by meteorologists (Kittredge et al. 86) is currently being equipped with French as second target language.
- Kukich's ANA, a system generating English stock market reports from Dow Jones data (Kukich 83), has a second tongue as well: The generation of French bulletins has been possible by replacing ANA's "linguistic module" with a French version - called FRANA (Contant 86) - while leaving ANA's other modules untouched (i.e. Fact Generator, Message Generator, Discourse Organizer).

But: Simply replacing linguistic modules will not always be sufficient. Since conventions of textual organization are in part culturally determined the relative ease in switching from English to French may simply reflect cultural "closeness". A case in point: The experience from generating Japanese news from a text representation derived by analyzing Spanish news on terrorism (Ishizaki 83). Ishizaki reports that he had to reorganize the representation of the story since according to Japanese text conventions temporal ordering of events is preferable.

References

Becker, J.D. "The phrasal lexicon", in: Schank & Webber (Eds.) "Theoretical Issues in Natural Language Processing", Cambridge, 1975

Contant, C. "Generation automatique de texte: application au sous-language boursier", M.A. thesis, Dept. de Linguistique, Univ. de Montreal, 1986

Emele, M. "FREGE - Entwicklung und Implementierung eines objektorientierten FRont-End-GEnerators für das Deutsche", Diplomarbeit, Institut für Informatik, Uni Stuttgart, 1986

Gabriel, R.P. "An Organization for Programs in Fluid Domains", Stanford University, Computer Science Department, AIM-342, May 1981

Hoenkamp, E. "Een Computermodel van de Spreker: Psychologische en Linguistische Aspecten", Dissertation (in Dutch, some chapters in English), University Nijmegen, 1983

Ishizaki, Sh. "Generation of Japanese Sentences from Conceptual Representation", in: IJCAI 83, Proceedings, Karlsruhe, 1983

Jacobs, P.S. "PHRED: A Generator for Natural Language Interfaces", Berkeley, Computer Science Division (EECS), Report No. UCB/CSD 84/189, June 1984

Kehl, W. "GEOTEX - Ein System zur Verbalisierung geometrischer Konstruktionen", Diplomarbeit, Institut für Informatik, Uni Stuttgart, 1986

Kempen, G., K. deSmedt "Incremental sentence generation", in: Kempen, G. (Ed.) "Natural language generation: New results in Artificial Intelligence, Psychology, and Linguistics" Kluwer Academic Publishers, Dordrecht/Boston, 1987

Kittredge, R., A. Polguere, E. Goldberg " Synthesizing Weather Forecasts from formatted Data", in: COLING-86, Proceedings, Bonn, August 1986

Kukich, K. "Design and Implementation of a Knowledge-Based Report Generator", ACL Annual Meeting, Proceedings, 1983

Mann, W.C. "Discourse Structures for Text Generation", in: COLING-84, Proceedings, Stanford, 1984

McDonald, D.D. "Natural Language Generation as a Computational Problem: an introduction", in: Brady & Berwick (eds.) "Computational Models of Discourse", MIT Press, 1983

McDonald,D.D., J.D. Pustejovsky, M.M. Vaughan "Factors contributing to efficiency in natural language generation", in: Kempen, G. (Ed.) "Natural language generation: New results in Artificial Intelligence, Psychology, and Linguistics" Kluwer Academic Publishers, Dordrecht/Boston, 1987

McKeown, K.R. "Focus constraints on language generation", in: IJCAI 83, Proceedings, Karlsruhe, 1983

Rösner, D., J. Laubsch "Formalization of Argumentation Structures in Newspaper Texts", in: COLING-82, Proceedings, Prague, 1982

Rösner, D. "Schemata for Understanding of Argumentation in Newspaper Texts" in: Steels & Campbell (Eds.), "Progress in Artificial Intelligence", Chichester, 1985

Rösner, D. "When Mariko talks to Siegfried - Experiences from a Japanese/German Machine Translation Project", in: COLING-86, Proceedings, Bonn, August 1986a

Rösner, D. "Ein System zur Generierung von deutschen Texten aus semantischen Repräsentationen", Dissertation, Institut für Informatik, Universität Stuttgart, 1986b

Rösner, D. "The automated news agency: the SEMTEX text generator for German", in: Kempen, G. (Ed.) "Natural language generation: New results in Artificial Intelligence, Psychology, and Linguistics" Kluwer Academic Publishers, Dordrecht/Boston, 1987

Swartout, W.R. "Producing Explanations and Justifications of Expert Consulting Programs", MIT, Laboratory for Computer Science, MIT/LCS/TR-251, Jan. 1981

Ein erster Blick auf POPEL –
Wie wird was gesagt?

Norbert Reithinger
SFB 314: Künstliche Intelligenz – Wissensbasierte Systeme
FB 10 - Informatik IV, Universität des Saarlandes
D-6600 Saarbrücken 11
Usenet/Eunet: bert@sbsvax.uucp

Zusammenfassung

Für XTRA, ein natürlichsprachliches Zugangssystem zu Expertensystemen, wird derzeit die Generierungskomponente POPEL[1] entwickelt. In diesem Artikel wird die Konzeption des Systems POPEL beschrieben, auf welche Wissensbasen es sich stützt und wie der inhaltsfestlegende ("what to say") und der inhaltsrealisierende ("how to say") Teil interagieren.

1. Einleitung

Der Entwurf einer Generierungskomponente für natürliche Sprache hängt von vielen Kriterien ab – u.a. von welchen Strukturen ausgegangen werden kann, welche Restriktionen das Gesamtsystem setzt, wie die Wissensbasen aussehen, ob isolierte Texte erzeugt werden sollen oder ob die Integration in ein Dialogsystem vorgesehen ist.

Zudem sieht sich der/die Systemdesigner(in) mit der Schwierigkeit konfrontiert, daß Menschen, deren natürliches Kommunikationsmedium Sprache ist, die sprachliche Qualität des Ergebnisses beurteilen. Um dem Benutzer und der Situation angepaßte Sprache zu erzeugen, muß Wissen des allgemeinen und dialogspezifischen Kontextes mit einbezogen werden.

In diesem Beitrag sollen einige Ideen, die die Architektur von POPEL beeinflußt haben, dargestellt werden. POPEL ist der Generierungteil des Systems XTRA, einem natürlichsprachlichen Zugangssystem für Expertensysteme [XTRA 87]. Im folgenden Abschnitt werden die Architekturen existierender Generierungssyteme kurz dargestellt und anhand einer Grobklassifikation eingeteilt. Abschnitt 3 beschreibt die Konzeption von POPEL. Auf den Stand der Implementation geht der abschließende Abschnitt ein.

2. Architektur von Generierungssystemen

Traditionellerweise unterscheidet man in Generierungssystemen zwischen einem inhaltsfestlegenden Teil ("what to say") und einem inhaltsrealisierenden Teil ("how to say"). Die Architektur von Generierungssystemen kann man unter dem Gesichtspunkt des Datenflusses in drei Klassen einteilen:

- *sequentielle Modelle*: zwischen den Verarbeitungsschritten besteht nur ein unidirektionaler Datenfluß vom inhaltsfestlegenden zum realisierenden Teil.

- *Modelle mit Rückwirkungen*: eine bidirektionale Kommunikation zwischen beiden Teilen findet über eine begrenzte, fest definierte Schnittstelle statt.

- *integrierte Modelle*: zwischen beiden Teilen besteht keine Trennung, sie sind beide Facetten ein- und desselben Prozesses.

Beispiele für Systeme, die dem sequentiellen Modell folgen, sind MUMBLE [McDonald 85], TEXT [McKeown 85] und SEMTEX/GEOTEX [Rösner, in diesem Band]. Dabei ist mit MUMBLE nur der "how to say"-Teil realisiert, der von einem Planer eine "Message" erhält, die in einen Text

---

Die hier vorgestellte Arbeit entstand im Sonderforschungsbereich 314, Projekt XTRA. Ich danke Jürgen Allgayer, Christel Kemke, Carola Reddig und Gudula Retz-Schmidt, die mich davon überzeugt haben, diesen Artikel doch noch fertigzustellen, und Dagmar Schmauks für das ausdauernde Korrekturlesen.
[1] POPEL ist die Abkürzung von "Production Of { Perhaps, Perfect, ... } Eloquent Language"

übersetzt wird. In TEXT sind beide Teile realisiert, wobei der Schwerpunkt der Implementierung auf der Entwicklung des "what to say"-Teils lag.

Ein System mit Rückwirkungen ist PAULINE [Hovy 87]. Die Interaktionen erfolgen an fünf Entscheidungspunkten – Themawahl, Satzinhalt, Satzorganisation, Satzteilorganisation und Wortwahl. Vom "what to say"-Teil wird ein Teil der Antwort vorgeplant und an den "how to say"-Teil weitergegeben. Trifft dieser auf einen der angegebenen Entscheidungspunkte, wird die Kontrolle wieder an die Inhaltsplanung übergeben.

KAMP [Appelt 85] ist ein Beispiel für ein integriertes Modell. Entscheidungen, was zu sagen ist und wie, werden als unterschiedliche Aspekte eines einzigen, hierarchischen Planungsprozesses angesehen, der sich gleichermaßen des Kontextwissens bedient, z.B. eines Benutzermodells, wie sprachlicher Informationen, beispielsweise einer Unifikationsgrammatik, um diese in die Planung der Äußerung einzubeziehen.

Die Texte, die die vier erstgenannten Systeme erzeugen, beziehungsweise die Einzelsätze des letzten Systems, werden jeweils isoliert generiert, ohne Bezugnahme auf Textteile, die aus vorangegangenen Generatorläufen oder von einem Dialogpartner stammen.

Vergleichbare Modelle zu den oben genannten werden auch in der psycholinguistischen Forschung aufgestellt (sequentiell [Garrett 80], interagierend [Bock 87], integriert [Danks 77]).

3. Architektur von POPEL

3.1 Anforderungen

Aus der Einsatzumgebung von XTRA ergeben sich u.a. folgende Anforderungen:

– Generierung von dialogspezifischen Ausdrücken

– Texte im Umfang von Erklärungen

– Verwendung der Wissensbasen des Gesamtsystems

Die gemeinsame Verwendung der Wissensbasen des Gesamtsystems erfolgt hauptsächlich aus zwei Gründen: das Wissen in einem Dialogsystem sollte allgemeingültig sein, sodaß es sowohl für Analyse als auch für Generierung verwendet werden kann. Außerdem findet in Dialogen ein gegenseitiges Referieren auf die Beiträge der Dialogteilnehmer statt. Der Analysekomponente muß also die Ausgabe des Systems zugänglich sein, damit die auf Systemausgaben referierenden Ausdrücke des Benutzers analysiert werden können, und umgekehrt.

3.2 Wissensbasen für POPEL

Folgende Wissensbasen des Gesamtsystems sind für den Generatorteil besonders relevant:

a) Die konzeptuelle Wissensbasis (Conceptual Knowledge Base, CKB)

In der konzeptuellen Wissensbasis wird Allgemein- und Sachwissen des Systems mithilfe des Repräsentationsformalismus SB-ONE dargestellt [XTRA 87], einer Weiterentwicklung von KL-ONE. Die Vererbungshierarchie der Konzepte und die Individualisierungen sind in Partitionen eingeteilt, die die Pläne und Überzeugungen des Systems und des Benutzers widerspiegeln. Für die Generierung von besonderem Interesse ist die Partition SWMB (System Wants that Mutual Belief exist), die Ziele des Systems enthält, die durch eine Benutzer- oder Systemaktion erreicht werden sollen. Der Generator wird dann aktiviert, wenn entschieden worden ist, daß eine Ausgabe des Systems an den Benutzer notwendig ist.

b) Die Funktionalsemantische Struktur (Functional Semantic Structure, FSS)

Die funktionalsemantische Struktur, ebenfalls in SB-ONE implementiert, enthält in ihrem generellen Teil Wissen über semantisch wohlgeformte Ausdrücke der deutschen Sprache , d.h. es wird definiert, welche Prädikate zu sinnvollen Ausdrücken kombiniert werden können.

c) Das Dialoggedächtnis (Linguistic Dialog Memory, LDM)

Diese Wissensbasis, die den bisherigen Verlauf und die Struktur des Dialogs enthält, besteht aus drei Teilen:

– den referentiellen Objekten: für jedes neu eingeführte Objekt oder Ereignis in der konzeptuellen Wissensbasis wird ein solches Objekt angelegt. Bei jeder Erwähnung erhält es einen Eintrag, der aus der funktionalsemantischen Struktur und der Position im Dialogfolgegedächtnis besteht.

– dem Dialogfolgegedächtnis: in ihm wird die zeitliche Abfolge der referentiellen Objekte im Dialog vermerkt, welcher Dialogpartner es an dieser Stelle geäußert hat, welchen Fokuswert das Element hat und zu welchem Kontextraum es gehört.

– dem Dialogkontextmodell: mit Kontexträumen wird der Dialog thematisch und rhetorisch strukturiert (vgl. [Reichman 85]).

Für den Übergang zwischen den einzelnen Repräsentationsebenen stehen das semantische Lexikon (zwischen dem Ergebnis der syntaktischen Analyse und der funktionalsemantischen Struktur) und Interpretationsregeln (zwischen funktionalsemantischer Struktur und konzeptueller Wissensbasis) zur Verfügung.

3.3 Aufteilung des Generierungsprozesses: POPEL-W und POPEL-H

Ausgehend von der Partition SWMB der konzeptuellen Wissensbasis besteht die Aufgabe von POPEL in der Auswahl und Zeitlinearisierung von Teilen der konzeptuellen Wissensbasis sowie deren Verbalisierung. Zunächst wird die funktionalsemantische Struktur der Ausgabe erstellt, parallel dazu erfolgt die Wortwahl. Danach wird die dependenzgrammatische Struktur erzeugt, in der die Wortstämme mit den entsprechenden syntaktischen Merkmalen versehen werden. Diese Informationen erhält der Flexionsteil, der die morphologische Synthese durchführt.

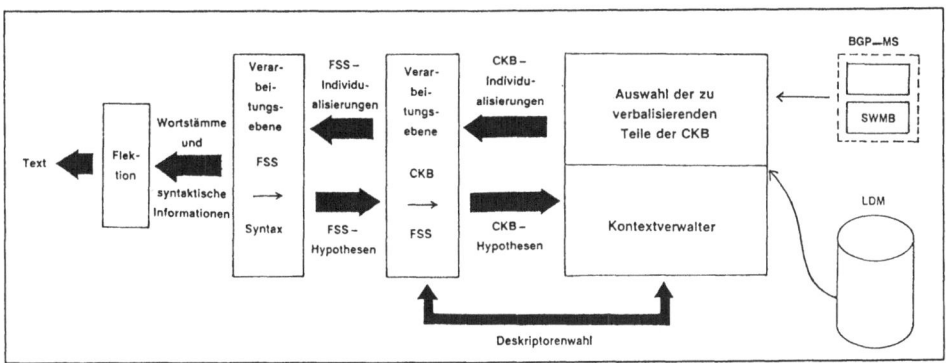

Figur 1: Architektur von POPEL

Es stellt sich die Frage, nach welchem der in Abschnitt 2 genannten Generierungsmodelle POPEL strukturiert werden soll. Das integrierte Modell hat den Nachteil, daß eine naheliegende Aufgabentrennung nicht mehr möglich ist und Wissen unterschiedlicher Art (z.B grammatikalisches und konzeptuelles) vom gleichen Planungsprozeß bearbeitet wird. Beim sequentiellen Modell wiederum erfolgt die Bestimmung des Inhalts ohne Rücksicht auf die Sprachstruktur. Die Umsetzung in einen Text kann dann z.B. aus syntaktischen Gründen eine Umordnung des Inhalts notwendig machen. Auch um dieses zu vermeiden, folgt POPEL dem *Modell mit Rückwirkungen* des realisierenden Teils auf den inhaltsfestlegenden. Ein wichtiges Prinzip der deutschen Sprache ist die *kommunikative Dynamik* [Sgall et al. 87]. Die Reihenfolge der Phrasen im deutschen Satz ist wesentlich vom aktuellen Dialogkontext beeinflußt. In einem Satz, der bereits teilweise verbalisiert wurde, restringieren aber auch die noch syntaktisch möglichen Leerstellen des Satzes die weitere Reihenfolge. In POPEL soll es Rückwirkungsmöglichkeiten des realisierenden Teils auf den inhaltsfestlegenden Teil geben, damit diese Restriktionen berücksichtigt werden können.

Die Schnittstelle ergibt sich aus den Strukturen, die verarbeitet werden: POPEL-W, der für die Auswahl und Linearisierung zuständige Teil, arbeitet über der konzeptuellen Wissensbasis, dem darin integrierten Benutzermodell und dem Dialoggedächtnis. POPEL-H, der Realisierungsteil, erhält diejenigen Teile der konzeptuellen Wissensbasis, deren Inhalte in der Ausgabe enthalten sein sollen, und erzeugt die entsprechenden natürlichsprachlichen Ausdrücke.

3.4 Interaktionsmöglichkeiten

Auf die Interaktionsmöglichkeiten in folgenden zwei Punkten soll in den nächsten beiden Abschnitten näher eingegangen werden:

– Inhaltsfestlegung

– Wahl der Deskriptionen

Interaktionen bei der Wortwahl und der Struktur der Sätze werden derzeit noch untersucht.

3.4.1 Satzinhalt

Um sprachstrukturelle Restriktionen berücksichtigen zu können, darf die Ausgabe nicht vollständig fertiggeplant an POPEL-H weitergegeben werden. Vielmehr soll das Vorgehen inkrementell sein.[2] Zu jedem Zeitpunkt während der Generierung muß festgelegt werden, welche Teile der konzeptuellen Wissensbasis an POPEL-H zur Verbalisierung übergeben werden sollen. Für diese Teile werden dann die entsprechenden funktionalsemantischen und syntaktischen Beschreibungen erzeugt. Falls dieser Vorgang nicht fortgesetzt werden kann, weil Informationen fehlen (z.B in der funktionalsemantischen Struktur ein notwendiger Teil eines Prädikats), werden für die fehlenden Teile Hypothesen erzeugt. Diese werden durch die Repräsentationsebenen, in deren entsprechenden Darstellungen, weitergegeben. Am Ende des Prozesses verfügt dann POPEL-W, in Form von Hypothesen der konzeptuellen Wissensbasis, über diejenigen Teile, die unter Beachtung sprachlicher Restriktionen in diesem (Teil-) Satz noch verbalisiert werden können oder müssen. Wichtig ist, daß die Information in einem Formalismus vorliegt, der sich nicht außerhalb der POPEL-W zugänglichen Wissensbasen befindet.

Zusätzliche Entscheidungskriterien, welche Teile der konzeptuellen Wissensbasis überhaupt an POPEL-H weitergegeben werden und in welcher Reihenfolge, sind die bisherige Dialogstruktur, das Wissen des Benutzers und eventuell Wissen darüber, wie die noch zu bearbeitenden Teile der konzeptuellen Wissensbasis strukturiert werden sollen.

3.4.2 Wahl der Deskriptionen

Für die Struktur und Form einer Deskription ist maßgebend, welches thematische Umfeld vorhanden ist und auf welche vorangegangenen Dialogteile sie sich möglicherweise beziehen kann. Diese Entscheidungen trifft der Kontextverwalter von POPEL-W, der im Gegensatz zu POPEL-H Zugriff auf das Dialoggedächtnis und das Benutzermodell hat. Trifft POPEL-H auf einen solchen Entscheidungspunkt, stellt er eine Anfrage an POPEL-W.

Mithilfe des Benutzermodells kann der Kontextverwalter von POPEL-W feststellen, ob die Deskription einer konzeptuellen Repräsentation dem Benutzer bekannt oder unbekannt ist. Ist sie nicht bekannt, erhält POPEL-H die Nachricht "unbekannt" und muß dann die funktionalsemantische Struktur und die Wörter neu berechnen. Die resultierende Phrase wird i.a. einen unbestimmten

---

[2] Im Unterschied zur inkrementellen Generierung in SOCCER [André et al., in diesem Band] soll in POPEL bereits vorliegendes Wissen strukturiert werden, wobei dieses unter Berücksichtigung sprachlicher Restriktionen auf Satzebene erfolgt. Im Gegensatz dazu reagiert SOCCER auf neu eintreffende Informationen in der zugrundeliegenden Repräsentation der Szene.

Artikel erhalten.

Bekannt ist die Deskription dann, wenn sie explizit oder implizit im Dialog erwähnt wurde, oder falls sie aus dem visuellen Kontext stammt. Der visuelle Kontext in XTRA ist die auf dem Bildschirm dargestellte Graphik, z.B. ein Lohnsteuerausgleichsformular. Bei visuell vorhandenen Objekten besteht also zusätzlich die Möglichkeit, Zeigegesten auf dem Bildschirm zu generieren. Einige Probleme, die sich daraus ergeben, sind in [Reithinger 87] dargestellt.

Für alle Deskriptionen aus dem impliziten verbalen Kontext müssen, wie bei unbekannten Deskriptionen, die funktionalsemantische Struktur und die Wörter berechnet werden. Allerdings kann ein definiter Artikel verwendet werden. Für Deskriptionen im expliziten verbalen Kontext, d.h. für solche die bereits erwähnt wurden, wird zunächst festgestellt, ob eine Anapher möglich ist. Dazu stellt der Kontextverwalter an POPEL-H die Anfrage, ob es aus syntaktischer Sicht überhaupt noch möglich ist, im gerade aktuellen Satz ein Prowort zu generieren. Falls nein, erhält POPEL-H die Nachricht, daß die bekannte Deskription, eventuell modifiziert, erneut verwendet wird. Ausgangspunkt in diesem Fall ist die bereits bekannte funktionalsemantische Struktur. Ist ein Prowort aus syntaktischer Sicht noch möglich, muß der Kontextverwalter bestimmen, ob es auch vom Dialogkontext her möglich ist. Die jeweilige Entscheidung wird POPEL-H mitgeteilt.

4. Derzeitiger Stand der Arbeiten

Nachdem die Grundlagen herausgearbeitet sind, konzentriert sich die derzeitige Arbeit an POPEL auf die Implementierung auf einer Symbolics Lispmaschine. POPEL-H wird im Rahmen von zwei Diplomarbeiten in einer Grundversion realisiert. Die Grundlage ist ein simulierter Parallelprozessor. Die Generierung soll als parallele Kaskade im Sinne Butterworth's [80] ablaufen. Der Autor arbeitet an der Implementierung von POPEL-W und der Dialogkontextwissensbasen.

5. Literatur

Appelt, D.E. (1985): Planning English Sentences. Cambridge, Cambridge University Press.

Bock, J.K (1987): Exploring Levels of Processing in Sentence Production. In: G. Kempen, ed.: Natural Language Generation. Dordrecht, Nijhoff.

Butterworth, B. (1980): Evidence from Pauses in Speech. In: B. Butterworth, ed.: Language Production (Vol. 1). London, Academic Press.

Danks, J.H. (1977): Producing Ideas and Sentences. In: S. Rosenberg, ed.: Sentence Production. Hillsdale, NJ., Lawrence Erlbaum Associates.

Garrett, M.F. (1980): Levels of Processing in Sentence Production. In: B.Butterworth, ed.: Language Production (Vol. 1). London, Academic Press.

Hovy, E.H. (1987): Some Pragmatic Decision Criteria in Generation. In: G. Kempen, ed.: Natural Language Generation. Dordrecht, Nijhoff.

McDonald, D.D. (1985): Surface Generation for a variety of applications. In: National Computer Conference 1985, 105-110.

McKeown, K.R. (1985): Text generation. Cambridge, Cambridge University Press.

Reichman, R. (1985): Getting Computers to Talk Like You and Me. Cambridge, MA., MIT Press.

Reithinger, N. (1987): Generating Referring Expressions and Pointing Gestures. In: G. Kempen, ed.: Natural Language Generation. Dordrecht, Nijhoff.

Sgall, P., Hajicova, E., Panevova, J. (1987): The Meaning of the Sentence in its Semantic and Pragmatic Aspects. Dordrecht, Reidel.

XTRA (1987): Abschlußbericht des Projekts XTRA für die Periode vom 1.4.1985 - 31.12.1987. Universität des Saarlandes.

How to say WHAT

—

IT or SOMETHING ?

Helmut Horacek

Research Unit for
Information Science and
Artificial Intelligence
University of Hamburg
2000 Hamburg 13
Mittelweg 179

Abstract

This paper deals with the nearly classical dichotomy whether or
not to partition the entire generation process into *'What to
say'* and *'How to say it'*. Evidence from practical systems is
collected in order to detect those properties which are inconsistent with the chosen approach of the system with respect to
the dichotomy. The reason for these failures is examined
which, in our view, lies in various aspects of limitations of
the representation and availability of knowledge. An attempt
is made to formulate necessary conditions that enable a strict
partition into *'What'* and *'How'* and the potential benefit of
such a design is sketched out.

Introduction

The topic of this workshop is a discussion of the nearly classical
paradigm of partitioning the entire process of natural language generation into two sections concerned with 'What to say' and 'How to say
something'. It is not clear whether this neutral form has been chosen
consciously in the announcement of the workshop. The commonly used
form, 'How to say *it*', explicitly expresses a separation of these two
sections, a principle, which actually is adopted by most of the
researchers in the field. In particular, the design of the most ambitious natural language generators MUMBLE [10] and TEXT [11] is oriented
on this principle.

In practice, however, the envisioned separation has not been consequently followed in all detail by these and many other systems. There
exists comparatively few works in which an intertwined schema is
favoured with conceptual and linguistic knowledge mixed up to some extent. Apart from early programs working in a very narrow domain with
only a small coverage (for instance LUNAR [18]), mainly Appelt [2] has
taken a counter position to the currently dominant view.

WHAT TO SAY   **HOW TO SAY SOMETHING**

cognitive domain   *linguistic domain*

```
+--------------------------+
|determine       discourse |
|goals    to  be  achieved |
+--------------------------+

+--------------------------+
|select   speechacts    to |
|express  discourse  goals |
+--------------------------+

+--------------------------+
|select      propositional |
|content   to be  conveyed |
+--------------------------+

   +--------------------------+
   |choose        appropriate |
   |rhetorical    constructs  |
   +--------------------------+

   +--------------------------+
   |categorize    the    con- |
   |tent    into    relevant  |
   |and    optional     parts |
   +--------------------------+

      +--------------------------+
      |determine    the   proper |
      |order      of      output |
      |(what   to   say   next)  |
      +--------------------------+

         +--------------------------+
         |determine        suitable |
         |parameters    of    style |
         +--------------------------+

            +--------------------------+
            |choose   lexical    items |
            |and grammatical functions |
            +--------------------------+

               +--------------------------+
               |determine sentence topic  |
               |and    voice    according |
               |to   the   intended focus |
               +--------------------------+

                  +--------------------------+
                  |perform a partition into  |
                  |sentences   and   clauses |
                  +--------------------------+

                  +--------------------------+
                  |create    anaphora    for |
                  |multiple       references |
                  +--------------------------+

                     +--------------------------+
                     |verify the overall gram-  |
                     |maticality of the result  |
                     +--------------------------+

                     +--------------------------+
                     |linearize   syntax   tree |
                     |(establish   word  order) |
                     +--------------------------+

                     +---------------------------+
                     |consider        morphology |
                     |(establish word endings)   |
                     +---------------------------+
```

Figure 1:

    Subtasks / decisions in the generation pro-
cess grouped according to the degree of dominance of cognitive or linguistic aspects

In this paper we will start with a characterization of the numerous subtasks of the complex generation process with respect to our thematic distinction. Examples from several generators are consulted in order to collect evidence for the reasons for the difficulties they are facing in the attempt to properly separate *'What'* from *'How'*. Methodological inconsistencies in this respect are caused, in our view, by various aspects of limitations in the adequate representation of knowledge, and by incompleteness or unavailability of knowledge in a given environment. A contribution to the dispute is constituted by an attempt to intuitively formulate necessary conditions which justify a strict separation into the two main processes and by sketching out the expected benefit.

Subtasks of generation

A wide range of subtasks involving plenty of decisions has to be performed before the production of text from a conceptual representation is completed. When a certain decision has been made, this can put further constraints on some other decisions to be made later in the entire generation process. This situation suggests the impression of a complex network of dependencies whose influence on single components may differ quite significantly.

In Figure 1 an enumeration of the major subtasks is presented. The order in which they are listed corresponds to their usual order of activation in a purely sequential process. This correlates quite naturally with the dominance of the conceptual viz. linguistic domain associated with each of them. The distance from the margins in placing the subtasks is intended to indicate the degree of dominance of either the cognitive or the linguistic aspects.

In the extreme cases there is no doubt about the categorization of a certain subtask. For instance, the selection of discourse goals is a purely cognitive task, while the consideration of morphology concerns only the linguistic domain.

In other cases the points of decision can be selected in such a way that they can be placed conveniently in a specific domain. Nevertheless, there is a good deal of influence from conceptual decision points on potential choices in the linguistic part. A typical example is the (conceptual) selection of the focus (of an utterance) which is the basis for a decision about a topicalization or the selection of the passive voice in the linguistic part, among others. In fact, there almost exists a direct influence, but a clear separation is still possible in this case.

The key problems are more or less concerned with the selection of lexical items (and grammatical functions) which is a manifestation of the transition from the cognitive to the linguistic domain. This is also one of the 'decision points' in Hovy's model [4] , when the control is temporarily passed from the 'production' component back to the 'planning' component. Other points of decision concern the content and the organization of sentences, which is pretty much related to the choice of words. A similar system architecture is sketched out in this workshop [15] .

A big difficulty in the transition from the cognitive to the linguistic level is constituted by different formalisms which have proved useful (for instance, semantic networks versus functional descriptions) and by the different information content of the primitives in either level.

Evidence from practical systems

The generator MUMBLE written by McDonald [10] , which is a linguistic component, produces text from a plan consisting of 'messages'. It assumes all conceptual decisions to be made by a previously run planning component. This component, however, is allowed to occasionally select lexical items already in the planning phase, thus anticipating and preempting later choices. This procedure is described in [8] McDonald states that this feature is applied most sensitively when basic information units can be combined into a useful 'package'. He mentions the realization of an object's beginning and ending by the word 'between' and the selection of a term such as 'get revenge' instead of simply stating the underlying events.

One might think that the option of such an early lexical decision may be useful in order to arrive quickly at a reasonable verbalization. Unexpectedly, the use of this option proves to be absolutely necessary in the actual system, which becomes clear after a view on the structure of plans actually used. They are represented in form of scripts, which makes it impossible to adequately express and maintain the internal relations between objects of different granularity. McDonald also identifies the considerable difference in 'packaging' as a key problem to bridge the gap between elements of the knowledge base and possible wordings in natural language.

We will perform a closer examination of the two examples mentioned before which, in fact, present rather different examples of 'packaging'. Intuitively, it does not seem to be too difficult to pass the option of selecting the word 'between' to the linguistic component. However, we suspect that the problem in this case lies in the missing possibility to specify in the planning language a preference of this lexicalization over the other feasible choices. Moreover, this preselection puts severe constraints on the potential realizations of the temporal beginning and ending (they must be mapped onto NP's), a fact which the planner must foresee.

The way of selecting a term like 'get revenge', on the other hand, points to the difficulty of representing in a sufficiently accurate manner the relations between events and emotional states and their (potential) consequences. Facing such a constellation it is very hard to imagine a mapping mechanism which exhibits a minimal degree of generality rather than being valid for particular lexemes or certain chunks of a conceptual representation only. The precise definition of overlaps and gaps in such a mapping presents a considerable problem. Consequently, it seems to be a feasible assumption that the information in the knowledge base is not organized subtle enough so that the selection of a lexeme bearing such a complex meaning could be left to the linguistic component.

Several approaches have particularly addressed the problem of mapping some kind of conceptual representation onto words that express a different amount of propositional content. Unlike many other systems, VIE-LANG [3] makes a clear distinction between the conceptual and the linguistic level. The general idea has been elaborated accurately for the concept denoting an 'object transfer', thus providing the potential to sensitively discriminate between possible verbalizations. According to the context in the actual instance a verb like 'to get', 'to sell' or 'to exchange' may be chosen. A strong point in this work is the (at least partial) symmetry that is present in the mapping from and onto the conceptual representation. Unfortunately, there is no evidence up to now, to what extent this kind of representation is beneficial when confronted with the evaluation of a certain request.

There is an even more detailed elaboration of this mapping process in the system NAOS [13] and [14] whose aim is the description of a filmed traffic scene with emphasis on the selection of appropriate motion verbs. The starting point of the entire process is the primary data which is available in a form that indicates the position and orientation of single objects over a certain time interval. Event models which are associated with verbs are matched against this primary data. This is done recursively, so that verbs expressing quite complex actions can be used to describe compound events.

In this domain and at the chosen level of accuracy it apparently has been possible to associate all event models with a suitable motion verb. We suspect that the selection process would be more complicated if such a direct correspondence is not always available. In the actual approach only the first step in this mechanism is the transition from purely cognitive information to information which is, at least, associated with linguistic information. In the following steps a motion verb associated with an event model serves two purposes:

- indicating an appropriate verbalization (a linguistic choice)

- being a key for the matching process to address more complex event models (a conceptual purpose)

Additionally, it would be very interesting to imagine an enhancement of this system where the use of several levels of granularity is required in order to draw inferences or to make some other kind of evaluation rather than only mapping between levels of expressibility. For instance, the system is able to produce a description like 'A red BMW overtook a yellow VW on Schlueterstreet and stopped in front of the traffic light'. It is not evident, how this mechanism is sensitively augmented so that it prefers this utterance to an almost identical one where 'stopped' is replaced by 'was standing'. When the original description is extended by 'and it got into a parking space', the clause expressing the 'stopping' event is inferable and can therefore be left out. The inference to be drawn in this case is clearly on the level of events, i. e. on the conceptual level, but not on its primary data which is object centred.

In any case, the (primary) knowledge is organized according to the nature of the domain which is completely different to the linguistic need. This way, several levels of granularity have been bridged in the entire mapping process maintaining a clear separation of linguistic and conceptual knowledge.

The transition from conceptual structures to linguistic descriptions also is treated very explicitly in Mellish's work [12] . His program is able to generate natural language instructions from plans which consist of non-linguistic objects called messages. The transition, which he calls compositional structure building, is done by using a set of rules that map from local message patterns to functional descriptions, the chosen linguistic representation. The task of optimizing the output is performed on the level of messages. It is done by applying the established method of algebraic operations expressed by a set of rewrite rules.

While it is clear that not all kind of optimization can and should be done at this stage, it contributes to the task of specifying what is possible (and desirable) on the merely conceptual level. Whereas the generated text is fairly comprehensible, its informativeness has been judged to be comparatively low. This is, at least partially, caused by missing causal relations in the plans. Moreover, they frequently do not express the right level of detail to be really useful to a human being. This again is in the responsibility of an adequate representation of knowledge.

A further example for a clear transition from the conceptual to the linguistic level is presented by Roesner [16] in this workshop. The rhetorical predicate 'EMPHASIZE-NEGATIVE' can be expressed by 'trotz', 'zwar - aber' or other connectives. Additionally, this involves restrictions on the category of the respective fillers (a clause or a noun phrase).

In order to address the optimization problem Mann and Moore use a wide variety of aggregation and preference rules in their Knowledge Delivery System KDS [7] . The former look similar to the algebraic simplification rules used by Mellish. The latter produce or modify numerical estimates for (parts of) the resulting text thus guiding a sensitive selection of the aggregation rules. Unlike in the previously discussed approach it is not clear to what extent the aggregation rules operate on conceptual or linguistic data, nor if there is some clear transition. The rules cover a wide range of operations. In the simplest form, they denote purely algebraic changes like combining two conditions with logically inverse premises into a 'then-otherwise' construct. On the other hand, the presented examples contain the semantically complex conjunction 'whenever'; it is not clear, how it is distinguished from 'if' or 'then' in the knowledge base other than by denoting the respective lexeme. Furthermore, there is a fairly complex rule which contains 'determine' on both sides and 'decide' on the right side. These observations create the impression that this set of rules, in fact, works on the linguistic level rather than on the conceptual one.

The TEXT system [11] , written by Kathy McKeown consists of a strategic and a tactical component which reflect, in general, the partition in 'What to say' and 'How to say it'. For instance, the availability of purely semantic information can influence the selection of the most suitable rhetorical schema. However, there is an inaccuracy in this respect concerning the selection of lexical items again. McKeown admits that 'the predicate semantics thus defined for TEXT are particular to a data base system and would have to be redefined if the schemata were to be used in another type of system'. Thus, TEXT relies on the possibility of an easy and straightforward mapping from the database attributes onto appropriate lexemes. Therefore, it is hard to imagine the system reacting adequately to requests whose evaluation involves some inferencing on the semantics of the database attributes.

So far, we have merely considered the work based on the separation of conceptual and linguistic decisions. In his work on 'Planning English Referring Expressions' Appelt [2] argues that no such modularization seems to be obvious to him, since the distinction between 'What' and 'How' becomes merely two points on a continuum between goal-satisfaction and rule-satisfaction processes. However, we feel that the continuum view intuitively does not look very convincing. We think that the traditional view assuming a series of subtasks including a separation between 'What' and 'How' occurring somewhere seems to be more plausible.

Appelt's view is realized in a smooth and natural control mechanism that mainly determines 'What to say'. At certain points a transition to lexical items and syntactic structures (only partially filled at the same time) is performed which, somehow disappointing, is straightforward in all occurrences presented. For instance, a 'remove' action is expressed by the identical verb and the instrument of this action is mapped onto the respective case slot. The planning language looks conceptually well organized according to the modelled processes, also at intermediate levels. However, the ontology of the planning language seems to be pretty well accomodated to the envisioned verbalization. The goal state 'not attached' triggers the demand for a 'remove' action which is further specified as 'unfasten' by a particular instrument. It is not clear how these primitives can be sensibly combined in the phase of plan generation. Furthermore, it seems to be quite significant that 'English' as the target language is explicitly mentioned in the title.

Thus, the system does not really represent a convincing counter position to the work oriented on the separation of 'What' and 'How'. Appelt's contribution lies, in our view, mainly in the design of a flexible control mechanism including, in particular, satisfaction of multiple goals.

Prerequisites and design criteria for a clear partition

So far, we have collected evidence from practical systems where various approaches were confronted with different problems concerning the transition from the cognitive to the linguistic level. Apart from NAOS and Mellish's program (and VIE-LANG, to some extent) none of the examined approaches has significant ontological differences between the representation on the cognitive and on the linguistic level. The effort spent on these systems creates the impression that the difficulty to produce a clear mapping mechanism is comparable to the complexity of present approaches to the subtasks of 'What' or 'How'.

In many systems, it is not clear where the content words really come in, be it in MUMBLE's 'messages' or in the 'protosentences' used by KDS. Slightly exaggerated, one might say that the effectively dominant approach is the determination of 'What to say' in an environment where a part of 'How to say something' (in terms of the content words) has already been decided upon.

When such a clear partition is envisioned in a convincing way we have to distinguish carefully two disjoint aspects:

- a separation into two components and a precise definition of the intermediate representation

- the execution of the associated processes in a strictly sequential order

The second aspect is not necessarily a consequence of the first one. On the contrary, it is desirable to adopt a more flexible control mechanism which greatly can enhance the efficiency in a fairly complex system. For instance, flexibility is of importance in case a paraphrase for a certain object or event is to be generated. The need ultimately is recognized by linguistic processes, whereas the necessary information must be accessed from the cognitive representation level. In principle, it is possible to provide all eventually required information in advance, but this includes a considerable overhead. On the other hand, when only the actually required information is provided (at a later stage), the result is a reduction of the overall effort. The preparation of optional information, that proves to be of no relevance later, simply has been cut off at an early stage.

The partitioning paradigm, however, has been adopted as a matter of convenience and as a heuristic from the engineering point of view, but its application surely is of more importance. When adopting the text quality as the main criterion for a preference or refusal of a strict partition, the decision (in a *theoretical* sense) can be transferred to the answer of the key question:

- Can a good overall result be achieved by selecting the most promising content and rhetorical turns to express the present discourse goals irrespective of the available linguistic capability to realize them, or

- can limitations and unbalanced skill in the linguistic part cause a revision of the results coming from the planning phase?

In other words, can the best realization of the plan occasionally be so bad that the realization of the second or third best plan is superior? Unfortunately, evidence from human behaviour does not clarify this question: People usually produce a great variety of text in comparable situations, which may differ significantly in the selection of information and application of rhetorical turns. But it is far from clear to what extent their behaviour is motivated by the difference in linguistic skill or by personal preferences concerning style, argumentation or even discourse goals.

In any case, the *practical* problems in partitioning the generation task must be solved which seems to be a very hard task. This part of the problem correlates with the possibility to precisely define the information derivable from the cognitive knowledge that has an effect on the linguistic decisions. In the first section, only the consequences of purely cognitive decisions have to be completely executed, while those involving linguistic decisions as well have to deliver appropriate specifications to the intermediate representation. Finally, an adequate intermediate representation for that purpose has to be found following the guidelines sketched out previously.

The representation on its own has been tackled very differently in the whole area of text generation. A lot of effort has been spent on designing and representing grammars, but comparatively few has been done concerning the representation of cognitive knowledge, knowledge about the user and about discourse. The same applies to the representation of knowledge concerning the transition from the cognitive to the linguistic level. The work in this subfield has been concentrated on defining the suitable data and designing appropriate processes rather than on the *representation* of the involved knowledge. In most cases, it has been fairly accomodated to the main goal of the respective system, neglecting the option to serve multiple purposes.

Among others, the representation problem has been identified as a considerable shortage in a workshop on generation chaired by Mann [5] . Unlike some other kind of evaluation processes which may work successfully on the basis of only shallow knowledge, generation of good quality text seems to be a subtle task which needs a rich knowledge representation. Therefore, most work that is intended to adopt a strict partition does not consequently obey to it in every detail. Conceivably, none of the existing generators is able to produce a considerably rich variety of verbalizations and has a reasonable amount of discourse knowledge and capability. Therefore, it is hard to believe that a revision of the discourse strategy really can be caused by the capability of the linguistic component.

Goals of generation in a broader context

As a working hypothesis we assume that neither the actual coverage nor the specific language used in the linguistic component of a generator significantly influence the conceptual and rhetorical decisions in the challenge of optimizing the overall quality of the produced text. This is consistent with Roesner's view [16] who argues that further progress in generation can only be achieved by improving the generation of content. Consequently, he considers the 'tactical' components to be the strong(er) part. When we are able to define a priori an adequate intermediate representation we can concentrate our effort in the separate design of two processes:

- a (really) language independent planning component that determines 'What to say'

- a domain independent linguistic component that determines the best way of 'How to say *it*' (rather than something)

The effort can then be concentrated on finding general discourse capabilities and common properties in different domains of application in order to reduce a duplication of effort in the first component. Adequate solutions for language specific problems and identification of common properties of several languages are the aims of the second part. When the development of separated components with a well-defined link can be achieved the complexity introduced by different domains and languages is greatly reduced.

Another challenge is the design of an efficient flow of control between the two components. This is also a field to model human behaviour, be it in producing online text (modelling spontaneous speech like McDonald [9] does) or in producing stepwise refined text (modelling the process of writing, the approach favoured by Mann [6] and also by McDonald [17], more recently). Particular control problems (for instance, only partially instantiated case frames) arise in a time-dependent environment like the description of time-variant scenes which is the domain of the SOCCER system [1] .

To summarize, progress in achieving a strict partition into *'What'* and *'How'* (envisaging more coverage of the components and, consequently, of a complete system) involves the following tasks:

- a (conceptual) representation of an utterance, including parameters that express conceptual decisions

- a representation of the transition from the conceptual to the linguistic level by defining a mapping from conceptual units onto lexical items and grammatical functions

- the evaluation of conceptual parameters for linguistic decisions

- an evaluation method by which a judgement of the (possibly conflicting) satisfaction of rhetorical needs and stylistic preferences can be obtained

- the design of a convincing architecture, putting special emphasis on an efficient flow of control

References

1. E. Andre, T. Rist, and G. Herzog, "Generierung natuerlichsprachlicher Aeusserungen zur simultanen Beschreibung von zeitveraenderlichen Szenen," in *GWAI-87*, ed. K. Morik, Springer Verlag, Berlin, 1987.

2. D. Appelt, "Planning English Referring Expressions," *Artificial Intelligence*, vol. 26, no. 1, pp. 1-33, North-Holland, Amsterdam, 1985.

3. E. Buchberger, E. Leinfellner, I. Steinacker, R. Trappl, and H. Trost, "VIE-LANG, A German Language Understanding System," *Cybernetics and Systems Research*, pp. 851-856, North-Holland, Amsterdam, 1982.

4. Eduard H. Hovy, "Integrating Text Planning and Production in Generation," in *Proceedings IJCAI-85*, pp. 848-851, Los Angeles, 1985.

5. W. Mann, "Proceedings of the Workshop - Text Generation," *AJCL*, vol. 8, no. 2, pp. 62-69, 1982.

6. W. Mann, "An Overview of the Penman Text Generation System," in *AAAI-83*, pp. 261-265, 1983.

7. W.C. Mann and J.A. Moore, "Computer Generation of Multiparagraph English Text," *AJCL*, vol. 7, no. 1, pp. 17-29, 1981.

8. D. McDonald and J. Pustejovsky, "Description-Directed Natural Language Generation," in *Proceedings IJCAI-85*, pp. 799-805, Los Angeles, 1985.

9. D. McDonald and J. Pustejowsky, "A Computational Theory of Prose Style for Natural Language Generation," in *Proceedings EACL-85*, pp. 187-193, Genf, 1985.

10. D.D. McDonald, "Language Generation: The Linguistics Component," *IJCAI-77*, vol. 1, p. 142, Cambridge, Massachussets, 1977.

11. K.R. McKeown, "Discourse Strategies for Generating Natural-Language Text," *Artificial Intelligence*, vol. 27, no. 1, pp. 1-41, 1985.

12. C. Mellish, "Natural Language Generation from Plans," Proceedings of 1st European Workshop on Natural Language Generation, M. Zock, 1987.

13. H.-J. Novak, "Language and Vision," in *GWAI-83*, ed. B. Neumann, pp. 100-107, Springer-Verlag, Berlin, 1983.

14. H.-J. Novak, "A Relational Matching Strategy for Temporal Event Recognition," in *GWAI-84*, ed. J. Laubsch, pp. 109-118, Springer-Verlag, Berlin, 1984.

15. N. Reithinger, "Ein erster Blick auf POPEL - Wie wird was gesagt?," in *GWAI-87*, ed. K. Morik, Springer Verlag, Berlin, 1987.

16. D. Roesner, "Generation of content vs. generation of form: A review of recent work in the SEMSYN project," in *GWAI-87*, ed. K. Morik, Springer Verlag, Berlin, 1987.

17. M. Vaughan and D. McDonald, "A Model of Revision in Natural Language Generation," in *ACL Proceedings*, pp. 90-96, New York, 1986.

18. W. Woods, "The Lunar Sciences Natural Language System," BBN report 2378, Cambridge, MA., 1972.

Generierung natürlichsprachlicher Äußerungen zur simultanen Beschreibung von zeitveränderlichen Szenen

Elisabeth André, Thomas Rist, Gerd Herzog

Fachbereich 10 - Informatik IV
Universität des Saarlandes
Im Stadtwald 15
D-6600 Saarbrücken 11

Abstract

Die automatische Erzeugung simultaner Beschreibungen zeitveränderlicher Szenen bringt eine in bisherigen Generierungssystemen nicht berücksichtigte Problematik zum Vorschein. Da die Beschreibung nicht a posteriori, sondern simultan zum Ablauf der Szene erfolgt, ist der vollständige Verlauf der Szene zum Zeitpunkt der Sprachproduktion unbekannt. Bei der Koordination von Wahrnehmung und Sprachproduktion sind zeitliche Aspekte wie Dauer der Textgenerierung und Dekodierzeit des Hörers bzw. Lesers zu berücksichtigen.

Der vorliegende Bericht* untersucht die sich durch die Situation der Simultanbeschreibung ergebenden Konsequenzen in bezug auf die Frage, welche Information über die Szene in welcher Form mitgeteilt werden soll. Anhand zweier Beispielszenen wird das Zusammenwirken von Ereigniserkennung und Sprachproduktion in dem von uns entwickelten System SOCCER erläutert.

1. Motivation

Die vorliegende Arbeit befaßt sich mit der simultanen Generierung natürlichsprachlicher Beschreibungen zeitveränderlicher Szenen. In Analogie zur simultanen Berichterstattung soll eine Szenenfolge, bereits während sie beobachtet wird, in natürlicher Sprache beschrieben werden.

Charakteristisch für die simultane Berichterstattung ist die Tatsache, daß während der Sprechzeit neue Information über die Szene gewonnen wird. Aus Analysen von Fußballdirektreportagen (vgl. [Rosenbaum 69] oder [Brandt 83]) sind u.a. die folgenden Phänomene bekannt: Kann ein Reporter mit seinen Äußerungen dem aktuellen Szenengeschehen nicht folgen, so reagiert er zur Minimierung dieser zeitlichen Differenz häufig mit Raffung (statt wohlgeformter Sätze werden nur Satzfragmente verwendet), Erhöhung der Sprechgeschwindigkeit, Auslassung ganzer Teilszenen oder unerwartetem Themenwechsel. Für den Fall, daß wenig neues über das Szenengeschehen zu berichten ist, wird entsprechend mit Dehnung, Sprechpause bzw. Nachdokumentation reagiert.

---

* Die hier beschriebene Arbeit wurde teilweise unterstützt vom SFB 314 "Künstliche Intelligenz und Wissensbasierte Systeme" der DFG, Teilprojekt NS2: VIsual TRAnslator.

Die Konzeption eines Systems, das in Analogie zur simultanen Berichterstattung eine sukzessiv gegebene Szenenfolge analysieren und das aktuell erkannte Geschehen mittels Sprache beschreiben soll, wird sich von Systemen zur Erstellung einer natürlichsprachlichen A-posteriori-Beschreibung zeitveränderlicher Szenen (vgl. u.a. [Novak 86]) mindestens in bezug auf die folgenden beiden Punkte unterscheiden:

(1) Bei der simultanen Beschreibung zeitveränderlicher Szenen ist zum Zeitpunkt der Textgenerierung der vollständige Verlauf der Szene noch unbekannt.

(2) Zeitliche Aspekte wie Dauer der Textgenerierung oder Dekodierzeit des Hörers bzw. Lesers spielen eine grundlegende Rolle bei der zeitlichen Koordination von Wahrnehmung und Sprechen.

Für die Prozesse, die entscheiden, welche Information über die Szene in welcher Form mitgeteilt wird, ergeben sich hieraus unmittelbar die folgenden Konsequenzen:

- Die Planung von Äußerungen kann sich immer nur auf einen zeitlich begrenzten Szenenausschnitt beziehen. Die Entwicklung von Strategien zur Strukturierung größerer Texteinheiten (vgl. [McKeown 85] oder [Novak 86]) ist daher nicht möglich.

- Bereits getroffene Entscheidungen müssen unter Umständen zurückgenommen werden.
Bei der simultanen Berichterstattung ist von einer starken Beeinflussung des Sprachproduktionsprozesses durch das unmittelbar Wahrgenommene auszugehen. Durch das Eintreten neuer herausragender Ereignisse können frühere Ereignisse, die selektiert wurden, um eventuell mitgeteilt zu werden, in so hohem Maße an Relevanz verlieren, daß sie nicht mehr genannt werden sollten.

- Der genaue Inhalt einer Äußerung ergibt sich häufig erst während des Sprechens.
Die von Kempen und Hoenkamp (vgl. [Kempen 77], [Kempen/Hoenkamp 82]) beobachtete und maschinell simulierte inkrementelle Sprachproduktion auf Satzebene ist bei Simultanreportagen oftmals dadurch zu erklären, daß ein Sprecher bereits über ein Ereignis berichtet, während es sich gerade erst entwickelt. In diesem Fall muß u.U. der Enkodierprozeß solange unterbrochen werden, bis die restliche Information (z.B. das Ziel einer Bewegung) vorliegt.

In dem System SOCCER [André et al. 87], das in Form von Bildfolgen gegebene Szenen aus Fußballspielen mittels natürlichsprachlicher Äußerungen simultan zum Szenenablauf beschreibt, können die bei der simultanen Berichterstattung durch zeitliche Restriktionen auftretenden Phänomene genauer untersucht werden. Im Gegensatz zu realen Fußballreportagen sind die von SOCCER erzeugten Beschreibungen rein sachlich; charakteristische Merkmale des Jargons der Fußballreportage bleiben unberücksichtigt. Die Diskurssituation ist dadurch gekennzeichnet, daß das Szenengeschehen einem Hörer mitgeteilt wird, der die Szene nicht selbst beobachten kann, wobei jedoch der statische Szenenhintergrund als prototypisch bekannt vorausgesetzt wird. Bevor wir näher auf die in SOCCER vorhandenen Komponenten zur Sprachproduktion eingehen, soll zunächst geklärt werden, welche Annahmen über Wahrnehmung und Sprachproduktion bei der Konzeption des Systems SOCCER zugrundegelegt wurden.

2. Wahrnehmung und Sprachproduktion

Unter dem Begriff Wahrnehmung verstehen wir in diesem Rahmen die Erfassung und Verarbeitung visueller Information bis hin zur Interpretation und Aggregation des Wahrgenommenen zu konzeptuellen Einheiten. Der *Wahrnehmungsprozeß* leistet insbesondere die Wahrnehmung von Ereignissen. Grundlegend für diesen Prozeß ist die auch aus psychologischer Sicht vertretbare Annahme, daß in der Szene gleichzeitig auftretende Ereignisse bis zu einem gewissen Grad gleichzeitig wahrgenommen werden. Bei unserer Arbeit sind wir von einer propositionalen Repräsentation [1] des Wahrgenommenen ausgegangen.

---

[1] Möglichkeiten zur Repräsentation visuell wahrgenommener Information werden in [Norman/Rumelhart 78] diskutiert.

Für den *Sprachproduktionsprozeß* wird in mehreren sprachpsychologischen Modellen eine Aufteilung in die Teilprozesse *Fokussierung*, *Selektion/Linearisierung* und *sprachliche Enkodierung* vorgeschlagen (vgl. [Herrmann 85]).

- Der *Fokussierungsprozeß* aktiviert die nichtverbalen Strukturen, über die gesprochen werden soll. Hierunter fällt sowohl die Bereitstellung von unmittelbar aus dem Wahrnehmungsprozeß gewonnener Information als auch die Aktivierung von Gedächtnisinhalten (z.B. wenn zur Objektreferenzierung Hintergrundwissen herangezogen werden muß).
- Die Auswahl und Anordnung der fokussierten Strukturen erfolgt durch *Selektions* - bzw. *Linearisierungsprozesse.*
- Unter *sprachlicher Enkodierung* wird die Kodierung nichtverbaler Information mittels Sprache verstanden. Ergebnis dieses Prozesses kann eine akustische Sprachausgabe oder geschriebener Text sein.

Obwohl in verschiedenen psychologischen Arbeiten die Beziehung zwischen Wahrnehmung und Sprachproduktion untersucht wird (z.B. in [Osgood 71] oder [Ertel 77]), werden in der Regel keine konkreten Aussagen über die zeitliche Koordination dieser Prozesse gemacht.[2] Für die maschinelle Erzeugung einer simultanen Szenenbeschreibung ist es jedoch unerläßlich, den Wahrnehmungsprozeß und den Sprachproduktionsprozeß zeitlich zu koordinieren.

Beim Wahrnehmungsprozeß vernachlässigen wir zur Vereinfachung die Zeit für Reizleitung und Reizverarbeitung. Das Szenengeschehen wird also simultan zu seinem realen Ablauf wahrgenommen; die Dauer des Wahrnehmungsprozesses wird somit als unmittelbar zur Szenendauer korrespondierend angenommen.

Für den Sprachproduktionsprozeß bietet sich eine Untersuchung der zeitlichen Dauer des sprachlichen Enkodierprozesses an. In der Regel wird ein Sprecher seine akustische Artikulation zeitlich so koordinieren, daß seine Äußerungen für den Hörer verständlich sind. Für den Fall der verbalen Kommunikation läßt sich der zeitliche Aspekt des Enkodierprozesses mittels empirischer Methoden konkretisieren (z.B. durch Messung der Sprechzeit [3]). Wird als Kodierungsform geschriebener Text gewählt (z.B. Wiedergabe des Textes auf einem Bildschirm), so ist auch hier die Dekodierzeit des Rezipienten als Grundlage einer sinnvollen Festlegung der zeitlichen Dauer eines maschinellen Enkodierprozesses zu berücksichtigen. An dieser Stelle sei auf psychologische Untersuchungen zur Wahrnehmung von Wort und Text verwiesen (vgl. [Carpenter/Just 86]).

Im Gegensatz zu dem von einer ähnlichen Problemstellung ausgehenden System COMMENTATOR [Sigurd 84] liegt der Schwerpunkt unserer Arbeit nicht in der Realisierung eines Sprachsyntheseprozesses, sondern in der Erarbeitung eines Modells zur Koordination von Wahrnehmung und Sprache, das die Computersimulation typischer bei Direktreportagen auftretender Phänomene erlaubt.

3. Das System SOCCER

Bei der Kopplung von bildverstehenden mit natürlichsprachlichen Systemen wurden bisher nur Ansätze verfolgt, die eine retrospektive Beschreibung der analysierten zeitveränderlichen Szene zum Ziel haben. Der Schritt von einer solchen A-posteriori-Vorgehensweise zur simultanen natürlichsprachlichen Beschreibung erfordert zum einen die Anwendung einer inkrementellen Ereigniserkennungsstrategie, zum anderen müssen Ereigniserkennung und Sprachproduktion entsprechend koordiniert werden. Diesen Anforderungen wurde bei der Konzeption des Systems SOCCER Rechnung getragen.

---

[2] Eine Ausnahme bildet die Arbeit von Pechmann (vgl. [Pechmann 84]), die sich mit den kognitiven Vorgängen bei der Referenzierung von Objekten befaßt. Die dazu entwickelten Überlegungen werden in einem Modell zusammengefaßt, das sowohl Wahrnehmung als auch Sprachproduktion als Komponenten integriert.

[3] Diesbezügliche Untersuchungen für Fußballdirektreportagen werden in [Rosenbaum 69] beschrieben.

Ausgehend von einer in Form einer Kamerabildfolge gegebenen zeitveränderlichen Realweltszene erzeugt ein *Bildfolgenanalysesystem* eine geometrische Beschreibung der in der Szene sichtbaren Objekte und deren Trajektorien. Zusammen mit dem Wissen über den statischen Szenenhintergrund bildet diese geometrische Bildfolgenbeschreibung die Eingabe für das System SOCCER. Derzeit werden diese Daten noch mit Hilfe eines speziell entwickelten *Trajektorieneditors* [Herzog 86] manuell erzeugt.

Ereignisse werden konzeptuell durch *Ereignismodelle* beschrieben - das Auftreten eines Ereignisses entspricht einer Instantiierung des entsprechenden generischen Ereignismodells (vgl. [Neumann 82]). In SOCCER umfaßt ein Ereignismodell neben Restriktionen für die an einem Ereignis beteiligten Objekte ein Ablaufschema. Das Ablaufschema spezifiziert sowohl die Sub-Ereignisse als auch den situativen Kontext, der in einer Szene beobachtbar sein muß, um von einem Auftreten des entsprechenden Ereignisses sprechen zu können. Um auch teilweise erkannte Ereignisse in propositionaler Form repräsentieren zu können, wurden entsprechende Prädikate definiert. Während beispielsweise das Prädikat $ACTIVE(\langle timemark\rangle \langle event\rangle)$ dann erfüllt ist, falls das Ereignis $\langle event\rangle$ zum Zeitpunkt $\langle timemark\rangle$ auftritt, markieren die Prädikate *TRIGGER* und *STOP* den Beginn bzw. das Ende eines Ereignisses (vgl. [Rist et al. 87]).

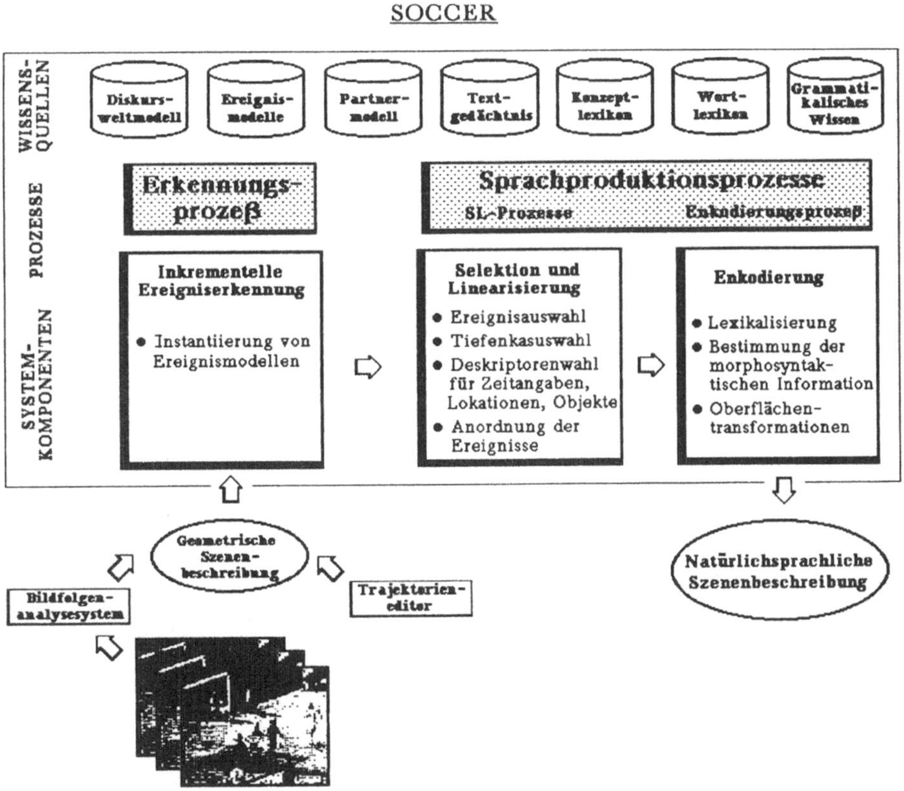

SOCCER

Abb.1: Systemarchitektur von SOCCER

Durch den *Ereigniserkennungsprozeß* wird von der inkrementell arbeitenden *Ereigniserkennungskomponente* ständig Information über die gerade auftretenden Ereignisse zur Verfügung gestellt. Da das Ziel von SOCCER darin besteht, den Hörer über das aktuelle Szenengeschehen zu unterrichten, ist diese Information als fokussiert zu betrachten (vgl. Abschnitt 2). Daraus wählt die *Selektions/Linearisierungskomponente* (im folgenden als SL-Komponente bezeichnet) die mitzuteilende Information aus, ordnet sie an und übergibt sie dann an die *Enkodierungskomponente*. Fehlt der Enkodierungskomponente noch Information, z.B. eine geeignete Deskription für ein zu referenzierendes Objekt, so wird ein entsprechender Selektionsprozeß angestoßen. Um zu gewährleisten, daß neu aufgenommene Information sich unmittelbar auf die Sprachproduktionsprozesse auswirken kann, arbeiten die Prozesse zur Ereigniserkennung und Ereignisselektion parallel zum Enkodierungsprozeß. Auch im Hinblick auf das Abbrechen einer Äußerung aufgrund neuer Information (zur Zeit in SOCCER noch nicht realisiert) scheint diese Konzeption der parallelen Prozesse adäquat.

4. Sprachproduktion in SOCCER

Im folgenden werden wir anhand typischer Beispielszenen die Zusammenarbeit zwischen Ereigniserkennung und den für die Sprachproduktion verantwortlichen Systemkomponenten in SOCCER demonstrieren.

4.1. Änderung des Textplans

Während das Geschehen der Szene beschrieben wird, können Ereignisse fortschreiten, enden oder neue Ereignisse auftreten. Das fortlaufende Szenengeschehen erfordert eine fortlaufende Selektion. Zu jedem Zeitpunkt muß untersucht werden, welche Information dem Hörer mitgeteilt werden muß, damit dieser dem Szenengeschehen folgen kann. Zum einen sollte der Hörer über alle relevanten Ereignisse informiert werden, zum anderen sollte Redundanz vermieden werden. Zur Bestimmung der Relevanz eines Ereignisses wird in SOCCER sowohl seine Spezifität als auch sein zeitlicher Bezug zum aktuellen Szenengeschehen berücksichtigt. Zur Vermeidung von Redundanz werden bereits mitgeteilte Ereignisse nur noch zur Objektreferenzierung herangezogen. Eine qualitative Verbesserung der Ereignisselektion soll in einer weiteren Ausbaustufe von SOCCER dadurch erreicht werden, daß sowohl die beim Hörer durch die bisherige Beschreibung entstandene Vorstellung von der Szene berücksichtigt wird, als auch dadurch, daß das zum Verstehen des Spielverlaufs notwendige Wissen explizit repräsentiert wird und somit zur Formulierung entsprechender Selektionskriterien herangezogen werden kann.

Werden zu einem Zeitpunkt mehrere relevante Ereignisse selektiert, so muß entschieden werden, in welcher Reihenfolge die Enkodierung erfolgen soll. Bei der Linearisierung von Ereignissen können berücksichtigt werden:

- temporale Aspekte (z.B. Dauer der Ereignisse)
- Relevanz der Ereignisse (Relevantere Ereignisse sollten möglichst früh mitgeteilt werden.)
- kausale Beziehungen zwischen Ereignissen (in SOCCER zur Zeit noch nicht realisiert)
- kohärenzstiftende Maßnahmen (z.B. Vermeidung unnötiger Fokusverschiebungen)

Gemäß dieser Kriterien werden die selektierten Ereignispropositionen in einem Puffer angeordnet, der somit als vorläufiger Textplan aufzufassen ist. Eine Änderung dieses Textplans kann ausgelöst werden, zum einen aufgrund des fortschreitenden Szenengeschehens, zum andern aufgrund von sich während der Enkodierung ergebenden Restriktionen. Beispielsweise entscheidet SOCCER erst während der Enkodierung, ob weitere Information über ein zu referenzierendes Objekt in einem Relativsatz mitgeteilt werden soll. Handelt es sich bei dieser Information um ein neu erkanntes Ereignis, könnte eine solche Entscheidung nicht früher getroffen werden. Die Enkodierung des Puffers unterliegt starken zeitlichen Beschränkungen. Bei schneller Szenenfolge hinkt der Sprachproduktionsprozeß deutlich gegenüber dem Szenengeschehen nach. Für SOCCER erweist es sich daher als notwendig, bei der Selektion die zur Verfügung stehende Zeit zu berücksichtigen, d.h. es werden nur Textpläne begrenzter Länge erstellt. Nach signifikanten Veränderungen in der Szene ist damit zu rechnen, daß sich die Relevanz früher erkannter Ereignisse verändert. In einigen Fällen führt dies sogar so weit, daß bereits selektierte, aber noch nicht enkodierte Propositionen aus dem Puffer wieder entfernt werden, während die zur Beschreibung des aktuellen Szenengeschehens relevanteren Ereignisse neu hinzukommen. Eine sich hieraus ergebende Änderung des Textplans äußert sich dann meistens durch einen für den Hörer überraschenden Themenwechsel.

Zur Demonstration betrachten wir die Situation eines mißglückten Zuspiels. Zum Zeitpunkt t_1 enthalte der Puffer folgende Einträge:

(P1) $ACTIVE(t_1 [EVENT$:Type *ball-transfer*
:Agent *sp5*
:Object *ball1*
:Goal $[LOCATION$:Relation *spatial-in*
:Ref–Object *strafraum1*]])

(P2) $ACTIVE(t_1 [EVENT$:Type *stehen*
:Agent *sp4*
:Place $[LOCATION$:Relation *spatial-in*
:Ref–Object *strafraum1*]])

Während der Enkodierung von (P1) werde erkannt, daß der Ball abgewehrt wird, d.h. zu einem späteren Zeitpunkt t_2 liefere die Ereigniserkennungskomponente die Proposition:

(P3) $ACTIVE(t_2 [EVENT$:Type *abwehren*
:Agent *sp13*])

Eine erneute Überprüfung des Pufferinhaltes hinsichtlich der Relevanz der Einträge führt zur Löschung von (P2) und zur Hinzunahme von (P3). Diese Situation würde beschrieben werden durch:

(S1) *Meier schießt den Ball in den Strafraum.*
(S2) *Breit vom FC-SOCCER wehrt ab.*

Es stellt sich das Problem, wie ein unerwarteter Themenwechsel sprachlich markiert werden kann. Eine Möglichkeit besteht in der Verwendung von Temporaladverbien wie *"jetzt"* oder Modaladverbien wie *"aber"*. Während Temporaladverbien bereits von SOCCER generiert werden können, erfordert die Verwendung von Modaladverbien zusätzliches Wissen (z.B. über mögliche Intentionen der einzelnen Spieler).

4.2. Inkrementelle Sprachproduktion auf Satzebene

Bei syntaktischen Untersuchungen von Fußballdirektreportagen stellte Rosenbaum (vgl. [Rosenbaum 69]) fest, daß Sprecher Konstituenten eines Satzes oft in einer Reihenfolge anordnen, die der Sukzession des Erkennens entspricht. Durch diese Anordnung bringen sie ihre Äußerungen in Kongruenz mit dem Szenengeschehen. Hierzu betrachten wir folgende Situation:

(S3) *Meier schießt den Ball – [Pause] – in den Strafraum.*

Zwischen dem Abspielen des Balls und dem Erreichen des Ziels liegt eine größere Zeitspanne; der Reporter beginnt bereits mit der Enkodierung, bevor er das Ziel des Schusses erkannt hat. Wie bereits erwähnt stellt die Ereigniserkennungskomponente in SOCCER nicht nur vollständig, sondern auch teilweise erkannte Ereignisse zur Sprachproduktion bereit. In Analogie zu obigem Beispiel wollen wir annehmen, daß die Ereigniserkennung das Konzept *ball-transfer* aktiviert, nachdem der Agent den Ball gespielt hat. Die Aktion *ball-transfer* ist zu diesem Zeitpunkt noch nicht beendet; daher ist der obligatorische Tiefenkasus :Goal noch nicht instantiiert. Intern sei das Ereignis repräsentiert durch die Proposition:

(P4) $ACTIVE(t_1 [EVENT$:Type *ball-transfer*
:Agent *sp5*
:Object *ball1*
:Goal *?goal*])

Die Enkodierungskomponente muß zunächst anhand der bereits verfügbaren Information ein geeignetes Verb selektieren. Unter Zugriff auf das Konzeptlexikon wird für das Konzept *ball-transfer* das Verb *"schießen"* selektiert. Nach der Instantiierung des Verbrahmens wird mit der Enkodierung der Konstituenten begonnen. Zur Bestimmung von Deskriptionen für die Objekte *sp5* und *ball1* wird die Kontrolle an die SL-Komponente zurückgegeben, die unter Zugriff auf das Partnermodell und das Textgedächtnis für den Spieler den Eigennamen und für den Ball den Klassenbezeichner liefert. In einigen Fällen liegt der SL-Komponente die von der Enkodierungskomponente angeforderte Information noch nicht vor. Im Beispiel signalisiert die ungebundene Variable *?goal* , daß der für das Konzept *ball-transfer* obligatorische Tiefenkasus :Goal noch nicht instantiiert ist. Der Enkodiervorgang kann daher erst dann fortgesetzt werden, wenn die Ereigniserkennung das Konzept *ball-transfer* vollständig erkannt hat.

Das Ziel des Reporters, die Hörer möglichst direkt über die Entwicklung des Szenengeschehens zu informieren, bedingt das Auftreten ungewöhnlicher oder sogar unkorrekter syntaktischer Konstruktionen. Beginnt ein Sprecher mit der Enkodierung, bevor Information über sämtliche Konstituenten vorliegt, sind seine Möglichkeiten zur Vorausplanung der Satzstruktur eingeschränkt.

(S4) *Müller spielt zu Meier -[Pause]- vom Mittelkreis aus.*

In (S4) hat der Sprecher bereits mit der Enkodierung begonnen, als er sich entschließt, zusätzlich den :Source-Kasus der Aktion mitzuteilen. Diese Information wird an den bereits enkodierten Teil der Äußerung angehängt, obwohl dies zu einer unkonventionellen, wenngleich verständlichen Satzstellung führt.

Diese Beispiele zeigen, daß in SOCCER bei der Oberflächengenerierung kein vollständig vorliegender Inhalt vorausgesetzt werden kann. Vielmehr ist es notwendig, die während der Enkodierung eintreffende Information in Abhängigkeit von bereits geäußerten Satzfragmenten zu realisieren. In SOCCER existiert derzeit zur Oberflächengenerierung erst eine Vorversion, bei der zur Ausführung der morphologischen Prozesse auf entsprechende Teile des Systems SUTRA [Busemann 83] zurückgegriffen wird.

5. Zusammenfassung

Bei der simultanen Beschreibung zeitveränderlicher Szenen sehen wir die Möglichkeiten zur Planung von Inhalt und Form erheblich eingeschränkt, sowohl durch den zum Zeitpunkt der Sprachproduktion unbekannten Fortgang der Szene als auch durch die Tatsache, daß die Dauer der sprachlichen Enkodierung nicht zu vernachlässigen ist. Es erscheint uns bei der Konzeption eines Systems zur Erzeugung simultaner Szenenbeschreibungen als eine grundlegende Voraussetzung, Wahrnehmung und Sprachproduktion durch zum Teil parallel arbeitende Prozesse zu realisieren. Nur auf diese Weise ist gewährleistet, daß sich neu aufgenommene Information direkt auf den Sprachproduktionsprozeß auswirken kann. Hierzu wurde gezeigt, daß unmittelbar Wahrgenommenes zu unerwarteten Themenwechseln führen kann; d.h. bestehende Textpläne werden zugunsten einer aktuellen Situationsbeschreibung abgeändert. Desweiteren führt die Konzeption paralleler Prozesse dazu, daß Enkodierungsprozesse in manchen Fällen unterbrochen werden, weil der weitere Verlauf der Szene erst abgewartet werden muß.

Das in Abschnitt 3 vorgestellte System SOCCER ist auf SYMBOLICS LISP-Maschinen vom Typ 3600 bzw. 3640 unter Release 6.2 implementiert. Durch den zur Verfügung stehenden Multitaskingmechanismus wurde Parallelität zwischen Enkodierung und Erkennung bzw. Selektion realisiert.

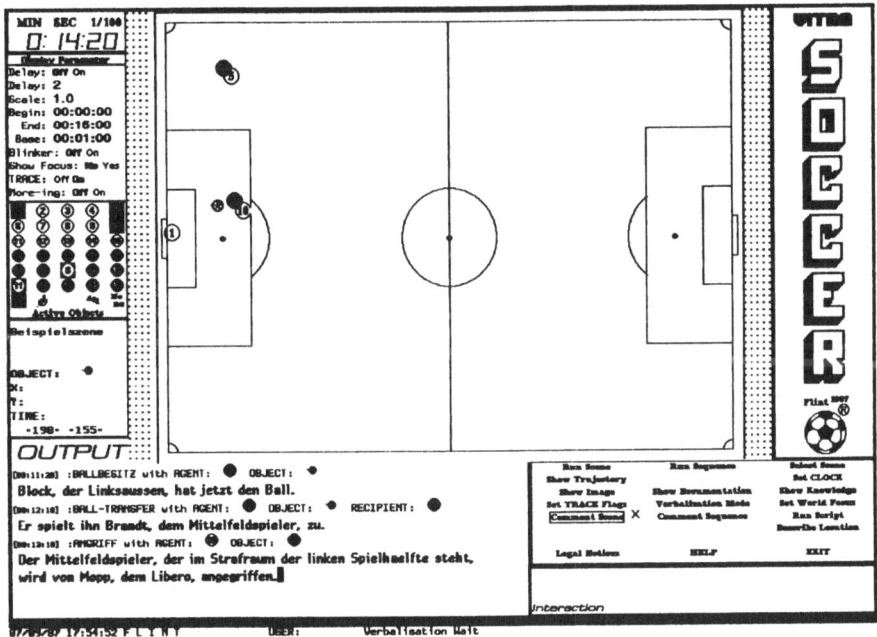

Abb.3: Bildschirmmaske des Systems SOCCER

Im Graphikausgabefenster des Systems können die mittels des Trajektorieneditors erstellten Szenen visualisiert und dazu simultan natürlichsprachlich beschrieben werden. Insbesondere können die auch in Fußballdirektreportagen auftretenden Phänomene wie inkrementelle Erzeugung natürlichsprachlicher Äußerungen, Nachhinken der Sprachproduktion in bezug auf das aktuelle Szenengeschehen und unerwartete Themenwechsel simuliert werden.

Literaturverzeichnis

André, E., Herzog, G., Rist, T. (1987): *SOCCER: Ein System zur simultanen natürlichsprach-lichen Beschreibung zeitveränderlicher Realweltszenen*. Universität des Saarlandes, SFB 314, Bericht, in Vorbereitung.

Brandt, W. (1983): *Zeitstruktur und Tempusgebrauch in Fußballreportagen des Hörfunks*. Marburg: Elwert Verlag.

Busemann, S. (1983): *Oberflächentransformationen bei der automatischen Generierung geschriebener deutscher Sprache*. Diplomarbeit, Fachbereich Informatik, Universität Hamburg.

Carpenter, P.A., Just, M.A. (1986): *Cognitive Processes in Reading*. In: Orasanu, J. (Hrsg.): Reading Comprehension: From Research to Practice. Hillsdale, New Jersey: Lawrence Erlbaum, S. 11-29.

Ertel, S. (1977): *Where do the Subjects of Sentences come from?* In: Rosenberg, S. (Hrsg.): Sentence Production: Developments in Research and Theory. Hillsdale, New Jersey: Lawrence Erlbaum, S. 141-167.

Herrmann, T. (1985): *Allgemeine Sprachpsychologie*. München, Wien, Baltimore: Urban und Schwarzenberg.

Herzog, G. (1986): *Ein Werkzeug zur Visualisierung und Generierung von geometrischen Bildfolgenbeschreibungen*. Universität des Saarlandes, SFB 314, Memo Nr. 12.

Kempen, G. (1977): *Conceptualizing and Formulating in Sentence Production*. In: Rosenberg, S. (Hrsg.): Sentence Production: Developments in Research and Theory. Hillsdale, New Jersey: Lawrence Erlbaum, S. 259-274.

Kempen, G., Hoenkamp, E. (1982): *Incremental Sentence Generation: Implications for the Structure of a Syntactic Processor*. In: Proc. COLING-82, S. 151-156.

McKeown, K.R. (1985): *Text Generation*. London: Cambridge University Press.

Neumann, B. (1982): *Knowledge Sources for Understanding and Describing Image Sequences*. In: Wahlster, W. (Hrsg.): GWAI-82. Berlin, Heidelberg, N.Y.: Springer, S. 1-21.

Novak, H.-J. (1986): *Textgenerierung auf der Grundlage visueller Daten: Beschreibungen von Straßenszenen*. Dissertation, Fachbereich Informatik, Universität Hamburg.

Norman, D.A., Rumelhart, D.E. (1978): *Strukturen des Wissens: Wege der Kognitionsforschung*. Stuttgart: Klett-Cotta.

Osgood, C.E. (1971): *Where do Sentences come from?* In: Steinberg, D.D., Jakobovitz, L.A. (Hrsg.): Semantics: An Interdisciplinary Reader in Philosophy, Linguistics and Psychology. London: Cambridge University Press, S. 497-529.

Pechmann, T. (1984): *Überspezifizierung und Betonung in referentieller Kommunikation*. Dissertation, Philosophische Fakultät, Universität Mannheim.

Rist, T., Herzog, G., André, E. (1987): *Ereignismodellierung zur inkrementellen High-level Bildfolgenanalyse*. Universität des Saarlandes, SFB 314, Bericht Nr. 19. Erscheint auch in: Proc. ÖGAI-87.

Rosenbaum, D. (1969): *Die Sprache der Fußballreportage im Hörfunk*. Dissertation, Philosophische Fakultät, Universität des Saarlandes.

Sigurd, B. (1984): *Computer Simulation of Spontaneous Speech Production*. In: Proc. COLING-84, S. 79-83.

Repräsentationssysteme für Grammatik und Lexikon
—Einleitung—

G. Görz, Universität Erlangen-Nürnberg

In der Linguistik und linguistischen Informatik vollzieht sich seit einigen Jahren ein Wandlungsprozeß, der zu einer Reihe neuartiger Grammatiktheorien, -formalismen und Verarbeitungsmodellen geführt hat. Viele Linguisten sind sich heute —von durchaus unterschiedlichen Annahmen ausgehend— einig, daß der Begriff der sequentiellen, regel-basierten Ableitung, der für 25 Jahre linguistischer Theoriebildung eine zentrale Rolle spielte, für die Charakterisierung wohlgeformter Äußerungen in den Hintergrund zu treten habe. Diese Schlüsselrolle übernimmt nun der Begriff der partiellen Information und eine Menge wechselseitig unabhängiger Restriktionen und Prinzipien. Die Entwicklung der Generativen Transformationsgrammatik gibt hierfür das beste Beispiel mit ihrer neuesten Revision als Rektions- und Bindungs-Theorie, in der Konstituentenstrukturregeln nahezu vollständig eliminiert sind. Aus der Sicht der Informatik wird an zentraler Stelle der "Constraint"-Begriff thematisiert und die (Graphen-) Unifikation als ein Verfahren zur Lösung von Constraint-Gleichungen, welche die Übereinstimmung linguistischer Attribute ausdrücken.

Für diesen neuen Typ von Grammatikformalismen sind die Bezeichnungen "unifikations-basiert" oder "merkmals-basiert" ("complex feature based") üblich geworden. Während die letzte Bezeichnung anzeigt, daß der Schwerpunkt dieser Formalismen in der Darstellung komplexer Systeme von Merkmalen liegt, betont die erste das Verfahren, mit dem solche Merkmals-Systeme verarbeitet werden. Die Unifikation ist eine Operation, durch die partielle Information —hier Merkmalsmengen— monoton erweitert wird, solange sie konsistent bleibt.

Die Wahl eines bestimmten Grammatikformalismus wird von einer Reihe von Kriterien beeinflußt, deren wichtigste sind:

- *linguistische Adäquatheit*: inwieweit Beschreibungen linguistischer Phänomene in einer der zugrundeliegenden Theorie angemessenen Form ausgedrückt werden können;

- *Ausdruckskraft*: welche Klassen von Analyse-Strukturen überhaupt formulierbar sind;

- *Algorithmische Effektivität*: welche algorithmischen Mittel verfügbar sind, um in dem Formalismus notierte Grammatiken effektiv zu interpretieren, und sofern solche Mittel existieren wo ihre Grenzen liegen.

Das Ziel unserer speziellen Sektion besteht in der Diskussion dieser neuen Konzeption für Grammatik und Lexikon im Rahmen der maschinellen Sprachverarbeitung. Sie vereinigt Beiträge, die den unifikations-basierten Ansatz exemplarisch anhand seiner konkreten Ausprägungen in einigen Systemen zur Analyse und Generierung natürlicher Sprache vorstellt. Paulus zeigt seine Anwendung in einem System zur morphologischen Analyse und Generierung deutscher Verbformen. Im Beitrag von Heid wird die funktional orientierte lexikalische Wissensquelle des Generierungssystems SEMSYN vorgestellt. Busemann präsentiert ein Generierungssystem auf der Grundlage der "Generalized Phrase Structure Grammar" (GPSG) als einem prominenten Repräsentanten unifikations-basierter Grammatikformalismen.

Endliche Automaten zur Verbflexion und ein spezielles deutsches Verblexikon

Dietrich Paulus
Universität Erlangen-Nürnberg
Institut für Mathematische Maschinen und Datenverarbeitung (IMMD 5)

Es wird ein allgemeiner und weitgehend sprachunabhängiger Ansatz vorgestellt, der die Morphologie einer Sprache in endlichen Automaten darstellt. Die Allgemeinheit des Modells wirkt im speziellen Fall der Verbmorphologie des Deutschen erschwerdend. Daher wird ein erweitertes Konzept angegeben, das eine vollständige Behandlung aller deutschen Verbformen gestattet und sich effizient implementieren ließ. Dabei erfährt der Stammvokal eine besondere Behandlung im Lexikon und im Automaten.

1. Primitive für die Modifikation von Zeichenketten

Ausgangspunkt für das Modell sind Zeichenketten. Diese müssen – möglicherweise in mehreren Schritten – verändert werden. In der Analyse führt eine solche Veränderung zu einer Grundform, in der Generierung zu einer flektierten Wortform.

"Rewriting Rules" [1] werden als allgemeines System zur Ersetzung von Zeichenketten verwendet. Dazu wird eine Menge von Regeln R_i verwendet, die als Paare von Zeichenketten angegeben werden. Die Regel $R_i = (a,b)$ ist auf das Wort w anwendbar, wenn es ein Unterwort a in w gibt (also $w = w_1 a w_2$); das Ergebnis ist eine Zeichenkette, in der das Unterwort a durch b ersetzt wurde: $R(w) = w_1 b w_2$.

(Dabei sind $a, b, w, w_1, w_2 \in \Sigma^*$; Σ ein Alphabet.)

Beispiel 1:
   Konvention: alle Wörter werden durch spitze Klammern eingerahmt.
   $R_1 = ("ab","att")$; $R_1 ("\langle haben \rangle") = "\langle hatten \rangle"$
   $R_2 = ("\langle","\langle er")$; $R_2 ("\langle haben \rangle") = "\langle erhaben \rangle"$

2. Verknüpfung von Regeln

Wortveränderungen werden durch mehrmalige Anwendung von Regeln erreicht. Zur Steuerung der Abfolge wird ein gerichteter Graph verwendet, dessen Kantenbeschriftung die Regeln sind. Dem Übergang entlang einer Kante entspricht die Anwendung der Regel. Jede Regel läßt sich als Automate ("Finite State Transducer" (FST)) darstellen. Dabei sind leere Eingaben und Ausgaben erlaubt, um verkürzende und verlängernde Regeln zu erhalten. Die Kombination von Graph und Automaten ergibt erneut einen Automaten. (Zu den Eigenschaften dieses Automatennetzes vgl. Aiserman [2] . Im Folgenden wird dieses Automatennetz mit einfach mit "Automat" bezeichnet.)

Die Kanten erhalten als weitere Beschriftung noch eine Merkmalsliste. In jedem Zustand des Automaten sind die aktuelle Merkmalsliste und Zeichenkette bekannt. Der Übergang zu einem anderen Zustand wird an zwei Bedingungen geknüpft:

- die Regel muß anwendbar sein; das Ergebnis ergibt das neue Wort;
- die Unifikation der Merkmale an der Kante mit den bereits bekannten muß erfolgreich sein; dabei wird eine einfache (nicht rekursive) Form der Unifikation verwendet; das Ergebnis ergibt die neue Merkmalsliste.

In der Analyse enthält die Merkmalsliste beim Erreichen des Endzustandes die gewünschte Information. Die Merkmalsliste ist zu Anfang leer.

Beispiel 2: Automat zur *Analyse*

Dieser Automat analysiert alle regelmäßigen Formen des Indikativ Präsens von französischen Verben mit der Endung "- er".

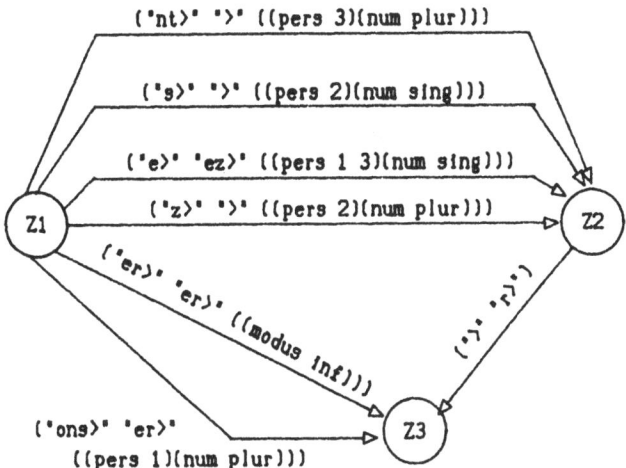

Zur Generierung müssen die Regeln rückwärts angewendet werden, und ein Pfad vom End- zum Anfangszustand gefunden werden. Ausgangsinformation ist eine Beschreibung der gewünschten Wortform als Merkmalsliste. Im Automaten zeigen alle Kanten zum Ziel *hin.* Daher wird zunächst ein Pfad vom Start zum Ziel gesucht, wobei als Kriterium für die Zulässigkeit eines Übergangs nur die Unifikation entscheidend ist. Dann wird dieser Pfad zum Anfang hin zurückverfolgt, wobei die Regeln rückwärts angewendet werden. Dieses

Verfahren ist praktikabel, da die Unifikation eine kommutative Operation ist.
Der Automat ist also für die Generierung ebenso wie für die Analyse geeignet.

3. Historie der endlichen Automaten für Morphologie

Der soweit vorgestellte Ansatz stammt in seinen Grundzügen von M. Kay[3]
Kennzeichnend für ihn ist die Verwendung der Unifkation, die eine Einbindung in viele
Verfahren erlaubt, die ebenfalls die Unifikation verwenden. (Ein Beispiel sind
Unifikationsgrammatiken vgl. Shieber [4]). Ein weiterer Ansatz zur Morphologie mit end-
lichen Automaten geht auf K. Koskenniemi zurück [5] . Ein Vergleich der Ansätze findet
sich bei Gazdar [6] .

4. Das Lexikon

Der Automat kann nur in Verbindung mit einem Lexikon sinnvoll verwendet werden. (Im
Beispiel 2 wird die Futur Form "aimerez" fehlerhaft als 1. Person Indikativ Präsens Plural
vom Infinitiv "aimerer" analysiert.) Jede als Infinitiv vorgeschlagene Form muß in der
Analyse anhand eines Lexikons überprüft werden.

5. Stammveränderungen

Bislang wurden nur Veränderungen betrachtet, die am Wortende stattfanden. In manchen
flektierten Formen ändert sich jedoch auch der Stamm des Verbs.
Einfach zu behandelnden ist die Reduplikation eines Konsonanten (z.B. in "je jet-te" von
"jeter"). Es genügt eine Kante zu haben, die den entsprechenden Konsonanten verdoppelt
(z.B. ("t-","tt-")), und ein Merkmal, das die Notwendigkeit der Verdoppelung anzeigt. Der
Wert dieses Merkmals wird dem Lexikon zu Beginn der Generierung entnommen. Damit
erweitert sich der Algorithmus wie folgt:

- Generierung: Die Merkmalsliste im Startzustand des Automaten ergibt sich aus der Uni-
  fikation des Lexikoneintrags mit der Darstellung der gewünschten flektierten Form.
- Analyse: Zur erfolgreichen Analyse muß auch die Unifikation der
  Ergebnismerkmalsliste mit dem Lexikoneintrag erfolgreich sein.

Bei umfangreicheren Veränderungen des Stamms ist es in vielen Fällen möglich,
unregelmäßige Flexionsformen durch regelmäßige Beugung nicht vorhandener
"Pseudoinfinitive" zu erhalten, die dem Lexikon entnommen werden.

Beispiel 3:

Um "aller" im Subjonctif Présent zu konjugieren, wird der nicht vorhandene Infinitiv
"ailler" regelmäßig flektiert. "haben" läßt sich im Imperfekt durch regelmäßige
Flexion von "haten" darstellen.

6. Übertragung des Modells auf das Deutsche

Das bisher Dargestellte trifft ebenso für deutsche Verben zu. Erhebliche Schwierigkeiten ergeben sich jedoch bei der Behandlung starker Verben. Als Stammvokale können a, e, i, o, u, ä, ö, ü, ei, ai, au, äu, eu und ie auftreten. Der Stammvokal kann in einer Konjugation bis zu sechs mal wechseln:

Beispiel 4: Das Verb "helfen":
  helfen: ich helfe, du hilfst, ich half, ich hälfe/hülfe, geholfen

Um die möglichen Kombinationen mit Ersetzungsregeln darzustellen, ist eine erhebliche Anzahl Kanten im Automaten erforderlich. Zudem ist es schwierig, den richtigen Vokal zu ersetzen. (Wo soll beispielsweise die Regel ("e","o") im Verb "verweben" angewendet werden?)
Prinzipiell lassen sich diese Probleme mit dem Modell bewältigen. Wegen der Größe des benötigten Automaten wird das Programm aber zu langsam. (Vgl. Paulus [7])

7. Erweiterung des Modells auf die Gegebenheiten des Deutschen

Da sich Prä- und Suffixe elegant mit dem Automatenmodell behandeln lassen, der Stammvokal jedoch Probleme bereitet, wurde eine Erweiterung speziell für deutsche Verben vorgenommen. Die Endungen werden vom Automaten verändert; der Stammvokal wird tabellengesteuert ersetzt. Die Tabelle besteht aus fünf Spalten, die den fünf Fällen im Beispiel 4 entsprechen. Die Zeilen sehen alle Vokalkombinationen vor. (z.B. die Eintragszeile zu "helfen" ((e) (i) (a) (ä,ü) (o))). Der Spaltenindex wird den Merkmalen im Zuge der Unifikation zugefügt. Der Zeilenindex ist im Lexikon eingetragen.

8. Ein neuartiger Lexikonaufbau

Diese Erweiterung bedingt einen neuartigen Lexikonaufbau. Verbstämme werden vor ihrem Eintrag in das Lexikon in eine interne Darstellung umgewandelt. Dabei wird der Stammvokal durch einen neutralen Platzhalter ersetzt und an das Wortende verschoben. Die Lokalisierung des Stammvokals ist mit einem einfachen Verfahren möglich, das bei Paulus angegeben ist [7] .

Beispiel 5: Buchstabenbaum für "wiegen", "wagen" und "wägen"
  (* (w (X (g (- (I ((gruppe 2))) ; *ie ist zusätzlich als I*
          (a ((gruppe 3))) ; *codiert*
          (ä ((gruppe 4)))))))))

9. Auswirkung des Lexikonaufbaus auf den Algorithmus

Der neue Lexikonaufbau beschleunigt die Analyse erheblich. Nun kann aus der Wortform durch Abtrennen der Endung und Ignorieren des Stammvokals (vgl. dazu Paulus [7]) sofort eine sehr kleine Anzahl möglicher Stämme ermittelt werden, die für die Analyse überhaupt nur in Frage kommen.

Beispiel 6: Analyse von "wog"
> "wog" → "wXg": Nachschlagen von "wXg" im Lexikon reduziert die möglichen Stämme auf den Unterbaum unter "wXg", in dem sich die Einträge für "wiegen", "wagen" und "wägen" befinden.

Die Lexikoneinträge zu diesen Infinitiven können nun als Startinformation an den Automaten mitgegeben werden. Die so gewonnene Merkmalsliste reduziert die Zahl der möglichen Pfade (und damit der Fehlversuche) durch den Automaten drastisch.

10. Ergebnisse

Zu dem ersten, sprachunabhängigen Ansatz existieren drei Sprachbeschreibungen, die eine große Zahl französischer Verben und exemplarisch einige deutsche und spanische Verben abdecken. Mit dem erweiterten Ansatz können *sämtliche* deutsche Verbformen verarbeiten werden. Dabei werden auch zusammengesetzte Verben und die Unterscheidung von transitivem und intransitivem Gebrauch ("er schrak" - "er erschreckte mich") sowie mehrfache Formen ("er buk" - "er backte") berücksichtigt. Das Programm dazu wurde auf einem PC in LISP geschrieben.

LITERATUR

1. Kay, M., Two-Level Morphology with Tiers, Paper presented to the CSLI Workshop on Finite-State Morphology July 1985 (1985).

2. Aiserman, M.A.; Gussew, L.A.; Rosonoer, L.I.R.; Smirnowa, I.M; Tal, A.A., Logik - Automaten - Algorithmen, R.Oldenburg Verlag, München und Wien (1967).

3. Kay M., Kaplan, R., unveröfferntlichter Vortrag beim LSA Treffen in New York im Winter 1981,

4. Shieber, S., An Introduction to Unification-based Approaches to Grammar, in *CSLI Lecture Notes*, Stanford University, Stanford, Cal. (1986).

5. Koskenniemi, K., Two-level Morphology: A General Computational Model for Wordform Recognition and Production, University of Helsinki, Department of General Linguistics, Helsinki (1983).

6. Gazdar, G., Finite State Morphology, A Review of Koskenniemi, Report No. CSLI-85-32, Stanford University, Stanford, Cal. (1985).

7. Paulus, Dietrich, Ein Programmsystem zur morphologischen Analyse, Diplomarbeit , Universität Erlangen-Nürnberg, RRZE, RRZE-IAB 259, Erlangen (1986).

Zur lexikalischen Wissensquelle
des Generierungssystems SEMSYN

Ulrich Heid

Projekt SEMSYN, Inst. für Informatik
Universität Stuttgart, Herdweg 51
7000 Stuttgart 1

1 Einleitung

Der Generator des SEMSYN-Systems nimmt semantische Repräsentationen als Eingabe, die in einer erweiterten Kasusrahmennotation vorliegen. Realisierungsregeln steuern die Abbildung der semantischen Strukturen auf funktionale grammatische Strukturen. Aufgabe des Generator-Front-Ends ist es dann, aus solchen funktionalen Strukturen deutsche Sätze oder Nominalphrasen zu erzeugen [EMELE 1987].

Die Generierung greift derzeit auf zwei verschiedene Lexika zu: zum einen auf ein Lexikon, das semantische Symbole auf deutsche Lexeme abbildet (z.B. 'PROJECT' auf *Projekt*, *Vorhaben*, *Forschungsprojekt*, etc.) und bei der Lexikalisierung der in den semantischen Netzen enthaltenen abstrakt gedachten Begriffe verwendet wird. Zum anderen wird ein morphologisch-syntaktisches Wörterbuch verwendet, das zum Beispiel Flexions- oder Steigerungsinformation enthält.

Insgesamt greift der Generierungsprozeß auf lexikalische Information zu, die ganz verschiedenen linguistischen Beschreibungsebenen zuzuordnen ist: außer der Abbildung der semantischen Symbole auf Lexeme auch syntaktische (z.B. Subkategorisierungs-) Information und morphologische Angaben.

Der folgende Vortrag beschreibt zuerst die bisherige Struktur der lexikalischen Wissensquellen von SEMSYN. Der zweite Teil soll Beispiele geben für einen (noch nicht in dieser Form implementierten) Vorschlag zur Organisation der lexikalischen Wissensquelle eines objektorientierten Generierungssystems, wie es SEMSYN ist. Gezeigt werden soll, wie in einer solchen Programmierumgebung Informationen zu verschiedenen Beschreibungsebenen getrennt und möglichst redundanzfrei abgelegt werden können, und wie die 'Einzel-Lexika' bei komplexen Aufgaben interagieren könnten. Solche Zusammenhänge betreffen

- die Interaktion von semantischer und syntaktischer Klassifikation, das heißt die Erschließbarkeit syntaktischer Konstruktionen auf der Basis von Kenntnissen über die Zugehörigkeit eines Verbs zu einer semantisch motivierten Verbklasse,

- die Funktionsweise von syntaktischen Redundanzregeln für die Konstruktion von deverbalen Nomina, das heißt die Vererbung der Verbvalenzkomplemente an die Nominalisierungen.

2 Die lexikalische Wissensquelle von SEMSYN

Der Aufbau der bisher vom SEMSYN-Generator verwendeten Wörterbücher ist durch eine Zweiteilung in onomasiologische und morphosyntaktische Information gekennzeichnet.

2.1 Das 'semantisch-deutsche' Lexikon: Abbildung von semantischen Symbolen auf Lexeme

Die semantischen Repräsentationen, die SEMSYN als Eingabe nimmt, stammen aus zwei Typen von Anwendungen:

- Parsing-Ergebnisse

- nicht sprachlich realisierte Daten

Die ersten Strukturen, die verarbeitet wurden, waren vom Analysesystem des japanischen Computerherstellers FUJITSU aus Titeln von japanischen informationstechnischen Aufsätzen gewonnen worden [RÖSNER 1986a]. Inzwischen wurden Experimente zur Generierung aus Analysestrukturen angestellt, die der TOMITA-Parser [TOMITA/CARBONELL 1986, RÖSNER 1987b] aus japanischen Sätzen ableitet, sowie zur Generierung aus Strukturen der Pre-Transfer-Phase des japanischen nationalen Projekts zur maschinellen Übersetzung [HOSAKA 1987] und aus Strukturen, wie sie die deutsche Gruppe von EUROTRA vorschlägt (keine Parsing-Ergebnisse) [HEID/RÖSNER/WECK 1987, HEID/WECK 1987]. Die semantischen Symbole, die in diesen Strukturen vorkommen, sind aus quellsprachlichen Lexemen gewonnene begriffliche Abstraktionen. Im 'semantisch-deutschen' Lexikon werden für diese Symbole mögliche, quasisynonyme Lexikalisierungen zusammengestellt, z.B. sind für das Symbol 'APPLY' die Lexeme *anwenden, verwenden, benutzen* denkbar, aber auch Wortbildungsprodukte wie *Anwendung, angewandt* (adj.) oder Mehrwortlexeme wie die Kollokation *zur Anwendung bringen* [RÖSNER 1986b].

Einen zweiten Bereich von SEMSYN-Anwendungen stellt die Generierung aus Laten dar. In [RÖSNER 1986b] wurde gezeigt, wie aus Daten zur Arbeitsmarktlage mit SEMSYN Zeitungstexte zur Beschäftigungssituation (Arbeitslosenquote, Männer- und Frauenarbeitslosigkeit, Vergleich mit Vormonat und Vorjahr, Stellungnahmen von Politikern) generiert werden können [auch RÖSNER 1987a]. Aus den Kommandos einer Geometriesprache hat [KEHL1986] Konstruktionstexte zu geometrischen Objekten generiert. Die aus solchen Daten gewonnenen semantischen Symbole können zum Teil als Archilexeme aufgefaßt werden: [KEHL 1986] lexikalisiert das Symbol 'DRAW' defaultmäßig mit *zeichnen*, setzt jedoch *ziehen*, wenn von einer *Linie* die Rede ist, bzw. *ein Lot* fällen, *einen Kreis* schlagen. Die Möglichkeiten der kontextsensitiven Lexikalisierung wurden dort exemplarisch vorgeführt, im Sinne einzelner Kollokationsangaben.

Zur Abbildung von semantischen Relationen auf syntaktische Funktionen sind in SEMSYN sogenannte 'Realisierungsregeln' formuliert und implementiert, die für eine semantische Rolle (z.B. Tiefenkasus) festlegen, welche interne Realisierung (Nominalgruppe, *daß*-Satz, Infinitiv) gewählt werden soll und welche syntaktische Funktion die Realisierung des Füllers dieser Rolle in der übergeordneten Struktur erhalten soll. Die Realisierungsregeln legen Standardabbildungen fest. Weicht die syntaktische Konstruktion eines Lexems, auf das ein semantisches Symbol abgebildet werden soll, von der Standardrealisierung der Rollen ab, die von diesem Symbol ausgehen, so muß im 'semantisch-deutschen' Lexikon angegeben werden, wie der Füller der betreffenden Rolle realisiert werden soll. Wenn beispielsweise ein Symbol 'MEET' alternativ durch *jemanden treffen* und *jemandem begegnen* realisiert werden soll, so muß neben der Standardrealisierung der OBJECT-Rolle (vgl. PATIENS bei FILLMORE) als direktes Objekt, im 'semantisch-deutschen' Lexikon angegeben werden, daß die OBJECT-Rolle beim Verb *begegnen* als indirektes Objekt zu realisieren ist.

347

Deswegen soll im zweiten Teil des Beitrags vorgeschlagen werden, Informationen zur syntaktischen Konstruktion (Subkategorisierung) separat abzulegen.

2.2 Das morphosyntaktische Lexikon

Das von SEMSYN benutzte morphosyntaktische Lexikon [EMELE/MOMMA 1985] beruht auf einer Einteilung der Lexeme in Flexionsklassen (zuerst [BROCKHAUS 1975]): im morphosyntaktischen Lexikon sind nur bestimmte 'Schlüsselformen' einzutragen, aus denen bei Bedarf durch die Anwendung von Redundanzregeln alle flektierten Formen erzeugt werden können. Dies erspart die Haltung eines Vollformenlexikons. Bei der Generierung eines aktuellen Satzes werden auf Grund von morphologischen Attribut-Wert-Paar-Angaben (z.B. Kasus, Numerus, Tempus, Person) die notwendigen Formen mit Hilfe der entsprechenden Regel generiert. 'Schlüsselformen' für Verben sind als Beispiel in der folgenden Abbildung zusammengestellt.

- Regelmäßige Verben: Infinitiv Präsens, Hilfsverb
- Unregelmäßige Verben: Infinitiv Präsens,
  1. Pers. Imperf. Ind.,
  Partizip Perfekt.
  - *Untergruppe 1:* zusätzlich 1. Pers. Sg. Imperfekt Konjunktiv
  - *Untergruppe 2:* zusätzlich 2. Pers. Sg. Präsens Indikativ
  - *Untergruppe 3:* zusätzlich 1. Pers. Sg. Imperfekt Konjunktiv,
    zusätzlich 2. Pers. Sg. Präsens Indikativ
  - *Untergruppe 4:* zusätzlich 1. Pers. Sg. Präsens Indikativ

Dieses Lexikon enthält auch einige lexemspexifische syntaktische Angaben, wie z.B. Hinweise auf die Möglichkeit des Anschlusses von Infinitiv-Konstruktionen.

3 Vorschläge zur Organisation der Lexikalischen Wissensquelle

Nachfolgend sollen Vorschläge zur Organisation der lexikalischen Wissensquelle von SEMSYN gemacht werden, die die bereits angelegte Tendenz zur redundanzfreien Speicherung lexikalischer Information weitertreiben und es gleichzeitig erlauben, Information verschiedener linguistischer Beschreibungsebenen auseinanderzuhalten.

3.1 Komponenten einer lexikalischen Wissensquelle

3.1.1 Abbildung der semantischen Symbole auf Lexeme

Für den Prozeß der Lexikalisierung von semantischen Symbolen bedarf es eines Lexikons, das relativ allgemeine Begriffe (wie sie durch die semantischen Symbole dargestellt werden) mit mehr oder minder spezifischen Lexemen in Relation setzt. Um einen modularen Aufbau des Lexikons sicherzustellen, ist an bereichsspezifische Oberbegriff-Unterbegriff-Hierarchien zu denken, wie sie in nuce bei der Lexikalisierung von 'DRAW' verwendet werden.

Nominalklassifikationen, wie sie in der 'Terminologie [WERSIG 1978] und der Fachsprachenlexikographie, aber auch in der Forschung zur Künstlichen Intelligenz [HABEL 1985] verwendet werden, können auf Objektklassenhierarchien abgebildet werden. Die Nutzung der Hyperonymierelation erleichtert das Auffinden von Oberbegriffen, z.B. bei der Generierung von Sätzen, in denen ein vorher eingeführtes Nomen durch ein Demontrativpronomen und Generikum wiederaufgenommen werden soll, wie in 'wir haben Indigo verwendet. *Dieser Farbstoff* eignet sich gut für Baumwollfärberei.'

Für den (weniger gut dokumentierten) Bereich der Verben kann mit einer semantisch motivierten Klassifikation wie derjenigen von [SCHUMACHER et al. 1986] gearbeitet werden, die sieben Klassen unterscheidet, von denen die meisten wiederum unterteilt sind in [ZUSTANDSVERB]-[VORGANGSVERB]-[KAUSATIVVERB]. Die folgende Abbildung stellt die Verbklassen zusammen:

```
-----------------------------------------------------------
|                                                         |
|   - Existenz                                            |
|      - allgemeine Existenz                              |
|          - Zustand                                      |
|          - Vorgang                                      |
|          - Kausativ                                     |
|      - spezielle Existenz                               |
|          - Existenzsituierung                           |
|          - Existenz in e. speziellen Kontext            |
|          - (kausative V. d. Ex. in e. spez. Kont.)      |
|                                                         |
|   - Differenz                                           |
|      - allgemeine V. d. Differenz                       |
|      - Einfache Änderungsverben                         |
|      - Kausative Änderungsverben                        |
|                                                         |
|   - Relation, Geistiges Handeln                         |
|      - Allgemeine Relationsverben                       |
|      - Identität und Äquivalenz                         |
|      - V. des Strukturierens                            |
|      - V. d. Bestandteilrelation                        |
|      - V. d. Grundlegung                                |
|      - V. d. Folgens und der Folgerung                  |
|      - V. d. Zielens                                    |
|      - V. d Berührung                                   |
|      - V. d. Evaluation                                 |
|      - V. d. Orientierung                               |
|      - V. d. Aufmerksamkeit                             |
|      - V. d. Außerachtlassens                           |
|      - V. d. geistigen Beschäftigung                    |
|      - V. d. Untersuchens                               |
|      - V. d. Prüfens                                    |
|                                                         |
|   - V. d. Handlungsspielraums                           |
|                                                         |
|   - V. d. sprachlichen Ausdrucks                        |
|      - V. d. Mitteilens                                 |
|      - V. d. Übermittelns                               |
|      - V. d. Diskutierens                               |
|                                                         |
|   - V. d. vitalen Bedürfnisse                           |
|      - Besitz und Besitzwechsel                         |
|      - Konsumation                                      |
|      - Schlafen und Wachsein                            |
|                                                         |
|---------------------------------------------------------|
|   Die Verbklassen von SCHUMACHER et al. 1986            |
-----------------------------------------------------------
```

3.1.2 Realisierungsklassen — Darstellung von Subkategorisierungsinformation

Das oben mit der Lexikalisierung von 'MEET' gegebene Beispiel zeigt, daß man bei der verbklassenunabhängigen Definition der Realisierung von Füllern semantischer Rollen ([OBJECT] —→ direktes Objekt) eine relativ hohe Anzahl von Abweichungen (wie bei *begegenen* + DAT.) gesondert behandeln muß.

Im Rahmen des EUROTRA-D/SEMSYN-Experiments wurde mit verbklassenspezifischen Regeln zur Realisierung von Füllern semantischer Rollen gearbeitet [HEID/RÖSNER/WECK 1987]. Die Verbklassen stammen aus der Systemic Functional Grammar [HALLIDAY 1985] und wurden bei EUROTRA-D für das Deutsche überarbeitet [STEINER 1986].

Das in diesem Experiment verwendete Verbklassensystem ist hierarchisch organisiert: es kennt vier Verbklassen, die jeweils Unterklassen haben. Im Sinne der Dependenzgrammatik wird innerhalb der Unterklassen nach der Anzahl der (obligatorischen und fakultativen) Verbkomplemente unterschieden (bezeichnet durch 1rp (= Einrollenprozeß), 2rp, 3rp). Die folgende Abbildung gibt einen Überblick über die Klassenhierarchie (PR-OR = Processor-Oriented, PH-OR = Phenomenon-Oriented, 2-PH = Two Phenomena):

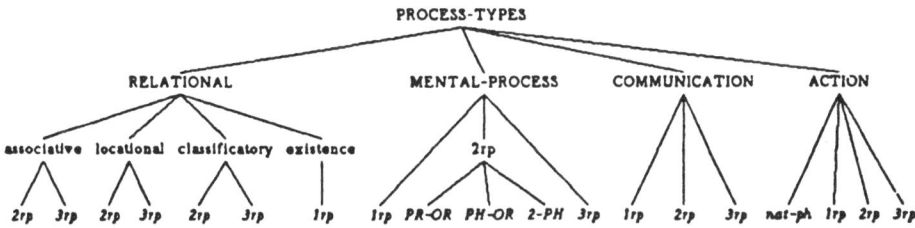

Damit wird die Realisierung der semantischen Relationen von der jeweiligen Verbklasse abhängig, der das zur Lexikalisierung der semantischen Symbole gewählte Lexem angehört. Solche verbalen Realisierungsklassen können auch abstrakt definiert werden (z.B. Verben, die Subjektsatz erlauben, Verben die Objekts-Prädikativ subkategorisieren, etc...).

Diese Verbklassen sind in einem objektorientierten System leicht auf Objekthierarchien abbildbar. Damit läßt sich weitgehende Redundanzfreiheit des syntaktischen Wörterbuchs erreichen: Generalisierbare Informationen über die syntaktische Konstruktion der Verben einzelner Verbklassen sind Bestandteil der Definition der Klassen und werden vererbt. Beim einzelnen Lexem werden nur die relativ wenigen Abweichungen von den für die Klasse gültigen Standardannahmen und valenzbedingte (semantisch 'leere') Präpositionen eingetragen.

3.1.3 Flexions- und Derivationsklassen – Darstellung morphologischer Information

Analog zur Darstellung von flexionsmorphologischer Information in Klassen, wie sie bereits in SEMSYN erfolgt, lassen sich auch für derivationsmorphologische Angaben Regelmäßigkeiten formulieren und für die Lexikonorganisation nutzen. Das Vorhandensein eines Inventars von Suffixen erschließt die flexionsmorphologischen Eigenschaften von Suffigierungen: für das Suffix *-ung* kann angegeben (und vererbt) werden, daß es feminine Nomina bildet, die einer regelmäßigen Pluralklasse angehören. Soweit die Derivation produktiv ist, können Regeln für die Kombinierbarkeit von Stämmen mit Affixen geschrieben werden. Für valenztragende Adjektive (z.B. *reich an* oder *nahe* (+ DAT)) und für Partizipien können Regeln formuliert werden, die als Varianten von *reich an Nährstoffen, der Regierung nahe, von der CDU regiert, den Verkauf fördernd* auch Komposita *nährstoffreich, regierungsnah, CDU-regiert, verkaufsfördernd* erzeugen [WILSS 1986]. An der Formulierung solcher Regeln wird derzeit gearbeitet. Entscheidungsparameter sind außer der Subkategorisierungsinformation auch die thematischen Rollen (AGENT, OBJECT,...).

3.2 Interaktion zwischen den Wörterbüchern einzelner Beschreibungsebenen

Bei der Generierung von Sätzen oder Nominalphrasen wird nacheinander auf verschiedene Typen lexikalischer Information zugegriffen. Komplexe Aufgaben, wie z.B. die Generierung verbaler und nominaler Varianten aus derselben semantischen Eingabestruktur, machen es nötig, daß die Einzellexika miteinander interagieren. Diese Interaktion kann bedeuten,

(1) daß von einem Lexem (z.B. im semantisch-deutschen Wörterbuch) auf eine (z.B. morphologische oder syntaktische) Klasse explizit verwiesen wird (Verweis),

(2) daß es zwischen verschiedenen Klassen (z.B. einer semantischen und einer syntaktischen Verbklasse) definierte Beziehungen gibt, so daß von einer Klasse auf eine andere verwiesen werden kann (= 'Klassenverweis'),

(3) daß über einzelne Klassen der Teilwörterbücher Redundanzregeln operieren, die klassenweise (oder global) aus vorhandenen Lexikoneinträgen neue Einträge erzeugen.

Fall (2) soll im Folgenden anhand des Zusammenhangs zwischen semantischen Verbklassen und Subkategorisierungsklassen, Fall (3) am Beispiel des syntaktischen Verhaltens von deverbalen Substantiven dargestellt werden.

3.2.1 Semantische und syntaktische Verbklassen

Das Inventar der von [SCHUMACHER ET AL. 1986] beschriebenen semantischen Verbklassen ist oben in Abbildung 1 angegeben worden. Für SEMSYN wurde versucht, eine linguistisch motivierte und unter Generierungsgesichtspunkten effizient ausnutzbare Abbildungsbeziehung zwischen diesen Klassen und den von [STEINER 1986] aufgestellten syntaktischen Verbklassen zu formulieren. Stark vereinfacht, trennt [STEINER 1986] Verben mit den folgenden Typen von Argumenten (d.h. folgende Realisierungsklassen):

- Satzförmige Argumente (MENTAL PROCESS- und COMMUNICATION-Verben)
    - mit Subjektsatz: PHENOMENON-ORIENTED
    - mit Objektsatz: PROCESSOR-ORIENTED
    - mit Subjekt- und Objektsatz: TWO PHENOMENA
    - mit direkter Rede: COMMUNICATION
- Prädikative Argumente (RELATIONAL-CLASSIFICATORY-Verben)
- Adverbiale Argumente (RELATIONAL-CLASSIFICATORY-Verben)

- [LOKAL-] oder [DIREKTIONAL-] Angaben als Argument
  (RELATIONAL-LOCATIONAL-Verben)
- Direkte Rede als Argument (COMMUNICATION-Verben)

Der Unterschied zwischen propositionalen und nicht-propositionalen Verbergänzungen, der in semantischen Netzen direkt ablesbar ist, kann als Kriterium für die Abbildung verwendet werden: auf dieser Basis läßt sich für jede semantische Klasse eine Standard-Realisierungsklasse ermitteln, in vielen Fällen ist die Abbildung eindeutig. Die folgende Illustration stellt dar, auf welche Realisierungsklassen die Klasse der Differenzverben abgebildet wird:

- Allgemeine Verben der Differenz
  - *[+propositional]*: MENTAL PROCESS
  - *[-propositional]*: RELATIONAL-LOCATIONAL (zweistellig)
- Einfache Änderungsverben
  - *[-propositional]*:
    - *Reflexives Verb*: RELATIONAL-LOCATIONAL (dreistellig)
    - *ohne refl. Verb*: ACTION (zwei- oder dreistellig)
- Kausative Änderungsverben
  - *[+propositional]*: PHENOMENON-ORIENTED (default)
  - *[-propositional]*: RELATIONAL-CLASSIFICATORY (dreistellig)

Beispiele für Default-Klassenverweise sind:

- Verben der *Berührung*: PHENOMENON-ORIENTED
- Verben der *Evaluation*: CLASSIFICATORY (dreistellig)
- Verben der *Aufmerksamkeit*: PROCESSOR-ORIENTED
- Verben des *Untersuchens*: PROCESSOR-ORIENTED
- Verben des *Prüfens*: PROCESSOR-ORIENTED
- Verben der *Konsumation*: ACTION

Bezieht man Unterklassen bzw. die Unterscheidung zwischen Zustands-, Vorgangs- und Kausativverb mit ein, so lassen sich die folgenden Regeln formulieren:

- Existenz im speziellen Kontext, [KAUSATIV]: RELATIONAL-ASSOCIATIVE
- Sprachlicher Ausdruck, *Mitteilung*: COMMUNICATION
- Sprachlicher Ausdruck, *Diskussion*: PROCESSOR-ORIENTED
- Vitale Bedürfnisse, *Schlaf* [ZUSTAND] oder [VORGANG]: ACTION
- Vitale Bedürfnisse, *Besitz*: RELATIONAL-ASSOCIATIVE

Die Verwendung klassenweiser Verweise erlaubt es also, aufgrund der Zugehörigkeit einer Verblesart zu einer semantischen Verbklasse nach SCHUMACHER ET AL. 1986, kombiniert mit der direkt aus dem aktuellen semantischen Netz ablesbaren Unterscheidung von Verbargumenten in Sachverhalte oder Entitäten/Qualitäten, in den meisten Fällen die Realisierungsklasse zu erschließen, der die betreffende Lesart zuzuordnen ist. In analoger Weise kann von einer Oberklasse des onomasiologischen Wörterbuchs auf eine abstrake Realisierungsklasse verwiesen werden. Wie für alle "Schlaf"-Verben die intransitive Konstruktion vorhergesagt werden kann, so wäre z. B. bei der SEMSYN-Anwendung auf Strukturen, die der TOMITA-Parser liefert, ein Verweis von "INGEST-MEDECINE"-Symbolen auf eine Realisierungsklasse von Verben denkbar, die Subjekt und direktes Objekt als Argumente nehmen (*nehmen, einnehmen, zu sich nehmen, schlucken, (zer)kauen,...*).

3.2.2 Generierung von Varianten: Redundanzregeln für die syntaktische Konstruktion von deverbalen Nomina

Der Generator von SEMSYN ist in der Lage, aus einer semantischen Struktur wahlweise einen Satz oder eine Nominalgruppe zu generieren. Die Entscheidung über die Wahl des Realisierungstyps wird durch globale Stilvorgaben (z.B. Text vs. Titel) getroffen [RÖSNER 1986b].

Die syntaktische Konstruktion der Nominalisierungen von Verben scheint von der semantischen Klasse, der das Basisverb zugehört, unabhängig zu sein. Sie kann vielmehr über Redundanzregeln gesteuert werden: für die von Verben subkategorisierten syntaktischen Funktionen lassen sich Regeln angeben, die festlegen, wie diese syntaktischen Funktionen beim deverbalen Substantiv realisiert werden. Für die Konstruktion regelmäßiger deverbaler Nomina muß deswegen kein eigener syntaktischer Wörterbucheintrag angelegt werden: die entsprechenden Einträge können, analog zu Flexionsformen, über Regeln erzeugt werden. Nachfolgend einige wichtige Regeln in vorläufiger, informeller Formulierung:

- valenzbedingte Präpositionalergänzungen sind bei Verb und Nominalisierung gleich

- propositionale Argumente sind bei Verb und Nominalisierung gleich

- Prädikativa können nur als Ergänzungen von Nominalisierungen auftreten, wenn sie durch die Präposition *als* eingeleitet werden

- treten Subjekt oder Objekt bei einem Verb auf, jedoch nicht gemeinsam im selben semantischen Netz, so werden sie bei der Nominalisierung als Genitivattribut realisiert

- treten Subjekt und Objekt beim Verb gemeinsam auf, so wird bei der Nominalisierung das Objekt als Genitivattribut, das Subjekt als *durch*-PP realisiert

Mit derartigen Regeln ist es möglich, aus der syntaktischen Struktur, die aus einer (wie auch immer gearteten) Kasusrahmennotation bei verbaler Realisierung erzeugt würde, die entsprechende Realisierung bei nominaler Ausdrucksweise direkt abzuleiten. Da die Regeln auf der syntaktischen und nicht auf der Ebene der semantischen Relationen ansetzen, können sie unverändert für die Variantengenerierung aus semantischen Repräsentationen unterschiedlichen Typs verwendet werden.

4 Ergebnisse, mögliche Erweiterungen

In diesem Beitrag sollte die lexikalische Wissensquelle des Generierungssystemes SEMSYN vorgestellt werden; gleichzeitig wurden Vorschläge diskutiert, die es erlauben sollen, Information zu verschiedenen linguistischen Beschreibungsebenen getrennt und weitgehend redundanzfrei abzulegen. Zu dieser Platzersparnis tragen die konsequente Verwendung von Lexemklassen mit Unterklassen, d.h. die Ausnutzung der Vererbungsmechanismen des Systems, und die Benutzung von Redundanzregeln (z.B. für die syntaktische Konstruktion von Nominalisationen) bei.

Die Trennung der linguistischen Beschreibungsebenen ermöglicht es, die jeweiligen Beschreibungen deklarativ zu formulieren. Außerdem sind einzelne Teile des Wörterbuchs austauschbar, ohne daß die anderen Teile deswegen angepaßt werden müßten. So liegt z. B. für die syntaktische (Subkategorisierungs-) Komponente ein Entwurf für das Französische vor, der, gegeben eine französische Morphologie- und Grammatik-Komponente, die Generierung von französischen Sätzen und Nominalgruppen aus den semantischen Repräsentationen erlauben würde, die bei EUROTRA-D verwendet werden. Eine französische Flexions-Morphologiekomponente, die analog zur deutschen organisiert sein soll, ist in Arbeit. Experimente zur Generierung englischer Arbeitsmarktbulletins wurden bereits erfolgreich durchgeführt. Von dem modularen Aufbau des Lexikons kann man eine relativ einfache Austauschbarkeit der als Eingabe verwendeten semantischen Repräsentationen erhoffen. Wie die Variantengenerierung dürfte auch die Parallelgenerierung in verschiedenen Sprachen durch die vorgeschlagene Modularisierung erleichtert werden.

Literatur

[BROCKHAUS 1976]
Klaus Brockhaus et al.: *Forschungsbericht 1.11.73/31.3.76. Sonderforschungsbereich 99 ('Linguistik'). Teilprojekt A2 (Automatische Übersetzung)*, Heidelberg.

[EMELE/MOMMA 1985]
Martin Emele / Stefan Momma:*SUTRA-S - Erweiterungen eines Generator-Front-End für das SEMSYN-Projekt*, Studienarbeit (Stuttgart: Institut für Informatik) 1985.

[HABEL 1985]
Christopher Habel: 'Das Lexikon in der Forschung der künstlichen Intelligenz', in: SCHWARZE, Christoph/WUNDERLICH, Dieter (Hrg.): *Handbuch der Lexikologie*, (Königstein: Athenäum) 1985: 441-474.

[HALLIDAY 1985]
M.A.K. Halliday: *Introduction to Functional Grammar* (London: Arnold) 1985.

[HEID/RÖSNER/WECK]
Ulrich Heid / Dietmar Rösner / Birgit Weck: 'Das EUROTRA-D/SEMSYN-Experiment: Generierung deutscher Sätze aus semantischen Repräsentationen', in: TILLMANN, Hans G./WILLEE, Gerd (Hrsg.): *Analyse und Synthese gesprochener Sprache. Vorträge im Rahmen der Jahrestagung 1987 der Gesellschaft für Linguistische Datenverarbeitung e. V. , Bonn, 4.-6. März 1987* (Hildesheim: Olms) 1987: 172-178.

[HEID/WECK 1987]

Ulrich Heid / Birgit Weck: 'Die Verbklassifikation von STEINER 1986 als Basis für die Generierung deutscher Sätze.' erscheint in: *Proceedings First International Conference on Terminology and Knowledge Engineering*, Trier, 1987.

[HOSAKA 1987]

Junko Hosaka: 'Probleme bei der maschinellen Übersetzung Japanisch-Deutsch', Vortrag bei der Jahrestagung 1987 der Gesellschaft für Angewandte Linguistik (GAL), Heidelberg, 1.-3.10.1987, manuscript.

[KEHL 1986]

Walter Kehl: *GEOTEX – Ein System zur Verbalisierung geometrischer Konstruktionen*, Diplomarbeit (Universität Stuttgart, Institut für Informatik) manuscript.

[RÖSNER 1986a]

Dietmar Rösner: 'When Mariko talks to Siegfried - Experiences from a Japanese/German Machine Translation Project', in *Proceedings of COLING 1986*, (Bonn: IKP) 1986: 652-654.

[RÖSNER 1986b]

Dietmar Rösner: *Ein System zur Generierung deutscher Texte aus semantischen Repräsentationen*, Diss. (Stuttgart: Institut für Informatik) 1986.

[RÖSNER 1987a]

Dietmar Rösner: 'The automated news agency: The SEMTEX text generator for German', in: KEMPEN (Ed.) 1987, soll erscheinen.

[RÖSNER 1987b]

Dietmar Rösner: 'Semantik als Basis multilingualer Maschineller Übersetzung: Bericht über ein Experiment', Vortrag bei der Jahrestagung 1987 der Gesellschaft für Angewandte Linguistik (GAL), Heidelberg, 1.-3.10.1987, manuscript.

[SCHUMACHER 1986]

Helmut Schuhmacher (Hrg.): *Verben in Feldern -Valenzwörterbuch zur Syntax und Semantik deutscher Verben*, (Berlin: de Gruyter) 1986 [= Schriften des Instituts für deutsche Sprache, Bd. 1].

[STEINER 1986]

Erich Steiner: 'Generating semantic Structures in EUROTRA-D', in *Proceedings of COLING 1986* (Bonn: IKP) 1986: 304-306.

[TOMITA/CARBONELL 1986]

Masaru TOMITA / Jaime G. CARBONELL: 'Another stride towards knowledge-based Machine-Translation', in *Proceedings of COLING 86* (Bonn: IKP): 633-638.

[WILSS 1986]

Wolfram Wilss: *Wortbildungstendenzen in der deutschen Gegenwartssprache*, Tübingen 1986.

[WERSIG 1978]

Gernot Wersig: *Thesaurus-Leitfaden. Eine Einführung in das Thesaurus-Prinzip in Theorie und Praxis*, (München/New York: Saur, Verlag Dokumentation), 1978.

Generierung mit GPSG

Stephan Busemann

Technische Universität Berlin
Computergestützte Informations-Systeme (CIS)
Projektgruppe KIT
Sekr. FR 5-8
Franklinstraße 28/29
D-1000 Berlin 10
BUSEMANN@DBOTUI11.BITNET

1 Einleitung

Im Berliner Projekt KIT/NASEV [1] wird die Theorie der Generalisierten Phrasen-struktur-Grammatiken (GPSG) in ihrer neuesten Version (Gazdar, Klein, Pullum, Sag 1985; Abk.: GKPS) für die syntaktische Analyse und Generierung natürlichsprachlicher (NL) Sätze bei der maschinellen Übersetzung (MÜ) nutzbar gemacht. Die Generierung geht von einer oberflächennahen semantischen Repräsentation eines Satzes aus und erzeugt auf der Grundlage von GPSG einen syntaktischen Baum, dessen Blätter terminale Wortformen ergeben. Dabei erweist es sich als notwendig, die deklarative Sicht von Grammatik in GKPS als eine Relation zwischen syntaktischen Strukturen und Sätzen durch eine konstruktive Sicht zu ergänzen, mit der es erst möglich wird, sprachliche Prozesse auf der Grundlage von GPSG zu definieren (Kap. 2).

Eine solche Operationalisierung liegt dem Berliner GPSG-System (Kap. 3) zugrunde, das neben dem Generator einen komfortablen Grammatik-Editor und zwei Parser umfaßt. Durch die strikte Trennung zwischen einzelsprachlichem Grammatikwissen und Prozeßwissen kann es als integraler Bestandteil eines MÜ-Systems aufgefaßt werden.

Auf dieser Grundlage wird in Kap. 4 das Zusammenwirken der GPSG-Komponenten bei der Generierung beschrieben.

----

[1] Dieser Aufsatz entstand im Rahmen des Projekts KIT/NASEV, das als Teilprojekt der EUROTRA-D-Begleitforschung vom Bundesminister für Forschung und Technologie unter dem Kennzeichen 10 13207-1 gefördert wurde.
Mein besonderer Dank gilt Christa Hauenschild für zahlreiche Hinweise und Anregungen.

2 Eine Operationalisierung der GPSG

Kennzeichnend für GPSG ist die ungewöhnliche Vielfalt an zusammenwirkenden Komponenten, die es erlauben, universelle linguistische Generalisierungen im Formalismus und einzelsprachliche in der Grammatik auszudrücken [2]:   ID-Regeln und LP-Aussagen (Wissen über unmittelbare Dominanz in Regeln und lineare Präzedenz in der Grammatik), Metaregeln, Verwendung einer X-Bar-Syntax, syntaktische Merkmale und Kategorien, ausgezeichnete Merkmalmengen (z.B.   HEAD, FOOT), Heads, semantische Typen, FCRs (Feature Cooccurrence Restrictions), FSDs (Feature Specification Defaults) und die universellen Merkmalsverteilungsprinzipien (FFP: Foot Feature Principle; HFC: Head Feature Convention; CAP: Control Agreement Principle).

Das Zusammenwirken der einzelnen Elemente läßt sich als Merkmalsverteilungstest auffassen: Ein syntaktischer Baum entspricht irgendeinem NL Satz, wenn er zulässig ist. Er ist zulässig, wenn seine Blätter aus terminalen Symbolen (Wörtern) bestehen und wenn sämtliche lokale Teilbäume (d.h. der Tiefe 1) zulässig sind. Ein lokaler Baum ist zulässig, wenn er aus einer Projektion (vgl. GKPS:78) einer ID-Regel hervorgeht und den FSDs, den Merkmalverteilungsprinzipien und den LP-Aussagen nicht widerspricht oder wenn er aus dem Lexikon generiert wird (seine Blätter bestehen aus terminalen Symbolen).

Diese Wohlgeformtheitsbedingungen für lokale Bäume operieren als Filter, indem sie für jede erzeugbare Projektion feststellen, ob sie zulässig ist. Solche Filter setzen die Generierung aller Projektionen zu einer ID-Regel voraus und sind daher für maschinelle Sprachverarbeitung ungeeignet. Aus konstruktiver Sicht sollten die Prinzipien der Merkmalsverteilung als Prinzipien des Merkmalstransports wirken, die nur zulässige Projektionen erzeugen. Das in ihnen kodierte universelle sprachliche Wissen dient dann weniger zum Überprüfen von Merkmalspezifikationen sondern vor allem als Anweisung, wie ein unspezifiziertes Merkmal zu instanziieren ist.

Analog verhält es sich mit den FCRs. Als Prädikate über Kategorien können sie nicht nur für ein Merkmal M einen bestimmten Wert W fordern; sie können auch verlangen, daß M undefiniert ist oder irgendeinen Wert hat. Diese implizite Disjunktion aller möglichen Werte und die Forderung der Undefiniertheit filtern unzulässige Kategorien aus, sie sind aber nicht geeignet, Merkmale zu instanziieren. Um FCRs in der konstruktiven Version einheitlich als Instanziierungsanweisungen aufgrund bestimmter Merkmalspezifikationen benutzen zu können, wird ein Merkmalwert für 'undefiniert' angenommen ('~').

Die deklarative Definition der GPSG macht keine expliziten Annahmen über eine Reihenfolge, in der die Tests durchzuführen seien. Die konstruktive Sicht erfordert hingegen eine Abarbeitungsreihenfolge, in deren Verlauf ein anfänglicher Zustand der

----

[2] Die Kenntnis des Formalismus wird im folgenden vorausgesetzt; wem die Lektüre von (GKPS Kap. 1-5) zu aufwendig ist, dem sei (Sells 1986, Kap. 3) empfohlen.

Unterbestimmtheit von Kategorien in einen Zustand maximaler Spezifikation überführt wird.

Shieber hat eine strikte Abfolge aus GKPS extrahiert (vgl. Shieber 1986:213), aus der die Ordnung CAP -- FFP -- HFC -- LP hervorgeht. Bei einer solchen Reihenfolge ergeben sich derzeit ungeklärte Probleme hinsichtlich der wechselseitigen Abhängigkeiten zwischen CAP und HFC (vgl. Shieber 1986:215). Außerdem schränkt CAP in der Definition aus GKPS die Möglichkeiten von LP-Generalisierungen gerade in einer Grammatik für eine Sprache mit relativ freier Wortstellung wie das Deutsche durch die Annahme binärer Strukturen stark ein [3]. Dies motivierte die Ersetzung von CAP in der Berliner Version durch ein rein syntaktisch gesteuertes Kongruenzprinzip (AP: Agreement Principle; Weisweber 1987). AP realisiert Kongruenzrelationen durch die Unifikation [4] einer Anzahl grammatikabhängig zu definierender Merkmale (AGR; z.B. Numerus, Kasus, usw.) an der Mutter und an Töchtern, wobei undefinierte Spezifikationen ausgenommen werden. Mißlingt die Unifikation, ist die Kongruenz nicht herstellbar, und der lokale Baum ist unzulässig. Welche Töchter vom AP betroffen sind, wird von FCRs durch die Instanziierung eines binären Merkmals (agr) festgelegt. Wenn z.B. Töchter mit Kasus Nominativ (cas: nom) oder finiter Verbform (vf: fin) die Spezifikation (agr: +) erhalten, kann das AP Subjekt-Verb-Kongruenz realisieren.

Das FFP wird für den Transport von Informationen über Long-Distance-Phänomene und anaphorische Bindungen genutzt. Es sorgt in der Berliner Version für die Unifikation der nicht in den ID-Regeln spezifizierten FOOT-Merkmale (z.B. slash, reflexiv) in allen Töchtern und der Mutter. Ist ein FOOT-Merkmal an einer Tochter undefiniert, ignoriert das FFP diese Spezifikation; nur wenn es an allen Töchtern undefiniert ist, wird es an der Mutter auch als undefiniert instanziiert. Mißlingt die Unifikation, liegen inkompatible grammatische Informationen vor, und der lokale Baum wird abgelehnt.

HFC bildet in der Berliner Version die Menge unifizierbarer HEAD-Merkmale aller Head-Töchter [5] und versucht, sie mit der Mutter zu unifizieren. Mißlingt die Unifikation, so hat HFC keine Auswirkungen, weist also keinen lokalen Baum zurück. Die Head-Töchter werden in den ID-Regeln durch ein entsprechendes binäres Merkmal

----

[3] Hätte ein lokaler Baum mehr als zwei Töchter, wäre das den Funktor kontrollierende Argument nicht immer eindeutig aufgrund der semantischen Typen identifizierbar (Hauenschild in Vorb.).

[4] Die Unifikation entspricht der in Prolog, wobei Kategorien mit allen n Merkmalen der Grammatik in der Form 'cat(W1,W2,...,Wn)' notiert werden. Der Wert W_j des Merkmals M_j steht in Position j. Die W_j können auch variabel sein und stehen dann für uninstanziierte Merkmale. Die Unifikation von Variablen bewirkt Identität der Werte bei einer späteren Instanziierung.

[5] Mehr als eine Head-Tochter erscheint nur für Koordination sinnvoll.

(head) gekennzeichnet. Beispielsweise bewirkt HFC zusammen mit passenden Spezifikationen des HEAD-Merkmals vf in den ID-Regeln die korrekte Kennzeichnung von Head-Verben als finite Formen, Partizipien oder Infinitive.

Die konstruktive Version der GPSG legt die Abarbeitungsfolge FFP -- AP -- HFC -- LP für die Merkmalinstanziierungsprinzipien (MIPs) nahe (Weisweber 1987). Nach jeder Instanziierung im lokalen Baum können FCRs anwendbar sein, die Voraussetzungen für die Anwendbarkeit nachfolgender Prinzipien herstellen. Da das Merkmal agr durch FCRs instanziiert wird, sollte das AP möglichst spät wirken. AP muß aber vor der HFC wirken, die die Arbeit der anderen Prinzipien voraussetzt (in Analogie zu GKPS:95). Die Definition der HFC basiert also auf dieser Abarbeitungsreihenfolge und der Annahme, daß HFC anders als in GKPS nie unzulässige Projektionen zu bearbeiten hat.

LP-Aussagen instanziieren keine Merkmale, aber sie beruhen auf Merkmal-spezifikationen. Daher sind sie zum Zeitpunkt maximaler Spezifikation, also zuletzt, einzusetzen. In der Analyse überprüfen sie die gegebene Wortstellung in einem lokalen Baum auf Zulässigkeit, während bei der Generierung erst eine zulässige Wortstellung erzeugt wird [6].

Die hier vorgestellte Operationalisierung des Formalismus der GPSG erhebt nicht den theoretischen Anspruch, daß die sprachlichen Universalien aus dem Formalismus als Theoreme hervorgehen (vgl. GKPS:4f). Sie beschränkt sich darauf, die wesentlichen Elemente des Formalismus für die Sprachverarbeitung zu erschließen und eine explizite Rekonstruktion theoretischer Aspekte zu ermöglichen. Dies könnte z.B. durch die Angabe von Regeln erfolgen, wie GPS-Grammatiken zu formulieren sind. In der Berliner Version (wie übrigens auch in GKPS) darf nämlich alles, was die MIPs evtl. nicht leisten könnten, a priori in den ID-Regeln spezifiziert werden; natürlich auf Kosten der linguistischen Aussage des Formalismus und der Ökonomie der Grammatik.

3 Das Berliner GPSG-System

Die skizzierte Operationalisierung der GPSG bildet die Grundlage für die Sprachverarbeitung im Berliner GPSG-System. Das System (vgl. Abb. 1) ermöglicht die Analyse und Generierung mit ein- und derselben Grammatik. Dies wird durch die strikte Trennung des im GPSG-Formalismus repräsentierten sprachlichen Wissens von dem Verarbeitungswissen des Parsers bzw. Generators erreicht. Das System ermöglicht auch den Austausch von Grammatiken, ohne den Parser oder den Generator zu tangieren. Dies ist entscheidend für seine Verwendbarkeit in einem MU-System und wird erreicht, indem einzelsprachliches und universelles sprachliches Wissen strikt getrennt sind.

----

[6] Strenggenommen arbeiten die MIPs bei der Generierung also auf ungeordneten, baumförmigen Graphen, die erst durch die Anwendung der LP-Aussagen zu zulässigen lokalen Bäumen werden.

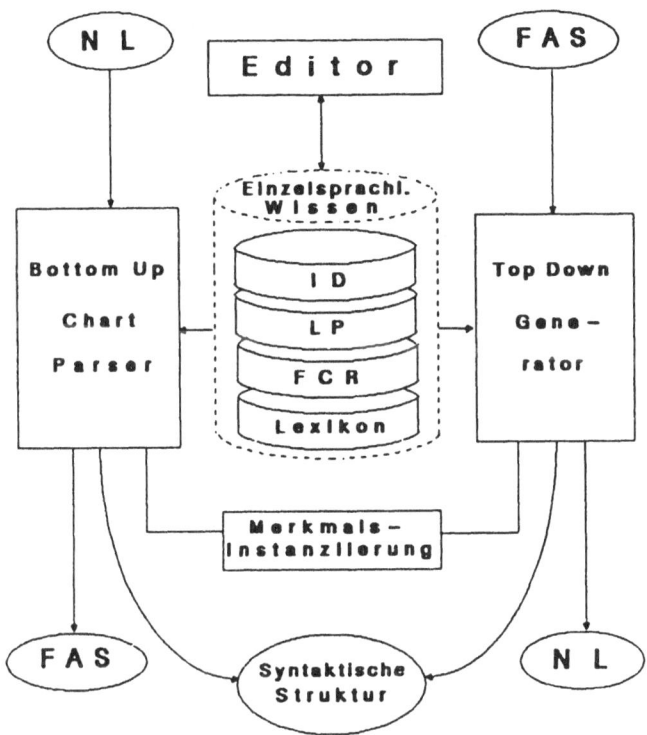

Abb. 1: Das Berliner GPSG-System

Universell sind die prozedural repräsentierten MIPs, die sowohl vom Parser als auch vom Generator benutzt werden. Einzelsprachabhängig ist die deklarativ repräsentierte Grammatik mit ihren ID-Regeln, LP-Aussagen und FCRs sowie das Lexikon.

Im GPSG-System arbeiten alternativ zwei Parser, ein Earley-basierter von Kilbury und Keller (Kilbury 1985) und ein Parser auf der Grundlage von Dominanzrelationen (Weisweber 1987). Die Parser und der Generator erzeugen syntaktische Strukturen; erstere aus NL Sätzen und letzterer aus oberflächennahen semantischen Strukturen, die eine Verallgemeinerung von Funktor-Argument-Strukturen (FAS) sind (vgl. Kap. 4). Mithilfe der syntaktischen Struktur generiert der Earley-Parser eine semantische Repräsentation [7], während der Generator sukzessive jedes Blatt des syntaktischen Baumes morphologisch transformiert und so einen NL Satz erzeugt.

Dies erlaubt dem Generator, Stammformeneinträge des Lexikons zu verwenden. Ein Lexikoneintrag weist einem Wort(stamm) eine syntaktische Kategorie (und ggf. eine semantische Struktur) zu.

---

[7] Er erzeugt mit einer Grammatik des Englischen Ausdrücke in intensionaler Logik (Dowty et al. 1981). Der Dominanz-Parser wird für die Erzeugung von Funktor-Argument-Strukturen nach (Sgall et al. 1973) erweitert.

Die Komplexität einer GPSG erfordert komfortable Entwicklungs- und Erweiterungs-
möglichkeiten. Der linguistisch orientierte Editor des GPSG-Systems (Kindermann,
Quantz 1987) akzeptiert Grammatikwissen in einer leicht lesbaren, 'externen'
Notation und erzeugt eine 'interne' Version der Grammatik, auf die Parser und
Generator zugreifen. Die Expansion von Metaregeln gehört ebenso zu dieser
Aufbereitung wie die Anwendung von FCRs auf ID-Regeln und das Lexikon.

Das GPSG-System wurde an Grammatiken für Fragmente des Englischen und des
Deutschen getestet. Die Grammatik des Deutschen (Preuß 1987) erfaßt typische
Wortstellungsphänomene und behandelt, teilweise in Anlehnung an (Uszkoreit 1984),
subkategorisierte nominale und infinitivische Verbargumente, Verberst-, -zweit- und
-endstellung, Vorfeldstellung der meisten Konstituenten, die üblichen Hilfs- und
Modalverbkonstruktionen sowie eine relativ komplexe Nominalgruppensyntax mit
subkategorisierten Argumenten und (eingeschränkt) Relativsätzen [8].

Das GPSG-System ist vollständig in WC-Prolog auf einer IBM 4381 implementiert.

4 Generierung mit GPSG

Aufgabe einer GPSG-basierten Generierungskomponente ist es, aus einer
Ausgangsstruktur (AS) einen zulässigen syntaktischen Baum und daraus einen Satz zu
erzeugen. Die im Berliner System zur Zeit verwendeten AS spiegeln im wesentlichen
die Anforderungen der Generierung mit GPSG wider und sind nicht von einer
Transferkomponente eines MÜ-Systems generiert worden. Allerdings enthalten sie keine
Informationen, die nicht von typischen semantisch-pragmatischen Verfahren erwartet
werden dürfen. Für den Einsatz in einem MÜ-System ist geplant, Funktor-Argument-
Strukturen auf der Grundlage von (Sgall et al. 1973) als AS zu entwickeln, die
jedenfalls stärker strukturiert als die im folgenden skizzierten sind.

Jede AS enthält lexikalisches Material und syntaktisch relevante Merkmal-
spezifikationen (im folgenden 'Featspec' genannt; vgl. Abb. 2) in einem baumförmigen
Graphen. Zeiger auf Lexikoneinträge erlauben den Zugriff auf Wortstämme und die
ihnen assoziierten lexikalischen Kategorien. 'lex(*verb_uebersetzen*)' in Abb. 2
erzeugt so den Verbstamm 'uebersetz' und eine verbale Kategorie mit der
Spezifikation (subc: 6), die transitive Verben subkategorisiert.
'lex(*verb_futur*)' generiert das Hilfsverb für Futur (Analoges gilt für Passiv und
Perfekt). Modalverben sind durch ihre Position auf einer höheren Ebene der AS
gekennzeichnet (die tiefere Ebene ist in Abb. 2 durch 'embed' markiert). Die
Anordnung und Form der Verben auf einer Ebene wird durch die Grammatik eindeutig
vorgeschrieben. Für das Deutsche gilt (und wurde in der Grammatik kodiert), daß
höchstens je eine Futur- und Passivspezifikation in einem Verbkomplex auftreten

----

[8] In Zahlen: 36 ID-Regeln, 27 FCRs, 9 LP-Aussagen; Kategorien haben 23 Merkmale.

darf, wobei das Futur am obersten und das Passiv am tiefsten Verb stehen muß.

Featspecs in der AS enthalten syntaktische Informationen über den zugeordneten Teilgraphen in Form von Merkmalen der verwendeten Grammatik. Die Spezifikationen zu Beginn in Abb. 2 legen z.B. fest, daß ein Hauptsatz generiert werden soll, was die Zweitstellung eines finiten Verbs erfordert. Andere Featspecs spezifizieren Vorfeldstellung (top), Kasus (cas) und Numerus (plu) für den zugehörigen Teilgraphen.

```
featspec(zweit: +, ac: +)
        lex(*verb_koennen*)
        lex(*futur*)
        embed
            lex(*verb_uebersetzen*)
            featspec(top: -, plu: +, cas: nom)
                lex(*det_def*)
                lex(*noun_kind*)
            featspec(top: +, plu: -, cas: acc)
                lex(*noun_satz*)
                lex(*det_dies*)
```

Abb.2: (Vereinfachte) Ausgangsstruktur für die Generierung von 'Diesen Satz werden die Kinder übersetzen können'

Der Generierungsalgorithmus bildet die syntaktische Struktur im rekursiven Abstieg (top-down) und wendet die MIPs, FCRs und LP-Aussagen beim Wiederaufstieg an (bottom-up). Die Verbalisierung der AS erfolgt durch Unifikation von lexikalischem Material und von Featspecs mit Kategorien im lokalen Graphen. Featspecs in der AS beschränken die Auswahl passender Regeln und damit die Expansion eines lokalen Graphen an einer nicht-lexikalischen Tochter. Eine Regel paßt, wenn die Mutter sowohl mit der Tochter im lokalen Graphen als auch mit den Featspecs unifiziert. So wird die AS nach und nach abgearbeitet und eine syntaktische Struktur aufgebaut.

Der Algorithmus wählt zunächst eine passende ID-Regel aus und betrachtet eine Tochter, die nun mit Material aus der obersten Ebene des fokussierten Anteils der AS (d.h. zunächst aus der gesamten Struktur) unifiziert werden soll. Ist sie mit lexikalischem Material unifizierbar, wird damit ein terminaler Knoten des Syntaxbaums erzeugt.

Ist sie mit einem Featspec unifizierbar, arbeitet das Verfahren rekursiv: Für die Tochter wird eine passende ID-Regel ausgewählt und der dem Featspec zugehörige Teil der AS (in Abb. 2 durch Einrückung markiert) fokussiert. Ist keine Unifikation erfolgreich, wird der Graph an der Tochter expandiert und mit dem betrachteten Teil der AS fortgefahren.

Aus Effizienzgründen sollten zuerst jene Töchter betrachtet werden, die nach möglichst wenigen Expansionsschritten mit lexikalischem Material unifizieren. Daher wird die Heuristik angewendet, zuerst die Tochter mit der niedrigsten Bar-Spezifikation zu betrachten (denn die lexikalischen Kategorien sind mit 'bar: 0' spezifiziert) [9]. Unabhängig davon werden 'rekursive' Töchter zuletzt betrachtet, um Endlosrekursionen auszuschließen.

Ist kein Material mehr für die Tochter vorhanden, war die gewählte Regel ungeeignet, und es erfolgt Backtracking. Der hierdurch verursachte Aufwand wird durch die Zwischenspeicherung generierter Teilbäume eingeschränkt. Sind alle Töchter abgearbeitet, instanziieren MIPs und FCRs den lokalen Graphen. Die endgültige Anordnung der Töchter und damit den lokalen Baum erzeugen dann die LP-Aussagen. Danach wird der lokale Baum verlassen und mit der Betrachtung der Töchter des Muttergraphen fortgefahren. War die Mutter der Startknoten, ist das Verfahren beendet, sofern die AS vollständig verbalisiert wurde.

Ist dies nicht der Fall, wurde zwar ein zulässiger Baum erzeugt, der aber nicht dem zu generierenden Satz entspricht. Das erforderliche Backtracking wird beschränkt, indem der Generator 'embed'-Konstituenten als letzte auf der fokussierten Ebene verbalisiert und bei Featspecs fordert, daß alles zugehörige Material verbalisiert wird. Sonst jedoch darf bei der Unifikation mit der letzten Tochter eines lokalen Graphen durchaus Material übrig bleiben, mit dem eine weitere Konstituente (in einem 'höheren' lokalen Graphen) unifiziert werden soll. Ob aber diese Unifikation gelingt, stellt der Algorithmus erst beim weiteren Wiederaufstieg fest. Hier ist ein Preis für die vollständige Unabhängigkeit der AS-Sprache und des Generators von der Grammatik zu zahlen.

Das Verfahren wird nun am Beispiel veranschaulicht. Abb. 3 zeigt einen Ausschnitt einer zulässigen syntaktischen Struktur für den Satz *Diesen Satz werden die Kinder übersetzen können,* wobei nur wenige Merkmale berücksichtigt sind [10]. Folgende ID-Regeln liegen den numerierten lokalen Bäumen zugrunde (agr und head wie in Abb. 3):

```
(1) s(slash: ~) --> (top: +, slash: ~), s(vf: fin) / (top: +, slash: ~)
(2) s(vf: fin) --> v(subc: 4, vf: fin), s(vf: inf)
(3)          s --> v(subc: 2), s(vf: inf)
(4) s / np(top: +, slash: ~, cas: acc)
             --> np(slash: ~, cas: nom), v(subc: 6)
```

Regel (1) realisiert die Vorfeldstellung einer Konstituente in finiten Sätzen, indem sie die Identität der ersten Tochter mit dem slash-Wert der zweiten in allen Merkmalen fordert. Die Regeln (2) und (3) führen das Futur-Hilfsverb bzw.

----

[9] Die exakte Präferenzreihenfolge der Bar-Werte lautet (für die Grammatik des Deutschen): ⟨0,1,2,3,X,~⟩. Dabei gilt z.B. S = V(bar: 3) und NP = N(bar: 2).

[10] Zur Abkürzung werden konventionelle Kategoriensymbole (S, NP, V) verwendet und die Spezifikationen von agr und head *unter* den Kategorien notiert, deren Bestandteil sie sind. In allen S sind cas und subc undefiniert, in allen NP vf und in allen V cas und slash. Wird top nicht angegeben, gilt (top: -); fehlen andere Merkmale, haben sie variable Werte. Die Notationen 'x(slash: y)' und 'x / y' sind äquivalent.

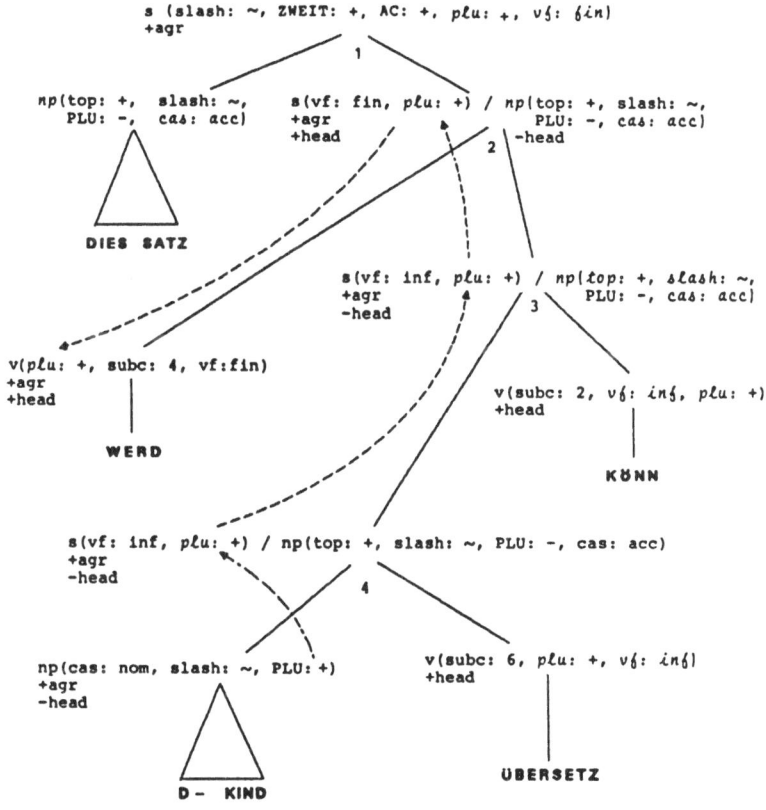

Abb. 3: Syntaktischer Baum (Auszug) für
'Diesen Satz werden die Kinder übersetzen können'

Modalverben ein. Das abhängige S ist stets infinitivisch. In der vierten Regel werden transitive Verben erfaßt, wobei das Objekt nicht lokal präsent ist (slash).

In Abb. 3 sind alle Spezifikationen, die durch ID-Regeln und durch Expansion in lokale Graphen gelangt sind, klein geschrieben. Alle kursiv notierten Merkmale werden durch MIPs instanziiert (FCRs sind für das Beispiel nicht wesentlich). Die Bestandteile in Versalien entstammen der AS (vgl. Abb. 2).

Die Generierung des Baums in Abb. 3 beginnt mit der Auswahl von Regel (1) aufgrund der AS-Spezifikation der Merkmale zweit und ac (die im Beispiel ausgelassen sind). Die S-Tochter wird mit Regel (2) expandiert (der Versuch mit Regel (3) scheitert, weil deren S-Tochter mit (vf: inf) spezifiziert ist, womit kein Futur mehr erzeugt werden kann). Im neuen lokalen Graphen wird das Futur-Hilfsverb (werd) verbalisiert und die S-Tochter mit Regel (3) expandiert, weil das Modalverb nur mit deren V-Tochter unifiziert (subc). Die in der AS verbliebene 'embed'-Konstituente wird als S verbalisiert, das nur durch Regel (4) erfolgreich expandiert wird. Der entstandene vierte lokale Graph nimmt das Hauptverb auf und erzwingt die Verbalisierung des dem Featspec mit (cas: nom) zugeordneten lexikalischen Materials

als NP. Danach sind beide Töchter abgearbeitet, und die MIP's werden aktiviert (die Menge FOOT enthalte das Merkmal slash, AGR die Merkmale cas und plu und HEAD die Merkmale cas, plu und vf).

Das AP transportiert nun die Spezifikation (plu: +) an die Mutter, von wo sie zusammen mit (vf: inf) durch HFC an die Head-Tochter gelangt. Der Infinitiv folgt gemäß den LP-Aussagen als letzte Konstituente im zulässigen lokalen Baum. Auch im dritten Graphen sind alle Töchter abgearbeitet, und das FFP transportiert den slash-Wert der S-Tochter an die Mutter; AP, HFC und LP wirken wie bei Graph (4). Am vollständig abgearbeiteten zweiten Graphen ergänzt dann das FFP den slash-Wert der Mutter und instanziiert damit indirekt auch die noch nicht bearbeitete Tochter im ersten lokalen Graphen. Das AP transportiert (plu: +) an das finite Verb (die Realisierung der Numeruskongruenz zwischen Subjekt und Verb ist durch gestrichelte Pfeile angedeutet). Den LP-Aussagen zufolge steht das finite Verb zuerst.

Das restliche Material aus der AS kann nun mit der verbliebenen Tochter in Graph (1) als NP verbalisiert werden, wodurch (plu: -) an verschiedenen Stellen des Baumes instanziiert wird. AP und HFC wirken an der Mutter, und durch die LP-Aussagen gelangtdie (top: +)-Konstituente an den Anfang. Die Bedingungen für den erfolgreichen Abbruch des Verfahrens sind erfüllt.

Zitierte Literatur

Dowty, David, R.; Wall, Robert; Peters, Stanley (1981): Introduction to Montague semantics. Dordrecht

Gazdar, Gerald; Klein, Ewan; Pullum, Geoffrey; Sag, Ivan (1985): Generalized phrase structure grammar. Blackwell, Oxford

Hauenschild, Christa (i.V.): A constructive version of GPSG for machine translation. Erscheint in: Steiner, E.; Schmidt, P.; Zelinski-Wibbelt, C. (Hg.): From syntax to semantics - insights from machine translation! Frances Pinter, in Vorbereitung

Kilbury, James (1985): A modification of the Earley-Shieber algorithm for direct parsing of ID/LP grammars. In: Laubsch, J. (Hg.): GWAI-84. 8th German Workshop on Artificial Intelligence. Springer 1985, 39-48

Kindermann, Carsten; Quantz, Joachim (1987): Entwurf und Implementierung eines Editors mit integriertem Präprozessor für ein GPSG-basiertes natürlich-sprachliches System. TU Berlin, CIS, Studienarbeit, April 1987

Preuß, Susanne (1987): GPSG-Syntax für ein Fragment des Deutschen. TU Berlin, CIS, KIT-Interner Arbeitsbericht Nr. 19

Sells, Peter (1986): Lectures on contemporary syntactic theories. CSLI lecture notes No. 3

Sgall, Petr; Hajicova, Eva; Benesova, Eva (1973): Topic, focus and generative semantics. Kronberg

Shieber, Stuart M. (1986): A simple reconstruction of GPSG. In: Proc. COLING-86, Bonn, 211-215

Uszkoreit, Hans (1984): Word order and constituent structure in German. Ph.D. Dissertation, University of Texas, Austin

Weisweber, Wilhelm (1987): Ein Dominanz-Chart-Parser für Generalisierte Phrasen-strukturgrammatiken. EWH Koblenz, Diplomarbeit, Mai 1987. Auch: TU Berlin, CIS, KIT-Report Nr. 45

Sektion "Künstliche Intelligenz und Datenbanksysteme - Konzeptuelle Modellierung und Systemarchitektur"

Rudi Studer
IBM Deutschland GmbH
Bereich Wissenschaft - LILOG
Postfach 80 08 80
7000 Stuttgart 80
STUDER at DSOLILOG.EARN

Rückblickend gesehen haben sich die Forschungsgebiete "Künstliche Intelligenz (KI)" und "Datenbanksysteme (DBS)" über lange Zeit hinweg ohne nennenswerte Interaktion parallel zueinander entwickelt. Dies ist insofern nicht weiter verwunderlich, als die Bereiche KI und DBS ursprünglich sehr unterschiedliche Fragestellungen als zentrale Forschungsgebiete hatten, wie z.B. Repräsentation von Wissen oder Inferenzprozesse auf der KI-Seite bzw. Methoden für effizienten Zugriff auf große Datenmengen auf der DBS-Seite.

Ein erster Anknüpfungspunkt ergab sich Ende der 70er-Jahre durch die Entwicklung der sogenannten Semantischen Datenmodelle im DBS-Bereich, da die Modellierungskonzepte semantischer Datenmodelle große Ähnlichkeiten zu den Wissensrepräsentationskonzepten der KI-Formalismen aufweisen. Nachdem man mit einiger Verzögerung die enge Verknüpfung dieser beiden Gebiete erkannt hatte, hat sich seit Beginn der 80er-Jahre eine immer enger werdende Verbindung dieser beiden Bereiche enwickelt und werden heute beide Bereiche unter dem Begriff "Konzeptuelle Modellierung" zusammengefaßt. Ein Markstein in dieser Entwicklung war sicher der Intervale-Workshop über "Konzeptuelle Modellierung" im Jahre 1982 (/BrMS84/).

Ein zweiter Anknüpfungspunkt ergab sich in der vergangenen drei bis vier Jahren dadurch, daß wissensbasierte System im KI-Bereich immer umfangreichere Wissensbasen zu verwalten haben, andererseits im DBS-Bereich eine Entwicklung einsetzte, Datenbanksysteme "intelligenter" zu machen, d.h. die Durchführung von Inferenzprozessen sowie die Verwaltung von komplexen Objekten zu unterstützen. Daraus entwickelte sich das Forschungsgebiet "Wissensbasismanagementsysteme" (siehe /BrMy86/), dessen zentrale Fragestellung die Entwicklung geeigneter Systemarchitekturen ist, die die effiziente Manipulation großer Wissensbasen durch eine Vielzahl von Benutzern ermöglichen.

Die in dieser Sektion enthaltenen Beiträge sind dabei in dieses zweite Themengebiet einzuordnen.

Literaturverzeichnis:

/BrMS84/ Brodie, M.; Mylopoulos, J.; Schmidt, J.W. (eds): On Conceptual Modelling, Springer Verlag, 1984

/BrMy86/ Brodie, M.; Mylopoulos, J. (eds): On Knowledge Base Management Systems, Springer Verlag, 1986

Architectural Concepts for Large Knowledge Bases

Gio Wiederhold, Surajit Chaudhuri, Waqar Hasan,

Michael G. Walker, and Marianne Winslett

Computer Science Department, Stanford University
Stanford, California, 94305

ABSTRACT We describe experience in structuring knowledge gained in two parallel projects. Earlier KBMS projects focused on simplifying access and improving the performance of databases using concepts from artificial intelligence. The RX project developed methods to extract knowledge from databases. Current research (KSYS) exploits this experience to develop and demonstrate new concepts and techniques for managing large collections of knowledge and data.

1. Introduction

As systems using artificial intelligence grow in size and importance, it behooves us to consider the engineering required to implement substantial such systems. Since the newer systems are distinguished by having large amounts of knowledge we consider techniques which now are being classified as *data engineering* [Shuey 86]. We define here *data engineering* as the approach which focuses on the structure of the data, while *software engineering* focuses on the computing procedures. In artificial intelligence (AI) systems, these two aspects of system design are characterized on one hand by a concern about the representation of knowledge and on the other hand by the capabilities of the the interpreters which operate on the knowledge [Barr 81].

Knowledge representation is recognized as a major concern in AI systems. The encoding of knowledge is difficult because of the intrinsic complexity of knowledge. This complexity is evidenced by the many and varied relationships we can define among the conceptual units needed to represent knowledge. On the other hand, structures intended to deal with large quantities of factual data tend to be simple and regular; and much of the recent progress in dealing with large databases is due to the structural simplification provided by the relational model [Codd 70].

In order to deal with demands posed by growing AI systems, a substantial research effort is now devoted to introducing more flexible support structures into databases, as indicated by the collections in [Kim 85], [Brodie 87]. Some researchers in the intersection of AI and databases expect that integrating database techniques into AI systems will provide the necessary assistance to deal with the problems encountered as knowledge bases grow, as seen in some papers presented in [Kerschberg 86]. No convincing demonstration of the benefits of such an integration can yet be shown.

1.1 Motivation

Why should problems arise with large knowledge-based systems? Let us visualize a knowledge base as a graph. Nodes in knowledge-bases represent objects, either conceptual nodes that define abstractions as classes and descriptions, or factual nodes that are typically instances of objects. The important semantics of the nodes are represented by the linkages that connect them to other nodes.

Conceptual nodes represent abstractions at a variety of levels and classifications. Often conceptual nodes apply to many instances. In a database the schema may contain an entry SHIP, and this concept is linked to a list of hundreds or thousands of ship recordss. Associated with each ship record are a number of attributes. A given value in the database, say 1031, is only linked to the identifier QueenElisabeth and the attribute LENGTH.

The nodes we classify as being conceptual can be linked to many other concepts. In an AI system we find relatively more conceptual nodes than in databases, and also a richer set of linkages. While the nodes classified as being factual need only be linked to their descriptor nodes, a ship, say the QueenElisabeth, is also linked to GreatBritain, to the concepts LUXURY, CRUISE, COMMERCE, etc. It is clear that the number of candidate relationships grows rapidly with the number of conceptual nodes.

Traditional databases, being concerned with facts, can use relational tables effectively for the representation of their contents. The relational table provides a regular linkage structure in two dimensions, namely to the attribute and to the entity represented by the key. Maintenance of such a database is fairly straightforward [Schkolnick 85]. Updating is a routine process, and typically performed by clerical personnel. Some checking of constraints may be imposed during update, substantial checking demands knowledge-based techniques [Qian 87].

But traditional databases present only a simple snapshot of a complex world. Not represented are the various levels of abstraction which permit us to manage the real world, nor the constant change that occurs over time, the history that constantly being created, and the change in knowledge which derives from changes over time.

In time-oriented databases a third dimension, *time*, is added, and this seemingly simple extrapolation, although long recognized as being useful [Weyl 75], is just now being dealt with formally [Gadia 86], [Martin 87]. Things get yet worse when more structural relationships are to be considered, such as derived views which join multiple database structures [Bancilhon 81].

Updating of the arbitrary structures used in AI is more difficult yet, in general it is probably n.p. hard as discussed by [Sowa 82] for rule-based representations. Once the expertise needed for an AI system has been extracted from the experts it must be verified by a suite of tests. Of course, no amount of testing can prove correctness in substantial systems. Furthermore, knowledge changes, as systems are expanded in scope and as the world changes. Such continuing development means that they are updated throughout by the experts. The changes in the knowledge base demand considerable retesting, and typically receive less than needed. When AI knowledge bases are placed into production situation without experts being present, they are expected to be stable.

1.2 Restatement of Definitions

In the discussion above we have casually introduced our definition of what is knowledge versus data. We will restate this definition now, since it is the basis for one of the two strategies we are trying to exploit in the research described in this paper. We define *data* as the factual, observable and verifiable descriptions of real-world events, and *knowledge* as the higher level concepts used to structure, classify, and relate such real world events. When the two are brought together, we can produce information [WiederholdWB 87]. A system which applies encoded knowledge to formalized collections of data, or databases, is defined to be a *knowledge-based system*.

These definitions have to be interpreted with some practical engineering sense. For instance, the data describing the contents of a bank account are not visually verifiable: there is no pile of money in the bank with a name on it, and yet, this information is certainly best classified as data. Also, records of events which occurred in the past are no longer verifiable, but are still considered to be data. Some other examples will be harder to classify. For instance, derived data are not dealt with in this classification. This issue is not discussed in this paper, although it is of concern to us.

1.3 A Roadmap

The remainder of this paper has four major sections:

Sec. 2 A description of some of approaches demonstrated in the past within the KBMS project, which focused on simplifying access and improving the performance of databases using concepts from artificial intelligence.

Sec. 3 A discussion of the knowledge base structure used within the RX project, which attempts to extract knowledge from databases.

Sec. 4 The concepts of current research under the KSYS banner which exploits this experience to develop and demonstrate new concepts and techniques for managing large collections of knowledge and data.

Sec. 5 A sketch of the implementation structure of a demonstration system.

2. Work on AI and Data Engineering in the KBMS Project

The application of knowledge about databases has been a focus of our KBMS project. Notice that today databases are rarely used by the users directly, although many languages for direct end-user access have been publicized. Instead, most use is by invoking transaction programs, that are prewritten by programmers or at least technical intermediaries, who understand the semantics and structure of the database. By having processable descriptions of the knowledge that such intermediaries have direct access by end-users should become feasible. The tools made available by researchers in Artificial intelligence provided the basis for the initial phases of our research.

Over the past ten years, our work related to AI and data engineering fell into four main areas:

1 intelligent database interfaces for queries and updates
2 cooperative processing of results for presentation
3 intelligent query optimization
4 techniques to abstract databases statistically

Problems which arose while addressing data engineering issues of knowledge-based systems caused us to formulate our KSYS project, the architecture of which will be sketched later in this paper. Some examples of earlier work are described below; an broader overview of earlier KBMS work is provided in [Wiederhold 84].

The provision of an intelligent database interface to end-users is important because of the potential of the interface to reduce the amount of programming and specialized knowledge required of the database user. For example, the provision of a natural-language interface allows easy access to the database by persons not familiar with the details of the structuring of the data. Similar arguments hold for improving the management of updates to the database. The provision of cooperative responses to queries, in which the system returns not just what the user asked for but also what the user really wanted, is another way to increase productivity.

A query optimizer equipped with specialized knowledge about the domain of inquiry has the potential to produce more efficient executable queries and updates than an optimizer equipped only with domain-independent optimization guidelines. And the use of statistical summary information in a database setting has the potential to speed up response time for queries asking for database statistics. We now look at these three areas in more detail.

2.1 Intelligent Language Interfaces

In the area of natural language interfaces, we have worked on problems associated with ambiguous queries and updates. For example, a practical natural language system must handle realistic database queries containing terms identifying stored entities, such as names of towns, ships, and people. Traditional database-query languages require that such terms appear only in a highly stylized format; for example, "List SHIPS in NameOfPort = 'San Francisco'" is the common method of referring to San Francisco in a database query. To avoid use of awkward, stylized formats for entity references, natural language systems store all such identifying names within a lexicon, along with common verbs and nouns. Now we can ask for "List SHIPS in San Francisco".

The database lexicon is not just a table attached to the query parser, however. A large database may require a lexicon large enough to need database-style utilities to ensure efficient access. In addition, updates to the database require changes in the lexicon, implying that the lexicon should use database technology for its efficient maintenance. By sharing the lexicon with the database, we can also assure that the lexicon is maintained synchronously with the database. If Alviso were to become a port that SHIPS visit, we can immediately ask to "List SHIPS in Alviso".

Ambiguities remain. New York is both a port and a state, and some objects of different classes can have the same identifier, as Kennedy: a ship, a spaceport, an airport, and a president. Within the KBMS project, [Davidson 80] developed and implemented a technique for reducing the number of lexical ambiguities for unknown terms by deferring lexical decisions as long as possible. The database itself is then accessed to try to resolve the ambiguities and complete the parsing. A simple cost model was used to select an appropriate method for resolving any remaining ambiguities.

Although considerable research has been devoted to the problem of processing queries expressed in natural language, the issues and techniques for performing natural-language database updates have had little attention. When attempting to process updates couched in natural language, problems arise that are conceptually similar to the problems associated with updates through database views. The difficulty is that casual users of a natural language system understand neither the scope nor the details of the underlying database, and so may make requests that:

a are reasonable, given their view of the domain, but are nevertheless not possible in the underlying database;
b are ambiguous with respect to the underlying database; or
c have unanticipated collateral effects upon the responses to earlier questions or upon alternative views of the database.

The problem of ambiguity is more severe in the case of natural language updates than in updates through traditional views, because the view of the database implicit in a natural language query is dynamic, varying from moment to moment. In contrast, traditional database views are static, predefined by a database administrator;

reasonable semantics for updates through static views can be given at view definition time, as shown by [Keller 86] within the KBMS project.

To address the problem in a dynamic context, Davidson and Kaplan applied AI techniques to select a plausible natural language update interpretation, based on the user's previous interactions with the database, database semantic constraints, and a goal of minimal side effects [Davidson 83]. If one update interpretation is clearly preferable, then it is chosen; otherwise the user is engaged in a disambiguation dialog.

To control the interpretation, a theory was developed to help identify a particular user's view of the database and to determine the legality, ambiguity, and potential side effects of updates expressed in natural language. A formal analysis of the problems associated with updates expressed on views is central to this work. A system that processes natural language updates using this approach, PIQUE, was implemented. PIQUE explains problems or options to the user in terms the user can understand, and makes changes in the underlying database with a minimal disruption of other views.

2.2 Cooperative Responses to Queries

Cooperation in our KBMS project has addressed looking at the results produced by the database system in response to user queries. The result is processed to give the right ammount of information, not too little and not too much.

In an environment where a user may have incomplete or incorrect knowledge of the structure of available data, queries or updates may be posed that are either unanswerable, impossible to perform, or are otherwise misguided. Our work has shown that such misconceptions can often be detected directly from the phrasing of the user's request and a knowledge of the structure of the database [Kaplan 80]. This information can be used to correct the user's misconceptions and inform the user about the nature of the database and database system. The usefulness of our techniques for cooperative processing of transactions has been demonstrated in a library environment [Corella 84]. These techniques need to be extended to distributed environments, where the knowledge necessary to aid users in use of the database may partially reside at remote sites.

We have also worked on the problem of presenting the information that the poser of a query *really* wants, rather than what was literally requested. In general, users cannot predict the volume or structure of a response, unless they are already quite knowledgeable about the database content. The traditional response to a database query is a list of the set of items from the database that satisfy the conditions presented in the query. This list can be excessively long and is then inappropriate for a conversational system. Often, a more appropriate response to such queries is a description of the set, rather than a listing of its elements. For example, the response "All corporate officers" may be more concise and informative in response to "Which employees profit share?" than a list of a thousand names.

[Kaplan 82] implemented practical techniques for producing a significant class of such responses from existing database systems without using a separate world model or knowledge base. Knowledge available in the structural specification of thge database, as given in structural, entity-relationship, or network models suffices [ElMasri 80].

2.3 Semantic Query Optimization

A request for information can often be formulated in more than one way, depending on knowledge about the subject domain and the ingenuity employed in determining the best access path to the desired information. A question about all SHIPS currently carrying IronOre, for example, can be answered by looking only at information about BulkOreCarriers, assuming that it is known that BulkOreCarriers carry all or most of the IronOre being shipped. Semantic query optimization is a method of improving the performance of database queries by automatically using such domain knowledge. The objective is to transform a query into a semantically equivalent one (i.e., one that produces the same answer but can be processed more efficiently).

A system, QUIST, was implemented within the KBMS project to explore this approach [King 80]. An evaluation of QUIST demonstrated that semantic knowledge about the database can be used in a new way to achieve efficient data retrieval. The method supplements conventional query optimization methods. Drawing on semantic, structural, and processing knowledge, it makes use of the heuristics of query processing developed in prior research.

Performance improvements were demonstrated in a range of query types, by means of transformations that add or delete constraints on attributes or even entire files, as warranted by the database and query structure. In other cases, the system detected unsatisfiable query conditions without inspecting the database, or aborted inference when it determined that no improvement could be expected. Analysis overhead was acceptably low in all cases.

Another optimization technique involves the reuse of information computed by earlier queries. Within the KBMS project, [Finkelstein 82] showed that common expression analysis can be applied in three different settings for optimization of database requests:

1 In an interpretive system, the reuse of answers to previous queries, or temporaries formed in the process of obtaining those answers, may significantly reduce processing time for subsequent queries. Finkelstein defined a methodology, based on the query graph representation, for deciding cheaply whether such temporaries are helpful.

2 A transaction that contains multiple queries may perform redundant database operations. Finkelstein described a procedure for optimization of a collection of queries, that involves computing least upper bounds on query graph nodes (which correspond to scans through relations which might profitably be combined). These are extended to maximal subexpressions between queries, and a heuristic procedure examines possible query revisions to find the best execution procedure.

3 The concept of optimization of generated code was extended to languages with embedded queries (such as SQL in PL/1). For instance, queries in loops can be optimized differentially, and global flow analysis can be used to determine available database expressions at places in the program.

The query graph representation of queries was originated for this work. It represents the structure of requests in an intuitively clear manner. Its decomposition of queries into nodes (relation occurrences in queries labeled with internal selection predicates and projected attributes) and edges (join predicates) serves as a convenient structure for automatic analysis in query optimization.

2.4 Use of a Statistical Abstract of a Large Database

The size of data sets subjected to statistical analysis is increasing as computer technology becomes more sophisticated. It is an attractive alternative for analysis to have quick estimates of descriptive statistics rather than exact values obtained with considerable delay. [Rowe 83] demonstrated within the KBMS project a new technique for estimating database statistics that is a *top-down* alternative to the *bottom-up* method of sampling. This approach precomputes a set of general-purpose database statistics (a *database abstract*) and then uses a set of approximately 400 inference rules to make bounded estimates of other, arbitrary statistics requested by users. The inference rules comprised a new example of an artificial-intelligence expert system. There are several important advantages of this approach over sampling methods, as was demonstrated experimentally in estimating a variety of statistics on two different databases.

Class frames can contain the procedures required to evaluate the statistics, and intermediate concept instance frames can inherit the computation. That way consistency of procedures is assured, complementing consistency of facts in the database.

3. Knowledge Structure for Learning from Data

At the same time a parallel research project, RX, managed jointly with Dr. R.L. Blum, addressed the problem of generating new knowledge. Here the underlying hypothesis is that databases which record faithfully the events in some domain contain valuable experience. Such experience should be extracted to serve as the basis for expert systems, complementing and validating knowledge directly acquired from the expert.

The relative benefits of knowledge acquisition from data versus knowledge acquisition from experts are:

1 Access to experience gathered by many practioners over time; in the RX example we are talking about hundreds of medical residents in an immunology clinic observing and treating patients.

2 No loss of information due to forgetfullness over a long period; the ARAMIS database, used for our experiments, preserves data collected from 1969 to today.

3 No bias, because the outcome is known by the expert, is applied to past information during current recall.

4 There is no excessive emphasis on recent occurrences, as is common when summarized experience is being reported rather than elemental facts.

Not everything favors this mode however:

1 Any form of automated learning is hard, so that each piece of knowledge is acquired at a high computational cost.

2 There are many aspects of learning. RX currently only establishes new causal relationships between predefined concepts. Other learning tasks appear feasible, but require major research efforts.

3 Few databases exist which are sufficiently comprehensive to permit learning other than on a very superficial level. We are relatively lucky here; the ARAMIS researchers were also motivated by a need for a deep understanding of puzzling disease manifestations.

4 Realistic large database have missing data. Our database is more than 85% sparse. Techniques to deal with missing data can be developed but complicate the analysis greatly.

5 Realistic large database have errors. Medical database such as ours have been validated to have fewer than 6% errors, databases in finance have been measured at less than 0.6% [Wiederhold 87]. But any errors can wrack havoc with formal logic, so that uncertainty-based techniques are needed to deal with the data.

RX deals with many of these issues and has discovered some new findings which are being reported in the medical literature [Blum 86]. In this paper however we will focus only on the architectural implications of this research.

3.1 The RX Knowledge Base

The original RX knowledge representation was influenced greatly by the frame methods developed in the MOLGEN project resulting in the UNITS package ([Stefik 79]). In our *ex post facto* analysis of the structures developed to serve the RX applications we were able to semantically classify several forms of knowledge. These semantics have structural implication at a higher level.

In RX the medical knowledge was contained in sizeable nodes implemented as frames, with linkages among them. Statistical knowledge was also represented, but here rules were used, although the rules were bound into frames to control their execution. The structural difference in representation can be related to the goals of RX:

1 Deep medical knowledge, at many levels of abstraction, was needed for the knowledge acquisition task.

2 Surface knowledge of statistics was sufficient to control the analysis operations. Essentially we believed our cooperating statisticians and never needed to justify the rules be referring to the underlying sciences, as for instance probability theory.

The frames establish the concepts and attributes of our medical information. The linkages among the frames are the essential knowledge. The knowledge was initialized by Dr. Blum and some medical collaborators, with extensive reference to textbooks. The aggregate knowledge architecture forms a network; represented by frames with references to each other:

In terms of the linkages we found three types of knowledge representation:

1 Categorical knowledge is hierarchically organized

2 Definitional knowledge relates concepts to factual findings, often reaching outside of its hierarchy

3 Causal knowledge consists of crosslinks in the hierarchy

3.1.1 Categorical Knowledge

The major hierarchy starts with a root frame: ALL-UNITS. Three distinct hierarchies sprout from it:

1 The description of patient state, i.e. the diseases and their symptoms

2 The description of actions, that is the treatments applied to alter the natural progression of state

3 The description of statistical analysis methods used to obtain new knowledge.

Frames at the top levels are illustrated in Figure 1.

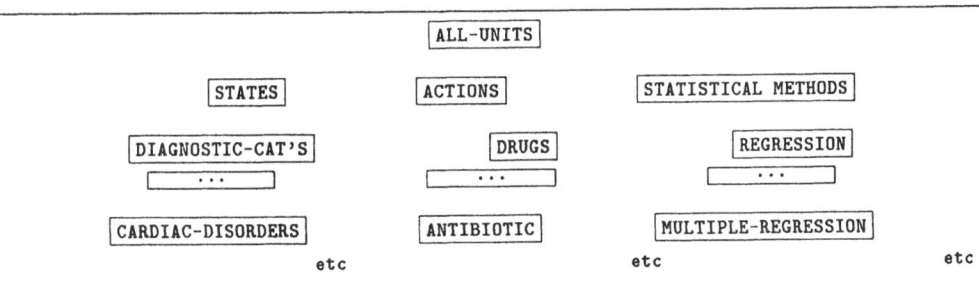

Figure 1   The Top Levels of the RX Hierarchy.

To implement the hierarchical classification of diseases each frame has

1 a generalization slot with one entry and

2 a specialization slot with a variable number of entries

Figure 2 shows frames with their hierarchical linkage slots at two leves of a subtree in the STATES tree.

Having a hierarchical categorization is extremely important; it permits establishment of two computational techniques:

1. Recognition of completeness, so that we can satisfy the state of a node higher in the hierarchy by exhaustively processing all dependent nodes on a lower layer. This argument is of course based on the *closed world* assumption and also exploited in the *negation by failure* rule employed by PROLOG. The hierarchical structure of STATES, for instance, matches the presentation in terms of chapters, sections, and subsections in a textbook, and gives as confidence that the assumption is valid in our case.

2. Inheritance, which permits us to use the knowledge even though we do not have all of medical knowledge in our base. The frames in the disease area represented in the database are fairly completely filled in. Beyond its reach we depend on inheritance to provide information on, say drugs belonging to drug classes which are not appropriate for our range of diseases, but which a patient may receive for other reasons.

While knowledge-bases to deal with classification problems may need no further structure, for our application the categorical knowledge only provides a framework for other types of knowledge.

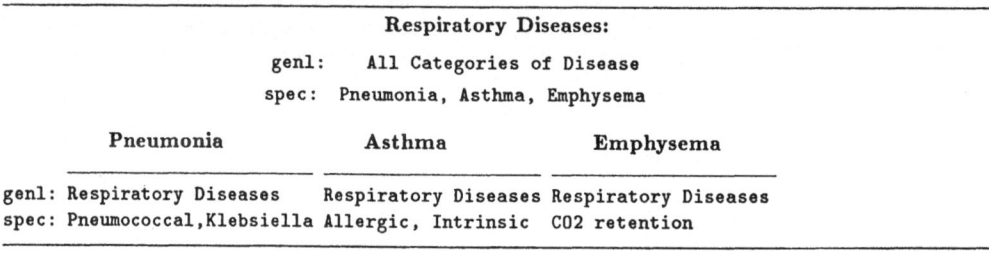

Respiratory Diseases:

```
        genl:   All Categories of Disease
        spec:   Pneumonia, Asthma, Emphysema

     Pneumonia              Asthma              Emphysema

genl: Respiratory Diseases  Respiratory Diseases  Respiratory Diseases
spec: Pneumococcal,Klebsiella Allergic, Intrinsic   CO2 retention
```

Figure 2   Linkage Slots to Implement the Hierarchy.

3.1.2   Definitional Knowledge

Many frames contain values to be instantiated based on conditions at lower levels, but not constrained to the same hierarchy. Definitions are in terms of other attributes in other frames. It is important that knowledge is available at the user and expert level of abstraction. Now the expert can formulate a relationship in terms of disease concepts that are at the same level used in teaching and discussion, rather than at the level that data is being acquired for the database. The definitions are hence typically in terms of lower level frames, eventually terminating at frames which can be bound to the database as shown in Figure 3.

This technique overcomes a rarely expressed, but important problem in the interface between high-level conceptualizers, and people used to working with data, including statistical and data-processing people. It separates

1. the mapping from low level data onto concepts,

from

2. the expression of relationships between concepts.

In current knowledge acquisition techniques both are gathered simultaneously, and the knowledge engineer may be frustrated by the problems the expert has in expressing the issues 'precisely.

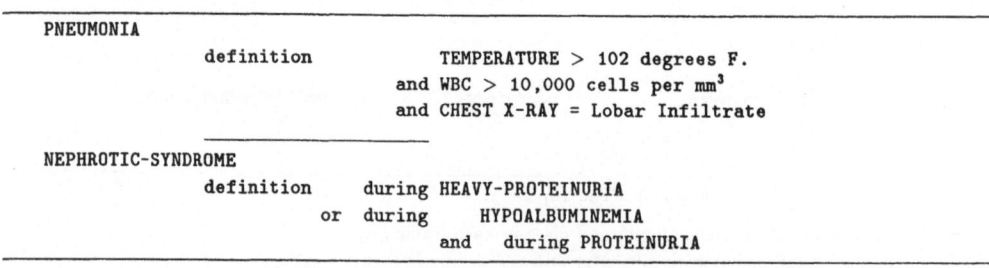

```
PNEUMONIA
                definition              TEMPERATURE > 102 degrees F.
                                  and WBC > 10,000 cells per mm³
                                  and CHEST X-RAY = Lobar Infiltrate

NEPHROTIC-SYNDROME
                definition      during HEAVY-PROTEINURIA
                        or  during    HYPOALBUMINEMIA
                                and   during PROTEINURIA
```

Figure 3   Contents of Two Definitional Frames.

The database we use is structured for efficient access by attribute, rather than by record. This *unnatural* internal arrangement is based on the observation that inference, whether statistical or logical, is by attribute, say Temperature, rather than by object or event, here perhaps Visit 10 of Patient 301. Such a transposed database then stores all values of an attribute for all patients in one, potentially very long record, followed by the data for the next attribute. For a question on how two attributes are related for all patients which satisfy a predicate condition on a third attribute, only three records need to be retrieved.

More precisely, the transposed data is linked to lower level frames as follows:
by FRAME (States, Actions)
   by PATIENT
     by VISIT

An example of the data attributes, as attached to the frames in list notation, is given in Figure 4. The user is unaware of this physical arrangement, unless there is a technical interest due to the good performance of database access. We explain the database to users in relational terms.

```
(Cholesterol

(    (Patient1 (31 29 24 30 31 29))
     (Patient3 (23 - 27 25 ))
     (Patient6 (20 22 ...))
     .  .  .
     (Patient78 (32 34 ...

Prednisone
     (.  .  .
  .  .  .
```

Figure 4   Transposed Database Storage.

3.1.3   Causal Knowledge Links Nodes

But the important knowledge which distinguishes the medical practioners from a generator of medical taxonomies or dictionaries is a grasp of causality. Any treatment or ACTION given the patient will have a multiplicity of effects on the patient's STATE. We must note such relationships in the knowledge base:

```
DE PREDNISONE MODE
     PREDNISONE, at a level of 30 mgms/day,
          usually increases CHOLESTEROL
               by 50 to 130 mgms/dl,
          regularly attenuates NEPHROTIC-SYNDROME
               by 1.0 to 2.0 gms protein/24 hrs,
          regularly attenuates GLOMERULONEPHRITIS
               by 10.0 to 30.0 percent,
          commonly attenuates SLE
               by 10.0 to 30.0 percent activity,
          regularly decreases ANTI-DNA-HEMAGGLUT
               by 50 to 90 percent,
          regularly increases IMMUNOSUPPRESSION
               by 16 to 32 percent activity,
          regularly decreases EOS by 2 to 3 % of WBC,
          occasionally increases KETOACIDOSIS
               by 20 to 100 mgms/dl of glucose,
```

Figure 5   Nodes Directly Effected by One Node.

Of course, with some time delay, changes in STATE nodes will cause changes in other STATE nodes as well.

```
TEMPERATURE
          regularily increases PERSPIRATION
               after 1 hour
```

Figure 6   Causal Relationship within a Subtree.

Each causal relationship is represented as a set of features:

    1 computational: intensity, frequency, direction
    2 descriptive: setting, functional form, validity, evidence

These features are also specified with the slot defining a causal link. For example, the relationship

```
PNEUMONIA
          increases TEMPERATURE
          intensity: to 104 degrees F.
          frequency: common
          direction: +
          setting: studied in middle-aged patients with pneumococcal pneumonia
          functional form: .5log (severity pneumonia) + 98
          validity:  widely confirmed
          evidence:  citations to medical literature
```

Figure 7   Descriptors of a Causal Relationship.

Note that all the terms are represented by numerically encoded values. Furthermore, the interpretation of the frequencies shown is not linear over the range of terms:

Cell	Adverb	Probability	Cell	Adverb	Probability
1	never*	.001	6	commonly	.32
2	very-rarely	.005	7	regularly	.64
3	rarely	.01	8	usually	.95
4	infrequently	.04	9	almost-always	.99
5	occasionally	.16	10	always	1.00
		* well-- hardly ever			

Figure 8   Value to Term Relationship.

The relationship we have used follows a hysteresis curve. We have not formally established its validity. Research to provide a basis for validating terms used in knowledge bases with numerical estimates is now in progress under sponsorship of IBM DPD (KBS).

HEMOGLOBIN	slot	type	*explanation*
Computational	attribute-type	point-event	*represented as a time:value pair*
	value-type	real	*i.e. a real-valued number*
	range	0 < value < 25	*the legal range of values*
	units	grams per deciliter	*measurement units*
	significance	.1	*used for rounding off values*
Real World Knowledge	function	oxygen transport	
	molecular-weight	67,000 daltons	
	structure	Fe + heme + 4 polypeptide chains	
	part-of	red blood cell	
	affected-by	high altitudes, genetic make-up	
	clinical-effects	deficiency causes fatigue	
		severe deficiency may cause cardiac failure	

Figure 9   Other Knowledge in Frame Slots.

3.2 Other Knowledge in the Frames

The frames do of course contain also values to help the inferencing computations. Note that RX does not have a single inference engine. A variety of interpreters share the knowledge base and have their own methods and goals. Further slots in the frames define computational parameters that are needed. Figure 9 shows the frame schema with sample values for Hemoglobin and Figure 10 displays a complete property list of slots relevant for inferencing.

```
PL NEPHROTIC-SYNDROME
    GENL: RENAL-DISORDERS
    SPEC: (PROTEINURIA HEAVY-PROTEINURIA)
    DEFINITION: (OR (DURING & --) (AND & --))
    TYPE: INTERVAL               /* -- marks detail omitted */
    EFFECTS: (URINE-PROTEIN-RANGE ALBUMIN 24-HR-URINE-PROTEIN --)
    MINIMUM-DURATION: 30
    MINIMUM-POINTS: 2
    INTERVALFN: MEAN-DURING-INTERVAL
    VALUE-TYPE: BINARY
    INTRA-EPISODE-GAP: 100
    INTER-EPISODE-GAP: 180
    RECORDS: INVERTED        /* These data are transposed */
    AFFECTED-BY: ((PREDNISONE &) (GLOMERULONEPHRITIS &) (SLE &))
    PARTITION: (0 .5 1 --)
    UNITS: "gms proteinuria/24 hrs"
    PROXIES: (ALBUMIN 24-HR-URINE-PROTEIN URINE-PROTEIN-RANGE)
    ONSET-DELAY: 7          /* days */
    MINIMUM-INTERVAL: 30   /* days */
    CARRY-OVER: 30         /* days */
```

Figure 10   Slots Used for Inferencing Control.

We see in the frames some time-oriented knowledge. This knowledge is critical to establishing potential causality. It is also used to bridge missing data. In this paper we will not follow on the important issues dependent on a time-oriented data and knowledge base, [Blum 82] provides more detail.

3.3 Operational Cycle

To clarify the motivation for the structural detail we have shown we will here list the major phases in RX operation:

1 Initially:
    1.1 Collect data (pre RX: ARAMIS)
    1.2 Define frames from 'textbook' knowledge

2 Discovery: generate hypothesis
    2.1 May be known and initially overlooked
    2.2 May be trivial
    2.3 Are worthy of study

3 Study Module
    3.1 Use knowledge to build model for statistical analysis
    3.2 Use data estimates to select statistical procedures
    3.3 Extract required data from database
    3.4 Perform analysis
    3.5 Inspect result

4 Learning
    4.1 If significant - insert into knowledge base

Another study will now take the new knowledge into account; the scientific loop has been closed.

3.3.1 Use of Data and Knowledge

To summarize we can list the functions that must be supported. Data is used in three phases:
    1 Generate hypotheses
    2 Assure that the data quantities are adequate for a validation study

3 Provide the input to the statistical analyses

Knowledge is used in RX to:

1 Build the model for validation of a hypothesis
2 Select the appropriate statistical procedure for the volume and type of observations held in the database
3 Describe the database for data retrieval

Other projects associated with RX have used the knowledge to summarize voluminous data to reduce the information overload for users faced with long-term medical records [Wiederhold 86]. In current research the data will be used to validate expert provided knowledge as well.

3.3.2 Model Building

Hypothetical relationships, either generated automatically ([Walker 87]) or explicitly stated by an investigator can be processed by the study module. Since this module uses the knowledge base we will sketch its tasks.

To build a model for a hypothetical relationship the interpreter has to collect information on the frequency and strength of known causal relationships. This model is generated by tracing all linkages given in the knowledge base between the nodes involved in the hypothetical relationship. Once all linkages have been located, and pruned for dominants, then it remains to be seen if the known causes fully explain the data, or if there is an additional, direct relationship.

A display of all paths above a threshold can be used to collect significant causes.

```
DP SLE CHOLESTEROL     (default 0.1 ?)

    SLE {30 percent activity} increases
            NEPHROTIC-SYNDROME
                {1 gms proteinuria/24 hrs } increases
                CHOLESTEROL {24 mgms/dl}

    SLE {30 percent activity} is treated by
            PREDNISONE {182 % of baseline} increases
                CHOLESTEROL {14 mgms/dl}

    SLE {30 percent activity} increases
            NEPHROTIC-SYNDROME
                {1 gms proteinuria/24 hrs } is treated by
                    PREDNISONE {143 % of baseline} increases
                    CHOLESTEROL {8 mgms/dl}

    SLE {30 percent activity} increases
            IMMUNOSUPPRESSION
                {18 percent activity} increases
                HEPATITIS {5 Iu/ml of SGOT} increases
                    CHOLESTEROL {6 mgms/dl}
```

Figure 11   Paths through the Knowledge Base.

3.3.3 Causal Inference

Generating new knowledge in RX means establishing and quantifying new causal linkages. Simple correlation, as used in the early discovery modules, does not by itself establish

1 Causality
2 Directness

For causality: "does A cause B ?" we use the heuristic: "if events of class B consistently follows in time events of class A, then B does not cause A". It is possible, of course, that there is an unknown covariate C, causing both with different delays. But this heuristic permits us to break loops using the evidence in the database.

For directness we investigate if the correlation may be due to known causes, using the model as described earlier.

But, to build a model we have also have to consider what other factors can affect the outcome, here changed levels of Cholesterol. These are candidate covariates in a statistical model.

We show a search for a change in Cholesterol Level, i.e., the set of nodes that affect it:

```
DC CHOLESTEROL
CHOLESTEROL
      always is increased by PREDNISONE
      regularly is increased by HEPATITIS
      regularly is increased by KETOACIDOSIS
      usually is increased by NEPHROTIC-SYNDROME
```

Figure 12   Other Causes of the Effect.

3.3.4 Model for the Relationship

If a computable relationship exists, and is valid by statistical tests then we have learned something new. The example below was produced by an RX analysis

```
DM PREDNISONE CHOLESTEROL

      Statistical Model for Prednisone/Cholesterol effect:

      cholesterol =  - 59.17575 albumin
                     + 23.13479 log(prednisone)
                     + 188.1984
                     + error term
      Setting of Effect:
                      not during KETOACIDOSIS
          and         not during HEPATITIS
      Validity of and Evidence in Support of the Causal Relationship:
          PREDNISONE influences CHOLESTEROL.
                      Other details can also be reported and are shown in [Blum 86].
```

Figure 13   Results of a Knowledge-driven Study.

The example above was actually discovered and validated by RX and entered into the knowledge base.

4. Current Research Directions for KBMS

The experience we have gained in the projects described above, as well what we are learning from others, is driving our current research directions. We will first present the principles of our approach, and then sketch its implementation, KSYS.

4.1 Our Approach

To manage large knowledge bases we follow the traditional engineering paradigm of partitioning the problem and trying to conquer the pieces. To defines the partitions we make some operational distinctions.

4.1.1 A model of knowledge and data usage

We view that end-objective of our systems is to deliver Information to decision-makers, and that such information is created due to an interplay of knowledge and data. Clerical staff can enter data, store data, and process data. Selecting the right data for processing, and performing data analysis requires knowledge. Knowledge is acquired by people through training and experience, and is encoded for automated management in expert or knowledge-based systems.

When the data are used to initiate actions and perform actions with a higher degree of confidence than would otherwise be possible, then we have created and used information. Information and the actions effected by information are the end-objective of information systems. There are many paths to obtain information, but a system designer must keep objectives at this level in view.

We believe that it is rare that the simple retrieval of a fact, as John is the Manager of the Toy-department, or a set of facts, as Max and Moritz are the descendants of Johann, provides much information. Information typically requires processing of many selected and retrieved data. Many processing rules are strongly bound to the system, and can be automatically retrieved as well as the data, and executed as needed. Leaving all processing method decisions to the intermediaries has risks of inconsistency. More serious yet is the loss of information if the user must depend on what the intermediaries present.

It is the end-user who initiates real-world actions based on the information. In order to generate an action, there has to be a decision-maker with the authority to carry out the activity. Providing information to a person who cannot effect change is only frustrating. In information system design, it is necessary to identify the person who will benefit from the information.

The actions initiated by the decision-maker will change the state of the world. These changes will be observed, recorded, and entered as data into the systems. Subsequent requests for information will reflect those changes, and cause new decision to be made.

There is also a knowledge loop. As the decision-maker learns from the effect of the actions the actions may change as well. If the knowledge is transmitted to others, by memos, papers, books, or perhaps by encoding in knowledge-based systems, the new knowledge can by applied to instances outside of the local system.

4.1.2 Feedback for evaluation

In order to improve a system, feedback must be encouraged from the users. Users adapt rapidly to awkwardnesses and failures in the system, so an attempt at an evaluation after a long interval of system operation, by sending a questionnaire to the users, will not provide very useful insights. Evidence of system responsiveness will also provide immediate benefits in terms of acceptance and cooperation.

This model of knowledge and data management provides the environment in which knowledge-based *information* systems should function. Direct interaction is needed so that the information users can improve their effectiveness.

4.2 Demonstration of methods

Our Knowledge SYStem project (KSYS) is intended to demonstrate methods towards a systematic approach to deal with large knowledge bases. Given the semantic distinction we make between knowledge and data, we make a corresponding engineering distinction. The notions underlying our current approach are largely based on the research experience in the KBMS and RX groups.

4.2.1 Partitioning Knowledge and Data

First of all, we will use in KSYS simple, regular structures for data, while supporting the complexity of the stored knowledge with a more general structure. The benefits expected from this dichotomy are that now the costly maintenance of complex structures is only required for a fraction of the stored information, and that well-established, efficient algorithms can be applied to the database. This benefit is only significant if the volume of information that can be classified as data is large. Our understanding of the few large knowledge-bases now in existence, such as R1/XCON [McDermott 82] is that this is indeed the case. We believe in fact that for all large AI systems the amount of complex stored knowledge, by our definition, is quite modest, especially in systems which require regular updating.

There are obviously also liabilities associated with the use of two distinct representations. The processing system has to provide an interface so that for a user needing information from the system, the knowledge and data are tightly coupled.

Since the user will always access the data via the knowledge-base, we believe we will find solutions to the user interface issue. In current database management systems, all accesses are already mediated by the a database schema. The traditional schema focuses on data attributes, their representation, and on access paths. Stored knowledge in the knowledge base can be viewed as a generalization of such a schema. The extension to the schema in a knowledge-based system can encompass concepts not directly represented in the database, for example overall health-status in a medical record. The knowledge base will also permit effective storage of interrelational constraints and processing rules.

The interface must also not reduce performance excessively, so that the benefits obtained from the specialized storage management can overcome this potential liability. We are not addressing in KSYS the problems of persistent storage of the conceptual frames within a DBMS. This is a real issue, and is being addressed by many researchers [Stonebraker 87]. We expect these efforts to be successful and solve the problem we foresee.

The problem of operational efficiency in access is being addressed by keeping the knowledge in real memory. We assume that the memory capacity of modern computers is adequate to hold all of the required knowledge once the more voluminous data are separated. For transactions where accessed data is reused, such data can be cached, and also retained in memory. For best use, the data, once retrieved, should be bound into the knowledge structure, as explored in [Ceri 86].

4.2.2 Conceptual Partitioning of Knowledge

We now come to the second of the two strategies for knowledge management: the use of multiple hierarchies. Although computer memory hardware is now adequate to store large amounts of knowledge, this does not address the problem of how to manage that knowledge. The complexity of interactions among the knowledge grows rapidly with the size of the knowledge, eventually overwhelming the access advantage gained from the use of a large memory. Much of this complexity of interaction can be mitigated through the use of a hierarchical organization, in which all interactions flow through well defined parent-child links. However, a single hierarchical organization is an inadequate paradigm for the representation of knowledge bases, especially those which involve sharing of knowledge.

4.2.3 Sharing Partitioned Knowledge

A large system, and hence the representations used to demonstrate KSYS, must support a diversity of usage. It is desirable to share knowledge as well as data, since knowledge acquisition is even more costly than data collection [Duda 83]. Sharing of knowledge is also motivated by the objective of consistency. We expect many applications to work on different aspects of the problem. Database technology has enabled data sharing, so that factual observations used by distinct applications will be identical. But if these applications interpret the same facts differently, because of differences in their encoded knowledge, we will not have achieved the objective of consistency among applications.

To enable sharing we see multiple hierarchical classifications of knowledge structures as a solution. Specific AI and database systems, which use general processing strategies, most often are constrained to operate in hierarchical structures, and have great difficulty in dealing with cycles. These hierarchies are closely related to the concepts of views, as further discussed below.

4.3 KSYS research projects

We now illustrate some research projects within the KSYS project, and describe the structure to support them. Each project addresses an aspect of the theme such as simplifying the design, implementation, or maintenance of databases, knowledge bases, or programs, or providing user interfaces that reduce the need for programmer involvement.

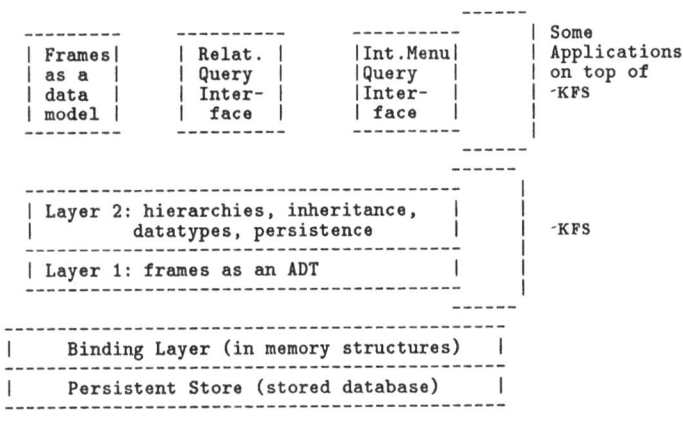

Figure 14 The KSYS Architecture.

The overall KSYS architecture is shown in Figure 14. The persistent store is a relational database (RDB from DEC in our prototype). The KSYS Frame System (KFS) is described first after an introduction. The binding layer seeks to make efficient use of a moderately large main memory (8 megabytes), and is not described here. Components of KSYS that use knowledge for dealing with views, semantic mediation of operations across disparate domains, integrity control and constraint management, and natural language interfaces, are in development and will be described in other publications.

5. The KSYS Frame System

The KSYS Frame System (KFS) is intended to be part of an experimental Knowledge Base Management System (KBMS). The KFS will provide a base on which intelligent database applications may be built. We plan to use the frame system with connections to a persistent store as the bottom layer for supporting such applications.

5.1 Frame Hierarchies

Frames were proposed by Minsky [Minsky 81] as part of a scheme for making intelligent machines. Commercial frame-based systems like KEE [Fikes 85] are widely available and familiar to most system developers. Since we wish to experiment with various novel concepts, we are building our own frame system rather than use one of the commercial systems. The most significant difference is formal support for multiple hierarchies, intended to help in the formulation of multiple views and object structures. The hierarchies are also expected to constrain interpretation. We will start with the basics.

5.2 Architecture of KFS

The KI 3 consists of two layers.

1 Layer 1 provides a very general and flexible framework on top of which layers with a tighter semantics may be built. It implements frames as an abstract data type and supports object-identity in the standard way. A KSYS frame can be viewed as an extensible record structure. It has a name and consists of a set of *slots*. Each slot has a set of *facets*. Facets contain data or metadata. The semantics of the representation depend on how the higher layers or programs interpret the data in the facets. Data in a facet may be interpreted as values, references to other frames or procedures, to mention some possibilities.

2 Layer 2 organizes frames into hierarchies and provides data-types and support for persistence.

The hierarchical structuring helps control the complexity of the design process [Dijkstra 68]. We will now briefly discuss our design decisions and contrast them with alternative approaches.

5.2.1 Class, Instance, and System frames

Frames may be of two kinds, *class* and *instance*. As an example, a class frame may define the class Ships and its properties, an instance frame may represent the ship QueenElizabeth, see Figures 15 and 16).

```
( G582
    (Shipname
        ( Value QueenElizabeth )))
```

Figure 15   The Instance Frame for the QueenElizabeth.

A given frame is of exactly one kind. *Class* frames are defined by the user to model the prototypical objects in the world being represented. Slots in a class could represent properties of either the class as a whole or that of its instances. For example the Ships class may have the slot ShipName which specifies the structure of the instances and the slot NumberofShips which is an exclusive property of the class. Any slot in a Class frame is required to have the type, value and inheritance facets. We expect that there will be a moderate number of class frames. We also find it useful to distinguish certain frames as *system frames*. *System frames* are those class frames which define the system. For example definitions of data types and hierarchy types are system frames. View definitions are another example of system frames. The *Instance* frames represent individuals or the instances of the prototypes. In instance frames, the only facet a slot is required and permitted to have is the value facet. It is expected that there will be a large number of such frames. They may be generated as needed from information in the database. The *instance* frames need to be implemented carefully from both space and access-time viewpoints.

5.2.2 Inheritance Hierarchies

Frames may reference each other. Through these references the class frames may be organized into *hierarchies*. A frame may belong to more than one hierarchy at the same time. The Ship hierarchy is shown in Figure 16. In it NavyShips and CommercialShips are subclasses of Ships class and may inherit slots from it. Note that each frame in the hierarchy has the slots ships-parent and ships-children. These are used by the system to store the links to the ancestor and children and are modifiable only through certain functions.

A hierarchy is defined by creating a hierarchy definition frame in the special hierarchy called Hierarchies. A hierarchy definition frame has the following slots: The parent-slot stores the name of the parent slot. This slot is required to contain exactly one frame with the exception of the root frame in which it is empty. The children-slot gives the name of the children slot. The root-frame-slot provides the name of the root frame of the hierarchy. The `hierarchy-slots` are the definitions of all slots which may be inherited through this hierarchy. The `required-instance-slots` are the names of slots which every frame in the hierarchy must possess. Instance frames which are instances of classes in the hierarchy must have values for these slots as a necessary condition for being instances. The `class-slots` give the names of slots which may not be inherited by instance frames. A class-slot cannot be a required-instance-slot. The defining frame for the `Ship` hierarchy is shown in Figure 17. Any frame belonging to a hierarchy possesses the parent-slot, children-slot and all the required-instance-slots for that hierarchy.

```
                        Ships
                       /    \
                      /      \
                     /        \
                NavyShips    CommercialShips
               /    |    \
              /     |     \
             /      |      \
    Destroyers  NuclearSubs  Frigates

( Ships
      ( Ship-parent
              ( Value ))                ; since no parents
      ( Ship-children
              ( Value NavyShips CommercialShips ))
      ( ShipName
              ( Type Symbol )
              ( Value )
              ( Inheritance Yes ))
      ( NumberOfShips
              ( Type Integer )
              ( Value 1105 )
              ( Inheritance No ))
      ( Instances
              (value  G582)
              (persistence ship-persistence)))

( NavyShips
      ( Ship-parent
              ( Value Ships ))
      ( Ship-children
              ( Value Destroyers Frigates))
      ( #Marines
              ( Type Integer )
              ( Value )
              ( Inheritance Yes )))

( CommercialShips
      ( Ship-parent
              ( Value Ships ))
      ( Ship-children
              ( Value ))
      ( CargoCapacity
              ( Type Integer )
              ( Value )
              ( Inheritance Yes ))
```

Figure 16   The Ship Hierarchy and Class Frames.

5.2.3 Hierarchy types

Hierarchies may have various semantics. For example, a hierarchy may be a generalization hierarchy. We may further specify properties like disjointness and completeness of subclasses. Hierarchies need not always be generalization hierarchies. For example, a hierarchy could be an aggregation (part-of) hierarchy or a view hierarchy. Such semantics will be enforced by the upper layers of the KBMS.

5.2.4 Inheritance

Any hierarchy-slot may be inherited by a child from its parent in the hierarchy. Inheritance makes it easier to specify similar classes. It often saves the trouble of redefinition, resulting in space saving and ease of maintenance. When we say "slot S is inherited" it means that the slot, all its facets and the data in the facets are also applicable to the child. In general, it may not be appropriate to inherit the slot exactly as it is; we may wish to make changes to the data in some of the facets. This is achieved by updating the desired facets in the child to override the inherited value. The Inheritance facet of the slot specifies whether the slot is to be inherited or not. The possible values for this facet are "Yes" and "No".

We now consider the question that at which level the inheritance facet should be specified. There are several choices. The inheritance could be specified Globally with the slot definition, at the parent frame or at the child frame. We will opt for thev generality of a Hybrid scheme, such that inheritance is specified in the parent frame, which may be overridden by specification at each child. Since a frame may be a child as well as a parent at the same time, an additional Inheritance-Override facet is needed to implement the hybrid scheme. In some hierarchies the inheritance may be globally controlled, to simplify automatic interpretation.

A frame may simultaneously belong to multiple hierarchies. However, slots are local to a hierarchy. This defines away the problem of multiple inheritance. The restriction that the hierarchy be a tree structure ensures that there is a single parent of a frame in a hierarchy. An interpreter can switch among the multiple hierarchies, in effect changing interpretive strategy. Such a switch would typically take place when some subgoal has been satisfied: some data have been located, or an intermediate conclusion has been drawn.

```
( Ship-hierarchy
    ( parent-slot
            ( Type Symbol )
            ( Value ship-parent )
            ( Inheritance Yes ))
    ( children-slot
            ( Type Symbol )
            ( Value ship-children )
            ( Inheritance Yes ))
    ( root-frame
            ( Type Frame )
            ( Value ships )
            ( Inheritance Yes ))
    ( hierarchy-slots
            ( Type Symbol )
            ( Value ShipName NumberOfShips #Marines
                    CargoCapacity)
            ( Inheritance Yes ))
    ( required-instance-slots
            ( Type Symbol )
            ( Value ShipName )
            ( Inheritance Yes ))
    ( class-slots
            ( Type Symbol )
            ( Value NumberOfShips )
            ( Inheritance Yes )))
```

Figure 17   The Definition of the Ships hierarchy.

5.2.5   What happened to Multiple Inheritance?

Multiple inheritance in its full generality is that a frame may have several parents and the value of a slot in a frame is a function (call this function the *inheritance policy*) of the value of the slot in all ancestors of the frame and some other factors (e.g, distance from an ancestor etc.). For example, the value of the completion-date slot in a projects hierarchy may be specified to be the minimum of the values in all superclasses.

However, multiple inheritance adds dangerous complexity to the system. The attempt to isolate functions which are useful as inheritance policies is an open ended process and degenerates to allowing the user to write his own inheritance policies as LISP functions, to be executed by a non-sharable interpreter. In general, a dividing line has to be found between what inheritance policies are sharable and defined and and those that are left to an interpreter implementing higher level view definitions or application programs. A problem with arbitrary functions as inheritance policies is that they make optimization by the system difficult.

These problems are better dealt with at a higher level. On the other hand, there are often cases when the same object has different and perhaps apparently contradictory values for a query depending on how we look at it. As an example we may consider an individual's financial-condition to be poor when he is accessed through the UniversityEmployees hierarchy. But it makes sense for his financial-condition to be considered rich when accessed through the Students hierarchy. The problems of management of such information¿ motivated the design decision to consider slots to be local to a hierarchy.

5.2.6 The Class-Instance Connection

We now define slots more precisely.

Instance slot: Class and Instance frames are connected by the Instances slot in the class frame. Let i be an *instance* frame and c be a *class* frame. A sufficient condition for i to be an *instance-of* c is the occurrence of *i* in the value facet of the instances slot of c A necessary condition for i to be an *instance-of* c is that in i values are assigned (*not* inherited) to all the required-instance-slots of the hierarchy to which c belongs. Another useful facet of the instances slot is the persistence facet which is discussed below.

Class-Instance inheritance: The value facet is the only facet of slots in instance frames. However, we would like an instance frame to inherit the default value from the class frame. But inheritance should be suppressed if the null value has the interpretation *not applicable*. Such values may be retrieved from the database due to the specific structure of the information.

The model we use often permits recognition of such structural-nulls. They occur for instance when a perfect normalization is not feasible because too many subclasses would be required.

As far as this layer is concerned the only relevant semantics of the structural nulls is that they suppress inheritance and therefore it suffices to *not* distinguish them from normal data values. We permit the specification of the inheritance-nulls as a facet called inheritance-nulls with each slot. The operational interpretation of this facet is: If the value of a slot in an instance frame is an inheritance-null then replace value with inherited value.

5.2.7 Persistence

We need to provide a mechanism to store and materialize frames from a persistent secondary store. One could use various storage systems for persistence, like files or relational databases. A Persistence Hierarchy provides the information about different available storage systems. As indicated earlier, the implementation of persistence for instance and class frames will be different. We will have a simple mechanism to store and materialize the class frames. However, the structures of instance frames for different classes may vary widely. Therefore, the information about the persistence mapping is best kept on a class by class basis. The persistence facet in the instance slot of the class frame refers to a persistence-frame which stores this information.

```
(Ship-persistence

  ( persistence-parent
            (Value Rdbmap))
  ( mapping
            ( Type slotattributemap)
         ( Value
            (shipname = ships. shipname)))
```

Figure 18   Example of a Persistence-frame.

Postscript

The engineering of AI systems remains a major problem. We have gathered in our research a fair amount of experience, and also listened carefully to the experience of others. In fact, actual quantitatively large projects cannot be implemented and operated in a university environment, and experience, especially when well circumscribed and quantified, is essential to our understanding and direction. Our new KSYS project is intended to elucidate and demonstrate methods to deal with the encoding and interpretation of conceptual knowledge and factual data.

Knowledge acquisition and validation is a time-consuming and expensive activity. It is important to develop techniques that will engender trust in systems using knowledge-based techniques. Shared use of knowledge is important for economy, but also as a means of sharing our concepts, and assuring consistency of interpretation of the large database on which modern planning systems are based.

We have learned that from our experience in dealing with large quantities of factual data that, to have any hope of success, the structures must be composed of a small number of conceptualizable components. The knowledge problem is harder. Yet, the methods chosen must not depend on a model which is beyond the users understanding.

We plan to always restrict maintenance and control effort to one active hierarchy or view at a time. We hope to able to demonstrate within KSYS that such a partitioning will permit retention of most of the power of fully general knowledge networks, while improving maintainability of the information structure,

Acknowledgements

Many of these ideas have been developed through interaction with the many collegues from academia and indudstry, and the students who collaborated in these projects. A precis of KBMS research, listiong about 140 papers, is available. Basic research in the Management of Knowledge and Databases is supported by ARPA under contract N39-84-C-211 and its predecessors, managed by SPAWAR. Research on natural language processing was supported by NSF-IST grant 8023889. Work on RX and RADIX was supported by the National Center for Health Services Research through grant HS-04389 and by the National Library of Medicine through grant LM-04334.

Computing resources are partially supported DEC ISTG and by SUMEX-AIM, which is funded by NIH grant RR-00785 from the Biomedical Research Technology Program. As always, our conclusions do not reflect official positions of any of our sponsoring agencies.

References

[Bancilhon 81] F.B. Bancilhon and N. Spryatos: "Update Semantics of Relational Views"; *ACM TODS*, Vol.6 No.4, December 1981, pages 557–575.

[Barr 81] Avron Barr and Edward A. Feigenbaum: *The Handbook of Artificial Intelligence*; HeurisTech Press, 1981.

[Blum 82] Robert R. Blum; *Discovery and Representation of Causal Relationships from a Large Time-oriented Clinial Database: The RX Project*; Vol. 19 in the Medical Informatics series edited by Lindberg and Reichertz, Springer-Verlag, 1982.

[Blum 86] Robert L. Blum: "Computer-Assisted Design of Studies Using Routine Clinical Data: Analyzing the Association of Prednisone and Serum Cholesterol"; Annals of Internal Medicine, Vol.104 No.6, June 1986, pages 858–868.

[Brodie 87] Michael Brodie, John Mylopoulos, and Joachim Schmidt (editors): *On Knowledge Base Management Systems: Integrating Artificial Intelligence and Database Technologies*; Springer-Verlag, 1987.

[Ceri 86] S. Ceri, G. Gottlob, and G. Wiederhold: "Interfacing Relational Databases and Prolog Efficiently"; in [Kerschberg 86], pages 141–153.

[Codd 70] Edgar F. Codd: "A Relational Model for Large Shared Data Banks"; CACM, Vol.13 No.6, June 1970, pages 377–387.

[Corella;84] F. Corella, S.J. Kaplan, G. Wiederhold and L. Yesil: "Cooperative Responses to Boolean Queries"; *Proc. IEEE Data Engineering Conference*, April 1984, Los Angeles CA, pages 77–93.

[Davidson 80] J. Davidson and S.J. Kaplan: "Parsing in the Absence of a Complete Lexicon"; *Proceedings of the 18th Annual Meeting of the Association for Computational Linguistics*, Philadelphia PA, June 1980, pages 105–106.

[Davidson 83] J. Davidson and S.J Kaplan: "Natural Language Access to Databases: Interpreting Update Requests"; *American Journal of Computational Linguistics*, April-June 1983, pages 57–68.

[Dijkstra 68] E.W. Dijkstra: "The Structure of the THE MultiProgramming System"; CACM, Vol.11 no.5, May 1968, pages 341–346.

[Duda 83] R.O. Duda and E.H. Shortliffe: "Expert Systems Research"; *Science*, Vol.220, 1983, pages 261–276.

[ElMasri 80] Ramez ElMasri and Gio Wiederhold: "Properties of Relationships and their Representation"; Proceedings of the National Computer Conference, AFIPS Press, May 1980, pages 319–326.

[Fikes 85] R. Fikes and T. Kehler; "The Role of Frame-Based Representation in Reasoning"; CACM, Vol.28 no.9, September 1985, pages 904–920.

[Finkelstein 82] Sheldon Finkelstein: "Common Expression Analysis in Database Applications"; *ACM SIGMOD International Conference on Management of Data*, June 1982, pages 235–245.

[Gadia 86] S.K. Gadia; "Towards a Multi-Homogeneous Model for a Temporal Database"; *Proc. Second IEEE Data Engineering Conference*, February 1986.

[Kaplan 80] S.J. Kaplan: "Appropriate Responses to Inappropriate Questions; in *Formal Aspects of Language and Discourse*, Joshi, Sag and Webber (eds.), Cambridge University Press, 1980.

[Kaplan 82] S.J. Kaplan; "Cooperative Responses from a Portable Natural Language Query System"; *Artificial Intelligence*, Vol.19, October 1982, pages 165–187.

[Keller 86] Arthur M. Keller: "The Role of Semantics in Translating View Updates"; IEEE Computer", Vol.19 no.1, January 1986, pages 63–73.

[Kerschberg 86] Larry Kerschberg (editor): *First Symposium on Expert Database Systems (EDBS)*; Institute of Information Management, Technology and Policy, Univ. of South Carolina, 1986; to be republished by Benjamin Cummins.

[Kim 85] W. Kim, D. Reiner and D. Batory: *Query Processing in Database Systems*; Springer-Verlag, New York, 1985.

[King 1980] Jonathan King: "Intelligent Retrieval Planning"; *Proceedings of the First National Conference on Artificial Intelligence*, August 1980, pages 243–245.

[McDermott 82] John McDermott: "R1: A Rule-Based Configurer of Computer Systems"; *Artificial Intelligence*, Vol.19 No.1, 1982, pages 39–88.

[Martin 87] N. Martin, S. Navathe, and R. Ahmed: "Dealing with Temporal Schema Anomalies in History Databases"; VLDB 13, Brighton England, Sep.1987.

[Minsky 81] Marvin Minsky: "A Framework for Representing Knowledge"; in *Mind Design*, Hangeland (editor), The MIT Press, 1981, pages 95–128.

[Qian 87] XioaLei Qian and D.R. Smith; "Constraint Reformulation for Efficient Validation"; *Proceedings 13th VLDB Conference*, Morgan-Kaufman, Los Altos, 1987.

[Rowe 83] Neil Rowe: "An Expert System for Statistical Estimates on Databases"; *National Conference on Artificial Intelligence*, March 1983.

[Schkolnick 85] Mario Schkolnick and M. Tiberio: "Estimating the Cost of Updates in a Relational Database"; *ACM TODS*, Vol.10 No.2, June 1985, pages 163–179.

[Shuey 86] Richard Shuey and Gio Wiederhold: "Data Engineering and Information Systems"; IEEE Computer, vol.19 no.1, January 1986, pages 18–30.

[Stefik 79] Mark J. Stefik: "An Examination of a Frame Structured Representation"; *Proceedings of the Sixth International Joint Conference on Artificial Intelligence*, 1979, pages 845–852.

[Stonebraker 87] Michael Stonebraker: "The Design of the POSTGRES Storage System"; Proceedings 13th VLDB Conference, Morgan-Kaufmann Los Altos, 1987.

[Suwa 82] M. Suwa, A.C. Scott, and E.H. Shortliffe: "An Approach to Verifying Completeness and Consistency in a Rule-Based Expert System"; *The AI Magazine* Vol.1 Fall, 1982, pages 16–21.

[Walker 87] Michael G. Walker: "How Feasible is Automated Discovery?"; *IEEE Expert*, Vol.2 No.1, spring 1987, pages 70–82.

[Weyl 75] S. Weyl, J. Fries, G. Wiederhold, and F. Germano:, "A Modular Self-Describing Databank System"; *Computers and Biomedical Research*, Vol.8, 1975, pages 279–293.

[Wiederhold 84] Gio Wiederhold: "Knowledge and Database Management"; *IEEE Software*, Vol.1 No.1, pages 63–73, January 1984.

[Wiederhold 86] Gio Wiederhold, M.G. Walker, R.L. Blum, and S.M. Downs: "Acquisition of Knowledge from Data"; *Proceedings of the International Symposium on Methodologies for Intelligent Systems*, Ras and Zemankova (editors), University of Tennessee, October 1986.

[WiederholdWB 87] Gio Wiederhold, M.G. Walker, and R.L. Blum: "An Integration of Knowledge and Data Representation"; in [Brodie 87].

[Wiederhold 87] Gio Wiederhold: *File Organization for Database Design*; McGraw-Hill, 1987.

Interfacing Prolog and External Data Management Systems:

A Model

Heinrich Jasper[1]
ETH Zürich
Institut für Informatik
CH-8092 Zürich

Abstract

Interfacing Prolog and external data management systems causes problems as a result of the different semantics of Prolog and the data manipulation language, offered by the data management system. These problems arise especially when backtrackable predicates in Prolog for accessing externally stored data are provided. In this paper, the problems regarding these backtrackable predicates are identified. The predicates must be managed in coordination with updates and non-complete backtracking (occurrences of cut), by some interface between Prolog and the external data management system. The solution to the problems is given in terms of a communication module, which is able to handle the accesses to the external data management system, while preserving the semantic of the programming language Prolog.

1. Introduction

The coupling or integration of Prolog and data management systems, i.e. relational database management systems (RDMS), may be approached in several ways; see for example [EDS86] and [WLD86]. These approaches have different aims. An initial aim is that of enhancing the functionality of a relational data manipulation language (RDML), in order to enable the handling of recursively defined queries, e.g. as described in [Ullm85], subsequently coming up with systems generally referred to as deductive databases. Other approaches make external data, i.e. ground facts, available to Prolog, either by providing a RDML in Prolog (e.g. [Chan86]), or by providing a translation mechanism for Prolog goals into a RDML ([Deno86], [Nejd86] and [Zani86]).

In addition, other architectures for efficient interfacing Prolog and databases are described in [Ceri86] and [Cupp86]. Both propose the preloading of externally stored data before starting a proof. In [Ceri86], a buffering mechanism to be used at proof-time is also described. Initial attempts to manage complex Prolog clauses have been described in [Bocc86] and [Appe86a].

Our approach - that of interfacing Prolog to external data management systems - is aimed at supporting a Prolog software engineering environment. This environment is to be built up in the EUREKA project PROTOS [Appe87]. In this project, the external data manager is intended to serve as a backend for storing Prolog programs. This backend server is meant to replace the internal clause base of the Prolog system.

The advantage of this approach is twofold: Firstly, only necessary parts of Prolog programs need be loaded into main memory. Those are such parts of a set of Prolog programs, used for the proof of the actual goal. Therefore, we think that very large Prolog programs can be managed more efficiently in time and space. Secondly, in such a system, all changes to the Prolog source code are stored in the external data management system. Thus, contrary to standard Prolog systems, they remain permanently available. This is especially useful for systems that generate their own code or program.

Those problems that have to be solved in such an approach regard the differences between the functionality of the data manipulation language of the external data management system and the needs of Prolog. The latter are specified by the syntax and the semantic of Prolog, e.g. as defined in [Cloc84]. Since the semantic of Prolog must be preserved in our system, the functionality of the external data management system must

---

[1] Author's Present Address: Heinrich Jasper, Universität Oldenburg, Fachbereich Informatik, Postfach 2503, D-2900 Oldenburg

be adapted to Prolog's needs. These regard especially the management of complex objects (clauses), ordering of clauses and intermixed update and retrieval on the clause base. Furthermore, set-wise answers must be translated into one tuple at a time accesses for the Prolog system.

In this paper, we will be concentrating on a part of these problems, viz., those arising as a result of the differences existing between the procedural semantic of Prolog and the functionality of data management systems. We will adapt the functionality of some abstract data manipulation language to Prolog, by specifying a communication module. This module is capable of handling accesses to externally stored data (not only programs), while preserving the procedural semantic of Prolog. It is particularly able to handle backtrackable accesses in coordination with the management of proof-trees.

In our opinion, none of the approaches mentioned above offers a satisfactory and complete solution suited to our requirements. In particular, those problems caused by the intermixed update and retrieval, and the occurrence of cuts in Prolog programs have so far remained unsolved.

Following this introductory section, some architectural preliminaries to the discussion of our model have been handled under section 2 below. Section 3 introduces the problems to be solved. In section 4, our model for the desired part of the communication module is presented. This is followed by a description of its integration into a Prolog environment. Before concluding with some comments on the implementation and an outlook for further research, a discourse regarding our approach is given in section 6.

2. The Architectural Environment

The interface discussed in this paper is defined in terms of a communication module (CM). The CM connects Prolog and the external data management system. It can be viewed as an extension to the external data management system. The generalized architecture of such a coupling is illustrated in Figure 1. The arrows indicate the bi-directional flow of control and exchange of data:

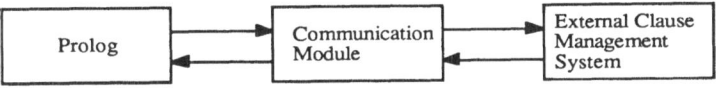

Figure 1: Architecture for the coupling of Prolog and external data management systems

In PROTOS the CM together with the external data management system (in the sequel called ECM, external clause management system) must be able to handle arbitrary prolog clauses. These are represented as tree type structures of dynamic shape and size. In this paper, we shall not consider the problem of storing complex objects. In particular, it is all the same to the CM introduced here, whether the ECM is able to handle arbitrary clauses, or only ground facts like a relational data management system. Nevertheless, the CM must fit the Prolog semantic, i.e. with the leftmost depth first proof strategy, in both cases.

In the sequel, we will concentrate on the elementary part of the CM between Prolog and the ECM regarding the problems due to backtrackable predicates. These problems will be identified, and we propose a model which is able to solve the problems. There are three conditions that must be fulfilled, in order to get the model to work correctly. These are the requirements that must be met by other parts of such an interface between Prolog and the ECM:

1. Firstly, the transparency of the ECM must be defined. We assume that predicates are the same for the management of externally stored data as for the internal clause base. These are four predicates: two predicates for asserting new clauses, one at the beginning, and one at the end of the clause base, one predicate for the deletion of clauses and one predicate for the retrieval of subsets of the clause base. The latter two are the only backtrackable predicates.

Access to externally stored data during a proof process is described in means of the predicate for the retrieval of clauses. Thus, proof time access is not explicitly described here, but the interface copes with enough functionality to simulate this in Prolog. Since we leave all interpretation to be done to Prolog (and thus change no semantic), the retrieval of clauses during proof processes will result in establishing facts or expanding the proof-tree.

2. The other two assumptions must be made about the external data management system. It must be able to provide the ordering of the clauses, which is defined by the chronology of the use of the two different predicates for insertion while establishing the clause base. Answers to queries must always observe this ordering. The same mechanism must be provided for the deletion of objects: observing the ordering all unifiable objects are deleted one after the other. (Interfacing Prolog to existing databases normally violates the ordering requirement. But applications might exist, where the Prolog semantic is not necessary for accessing externally stored data. Of course, our model works in those cases, but without guaranteeing the Prolog semantic.)

3. The third preliminary refers to the power of the query language of the ECM. The query language must support some specific type of access to the objects. This type of access regards to the Prolog unification mechanism. Because accesses to the ECM mirror some Prolog goal, unifiable objects for his goal must be provided by such an access.

    Since data management systems do not offer a data manipulation mechanism based on unification, we assume that the ECM is at least able to handle partial match access for a given tree type structure. Arbitrary leaves of this structure can be variables. Those objects having arbitrary data at these leaves are the answeres of a partial match query. Thus, a partial match access will result in a (at most small) superset of the requested set of unifiable clauses. The way of meeting these requirements in some implementation of the ECM has not been discussed here, but reserved instead for the EUREKA project. Translating Prolog goals to (relational) data manipulation languages is discussed e.g. in [Deno86], [Nejd86] and [Zani86].

As mentioned above, the coupling described in this paper is a solution to a general problem of accessing data stored in databases by Prolog systems. We need not limit ourselves to the handling of clauses; however, we are also able to access e.g. arbitrary relations of a relational database management system. Hence, the model gives hints for the coupling of existing databases to Prolog systems.

3. Identification of the Problems

We have identified at least four problems which will always come up, when defining an interface between Prolog and an external data management system. They originate from the navigational one-tuple-at-a-time proof strategy of Prolog together with backtrackable predicates. We will concentrate on queries, since we think of this case to be the most commonly used. The backtrackable predicate for the deletion of clauses can be simulated by a query together with a predicate for the deletion of just one object, using first fit with regarding to the ordering of the clauses. Thus, these four problems can be detailed as follows:

Multiple Queries
Prolog's leftmost depth first proof strategy works in a one-tuple-at-a-time manner. In order to get all solutions to a given goal, it uses backtracking. This might result in more than one node of the actual proof-tree representing some operation to the external data management system. Thus, there are multiple queries known at a time. These must be correctly handled in coordination with the dynamic behavior of the proof-tree.

Updates
During the proof of a Prolog goal, updates on the ordered set of clauses might be established. This regards both the insertion of a clause, as well as the deletion of a clause. The insertion of a clause is possible at the beginning or at the end of the database. Insertions at the end must be observed by already established queries, i.e. these clauses must be provided by all existing queries they fit to. The delete operation is backtrackable and always deletes the first unifiable clause. Since multiple copies of one clause are possible within a Prolog data base, exactly the first of these has to be deleted and should no longer be provided by any established query.

Non-Complete Backtracking / Cut
Non-complete backtracking occurs when not all answers to a backtrackable predicate are required during the proof process. This occurs either when a cut occurs in the proof-tree, or not all answers to the actual prolog goal are requested by its caller. In the first case, all brothers and the father of the actual node (this is of course the cut) are deleted from the proof-tree. The second case, for example, occurs when the user of the Prolog interpreter wants to prove a new goal, but did not request all answers to the previous one.

One-Tuple-at-a-Time / Ordering

Existing database systems often provide a set-oriented data manipulation language. Since Prolog requires one-tuple-at-a-time, the interface must convert set-wise answers into tuple-wise answers. Although most database systems today allow access to their internal tuple-oriented interface, we think that our model must be able to handle this problem, especially in those cases where the backend database can do some optimization on given queries. These optimizations can e.g. address the use of the joins. For example, the internal buffers of a RDMS, holding sets of answers, might be joined, in order to get a quicker response to some query.

The semantic of a Prolog program directly relies on the ordering of the clauses establishing the program. In the introduction, we established this as a requirement that the ECM has to cope with. Thus, our model must preserve the ordering, when converting set-wise answers into tuple-oriented ones.

4. A Model for Solving the Problems

A model is proposed to solve the four problems described above. Since this model must cope with ECMs providing both a set-wise, as well as a tuple-oriented interface, there are two solutions for the problem of one-tuple-a-a-time access to externally stored data. The solutions to the rest of the problems depend on the solution for this two cases. Thus, we will first concentrate on the fourth problem, and then on the other three in the sequence given in section 3.

One-Tuple-at-a-Time / Ordering

Having a one-tuple-at-a-time interface the ECM must handle a descriptor for each query. This descriptor points logically to the next clause to be provided by the desired query. Since the ECM satisfies the requirements described in the second section, the ordering of the answers is not a problem. [Zani86] proposes this navigational solution as the natural one for an integrated Prolog database system.

On the other hand, having a set-wise access to externally stored data requires the conversion of these sets into a one-tuple-at-a-time-oriented interface. In this case, we propose the intermediate storing of the answers of some query in a buffer, as illustrated in figure 2.

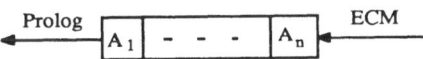

Figure 2: A Buffer connecting Prolog and the ECM, the arrows indicate the flow of data.

The buffer has a first-in first-out property in order to preserve the ordering of the clauses. The interface of the buffer is like the following:

- Prolog side: - Initialize a buffer B for a given goal G (G is a clause describing the unifiable objects),
  - get next clause C from a buffer B and
  - discard the buffer B.
- ECM side: - calls the ECM with a partial match query and
  - awaits the set of answers to the query.

Such a buffer connects a node of the actual Prolog proof-tree with the ECM. A practical solution of such a buffering mechanism are UNIX pipes, e.g. as described in a slightly different form in [Bocc86]. If such a mechanism is not available, explicitly storing the answers of a query in main memory requires the implementation of a dynamic buffer manager.

Another solution is the use of buffers of fixed size and a demand query processing which looks at the ECM for the next answers, in the event that the buffer runs out of clauses. From Prolog's point of view, the buffer must contain all unifiable clauses in the actual ECM instantiation. This might change during the lifetime of the buffer, see the update problem mentioned in section 3. The interface must be able to handle an arbitrary set of those buffers, as described in the sequel.

Multiple Queries

More than one backtrackable predicate working on the ECM might exist at some time as described in section 3. Since Prolog's leftmost depth first proof strategy can be simulated by a stack (i.e. as long as no explicit control of the backtracking is done), we use a single stack to manage multiple instantiations of buffers (set wise ECM) or query descriptors (tuple wise ECM), see figure 3.

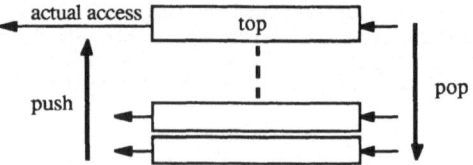

Figure 3: The query stack

The stack is initially empty. Each time a buffer or query is successfully initialized the buffer or the descriptor respectively is pushed on the stack. Access to the ECM is always done by the top element of the stack. On the other hand, if no more unifiable clauses are provided by the buffer or the query, the top element is popped from the stack. It can be shown that this way of managing the buffers/ descriptors copes with Prolog's proof strategy as long as no explicit control of backtracking is done, e.g. by a cut . The stack introduced here is called query stack in the sequel.

Updates

Updates on an ECM having a one-tuple-at-a-time interface cause no problems, if this ECM is at least able to do update and retrieval simultaneously, i.e. existing queries are not regarded by updates and the updates get known to existing queries. Extensions to the model described so far must be made for the handling of ECMs having a set-oriented interface. These extensions are different for the three types of updates mentioned above (see also the algorithms for handling updates by the CM given below in a PASCAL like pseudo code).

The insertion of clauses at the beginning of a database need not be considered by any established query. No extension to the CM is necessary in this case. Of course, the ECM itself must handle these insertions with respect to the ordering of clauses. Therefore, the insertion of a clause at the beginning of the set of clauses will result in the immediate update of the external clause base.

Contrary to the first case, insertions at the end of the database must be considered by both the ECM and the CM. In addition to their insertion into the ECM, they have to be inserted into all those buffers to whose goal they can be unified. Since this insertion must be done at the end of the buffers, updates at the end of the clause base easily fits into our model.

```
PROCEDURE InsertClause (Clause, At_End)
    InsertClauseIntoECM (Clause, At_End);
    IF At_End THEN
        FOR ALL Buffers DO
            IF Unify (Clause, Buffer) THEN
                AddClause (Clause, Buffer)
            END;
        END;
    END;
END; (* InsertClause *)
```

```
PROCEDURE DeleteClause (Clause)
    DeleteClauseOutOfECM (Clause, Surrogate);
    FOR ALL Buffers DO
        IF IsIn (Surrogate, Buffer) THEN
            DeleteClause (Surrogate, Buffer)
        END;
    END;
END; (* DeleteClause *)
```

Algorithm for insertion of clauses   Algorithm for deletion of clauses (backtrackable)

The third type of update is the delete operation which removes unifiable clauses from the ECM with respect to their ordering. Each time a clause is deleted, it must be discarded out of all existing buffers. Since multiple copies of a clause might exist in the ECM, we must be able to identify the single object, in order to discard it (and not a copy) out of the buffers. This identification can easily be done when using a surrogate for each object, see the algorithm given above.

A delete operation called by Prolog will result in the deletion of the first (with regard to the ordering) unifiable clause in the ECM. In addition, the ECM provides the surrogate of this clause. Now each buffer is searched for this surrogate. If a surrogate is found in some buffer, it will be deleted.

Non-Complete Backtracking / Cut

The two cases of non-complete backtracking must be handled in different ways. The cut (!) is an extra-logical primitive in Prolog to avoid unnecessary backtracking. In particular, it is a goal which succeeds immediately and can not be resatisfied. Furthermore, it discards all choice points made since the parent goal was invoked the first time. This can cause several queries to the ECM to become obsolete. In addition, the defined access strategy for multiple queries will no longer fit, since there is no way to pop the appropriate elements from the stack so far. These are some top elements of the query stack.

The other problem is that a user of Prolog does not require all solutions to a goal. This results in a fully established proof-tree, which is not needed any longer. Thus, all accesses to the external clause manager become obsolete.

We have to add some functions to the Prolog interpreter to solve these two problems. Regarding the cut, we propose two solutions:

1. The first solution requires a complex change of the Prolog interpreter, but offers a general approach to the problem, since it can be used for all predicates realized externally. Each externally defined predicate will be called with an appropriate message, if it is no longer needed in the actual proof. This reduces the effort to be made by the interface. An example of such a mechanism has been implemented in IF/Prolog ([IFMa84]).

2. The other solution must imitate the management of choice points done by Prolog, as far as information necessary for the cut handling is concerned. This is done by providing an additional stack which counts for each parent goal in a proof-tree the number of existing (backtrackable) accesses to the ECM by its child nodes. Furthermore, for each stack entry, the level of the corresponding goal in the actual proof-tree is known. In the sequel, this stack is called count stack. This stack is visualized in figure 4:

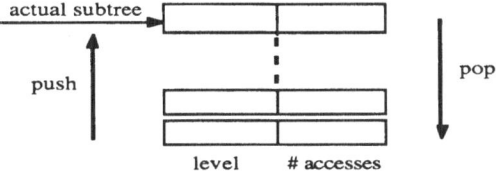

Figure 4: The count stack

The count stack is initially empty. Each time a rule is found in the prove process a new element is pushed on the stack. These elements contain the number of predicates accessing the ECM. This number is initially equal to one if the parent goal is an access to the ECM itself, otherwise it is equal to zero. Therefore, pushing one element on the query stack will result in incrementing the number of accesses in the top element of the count stack, and popping one element from the query stack will result in decrementing this entry in the top element of the stack. Discarding a parent goal will result in popping the top element from the count stack. (This is, of course, some "brute force" algorithm, since we do not perform any look ahead, which can be used to optimize the cut handling.)

```
REPEAT
    WHILE top (count-stack.#accesses) > 0 DO
        DEC (top (count-stack.#accesses) );
        DiscardBuffer (top (Buffer) );
        pop (Buffer);
    END;
    pop (count-stack);
UNTIL top (count-stack.level) = actual_level ;

IF "father of the cut accesses Buffer" THEN
    DiscardBuffer (top (Buffer) ) ;
    pop (Buffer);
    DEC (top (count-stack.#accesses) ) ;
END;
```

Now this stack is used to control the number of elements to be popped from the query stack, if a cut occurs. This number is exactly the sum of all numbers provided by those first (top) elements of the stack having a level at least equal to the level of the parent goal of the cut. These number of elements are popped from the query stack. In addition, all elements involved in the summation described above are popped from the count stack. The algorithm given in the box above will do the appropriate handling of the buffers. It is called each time a cut occurs as the actual node in the proof-tree.

The problem of managing the case when the user does not require all solutions to a goal causes another extension of the Prolog interpreter. Before returning to the top interpreter level (i.e. before printing the next '?-'), the query stack and the count stack must first be emptied.

Architecture of the model
Above we gave a verbal description of the model. Figure 5 is meant to illustrate the model and its connections to Prolog and to the external data management system.

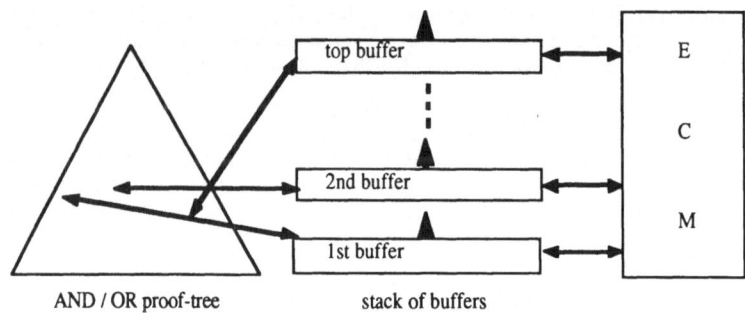

Figure 5: Connection of the proof-tree and the ECM by the CM (stack of buffers)

Each buffer represents a connection between a node in the actual proof-tree and the ECM. The Prolog proof-tree always accesses the ECM by the top buffer. The darkened triangles denote the possibility of deleting clauses in each buffer. The count stack is neglected, since we did not show the internals (the cuts) of the proof-tree.

5. Integration of the Model into Prolog

So far, we have established a model suitable to handle answers of backtrackable predicates in a Prolog-database environment. Now, we have to describe how this model fits to Prolog, i.e. how it is connected into the Prolog interpretation mechanism. To do this, we describe Prolog predicates using the box model propagated by [Cloc84]. We will exemplify this translation / connection for the predicate 'extclause(X)', being the hypothetically most general query predicate. Its semantic is to get all clauses unifiable with X from the external data management system.

The box model describes a predicate as a frame having four connections to other predicates occurring in a proof-tree. These connections are two entries into the proof of the predicate and two exits to leave the proof of a predicate. One entry is for the first call (called CALL), the other for each recall (called REDO). The two possible exits of a proof are one, for a successful call or recall (called EXIT), the other, in the event that a proof failed (called FAIL).

We assume that the ECM provides a set-oriented interface, thus, we require the buffering mechanism described above. In addition the solution for the cut problem using the count stack is provided for the interface. Consequently, the frame for 'extclause(X)' looks like the following, where the internal semantic of the box is defined by a procedural (PASCAL like) type of language. The procedures used for the query stack, as well as the count stack, are named according to their description given above.

```
CALL    CALL ( extclause (X) )                                                      EXIT
  →              InitializeBuffer (X, B);
               IF  GetNextElement (B, C) THEN
                  REPEAT
                  UNTIL  Unify (X, C)  OR  NOT  GetNextElement (B, C) ;
                  IF Unify (X, C)  THEN
                     PushBuffer  (B) ;
                     INC ( top (count-stack.#accesses) ) ;
                     EXIT  ;
                  ELSE
                     DiscardBuffer (B) ;
                     FAIL ;
                  END ;
               END ;

        REDO  ( extclause (X) )
               IF  GetNextElement (top (Buffer), C) THEN
                  REPEAT
                  UNTIL  Unify (X, C)  OR  NOT  GetNextElement (top (Buffer), C) ;
                  IF  Unify (X, C) THEN
                     EXIT  ;
                  ELSE
                     DiscardBuffer (top (Buffer) ) ;
                     DEC ( top (count-stack.#accesses) ) ;
                     pop (Buffer);
  FAIL         FAIL ;                                                               REDO
  ←              END ;                                                               ←
               END ;
```

Since the partial match queries of the ECM possibly provide supersets of the set of unifiable answers, the translation of the answers to Prolog must be done in a loop. This is designated by the REPEAT UNTIL construct used in the picture above.

The Prolog system must provide the possibility to unify an element managed externally with a given structure. This might be done by a unification procedure, e.g. as used in the description above, which calls the Prolog unification mechanism.

Invoking a query to some external database and managing the subsequent delivered set of answers is no problem, when using standard programming techniques. However, updating the external database might cause subsequent updates on some buffers or descriptors. Using an object-oriented approach will result in small and lucid implementations of the search through the stack of buffers / descriptors for those suited to some request.

6. Discussion

Most of the problems described above are mentioned in the papers given in the literature list at the end of this paper. Although most of them use some sort of communication module between Prolog and the ECM, none of the approaches solves all problems identified in the section 3.

The problems arising as a result of multiple queries, are described in detail in [Bocc86]. Solutions are given in most of the systems. The approaches given in [Deno86], [Cupp86] and [Ceri86], which propose the preloading of externally stored data into Prolog's internal clause base, are worthy of mention. Therefore, they need not consider the problem of multiple queries at proof-time. Our approach regarding the use of a stack can be optimized by the mechanisms described in [Ross86], who proposes a top-of-stack paging strategy for Prolog's run time structures.

The problems owing to intermixed update and retrieval and the semantic of updates in Prolog are not mentioned in any of the approaches known to us. The approaches either neglect the problem, or state that offering the update capabilities of the RDML will give a sufficient solution. Subsequently, we consider our approach to be among the neatest known to us for the handling of this particular problem in the context of externally defined backtrackable predicates.

The problem of ordering externally managed data in order to cope with Prolog's semantic has been mentioned in nearly all of the papers, but solutions are only given in [Appe86a] and [Bocc86], the latter however only with regard to rules. Since most of the approaches discuss the coupling to RDMS, conversion of set-wise answers into tuple-oriented suitable for Prolog has been solved either by asserting the set of answers to Prolog ([Deno86], [Cupp86] and [Ceri86]), or by using the UNIX pipe mechanism [Bocc86]. Others navigate on the tuple-oriented interface through the DBMS. Set-wise handing back of answers to Prolog (e.g. as a Prolog list) is not considered at all.

None of the approaches known to us solve the cut problem, with the exception of [Appe86a] (because they implemented an integrated system rather than a coupling of Prolog and a RDMS). [Deno86] mention the cut problem, but they spare a solution for further investigations.

Although our approach solves the problems, it seems to be a rather naive approach in terms of efficiency, regarding space as well as execution time. Other approaches spend a lot effort on optimization issues, that have so far not been mentioned in our approach. We think that further investigations have to consider three types of optimization:

1. Source level optimization for Prolog programs will cut down the proof-tree. This is discussed together with a subsequently done query optimization in [Venk84].

2. Leaving work to the external database, which can be done there efficiently. This often regards the use of joins. Generalizing components of database systems and adding them to Prolog is proposed in [Scio86].

3. Optimizing the model described here, where there are
    - taking advantage of possible subsumption relations holding between queries ([Ceri86]),
    - logically caching clauses ([Appe86a]) and
    - preloading of externally stored clauses by precompilation of Prolog programs, e.g. as described in [Ceri86] and [Cupp86],
    all of them minimizing access to the ECM. The three techniques mentioned will work independently, but when using them simultaneously, gaining a better result seems feasible. Such a combined solution avoids the generation of redundant queries. Other techniques, that can be used for preloading subsets of databases, can be taken over from the proposals given in [Wede86].

Using indexing or hashing to access unifiable clauses in an efficient manner is not a subject of this paper. However, an effecive implementation of an integrated Prolog database system must obviously pay close attention to this topic, as described e.g. in [Deer85] and [Wise84].

7. Conclusion

There are many proposals for the coupling of Prolog and databases. Most of those known so far concentrate on enabling access to externally stored data, i.e. ground facts, into the Prolog environment. Therefore, they can be considered as systems extending a query language by Prolog rather than systems enabling the programming language Prolog to manage its clause base externally.

Our approach towards supporting the programming language Prolog with a backend database server has been discussed. Several problems owing to the procedural semantic of Prolog regarding backtrackable predicates were identified and solutions for these problems were given. We think of our model as being a natural approach to these problems. Some optimization must be done to make this model more efficient in terms of time and space.

Nevertheless this approach must still be proven by some implementation. Until now, only the query stack has been implemented in the project KOFIS [Appe86b]. In KOFIS, a Prolog system is supported by a backend fact server implemented on top of the GridFile ([Niev84]). Multiple queries for the retrieval of facts are provided within the KOFIS system. An implementation of the entire model constitutes the subject-matter of the EUREKA project PROTOS mentioned above.

I am greatly indebted to Messrs. H.-J. Appelrath, M. Ester, H. Lorek, M. Nussbaum and A.Ultsch for the many fruitful discussions which motivated me in writing this paper.

8. Literature

[Appe86a] Appelrath, H.-J.; Bense, H.; Rose, T.: "Controlled Prolog - A Front-End to Prolog incorporating meta-knowledge", in Proceedings "10. GWAI 1986 u. 2. österr. AI-Tagung 1986", Informatik Fachberichte Nr. 124, Springer Verlag, September 1986.

[Appe86b] Appelrath, H.-J.; Ester, M.; Jasper, H.; Ultsch, A.: "KOFIS: An Expert System for Information Retrieval in Offices", in: Proc. of the "2nd Intern. Conf. on the Appl. of Micro-computers in Information, Documentation and Libraries", North Holland Publ. Co., 1986.

[Appe87] Appelrath, H.-J.: "PROTOS- Prolog Tools for Building Expert Systems", to appear in "GI-Kongress 1987, Wissensbasierte Systeme", Informatik Fachberichte, Springer Verlag, October 1987.

[Bocc86] Bocca, J.: "On the Evaluation Strategy of EDUCE", in ACM SIGMOD '86, 1986.

[Ceri86] Ceri, S.; Gottlob, G.; Wiederhold, G.: "Interfacing Relational Databases and Prolog Efficiently", in [EDS86].

[Chan86] Chang, C. L.; Walker, A.: "PROSQL: A Prolog Programming Interface with SQL/DS", in [EDS86].

[Cloc84] Clocksin, W. F.; Mellish, C. S.: "Programming in Prolog", Springer Verlag, 2nd edition, Berlin Heidelberg New York Tokyo, 1984.

[Cupp86] Cuppens, F.; Demolombe, R.: "A PROLOG-Relational DBMS interface using delayed evaluation", in [WLD86].

[Deer85] Deering, M.: "Database Support for Storage of AI Reasoning Knowledge", in [EDS86].

[Deno86] Denoel, E.; Roelants, D.; Vauclair, M.: "Query Translation for Coupling Prolog with a Relational Database Management System", in [WLD86].

[EDS86] Kerschberg, L. (ed.): "Expert Database Systems", proceedings of the 1st intern. workshop on Expert Database Systems, Benjamin/Cummings Publ. Inc., 1986.

[IFMa84] IF/Prolog Manual, Version 2.0, InterFace Computer GmbH, Munich, December 1984.

[Nejd86] Nejdl, W.; Neuhold; E. J.: "The PROLOG-DB System: Integrating Prolog and Relational Databases", in ÖGAI-Journal, 5/1, 1986.

[Niev84] Nievergelt, J.; Hinterberger, H.; Sevik, K.C.: "The GridFile: An Adaptable, Symmetric Multikey File Structure", ACM TODS, Vol. 9, No. 1, pp. 38 - 71, 1984.

[Scio86] Sciore, E.; Warren, D. S.: "Towards an Integrated Database-Prolog System", in [EDS86].

[Ross86] Ross, M. L.; Ramamohanarao, K.: "Paging Strategy for Prolog Based on Dynamic Virtual Memory", Technical Report, University of Melbourne, Australia, August 1986.

[Ullm85] Ullman J. D.: "Implementation of Logical Query Languages for Data Bases", in ACM TODS, Vol. 10, No. 3, pp. 289 - 321, September 1985.

[Venk84] Venken, R.: "A Prolog Meta-Interpreter for Partial Evaluation and its Application to Source to Source Transformation and Query-Optimization", in proceedings ECAI '84, "Advances in Artificial Intelligence", T. O'Shea (ed.), North-Holland, 1984.

[Wede86] Wedekind, H.; Zoerntlein, G.: "Prefetching in Realtime Database Applications", in ACM SIGMOD '86, 1986.

[Wise84] Wise, M. J.; Powers, D. M. W.: "Indexing PROLOG Clauses via Superimposed Code Words and Field Encoded Words", Intern. Symposium on Logic Programming, IEEE Comp. Society, pp. 203 - 210, 1984.

[WLD86] Proceedings of the "Workshop on Integration of Logic Programming and Data Bases", Commission of the Europ. Com., Esprit Project 530, Venice, December 1986.

[Zani86] Zaniolo, C.: "Prolog: A Database Query Language for All Seasons", in [EDS86].

Abbildung von Frames auf neuere Datenmodelle

Th. Härder, N. Mattos, B. Mitschang
Universität Kaiserslautern

Übersicht

Es wird die Abbildung von Frames mit ihren Modellierungskonzepten und charakteristischen Operationen auf objekt-orientierte Datenmodelle untersucht, um Wissensrepräsentation in sogenannten Non-Standard-Datenbanksystemen - beispielsweise für Expertensystem-Anwendungen - unterstützen zu können. Nach einem Vergleich der Eigenschaften von Relationenmodell, NF^2-Modell und MAD-Modell für diese Aufgabe wird eine Bewertung der verschiedenen Ansätze vorgenommen, um ihre Tauglichkeit für die Frame-Modellierung deutlicher herauszukristallisieren.

1. Einleitung

Praxistaugliche Expertensysteme (XPS) erfordern eine effiziente Verwaltung sehr großer Wissensbasen auf Sekundär-speicher, Mehrbenutzerfähigkeit und ein gewisses Maß an Fehlertoleranz. Diese Aspekte werden bereits in Datenbank-systemen (DBS) realisiert, die seit Jahren zur Verwaltung großer Datenmengen vor allem in kommerziellen Bereichen erfolgreich eingesetzt werden. Eine bloße Übernahme solcher konventioneller DBS für den Einsatz bei XPS-Anwendungen würde zumindest zu schwerfälliger Wissensmodellierung und erheblicher Leistungseinbuße führen, da herkömmliche Da-tenmodelle - ihre Datenstrukturen, Operationen und Konzepte zur Integritätssicherung - sowie ihre unterstützenden Maß-nahmen in einer DBS-Implementierung nicht für solche Non-Standard-Anwendungen [HR85] entworfen wurden. Deshalb wird in der DB-Forschung momentan auf breiter Front die Frage untersucht, wie die Architektur und Implementierung künftiger DBS für Non-Standard-Anwendungen (NDBS) aussehen soll. Die DBS-Kern-Architektur, die als aussichtsreicher Lösungsvorschlag gilt, wird im Moment in mehreren Prototyp-Implementierungen erprobt [Da86,HMMS87,PSSWD87]. Für unsere Diskussion benutzen wir diese Architektur als Rahmenvorstellung, wie in Bild 1 gezeigt. Sie besteht grob ge-sprochen aus einem anwendungsunabhängigen Kern und einer Zusatzschicht - Modellabbildung genannt -, in der eine Anwendungsorientierung erreicht wird. Neben einer Reihe von Vorteilen [HR85] soll diese Architektur durch ihre Zwei-teilung auch die Abbildung des NDBS auf Workstation und Server unterstützen.

Als Datenmodelle, die für den Kern in Frage kommen, stellt man sich solche vor, die bereits eine Objektorientierung auf-weisen und damit die Abbildung komplexer Anwendungsobjekte erleichtern [BB84,Mi87,SS86]. Aufgabe der Modell-abbildung ist die Bereitstellung von Anwendungsobjekten an der NDBS-Schnittstelle, deren Repräsentationsformen, Operationen und Integritätsbedingungen letztlich mit Hilfe der Primitive des Datenmodells realisiert werden müssen.

Die speziell auf das Anwendungsgebiet Expertensysteme zugeschnittene Modellabbildung - auch als Wissensadministrator bezeichnet - stellt ein Modellierungswerkzeug zur Unterstützung der XPS-Arbeit zur Verfügung. Dieses soll beispiels-weise allgemeine Modellierungskonzepte umfassen, mit denen die verschiedenen Formen der Wissensrepräsentation leicht nachgebildet werden können. Es sollen daher zumindest die vier in vielen Wissensrepräsentationsformen implizit exis-tierenden grundlegenden Abstraktionskonzepte unterstützt werden: Generalisierung (is-a), Klassifikation (instance-of), Aggregation (part-of) und Assoziation (member-of). Neben diesen Konzepten bietet der Wissensadministrator noch zusätz-lich spezielle Objektdarstellungen und Operationen an. Für das Frame-Konzept [Mi75,FK85] sind beispielsweise Units, Slots und Aspekte als Objekte sowie die darauf definierten Operationen Einfügen eines Frames, Lesen von Slotwerten, Ausführung von Methoden usw. anzubieten. Die Aufgabe des Wissensadministrators besteht nun darin, diese Objekte und Operationen geeignet auf das Datenmodell des NDBS-Kerns abzubilden. Der Wahl des richtigen Datenmodells kommt hierbei eine entscheidende Bedeutung zu.

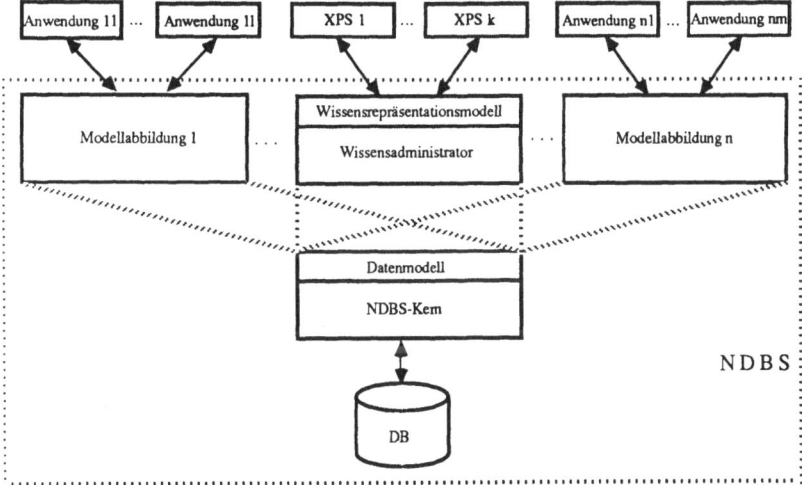

Bild 1: Grobarchitektur von DBS für Non-Standard-Anwendungen

Ziel dieser Arbeit ist, die Tauglichkeit von Datenmodellen zur Frame-Abbildung zu belegen. Es wird zunächst ein an [Mi75,FK85,BS83] angelehntes Frame-Modell vorgestellt. Anschließend wird eine vergleichende Betrachtung einiger Datenmodelle (Relationenmodell, NF^2-Modell [SS86] und das Molekül-Atom-Datenmodell (MAD-Modell) [Mi87]) hinsichtlich ihrer Modellierungs- und Manipulationsmöglichkeiten zur Abbildung des eingeführten Frame-Modells durchgeführt.

2. Das Frame-Modell

Im Bereich der XPS stellt die Repräsentation von Wissen, bestehend aus Daten und Programmen, den Versuch dar, die Vorgehensweise von Spezialisten (Experten) bei der Lösung von Problemen zu formalisieren. Je nachdem, ob man Wissensinhalte für einen passiv-deklarativen Gebrauch oder für einen aktiv-prozeduralen Gebrauch beschreibt, gelangt man zu verschiedenen Formen der Wissensrepräsentation - deklarativ oder prozedural [Ra82]. Viele der verschiedenen Wissensrepräsentationen enthalten jedoch sowohl deklarative als auch prozedurale Aspekte. Dies gilt auch für Frames [Mi75,FK85], mit denen in meist deklarativer Weise stereotypische Situationen und Objekte beschrieben werden [Pu86]. In dieser Arbeit werden die prozeduralen Aspekte von Frames (Programme, Methoden und Regelmengen) nicht berücksichtigt, da es hier mehr um die Abbildung des deklarativen Bestandteils von Frames geht. Daher beschränken wir uns in diesem Kapitel auf die Beschreibung eines Frame-Modells unter dem Aspekt der Repräsentation von deklarativem Wissen.

Dieses Frame-Modell (siehe Tabelle 1) kennt zunächst nur Objekte (hier als Unit bezeichnet), die die Grundelemente für die Wissensrepräsentation sind. Eine Unit setzt sich aus einer Liste von Attributen (Slots) mit Attributwerten (Werte) zusammen (Konzept der Aggregation) und wird durch einen Unit-Namen eindeutig identifiziert. Jedem Slot ist eine Liste von Aspekten mit den zugehörigen Aspektwerten zugeordnet, die dazu dienen, den Slot mit seinem Wert genauer zu spezifizieren (Bild 2). Mögliche Aspekte sind beispielsweise "Comment", den der Benutzer als Kommentar verwenden kann, "Default" zur Definition eines Standardwerts im Fall eines undefinierten Slotwerts und "Wertmenge" zur Festlegung einer Menge von Werten, aus denen der Wert des Slots ausgewählt werden muß.

Die Units entsprechen den Objekten (auch Entities genannt) eines Ausschnitts der realen Welt, die zu modellieren sind. Dabei unterscheidet man zwischen Units, die eine Menge von Entities repräsentieren und daher als Klasse bezeichnet werden, und Units, die Entities einer Klasse repräsentieren und daher als Member einer Klasse bezeichnet werden. Die Unterscheidung zwischen Klassen, die den Ausprägungstyp von Member-Objekten (d.h. Instances) darstellen - entsprechend dem Abstraktionskonzept der Klassifikation -, von denen, die eine Menge von Objekten im streng mengentheoretischen Sinn beschreiben - entsprechend dem Abstraktionskonzept der Assoziation - wird jedoch nicht gemacht. Ebenso unterscheidet man nicht zwischen Member, die Instances eines Ausprägungstyps darstellen, von denen, die die Elemente einer Menge repräsentieren. Daher entspricht die Unterteilung der Units (Objekte) in Klassen und Member sowohl dem Konzept der Assoziation als auch der Klassifikation, mittels denen sogenannte Member-Objekte über eine "member-of" Relation mit Klassenobjekten in Beziehung gesetzt werden. Weiterhin ist es möglich, daß eine Unit sowohl Member als auch Klasse sein kann bzw., daß eine Unit gleichzeitig Member verschiedener Klassen sein kann. Neben dieser Beziehung zu ihren Member haben Klassen Beziehungen mit anderen Klassen. Diese entsprechen dem Abstraktionskonzept der Generalisierung, durch das eine Hierarchie von Objektklassen gebildet wird, zwischen denen eine "is-a" Relation existiert.

Diese Hierarchie macht die wichtige Bedeutung der Unit-Beziehungen deutlich: Informationen über Units werden entlang dieser Hierarchie transportiert. Slots (Eigenschaften) von übergeordneten Units können an untergeordnete Units übertragen werden. Man unterscheidet dabei zwischen zwei Arten von Slots: "Klassen-Slots" und "Member-Slots". Klassen-Slots bezeichnen Eigenschaften der Unit, während Member-Slots die Eigenschaften der zugehörigen Member beschreiben. Daher werden die Member-Slots an die untergeordneten Units übertragen. Da sie zur Spezifikation der Member-Eigenschaften dienen, besitzen sie keinen Wert. Erst wenn der Slot an die Member-Units vererbt wird, wird ihm ein Wert zugeordnet (siehe Bild 4). Unter Umständen ist es jedoch sinnvoll einen Standard-Wert zu definieren, der generell weitervererbt werden soll. Dies wird mit Hilfe des Default-Aspekts modelliert. Klassen-Slots werden dagegen nicht übertragen. Sie spezifizieren entweder Eigenschaften, die für alle Member der Klasse gelten, oder Eigenschaften, die nur für die Klasse relevant sind. Die Zuordnung eines Wertes ist deshalb notwendig. Bei der Übertragung von Slots an untergeordnete Units, auch Vererbung von Eigenschaften genannt, wird dann wie folgt unterschieden: Member-Slots werden entlang der Klasse/Klasse-Beziehungen an alle untergeordneten Klassen (Units) als Member-Slots und entlang der Klasse/Member-Beziehungen an die untergeordneten Member (Units) als Klassen-Slots vererbt; Klassen-Slots werden überhaupt nicht vererbt. Diese Unterscheidung macht deshalb die Zuordnung sowohl eines Slot-Typs (Klassen-Slot, Member-Slot) als auch einer Kennung (eigener Slot, geerbter Slot) zu jedem Slot erforderlich. Um diese Klasse/Member- bzw. Klasse/Klasse-Beziehungen modellieren zu können, existieren spezielle Slots, die für jede Unit definiert sind. Die Slots ist_subklasse_von und hat_als_subklassen werden dazu benutzt die Klasse/Klasse-Beziehung zu modellieren, wobei ist_subklasse_von die "Super"-Klassen einer Klasse und hat_als_subklassen die "Sub"-Klassen einer Klasse referenziert. ist_member_von und hat_als_member stellen die Klasse/Member-Beziehungen dar; ist_member_von spezifiziert die Referenz zu den Klassen bei denen die Unit ein Member ist und hat_als_member gibt die Referenz zu allen Member dieser Klasse an.

Unitname			
ist_subklasse_von:		Liste von Units	
hat_als_subklassen:		Liste von Units	
ist_member_von:		Liste von Units	
hat_als_member:		Liste von Units	
Slot 1:	Typ1	Kennung 1	Wert 1
		Aspekt 11	Aspektwert 11
		Aspekt 12	Aspektwert 12
		Aspekt 1m	Aspektwert 1m
Slot n:	Typn	Kennung n	Wert n
		Aspekt n1	Aspektwert n1
		Aspekt n2	Aspektwert n2
		Aspekt nm	Aspektwert nm

Bild 2: Struktur der Units

Bild 2 zeigt die komplette Struktur einer Unit. Es wird deutlich, daß die vier oben angesprochenen Slots auf Grund ihrer speziellen Bedeutung, nämlich der Modellierung der Unit-Beziehungen, aus der Menge der übrigen Slots herausgehoben sind. Die zugehörigen primitiven Operationen des Frame-Modells umfassen einerseits allgemeine objektbezogene Operationen wie das Einspeichern, Löschen, Lesen und Modifizieren von Units. Andererseits existieren Operationen, die Slots und Aspekte direkt manipulieren.

Tabelle 1:

Einige Aspekte des

Frame-Modells

Sloteigenschaften		Modellierung	
		von	mittels
Typ	Klassen-Slot / Member-Slot	Generalisierung	ist_subklasse_von / hat_als_subklassen
Kennung	eigener / geerbter	Assoziation	ist_member_von / hat_als_member, Klassen-Slot
Aspekte	Default, Comment, Wertmenge	Klassifikation	ist_member_von / hat_als_member, Member-Slot
		Aggregation	nur von Aspekten / zu Slots / zu Units

3. Datenmodelle zur Wissensrepräsentation

Im folgenden werden verschiedene Datenmodelle für die Abbildung des eingeführten Frame-Modells verwendet. Damit soll die Adäquatheit bzw. Unzulänglichkeit dieser Datenmodelle zur Wissensrepräsentation aufgezeigt werden. Zur Vereinfachung wird vorab eine Zwischenabbildung mit Hilfe des Entity- Relationship-Modells (ER-Modell) durchgeführt.

3.1 Eine Entity-Relationship-Modellierung des Frame-Modells

Das ER-Modell [Ch76] dient zur Strukturierung der in einem Weltausschnitt enthaltenen Information. Die Gegenstände dieses Weltausschnitts werden auf "Entities", ihre Beziehungen auf "Relationships" abgebildet. Die Eigenschaften dieser Gegenstände und ihrer Beziehungen können durch Entity- und Relationship-Attribute dargestellt werden. Gleichartige Gegenstände bzw. damit assoziierte Entities werden zu sog. "Entity-Mengen" (Typen) zusammengefaßt; gleiches führt zu den sog. Relationship-Typen. Bei den Beziehungen unterscheidet man drei Arten: (1:1), (1:n) und (n:m); damit werden eindeutige, funktionale und komplexe Beziehungen zwischen Entities charakterisiert. Zur graphischen Darstellung des ER-Modells werden i.a. ER-Diagramme (Bild 3) verwendet.

Bild 3:

ER-Diagramm des

Frame-Modells

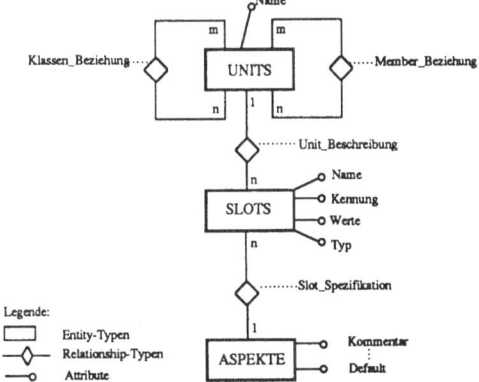

Zur Darstellung der Objekte des Frame-Modells scheint es auf den ersten Blick sinnvoll, für jede Klasse des abzubildenden Weltausschnitts einen Entity-Typ zu definieren. Diese Modellierungsweise offenbart allerdings größere Probleme: zum einen kann ein Objekt sowohl Member wie auch Klasse sein (d.h., ein Objekt ist als Typ und auch als Ausprägung zu modellieren); zum anderen kann es gleichzeitig Member von unterschiedlichen Klassen sein (d.h., ein Objekt ist gleichzeitig Ausprägung von verschiedenen Entity-Typen). Will man diese Abbildungsprobleme lösen, so muß man Redundanzen einführen, die allerdings auch ein erhebliches Maß an Overhead bedeuten.

Betrachtet man das Frame-Konzept jedoch etwas näher, so erkennt man, daß es von einem semantisch höheren Standpunkt aus nur abstrakte Objekte, die sog. Units, gibt. Deren Bedeutung als Klassen bzw. Member wird eigentlich nur durch die Beziehungen zwischen den Units realisiert und nicht durch die Units selbst. Eine Modellierung des Frame-Konzepts auf dieser abstrakteren Ebene vermeidet die oben beschriebenen Probleme. Man hat dabei einen Entity-Typ UNITS, der dazu benutzt wird, alle Objekte (Units) des zu modellierenden Weltausschnitts darzustellen. Alle diese Objekte, egal ob sie Member oder Klassen sind, werden dann als Ausprägung dieses Entity-Typs repräsentiert. Man erhält dadurch ein sehr generisches Schema, das es erlaubt, beliebige Frame-Anwendungen geeignet darzustellen.

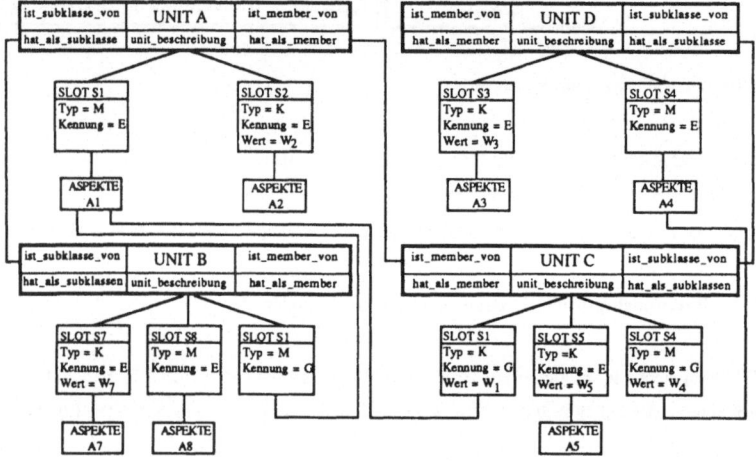

Bild 4: Ausprägungsbeispiel des Frame-Modells

In Bild 3 ist das resultierende ER-Diagramm der angesprochenen Frame-Modellierung dargestellt. Bild 4 zeigt ein dazu passendes Ausprägungsbeispiel. Die Semantik der Units (nämlich Member- und/oder Klassen-Unit) wird durch die beiden (n:m)-Beziehungen definiert: Die Klassen_Beziehung (mit den Teilbeziehungen hat_als_subklassen und ist_subklasse_ von) baut die Generalisierungshierarchie und die Member_Beziehung (mit den Teilbeziehungen ist_member_von und hat_ als_member) die Klassifikations- und Assoziationsstrukturen auf. Über die Beziehung Unit_Beschreibung werden die einzelnen Slotdaten zur Beschreibung der Units aggregiert (Aggregation). Ebenso führt die Beziehung Slot_Spezifikation eine aggregierende Beschreibung um die Aspektdaten des zugehörigen Slots durch. Dieser Entity-Typ realisiert eine generische Wertebereichs- bzw. Typdefinition der zugehörigen Slotwerte.

3.2 Modellierung unter Verwendung des Relationenmodells und des NF^2-Modells

Das Relationenmodell stellt für die Darstellung von Entity- und Relationship-Mengen nur ein Konstrukt - die Relation (Tabelle) - zur Verfügung. Daher entspricht ein Tabellenaufbau im wesentlichen dem Entity- bzw. Relationship-Typ, die Spalten dessen Attributbeschreibung und die Zeilen (auch als Tupel bezeichnet) konkreten Entities oder Beziehungen. Eine wesentliche Eigenschaft des Relationenmodells ist, daß alle Informationen - auch die Beziehungen zwischen Tupeln - explizit durch Attributwerte der Tupel ausgedrückt werden.

Die Modellierung des Frame-Modells mittels des Relationenmodells (RM) sieht dann wie folgt aus: Jedem Entity-Typ wird eine Relationenbeschreibung zugeordnet; die Attribute werden dabei übernommen. Die (1:1)- und (1:n)-Beziehungen werden durch entsprechende Attributwerte (Primär- und Fremdschlüssel) dargestellt, wohingegen alle (n:m)-Beziehungen über Hilfsrelationen beschrieben werden. Die im RM definierten Operationen erlauben ein deskriptives Ansprechen und Manipulieren einzelner Tupel bzw. Tupelmengen sowie eine mächtige tupelübergreifende Operation (Join-Operation). Modellierbar und ansprechbar sind nur homogene Tupelmengen. Daher führt jede Join-Operation eine Zusammenlegung der beiden beteiligten Tabellen durch, wobei allerdings auch Strukturinformation verloren geht. Der Versuch eine voll-ständige Unit-Aggregation aufzubauen, führt zu einer flachen Ergebnisrelation (Unit-, Slot- und Aspektdaten sind neben-einandergereiht und nicht aggregiert) aufgrund der zu verwendenden Join-Operationen. Noch schwieriger stellen sich die Operationen auf der Generalisierungshierarchie dar: z.B. erfordert die Vererbung eines Slot-Eintrags wegen der Abwesenheit von Rekursion das explizite, iterative Berechnen der Unit-Hierarchie. Insgesamt sind alle in unserem Frame-Modell enthaltenen Abstraktionskonzepte durch die Modellierung verloren gegangen und können durch die angebotenen Operationen auch nicht wiedergewonnen werden. Das bedeutet, daß die Abstraktionshierarchien sowie die Assoziations- und Aggregationseigenschaften durch externe Programmierung aufgebaut werden müssen. Dies bedeutet einen erheblichen Effizienzverlust, der aufgrund nicht adäquater Modellierungs- und Manipulationsmöglichkeiten entstanden ist.

Das NF^2-Modell (non-first normal form, [SS86]) ist eine Erweiterung des RM um relationenwertige, also nicht-atomare Attribute. Dadurch, daß damit die Attribute wiederum Relationen sein dürfen, wird die Kombination von Aggregation und Assoziation direkt unterstützt - die dem Modell inhärente "Schachtelung" von Relationen "materialisiert" sozusagen Aggregation und auch Assoziation. Durch unterschiedliche Anwendung dieses Schachtelungskonzepts können sehr ver-schiedene Frame-Modellierungen erzeugt werden: Verzichtet man gänzlich auf die Relationenschachtelung, so erhält man eine ähnliche Modellierung wie mit dem RM und damit einhergehend auch alle o.a. Nachteile. Zur Aggregation aller Unit-Informationen muß eine NF^2-Tabelle bestehend aus den ineinandergeschachtelten Relationenbeschreibungen von Units, Slots und Aspekten definiert werden. Diese Aggregation erzeugt eine Datenredundanz bzgl. der Aspektdaten, welche ein gewisses Maß an Verwaltungsoverhead zur Redundanzkontrolle verursacht. Unterstellt man, was sicherlich plausibel erscheint, daß die Änderungshäufigkeiten auf den Aspektdaten ziemlich gering sind, so kann der Aufwand zur Redundanz-kontrolle vernachlässigt werden. Das Schachtelungskonzept des NF^2-Modells kann in diesem Bereich also gewinnbringend eingesetzt werden. Zur Verarbeitung dieser geschachtelten Tabellen wird vom NF^2-Modell ein mächtiger Operationsvorrat zur Verfügung gestellt, den man durch die geschachtelte Anwendung der bisherigen Relationenalgebra erhält. Versucht man jedoch auch die typmäßig rekursiven Netzstrukturen der Generalisierung sowie der Klassifikation und Assoziation (d.h. Klassen- und Memberbeziehung) ebenfalls mit Hilfe des Schachtelungskonzepts abzubilden, so stößt man sowohl auf modellierungstechnische als auch auf operationale Schwierigkeiten: rekursive Strukturen sind im NF^2-Modell nicht darstellbar und müssen deshalb "flachgeklopft" werden; netzwerkartige Strukturen können entweder analog zum RM über Primär-/Fremdschlüsselbeziehungen oder teilweise redundant mit Hilfe des Schachtelungskonzepts (siehe Aspekt-modellierung) dargestellt werden. Die vom NF^2-Modell angebotenen Operationen erlauben nicht den nachträglichen Auf-bau der gewünschten typmäßig rekursiven Netzwerkstrukturen. Aktuelle Forschungsarbeiten [Li87] sehen nur eine Erweiterung der NF^2-Anfragesprache auf rekursive Anfragen, allerdings keine Erweiterung des Datenmodells vor.

Zusammenfassend läßt sich sagen, daß das RM deutliche Schwächen bei der Abbildung des Frame-Modells sowie der dort enthaltenen Abstraktionskonzepte offenbart. Im Gegensatz dazu erlaubt das NF^2-Modell aufgrund seines Schachtelungs-konzepts hier zumindest die direkte Abbildung der Aggregation, wobei allerdings häufig ein gewisses Maß an Datenredun-danz erzeugt wird, welche es zu kontrollieren gilt (Zusatzaufwand). Zur Abbildung der Operationen des Frame-Modells wird in beiden Fällen wenig Unterstützung angeboten. Die durch die Abstraktionsstrukturen definierten typmäßig rekursiven Netzstrukturen müssen extern, d.h. im Anwendungsprogramm, aufgebaut werden. Ebenso sind die auszuführenden Manipulationen auch extern durchzuführen bevor die aktualisierten Einzelteile wieder zurückgeschrieben werden.

3.3 Modellierung mit Hilfe des Molekül-Atom-Datenmodells

Beim Molekül-Atom-Datenmodell (MAD-Modell, [Mi87]) handelt es sich ebenfalls um eine RM-Erweiterung, dessen Ziel die konsistente Erweiterung der Verarbeitung von homogenen zu heterogenen Satzmengen ist (sprich: die Erweiterung von der bisherigen Tupelverarbeitung zur Molekülverarbeitung).

Die Grundelemente des MAD-Modells sind die Atomtypen. Sie sind vergleichbar mit den Relationen des Relationenmodells, d.h., sie fassen Attribute verschiedener Typen zusammen. Aus diesen Atomtypen können nun dynamisch Molekültypen gebildet werden. Ein Molekültyp ist die Zusammenfassung von Atomtypen zwischen denen definierte Beziehungstypen existieren. Die Spezifikation dieser Beziehungstypen basiert auf einem vom System unterstützten Primärschlüssel-Fremdschlüssel-Konzept, welches durch speziell dafür eingeführte Attributtypen (IDENTIFIER und REFERENCE) realisiert wird. Jeder Beziehungstyp wird immer symmetrisch (d.h. beide Teilbeziehungen) dargestellt, wobei sowohl (1:1)- als auch (1:n)- bzw. (n:m)-Beziehungen direkt und als Teil des Atomtyps beschrieben werden können (hierzu wird der Wiederholungsgruppentyp SET verwendet). Damit können auf Atomebene die geforderten Netzstrukturen aufgebaut werden. Molekültypen entsprechen folglich speziellen Sichten auf die Menge der im Schema definierten Atom- und Beziehungstypen (also Ausschnitte auf den Netzstrukturen). Sie können selbst wieder zum Aufbau noch komplexerer Molekültypen benutzt werden, was außerdem auch rekursiv geschehen kann. Jeder Molekültyp legt fest, wie die zugehörigen Moleküle (rekursiv) aus anderen Molekülen bzw. Atomen aufgebaut sind. Der Begriff "Molekül" soll dabei ausdrücken, daß Atome dynamisch verschiedene Bindungen eingehen können. Dieses allgemeine und variable "Bindungskonzept" kann nun einfach zur Realisierung der Abstraktionskonzepte verwendet werden: Aggregation, Assoziation, Generalisierung und Klassifikation (inklusive der netzwerkartigen Strukturen) werden direkt durch das Bindungskonzept, d.h. durch die Molekülbildung, unterstützt. Moleküle bzw. Molekültypen können damit vom Wissensadministrator so definiert werden, daß die Verarbeitung der Objekte des Frame-Modells möglichst effektiv abgewickelt werden kann.

Die Abbildung des Frame-Modells aus Kapitel 2 vereinfacht sich hier zu einer direkten Umsetzung des Entity-Relationship-Schemas in das äquivalente MAD-Schema. Jedem Entity-Typ wird ein Atomtyp zugeordnet und jeder Relationship-Typ wird als Beziehungstyp mit seinen beiden Teilbeziehungen dargestellt. Aufgrund dieser direkten Abbildbarkeit der Konzepte kann das Diagramm aus Bild 3 auch als MAD-Schema interpretiert werden; Bild 4 zeigt demnach ein Ausprägungsbeispiel des MAD-Schemas, d.h. Atome und deren konkrete Beziehungen (Teilbeziehungen sind benannt).

Die Datenmanipulation des MAD-Modells (DML) ist damit "molekül-mengenorientiert", d.h., sie erlaubt die Verarbeitung einer Molekülmenge, wobei jedes Molekül wiederum aus einer Menge von Atomen potentiell verschiedener Typen besteht. Der Typ der Moleküle entspricht dabei entweder einem bereits vordefinierten Molekültyp oder er wird dynamisch in der Manipulationsanweisung festgelegt. Die im MAD-Modell definierte Sprache MQL (Molecule Query Language) erlaubt eine recht komfortable Molekülverarbeitung. Sie ist an SQL angelehnt und besteht daher aus den drei Basiskonstrukten der FROM-Klausel (Spezifikation der für die Anweisung relevanten Molekültypen), der WHERE-Klausel (Spezifikation der Restriktionen/Qualifikationsbedingungen) und der SELECT-Klausel (Spezifikation der Projektionen).

Im folgenden wird exemplarisch für einige ausgewählte Frame-Operationen deren Umsetzung mit Hilfe der MAD-DML aufgezeigt. Bild 5 enthält die DML-Anweisungen sowie die zugehörigen Moleküldarstellungen zur näheren Erläuterung. Beispiel 1 zeigt das "Lesen einer Unit". Diese Frame-Operation umfaßt das Holen der Unit-Beschreibung inklusive der zugehörigen Slot- und Aspektdaten und kann in einer einzigen DML-Anweisung ausgedrückt werden. Die Molekül-definition innerhalb der FROM-Klausel umfaßt die zu aggregierenden Atomtypen (UNITS, SLOTS und ASPEKTE) und die entsprechenden Beziehungstypen (unit_beschreibung, slot_spezifikation), die die Aggregation spezifizieren. Jeder definierte Molekültyp ist ein zusammenhängender Teilausschnitt oder Teilgraph des DB-Schemas, dessen Knoten die Atomtypen und dessen Kanten die Beziehungstypen darstellen. Die Qualifikationsbedingung der WHERE-Klausel beschränkt die Ergebnismengen auf die Moleküle, die den Namen 'Eulen' besitzen. Der Ergebnisbereich der spezifizierten Projektion wird im Moleküldiagramm immer gestrichelt umrahmt. Das "Einfügen eines Member-Slots" ist eine sehr umfangreiche Operation, die in vier DML-Anweisungen aufzugliedern ist (Beispiel 2). Die erste Teiloperation fügt den Slot inkl. der zugehörigen Aspektdaten als Member-Slot bei der entsprechenden Unit ein. Dieses Einfügen umfaßt das Eintragen neuer Atome in die Atomtypen SLOTS und ASPEKTE sowie die Zuordnung zur entsprechenden Unit. Der Molekültyp der INSERT-Operation besteht aus dem aggregierten Unit-Molekül und legt die "Umgebung" fest, in die das zu speichernde Slot-Molekül eingefügt wird. Die zweite Teiloperation liefert den IDENTIFIER-Wert des neu eingefügten ASPEKTE-Atoms. Dieser Wert wird von Teiloperation drei und vier für das Attribut slot_spezifikation benötigt, um dort die Referenz auf das bereits gespeicherte ASPEKTE-Atom zu setzen. Hierdurch wird die Mehrfachbenutzung der Aspekt-daten gewährleistet. Die zugehörige Anfrage zeigt eine wichtige Eigenschaft der MAD-DML auf: die qualifizierte Projektion (Anfrageanweisung innerhalb der SELECT-Klausel) erlaubt ein wertabhängiges Projizieren; hier werden nur die Slots

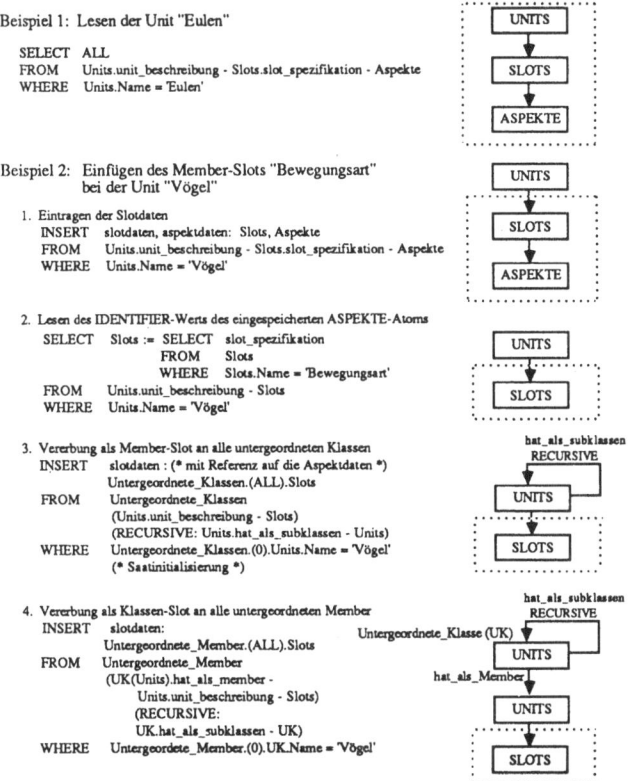

Bild 5: Umsetzung von FRAME-Operationen mittels der MAD-DML

in das Ergebnis aufgenommen, deren Name 'Bewegungsart' ist. Die dritte Teiloperation "vererbt" den Slot als Member-Slot an die untergeordneten Klassen. Hier wird ausgenutzt, daß das MAD-Modell eine rekursive Molekülbildung erlaubt. Die Subklassenstruktur wird durch die RECURSIVE-Klausel spezifiziert und im Sinne eines "transitiven Hülle"-Operators ausgewertet (im Relationen- und NF^2-Modell mußte dies extern programmiert werden). Ausgehend von der in der WHERE-Klausel qualifizierten Wurzel des Rekursivmoleküls werden in einer Rekursionsschleife alle untergeordneten Subklassen-Units über die 'hat_als_subklassen'-Teilbeziehung aufgesucht und deren Slots um den neuen Member-Slot ergänzt. Die vierte Teiloperation "vererbt" den Slot als Klassen-Slot an alle untergeordneten Member sowie an alle Member der untergeordneten Klassen. Die Umsetzung dieser Teiloperation geschieht dabei analog oben.

Auf eine ausführliche Diskussion von allen Frame-Operationen (siehe [Ma86]) muß hier aus Platzgründen verzichtet werden. Die Eignung des MAD-Modells sowohl hinsichtlich der angebotenen Modellierungskonzepte als auch hinsichtlich der verfügbaren Manipulationsmöglichkeiten kommt trotzdem sehr deutlich zum Vorschein.

3.4 Vergleichende Betrachtung

Eine Zusammenfassung der beiden vorigen Abschnitte wird in Tabelle 2 in Form einer vergleichenden Betrachtung der drei Datenmodelle hinsichtlich ihrer Eignung zur Frame-Modellierung aufgezeigt. Diese Gegenüberstellung soll zum Ausdruck bringen, wie einfach bzw. umständlich es ist, die Strukturen des Frame-Modells nachzubilden. Die Schwächen des RM kommen dabei sehr deutlich zum Vorschein. Die im RM enthaltenen Modellierungskonzepte reichen keinesfalls aus: sämtliche Abstraktionsstrukturen können zwar modelliert werden, müssen aber im Anwendungsprogramm explizit aufgebaut werden. Im NF^2-Modell können durch das Konzept der Relationenschachtelung einige Aspekte der Abstraktionsstrukturen bereits im Datenmodell integriert werden. Allerdings sind die Abstraktionshierarchien der Generalisierung und Assoziation analog zum RM wiederum explizit im Anwendungsprogramm zu realisieren. Das MAD-Modell bietet mit dem allgemeinen Konzept der Molekülbildung die Integration von Netzstrukturen und auch rekursiven Strukturen. Damit können dann alle Abstraktionsstrukturen in einfacher Weise dargestellt werden. Deren jeweilige semantische Interpretation bleibt natürlich den Ebenen oberhalb des Datenmodells (im Wissensadministrator) vorbehalten. Von der Datenmodellseite können immer nur allgemeine Abbildungskonzepte (z.B. Schachtelung oder Molekülbildung) angeboten werden.

Datenmodelle / Vergleichskriterien	RM	NF^2-Modell	MAD-Modell
Netzstrukturen	Nachbildung von (n:m)-Beziehungen über Verknüpfungsrelationen	Nachbildung teilweise durch Schachtelungskonzept unterstützt (ggf. Verzicht auf Symmetrie; Kontrolle etwaiger Redundanz)	darstellbar durch Modellkonstrukte
Rekursion	Modellierung flachgeklopft; Aufbau im AP	Modellierung flachgeklopft; Aufbau im AP	darstellbar durch Modellkonstrukte
Klassifikation	entspricht der Unterscheidung von Typ/Schema und Ausprägung	entspricht der Unterscheidung von Typ/Schema und Ausprägung	entspricht der Unterscheidung von Typ/Schema und Ausprägung
Aggregationsstrukturen	nur auf Attributebene; Aufbau höherer Strukturen im AP	durch Schachtelungskonzept unterstützt	durch Molekülbildung unterstützt
Assoziationsstrukturen	keine direkte Unterstützung; Aufbau der Strukturen im AP	durch Schachtelungskonzept unterstützt *	durch Molekülbildung unterstützt
Generalisierungsstrukturen	keine direkte Unterstützung; Aufbau der Strukturen im AP	keine direkte Unterstützung	durch Molekülbildung unterstützt

* rekursiv aufgebaute Hierarchien werden nicht unterstützt, d.h., diese sind im Anwendungsprogramm (AP) zu realisieren

Tabelle 2: Datenmodellvergleich

4. Zusammenfassung

Hier wurde die Abbildung von Frames mit ihren Modellierungskonzepten und charakteristischen Operationen auf objektorientierte Datenmodelle untersucht. Die Tauglichkeit der verschiedenen Ansätze ist in entscheidendem Maße von den verfügbaren Konzepten zur Modellierung und Verarbeitung der Abstraktionsstrukturen von Klassifikation, Aggregation, Assoziation und Generalisierung abhängig. Das Molekül-Atom-Datenmodell bietet, im Vergleich zu anderen untersuchten Datenmodellen, hierfür allgemeine Modellierungskonzepte an, die es erlauben

- Netzstrukturen direkt und symmetrisch darzustellen,
- rekursive Strukturen abzubilden und
- die Abstraktionsstrukturen mit dem Konzept der dynamischen Molekülbildung direkt zu unterstützen.

Durch die zugehörigen Datenmodelloperationen können die modellierten Strukturen entsprechend verarbeitet werden.

Die Ergebnisse dieser Arbeit sind auch übertragbar auf andere Wissensrepräsentationsmodelle, die ebenfalls die genannten Abstraktionskonzepte enthalten (etwa die Klasse der Semantischen Netze).

Literaturverzeichnis

[BB84]   Batory, D.S., Buchmann, A.P.: Molecular Objects, Abstract Data Types and Data Models: A Framework, in: Proc. 10th VLDB Conf., Singapore, 1984, pp. 172-184.

[BS83]   Bobrow, D., Stefik, M.: The LOOPS Manual, Palo Alto, California, Xerox, 1983.

[Ch76]   Chen, P.P.: The Entity-Relationship-Model - Toward a Unified View of Data, in: ACM TODS, Vol. 1, No. 1, 1976, pp. 9-36.

[Da86]   Dadam, P., et al.: A DBMS Prototype to Support Extended NF^2-Relations: An Integrated View on Flat Tables and Hierarchies, in: Proc. ACM SIGMOD Conf., Washington, D.C., 1986, pp. 356-367.

[FK85]   Fikes, R., Kehler, T.: The Role of Frame-based Representation in Reasoning, in: Communications of the ACM, Vol. 28, No. 9, Sept. 1985, S. 904-920.

[HMMS87] Härder, T., Meyer-Wegener, K., Mitschang, B., Sikeler, A.: PRIMA - a DBMS Prototype Supporting Engineering Applications, in: Proc. Int. Conf. on VLDB, Brighton, 1987.

[HR85]   Härder, T., Reuter, A.: Architektur von Datenbanksystemen für Non-Standard- Anwendungen, in: Proc. GI-Fachtagung "Datenbanksysteme in Büro, Technik und Wissenschaft", IFB94, Karlsruhe, 1985, S. 253-286 (eingeladener Vortrag).

[Li87]   Linnemann, V.: Non-First Normal Form Relations and Recursive Queries: An SQL-Based Approach, in: Proc. 3rd Int. Conf. on Data Engineering, Los Angeles, CA, 1987.

[Ma86]   Mattos, N.: Modellierung von FRAME-Konzepten mit dem MAD-Modell, Interner Bericht 164/86 des FB Informatik der Univ. Kaiserslautern, 1986.

[Mi87]   Mitschang, B.: MAD - ein Datenmodell für den Kern eines Non-Standard-Datenbanksystems, in: Proc. GI-Fachtagung "Datenbanksysteme in Büro, Technik und Wissenschaft", Darmstadt, 1987, S. 180-195.

[Mi75]   Minsky, M.: A Framework for Representing Knowledge, in: The Psychology of Computer Vision (editor: Winston, P.), McGraw-Hill Book Company, 1975.

[PSSWD87] Paul, H.-B., Schek, H.-J., Scholl, M.H., Weikum, G., Deppisch, U.: Architecture and Implementation of the Darmstadt Database Kernel System, in: Proc. SIGMOD, San Francisco, 1987.

[Pu86]   Puppe, F.: Expertensysteme - Übersicht und Exemplarische Einführung, in: Informatik-Spektrum, Vol. 9, No. 1, Februar 1986, S. 1-13.

[Ra82]   Raulefs, P.: Expertensysteme, in: Künstliche Intelligenz Frühjahrsschule, Teisendorf, März 1982, S. 61-98.

[SS86]   Schek, H.-J., Scholl, M.H.: The Relational Model with Relation-Valued Attributes, in: Information Systems, Vol. 2, No. 2, 1986, pp. 137-147.